The Open Mobile Alliance

The Open Mobile Alliance

Delivering Service Enablers for Next-Generation Applications

Michael Brenner, *Alcatel-Lucent, USA*
Musa Unmehopa, *Alcatel-Lucent, The Netherlands*

John Wiley & Sons, Ltd

Email (for orders and customer service enquiries): cs-books@wiley.co.uk
Visit our Home Page on www.wileyeurope.com or www.wiley.com

Other Wiley Editorial Offices

John Wiley & Sons Inc., 111 River Street, Hoboken, NJ 07030, USA

Jossey-Bass, 989 Market Street, San Francisco, CA 94103-1741, USA

Wiley-VCH Verlag GmbH, Boschstr. 12, D-69469 Weinheim, Germany

John Wiley & Sons Australia Ltd, 42 McDougall Street, Milton, Queensland 4064, Australia

John Wiley & Sons (Asia) Pte Ltd, 2 Clementi Loop #02-01, Jin Xing Distripark, Singapore 129809

John Wiley & Sons Canada Ltd, 6045 Freemont Blvd, Mississauga, Ontario, L5R 4J3, Canada

Wiley also publishes its books in a variety of electronic formats. Some content that appears in print may not be available in electronic books.

Library of Congress Cataloging-in-Publication Data

Unmehopa, Musa.
   The open mobile alliance : delivering service enablers for next-
generation applications / Michael Brenner, Musa Unmehopa
      p. cm.
   Includes index.
   ISBN 978-0-470-51918-9 (cloth)
  1. Mobile communication systems.   I. Brenner, Michael. II. Title.
   TK6570.M6U55 2008
   621.384 – dc22

                           2007042810

British Library Cataloguing in Publication Data

A catalogue record for this book is available from the British Library

ISBN 978-0-470-51918-9 (HB)

Typeset in 9/11 Times by Laserwords Private Limited, Chennai, India
Printed and bound in Great Britain by Antony Rowe Ltd, Chippenham, England
This book is printed on acid-free paper responsibly manufactured from sustainable forestry
in which at least two trees are planted for each one used for paper production.

Trademarks and Permissions

America Online™ and AOL™ are trademarks of AOL LLC.

BlackBerry™ is a trademark of Research In Motion Limited.

CableLabs® and PacketCable™ are trademarks of Cable Television Laboratories, Inc.

cdma2000® is a registered trademark of the Telecommunications Industry Association (TIA-USA) in the United States.

CORBA® and OMG™ are trademarks or registered trademarks of Object Management Group, Inc. in the United States and/or other countries.

DVB® is a registered trademark of the DVB Project.

eTOM® is a registered trademark of the TM Forum.

Google™ is a trademark of Google Inc.

iPod™ and iTunes™ are trademarks of Apple Inc., registered in the U.S. and other countries.

Java™, J2EE™, J2ME™, J2SE™, and Sun™ are trademarks of SUN Microsystems, Inc. in the United States and other countries.

Microsoft®, Outlook® and Windows Media Player™ are either registered trademarks or trademarks of Microsoft Corporation in the United States and/or other countries.

NEXTEL™ is a trademark of Sprint Nextel.

OASIS™ and SAML™ are trademarks of OASIS (Organization for the Advancement of Structured Information Standards).

UMTS™ and 3GPP™ are registered trademarks of ETSI in France and other jurisdictions.

W3C® is a registered trademark of the World Wide Web Consortium, registered in numerous countries.

WiMAX™ is a trademark of the WiMAX Forum.

Yahoo® is a registered trademark of Yahoo, Inc.

WiFi® is a registered trademark of the Wi-Fi Alliance.

3GPP(tm) TSs and TRs are the property of ARIB, ATIS, ETSI, CCSA, TTA and TTC who jointly own the copyright in them. They are subject to modifications and are therefore provided to you "as is" for information purposes only. Further use is strictly prohibited.

To Hedy – who challenged me to start the book, and Greta, Dan and Andrew – who challenged me to finish it. MB

To Odette and Aron, of course. MU

Contents

Trademarks and Permissions   v

Dedication   vii

Foreword   xxi

Preface   xxiii
    I. Who Should Read This Book?   xxiv
    II. What to Cover?   xxiv
    III. A Word on Timing   xxiv
    IV. A Disclaimer   xxv

Acknowledgements   xxvii

About the Authors   xxix

List of Figures   xxxiii

Part I   Background and Introduction   1

1   Introduction   3
    1.1   Service Enablers   3
    1.2   The Open Mobile Alliance (OMA)   4
    1.3   Service Enablers in OMA   5

2   The Silo Syndrome and its Solution   7
    2.1   Vertical Integration   7
    2.2   Re-use as First-Class Citizen   9
        2.2.1   *Service Enablers*   10
        2.2.2   *Interfaces*   11
        2.2.3   *Some Examples Using Interfaces* 12
        2.2.4   *Resources*   13
    2.3   The OSE   13
        2.3.1   *Policy Enforcer*   14
        2.3.2   *OSE Interface Categories*   15
        2.3.3   *Protocol Bindings*   17
        2.3.4   *Putting the Piece Parts Together* 17
        2.3.5   *What the OSE Isn't*   18
    2.4   Additional Features of the OSE   18
        2.4.1   *Protection of Resources*   18
        2.4.2   *End-user Experience*   18
    2.5   OSE and Related Technologies   19
    2.6   Summary   19

3   The Open Mobile Alliance – An Organizational Overview   **21**

    3.1   Overview of the OMA   21
        3.1.1   *Affiliation – A Historic Perspective*   22
    3.2   Principles of the OMA   23
    3.3   The OMA's Relationship with External Organizations   23
    3.4   OMA Organizational Structure   24
        3.4.1   *OMA Board of Directors*   25
        3.4.2   *Technical Plenary*   25
        3.4.3   *OMA Committees*   26
        3.4.4   *OMA Horizontal Working Groups*   27
        3.4.5   *OMA Vertical Working Groups*   28
        3.4.6   *OMA Birds of a Feather Groups*   33
    3.5   The Processes   33
        3.5.1   *Smooth Sailing, no Waterfalls or Gates*   33
        3.5.2   *Support for Off-line Progress and Decision Making*   34
        3.5.3   *Strive for Consensus*   34
        3.5.4   *Low Threshold for New Work*   34
        3.5.5   *Enabler Release Program*   34
    3.6   Interoperability in the Open Mobile Alliance   35
        3.6.1   *The Objectives of the OMA IOP*   36
        3.6.2   *Process and Documentation*   37
        3.6.3   *OMA Interoperability Recognition Program*   39
    3.7   Summary   40

4   Interoperability TestFests   **41**

    4.1   The Objective of Interoperability in the OMA   41
    4.2   The Organization of the Test Campaigns   42
    4.3   Planning   43
    4.4   Finances   44
    4.5   TestFest Statistics   44
    4.6   Comparison with Other Standards Development Organizations (SDOs)   44
    4.7   Summary   45

5   Service Provider – The Network Operator Perspective   **47**

    5.1   The Need for OMA   47
    5.2   Operators in the OMA   50
    5.3   OMA Challenges for the Future   53
    5.4   Summary   55

6   Service Provider – The Enterprise Perspective   **57**

    6.1   Enterprise Needs   57
    6.2   OMA Enterprise Awareness   59
    6.3   Summary   60

Part II   Horizontal Topics   **61**

7   The Policy Enforcer Details: Model, Architecture, Realization, and Impact   **63**

    7.1   Policy Enforcement Modeling in the OSE   63

	7.2	Beyond the OSE: Policy Enforcement as Service Oriented Architecture Composition	65
	7.3	Logical Architecture versus Deployment Considerations	68
	7.4	Relationship to Parlay and IP Multimedia Subsystem (IMS)	68
	7.5	Policy Modeling	69
	7.6	Policy Enforcer through OMA Enabler Realization	69
	7.7	Relationship of Policy Enforcer to IETF PEP/PDP	71
	7.8	Policy Assembly, Composition, and Orchestration	71
	7.8.1	Model and PEL Assembly	71
	7.8.2	Usage Considerations	72
	7.8.3	Policies in Service Provider Domain	73
	7.9	Summary – Next Steps	75

8   The Policy Evaluation, Enforcement, and Management Enabler   77

	8.1	Are Those Specifications Really Needed?	78
	8.1.1	Policy Control and Management Overview	79
	8.1.2	Standards Precursors to PEEM	80
	8.1.3	What Roles Are the PEEM Specifications Playing?	82
	8.2	PEEM Market Needs	82
	8.2.1	Use Case for Explicit Requests to PEEM	83
	8.2.2	Use Case for Intercepted Requests by PEEM	84
	8.2.3	PEEM Requirements	86
	8.3	PEEM Architecture and Technical Specifications	89
	8.3.1	PEEM in the OSE	89
	8.3.2	PEEM Logical Architecture	90
	8.3.3	Logical Flows for PEEM	93
	8.3.4	PEEM Policy Expression Language Details	94
	8.3.5	PEM-1 Interface Details	96
	8.3.6	PEM-2 Interface Specification	98
	8.4	PEEM Salient Points	99
	8.4.1	Usage Patterns	99
	8.4.2	Expert Topics for PEL	103
	8.4.3	Expert Topics for PEM-1	104
	8.4.4	Divergent Views and their Resolution	105
	8.5	Impact of Specifications on the Industry	107
	8.5.1	Impact on Service Providers	108
	8.5.2	Impact on Vendors	109
	8.5.3	Impact on Consumer Market	110
	8.5.4	Impact on Corporate Market	111
	8.5.5	Impact on Other Specifications	112
	8.6	Specifications Evolution and Future Direction	112
	8.7	Summary	113

9   Utilization of IMS in OMA   115

	9.1	Are Those Specifications Really Needed?	116
	9.2	Standard Precursors to IMSinOMA	117
	9.3	Architecture Overview	117
	9.4	Salient Points and Divergent Views	120
	9.5	Impact of Specifications	122

		9.5.1	Impact on the Industry	122
		9.5.2	Impact on Other Specifications	122
	9.6	Specifications Evolution and Future Direction		123
	9.7	Summary		123

10   Service Architectures – Parlay and the OSE   **125**

	10.1	A Quick Taster of Parlay		125
		10.1.1	Parlay X	126
	10.2	The Parlay in OSE Enabler		128
		10.2.1	Parlay as Network Resource	129
		10.2.2	Parlay X Web Service as the Enabler	129
		10.2.3	Parlay Service Capability Feature as the Enabler	130
		10.2.4	Hybrid Parlay and OMA Solution	130
	10.3	PIOSE Challenges		131
		10.3.1	Enforcing Service Provider Policies	131
		10.3.2	The Parlay Policy Management Service Capability Feature	132
	10.4	Impact of Specifications on the Industry		133
	10.5	Specifications Evolution and Future Direction		133
	10.6	Summary		133

11   A Web Services Technology Realization of the OSE   **135**

	11.1	Web Services Crash Course		136
	11.2	A Web Services Infrastructure Framework		137
	11.3	Mobile Web Services		139
		11.3.1	The Mobile Network as Content Source for the Web Service	139
		11.3.2	The Mobile Device as Web Service Requestor	139
		11.3.3	The Mobile Device as Web Service Provider	140
	11.4	The OMA Web Services Enabler Release		140
	11.5	The Technologies Specified by OWSER		142
		11.5.1	Transport	142
		11.5.2	Messaging	143
		11.5.3	Description	144
		11.5.4	Quality of Service	145
		11.5.5	Components	145
		11.5.6	Discovery	146
	11.6	Network Identity		146
		11.6.1	Identity Management Concepts Overview	146
		11.6.2	Identity Provider Introduction	148
		11.6.3	Identity Federation and Single Sign-On	149
		11.6.4	Name Registration	149
		11.6.5	Authentication Context	150
		11.6.6	Single Sign-Out	150
		11.6.7	Federation Termination Notification	150
		11.6.8	Attribute Query and/or Modification	150
		11.6.9	Usage Directive	151
		11.6.10	Interaction Service	151
		11.6.11	Bootstrapping Identity based Web Services Framework	151

		11.6.12	Discovery Service	151
		11.6.13	Liberty enabled User Agent	152
		11.6.14	Security	152
		11.6.15	Network Identity Conclusions	152
	11.7	OWSER and the OSE		153
	11.8	Divergent Views and their Resolution		154
	11.9	Specifications Evolution and Future Direction		154
		11.9.1	Web Services on Devices	155
		11.9.2	XML Usage Guide	155
		11.9.3	Common XML Dictionary	155
		11.9.4	Additional WS-I Profiles	155
		11.9.5	Other Industry Profiles	156
	11.10	Impact of the Specifications		157
		11.10.1	Impact on the Industry	157
		11.10.2	Impact on Other Specifications	157
	11.11	Summary		157

12   The OMA Service Provider Environment Enabler   159

	12.1	Are Those Specifications Really Needed?		160
	12.2	OSPE Use Cases		161
	12.3	OSPE Requirements		163
	12.4	Standard Precursors to OSPE		164
		12.4.1	OAM&P Standards in the Telecommunications Industry	164
		12.4.2	OAM&P Standards in the IT Industry	165
	12.5	OSPE Architecture and Technical Specifications		167
		12.5.1	OSPE Enabler in the OSE	167
		12.5.2	OSPE Logical Architecture	168
		12.5.3	OSPE Logical Flows	169
	12.6	OSPE Salient Points		172
	12.7	Impact of Specifications on the Industry		173
		12.7.1	Impact on Service Providers	174
		12.7.2	Impact on Vendors	174
		12.7.3	Impact on Consumer Market	174
		12.7.4	Impact on Corporate Market	175
		12.7.5	Impact on Other Specifications	175
	12.8	Specifications Evolution and Future Direction		175
	12.9	Summary		175

13   The Security Enablers   177

	13.1	Are Those Specifications Really Needed?		179
		13.1.1	Wireless Public Key Infrastructure	180
		13.1.2	On-board Key Generation (OBKG)	180
		13.1.3	Online Certificate Status Protocol Mobile Profile	180
		13.1.4	Smart Card Web Server (SCWS)	180
	13.2	Security Common Functions Enabler		180
		13.2.1	SEC-CF Use Case	181
		13.2.2	Security Common Functions Requirements	182

	13.2.3	Standards Precursors to Security Common Functions	182
	13.2.4	SEC-CF Architecture and Technical Specifications	182
	13.2.5	SEC-CF Technical Specifications	186
13.3	SEC-CF Salient Points		188
	13.3.1	Divergent Views and their Resolution	189
13.4	Impact of Specifications on the Industry		189
	13.4.1	Impact on Service Providers	190
	13.4.2	Impact on Vendors	190
	13.4.3	Impact on Consumer Market	191
	13.4.4	Impact on Corporate Market	191
	13.4.5	Impact on Other Specifications	191
13.5	Specifications Evolution and Future Direction		192
13.6	Summary		192

Part III   Selected OMA Service Enablers   **193**

14   The Presence and List Management Enablers   **195**

14.1	Presence – What is it?		195
14.2	A Constructionist View of Presence Architectures		196
	14.2.1	Basic Elements	196
	14.2.2	Presence Service Interfaces and the Resource List Server	197
	14.2.3	Presence Authorization Policies	198
	14.2.4	Presence-related Event Packages	199
	14.2.5	Presence Optimizations	199
	14.2.6	Presence Standards	200
	14.2.7	The 'Three-Layer Brick' Model	200
	14.2.8	The IETF Presence Model and Standards	201
	14.2.9	A Summary of IETF Presence Standards	202
	14.2.10	The 3GPP2 Presence Model and Standards	202
	14.2.11	The 3GPP Presence Model and Standards	203
	14.2.12	The OSA PAM SCF Model	204
14.3	The OMA Presence Model and Specifications		205
	14.3.1	Presence, XDM, and IMPS Enablers in the OSE	205
	14.3.2	Wireless Village and OMA Instant Messaging and Presence Service	205
	14.3.3	OMA Presence SIMPLE	207
	14.3.4	OMA XML Document Management	209
14.4	A Deployment Example – Deploying Presence and XDM Enablers in an IMS or MMD environment		213
14.5	Impact of Specifications on the Industry		215
14.6	Specifications Evolution and Future Direction		215
14.7	Summary		215

15   The Push-to-talk over Cellular Enabler   **217**

15.1	Are Those Specifications Really Needed?		218
15.2	Standard Precursors to OMA Push-to-talk over Cellular		218
15.3	Architecture and Technical Specifications Overview		219
	15.3.1	PoC V1.0 Architecture and Functional Description	219
	15.3.2	Enhancements for PoC V2.0 in Architecture and Functionality	227
15.4	Salient Points		233

15.5   Impact of Specifications on the Industry   233
        15.5.1   Impact on Service Providers, Vendors, Consumer, and Corporate
                 Market   233
        15.5.2   Impact on Other Specifications   234
15.6   Specifications Evolution and Future Direction   234
15.7   Summary   234

16 Mobile E-mail   237

16.1   Background   237
        16.1.1   Market Drivers   239
        16.1.2   The Standards Landscape   240
16.2   MEM Architecture   243
        16.2.1   Analysis   243
        16.2.2   Data Synchronization (DS) Realization   245
        16.2.3   LEMONADE Realization   247
16.3   Summary   250

17 The Charging Enabler   251

17.1   Are Those Specifications Really Needed?   252
17.2   Standards Precursors to Charging   253
        17.2.1   Mobile Commerce Four Party Model   253
        17.2.2   Convergence of Financial, IT, and Telephony Aspects of the Charging
                 Enabler   254
        17.2.3   Influence from Other Standards   255
17.3   Charging Requirements   255
17.4   Charging Architecture and Technical Specifications   255
        17.4.1   The Charging Enabler in the OSE   256
        17.4.2   Charging Logical Architecture   256
        17.4.3   Charging Logical Flows   258
        17.4.4   Charging Enabler Technical Specifications   261
17.5   Divergent Views and Their Resolution   265
17.6   Impact of Specifications on the Industry   265
        17.6.1   Impact on Service Providers   266
        17.6.2   Impact on Vendors   266
        17.6.3   Impact on Other Specifications   266
17.7   Specifications Evolution and Future Direction   266
17.8   Summary   267

18 The Device Management Enablers   269

18.1   Device Management Requirements   271
18.2   Device Management Architecture   271
        18.2.1   DM in the OMA Service Environment   271
        18.2.2   Generic DM Architecture – Components and Interfaces   272
        18.2.3   Initial Provisioning   273
        18.2.4   OMA Device Management Architecture   274
        18.2.5   Bootstrapping   276
        18.2.6   The DM Protocol   276
        18.2.7   The Management Tree   277

		18.2.8	Management Commands	278
		18.2.9	Client Responses and Alerts	279
		18.2.10	Aggregate Management Operations	279
		18.2.11	Configuration Data Storage Models	280
	18.3	Device Management Enabler Specifications		280
		18.3.1	History	281
		18.3.2	OMA Client Provisioning	281
		18.3.3	OMA Device Management	282
		18.3.4	Domain-specific Device Management Enablers	282
	18.4	Impact of DM Specifications on the Industry		286
		18.4.1	Impact on Service Providers	286
		18.4.2	Impact on Vendors	287
		18.4.3	Impact on Consumer Market	287
		18.4.4	Impact on Corporate Market	287
		18.4.5	Impact on Other Specifications	287
	18.5	Specifications Evolution and Future Direction		287
	18.6	Summary		288

19 The Digital Rights Management Enabler   **289**

	19.1	What Were the Drivers for Those Specifications?		290
	19.2	Are Those Specifications Really Necessary?		291
		19.2.1	Basic Download	292
		19.2.2	Multiple Device Usage	292
		19.2.3	Super-distribution (Peer-to-Peer Sharing)	293
		19.2.4	Preview	293
		19.2.5	Buying the Rights Object for another User	293
		19.2.6	Streaming Content	293
		19.2.7	Backup and Restore	293
		19.2.8	Export of Rights Object	293
	19.3	OMA DRM Requirements		294
		19.3.1	Types of Content	294
		19.3.2	Rights Objects	294
		19.3.3	Content and Rights Object Delivery	294
		19.3.4	Streaming	294
		19.3.5	Enhanced Security	295
		19.3.6	Export of Rights Object	295
		19.3.7	Super-distribution	295
		19.3.8	Backup and Storage	295
	19.4	Architecture and Technical Specifications Overview		295
	19.5	Salient Points		297
		19.5.1	Divergent Views and Their Resolution	297
	19.6	Impact of Specifications on the Industry		298
		19.6.1	Impact on Service Providers	298
		19.6.2	Impact on Vendors	299
		19.6.3	Impact on Consumer Market	299
		19.6.4	Impact on Corporate Market	300
		19.6.5	Impact on other Specifications	300
	19.7	Specifications Evolution and Future Direction		301
	19.8	Summary		302

20   The Broadcast Enabler   **303**

20.1   Are Those Specifications Really Needed?   304
20.2   Standards Precursors to BCAST Enabler   305
20.3   BCAST Architecture   306
        20.3.1   *BCAST Logical Architecture (Reference Points)*   307
        20.3.2   *BCAST Enabler Functions and Interfaces*   308
20.4   Impact of Specifications   319
20.5   Specifications Evolution and Future Direction   320
20.6   Summary   320

21   The Dynamic Content Delivery Enabler   **321**

21.1   Why Do We Need New Specifications for DCD?   322
        21.1.1   *DCD Use Cases*   323
21.2   Standards Precursors to DCD   325
21.3   DCD Architecture and Technical Specifications   325
        21.3.1   *DCD in the OMA Service Environment*   325
        21.3.2   *DCD Logical Architecture*   326
        21.3.3   *DCD Technical Specifications*   328
21.4   DCD Deployment Options   328
        21.4.1   *A DCD Deployment Example*   329
        21.4.2   *A DCD Service Example*   330
21.5   DCD Salient Points   332
21.6   Impact of Specifications on the Industry   333
        21.6.1   *Impact on Service Providers*   333
        21.6.2   *Impact on Content Providers*   333
        21.6.3   *Impact on Application Developers*   334
        21.6.4   *Impact on Vendors*   334
        21.6.5   *Impact on Consumer Market*   334
        21.6.6   *Impact on Corporate Market*   335
        21.6.7   *Impact on Other Specifications*   335
21.7   Specifications Evolution and Future Direction   335
21.8   Summary   335

22   The Global Permissions Management Enabler   **337**

22.1   Are Those Specifications Really Needed?   338
        22.1.1   *GPM Actors and Main Concepts in the Requirements Document*   339
        22.1.2   *A Typical GPM Flow*   340
        22.1.3   *Management of Permissions Rule*   342
22.2   Standards Precursors to GPM   342
22.3   GPM Architecture and Technical Specifications   343
        22.3.1   *GPM in the OSE*   343
        22.3.2   *GPM Logical Architecture*   344
        22.3.3   *Logical Flows for GPM*   346
        22.3.4   *GPM Technical Specifications*   347
22.4   GPM Salient Points   347
22.5   Impact of Specifications on the Industry   349
        22.5.1   *Impact on Service Providers*   349
        22.5.2   *Impact on Vendors*   349
        22.5.3   *Impact on Consumer Market*   349

| | 22.5.4 | Impact on Corporate Market | 350 |

22.5.4   Impact on Corporate Market   350
22.5.5   Impact on Other Specifications   350
22.6   Specifications Evolution and Future Direction   350
22.7   Summary   350

23   The Categorization Based Content Screening Enabler   351

23.1   Are Those Specifications Really Needed?   354
23.2   Standards Precursors to CBCS   356
23.3   CBCS Architecture and Technical Specifications   356
        23.3.1   CBCS Enabler in the OSE   357
        23.3.2   CBCS Logical Architecture   358
        23.3.3   Logical Flows for CBCS   362
        23.3.4   CBCS Technical Specifications   364
23.4   Impact of Specifications on the Industry   364
        23.4.1   Impact on Service Providers   364
        23.4.2   Impact on Vendors   365
        23.4.3   Impact on Consumer Market   365
        23.4.4   Impact on Corporate Market   365
        23.4.5   Impact on Other Specifications   365
23.5   Specifications Evolution and Future Direction   366
23.6   Summary   366

24   The Game Services Enabler   367

24.1   Are Those Specifications Really Needed?   368
24.2   Standards Precursors to Game Services   369
24.3   Game Services Specifications   369
        24.3.1   The Gaming Platform   370
        24.3.2   Game Services Architecture   371
        24.3.3   Game Services – Client/Server Interface Enabler   372
24.4   Impact of Specifications on the Industry   375
        24.4.1   Impact on Service Providers   376
        24.4.2   Impact on Vendors   376
        24.4.3   Impact on Consumer Market   377
        24.4.4   Impact on Other Specifications   377
24.5   Specifications Evolution and Future Direction   377
24.6   Summary   379

25   The Location Enabler   381

25.1   What is Location?   382
25.2   Location Architectures   383
        25.2.1   Control Plane Location   383
        25.2.2   User Plane Location   385
25.3   The Mobile Location Services Enabler   387
        25.3.1   OMA Mobile Location Protocol   387
        25.3.2   OMA Privacy Checking Protocol   387
        25.3.3   OMA Roaming Location Protocol   387

	25.4	The Secure User Plane Location	388
		25.4.1 *SUPL 1.0 Architecture*	389
		25.4.2 *SUPL 2.0 Architecture*	391
		25.4.3 *SUPL Technical Specifications*	393
		25.4.4 *SUPL Sequence Flow*	397
	25.5	Summary	400

26   The Mobile Application Environment   401

	26.1	The Mobile Web Architecture	402
	26.2	Mobile Browser	403
		26.2.1 *Precursors*	403
		26.2.2 *OMA Extensions*	403
	26.3	Mobile Content Data Formats	405
		26.3.1 *vObject*	405
		26.3.2 *SVG for the Mobile Domain*	406
		26.3.3 *SMIL for the Mobile Domain*	406
		26.3.4 *Where Browser and Content Meet*	407
	26.4	Multiple Interaction Modalities and Devices	407
	26.5	Summary	409

27   Recent Topics   411

	27.1	The General Service Subscription Management Enabler	411
		27.1.1 *Prior Work – Subscription Management*	412
		27.1.2 *New Work – General Service Subscription Management*	412
		27.1.3 *Related Activities*	413
	27.2	Device Profile Evolution	414
		27.2.1 *Prior Work – Static Properties*	414
		27.2.2 *New Work – Dynamic Properties*	415
		27.2.3 *DPE Examples*	415
		27.2.4 *DPE Related Activities*	416
	27.3	Converged IP Messaging Enabler	416
		27.3.1 *Multimedia Messaging Service*	416
		27.3.2 *Instant Messaging and Presence Service*	417
		27.3.3 *SIP and IMS introduce SIMPLE Instant Messaging*	417
		27.3.4 *Push-to-Talk over Cellular*	418
		27.3.5 *OMA's Approach to Enablers*	418
		27.3.6 *Converged IP Messaging*	418
		27.3.7 *CPM Summary*	421
	27.4	Mobile Advertising	421
		27.4.1 *Prior Work – Mobile Advertising Landscape*	423
		27.4.2 *New Work – Mobile Advertising*	424

Part IV   Conclusions   427

28   Concluding Remarks, and What's in Store Next?   429

	28.1	Project Post-mortem	429
	28.2	What's Next?	430

Annex A   **435**

Abbreviations and Acronyms   **441**

References   **455**

Index   **469**

Foreword

Communication, and the ability to interact in advanced and complex forms over great distances, is mankind's greatest differentiator with the other species. The ability to communicate has resulted in mankind becoming the dominating species, enabling us to record the past, engage in the present and prepare for the future.

With all our modern communication systems, it is difficult to imagine a world without the ability to communicate. So dependent is today's society on modern communications that a world without radios, televisions, computers, PDAs, Internet, and telephones and mobile phones would set us back hundreds of years and severely impact our ability to go about modern day life. The modern means of communication that we take for granted are expected to continue driving forward and further increase society's dependence in the future. Developing future communication methods is thus crucial to shaping the way we interact and evolve as a society.

The Open Mobile Alliance (OMA) resulted from the need to further evolve mobile communications. Early mobile communications in first generation analog mobile systems were superseded by the 1980s move towards second generation digital mobile systems, incorporating some ISDN telephony services. Enhancements to the second generation digital mobile systems provided enhanced data bandwidth and some additional services infrastructure. Development of third generation digital mobile systems began in the early 1990s to enable higher data rates for multimedia services. However, much more was needed to enable and promote interoperable data services to fulfill the multimedia expectations. It was this unsatisfied demand that resulted in the creation of OMA.

During late 2001 and early 2002, a grouping of companies (calling itself the Open Mobile Architecture Initiative) was formed to promote mobile interoperable data services. Their discussions resulted in the OMA mission to develop open specifications for multimedia services. OMA was created in Vancouver in June 2002 by modifying the WAP Forum articles, and incorporating several other organizations (Wireless Village, MGIF, SyncML, MWIF, MMS IOP and LIF). With its broad membership from across the entire mobile value chain, its focus on enabling multimedia services and major testing program to prove interoperability of its specifications, OMA is unique in the standardization landscape. In 2005, OMA's scope was broadened to support services in fixed networks based on the family of IP protocols.

Through its market-requirements oriented and contribution-driven approach, major specifications have been created to support Digital Rights Management, Download, Push, Browsing, Multimedia Messaging, Instant Messaging, Device Management, Client Provisioning, Presence, XML Document Management, Push-to-Talk Over Cellular, Mobile Location Services, Secure User Plane Location, Data Synchronization, Standardized Transcoding, Client Side Content Screening, Categorization Based Content Screening, Game Services, and many more. The industry-leading and successful TestFest program continues its commendable work proving interoperability of OMA specifications through members' implementations.

So where does OMA go from here? With the increasing capabilities of devices, fixed mobile convergence, closer integration with the Internet, always-on capability, service customization (e.g. user profiling, location, presence, etc.) and expansion of end-user and enterprise content, the multimedia services industry will continue to rapidly develop and provide an increasing revenue stream.

The success of OMA is due to its individual members' contributions, and this book is testament to their hard work. The individual members' efforts and the authors of this book are to be congratulated on their magnificent achievements.

Mark Cataldo
Senior Advisor
Orange SA
OMA Technical Plenary Chairman

Preface

'Next-Generation Applications, sounds interesting, but where are they defined?'

'Can't I get an overview of how things relate, rather than just traverse a bunch of individual enabler specifications?'

'Standards specifications make for such dry reading.'

'Only a seasoned standards veteran can navigate the websites of standards fora or industry consortiums.'

Many times colleagues have asked us questions or confronted us with statements very similar to the ones above. We've even uttered them ourselves on occasions. The fact of the matter is that standards organizations have as their objective to produce precise and unambiguous technical specifications for a given topic. A great deal of prior knowledge is assumed and a fair grounding in communications and software development technology is expected as a prerequisite. It is often notoriously hard to get an introductory overview at a non-technical level. Or even on a technical level to understand the greater picture, to put the individual piece parts into their collective perspective.

This book intends to provide a unique overview of the industry landscape for service enablers for Next-Generation Applications, as it is currently being developed by the Open Mobile Alliance™. The first part of the book provides an overall but concise introduction into the subject matter covered in this book, that is, service enablers for Next-Generation Applications. It describes the problems that service enablers are attempting to solve. It chooses to use the horizontal services architecture developed by OMA as the framework to introduce and describe a judiciously selected sample of OMA service enablers. Part I concludes by bringing to the fore the Open Mobile Alliance, an international specifications setting body that delivers open specifications for creating interoperable services that work across countries, operators, fixed and mobile terminals. Part II builds on the concepts introduced, and discusses a number of topics that are of horizontal interest in the OMA. In summation, the chapters in Part II of the book present the foundation upon which individual OMA service enablers can thrive. Part III then continues with an in-depth coverage of a carefully selected range of such OMA service enablers. Note that although the horizontal services architecture is used as a narrational tool to help weave the OMA fabric, each chapter in Part III and most in Part II can be consumed as stand-alone coverage of an individual OMA service enabler, or group of enablers. Readers interested only in one or a few specific enablers are invited to skip to the relevant chapters for the topic of interest. Having said that, however, looking at individual enablers without a thorough understanding of the larger environment may prove to be an exercise in flapping wings. Hence, the main objective of the book is to provide an overview, connect the dots, and give you the bigger picture that the standards themselves do not provide.

I. Who Should Read This Book?

The book is aimed at technical professionals. More specifically, the target audience for the book includes the following:

- Product managers who need to understand the direction of standards to support the product road map of their services and applications portfolio.
- Company CTOs who charter the future directions of their companies in the mobile industry.
- Network architects or planners who need to understand the standards landscape and available specifications in order to be able to design and deploy interoperable products in complex, differentiated networks.
- Standards managers who need to understand how the various industry fora and consortia, and standards development organizations tie together.
- Standards engineers who are starting to participate in the OMA.
- IT professionals who are interested in learning which communication enablers are available for integration with their enterprise solution.
- Technical university students in advanced telecommunication programs.
- Anyone else who is interested in an overview of what OMA does, without having to sift through the many detailed technical specifications.

This will be a technical book, though the book does not specifically address the developer community. Protocol specifications are discussed, with a focus on the architecture and function of service enablers, and developed based on market-driven requirements. As such, you will not find any source code fragments or XML angle bracket examples.

II. What to Cover?

This book describes a compilation of service enablers out of the vast and extensive pool of OMA enabler specifications. The following criteria are offered as justification for the selection we made. Using the OMA Service Environment as the narrative theme throughout the book, we purposely chose to describe those enablers that have a horizontal significance within this architecture. In addition, those enablers that have already been commercially rolled out in today's networks, or which have managed to capture their fair share of media attention as potential high runners for future deployment, warrant a description in our text. This is not to say that any of the OMA service enablers not covered are expected to be less successful, or are to be considered less critical or essential. Each of them is anticipated to play their own important role in the creation of value-added applications.

Let's use the vehicle analogy. Describing a car as consisting of four tires, two axles, and a steering wheel is not going to help you understand what makes it run. On the other hand, detailing every bolt in terms of size, width, thread count, and torsion parameters is definitely going to put you to sleep. What you want to do is to look under the hood to see some of the moving parts. A book can only have so many pages, and an author team can only claim (rightly or not) to be knowledgeable on so many topics. Despite these constraints, we have strived to choose an appealing angle. We hope to have composed an overview that is both consistent as well as comprehensive, which will be interesting and insightful to you, the reader.

III. A Word on Timing

Anyone who has ever bought a new, state of the art PC (and who hasn't) is familiar with the following irony. As soon as you walk out of the store with your latest purchase, it is outdated and a newer model is already available. Books on technology sometimes suffer from the same paradox. When describing technology that is still very much in the process of being defined or standardized, it is inevitable that one takes a snapshot of a moving target. The same holds true for this book, as new versions of OMA specifications are continuously being published.

So, although this section may read as a warning coming from a Lonely Planet travel guide, it is important to realize nevertheless. The information in this book may be subject to change, with new work items being approved and stale ones suspended, with individual enablers going through the specification development life cycle and the change request process, and with problem reports being issued after interoperability test events. Having said that, every attempt has been made to both describe the organizational aspects and architectural concepts in an as timeless a manner as possible, as well as select the latest stable and approved specifications available at the time of writing.

IV. A Disclaimer

Before we start in earnest, just a few words on the ideas expressed in the book. Although great care was put in the production of the text in order to present a view that is both technically correct, as well as fair and balanced, it is prudent to point out to the reader that the views and opinions presented here are solely those of the authors. They do not necessarily reflect an official OMA point of view, and the authors expressly do not speak in any capacity of an elected OMA officer. Furthermore, towards imparting a fair view, the two lead authors have strived to engage experts from all segments of the industry to collaborate as contributing authors, without editing their views on the topic assigned, even when those views might not completely match those of the lead authors. As a result, we hope to have provided the reader with a fair-minded and even-handed text on OMA and its enablers.

Acknowledgements

These are exciting times in the mobile applications space. Fundamental changes are taking place. And so we feel especially fortunate to work in an organization like the Open Mobile Alliance that helps drive and define many of these fundamental changes. For this book, we have had the privilege to work with a distinct selection of expert contributing authors in this field. But our gratitude goes well beyond. We are deeply indebted to all the people who have helped making this project come to fruition.

First and foremost, many reviewers have selflessly provided extraordinary feedback, generously offered many helpful suggestions, and above all, kept us honest. The following people have acted as expert reviewers for one or more sections or chapters of the book: Juan Cambeiro from Telefonica, Paulus Karremans from Ericsson, Paul Knight from Nortel Networks, Tero Lehtonen from TeliaSonera, Anders Lundqvist from BEA Systems, Hans Portschy from Siemens AG, Mark Pozefsky from IBM, Michael Shenfield from Research In Motion, James (Jie) Tang from Huawei Technologies, Larry Young from Sprint Nextel, Duan Xiang from China Mobile, and Jerome Marcon, Ramesh Pattabhiraman, Thomas Picard, Moh Torabi, and Indaka Weerasekera from Alcatel-Lucent. All gave us the benefit of their criticism, and reviewed various drafts with a sharp eye and even sharper red pencil. We have incorporated extensive revisions in response to their invaluable comments.

Our management chain in Alcatel-Lucent has provided us with the opportunity to embark on this endeavor. In particular, our gratitude goes to Michel Grech, Fran O'Brien, Cheryl Blum, and Didier Berthoumieux.

For a number of expert topics, we were fortunate to pick the brain of a long list of insightful and selfless colleagues. They may have been mildly puzzled, if not somewhat amused, by our seemingly random queries for often esoteric bits of information. But all subjected themselves kindly to our quizzes, and their insights have helped refine this book's content and presentation. Our appreciation is due to: Alastair Angwin from IBM, Peter Arnby from Ericsson, Ken Henriksen from Sprint Nextel, Ileana Leuca from AT&T, Bennett Marks from Nokia, Bindu Rao from Hewlett Packard, Patrick Slaats from Vodafone, Peter Thompson from Qualcomm, and Rick Hull, Terry Jacobson, Bharat Kumar, Mike Rudolph, Tom Strom, Jacky Tang-Taye, and Daping Wang from Alcatel-Lucent.

From Forapolis, Carole Rodriguez, Victoria Gray, and Gerry McAuley deserve special mention, for their support and insight. We would also like to acknowledge the support received from the staff of the OMA organization. In particular, the assistance of Seth Newberry, Stephen Jones and Ann Woodliff is greatly appreciated. From John Wiley & Sons, Birgit Gruber, Anna Smart, and Sarah Hinton our project editor, have been instrumental in helping two techies navigate through the process of manuscript writing and book publishing. We would also like to thank Mark Cataldo, the OMA Technical Plenary chairman, for providing the foreword to this book.

No idea evolves in a vacuum, no man or woman is an island. Many of the insights presented in this book have only taken on their final shape and form after various highly engaging and invigorating discussions with our peers from other companies. Our knowledge and understanding of OMA technologies have benefited tremendously from the many contributions of the participants in the OMA technical working groups. And as with any technology, they are the unsung heroes who tirelessly undertake the often tedious and mundane task of writing the input contributions and change requests, reviewing several iterations of draft specifications, and finally preparing those for review and publication. The entire industry should be grateful. We sure are.

And last but by no means least, a colossal 'thank you' goes to our families. Taking on an extra curricular activity on top of an already demanding job requires the love and understanding from one's family, in no small quantities. Spending hours pounding away on the keyboard, well into the wee hours of the morning, can only be done at the expense of other duties and responsibilities. Thank you for your unconditional support. From now on, we will take our turns again with mowing the lawn or starting the long-postponed painting project.

All these people have generously helped this project culminate into the book you now hold in your hand. Any remaining errors are of course strictly our own.

Michael and Musa

About the Authors

Like any project of a certain size and scope, the end deliverable is the fruit of the labor of many team members. This project was managed by two lead authors who wrote most chapters of the book, and co-ordinated the inputs from a team of contributing authors.

MICHAEL BRENNER is a Consulting Member of Technical Staff within the office of the CTO of Alcatel-Lucent's Applications division of the Carrier Business Group, with the role of Chief Architect for Converged Applications/Services Standards. Michael is the Alcatel-Lucent OMA delegation technical co-ordinator, a lead contributor in the OMA Architecture Working Group and a contributor in other OMA groups. In the past, Michael led software development and architecture teams in Lucent Technologies in his position as a Director with the company, in particular in the areas of Network and Service Management, Data Center Architecture, Mobile User Provisioning and Device Client Architecture. Prior to joining AT&T Bell Laboratories in 1989, Michael had a successful R&D career in the medical imaging industry, developing real-time data acquisition and processing software, as well as picture archiving and communication systems for nuclear cameras and Magnetic Resonance Imaging (MRI) systems. Michael has authored numerous technical journal and conference papers, has several pending patents applications and has obtained industry awards for innovative projects. In 2007, Michael has been awarded the OMA 'Contributor and Achievement Award' for his outstanding efforts and contributions to OMA's technical working groups. Michael holds an M.Sc degree in Computer Science from the Polytechnic University of Bucharest, Romania.

MUSA UNMEHOPA is a Distinguished Member of Technical Staff within the office of the CTO of Alcatel-Lucent's Applications division of the Carrier Business Group, where he serves as senior consultant for service delivery architectures and standards. His career in communications technology spans over a decade, at Lucent Technologies Bell Laboratories, and now Alcatel-Lucent. Musa has held several leadership positions in various standards organizations (3GPP, ETSI, Parlay, OMA), and currently serves in his second term as the chairman of the OMA Architecture Working Group. In the past, Musa also held the vice-chair position in the OMA Mobile Web Services Working Group, and prior to that the vice-chair position of 3GPP CT5. Musa is a co-author of the technical book 'Parlay/OSA: From Standards to Reality', also published by Wiley & Sons. In addition, Musa has authored numerous journal and conference papers, holds one patent and has several patents pending in the area of service delivery and service mediation. Musa holds an M.Sc degree in Computer Science from the Technical University of Twente in the Netherlands.

The ground covered in the book is so vast it's almost daunting. To do justice to the versatility of topics and the broad range of technologies covered, a number of subject matter experts have contributed specific sections or chapters to the book. In many cases, they have been intimately involved with the creation of the specifications they describe. Their biographies are included here in alphabetical order.

MILLER ABEL, author of Chapter 18, is a Standards Architect in Microsoft's Mobile Communications Business unit. He has represented Microsoft in the Open Mobile Alliance Device Management

Working Group since OMA's formation in 2002. Mr Abel brings 30 years of software design experience to his role in guiding the development of mobile device standards and their implementation in Microsoft products.

DIEGO ANZA, author of Chapter 22, is currently Senior Innovation Manager in Orange. Diego joined the Orange – France Telecom Group in 2000 where he has taken different positions based in France and Spain. Over the last few years Diego has been a very active contributor in international organizations such as the GSM Association and the Open Mobile Alliance where he has taken visible roles as vice-chair then chairman of the OMA Requirements Working Group and as Orange Head of Delegation. Diego convened several ad hoc working groups developing requirements specifications, including the "OMA Global Permissions Management" requirements. Prior to joining the Orange – France Telecom Group, Diego worked for Nortel (France) and for Schlumberger (US). Diego graduated with honors from the Ecole Supérieure d'Electricité (Paris, France) and from the Universidad Politécnica de Madrid (Madrid, Spain) and holds Master of Science degrees in Electrical Engineering from both schools.

GILBERT BUTY, author of Chapter 4, works for Alcatel-Lucent, and belongs to the Alcatel Group since more than 15 years. He worked first on EEC research projects (DIMPE – multi-media environment in the field of the press, TELEMED – applications of tele-diagnosis and tele-learning in the medical field, OSIRIS – interconnection of freight offers). After a two-year period at the European Commission in Brussels, where he was in charge of the follow-up of research projects within the DG XIII Telematics program, Gilbert came back in Alcatel as Standard manager within the Corporate Standardization Department in Alcatel HQ. Since then, Gilbert has been deeply involved in interoperability and certification related matters. He set-up the Alcatel Task Force on the Terminal Directive (R&TTE) and was a Member of the French Delegation to the European Commission in charge of the implementation of the R&TTE Directive in France. He participated in the launch of the Global Certification Forum back in 1999 and was the chairman of this Forum in 2002–2003. Since 2004, Gilbert is chairing the Interoperability group within OMA, in charge of ensuring the quality and interoperability of specifications and resulting implementations.

JUAN CAMBEIRO, author of Chapter 5, is a Telecommunications Engineer by the University of Vigo (Spain) and specializes in computing engineering and has been working in the Telecom industry ever since. After working in companies like Alcatel, Telefónica R&D and Ericsson, he was hired again by Telefónica as architect for the development of a Global Services Architecture and Infrastructure for the Telefónica Group, as well as for the local operator in Spain. In the meantime and during the last three years, he's been a Telefónica delegate in the Open Mobile Alliance in architecture and requirements related activities, where he contributed with the experiences learned in such job.

BETSY COVELL, author of Chapter 17, is a Distinguished Member of Technical Staff at Alcatel-Lucent. Betsy has over 12 years experience in wireless telephony standards development. She has been active in developing standards for many technologies, including TIA-41, WIN, IMT-2000, LMSD and MMD. She has been a leader in the wireless industry, holding vice-chair positions in TIA TR-45.2 and OMA MCC WG. She has also held chair positions in the ITU-T SG11 Joint Rapporteur's Group 4, 3GPP2 TSG-N, and is currently chair of 3GPP2 TSG-X.

MICHEL L. F. GRECH, co-author of Chapter 14, is an analyst in the Network Performance and Economic Analysis division of Bell Laboratories at Alcatel-Lucent, where his primary responsibility is working on business models for service providers and enterprises, examining their specific business and network issues and recommending solutions that meet their business objectives. Prior to Bell Labs, Mr Grech was responsible for a team of delegates in Alcatel-Lucent, driving service-related standards issues in several international organizations such as the Open Mobile Alliance (OMA) and the 3rd Generation Partnership programme (3GPP). Mr Grech holds a Bachelor of Science degree in Electronic Engineering from the University of Essex in Colchester, England, a Master of Science degree in Telecommunications Technology from Aston University in Birmingham, England and a Masters of Business Administration degree from London Business School, London, England. Mr Grech is also a member of The Institution of Engineering and Technology (IET), a Chartered Engineer in the United Kingdom's Engineering Council and has co-authored several patents/patents pending and technical papers in the field of telecommunications services and applications.

KEVIN HOLLEY, author of Chapter 27.3, is Manager of Application Standards for Telefonica O2 Europe, based in Ipswich, UK. He is responsible for Telefonica O2 Europe's engagement in standardization activities in the Open Mobile Alliance Ltd, and also works towards the development of 3GPP standards. Mr Holley has acted in the capacity of vice chair of the Technical Plenary of the Open Mobile Alliance since November 2006. Prior to that he was chair of the Requirements Group of the Open Mobile Alliance from 2002 to 2006. He was vice chair of 3GPP TSG-T from 1999 to 2005. Mr Holley has been with O2 since before it was demerged from BT in 2001. He has been working with mobile applications since 1985 and has participated in mobile standardization since 1988. He was one of the original designers of the GSM SMS Standard. Mr Holley holds a Bachelor of Science degree in Physics.

STÉPHANE H. MAES, author of Chapter 7, is Chief Architect and CTO at Oracle, Mobile, Voice and Communications, in charge of product architecture for SDP (Service Delivery Platforms) and end-to-end OSS/BSS/SDP integration, as well as technical strategy for SDP and end-to-end OSS/BSS/SDP vision targeting telecommunications service providers, as well as enterprise markets. At Oracle since 2002, Dr Maes has also been driving Oracle-wide standard activities related to mobility, voice and communications. In the past, Dr Maes has been responsible for architecture, technical strategy and evangelization successively for Oracle AS wireless, including Application server and E-Business Suite mobile development tools, OCS mobile and voice components, Oracle Light and Telco middleware, Oracle Collaboration Suite (OCS), Real Time Collaboration and Communications (OCS), and OCS 11g. Dr Maes is widely credited for the evangelization of the use of IT technology concepts in Telco's with work significant impact on industry wide standardization of the service layer (e.g. OSE, Parlay, 3GPP/2), Policy enforcement (e.g. OSE PE, PEEM), SOA for Telco's, OSS/BSS/SDP integration, Parlay/IMS/OSE integration, open standard based mobile e-mail etc. His work led to the widely adopted OSE (Open Mobile Alliance Service Environment) now endorsed by OMA, Parlay, 3GPP, 3GPP2, ETSI, TISPAN, ITU, TMF and more. Before Oracle, Stéphane was at IBM, T.J. Watson Research Center where he was driving R&D efforts in speech recognition and multi-channel, multimodal, multi-device and conversational middleware and tools. Prior to that, he had pursued similar topics as a Member of Technical Staff at AT&T Bell Laboratories in Murray Hill, NJ. Stéphane holds Bachelor, Master and PhD degrees simultaneously in Electrical Engineering and Physics from the UCL, Louvain, Belgium. He completed his PhD jointly at CAIP (Center For Computer Aids To Industrial Productivity), Rutgers University, NJ. He also successfully graduated from the International Space University. His academic work was sponsored by several grants from the European Union (Erasmus), the European Space Agency (ESA), DARPA and the prestigious National Funds for Scientific Research (FNRS). While at IBM, he also successfully completed the IBM MBA program.

Dr ANETT SCHÜLKE, author of Chapter 15, is Chief Researcher at NEC European Network Laboratories, Germany. She received her PhD in Physics in 1995 from Dresden University of Technology. From 1996 to 1998 she was awarded a DAAD fellowship for the LBNL, California/USA and worked until 1999 as a Postdoctoral Fellow. In July 2000 she joined NEC Network

Laboratories where her focus was on service creation and delivery technologies, IP Multimedia Subsystem (IMS) and content service management in telecom and data networking research, design and development. Anett has published in several international journals and conferences, presented tutorials on IMS and SDP at research and marketing events, and has been involved in TPC for IEEE conferences. She represents NEC in OMA standardization and is an active contributor in various OMA groups. From 2005–2007, she was elected as vice chair of the OMA PoC Working Group.

BRYAN SULLIVAN, author of Chapter 21, has been involved in the telephony and wireless data services for 25 years. Coming from a background in voice/data PBX, ISDN, ATM, and fixed wireless system development, Bryan has spent the last 12 years in the mobile data industry. Initially as a lead member of the AT&T Wireless team that launched the first mobile browser service in the USA (AT&T PocketNet), Bryan has since been a lead network and services architect for the WAP and Push based services of AT&T Wireless, Cingular Wireless, and now the new AT&T. Representing these companies in the WAP Forum and Open Mobile Alliance since 2000, Bryan is currently the chair of the OMA Content Delivery Working Group.

KUMAR VEMURI, co-author of Chapter 14, has worked on the research, architecture, systems analysis & engineering, design, and prototyping aspects of several projects dealing with new and exciting telecommunications and Internet technologies. Kumar has been an employee at Lucent Technologies Bell Labs Innovations (now Alcatel-Lucent) for over a decade, most recently in the CTO organization of the IMS Business Division. He has been actively involved as a technical lead in the design of several new systems, services, applications, and customer deployments, has authored and co-authored several papers, standards contributions, and a technical book, and holds two patents with several others pending with the US and EU PTO's. A winner of the Bell Labs President's Gold Award and twice recipient of the Core Bell Labs Teamwork Award while at Lucent, Kumar holds a BE degree in Computer Engineering, an MS in Computer Science, and is currently pursuing an MBA at the MIT Sloan School of Management.

INDAKA N. WEERASEKERA, author of Chapters 16 and 19, is a Systems Consultant for Alcatel-Lucent. Indaka originally joined Lucent Technologies in 1998 and as a full time delegate to the Open Mobile Alliance, he has previously held a vice-chair position of the OMA Requirements Working Group as well as a number of rapporteurships for OMA requirements documents. Indaka has been working in the telecommunications industry since 1991 and has been involved in various projects including the product development of GSM mobile handsets.

WAYNE ZEUCH, author of Chapter 24, is a Distinguished Member of Technical Staff in the Chief Technology Office of Alcatel-Lucent's Convergence Business Group in Murray Hill, New Jersey. Joining AT&T in 1985, he worked for Bell Laboratories in both the United States and international switching systems engineering organizations and the standards management organizations of both AT&T and Lucent Technologies. Wayne has led and contributed to telecommunications standardization since 1987 with ATIS Standards Committee T1 in the United States (serving most recently as T1 vice chairman from 2000–2004) and with the International Telecommunication Union (ITU) in Geneva (serving as Working Party Vice Chairman for Intelligent Network Applications and Protocols from 1997–2004). For the past five years, he has served on the Board of Directors of The Parlay Group (Application Interface and Web Services standards) and is currently Rapporteur for Standards Coordination in CITEL PCC.I (Organization of American States). Wayne holds a Bachelor of Science degree in Physics from the Illinois Institute of Technology, a Master of Science degree in Nuclear Science from The University of Michigan, and an MBA in Marketing and Finance from the University of Chicago.

List of Figures

2.1	Vertical silos	8
2.2	Layered architectures	10
2.3	Horizontal services architecture	14
2.4	The OMA Service Environment (OSE)	17
3.1	OMA organizational structure	24
3.2	Browser and Content Working Group (BAC WG) re-structuring	29
3.3	OMA documentation involved in defining tests	38
3.4	OMA documentation involved in the TestFests	39
5.1	End user perceives operators as the only responsible party for the services portfolio	49
5.2	Vertical design ('silos') in a service architecture	50
5.3	Will the OMA define interfaces toward back-end systems?	54
6.1	Enterprise user perceives the enterprise as the main responsible party for the services portfolio	58
7.1	Layers introduced in the OSE, not considering policy enforcement	64
7.2	Layers introduced in the OSE, including policy enforcement	65
7.3	Parameter P and I0+P mapped on the OSE. Reproduced by Permission of the Open Mobile Alliance Ltd.	66
7.4	Generalization of the OSE as an SOA-based environment	67
7.5	An example of a graph that describes the topology of a policy (composed of multiple policy rules)	70
7.6	Example of policy expressed by assembling multiple policy expression languages	72
7.7	Concept and deployment architecture of a service gateway	74
7.8	High-level TISPAN NGN architecture. © European Telecommunications Standards Institute 2006. Further use, modification, redistribution is strictly prohibited. ETSI standards are available from http://pda.etsi.org/pda/	75
8.1	IETF PEP-PDP model	81
8.2	Typical use case for explicit request to PEEM. Reproduced by Permission of the Open Mobile Alliance Ltd.	83
8.3	Typical use case for intercepted request by PEEM. Reproduced by Permission of the Open Mobile Alliance Ltd.	85
8.4	PEEM enabler in the OSE architecture – initial view	90
8.5	PEEM logical architecture. Reproduced by Permission of the Open Mobile Alliance Ltd.	91
8.6	A graph that describes the topology of a policy. Reproduced by Permission of the Open Mobile Alliance Ltd.	92

8.7   Logical flows for request via the PEM-1 interface   93
8.8   Logical flows for request via the Proxy interface. Reproduced by Permission of the
        Open Mobile Alliance Ltd.   94
8.9   Logical flows for request via the PEM-2 interface. Reproduced by Permission of
        the Open Mobile Alliance Ltd.   94
8.10   PEEM callable usage pattern. Reproduced by Permission of the Open Mobile
        Alliance Ltd.   100
8.11   PEEM architecture in callable usage pattern. Reproduced by Permission of the
        Open Mobile Alliance Ltd.   101
8.12   PEEM proxy usage pattern. Reproduced by Permission of the Open Mobile Alliance
        Ltd.   101
8.13   PEEM architecture in proxy usage pattern. Reproduced by Permission of the Open
        Mobile Alliance Ltd.   102
8.14   PEEM enabler in the OSE architecture – updated view   103
8.15   A simplified graph that describes the topology of a policy that involves only eval-
        uation. Reproduced by Permission of the Open Mobile Alliance Ltd.   104
8.16   A de-composition with separate policy evaluation/enforcement and policy man-
        agement components. Reproduced by Permission of the Open Mobile Alliance
        Ltd.   110
8.17   A further de-composition with separate policy evaluation and policy enforcement
        components. Reproduced by Permission of the Open Mobile Alliance Ltd. 110
8.18   A de-composition closely matching a pure policy decision point model. Reproduced
        by Permission of the Open Mobile Alliance Ltd.   111

9.1   IMS interfaces in the context of OSE   119
9.2   OSE and 3GPP/3GPP2 IMS services   120
9.3   Network capabilities provided by the IMS Core or another SIP/IP Core   121

10.1   The Parlay Architecture   127
10.2   The Parlay Gateway   127
10.3   Parlay X Web Service deployment options   128
10.4   Parlay as a network resource   129
10.5   Parlay X Web Service as the enabler   130
10.6   Parlay Service Capability Feature as the enabler   131
10.7   Hybrid Parlay and OMA solution   132

11.1   The Web Services triangle   136
11.2   The Web Services platform architecture   138
11.3   Direct and Indirect Architecture Model   141
11.4   The OWSER Web Services Stack   141
11.5   The OWSER Web Services Stack. Prop, proprietary specification   142
11.6   An Identity Management model in a Web Services environment   147
11.7   OWSER and the OSE   153

12.1   Deploying a new application in the Service Provider Environment   162
12.2   OSPE enabler in the OSE architecture   167
12.3   OSPE enabler architecture. Reproduced by Permission of the Open Mobile Alliance
        Ltd.   168
12.4   Deployed component modification. Reproduced by Permission of the Open Mobile
        Alliance Ltd.   170

12.5	Turning on Service Level Tracing (SLT). Reproduced by Permission of the Open Mobile Alliance Ltd.	171
12.6	Marking a component and starting an SLT session	172
13.1	Authentication using authentication proxy. Reproduced by Permission of the Open Mobile Alliance Ltd.	181
13.2	Security Common Functions in the OSE architecture	183
13.3	Security Common Functions in the OSE architecture – a variation	184
13.4	SEC-CF architecture for enablers in either home or visited network. Reproduced by Permission of the Open Mobile Alliance Ltd.	185
13.5	SECA initiated authentication via OSG. Reproduced by Permission of the Open Mobile Alliance Ltd.	187
14.1	The three-layer brick model. Reproduced by Permission of the Open Mobile Alliance Ltd.	201
14.2	XCAP usage for manipulating presence document contents. ESC, Event State Compositor; PUA, Presence User Agent	202
14.3	3GPP reference architecture to support a Presence service in an IMS environment. 3GPP(tm) TSs and TRs are the property of ARIB, ATIS, ETSI, CCSA, TTA and TTC who jointly own the copyright in them. They are subject to modifications and are therefore provided to you "as is" for information purposes only. Further use is strictly prohibited	203
14.4	The Presence, XDM, and IMPS enablers in the OSE architecture	206
14.5	OMA IMPS architecture. Reproduced by Permission of the Open Mobile Alliance Ltd.	206
14.6	OMA Presence architecture. Reproduced by Permission of the Open Mobile Alliance Ltd.	208
14.7	OMA XDM Architecture. Reproduced by Permission of the Open Mobile Alliance Ltd.	210
14.8	OMA Presence and XDM in a 3GPP/3GPP2 environment	213
15.1	Generic view of the Push-to-talk over Cellular enabler and related supporting enablers in the OSE representation	220
15.2	Logical high-level Push-to-talk over Cellular V1.0 architecture illustrating relationship to supporting enablers in the OSE view	221
15.3	Detailed Push-to-talk over Cellular V1.0 architecture. Reproduced by Permission of the Open Mobile Alliance Ltd.	222
15.4	PoC server roles of participating and controlling PoC functions illustrated in different networks. Reproduced by Permission of the Open Mobile Alliance Ltd.	223
15.5	Illustration of the pre-established and on-demand session models	224
15.6	PoC session establishment with confirmed indication. Reproduced by Permission of the Open Mobile Alliance Ltd.	225
15.7	Logical high-level Push-to-talk over Cellular V2.0 architecture with relation to supporting enablers in the OSE view	228
15.8	Detailed Push-to-talk over Cellular V2.0 architecture. Reproduced by Permission of the Open Mobile Alliance Ltd.	229
16.1	E-mail client/server options	238
16.2	MMS architecture elements	241
16.3	Simplified Internet messaging model	243

16.4   OMA MEM logical architecture representation. Reproduced by Permission of the
        Open Mobile Alliance Ltd.   244
16.5   OMA DS realization of OMA MEM   246
16.6   LEMONADE realization of OMA MEM   250

17.1   Mobile commerce reference model. Reproduced by Permission of the Open Mobile
        Alliance Ltd.   254
17.2   Charging enabler in OSE   256
17.3   Charging enabler functional architecture. Reproduced by Permission of the Open
        Mobile Alliance Ltd.   257
17.4   Offline charging flows in the event-based charging model. Reproduced by Permis-
        sion of the Open Mobile Alliance Ltd.   259
17.5   Offline charging flows in the session-based charging model. Reproduced by Per-
        mission of the Open Mobile Alliance Ltd.   259
17.6   Online charging flows in the event-based charging model. Reproduced by Permis-
        sion of the Open Mobile Alliance Ltd.   260
17.7   Online charging flows in the session-based charging model. Reproduced by Per-
        mission of the Open Mobile Alliance Ltd.   261
17.8   Charging messages hierarchy for offline charging   262
17.9   Charging messages hierarchy for online charging. Reproduced by Permission of
        the Open Mobile Alliance Ltd.   263
17.10   Charging interfaces protocol layers. Reproduced by Permission of the Open Mobile
        Alliance Ltd.   264

18.1   Device management in the OMA service environment   272
18.2   Mobile device management generic system elements   273
18.3   OMA DM architecture   275

19.1   OMA DRM logical model   292
19.2   OMA DRM logical architecture   296
19.3   OMA DRM protection element   296

20.1   BCAST logical architecture (reference points). Reproduced by Permission of the
        Open Mobile Alliance Ltd.   307
20.2   Service guide functional architecture   309
20.3   File distribution functional architecture   311
20.4   Stream distribution functional architecture   312
20.5   Service protection functional architecture   314
20.6   Content protection functional architecture   315
20.7   Service interaction functional architecture   316
20.8   Service provisioning functional architecture   317
20.9   Terminal provisioning functional architecture   317
20.10   Notification functional architecture   318

21.1   Dynamic content delivery in a ubiquitous service environment   324
21.2   Dynamic content delivery in the OMA service environment   326
21.3   DCD architecture. Reproduced by Permission of the Open Mobile Alliance Ltd.   327
21.4   Example DCD deployment in combined broadcast and 2.5G/3G environments   329
21.5   Example DCD-enabled service data flow   330

22.1   Global Permissions Management actor chain. Reproduced by Permission of the
        Open Mobile Alliance Ltd.   340

22.2   Typical GPM use case   341
22.3   GPM enabler in the OSE architecture   344
22.4   GPM logical architecture. Reproduced by Permission of the Open Mobile Alliance
        Ltd.   345
22.5   Typical GPM permissions checking flow   346
22.6   Permissions Rule management flow   347

23.1   Categorization-based content screening actor chain   355
23.2   CBCS enabler in the OSE   357
23.3   CBCS enabler logical architecture. Reproduced by Permission of the Open Mobile
        Alliance Ltd.   358
23.4   Typical CBCS flow in proxy usage pattern   362
23.5   Typical CBCS flow in callable usage pattern   363

24.1   Relations among session entities. Reproduced by Permission of the Open Mobile
        Alliance Ltd.   371
24.2   Game services enabler architecture. Reproduced by Permission of the Open Mobile
        Alliance Ltd.   372
24.3   Game services within a Service Provider domain. Reproduced by Permission of the
        Open Mobile Alliance Ltd.   372
24.4   Example of game services context model   373
24.5   Domain model relationships for game services CSI 1.0. Reproduced by Permission
        of the Open Mobile Alliance Ltd.   373
24.6   Example flows for real-time multiplayer gaming. Reproduced by Permission of the
        Open Mobile Alliance Ltd.   378
24.7   Game services context model supporting future features. Reproduced by Permission
        of the Open Mobile Alliance Ltd.   378

25.1   Control Plane Location in GSM/UMTS networks   384
25.2   Simplified Control Plane Location in GSM and CDMA networks   385
25.3   Control Plane Location and User Plane Location compared   386
25.4   Basic SUPL Architecture   389
25.5   Operation modes for the SLC and SPC   390
25.6   Network-Initiated Location Request   391
25.7   Completed SUPL 1.0 Architecture   392
25.8   Network-Initiated Location in SUPL V2.0   393
25.9   Internal Location Protocol – ILP   394
25.10   SUPL 2.0 Architecture   394
25.11   OMA Location sequence flow   399

26.1   Mobile Application Environment Proxy Architecture   402
26.2   Multimodal, Multidevice Enabler Architecture   408

27.1   Silo messaging: complex deployment and less-than-ideal user experience   419
27.2   Converged messaging: reduced complexity and improved user experience   420
27.3   Converged messaging: interworking with legacy messaging systems   420
27.4   Basic model for mobile advertisement delivery   426

28.1   The OMA Service Environment (OSE)   431
28.2   The OMA Service Environment (OSE) – recipe for an SDE?   432

Part I

Background and Introduction

This is a book about service enablers for next generation applications, a burgeoning space. As voice becomes commoditized and competition among service providers intensifies, applications become increasingly important. This first part will set the stage for the remainder of the book. We will spend a great deal explaining the problem of vertically integrated service silos and on a horizontal service architecture designed to overcome these problems. For some readers these may already be household concepts, but the power of the principles introduced is easy to underestimate, yet central to the approach taken by the Open Mobile Alliance. It is of the essence that the higher goal is swimming into view, before proceeding with a deeper coverage of a selection of individual service enablers.

Chapter 1 provides a gentle introduction into the subject matter of the book. In Chapter 2 we will then paint a detailed picture of the problem space, which goes by the name of silo syndrome, and will drive home the principles that underpin the solution. Chapter 3 is dedicated to the organization that has taken on the challenges introduced in the previous chapter. The Open Mobile Alliance will be described in terms of how the organization came into existence, how it is structured and does its work, and how it relates to other initiatives in the industry. The Interoperability TestFests, a key aspect of OMA, will be detailed in Chapter 4. Chapters 5 and 6 take the viewpoint of the Service Provider. What keeps them tossing and turning at night, what are their big ticket-line items? What are the things that not only prepare them for the future, but make sure they have one? The perspective of the Network Operator as well as that of the Enterprise is offered for good balance.

The Open Mobile Alliance   M. Brenner and M. Unmehopa
© 2008 Alcatel-Lucent. All Rights Reserved

1

Introduction

The advent of Third Generation (3G) networks has long been heralded, and the first commercial deployments are being rolled out today. While the various access technologies and the core network evolution are fascinating topics (and the subject of many good books), it is the innovative new value added services that will drive traffic across these 3G networks and hence generate the revenue for service providers. This book is about those services, or rather what building blocks they are made out of.

To date, there is little debate that mobile communication has become a commodity. Market research demonstrates this trend through empirical studies and market assessments, but you may have arrived at the same conclusion simply by looking around you and at your own communication behavior. Penetration of mobile subscriptions is in the double digit percentage range in most regions in the world, with some of the more developed countries showing penetration figures that exceed 100%. Opportunities for revenue growth through increased mobile subscriber numbers are thus greatly diminished, as there are only so many phones that can be sold in any given population. There are generally two ways to combat this stagnating growth condition. One is to grow the subscriber base by luring customers away from the competition. However, a characteristic of commodity goods is that the price margins are very slim. Therefore, another differentiator has to be identified to act as the carrot. The second approach is to generate more revenue out of the existing customer base, that is, increase the Average Revenue Per User (ARPU). There appears to be a single solution that addresses both approaches. Both subscriber retention and attraction, as well as ARPU upsurge, are sought through the introduction of premium services. These premium services are defined as services providing a value add on top of the voice commodity, for which the service provider may collect premium charges. The typical example of a premium service is the so-called killer service – one that appeals to a massive number of users. Killer services are far from abundant, but each of them will individually generate substantial revenue because of volume alone.

1.1 Service Enablers

So, is talking about increased revenue through services all about killer services? Yes and no. Killer services are few and far between. It is difficult, if not impossible, to predict which services have significant revenue potential, and thus which services will justify the large research and development investment that is required. Let us look at the characteristics of killer services instead. From current killer services, we see that they are both highly standardized as well as specified in a vertical manner. By vertical we mean that service component architecture and integration is performed per service. Supporting functions like operations and management, charging, and

The Open Mobile Alliance   M. Brenner and M. Unmehopa
© 2008 Alcatel-Lucent. All Rights Reserved

security are specifically designed and customized to facilitate smooth operation of the service. All performance and cost issues are methodically driven out of the service stack. As a result, these highly optimized services may handle a whopping million transactions an hour, barely breaking a sweat. However, and here we come to the point of all this, all these huge efforts and investments in vertical integration may have turned the service into a well-oiled moneymaker, and as a result there is surprisingly little ability for re-use between services. That is, for the next killer service, re-use of supporting functions may be hampered by the fact that the previous optimization created short-cuts that may not be adequate for the new use case. Hence, a certain amount of re-development and mainly testing will be needed, leading to vertical integration all over again. And as we've seen, what the next killer service will be is, like so much else, anybody's guess.

A vertical service, by its very nature requiring close coupling throughout the vertical service stack, is traditionally specified by a single standards body or industry forum. Evidently, this requires re-invention of the proverbial wheel and results in a disturbing lack of interoperability between services. Combined with the big wild card of what the next killer service will be, this has been cause for great concern and frustration among service providers and network operators. Consequently, the service standards world has witnessed a paradigm shift away from standardizing services toward standardizing service components. The idea being that one can aggregate, and mix and match such service components in order to build differentiated, value added services. Such components are referred to as 'Service Enablers'. There is less emphasis on the arcane quest for the next killer service. Rather, an environment is created that allows the proliferation of niche services, targeted at specific subscriber segments and specialized user groups. A large number of them are expected, collectively generating considerable revenue through economies of scale. The service environment, realized through generalized standard service components, facilitates shorter development cycles, lower integration efforts, and hence shorter time-to-market. New services developed in such a service environment have significantly lower up-front costs and the ability to bring the application online relatively quickly. So, to come back to the question whether talking about increased revenue through services is all about killer services, the answer is that it is all about service enablers in a horizontal services environment. And of course, such a horizontal service environment may also nurture the next killer service.

1.2   The Open Mobile Alliance (OMA)

This development, from services to service enablers, has enthused the service standards community to move away from vertical specification organizations. Smaller scale horizontal standardization efforts have seen the light of day, attempting to create standardized tool kits for service creation. The majority of these, however, have been very much targeted to a specific application area. Examples include the Intelligent Networking/Customized Applications for Mobile Network Enhanced Logic (IN/CAMEL) concepts for voice centric telephony, the Wireless Application Protocol (WAP) Forum for mobile-specific browsers, and Parlay/OSA for network operator capabilities. Enter the Open Mobile Alliance (OMA), which takes on a much broader perspective.

The OMA is the leading industry forum for developing market-driven, interoperable mobile service enablers to facilitate global user adoption of mobile multimedia services. Since its formation in 2002, OMA has made significant progress in delivering several enablers in areas such as Push-to-talk-over-Cellular, Presence, Location, and others, with plans to deliver much more in the years to come. As an industry organization that boasts well over 400 geographically dispersed member companies of various sizes, representing the entire industry value chain, giant strides are being made into the development of a service environment that will allow deployment of multi-vendor platforms and services while avoiding costly customized integration with the operator's network.

1.3   Service Enablers in OMA

So why a book on OMA service enablers, if you can go to the OMA public website and access the approved enabler specifications yourself? Well, there is a reason for that. Standards activities in the applications arena have traditionally been scattered around single technologies or single enablers. The OMA has brought these disparate and fragmented initiatives together under a single umbrella. Yet, the OMA itself is now working on over a hundred work items, resulting in as much as 70 enablers (a number that continues to rise), in a large number of technical working groups that mostly operate in parallel. And these numbers are growing. This book will use the horizontal service architecture developed within the OMA, the OMA Service Environment (OSE), as a framework to introduce and link together many of the service enablers published or still being developed by the OMA.

Within the OMA, the Architecture Working Group (ARC WG) has defined a horizontal services architecture in which the OMA service enablers can be developed and deployed in a consistent and interoperable manner. This architecture is termed the *OMA Service Environment*, or OSE. The book will introduce the OSE, outline the architectural principles underpinning it, discuss its key merits, and explain how it addresses the challenges that the OMA faces in the industry. The OSE will then serve as a framework to introduce and discuss a range of service enablers that have been specified by the OMA or are currently under development. The OSE will be the glue that ties these topics together, both from an architecture perspective, as well as for the narrative in the book. As such, the book will provide a unique overview of the industry landscape for service enablers for Next Generation Applications.

2

The Silo Syndrome and its Solution

The exponential growth and proliferation of attractive, data-rich content and applications is quite central to the viability of the 3G business case. Standardization focus in this area has settled on service enablers, with the promise that these can be mixed and matched, and cleverly bundled to offer yet-to-be imagined, compelling and innovative services to end-users. Anything less would generate glazed looks and stifled yawns. But why would anyone want to break services up into components, the service enablers, only to mix and match them and aggregate them again into such a cleverly bundled, blended service? In the previous chapter, we succinctly introduced the concept of service enablers as an approach to overcome the drawbacks of the vertical integration of services specifications and their implementations. But that was a mere preamble, and did not go much farther than the 'elevator pitch' level. This chapter will deepen those considerations by expanding on the so-called silo syndrome. Service enablers are brought to the fore as a core services function exposing a defined interface.

This will bring us only halfway through our story, since once we have all these service enablers at our disposal as components or building blocks, we need a model that allows us to compose these service enablers into revenue-generating applications that can be offered to end-users. Within the Open Mobile Alliance (OMA), the OMA Service Environment (OSE) is that model [OSE AD]. It provides a horizontal architecture (a term detailed later in this chapter) for the deployment of service enablers. The draw of such a horizontal service environment that allows service providers to nimbly roll out innovative applications that capture the eye and, of course, the spending of end-users is sure enough universally alluring. The ability to quickly and efficiently create, deploy, and deliver services, be they developed in-house or offered by third-party content vendors, will increasingly be a competitive differentiator for service providers. Finding an architecture model that solves this puzzle has been a relentless pursuit.

In what follows, a more detailed analysis of the problems of vertical integration will be presented, as well as how this challenge can be addressed by the introduction of a horizontal services architecture. At the end of this chapter the reader will have a better appreciation for the problems that the industry faces and the unique value that the OMA brings to the burgeoning space of next generation applications and service enablers.

2.1 Vertical Integration

This section will explain the problem of vertical integration. The problem also goes by several figurative names, such as the silo syndrome or stovepipe architecture. Metaphors aside, a vertically integrated system is a legacy system that is constructed of inter-related elements that are

The Open Mobile Alliance   M. Brenner and M. Unmehopa
© 2008 Alcatel-Lucent. All Rights Reserved

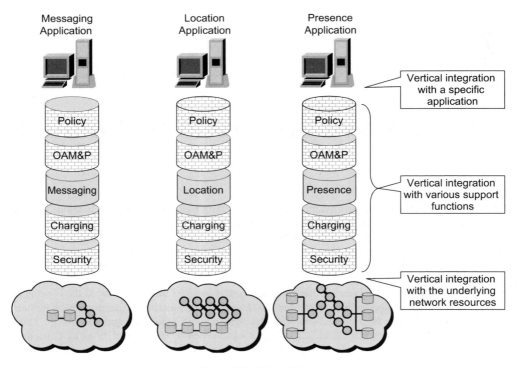

Figure 2.1   Vertical silos

tightly coupled together. The silo represents a finely tuned, vertically integrated stack of specialized resources running on a dedicated set of servers. The integrated elements often make assumptions about or are dependent on the knowledge of the other elements within the silo. Such assumptions, on issues like data formats, memory usage, security model, or functional behavior, allow for extensive optimizations that would otherwise not be possible.

Vertically integrated systems often yield dedicated, highly optimized, extremely efficient, high-performance solutions. As such, vertical systems are abundant and widely deployed in the industry. The architecture of a set of more-or-less independent silos, each responsible for a distinct service or application, is fairly commonplace in the industry. This is depicted in Figure 2.1.

Despite the obvious benefits, and the success of this architecture, there are several problems arising from this approach, the more important of which are listed below:

- As a result of the tight coupling, individual elements cannot be differentiated, upgraded, or replaced. The silo must be maintained until it can be entirely replaced by a new system. And if it takes the industry a long time to introduce and roll out a new system, it takes us even longer to phase it out.
- The silo system isolates itself, its function, its policies, and its data repository from other systems that might have taken advantage of it. Therefore, the effort that went into designing these elements cannot be re-used by other systems, and similar elements are repeatedly rebuilt, integrated, and independently maintained. This jacks up the overall cost of deploying new services, since the design and build stages as well as the integration efforts need to be repeated time and again.
- Optimization and fine tuning (e.g. in terms of assembly code optimizations, embedded software, or dedicated hardware) of the service performance is carried out within the silo. Again, these

efforts are to be repeated across each silo, and on top of that make the elements even more isolated and less suitable for re-use.

- Operational Expenditures (OPEX) are higher than they need to be. For example, each distinct silo more often than not requires specialized operations skills. Costly assets like software licenses or data back-ups are maintained per silo.
- Capital Expenditures (CAPEX) are higher than they need to be. For reasons of reliability (e.g. providing excess capacity for occasional peak loads) or engineering for growth, individual silos may be running idle or at lower utilization a large chunk of the time, without the possibility of sharing excess capacity with other silos.

Reducing CAPEX and OPEX is of course always a good idea, and a good reason to abandon the silo syndrome. But there is another sound reason for change. Service providers would like to respond more rapidly to changing business demands, and they require their deployed systems to be agile. The duplication of technology is costly and prevents service providers from easily bundling or combining services into new offerings. Rolling out attractive services more rapidly in order to attract and retain customers, calls for a flexible architecture. Rolling out a steady stream of cool applications becomes a must for service providers. If they don't, others well might, causing increased subscriber churn. An architectural approach needs to be identified to overcome the rigidity and brittleness introduced by silo systems.

Before we move on to the next section that introduces the concept of re-usable service enablers as a means to overcome the silo syndrome, let's look at why vertical architectures seemed to make so much sense at that time, and why some architects still find it difficult to abandon this design practice and persist on applying it.

Designing services silos is like re-inventing the wheel. You simply repeat a process you have successfully executed before. And there is a good reason why re-inventing the wheel is such a popular approach. Not only has the wheel been invented before, chances are it has been re-invented before as well. This is why software and design patterns are popular. An approach that has been tried and tested has a high likelihood for success when applied to the same or a similar problem space. So, if the similar problem space is the only problem space you are working with, then please by all means, re-invent the wheel. Or more formally, apply a suitable design pattern to your bounded and well-defined vertical problem space.

There is also the consideration that horizontal solutions do not necessarily yield local benefits. Or in other words, there likely have to be local penalties to obtain a globally improved solution. Solving problems vertically is often much simpler to understand, and frequently much easier (e.g. cheaper, quicker) to do on a per enabler basis. It is a proven approach, even if proven problematic for larger problem spaces. However, if every architect or service development team looks only after one's own turf, the performance of the services infrastructure as a whole will be significantly below what would be possible. Intentionally sacrificing local optimizations to achieve an increased overall cost/performance of the entire system as a whole, is what breaking silos is all about.

Thus the benefits are clear for environments in which multiple services are and will be deployed. But how about much simpler environments? The issue of local penalties for a global optimization may lead some architects of only a single enabler to believe that a vertical approach may be the best solution in their situation. For, why would you accept a penalty if you foresee no larger whole of which your enabler will be part. But as we will see in the next section, it is assumptions like these that make vertical solutions brittle.

2.2   Re-use as First-Class Citizen

The approach chosen in the industry and, in particular, in the OMA, to avoid the silo syndrome is to present the concept of service enablers and a horizontal services architecture in which they can be developed and deployed. A service enabler is a function (or set of closely related functions) in the domain of a service provider that is exposed through a defined interface, toward other resources. Service enablers are re-used through their interface. Re-use is the key concept here. In this section, we will gradually introduce all these concepts that together build up this architectural approach.

2.2.1 Service Enablers

We are all familiar with layered architectures. In telecommunication networks, the prevalent model is that of separating the Access Layer from the Core Network Layer, and the Core Network Layer from the Services Layer. This layering allows for separation of concerns. That is, the core network can be designed commonly across various access network technologies (such as a single Time-Division Multiplexing (TDM) core for Global System for Mobile Communication (GSM) and Integrated Services Digital Network (ISDN)), and the services can be deployed commonly across various core network technologies (such as a single Messaging Service across TDM and Internet Protocol (IP)-based networks). Each layer can then use the functions provided by a lower layer to in turn offer its own functions to yet a higher layer. The same layering principle can be applied again within the Services Layer, as demonstrated in Figure 2.2.

In this model, service enablers are separated from the applications using them, and from the resources that they make use of, thereby breaking the silos between these tiers. Service enablers are no longer integrated with the dedicated servers or network hardware platforms. Applications are no longer integrated with service capabilities in a given network. Service enablers no longer have to be duplicated. Enablers are not restricted to a single silo anymore. Service enablers become the basic technology building blocks for creating services.

Some models introduce a fourth tier, making a distinction between service enablers and common functions, where the latter tier consists of functions that are common across multiple services. The OMA does not use this distinction, for the simple reason that all enablers are designed for re-use and hence can be regarded as 'common'. Not one enabler can be considered more common than the next one beforehand. Common or not, it makes no difference from the perspective of how you define your enabler. It may make a difference in the environment that a service provider may wish to deploy in its network, but that's a different matter altogether.

One could try and predict what the common enablers would be. Or one could analyze previous architectures, standards initiatives, or successful commercial deployments, and try to extrapolate from there what the common enablers would be. But even if carefully done, prediction or extrapolation might introduce unnecessary restrictions that could stifle innovation and hamper creativity. A priori, there is no reason to assume that one enabler would be more common than the next. What might be a common function to one service provider, in an unexciting support role, might be the

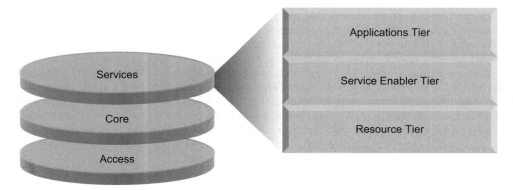

Figure 2.2   Layered architectures

bread and butter to another. And yet another service provider may not have a need for the function at all.

Service enablers, as introduced in this section, are re-usable service building blocks. But merely de-coupling service enablers from the resource and application tier alone does not necessarily make them suitable for re-use. The function they provide needs to be exposed through a defined interface. And even for these interfaces, considerations are at play to facilitate uninhibited re-use. We will review those in the next section.

2.2.2 Interfaces

A fundamental concept for defining re-usable service enablers is that of interface. Many architecture initiatives use the concept of interfaces, and hence its use may appear to be trivial. The concept, however, is as subtle as it is important, so its power is easy to underestimate. This section will demonstrate why interfaces are so pivotal.

An interface is defined as the means of exposing the function(s) of an enabler for use by a resource, or rather, for use by any resource. A defined interface tells a resource what services the enabler that offers the interface is prepared to provide. In other words, an interface is defined in terms of what the service enabler can do for another resource.

A concept related to interface is that of reference point. Although many definitions exist in the industry, for the purpose of this book there is one important distinction between interfaces and reference points. For a reference point, the resources at either end of the reference point are defined. A reference point exists *between* two (sets of) resources, for instance between the messaging client and the messaging server. This distinction is important for the OMA, because this notion of defining what resource can reside at either end of the reference point limits the use of that reference point to those resources only.

Interfaces only tell a resource how the functions of the service enabler can be used. The interface makes no assumptions on the resources that may use it. The interface may not even know. In fact, the fewer the assumptions that are made and the less the interface knows about the resources that may use it, the better suited it will be for re-use. Making no assumptions on potential consumers of the interface will broaden the applicability far beyond the original intent of the designers of the interface. Making no assumptions as an interface designer should, however, not be considered as being oblivious to the problem space or application domain. Instead, it should be considered as preparing for unanticipated use cases. What this means is that the designer of the interface should demand almost nothing of the resources using the interface. The designer is better off not to second-guess the resource that will be using the interface.

So why would I be better off if my enabler has a defined interface? If you are a service provider, just because your enabler implementation offers an interface doesn't make it more valuable. You cannot charge your end-users a premium just for that. The true value is elsewhere, and it shows when your enabler becomes part of a larger ecosystem of enablers that can be easily combined in creative ways to offer new applications. Along those same lines, the first enabler to deploy an interface doesn't experience any benefits. Imagine the first person who bought a telephone, sitting impatiently next to his latest purchase waiting for it to ring. There is hardly a point in owning a telephone if you cannot call someone else. The value is in the ability to connect and communicate. When considering each enabler individually, there is an additional effort required for an enabler to make it re-usable (i.e. provide an interface): a price tag for which the return may not be obvious when looking at a single enabler only. There is a justification however, as even though an additional investment over and above the development cost required for doing it the old way is needed, the cost involved is linear. That is, you do it only once, and you do not have to undergo a similar exercise for every single resource that wants to use your function. So the pay out comes when considering the enabler as part of a larger environment. Again, the value is in the ability to connect and communicate, and the savings one gains through re-use.

One might ask what exactly is 'being re-used'. Re-use in this model does not require re-usable or portable enabler implementations. Rather, it is the interface that is re-used. Applying the concept of interfaces in this way isolates a resource from implementation details (such as the vendor, the version, the execution environment, the programming language, or the operating system) of the enabler whose function(s) it uses. That is true as long as the defined interface remains unchanged, and as long as the enabler implementation offers the use of its function(s) through that interface. But for this, the interface must truly be limited to the enabler's intrinsic functionality. What this means is that the interface should expose only the function (or set of functions) that is core to the enabler. Any combining of functionality out of convenience or optimization for a given enabler means a move back toward vertical integration, and all the downsides that come with it. Here as well, absolutely key is that the interface makes no assumptions about which resource might use it. And this extends to assumptions about what combination of functions might make sense for other enablers to re-use.

These principles of re-use, being application agnostic, and being prepared for unanticipated use cases are at the basis of the concept of loose coupling. An excellent text on loose coupling and the use of interfaces can be found in [Kaye2003].

2.2.3 Some Examples Using Interfaces

This concept of loose coupling also introduces agility. Systems don't break when deployed in ways for which they weren't originally designed or intended. And this is only possible because features to support any particular use case or application were never part of the design or architecture. A resource using an interface should never make any assumptions on the behavior of the system behind the interface. It can only count on behavior exposed through the interface, based on receiving the messages that are carried by the interface.

The following example shows that making assumptions in your design might be very tempting. Consider resource A and resource B, where resource B performs a task for resource A. Resource A may know that resource B always reliably executes its tasks within a given amount of time (e.g. a given number of processor cycles), and may therefore use synchronous communication with resource B, locking its own thread while waiting for the response. This is easier and cheaper to implement than asynchronous communication with support for multi-threading, and hence may seem like a smart and efficient design. But if we look a bit beyond this simple use case, we see that the assumption about reliable execution within a given timeframe has introduced a certain brittleness that may cause the system to break down. Consider for instance the case where resource B is replaced with a cheaper, but less reliable version, or if the task performed by resource B over time becomes more involved and time consuming because of changed load characteristics and now requires more processor cycles. Such a situation, which isn't really that uncommon in real-life deployments, will inevitably cause the system to break, since resource A's thread may now be locked longer than expected or, in case resource B fails, may be locked forever.

The previous example shows that making assumptions introduces brittleness that may cause a system to break. So there are good reasons to avoid assumptions. But there is also a positive incentive. To illustrate the full potential of the concept of making no assumptions, let's use an analogy that we're all familiar with, that is, the Universal Serial Bus (USB) interface. The USB interface carries data at the rate of 12 Mbps (full speed rate), and is particularly well suited for medium- to low-speed Personal Computer (PC) peripherals. Just about any computer bought today comes with one or more USB connectors on the back. And just about every peripheral manufactured today comes in a USB version. The PC can be hooked up to the keyboard, mouse, modem, digital joystick, CD-ROM drive, external hard disk drive, digital scanner and printer, all using USB.

But the USB interface is so generic that it also accommodates a whole new generation of peripherals that were not conceived of during its design, such as mobile phones and digital cameras. This is only possible because the USB interface was not designed with a particular application in mind, or a particular resource using it. And to even further drive home this point of interfaces being ignorant of the application using it, consider such applications as the USB lava lamp, the USB lighted Christmas tree, the USB cup heater, and the USB pot noodle cooker. It only goes to show that there is no limit to the imagination of innovative application providers, and that the original interface designers should have no desire or intent to predict or prescribe the class of applications that will find a market.

The USB interface is a perfect example of an application agnostic interface, designed for re-use. Its design makes no assumptions on how it will be used, or by whom. It only specifies its own intrinsic function, that is, transport of data at a certain rate. What data and by whom is of no concern to the interface itself.

2.2.4 Resources

We have used the term 'resources' thus far in the chapter without defining it. Now that we understand the concept of service enabler, it makes sense to grasp the distinction between enabler and resource. A resource can be an application, component, function, or enabler that can send, receive, or process a request. It is this broad meaning that allowed us to understand the term before having introduced its definition. One interesting aspect of the definition however is that an enabler itself is also a resource, the implication being that enablers can use the function of another enabler, through its defined interface. This recursive aspect of enablers will prove quite valuable, as we will see later on.

2.3 The OSE

So far, we have introduced a three-tier model in the services plane. We have seen that service enablers, in the top tier, who expose their functions through defined interfaces, carefully designed to make no unnecessary assumptions, will greatly facilitate re-use. These concepts can now be put together to form a horizontal, logical services architecture. The horizontal services architecture for the OMA service enablers is called the OMA Service Environment, or OSE. This section will take the reader through how the OSE is built up.

There are many definitions of architecture around, prefixed with qualifiers like software-, system-, logical-, abstract-, etc. The term, qualified or not, means many things to many people. In fact, it is exceedingly difficult to get two architects to agree on what the term means. For the purpose of this book, we will first run through what we mean by architecture. The Telecommunications Information Networking Architecture (TINA) Consortium [TINA] defines an architecture as 'consisting of a set of concepts, principles, rules and guidelines for constructing, deploying, operating, and withdrawing services'. It also describes the environment in which such services operate. We have thus far used the term 'horizontal' as the reverse of 'vertical', which is somewhat helpful but not very exact. A horizontal services architecture, for our purposes, is an architecture that describes the essential components of an end-to-end services environment, an infrastructure framework of re-usable standards-based components that can be leveraged across multiple different networks and applications, and accessed by a range of resources, without imposing any particular combination of those components. Figure 2.3 depicts a horizontal services architecture.

According to the principles of re-use, this horizontal services architecture adopts the concept that all enablers are equal (i.e. there is no notion of 'common') and should have the ability to connect to any other resource, through their defined interface. It is very much a network of peers, or islands of enablers. The enablers are, by design, application-ignorant. Applications are designed using any combination of enablers as re-usable horizontal parts.

Let's see if we are done now. At the start of this chapter, we alluded that it is not sufficient to break the silos into service enablers, so that the service enablers can be bundled and blended into applications. We are not yet done by finishing at a three-layer model of a collection of service enablers that expose interfaces. The horizontal service architecture needs to provide explicit support for combining service enablers in a highly configurable manner, so as to carry out more

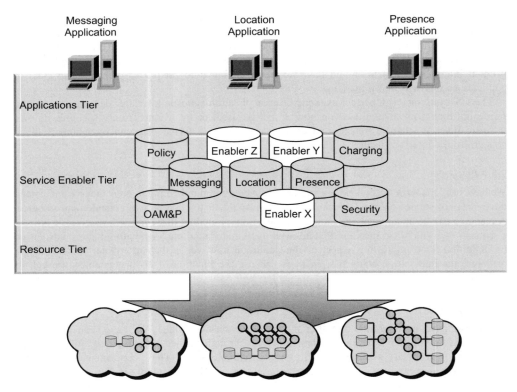

Figure 2.3   Horizontal services architecture

complex communication tasks, and a control infrastructure to facilitate delegated re-use. The control infrastructure allows a service provider to orchestrate its deployed service enablers, to bundle any number of them into a single real time, blended service experience for the end-user. For this, we introduce the concept of Policy Enforcer.

2.3.1 Policy Enforcer

What we now need to do after breaking the silos is to put the building blocks back together again. And this time around not tightly integrated into a silo, but fully utilizing all the good qualities of loose coupling that have been introduced in the previous sections. A mechanism that can flexibly string together any combination of enablers is needed. And the mechanism needs to be able to do it again and again, using creative new combinations as and when required.

The combination of enablers is what we used to refer to as the service logic. The service logic defines the behavior of the end-user application; it is the factor that differentiates one application from the next. This service logic is the property of the service provider. And the service provider expresses or codifies the service logic in terms of one or more service provider policies. An example of a service provider policy might be 'before sending this digital postcard to end-user Alice, first check Alice's account for sufficient credit to pay for this service'. In this simplest example, enforcing this service provider policy involves two enablers, a charging enabler (to perform the credit check) and a messaging enabler (to send the multimedia message). Such policies allow the service provider to specify service logic as a sequence of delegations to particular enablers, charging and messaging in this case. The idiom delegation is used here to capitalize on the concept of loose coupling introduced before. In other words, enablers offer access to their intrinsic function(s) only through their defined interface. In case more than one function is required for the service logic, the execution of that function will be delegated to another enabler, through its defined interface. The OMA has defined the Policy Enforcer as the mechanism of delegated re-use through the enforcement of service provider policies.

Note that the Policy Enforcer in the OSE is a logical concept. There may be many ways to deploy the concept in a real platform or system. The concept may be realized by hard-coding a limited set of policies in the enabler implementation platforms, by deploying an advanced and programmable policy engine, or a combination, etc. The OMA is defining one possible way to realize the Policy Enforcer logical concept, and that is the Policy Evaluation, Enforcement, and Management (PEEM) enabler. The PEEM enabler will be covered in a lot more detail in Chapter 8 later in the book.

2.3.2 OSE Interface Categories

The concept of interfaces has been introduced as a central element of horizontal service architectures. The OSE recognizes three categories of interfaces, each with their own characteristics that allow us to further model the horizontal architecture.

2.3.2.1 The Category of I0 Interfaces

First there is the obvious category of interfaces that are exposed by the OMA service enablers. This is the category of I0 interfaces (pronounced 'eye zero'). I0 interfaces offer all the good qualities we discussed previously in this chapter, that is to say they are application agnostic, prepared for unanticipated use cases, make no unnecessary or restricting assumptions, and limit themselves to the enabler's intrinsic function only. The notion of I0 is absolutely pivotal in the OMA. It is what makes the OMA enablers into re-usable components. It is what keeps the silo syndrome from re-emerging in the OMA.

2.3.2.2 The Category of I2 Interfaces

The OMA does not operate in a vacuum. In fact, in the next chapter we will see that the OMA is engaged in a whole slew of liaison relationships with numerable other standardization organizations and industry fora. Any implementation of OMA technology, be it a single enabler or an entire system of communicating enablers, will be deployed in a networked environment that is part of a larger ecosystem. Many other platforms will be deployed in that ecosystem, quite possibly built to other specifications and adhering to other architectures. For this reason it is useful to make a distinction between interfaces defined by the OMA and interfaces defined elsewhere. This category of interfaces, which may include both specified and standardized interfaces as well as proprietary technologies, is called the category of I2 interfaces. One may expect to find I2 interfaces in the resource tier, representing, for example, a Transport Layer protocol. But it is equally valid for the function, properties, and appearance of an I2 interface to be very similar to those of an I0 interface. The only genuine difference between these two categories is that I2 interfaces are defined elsewhere, and not by the OMA.

The category of I2 interfaces in addition allows you to stick to the principle of loose coupling, even if the function you wish to use or to delegate to, is not defined in the OMA, or for that matter in any other specifications fora. Consider the case where an enabler designer, intent on not falling into the silo trap, is set on delegating the functions that are not intrinsic to the enabler at hand. But no such delegated enabler happens to be available among the OMA enabler specifications. The concept of the I2 interface category lets the enabler designer designate an interface defined elsewhere (be it standardized or proprietary) to carry out the non-intrinsic functions, whilst keeping the enabler at hand constrained and focused on its intrinsic function. So with the benefit of a horizontal service architecture, an OMA enabler is no longer forced to define each and every function as part of its own specification in order to fulfill all its requirements.

2.3.2.3 The Category of I1 Interfaces

The last category of interfaces, that is I1, is described here out-of-sequence. The reason is that the distinguishing factor for this category is somewhat different. I1 interfaces are interfaces to those Operation, Administration, Maintenance, and Provisioning (OAM&P) functions of the OSE, which are as of yet undefined. And this makes the I1 category a bit different than the I0 and I2 interfaces. For, as soon as an OAM&P capability can be identified that has been defined outside the OMA, the interface by definition moves to the I2 category. And, in case no such OAM&P asset exists and the OMA decides to define one itself as an OMA service enabler, then of course the interface becomes a regular I0 interface. A good example of the latter case, an I1 moving to the I0 category, is the Open Mobile Alliance Service Provider Environment (OSPE) enabler, which will be covered in more detail in Chapter 12. Despite the somewhat awkward definition for the category of I1 interfaces, the usefulness of showing the I1 interfaces is to drive home the point that in any run-time deployment of the OSE, common interfaces for functions like life-cycle management and other capabilities exposed to Operations Support System (OSS) or Business Support System (BSS) are offered by each deployed service enabler.

2.3.2.4 Policy Enforcement Applied to I0 Interfaces

With the concept of the Policy Enforcer, the OSE has established a mechanism to set apart one application from another, while still using the same service enablers. Service offerings can be personalized, adapted to classes of users, and customized to a particular application domain. For example, a service provider may settle for the less stringent transport level security provided by the corporate Intranet for its own employees when accessing a resource, but insist on username and password authentication for service requests that originate from the public Internet. This then becomes the service provider policy to be enforced on any service request that is received.

But just because we want to give the service provider full flexibility and freedom to offer a creative, differentiating, and adaptable portfolio of applications, it does not imply that we need to equip the service enablers with all kinds of knobs, dials, and levers to be able to tune to the specific use case at hand. Nor should it mean that we require many very similar service enablers that are different only in some details (e.g. a messaging enabler for corporate Intranet security as well as a messaging enabler for username/password security). The enabler stays the same, or rather the enabler's I0 interface stays the same. It is the service provider policies that bring about the differentiation. The service provider policies need to be separated from the enabler definition. In the OSE, it is the Policy Enforcer that accomplishes this by adding so-called P parameters to the I0 interface, when exposed to applications.

We have seen that proper design of enablers implies exposing their intrinsic functionality only. Extending this model to the Policy Enforcer would mean that domain owner–specific parameters, associated with the service provider policies, must be separated from the parameters that are core to the enabler interface (I0). These domain owner–specific parameters are referred to as the P parameters, and the interface exposed toward applications by the Policy Enforcer is referred to as the I0+P interface. The distinction between interface I0 and interface I0+P allows the enabler developer to implement the enabler I0 interface, which requests only the parameters associated to the enabler intrinsic functionality, yet still allows the service provider to apply its domain-specific policies to any incoming request by mandating the addition of the P parameters. Differentiation is made possible while still using the same service enablers, and without extending the enablers' I0 interfaces with any additional, non-intrinsic, parameters. The P parameters encompass additional information (on top of the information in the I0 interface) that is required by the service provider policies and consumed by the Policy Enforcer.

For example, consider a service provider that offers access to its service enablers to third-party applications outside its own domain. In order to control and secure such access, the service provider imposes service provider policies, requiring authentication, authorization or charging. To comply with these service provider policies, the third-party application must deliver the necessary information (i.e. the P parameters) along with its original request (i.e. the I0 interface invocation). But of course, the enabler I0 interface only supports the enabler's intrinsic procedures and parameters. The concept of I0+P makes it possible for the service provider to request the additional information, such as charging tokens, identity credentials, or authentication assertions, as imposed by their policies. The I0 with these additional parameters constitutes I0+P, which is the interface exposed by the Policy Enforcer.

Depending on the protocol binding, these P additional parameters may be passed as extra parameters to existing messages, as separate dedicated messages, or as new headers added to the existing message envelope, etc. Bindings will be discussed in the next section.

2.3.3 Protocol Bindings

The I0 interfaces are abstract descriptions of how a resource can invoke the intrinsic function of the enabler. The I0 interface does not specify what is communicated 'across the wire'. In order to achieve such connectivity in a deployment, the abstract interface needs to be tied to a particular protocol. You need a way of saying 'here is how you pass the messages of the interface on top of an underlying protocol'. This is called the protocol binding. For each enabler I0 interfaces, multiple such protocol bindings may be specified. HTTP and Web Services are examples of possible OSE I0 protocol bindings.

2.3.4 Putting the Piece Parts Together

We have defined what we mean by horizontal services architecture, and we have introduced all the piece parts that make up the horizontal services architecture in the OMA, that is the OSE. So let

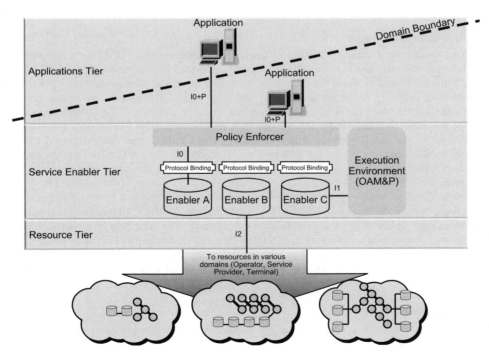

Figure 2.4   The OMA Service Environment (OSE)

us now overlay all those piece parts on top of the generic architecture model from Figure 2.3 to reveal the resulting OSE. Figure 2.4 shows the OSE consisting of Service Enablers, Applications, and Resources, connected through three categories of Interfaces that may support various protocol bindings, distributed across three tiers, and orchestrated through the Policy Enforcer.

In the remainder of the book, we will use this OSE diagram to position the various enablers that will be discussed in detail in the chapters that follow. It provides the tool to help put all the individual chapters into perspective, and to tie those back to the objective of breaking silo systems.

2.3.5 What the OSE Isn't

We have introduced the OSE as the horizontal service environment for the development and deployment of the OMA service enablers. We have gone to quite some length to explain what it is, what the key concepts are, and why those are useful. But since 'architectures' and 'concepts' are often fairly ethereal and elusive, perhaps it is helpful to also spend a few words on what the OSE isn't.

The OSE is not a run-time execution environment. It is also not a functional architecture, and it certainly is far from a physical architecture. Rather, it is a logical architecture or a reference architecture. OSE is not a platform, as elements of it may be deployed across domain boundaries and be provided by multiple vendors. The OSE also does not make any assumptions on whether enablers are deployed on servers in the Service Provider domain or on terminals that interact with other elements in the Service Provider's domain.

2.4 Additional Features of the OSE

The OSE avoids the design and deployment of silo architectures. It avoids the lock-in of monolithic applications in a constrained environment. Given the problems of vertical integration, this is a laudable goal. But there are more features of this horizontal service architecture. This section will outline some of the more eminent traits.

2.4.1 Protection of Resources

As we have seen, an interface is defined in terms of what the enabler can do for a resource. Put in a different way, the interface exposes the function provided by the enabler. Coupled with the Policy Enforcer logical component, the service provider now has at its disposal an instrument for the controlled exposure of the resources and capabilities within its domain. The service provider can manage, secure, and bill for access to its resources. This is particularly important when service requests are received from outside the Service Provider domain. With the growing popularity of the third-party application provider business model, where third parties are contracted to offer applications that make use of and are delivered across capabilities in the Service Provider domain, controlled exposure is of key significance. Contracts between a service provider and a third-party application provider involve Service Level Agreements (SLAs) that may cover aspects like Quality of Service (QoS). In order to govern the SLA, the service provider requires control. Moreover, it is vitally important for the service provider to protect the integrity of the resources in its domain from harmful actions, malicious or otherwise, from any third party. The protection of resources within a domain from unauthorized, malicious or otherwise harmful service requests is an essential feature of the OSE. Other technologies that deal with controlled third-party access to service capabilities include Parlay. The reader is referred to [Unmehopa2006] for an in-depth coverage of the Parlay technology.

2.4.2 End-user Experience

We have covered the silo syndrome from the perspective of service providers who deploy service enablers, as well as from the point of view of architects who design service enablers. Key considerations here were the integration cost and deployment complexity. A stakeholder whose viewpoint we have not yet contemplated is the end-user. After all, it will be the end-user who consumes the application and who will ultimately have to be prepared to part with some money for that privilege. CAPEX and OPEX reductions are great, and will benefit the end-user as well, but there are further incentives.

One facet of vertical integration is the duplication of functionality across the smoke stacks. If such a duplicated function trickles through to the experience toward the end-user, this may reduce customer satisfaction. Consider for example Alice, who has subscribed to a Presence service (which alerts her when her buddies are in the neighborhood) and a Calendar service (which reminds her of her appointments). Alice wishes the alerts of both subscribed services to be sent using Short-Message Service (SMS). In a vertically integrated system, Alice would have to provision this preference once for the Presence service, and again for the Calendar service. Preferably, Alice would like to set her preferences, or any user data, only once. A user data enabler, which is re-used by both the Presence service and the Calendar service, as per the principles of the OSE, would make this a reality.

The OSE facilitates a consistent end-user experience when subscribing to multiple applications from a single service provider, through re-use of enablers that have some bearing on this experience. The OSE facilitates a consistent end-user experience when using the same application, but across environments. For example, accessing the application when registered to a different network while roaming, or accessing the application from a different device. This consistency is achieved by re-using the same enablers, which are, if you recall from Section 2.2.1, independent from the resources tier.

2.5 OSE and Related Technologies

Many of the concepts underpinning the OSE are not new. In fact, some are only the culmination of the excellent efforts carried out by other organizations and industries. OSE does however put these piece parts together in a structured and consistent way, and places them in a communications context. Before we wrap up this chapter, we will momentarily point out two related technologies available in the industry to better appreciate the place of OSE in the technology spectrum.

Parlay is a service architecture for controlled, manageable, and billable third-party access to abstracted network service capabilities, and a suite of Application Programming Interfaces to those network service capabilities. The relationship between Parlay and OSE is explored in Chapter 10.

Service Oriented Architecture (SOA) is in essence an architectural concept for composable and interoperable networked services, which lends itself to create applications in a dynamic manner. An SOA abstracts services from their realization using the concept of interface, which describes how interaction between parties will occur. Services in an SOA are relying on agreed-to properties, such as being discoverable, addressable, loosely coupled, interoperable (allowing them to be diversely owned), and composable. A popular technology to realize an SOA is Web Services. Chapter 11 discusses the relationship between Web Services and OSE.

2.6 Summary

OMA enablers are defined as independent service building blocks, sporting an I0 interface. The principle of loose coupling and the design characteristics of being application agnostic, prepared for unanticipated use without making any unnecessary or restricting assumptions, while limiting themselves to the enabler's intrinsic function only, together combat the problems brought forth by vertical integration. It is the OSE that promotes these principles and design characteristics across all the OMA enablers, allowing for architectural consistency and integrity, as well as interoperability. It is the OSE that guides how the OMA enablers are developed and deployed. The mechanism of delegated re-use, made possible by the Policy Enforcer, permits the OMA enablers to fulfill all their requirements without the necessity to provide for all functions for those requirements within their own specifications, and hence implementations. All these attributes coalesce to make the OSE the horizontal services architecture that delivers on the promise of unleashing the abundance of value added applications that will make next generation networks a success.

3

The Open Mobile Alliance – An Organizational Overview

The Open Mobile Alliance (OMA) is the leading industry forum for developing and specifying market-driven, interoperable mobile service enablers to facilitate global user adoption of mobile multimedia applications. This book is about these service enablers. Before presenting a carefully selected subset of them in the remainder of the book, let us first introduce the OMA organization, and the role it has set out for itself in the specification of these service enablers. Efforts have been made in the past to standardize service enablers. Some have been successful to a certain extent, others decidedly less so. And hence you might ask why the OMA should be any more successful.

What all these previous standards efforts have in common is that in some way they limit their scope to, or aim their focus at, if you will, a specific application area. The mission of the OMA is nothing less than to create specifications for 'mobile data services interoperable across different devices, geographies, service providers, operators, and networks, that are as easy and seamless to use as voice services today, and that provide value to all players in the mobile value chain'. A truly daunting undertaking, for sure. At the end of this chapter the reader will have a good appreciation of the OMA organizational structure, the scope and objectives, and the guiding principles underpinning the OMA specification efforts. And hopefully you will understand why the OMA is perfectly positioned to deliver its promises.

3.1 Overview of the OMA

The OMA defines as its mission 'to facilitate global user adoption of mobile data services by specifying market-driven mobile service enablers that ensure service interoperability across devices, geographies, service providers, operators, and networks, while allowing businesses to compete through innovation and differentiation'. That is quite a mouthful. This mission statement gives a good indication of what the OMA is trying to achieve. However, it doesn't say exactly what the OMA does, how it does it, and why. In this chapter, we will attempt to address these aspects.

The OMA undertakes the development of specifications for service enablers that are independent of the underlying bearers, predominantly to address the needs of a mobile user but not necessarily restricted to cellular or mobile network domains. Since its formation in 2002, the OMA has made significant progress in delivering several enablers in areas such as Device Management (DM), wireless browsing, Mobile Web Services (MWS), Push-to-talk over Cellular (PoC), and presence, and it plans to deliver many more enablers in the coming years. In the 5 years of its existence, the OMA has established itself as the leading forum for generating specifications for mobile service enablers.

The Open Mobile Alliance   M. Brenner and M. Unmehopa
© 2008 Alcatel-Lucent. All Rights Reserved

As an industry organization that includes over 400 geographically dispersed member companies, the OMA is making giant strides in the development of specifications for a service environment that will represent a paradigm shift because it will make it possible to deploy multi-vendor platforms and services while avoiding costly customized integration with the operator's network.

The OMA is different from other standards organizations because it has made a conscious effort to attract as its member representatives, the widest possible range of interest groups throughout the mobile industry value chain, ranging from providers to end-users, thereby ensuring that everyone will benefit from their membership. In addition to the network operators and equipment and infrastructure vendors that are traditionally represented in communications standards organizations, the OMA includes representatives from throughout the value chain, including mobile terminal vendors, the service developer community, Information Technology (IT) infrastructure vendors, content providers, tool vendors, and certification bodies. The presence of representatives of these two final sectors of the value chain is indicative of the importance the OMA attaches to the interoperability of the specifications it produces, a concern that distinguishes the OMA from a significant number of organizations that set specifications and standards. The OMA has four member categories, namely sponsor member, full member, associate member, and supporter member. Membership category is determined through membership fees, and each category comes with a set of benefits.

The success of the OMA will be measured by how widely its specifications are adopted by the marketplace (which consists of the various stakeholders) and the commercial success of the applications built to these specifications. This success will largely depend on delivering interoperable services that foster multi-vendor environments and eliminate barriers to service integration and deployment.

3.1.1 Affiliation – A Historic Perspective

Prior to the OMA, industry consortiums and interest groups focusing on a single vertical enabler were abound. In keeping with the idea of re-use and reducing vertical integration, as introduced in Chapter 2, one of the stated goals of the OMA is to act as a catalyst for the consolidation of multiple fora under one umbrella organization. Affiliation is the OMA parlance used to describe the process by which organizations can reposition their activities, specification collateral, and membership under the banner of the OMA. Many of the individual standards fora and industry consortia subscribed to the compelling proposition of the OMA, and as a result the OMA was formed in June 2002 through the consolidation of the WAP Forum, Synchronization Markup Language (SyncML), Wireless Village, Location Interoperability Forum (LIF) and the Multimedia Messaging Service Interoperability (MMS-IOP) group. To date no fewer than seven organizations (adding the Mobile Game Interoperability Forum (MGIF) and the Mobile Wireless Internet Forum (MWIF)) have been affiliated with the OMA, and their work has been subsumed in the work of the OMA's technical Working Groups (WGs). These affiliates no longer exist as independent organizations. In most cases, the specifications that were in the process of being published by the affiliates are now published as the OMA specifications and care is taken to ensure that they are in line with other ongoing work in the OMA WGs. Such an approach reduces the likelihood of producing overlapping specifications within a single functional area.

Integration of processes and specifications takes some time and effort. However, an important consideration is that the drawbacks of this affiliation process do not negate any potential gains.

The OMA had to define itself as an organization with all its affiliated partners, without dropping the baton as it was being passed on to it; the OMA had to hit the ground running. It is not the intention of the affiliation program to just gobble up or totally eclipse these other organizations. It is rather, to join hands with others to create something stronger, more adaptive, and more creative than any individual organization was capable of. Affiliated partners can now channel their individual financial resources and intellectual capital toward the common OMA specification efforts. In return, the OMA commits itself to preserve the vested interest in the collateral of the affiliated organization. As an additional part of the integration process of affiliated organizations, the OMA mined its processes and procedures to harvest the most promising best practices and re-use these in the new alliance.

3.2 Principles of the OMA

The OMA has established a collection of principles to guide its work. These principles are set to ensure that all member companies benefit from their membership and participation and none are disenfranchised. In addition, the principles codify the OMA's mission statement into more practical guidelines for the specification development process.

If one thing defines the computer, IT, and communication industry, it is the sheer abundance of operating systems, programming languages, hardware platforms, execution environments, and end-user devices. The wide scope of the OMA, and the multiplicity of its membership, demands that the OMA specifications cannot be built toward any one particular technology, nor preclude any such technology. In order to maximize commercial success and widespread adoption of its standards, the OMA has embraced the principle of neutrality with respect to the operating system, execution environment, and programming language. This principle underscores the OMA's goal of achieving platform and device independence. A truly open environment in which a multi-vendor ecosystem thrives should result in greater innovation, healthier competition, lower costs, less market fragmentation, and a richer user experience.

A second neutrality principle is that the Applications Tier is agnostic of the bearer and access network technology. This means that applications that build toward the OMA specifications can be deployed in networks where the end-users connect through any mobile technology like GSM, General Packet Radio Service (GPRS), Enhanced Data Rates for GSM Evolution (EDGE), Code Division Multiple Access (CDMA), Universal Mobile Telecommunications System (UMTS), Wireless Fidelity (WiFi), or Worldwide Interoperability for Microwave Access (WiMAX). In order to adhere to this principle, the OMA specifications should not limit applications to use the lowest common denominator of network features among these access technologies. While optimizations related to specific underlying technologies are permitted (like content adaptation for low capacity networks), application developers must not be required to use them.

As for any engineering problem of any size in the mobile industry, or any other industry for that matter, there likely exist several solutions to the same problem. There may be many reasons for that. The solution may be driven more by technology than by the underlying needs of the market, the solution may be an adaptation of an existing solution to a similar problem, or the solution may be contributed by a different set of stakeholders. Whatever the reason, the end result is duplication. To avoid such duplication, one OMA architectural principle permits services to be built, managed, and deployed by leveraging existing industry standards, where they meet the OMA requirements. Any technology that currently provides features and functionality to the mobile industry in line with the OMA requirements is considered a candidate for re-use in the OMA specifications.

The last OMA principle is an important one, and prescribes that applications and platforms are interoperable, providing seamless geographic and intergenerational roaming. Interoperability is a fundamental principle in the OMA. To reflect the pivotal role, this chapter will devote a section to the topic of interoperability while the next chapter is entirely dedicated to the so-called OMA Interoperability TestFests.

3.3 The OMA's Relationship with External Organizations

The OMA does not operate in solitude within a cordoned-off environment, nor does it seek to affiliate every other organization that is active within the next generation application domain. Rather, the OMA seeks broad industry participation, putting together elements of solutions coming from many different sources. The OMA seeks to work closely with other established standards organizations (e.g. the International Telecommunication Union [ITU] and the European Telecommunications

Standards Institute [ETSI]) as well as with other organizations that generate Technical Specifications (TSs) (e.g. the Internet Engineering Task Force [IETF], the Third Generation Partnership Project (3GPP) [3GPP], and the Third Generation Partnership Project 2 [3GPP2]).

To this end, the OMA external liaison program was specifically created to establish relationships with the outside world. Because of the disparate nature of the various standards and industry organizations (e.g. some are legal entities while others are not), the OMA has two mechanisms for collaboration with other organizations: a cooperation framework that is an agreed-upon but unsigned set of guidelines and a cooperation agreement that is a formally signed agreement. Cooperation frameworks and cooperation agreements typically address issues like sharing of documents, how to deal with Intellectual Property Rights (IPR) and copyright, and whether members of one organization are allowed to attend and contribute to meetings hosted by the other. To date, the OMA has established cooperation frameworks and agreements with a large variety of organizations on topics spanning the entire spectrum of communications and IT. The liaison dialogue helps to avoid overlap or duplication of specifications efforts across standards organizations.

3.4 OMA Organizational Structure

The objectives of the OMA are ambitious and the ground they aim to cover is comprehensive. The job of slotting in the affiliated partners and the responsibility to assimilate and continue their technical legacy adds a further challenge. These considerations require an organizational structure tuned to the task at hand. Figure 3.1 shows how, at the time of writing this book, the OMA has organized itself to coordinate the technical work and manage the work program, and the following sections will elaborate on this structure. Although much of the information on the activities and responsibilities of the various WGs and committees can be obtained from the individual charters, this section presents the material in a coherent overview.

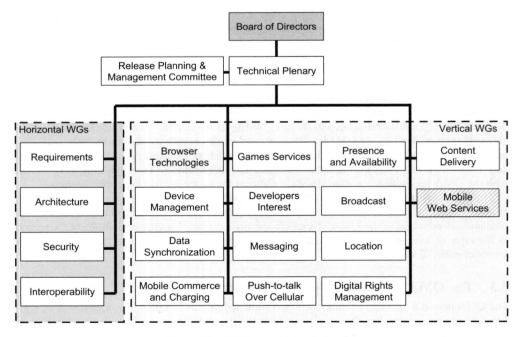

Figure 3.1   OMA organizational structure

3.4.1 OMA Board of Directors

The OMA is incorporated in the United Kingdom. Hence, it is effectively a company, with a Board of Directors (BoD). This BoD is made up of delegates of the sponsor members, and includes representatives of all market segments participating in the OMA (i.e. Mobile Operators, IT Companies, Wireless Vendors, and Content Providers). In addition to the sponsor members in each of these market segments, there are a small number of elected seats. Half of these elected seats are renewed every 2 years. The board is charged with the conduct and management of the affairs of the OMA, and has the general duty to run the OMA in the best interest of the members. The activities of the board are performed in a number of committees, some of which are described as follows:

- The board's external liaison committee develops strategic relationships with other industry bodies by engaging in cooperation frameworks or cooperation agreements. The latter are legal agreements defining the scope and boundaries to engage in information exchanges or joint activities.
- The board's finance committee is responsible for the OMA budget planning and strategy, as well as the budget control. The finance committee also engages with an external auditor to ensure that the annual audit of the OMA's financial statements takes place, as legally required by company law.
- The board's legal and trademark committee deals with all legal affairs related to the OMA. These include the articles of association, the IPR policy for the OMA technical activities, and such issues like copyright in specifications that may be developed jointly with other organizations.
- The board's interoperability committee oversees the organizational aspects with regard to the OMA interoperability program. These may include required funds for test tools, possible license agreements for the use of external test tools, and logistical arrangements for hosting a TestFest.
- The board's strategic planning committee oversees the long-term evolution of the OMA, addressing questions such as the vision, framework, and strategies for the success of the OMA deliverables in support of its member companies.

The BoD of the OMA has no involvement with the technical work of the organization. This responsibility lies with the OMA Technical Plenary (TP).

3.4.2 Technical Plenary

The OMA technical work takes place under the auspices of the TP. The TP is the governing technical body responsible for the OMA Work Program (OWP). In order to perform all its tasks, the TP distributes its work across the committees and the technical WGs, where the actual TS drafting activities take place. The WGs generate technical specifications; the committees, working documents related to the internal operations of the OMA or supporting documentation for the OMA enabler releases. WGs and committees are chartered by the TP. Charters are renewed on a yearly basis. Member companies may submit proposals for new work areas, or new versions of already published enablers. If approved by the TP, the work gets assigned to one of the WGs. New WGs may be spawned, as needed, while existing WGs may be closed down in case all committed deliverables have been completed and approved, or in case work has become obsolete or is no longer being progressed. The end responsibility for the technical work carried out by the WGs and committees resides with the TP, which oversees approval and maintenance of TSs, resolution of technical issues that cannot be resolved within the WGs, and submission of approved TSs and supporting documentation to the BoD for final approval and publication. It is the TP which ensures that the technical activities meet the goals of the OMA in terms of quality, consistency, completeness and timeliness, fulfilling market demand and satisfying business needs.

3.4.3 OMA Committees

At the onset of the OMA, there were two committees that supported the activities of the TP; the Operations and Processes (OPS) Committee and the Release Planning and Management (REL) Committee. Both played an important role in supporting the activities and internal operations of the TP. In an unremitting attempt to streamline the activities and operations of the OMA, the two committees merged their activities into a single committee that continues under the name REL Committee.

The REL Committee is responsible for the OWP. The OWP tracks Work Items from that point in time when they are approved by the TP and follows the work through the subsequent requirements, architecture, and specifications phases and up to the end when Enabler Release Packages are created and subsequently subjected to interoperability testing. The OWP is basically the equivalent of a project management function that is used to ensure that the work in the OMA can be performed in an efficient manner. Program management tasks like keeping track of time plans for and the dependencies between the OMA Work Items, keeping track of specifications and their dependencies (internal and external), and keeping track of releases, all fall under the remit of the REL Committee. Where it is the individual WGs which produce the technical deliverables (such as Requirement Documents (RDs), Architecture Documents (ADs), and Technical Specifications (TSs)), The REL Committee maintains and monitors supporting documents, such as Review Reports and Test Reports that are required to be produced and presented to the TP in conjunction to approval points for Work Item deliverables. As part of their program management reporting responsibilities, REL Committee keeps the TP, wider OMA membership, liaison partners, and non members informed of the overall progress of Work Items and releases. REL Committee manages and hosts the Consistency Reviews of Enabler Release Packages when the WGs have completed their enabler development activities.

The functions inherited through the merger with the OPS Committee include management of the OMA process, maintenance and publication of the OMA document templates, and management of the Open Mobile Naming Authority (OMNA). These functions are detailed below:

- The OMA Process Document defines the operations and process of the TP and all WGs operating under the TP umbrella. For any organization of the size of the OMA, with all its stakeholders, there are rules to be followed by the members in order to operate smoothly, transparently, and efficiently. The Process Document lays out some of the rules by which participants to the OMA TP are expected to adhere. It includes directives pertaining to the organizational structure, meeting procedures, work activities and document procedures, decision making and consensus reaching, election and dismissal of officers, as well as the responsibilities and tasks of those officers. Section 3.5 addresses some aspects of the OMA process itself.
- For each deliverable type (e.g. RD, Review Report, Liaison Statement), the OMA provides document templates. As per the OMA process, WGs are required to utilize the appropriate templates. The templates may contain notes on desired content, guidelines, best practices, and naming conventions as well as legal disclaimers and copyright notices. Adherence to the templates helps ensure consistency in published deliverables as well as in communication with external organizations.
- The OMNA is the body which establishes the operational procedures and rules for the OMA namespaces. As the number of names and objects grows within the large number of enablers specified by the OMA, the OMNA has the responsibility of managing uniqueness of such named objects among enablers and across WGs. The OMNA oversees the allocation of names for the OMA protocols and interfaces. Many of the OMA protocols have been carefully designed to allow for future extensions. New functionality can be added through content types, parameters, and access methods without any changes to the base protocol. The OMNA registration process is needed to ensure that the set of such variables is developed in a well-specified and centrally coordinated fashion.

3.4.4 OMA Horizontal Working Groups

There are four horizontal WGs that support the activities of the TP: horizontal, as their roles and responsibilities span all specification drafting activities across all the OMA WGs. The following sections succinctly explain the responsibilities of the horizontal WGs.

3.4.4.1 Requirements Working Group (REQ WG)

The OMA was born out of an unmistakable need in the marketplace. The desire to produce enabler specifications that are driven by commercial requirements rather than pushed by technological advances, is strongly embedded in the OMA's DNA. It is the OMA Requirements Working Group (REQ WG) which is responsible for collecting, identifying and understanding the market needs from the community of the OMA member companies. Note that the creation of requirements in the OMA is a shared activity across the OMA organization. REQ WG may develop requirements themselves (i.e. identifying and specifying use cases and requirements for services and identifying interoperability and usability requirements) as well as coordinate the requirements activities undertaken in other OMA WGs. Such coordination consists of consolidating all requirements, verifying consistency and avoiding duplication of requirements activity in all WGs. As the number of requirements grows, REQ WG may prioritize the different use cases and requirements to meet specific commercial demands. As the requirements expert group, REQ WG will host and conduct the formal review of each OMA RD. REQ WG also plays a role in the review of new work item proposals, to check for market consistency, terminology, and priority, as well as possible relationships with external organizations.

As one can see, the REQ WG is involved in many activities, spanning the whole breadth of the OMA. A number of the enablers that the REQ WG has worked on, or is still in the process of developing, are covered in more detail in later chapters. For example, General Service Subscription Management (GSSM) and Mobile Advertising (MobAd) are addressed in Chapter 27.

3.4.4.2 Architecture Working Group (ARC WG)

In Chapter 2 we have already been introduced to the OMA Service Environment (OSE), and the key architectural principles that underpin it. We have seen that many of the concepts are quite different from the way things used to be done. It is the responsibility of the OMA Architecture Working Group (ARC WG) to define and maintain the OSE in close cooperation with the other groups in the OMA. The ARC WG serves a coordinating role, producing an OSE architecture that provides for both current and future OMA needs. The OMA ARC WG assures, through review, consultancy and guidance, the adherence of specification work to the OSE, to the OMA Architecture Principles and to other applicable normative deliverables. Re-use and the avoidance of silos are among the main objectives and activities within the scope of the OMA ARC WG Group.

Similar to the REQ WG, the ARC WG hosts and conducts the formal review of each OMA AD, for technical soundness and consistency. ADs may be developed by the ARC WG itself, or in any of the other OMA WGs. In the latter case, the ARC WG manages the architectural overview of the OMA Enablers, monitors and reports on their dependencies, and identifies gaps and issues related to interworking among multiple enablers.

Also, like the REQ WG, the ARC WG's activities cover topics across the entire OMA spectrum. The OSE has already been introduced in Chapter 2. Other ARC WG activities are elaborated in subsequent parts of the book. The Policy Enforcer is detailed in Chapter 7, while the Policy Evaluation, Enforcement, and Management (PEEM) enabler which is one possible realization of the Policy Enforcer concept, is covered in depth in Chapter 8. Additional dedicated chapters are included for the Utilization of IMS in OMA (IMSinOMA, Chapter 9) enabler and Parlay in OSE (PIOSE, Chapter 10). For other enablers, in addition to the AD, ARC WG is also developing the TSs. These include the OMA Service Provider Environment (OSPE, Chapter 12), Global Permissions Management (GPM, Chapter 22), and Categorization Based Content Screening (CBCS, Chapter 23).

3.4.4.3 Security Working Group (SEC WG)

Security is a critical aspect for the success of any technology. It is a feature that cannot be added as an afterthought, it is not just some module you bolt on to your system as a final step before shipping. It has to be an integral part of the enabler design. At the same time, security is an expert topic, requiring well-trained, highly specialized and experienced practitioners. For these reasons, the Security Working Group (SEC WG) has been established as the third horizontal WG in the OMA. SEC WG ensures that all the OMA technical WGs have access to the latest and most up-to-date security technologies, by providing protocols for secure communication between mobile clients and servers at both the Transport Layer and the Application Layer. SEC WG offers consultancy on security considerations, trust services (e.g. authentication, confidentiality, and integrity), and smart card technologies. Furthermore, as part of the requirements and architecture reviews, SEC WG conducts security threat assessments of all OMA enablers. By virtue of acting as a horizontal group governing all security issues, SEC WG ensures that individual enablers do not have to resolve their security requirements on a per enabler basis, adding further rigor to the OSE concept of horizontal services architecture. Chapter 13 will do a lot more justice to the complex topic of security by delving deeper into the Application Layer Security Common Functions enabler and several other OMA security specifications.

3.4.4.4 Interoperability Working Group (IOP WG)

The Interoperability Working Group (IOP WG) is responsible for producing the interoperability material (e.g. test specifications with conformance tests and end-to-end interoperability tests) for all OMA enablers. IOP WG conducts and hosts the test events in order to improve the quality of the specifications produced and published by the OMA. In support of these tasks and responsibilities, IOP WG will maintain the required processes, policies and test programs. Section 3.6 will further elaborate on the fundamental role of interoperability in the OMA, while Chapter 4 will provide a deep dive into the OMA Interoperability TestFests.

3.4.5 OMA Vertical Working Groups

In the sections above, we presented the four horizontal WGs in the OMA. What follows are brief descriptions of each vertical WG. Some of these WGs' activities will be described in more detail later on in the book, when elaborating on a selection of individual OMA enablers.

3.4.5.1 Browser and Content Working Group (BAC WG)

The Browser and Content Working Group (BAC WG) started out as an amalgamation of a great many activities related to mobile browser agents, the base content formats they use, rendering of that content, and delivery technologies for the request and delivery of such content. As such, BAC WG was responsible for a large number of the enabler specifications published by the OMA. Although it had evolved since the beginning of the OMA, in many ways BAC WG was the continuation of the former WAP Forum within the OMA. BAC WG's activities were aimed at enabling the creation and use of data services on mobile hand held devices, including mobile telephones, pagers, and Personal Digital Assistants (PDAs). Because of the large diversity of topics BAC WG was responsible for, it had established a number of Sub Working Groups (SWGs), including Mobile Broadcast (BAC BCAST), Content Delivery (BAC CD), User Agent Profile (BAC UAProf), Download and Digital Rights Management (BAC DLDRM), Standard Transcoding Interface (BAC STI), and Mobile Application Environment (BAC MAE).

During a restructuring effort of the technical activities within the TP, a reorganization took place resulting in the promotion of a number of the BAC SWGs to full WGs. Figure 3.2 depicts both the previous as well as the new organizational structure. Since the restructuring, the BAC WG itself no longer exists.

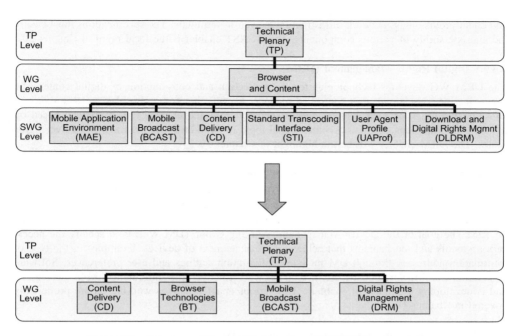

Figure 3.2   Browser and Content Working Group (BAC WG) re-structuring

3.4.5.2 Browser Technologies (BTs)

Browser Technologies (BTs) is one of the WGs created as a result of the BAC WG restructuring. BT specifically aims at technologies for browsing, content rendering, content formats, and device capabilities. The internal organizational structure of BT makes use of *Ad Hoc* Groups (AHGs), rather than SWGs. As AHGs typically are more transient in nature, the internal structure is not discussed here. It is worthwhile pointing out however, that it is BT which inherited the extensive legacy work from the Mobile Application Environment activity (BAC MAE). The more recent activities of the Mobile Application Environment SWG are reviewed in Chapter 26.

3.4.5.3 Content Delivery (CD)

CD refers to a broad range of capabilities, which addresses requirements of content packaging and delivery via point-to-point and broadcast bearers in a mobile environment. These requirements will include the basic delivery mechanisms necessary to support various CD paradigms. Chapter 21 will home in on the Dynamic Content Delivery (DCD) enabler, one of the enablers under development in the CD WG. The work on the Over-the-air Activation (OTA) and the various Push protocols is being reused by various other OMA enabler specifications. For more details on how OTA and Push specifications are reused, the reader is referred to Chapter 19 on Digital Rights Management (DRM) and Chapter 25 on Location.

3.4.5.4 Mobile Broadcast (BCAST)

The BCAST WG is working on the development of a single enabler, but it is a significant and very complex enabler. This enabler defines the environment needed for the delivery of BCAST services. Such an environment contains aspects like service discovery, electronic service guides, charging and content/service protection, and as such the enabler will have implications on service and client provisioning, network infrastructure as well as terminals. The specifications must ensure the interoperability of various components. The BCAST enabler is the focal point of Chapter 20.

3.4.5.5 Digital Rights Management (DRM)

The DRM WG develops technologies for the protection and consumption of digital content, be it personal or commercial, in a controlled manner. Aspects that come into play are techniques to constrain the usage of such content, and to securely store and exchange such content, based on associated permissions. DRM is a controversial topic in an industry that is fragmented over rights issues. The DRM enabler will be the highlight of Chapter 19.

3.4.5.6 Device Management Working Group (DM WG)

The field of DM is concerned with aspects such as setting initial configuration information in devices, and the subsequent installation and updates of persistent information in devices, the retrieval of management information from devices and the processing of events and alarms generated by devices. The goal of the Device Management Working Group (DM WG) is to specify the necessary protocols and mechanisms that achieve the management of devices. Examples of the type of information addressed through DM include configuration settings and user preferences. Software installation and firmware updates are in-scope as well. To cover this entire field, DM has developed and is developing a number of enablers. The various enablers DM is working on are proficiently covered in Chapter 18.

3.4.5.7 Data Synchronization Working Group (DS WG)

The Data Synchronization Working Group (DS WG) has subsumed the responsibility of the maintenance and further development of the SyncML Data Synchronization technologies, used for example, to synchronize e-mail or calendar applications. But the scope of the DS WG has expanded beyond SyncML. DS WG defines the eXtensible Markup Language (XML)-based SyncML, the Data Synchronization protocol, and several transport bindings that specify how to use a particular transport technology to exchange Data Synchronization protocol messages and responses. It looks at compression and enhanced security, as well as at real-time synchronization capabilities applicable in always-on environments. The Data Synchronization enabler serves as one possible technology realization of the Mobile E-mail enabler. For details on this realization, the reader is referred to Chapter 16.

3.4.5.8 Mobile Commerce and Charging Working Group (MCC WG)

The significant number of enablers being developed within the OMA calls for a consistent approach to deal with the commercial aspects of providing a service or delivering content. The Mobile Commerce and Charging Working Group (MCC WG) is the primary group for mobile commerce (m-commerce) and charging work inside of the OMA, with the objective of creating specifications for safe m-commerce. This is achieved through the specification of consistent interfaces for other OMA enablers to facilitate charging and the definition of a specific m-commerce and charging enabler. Chapter 17 will provide a deep dive into the specifics of the OMA Charging enabler.

3.4.5.9 Game Services Working Group (GS WG)

The Game Services Working Group (GS WG) continues the work originated in the now affiliated MGIF. The goal of the GS WG is to define interoperability specifications, interface specifications and protocols for single and multi-player, network-enabled gaming, delivered on mobile devices. Aspects like game distribution and rights management, user account management, and quality of experience (e.g. how the game is affected by network lapses) are addressed. Chapter 24 is dedicated to the requirements, architecture and technical details of the Game Services enabler.

3.4.5.10 Messaging Working Group (MWG)

The OMA Messaging Working Group (MWG) is responsible for the specification of enabling technologies for the various messaging paradigms. It is concerned with the specification of all the messaging protocols, and in addition may also develop requirements for affected components that are not directly specified by MWG itself (e.g. content or media formats, codecs, authentication methods). There are dedicated SWGs for specific messaging paradigms; MWG Instant Messaging (MWG-IM), MWG Mobile E-mail (MWG-MEM), and MWG Multimedia Messaging (MWG-MMSG). There is also an AHG for MWG Converged IP Messaging (MWG-CPM). This book contains a chapter on the Mobile E-mail enabler developed by MWG-MEM (Chapter 16) and a section on the Converged IP Messaging enabler developed by MWG-CPM (Section 27.3).

3.4.5.11 Push-to-talk over Cellular Working Group (POC)

The OMA Push-to-talk over Cellular Working Group (POC) is responsible for developing application enabling specifications for the deployment of an interoperable PoC enabler in mobile networks. The PoC specifications are built on top of various standards for lower-level protocols and architectures required for supporting the current and evolving PoC service. To this end, a strong liaison and close coordination with the groups responsible for those standards is essential for the working of the POC. The WG has instantiated AHGs for each version of the PoC enabler that is being developed or maintained. The PoC enabler takes center stage in Chapter 15.

3.4.5.12 Presence and Availability Working Group (PAG WG)

The OMA Presence and Availability Working Group (PAG WG) has inherited from the affiliated Wireless Village those activities from Instant Messaging and Presence (IMPS) that are not already covered by the activities of MWG-IM. PAG WG has the aim of specifying service enablers to permit the deployment of interoperable mobile presence and availability services, and is expected to specify the OMA service enablers for presence and availability and XML document management. These enablers are detailed in Chapter 14.

3.4.5.13 Mobile Web Services Working Group (MWS WG)

The objective of the Mobile Web Services Working Group (MWS WG) has been to develop a Web Services infrastructure that can readily be used by the OMA enablers that wish to expose their capabilities as Web Services. After successful completion and publication of enabler releases for both the core Web Services aspects, the (OMA Web Services Enabler Release, or OWSER) as well as the network identity aspects (OWSER Network Identity, or OWSER-NI), the WG has been closed and its technical activities and enabler maintenance responsibilities were folded under the wings of the TP. Chapter 11 provides a description of the OWSER and OWSER-NI specifications.

3.4.5.14 Location Working Group (LOC WG)

The Location Working Group (LOC WG) continues the work originated in the affiliated LIF and Location Drafting Committee of the WAP Forum. LOC WG covers the primary aspects of Location Services including an architectural framework with relevant application and content interfaces, privacy and security, charging and billing, and roaming. The enablers being developed and maintained in the LOC WG are the Mobile Location Service (MLS) enabler and the Secure User Plane Location (SUPL) enabler. Both MLS and SUPL are discussed in Chapter 25.

3.4.5.15 Developer Interest Group (DIG)

This section will be slightly more elaborate as this WG does not produce any enabler specifications and hence no detailed follow up chapter is included later in the book. Having said that, the OMA is in the business of developing and publishing specifications for service enablers. Standardized interfaces of such an enabler act as a contract through which a resource can access and use the functions provided by the enabler, and adhering to the specified interface ensures interoperable systems. So all you have to do is hand the interface specification to a software developer who will write the code for it, right? Well, it is not quite as easy as that, for a number of reasons. The requirements that software developers and engineers have may differ from the functional and system requirements for the enabler, which is driven by market needs. As the current structure of the OMA is generally organized around a collection of technical WGs, each focused on a particular topic, there is a need for a single governing body looking out for these developer requirements. The OMA Developer Interest Group (DIG) is that body, representing the interests of software developers.

The DIG is designed as a forum to support developers and users of the OMA specifications. The intent is to give software professionals technical guidance and a set of best practices to build more consistent, higher-quality OMA-conformant systems with less effort. The DIG does not provide common software assets or reusable source-code components, but rather artifacts like a common namespace and guidance on source-code organization. The goal is to provide everything a developer needs to build high-quality business solutions based on the OMA specifications. The DIG provides guidance to software developers for implementing on various OMA-based platforms. Being conscious of developer requirements goes a long way to ensure as broad a base of users as possible within the larger software developer community.

To achieve its objectives, the DIG has three primary activities. The foremost task is to collect and publish information that is relevant to developers. This information can be used in conjunction with the TSs to develop robust, extensible, and maintainable implementations. Secondly, the DIG identifies possible missing and inconsistent developer interfaces. Based on these findings, the DIG makes recommendations for additional or enhanced developer interfaces. And last of all, the interest group provides a channel for the software developer community to articulate and specify their needs back into the OMA. Such feedback and requirements may then serve as input to new enabler specifications or subsequent releases of existing OMA enablers.

So why is it so important to take developer requirements into account when developing standards? Chiefly because these requirements are often out of scope for market requirements, as well as system and functional requirements. In some instances they may even be at odds with the high-level principles. For example, several times now we have touched upon the OMA principle of neutrality toward operating systems and programming language. While this makes sure that no industry segment or user group is disadvantaged, shut out, or ignored, it does present developers with the challenge to translate language neutral concepts into a specific language realization, or operating systems neutral concepts into a realization meant to run with a specific operating system.

The DIG, as its name suggests, is an interest group rather than a technical WG. This implies that any output it creates and presents to the TP must have joint approval from an appropriate OMA WG. To this end, DIG will schedule joint sessions with other OMA WGs on a periodic basis. For example, if a specific developer interface has an impact on or relationship with the OSE, then the ARC WG would need to jointly approve this work. One such example is the white paper on developer guidelines for the OMA namespace encoding [DIG WP]. This white paper, jointly agreed with the ARC WG, provides informative recommendations for naming conventions to address programming language neutral identifications of software packages, classes, methods, metadata, configuration files, exceptions, and synchronous and asynchronous message exchange patterns to be used by developers while implementing the OMA specifications. The use of namespaces will resolve any conflict that may occur when two different OMA enabler specifications use the same element names in software products that contain implementations of both those enablers. The standard root namespace is 'org.openmobilealliance', a name that is registered through OMNA.

It may be interesting to note that there is another OMA activity outside of DIG that bears some relationship. Within the MWS WG, a deliverable called the Web Services Description Language

(WSDL) Style Guide was published as part of the OWSER enabler [OWSERWSDL]. This style guide provides informative guidance for the use of the WSDL that should be followed for the OMA-defined Web Services (see also Chapter 11). Although the intention is similar, that is, providing guidance, the target audience is different. Where DIG addresses the developer community interested in the OMA specifications (i.e. the specifications implementers), the OWSER WSDL Style Guide is aimed at participants in the OMA WGs that develop Web Service interface specifications for the OMA enablers (i.e. the specification writers).

Going forward, the DIG may address further topics such as a common versioning mechanism for the OMA interfaces, or common considerations for backwards compatibility of the OMA compliant implementations.

3.4.6 OMA Birds of a Feather Groups

Not all activities warrant a long-term organizational structure like a WG or fit within the charter of an existing group. Examples of such limited scope activities include feasibility studies, preparatory investigations, informal white papers for internal reference, or attempts to assess the level of interest in or support for a new topic. The OMA provides a lightweight, low threshold process for informal, short-lived groups that may examine issues that are not covered or addressed within a formally chartered group. Such groups are called Birds of a Feather (BoF) groups. The idea is to provide members that have a common interest with a flexible and *ad hoc* forum, without any of the process burden. BoF groups do not produce any normative documents. The outcome of a BoF group may include informative documents for subsequent referencing, such as informal white papers, or a recommendation to TP for a new work item or the creation and chartering of a new WG.

3.5 The Processes

As the OMA was certainly not the first specification development organization in existence, it had the distinct benefit to observe and learn from the processes in use by other bodies. An often-heard frustration of service providers is that the time taken to traverse the entire cycle from work item inception to specification approval and publication is simply too long. Obviously, any process that suffers from too much complexity does little to endear itself to specification developers, and even less to service providers. So, the OMA has set out to define a lightweight process, allowing for flexibility and parallel activities. The idea is to dramatically limit the number of approval gates, which only serve to serialize the specification development trajectory, resulting in extended timelines.

Despite that, the OMA Process Document has grown to a respectable size. It is certainly not the intention here to cover each and every aspect. Many members participating in the OMA have only familiarized themselves with those specific sections that are relevant to their activity of interest, for example, only requirements review, or only interoperability testing. Hence, only the general process and some specific aspects are outlined here, as well as some practices that set the OMA aside from their peers. Note that interoperability, one of the pivotal aspects in the OMA process, warrants its own spotlight and will be described in Section 3.6 and Chapter 4.

3.5.1 Smooth Sailing, no Waterfalls or Gates

One of the most notable characteristics is that the OMA process does not follow the classical waterfall model. That is, the various parts of an enabler may be developed in parallel, without one part having to be completed before commencing the next stage. Although the OMA deliverables typically fall in the three tiers of requirements, architecture, and TS, there is no notion of stages. For example, the work on a TS can start as soon as some of the main architectural concepts have stabilized. There is no need to wait for a reviewed and agreed AD. AD completion is not a gate in the process.

3.5.2 Support for Off-line Progress and Decision Making

A lot of the work that the OMA does takes place at the face-to-face meetings, where the WGs and committees meet and progress their deliverables. In order to help meet some of the aggressive deadlines demanded by commercial pressure and to deliver the promise of shorter specification development cycles, the OMA makes extensive use of off-line electronic means as well to progress their work. E-mail is used, not only for members to go off on their tangents, but to further the technical debates on thorny and often contentious issues. Electronic voting facilities are in place to force a decision in cases for which the instrument of debate has been exhausted and convergence of views can no longer be achieved.

For items requiring only a final cursory review after many rounds of revisions, or for some of the more straightforward administrative decisions, the OMA portal provides support for so-called Review and Approval (R&A). This R&A is an electronic means to agree and dispose of input contributions. Comments or objections can be submitted online, using a Web interface. R&A is also well suited for more extensive reviews with a focus on collecting large sets of comments and feedback from as many sources as possible. Such reviews may take up to 1 or 2 weeks, and are typically not very efficiently done on a conference call or face-to-face session.

3.5.3 Strive for Consensus

The OMA is a consensus driven organization, which fosters the participation from all stakeholders in the value chain and encourages contributions from the widest possible range of members. The cooperative process of specification development requires cooperative decision making. Technical input contributions are discussed, reviewed and subsequently assigned a disposition based on consensus in the WG. Consensus ensures the largest possible buy-in from the OMA community. Only in the case an accord cannot be reached, a formal voting mechanism is in place as a last resort to ensure progress.

3.5.4 Low Threshold for New Work

Any group of four member companies may propose a new Work Item Document (WID) for the OWP. There is no ballot committee or council of wise men to judge the validity of a proposal. Any body of work that has sufficient interest among some of the members may be brought forward as a proposal. New work item proposals are reviewed and agreed by the TP. Broad buy-in from member companies and the OMA WGs may be sought prior to submission of the proposed WID to the TP, through socializing the proposal. Socialization with REQ WG and ARC WG is a mandatory part of the process, as these horizontal groups have a wider visibility of ongoing and completed OMA enabler specifications. This puts them in a unique position to check for consistency, advocate re-use, and avoid overlap and duplication. But again, there is no gate that a WID proposal needs to pass, before submitting for consideration to the TP.

3.5.5 Enabler Release Program

Many organizations, whether they develop standards or any other product, know the concept of 'releases'. A release in this context is defined as a coordinated, self-contained suite of related enablers. Examples include 3GPP Release 99, or Microsoft Office 2000. The advantage of the release concept is that you obtain a bundle of related functions, each of which is perfectly tuned to play well with any of the other functions within the confines of that release. The main disadvantage is the flip side to the same coin. That is, it is a package deal. If you are only interested in the one function, you are stuck with the entire package. You have to wait until the entire package is available, and it may prove cumbersome to use the function in isolation of its often closely coupled buddies from the same release. To allow each enabler to be developed to its own time schedule and market demands, the OMA Process does not work with traditional releases. Instead, it has introduced the concept of the Enabler Release. The Enabler Release is a work package centered around a single enabler, and contains the entire documentation set relevant to the enabler, but nothing more.

The OMA supports two types of releases. The most common release is the Enabler Release. An Enabler Release is defined as a set of specifications (e.g. requirements, architecture, TSs) and white papers, which form a formal deliverable of the OMA that can be implemented in products and solutions and which can also be tested for interoperability. This release type applies to most of the work conducted in the OMA. However, not all of the activities fit this model. To account for that, a second release type was put in place, the Reference Release. A Reference Release, like an Enabler Release, is defined as a set of specifications and/or white papers, which form a formal deliverable of the OMA. The Reference Release can be referenced or otherwise used to support implementable enabler releases, but it cannot by itself be implemented in products. Therefore, there is also no interoperability testing involved. An example of a Reference Release would be an architectural analysis, such as the PIOSE enabler, detailed in Chapter 10.

There is a staged approval process for releases. Once all deliverables that make up the release package (i.e. RD, AD, TSs, and all supporting documentation such as Review Reports and Test Plans) are completed, a review is scheduled in order to determine the suitability of the material being advanced to the first stage of approval, that is, the Candidate state. This review is called the Consistency Review, and these reviews are held to address the full range of concerns that may be raised regarding the quality and suitability of the material to be published. Special attention is paid to the consistency across the entire package, which consists of deliverables that have already been reviewed individually, often by smaller groups. The Consistency Review will have participation of delegates who cover the full range of interests in the OMA to assure complete coverage. After successful completion of the Consistency Review, the release is promoted to the Candidate state. This applies to both Enabler Releases as well as Reference Releases. For the latter, the development cycle is now completed. For Enabler Releases however, a second stage of approval is sought, that is, the Approved state. This second stage consists of a validation phase carried out through a succession of interoperability test events. Interoperability is addressed in the next section, and in Chapter 4. A Candidate Enabler Release which has been subject to public review and interoperability validation process and has addressed all comments and subsequently resolved all problems shall be approved by the TP unless a substantial sustained objection is received from either a member company or any WG. Following the approval by the TP, the release is then to be ratified by the OMA BoD, after which it is published as an Approved Enabler Release. Recall that the OMA BoD is not involved in the technical decision making process, and hence ratification is mainly to ascertain that due process was followed in the creation of the release and that there are no legal issues (such as e.g. copyright infringement).

The concept of Enabler Releases in use by the OMA adds further rigor to the OSE principle of re-use of loosely coupled service building blocks. Enablers can be mixed and matched using best of breed components, to compose imaginative, value added, next generation applications. But since the OMA did away with the concept of traditional releases, it is imperative for the individual enablers to be interoperable. And that brings us to the topic of interoperability in the OMA.

3.6 Interoperability in the Open Mobile Alliance

One of the main purposes of standardization is to build open systems. Various components manufactured by different vendors can be assembled into a larger coherent system, as long as each component adheres to a previously agreed contract, the standardized interface specification. There may be various reasons why one would want to create systems comprising several components, ranging from practical, economical or performance considerations to regulatory requirements for multi-vendor solutions. One of the key aspects of open systems is interoperability among each of the interacting system components. That is, the ability to operate in concert in order to perform a common task or provide a uniform service. Interoperability results in reduced cost and complexity of larger systems and diminishes the risk of deploying compliant products.

Specifications, be they proprietary or endorsed by some Standards Development Organizations (SDOs), are a necessary condition for interoperability. But adherence to specifications alone in most cases is not sufficient to ensure interoperability among complex components in larger systems. Specifications may define options that may be mutually exclusive in a deployment (e.g. enabler implementation A requires Kerberos authentication, whereas enabler implementation B does not support that technology) or specific combinations of options from various specifications may cause interactions that were unforeseen at the time of writing of any of the individual specifications. Additionally, specifications may be ill-defined, where for instance, a given function is underspecified or ambiguously described, allowing for multiple interpretations. And of course, specifications may simply have been implemented incorrectly.

If we disregard implementation errors for a moment, it is desirable for any specifications committee to provide a level of confidence in the interoperability of the interface specifications they produce and publish. There are generally two ways to assess interoperability of interface specifications. One way is to proof interoperability by using formal methods to simulate or model the systems; perform design verification and validation; and test for conditions like deadlock, live lock, starvation (or dining philosophers problem), stale mates, race conditions, infinite loops, and the like.

The other method for ensuring interoperability is to perform interoperability testing with actual products (or early implementations and prototypes) that implement a given enabler specification. It is important to have a representative number of vendors participate in such interoperability events, to prevent a single vendor (or small group of vendors) to dictate the direction of a specification based on their interpretation of a specified function or peculiarity of their product.

There are also other approaches to interoperability in the industry, most notably profiling. Profiles limit the number of options provided in a given specification to only one, on the basis of a given set of use cases or a particular application domain. Usually, profiles are accompanied by guidelines, conventions or best practices for implementation and deployment. Adherence to a given profile guarantees interoperability with another implementation built to the same profile.

When introducing the topic of interoperability just now, we disregarded for the time being incorrect implementations as a cause for non-interoperable system components. However, this is of course an important item for consideration. Implementations need to be compliant to the specification as a necessary first condition to interoperability. Implementations need to be correct as well as complete (i.e. supporting all mandatory requirements). When testing for interoperability, one has to test for or assert compliance first.

Despite the key importance of interoperability, many standards organizations and consortia stop short at publication of standards and/or specifications. Interoperability testing may be undertaken as a bilingual effort on a case by case basis between two vendors, but is not considered an integral part of the specifications trajectory. The OMA departs from this common practice and has adopted interoperability as a fundamental part of its specifications process. Interoperability will be essential for the uptake of specifications produced by the OMA, and ultimately contributes toward the commercial success of the innovative mobile data applications built to those specifications. This section will outline the efforts undertaken as part of the OMA specification processes to ensure interoperability among its enabler releases.

3.6.1 The Objectives of the OMA IOP

At the highest level, the OMA IOP Testing Process consists of two main activities. The first activity is to produce test specifications for each enabler. These test specifications then serve as input to the second activity, the OMA Test Festivals, or TestFests (Chapter 4). Both activities contribute as follows toward the objectives for the OMA IOP Testing Process:

- Improve the OMA enabler specifications – The first main objective is to produce and publish interoperable specifications to reduce cost and increase revenue opportunities for all stakeholders in the next generation application space. Performing rigorous interoperability testing on enabler implementations generates invaluable feedback on implementation issues, and operational and deployment considerations to the OMA members involved in the development of the OMA enabler specifications. This feedback loop will enhance the quality of the specifications and the specification creation process, as well as enhance the credibility and confidence level of approved and published OMA specifications.
- Verify enabler implementations – The second main objective is to verify the interoperability of member company enabler implementations that are built conformant to the specifications. While conducting interoperability tests, other quality aspects like stability and feature support can be verified as well, in a multi-vendor environment.
- Facilitate testing for members – As an additional objective and as a service to its member companies, the OMA TestFests provide a peer-to-peer, heterogeneous production environment to subject their enabler implementations to comprehensive testing in a controlled and trusted setting. Testing is a necessary step in any product development cycle and requires specially configured infrastructure dedicated to handle test transactions and generate required stimuli as input to the system under test. Additionally required resources may include specially trained and skilled testing staff, customized testing tools, etc. Sharing these investments in the OMA TestFests provides significant benefits to the OMA member companies to improve their own implementations.

3.6.2 Process and Documentation

The OMA provides a whole range of documentation to support the complex process of testing. Part of the information is documented as an integral part of the enabler specifications themselves, whereas more specialized testing data requires dedicated records. This section offers a guide to navigate through the administrative infrastructure of the OMA IOP process by providing a description of the various document types involved, along with their purpose. Note that not all document types are covered, only the more significant ones are described.

The entire process obviously starts with the RD, which contains the market-driven functional requirements for the enabler, and hence describes the behavior a system under test is expected to expose. The AD typically describes the functional de-composition into architectural entities, each exposing a defined interface. Such de-composition may introduce additional requirements for interoperability.

The TS for the enabler includes the detailed message flows, the exchanged parameters, their data types and formats, and the state behavior of the various entities involved. Every feature of the enabler is defined in detail. Protocol binding information may be provided. As an appendix to the TS, the Static Conformance Requirement (SCR) provides a list of mandatory features of the enabler, which need to be supported by any compliant implementation, as well as any number of optional features. The list contains each individual feature that can be implemented by an enabler implementation. Any conformant enabler implementation must support the entire set of mandatory features to ensure interoperability and compliance.

The RD, AD, and TSs are of a more generic nature, whereas the Enabler Test Requirement (ETR) document is the first in the set of documents specifically dedicated to IOP. The ETR collects requirements from the RD and the AD, and supplements those where appropriate with any other requirement that may not have been explicitly identified but is considered critical from the perspective of interoperability. The test requirements include scenarios that validate normal working behavior for the enabler, as well as error conditions and exceptions. In addition to positive testing (does the enabler do what it is supposed to do?) the test requirements may also incorporate negative testing (does the enabler do only what it is allowed to do and nothing else?). Backward compatibility of the system under test, with implementations conformant to previous releases of the specification may also be part of the test requirements.

The ETR serves as an input to the Enabler Test Guidelines (ETG), which captures the infrastructure, operational, and participation conditions for a valid and successful TestFest. The ETG defines the test strategy and test methodologies for meeting the testing requirements recorded in the ETR. Such guidelines provide recommendations on minimal configurations of the enabler, minimal participation in a TestFest, any specific requirements on the infrastructure of the testing environment, tools and resources that need to be available, etc. Any legal requirements, such as software licensing obligations or confidentiality restrictions should be addressed by the ETG as well.

All this preparatory material leads to the Enabler Test Specification (ETS). The ETS documents the actual test cases that are to be executed at an OMA TestFest. There are two types of test cases: conformance test cases and interoperability test cases. The conformance test cases verify whether the enabler implementation adheres to the normative requirements contained in the TSs (RD, AD, and TSs). The interoperability test cases verify whether enabler implementations interoperate to collectively perform their common task. Both types of test cases are described in terms of a detailed, step-by-step test procedure along with pre-conditions and pass- and fail-criteria. All documentation involved in defining the tests is shown in Figure 3.3.

The following documentation set is related to the TestFests themselves. The Enabler Implementation Conformance Statement (EICS) is a check-list that allows vendors to indicate which features their implementation supports. These features correspond to the ones defined in the SCR collected from the TSs. Using the EICS, vendors can identify which of the high-level requirements, in terms of mandatory features and optional features of the TSs, they have implemented. This document is mainly used by the OMA to pair client and server implementations in the TestFests.

The Enabler Validation Plan (EVP) is created before any TestFest or Bi-lateral Testing is conducted. It defines the validation strategy and the validation methodologies for meeting the requirements defined by the technical WG that has developed the specification. It includes the definition of scope for testing of the enabler including interoperability testing details as well as possible prioritizations, and has a preliminary proposal on the high-level requirements for a test tool for the enabler. In addition to the above, the EVP is also used to identify the financial and legal requirements. It is really the document on the basis of which the recommendation for approved status is decided.

Companies who have participated in an OMA TestFest complete a Test Session Report (TS_RPT), recording the results of the event. For each test case, the company logs whether a test case passed or failed, or whether the result was inconclusive, or not obtained due to timing restrictions.

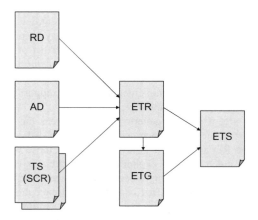

Figure 3.3 OMA documentation involved in defining tests

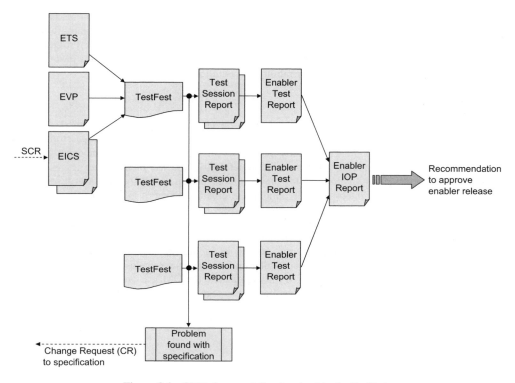

Figure 3.4 OMA documentation involved in the TestFests

The OMA, as the trusted party hosting the TestFest, will collate all the TS_RPTs for the TestFest for a given enabler, and create the Enabler Test Report (ET_RPT). This ET_RPT contains all relevant test information for the given enabler and the given TestFest. Such information includes the enabler being tested (name and revision), information on the tests themselves (e.g. version of ETS, version of test tool), any problems found (either with the specifications, or the test collateral like test tools or test specifications), and the participating companies.

In order to ensure that sufficient statistical data and test results have been gathered before considering approving the enabler release, a succession of TestFests will be conducted for any given enabler. Once that determination has been made, the IOP WG will assemble all ET_RPTs into an Enabler IOP Report (IOP_RPT), which will accompany the recommendation to approve the enabler release. All documentation involved in conducting the tests is shown in Figure 3.4.

3.6.3 OMA Interoperability Recognition Program

In some organizations, having successfully participated in a series of test events grants the system under test the right or privilege to claim compliance to the specification. In many cases, certification of products is required, either by the network operator deploying the systems, or by a regulatory body. Examples of certification programs include Network Equipment-Building System (NEBS) for network servers, and the Global Certification Forum (GCF) and Personal Communication Service (PCS) Type Certification Review Board (PTCRB) for mobile wireless terminal equipment.

The OMA, however, does not offer any such certification, as it does not provide any certification programs. External certification authorities are encouraged and invited to develop such certification programs related to the OMA enabler specifications. Nevertheless, in order to demonstrate the OMA's firm commitment and unremitting devotion to interoperability and to acknowledge the significant accomplishment of companies which successfully validated interoperability of their enabler implementation, the OMA has established an Interoperability Recognition Program. The OMA member companies who have successfully participated in the series of TestFests for the enabler are eligible for the OMA Interoperability Recognition Program.

3.7 Summary

This chapter has introduced the OMA, a specification development organization for market-driven, interoperable mobile service enablers. As we have seen, the OMA marks a change from earlier specification development approaches chiefly through its principles of neutrality, the departure from vertical integration, the emphasis placed on interoperability, and the membership representation across the entire value chain. Interoperability plays a pivotal part in the OMA standards development process. Ensuring seamless interoperability among the broadest range of independently developed, standards-based enabler implementations helps the OMA attain the objective to grow the market for the entire mobile industry. Interoperability helps remove barriers to the accelerated adoption of next generation applications for service providers.

A lot of ground has been covered in this chapter, including organizational aspects, processes, and documentation – not always the most exhilarating topics. Nevertheless, the information presented provides the necessary foundation to fully appreciate the OMA as an organization. We have described how the OMA has come into being, how it has organized itself, and the characteristics that has set it aside from other organizations. All these traits have propelled the OMA into the position of foremost industry organization, fueling the success of the mobile service enabler market.

4

Interoperability TestFests

One could undoubtedly write many chapters on the definition of interoperability. Several seminars dedicated to the topic have examined the manner possible to tackle this question. To take only one of them among the most important ones, European Telecommunications Standards Institute (ETSI) had to organize a series of workshops (S.O.S Interop I, II, and III) during which more than a hundred representatives of the ETSI members proposed definitions for the term, and discussed the frontiers between interoperability, open software, and regulation. Beyond the altogether academic discussion on a rigorous and exhaustive definition of the interoperability, the Open Mobile Alliance (OMA) has adopted an approach much more pragmatic, which is summarized in its vision: 'No matter what device I use, no matter what service I want, no matter what carrier network I'm using, I want to communicate, access and exchange information.'

4.1 The Objective of Interoperability in the OMA

The goal that the OMA is setting out to achieve regarding interoperability is twofold. First, the goal is to verify that the specifications produced by the working groups are sufficiently defined and non ambiguous so that they can be indeed implemented in products. This implies the testing of all the important functionalities provided in the specifications that are usually described as mandatory, as well as those which will be implemented in a selective way, which are named as optional. Secondly, the objective is to make it possible for member companies to test their products or advanced prototypes in order to be able to put mature products on the market as soon as the demand is there.

Broadly speaking, by participating in the OMA TestFests, companies can expand their market opportunities by ensuring that their products interoperate with other implementations of OMA specifications. Using TestFests to resolve specification issues in an early stage of the product life cycle (i.e. prior to commercial rollout) helps to avoid costs and delays in the product deployment process. Equipment manufacturers and software developers are invited to integrate their platforms in a trusted and secure environment, enabling testing and debugging. The events facilitate close interaction and exchange of ideas and experiences between the people drafting the specifications and the developer community implementing them, hopefully resulting in enhanced quality of the specifications.

The interest for a member is, of course, different depending on whether the member is a supplier of equipment or software, an operator, a test tool supplier, or a content provider. The most interested in the activities of interoperability are mainly the suppliers of equipment or software, the operators, and the test tool suppliers. The content providers' position is different in the OMA and their presence and participation in the activities of interoperability is relatively reduced.

The Open Mobile Alliance   M. Brenner and M. Unmehopa
© 2008 Alcatel-Lucent. All Rights Reserved

The suppliers of equipment and software are those that are the most active for obvious reasons. The question for them is to put on the market well-developed equipment, presenting the least possible number of residual problems and this preferably before any of the other competing manufacturers. Network equipment vendors can ensure that their server products are interoperable with an extensive range of clients or mobile devices from different manufacturers. Conversely, device manufacturers can verify whether their device is able to register and interact with a multitude of server implementations. Moreover, an active participation in interoperability testing is always an excellent commercial argument for a manufacturer to put forward to one's customers.

The operators are interested in interoperability because it makes it possible for them to evaluate the quality of the equipment they will see a few months later when they will issue their Request for Quotations (RFQ). Of course, they try to reinforce their presence in these activities of interoperability TestFests, in particular by trying to get access to the results of the tests, which are restricted only to the manufacturers.

To illustrate the respective involvement of these OMA member companies, the participation of the suppliers of equipment and software represents approximately 55% of the members and a little more than 58% of the contributions, whereas the figures for the operators indicate that approximately 21% of the participants in the activities of interoperability belong to this category and submit approximately 11% of the contributions.

4.2   The Organization of the Test Campaigns

Basically, the objective of the TestFest is to provide a confidential and neutral environment allowing inter-working between competitors. OMA TestFests are organized by the OMA Interoperability Working Group (IOP WG), making use of the resources provided by an OMA member company who acts as the hosting operator. The hosting operator provides a testing environment, which may consist of a complete mobile Second Generation (2G) and 3G network infrastructure (GSM, CDMA, W-CDMA) with the relevant equipment (e.g. WAP Gateway, Push Proxy Gateway (PPG), Short Message Service (SMS) Centers, IP Multimedia Subsystem (IMS) System), Radio Frequency (RF) coverage, a pool of test Subscriber Identity Modules (SIMs) to register devices to be tested, Internet or other type of network connectivity, dedicated test tools, etc. By alternating between hosting operators that support various access networks, implementers can validate whether their enabler can operate across various bearer technologies.

In order to participate in an OMA TestFest, the company must, of course, be a member of the OMA, irrespective of the membership class. Some amount of pre-testing is mandated to be allowed to participate in a TestFest, for instance to administrate any required local network configurations for the test environment and verify that basic connectivity can be established. Additionally, for the interoperability testing to be meaningful and effective, a certain level of implementation maturity and stability must be met by each client or server implementation before engaging in peer-to-peer test scenarios. The OMA member should have developed, or commissioned for development, their own client/terminal or server implementations of an OMA enabler specification. This latter constraint is put in place to make sure real products, developed by the company and which it intends to put on the market, are brought to the TestFest.

The participating company should also submit to the OMA, prior to the event, the test report demonstrating that their implementation can pass a set of defined conformance tests for that enabler. It should be noted that the demonstration of passing the tests will vary from enabler to enabler and may also vary from TestFest to TestFest. As explained in Chapter 3, an Enabler Implementation Conformance Statement (EICS) for each enabler to be tested should also be provided so that OMA staff can pair each implementation with an appropriate counterpart. All items that are mandated by this EICS document must be supported by the implementation before entering the TestFest. If this is not the case, this company could be prevented to participate. In practice though, it is exceptional that a participating company be refused for this reason.

At last, companies should have sent the signed Non Disclosure Agreement (NDA) prior to the start of the TestFest, otherwise they will not be permitted to participate and will be asked to leave the testing facility. Any successful test event requires a significant representation of the vendor and developer community to participate, commit resources, and bring their implementations. It is essential that vendors and implementers have a certain comfort level in bringing their products to a test event and submit them to extensive and rigorous testing. To this end, the OMA serves as the neutral party to schedule and host the test events, and handle any confidential information. The NDAs are in place to protect any competitive information from disseminating to competitors directly or the industry as a whole. Individual product test results therefore are held under strict confidentiality. Verification of specifications is done on the basis of the technical requirements defined for the enabler only. This implies that OMA interoperability testing does not address any commercial aspects of the systems under test, including performance attributes (such as transactional capacity, load characteristics, reliability parameters, etc.) or pricing considerations.

4.3   Planning

The organization of the TestFest is always a bit of a challenge although the OMA staff has acquired a lot of experience over the years. To minimize the problems when organizing this event, which could lead to a waste of time, bad conditions for the member, or even worse the obligation to cancel the event, the OMA has set deadlines that should be respected each time the forum has decided to set up such an event.

- Twelve weeks before the event, the host is decided. The host should be an OMA member and a well-balanced geographical distribution should be sought. In particular, OMA verifies that two successive TestFests cannot be organized in the same continent and that each continent is chosen at least once a year. At this stage, the TestFest website is also updated.
- Eight weeks before the event, the date and location of the TestFest are notified to OMA members and all TestFest documents are identified (EICS template, test cases, test tools, NDA template).
- Seven weeks before the event, the registration is open via an online web registration for the TestFest via the OMA website. The TestFest is officially announced and members are provided with the site information for the event (i.e. infrastructure description, travel information, etc.).
- Six weeks before the event, all final documentation is made available on the website, and will be used in the event.
- Early registration is closed five weeks before the event. After this date, the price of participation increases.
- Four weeks before the event, the last updates to the test tools are agreed and registration closes three weeks before the TestFest. At this stage, the participating companies should have provided both the EICS, proving that their implementations support the minimal functionalities and the NDA.
- Typically, a TestFest lasts one week. It starts with the pre-testing day during which the network infrastructure is set up and participants are provided with detailed onsite information for the TestFest event (i.e. IP numbers, test schedule, onsite logistics etc.).

During that one week, the TestFest is executed according to the schedule created by the OMA staff. Each team goes to a meeting room, passes the tests with their counterpart, writes down the results they have obtained (sometimes after a technical discussion with the other team to align their positions), and moves to another meeting room. At the end of the TestFest, all results are compiled in a report, which is sent to the OMA staff. The staff will then produce an overall summary of the results obtained during the TestFest and will distribute it within the OMA.

Table 4.1   Statistics on past IOP TestFests

Enablers tested	Companies	Implementations	Clients	Servers	Issues raised
IMPS 1.x testing	119	152	85	67	86
MMS 1.x testing	93	112	71	41	65
OCSP v1.0	5	8	6	2	0
PoC v1.0	110	143	94	49	37
Presence v1.0	67	82	49	33	13
Push v2.0	3	3	1	2	0
SUPL v1.0	17	24	11	13	3
XDM v1.0	69	86	55	31	29

4.4   Finances

The pricing structure for the TestFest is based on what a company has to pay per implementation. There is a fee for each product or implementation for a standard registration. In addition, each participating company in a TestFest shall pay an additional fee per engineer for a standard registration. Discounts are available for early bird registrations.

4.5   TestFest Statistics

Statistics gathered during the first couple of years of operation of the OMA show that typically, OMA interoperability events are held four or five times per year and gather between 120 and 200 engineers. In average seven to nine enablers are tested by 70–90 different test teams.

Obviously, the number of participants for each enabler depends on the interest of the market for that enabler. Table 4.1 gives some ideas on which enablers raised momentum. Instant Messaging and Presence (IMPS), Multimedia Messaging Service (MMS), and everything related to Push-to-talk over Cellular (PoC) (including XML Document Management (XDM) and Presence) attracted a lot of companies, while other enablers such as Online Certificate Status Protocol (OCSP) or Secure User Plane Location (SUPL) were of interest to a somewhat smaller group of members.

In total, since the existence of the OMA (statistics collected in June 2007), over 930 implementations have been tested and the number is increasing every year. These numbers break down as follows: 144 implementations were tested in the first year (November 2002–October 2003, five events), 178 in the second year (November 2003–October 2004, four events), 263 in the third year (November 2004–October 2005, four events) and 351 in fourth year (November 2005–June 2006, four events). During this period, 466 technical problems were raised and resolved by the various technical working groups.

After several TestFests, and provided that appropriate conditions are verified (no pending problem reports, all mandatory features tested, etc.), the IOP WG can propose the approval status for the enabler. This recommendation should be agreed by the Technical Plenary.

4.6   Comparison with Other Standards Development Organizations (SDOs)

The validation of draft specifications through interoperability testing is well defined and mature in the OMA. Based on open testing events during which a large variety of implementations can be tested against each other, a problem reporting tool allowing members to alert the technical working groups to necessary changes to be applied to the specifications, significantly increases the quality of these specifications.

Not all other Standards Development Organizations (SDOs) have defined such a process. ETSI has no formal feedback mechanism to take into account the results of its plugtest events. International Telecommunication Union – Telecommunication Standardization Sector (ITU-T) has also only limited facilities for validating recommendations before they are published. Digital Video

Broadcasting (DVB) lacks formal processes for drafting, validation, and change management. In the Institute of Electrical and Electronics Engineers (IEEE), the specification of interoperability and/or conformance test suites is not part of the standards development process. Moreover the complex hierarchy of management and the approval and auditing committees assure consensus, due process, openness, and balance in the development of standards but has the adverse effect of extending the development cycle.

4.7 Summary

Obviously, the more participants registering for the TestFest, the better. This increases the number of implementations tested, helps in discovering technical shortcomings or ambiguities in the specifications, and ensures that a higher number of mature products is available when the market takes off. The IOP WG is putting a lot of effort in promoting the benefits of participating in the TestFests, in particular by encouraging companies to apply as IOP champions, whose role is to take the lead in the preparation of the IOP documents. Operators are also willing to increase the value of the testing activities by proposing the creation of a certification program. This idea is still under discussion but is creating strong opposition from the equipment suppliers. The future will tell us if a consensus is possible on this concept.

5

Service Provider – The Network Operator Perspective

This chapter and the next one are meant to give you the service providers' perspective about the Open Mobile Alliance (OMA) work. This should be easy, right? Either they like and support the OMA, or they don't. But then we stopped for a moment, and thought, who are 'they'? In bland generic terms, a service provider is an organization supplying services or products to customers. In the OMA, a service is defined as a selection from a portfolio of offerings, utilizing one or more service enablers and made available by a service provider, which the user may subscribe to and be optionally charged for. The OMA prides itself in having its membership represent all the segments of the mobile industry, and more recently, even segments of the converged services industry, beyond the mobile industry. In such a value chain, lots of services are provided to a range of principals. Indeed, the OMA enablers serve in building such services. As a result, we will encounter in the OMA Network Operators (Mobile and/or Fixed), Content Providers, Application Providers, network equipment and IT vendors, and other categories of service providers, all offering services to other entities in the value chain, or to the individual consumers.

Since it is impractical to even try in a short chapter to get the perspective of every type of service provider in the value chain, we decided to focus first on the views of a Mobile Operator on OMA (after all, this is a book about the Open Mobile Alliance). The Mobile Operator has specific needs in its role as a service provider. Is the OMA responding to them?

5.1 The Need for OMA

Standards have proven to be of extraordinary impact on the Mobile Operators' business. A straightforward example is the GSM standard. The success of the European Telecommunications Standards Institute (ETSI) in developing the GSM specifications made possible the deployment of a global telecommunications system that operates all over the world today, as well as the development of a very strong industry around it. The same can be said about the development of CDMA in other parts of the world.

In the following sections of this chapter, we will explore the operator's point of view on the OMA, our experience in this specifications activity, and our expectations for the future. To fully understand this experience, it is important to keep in mind that when the Mobile Services ecosystem began to appear in the telecom industry, it had the GSM and 3GPP specifications as the base reference for their investments, deployments, and end-user core services.

The Open Mobile Alliance   M. Brenner and M. Unmehopa
© 2008 Alcatel-Lucent. All Rights Reserved

The term 'Mobile Services' is a very broad one. For convenience and for this section, it is being used as a generic shortcut to represent a range of value added services, other than plain voice and short messages, delivered to end-users over Mobile Operators' networks. Of course, and especially nowadays, a fairer definition of mobile services would include many others types of networks. Today's technology convergence and, more precisely, convergence between fixed and mobile telecommunication networks, is blurring frontiers formerly defined between them. Additional considerations are being given as well to the terms of mobility, availability, nomadic services, etc.

After years of business based mainly on voice and short messaging services, with a very stable business value chain and a consolidated customer base, the Mobile Services ecosystem was about to require significant changes. These changes refer not only to technology, but also to business relations, value chains, roles, and, of course, standards.

The beginning of the journey (where Parlay/OSA (Open Service Access) work had a leading role) was to open the Operator's network capabilities toward third parties. These third-party companies could then develop an innovative and varied set of services to be delivered to the end-user based on the Mobile Operator's network capabilities. Enterprise customers, some of which had their own IT departments, could also gain access more directly to the network functionalities, in order to obtain richer functionality and better performance.

This new ecosystem put in contact the network operators segment and the enterprise segment, two worlds that used different technologies, followed different standards, and have largely different major technology vendors. There was an important gap to bridge somehow.

In response to this gap, many proprietary solutions were developed by operators, especially incumbent ones (which could flex enough muscle in their markets) in order to offer proprietary interfaces toward third parties. Initially these third parties developed their services using the available proprietary solutions and interfaces. This created a problem for third-party developers as well as for operators: vendors could not easily reuse their applications for other operators (new integration efforts had to take place in order to adapt to a different proprietary technology), and operators would experience high cost and increased time-to-market for new services.

Choosing the best technology to bridge that gap was also something that needed thorough consideration. Technologies like Signalling System 7 (SS7) or ISDN User Part (ISUP) did not count on a general developer base, neither were they the best choice for modeling this type of Business-to-Business (B2B) relationships. Abstractions based on Common Object Request Broker Architecture (CORBA) did not prove to be friendly enough for third parties, and they encountered technical problems when used across the Internet, due to firewalls and proxies. Internet technologies on the other hand, mainly based on HTTP, were not perceived as a good match for the real-time/carrier grade performance that was considered a requirement in telecom systems. Finally, having different technology providers on both sides was another difficulty to surmount: to solve the same issues, they were using different terminology, methodology, approaches, architecture, etc.

An additional point is that the business scenarios and value chains were enriched with a multiplicity of new roles, which brought a whole new complexity in the B2B relationships held by the operator. Billing and general post-processing systems had to be adjusted to the new business reality. However, unlike the end-user's low expectations from fixed Internet service providers no matter how complex the Mobile Operators services may be, subscribers of a Mobile Operator tend to perceive it as the responsible entity for any problem in the service delivery, regardless of how many different actors are involved in it. This is shown in Figure 5.1.

In order to offer proper service delivery and support to the user, one needs to know what happens in every link of the delivery chain. Doing so in this new complex value chain brings about the necessity to horizontally expand the monitoring and operation systems, and carefully design Service Level Agreements (SLAs) in the operator's B2B relationships, so that the operator can achieve an accurate end-to-end view of its services portfolio's status. Achieving this end-to-end view becomes cumbersome and rather complex, given the lack of standards filling the gaps between technologies.

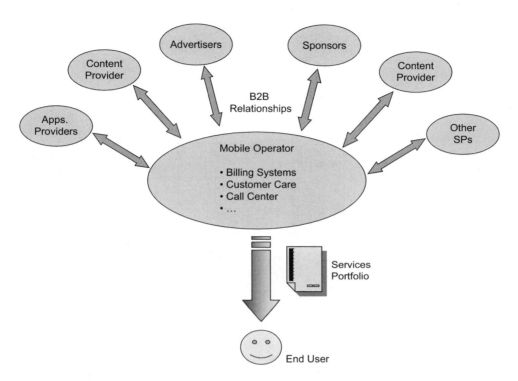

Figure 5.1 End user perceives operators as the only responsible party for the services portfolio

Mobile handsets, on the other hand, were no longer mere devices for voice communications and short messages. They began to be enriched with functionality: browsing, multimedia messaging, ring tones, wallpapers, games, etc. Many different services appeared on the market with very little interoperability among terminals of different vendors, requiring huge integration and testing efforts to make them available and serviceable, and increasing time-to-market for many innovative services. Some compelling services simply did not even get the opportunity to be generally available to end-users due to the difficulties in being deployed.

Architecturally speaking, the situation was becoming too complex, and difficult to manage. Various service architecture solutions appeared in the market in order to bring some consolidation and interoperability in this Mobile Services ecosystem. However, they were vertical architectures: messaging architecture, streaming architecture, browsing architectures, etc. They had the goal of solving the interoperability problems inherent to a multi-vendor environment, but only for a given type of service. Each one of them supported its own way of integration toward support back-end systems (billing, Operations, Administration, and Maintenance (OA&M), Customer Relationship Management (CRM), etc.) and network capabilities. This is depicted in Figure 5.2. However, this integration could not be reused for other services. We were falling back into vertical solutions for our infrastructures, going away from the horizontal principles that initiatives like the Parlay/OSA had introduced. Technology overlap, effort repetition, difficulty of combining capabilities into a single service, and inconsistent end-user and third-party experience were the direct consequences.

Finally, as a response of the industry, many different fora tried to individually address the technology gaps that were being created: WAP Forum, Location Interoperability Forum (LIF),

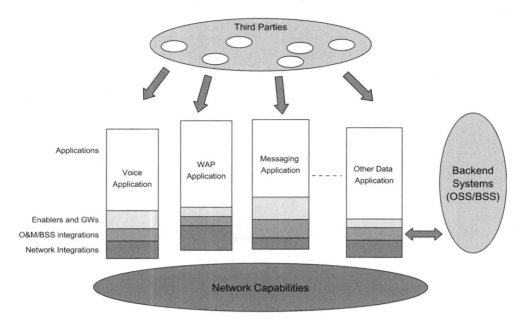

Figure 5.2   Vertical design ('silos') in a service architecture

Wireless Village, Synchronization Markup Language (SyncML) Forum, etc. The result was the multiplicity of fora, sometimes creating overlap, and lack of a broader view in order to properly develop a standardized services environment.

Hence, the effect was that new business rules, new business relationships, new roles in the value chain in an ecosystem where the number of services was continuously increasing while their life cycle was becoming shorter, and the technology divergence and lack of standards were imposing very high integration costs in service deployment. As a last remark, we should point out that in the years prior to the OMA, Mobile Operators were already growing globally. The result was that the global operators were faced with several local operations around the world, under the same management, using different telecom technologies and business models. Trying to find the desired technology synergy in the Mobile Services ecosystem that we have described so far was a tough challenge.

At this point in time, we could definitely say that a forum like the OMA was really needed.

5.2   Operators in the OMA

One of the first things that operators identified as a positive development in the OMA was the consolidation of different fora (LIF, WAP, Wireless Village, SyncML, etc.) into a single one. This made possible to get an end-to-end standards view in the industry while needing less resources and with a more consistent and coordinated participation.

Having said that, the operators had to soon realize that 3GPP and 3GPP2 on one hand (3GPP/2) and the OMA on the other hand, were different. Many delegates in the OMA were coming from a 3GPP/2 background, which meant that they were used to working in a certain environment. The major players in 3GPP/2 were coming from the mobile telecom industry, and the standardization efforts were pretty much addressed to support a very well-defined business model.

In the OMA we had to change our view and engage in discussions with different segments of the industry that had very different requirements than those of the traditional telecom industry. Other industry segments were used to different technologies, different business models, and were even employing a different terminology.

We could say that, at the beginning of our work, terminology differences were the cause of a big percent of the discrepancies, especially in groups like the Architecture Working Group (ARC WG), where it was so important to state clearly the basics, the principles and goals of our work. At the end of the day, those principles were going to be applied throughout the OMA by means of the architecture reviews and to all the Architecture Documents (ADs) made in the OMA. Needless to say, agreeing on a common terminology was important.

A massive attendance to an OMA meeting (over 500 people in general) equates to a significant number of people coming from the 3GPP/2, the WAP Forum, the Internet Engineering Task Force (IETF), the Organization for the Advancement of Structured Information Standards (OASIS), and from other backgrounds and used to different ways to develop specifications. Given this premise, it is easy to imagine the significant efforts that the Operations and Process Working Group had to invest in the beginning. This Working Group had to develop a process clear and concise enough to avoid ambiguities, and comfortable enough for everyone.

Nowadays, we can say that the different segments of the industry participating in the OMA have achieved a much better understanding of each other's circumstances. This will ultimately lead to more harmonized work in the standards environment, and to the specification of a Mobile Services Environment useful for everyone.

One of the main challenges for operators in the OMA consists of figuring out smooth ways to deploy products based on the OMA work over 3GPP/2 networks. Establishing a standard Mobile Services ecosystem in the OMA wouldn't be of much use to us if its deployment on 3GPP/2 networks was not feasible. In attacking this issue, specific technology realizations of the specifications were very useful. Specification realizations start with an OMA specification and specify how it should be implemented in a given environment and using a particular technology (abandoning, or rather complementing the OMA's network neutrality principle to get to a more implementable alternative).

Given the different business models represented in the OMA, specification realizations have special importance. The broader the community that has to be supported by a specification, the more general and less specific and detailed the specification becomes. While a generic and broad specification has its own advantages, stopping the work at a too abstract level however, leads to vague specifications that may generate a huge number of interoperability problems between the different vendors' solutions. In not so many words, the result is an ambiguous specification. By giving to each industry segment the opportunity to write down a technology realization of the specification, the OMA establishes a deployment reference to be followed and, hopefully, a basis for achieving the desired multi-vendor interoperability.

Another hot topic for the operators is the quest to reduce the number of specification options. The less options in the specifications the better. This is particularly important in the core functionalities. In our networks, which are a multi-vendor environment, the mix and match of products is a must. We have to be able to change, for example, a presence enabler by another presence enabler from another vendor and be able to activate the newly deployed enabler and have it functioning with minimum efforts, without impacting any service and without impacting the presence enabler's communications and dependencies with other enablers. This can only be achieved with very detailed specifications and a much reduced number of options.

However, technology options are the core of other industries, where different choices are made available to the market and end-users end up choosing the winner by means of a massive use of the preferred options, constituting a 'de facto' standard. While this may work in other industries, the GSM and CDMA industry however has been developed following different principles.

The clash between industry philosophies and, more precisely, between the Internet and the Telecom philosophies, is at the centre of many of the discrepancies in the OMA. Both worlds try to preserve their preferred business model, which proved to be successful for their respective industries. We could say that the key challenge in the OMA in the day by day activities is to find the common ground for both business models or, at least, to know how far we can reach without threatening anyone's business. Later realizations of the specifications will take care of the rest. One would think that this is quite a difficult task and, truly, it is. However, the OMA has very skilled and professional delegates that are aware of the issues and diligently work on resolving them every day.

One of the tasks that proved to be quite challenging was the definition of service architecture for the OMA enablers. Coming from the 3GPP/2 backgrounds, the natural impulse from the operator side was trying to define a full-fledged architecture in which all the OMA enablers would be represented, with plenty of detail and a limited number of options. However, this type of architecture tends to require a number of deployment assumptions. Due to the diverse nature of the companies participating in the OMA, it is preferable to avoid deployment assumptions, since the deployment options followed by the different sectors of the industry tend to be very different and, sometimes, contradictory.

An additional consideration to be taken into account is that the OMA does not publish synchronized releases as is the norm in 3GPP/2. Because of this, trying to create a snapshot of the overall architecture with a set of enablers that have their independent specification roadmap may be a very difficult task, and the resulting specification would possibly have a short-lived value, unless constantly maintained.

This situation led to the fact that a 'narrower focus' or 'granular' specifications are more feasible in the OMA. Of course you still have to find the common ground for all the participating companies, but you don't have to concentrate on the bigger picture or on general architectural functions. Nevertheless, this does not take value away from those specifications. Before the OMA, many of these vertical functionalities were designed *ad hoc* by innovative vendors, and could be used only with a subset of terminals in the market (generally, those from the vendor providing the network platforms). With the OMA specifications, we will hopefully ensure that all the OMA compliant networks solutions and terminals will interoperate smoothly. This circumstance, just by itself and for any given service, dramatically reduces the integration and terminal testing efforts.

There are already some success stories in the OMA worth mentioning, because they have a broad impact. Device Management (DM) is one such example. DM specifications (see Chapter 18) facilitate the management of a huge and diverse handset base for operators. Features such as remote configuration and handset information retrieval improve the service delivery and especially the customer care capabilities, by transparently supporting the configuration of the end-user's handset to allow successful access to the services, and by adapting the service delivery to the capabilities of the terminal. So far, this specification has been developed in such a way that any OMA enabler can reuse its functionality in order to configure the enabler parameters on the terminal side. Enablers like this are of extreme importance, because of their direct impact on the relationship between service providers and their customers.

Applying 'horizontalization' principles in service architecture in order to avoid silos has been one of the first goals of several service providers in the OMA. In this regard, much work has been done in the ARC WG.

Activities of great interest for operators in the ARC WG included the definition of a general architecture and principles for the OMA, the promotion of several horizontal enablers and the definition of realizations of the OMA enablers over existing and well-known specifications and technologies.

The OMA Service Environment (OSE) architecture (see Section 2.3), which is mainly defined by a set of architecture design guidelines and principles, helped a lot in redirecting the OMA specifications by means of the AD reviews. Compliance to the OSE principles is critical in order to avoid the development of silos, overlap, and lack of general visibility of the work in the OMA.

No details on the different horizontal functions that were promoted from the ARC WG will be mentioned here, since they are detailed in other chapters of this book. We will just say that important examples of those functions are Policy Evaluation, Enforcement, and Management (PEEM) specifications (see Chapter 8), Service Life-cycle Management and Service Level Tracing addressed by the OMA Service Provider Environment (OSPE) specifications (see Chapter 12), and General Service Subscription Management (GSSM) specifications (see Section 27.1). All these specifications are wide in scope, ambitious in goals, and carrying every operator's hope that they will deliver on their promise when completed.

Finally, reuse of former technologies and coexistence and cooperation of the OMA specifications with specifications from other standard bodies is another one of the very commendable activities the OMA ARC WG has undertaken. The two more representative cases are the Parlay in OSE (see Chapter 10) and the Utilization of IMS in OMA (IMSinOMA) (see Chapter 9) specifications. For the telecommunications industry, defining how the OMA specifications will coexist with (or be based upon) Parlay/OSA and the IP Multimedia Subsystem (IMS) infrastructure is vital. Vital for operators to smoothly and usefully deploy the OMA technology in our networks. Vital for the OMA specifications to be successful among operators.

5.3   OMA Challenges for the Future

Looking forward, the OMA has an interesting number of challenges lying ahead. Throughout all these years, there was a coexistence of two different standard development philosophies in the OMA. One is similar to the 3GPP/2 philosophy, which is based on an overall architecture that tries to keep coherence and consistency among the OMA specifications, while providing a comprehensive framework for them. The other approach is following more the IETF style, where interested companies develop certain functionality to be reused by whoever finds it appropriate, but without excessive concerns about overlapping or lack of integration in the overall environment.

Due to this coexistence of philosophies, avoiding overlap and creating synergy in the OMA is going to continue to be challenging and will require plenty of effort. What do we mean by overlap? The concern is less with respect to overlap of main functionality specified, but instead overlap and divergence in the integration with other systems. For example, different enablers have taken different approaches dealing with user subscription, user privacy, user information, charging, etc. Despite the efforts of some working groups (ARC WG is a good example) to promote reuse and avoidance of silos, local optimization at working group level combined with timing and communication still poses a challenge that needs to be overcome.

At the time this book lands in your hands, the OMA is developing specifications to support subscription management (see Section 27.1 on GSSM). This work is of extraordinary importance for operators, where the management of user and subscription information throughout the operator's infrastructure is quite distributed and complex. The main challenge will consist in contributing to the development of a solution that, once a user subscription request is received, is capable to provision all the necessary user information in the appropriate entities of our networks, and be able to ultimately notify the subscriber that 'your subscription is complete, and you may use the service'. Management of user data related to its subscriptions (in fact one could say that there's no user if there is no subscription) and its consistency during modifications and removals, is of utmost importance. If the OMA is able to develop a solution, flexible and good enough to automate the bulk of these processes, we will greatly benefit from it.

Something of similar importance is the OSPE, which is also in specifications development phase. Addressing any of the two key points covered in this work (service life-cycle management and service level tracing) would translate into key benefits for the operator and the end-user. Reducing the cost of services life-cycle management, as well as reducing their time-to-market, will possibly result into a richer and more dynamic service catalogue available to the user. In addition, enabling a better end-to-end tracing and monitoring of services will surely increase the quality of the service support given to the end-user. The complex ecosystem and value chain in which operators deliver their services these days make both these functions very important.

However, the OMA also needs to develop an enabler for the management of general end-user information. It needs to define a common way to identify the user, avoiding that each enabler chooses a different way to represent the user in the data it handles, which would lead to a severe interoperability problem among enablers. Equally, the lack of a directory or repository for user information will probably jeopardize the usefulness of work like GSSM, which is aiming to standardize the management of end-user subscriptions while de-coupling them from the user information itself. XML Document Management (XDM) specifications (see Chapter 14) have done quite a good job in specifying the management of end-user groups and lists. XDM has also extended its functionality to deal with much of the privacy information related to this group management, and it is looking into extending its functionality to cover even more user information. Global Permissions Management (GPM) specifications (see Chapter 22) also deal with the management of end-user privacy rules. However, we still need to define a general directory or repository that serves as reference for end-user information, with a well-defined data structure to be shared amongst the enablers in the OMA.

We should not forget technology and business convergence. Operators are facing an era of convergence between fixed and mobile networks, which will bring a perfect scenario to test the OMA network agnosticism philosophy. The OMA specifications will probably be some of the standards of reference for the service layer of operators wanting to offer converged services. Once again, the definition of technology realizations over the IMS infrastructure will play a major role here.

Another definite challenge for the OMA, and definitely a key point for operators, is the standardization of interfaces toward back-end Operations Support Systems/Business Support Systems (OSS/BSS). Integration toward the back-end systems is one of the most costly processes in a service deployment, and one of the less re-usable amongst services (Figure 5.3). Activities like OSPE and GSSM are starting to deal with the frontiers of these back-end systems, however much work is still to be done. The reuse of work provided by very prestigious bodies like the TM Forum is a thought not lost on the OMA companies, but it takes resources and commitment to apply the well-defined TM Forum models toward building a standard solution that fulfills the requirements discussed before.

In fact, one of the main challenges the OMA will face is the time when the operator infrastructure starts including the deployment of a significant number of products compliant with the OMA specifications, and the OMA 'ecosystem' becomes a reality. As operators, we will find out if the different realization specifications created in order to guarantee the correct inter-functioning of the OMA enablers in 3GPP/2 infrastructure were sufficient. Deploying the OMA enablers in our own infrastructure will show if the OMA enablers were developed in a consistent manner or as a set of independent building blocks that have difficultly to coexist and cooperate. The adherence to reference enablers like the OSE, Parlay in OSE and IMSinOMA will be of vital importance in order to achieve these goals.

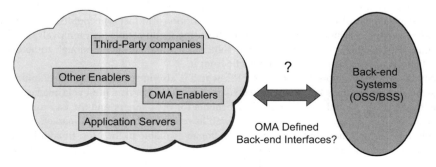

Figure 5.3   Will the OMA define interfaces toward back-end systems?

5.4 Summary

Difficult as all these challenges may sound, we are convinced that at this moment the OMA is the right place to address them. This forum has created a very good playground to sort all those issues out, with involvement from all the appropriate players in the industry. As it was already said, through hard work a good level of understanding between the different segments of the industry has been achieved in the OMA, and we all should benefit from it.

6

Service Provider – The Enterprise Perspective

Service providers come in many flavours. But apart from offering services to their customers, all of them have also something else in common, and that is that from a business perspective, they are enterprises. As enterprises they all have employees to whom the enterprise itself provides services, in order to support their work. So, by and large, one could say that there are two aspects of being a service provider, one focused on services offered to the market (market services), the other one on services provided to their employees (employee services). Examples of employee services, among many, include authentication, authorization, local and remote access to company's applications, databases, and collaboration tools based on presence, availability and location, and enterprise device management. The performance, value, and ultimately the cost of market services are dependent on the performance and cost of the work performed by the company's employees who develop and maintain those services. Therefore, employee services are as important, since they improve the ability of the company's employees to do their jobs. The use of standards has been proven to be a critical component in ensuring interoperability between different vendors' products, and key in delivering services with increased value and lower time-to-market, while also keeping under control capital expenditure (CAPEX) and operational expenditure (OPEX) for the service providers. That notion holds true regardless of whether we refer to market services or employee services. However, when looking for particular aspects in the use of standards, the need for employee services may be somewhat different from the need for market services. The next sections will explore some of those needs, as well as some of the differences, and how the Open Mobile Alliance (OMA) can help in addressing them.

An enterprise may or may not offer market services built using the OMA service enablers (they may offer products in different ways), to external principals. The enterprise relies on its employees to achieve its business goals, and it provides, or facilitates access to employee services in order to support them in their tasks. The enterprise has its own specific needs for the employee services it offers. Is the OMA responding to them?

6.1 Enterprise Needs

Enterprises may offer market services, built with service enablers, to other principals, and when doing so they may face issues like those of any other service provider. What makes an enterprise different then? Any enterprise, in order to be successful (i.e. sell their products and/or services) needs to make their employees as efficient as possible, and they do that by providing services to their

The Open Mobile Alliance   M. Brenner and M. Unmehopa
© 2008 Alcatel-Lucent. All Rights Reserved

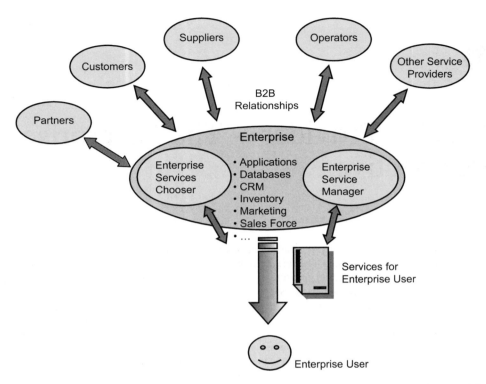

Figure 6.1   Enterprise user perceives the enterprise as the main responsible party for the services portfolio

employees. The enterprise becomes a service provider for its own employees, and its employees
become Enterprise Users (end-users that consume their enterprise's employee services). The needs
of the user as an employee might well differ from the needs of an end-user that enjoys the services
for her personal use.

Standards are needed in the enterprise as much as they are needed in any other business. Enterprises need to streamline their operations, and as they are being (or becoming) convinced that using
Service Oriented Architecture (SOA) and new technologies to implement it (e.g. Web Services)
they also become acutely aware of the importance of selecting the appropriate set of standards to
ensure success in their internal integration efforts.

Since this book is about the OMA work, and since we have presented the perspective of a
Mobile Operator, let's focus on issues related to mobility in an enterprise. A simple illustration of
the different actors involved in an Enterprise ecosystem dealing with mobile services needed by
enterprise employees is illustrated in Figure 6.1.

When focusing on services for their employees, enterprises do not face the issue of dealing with
millions of devices (one of the main challenges of a Mobile Operator). However, in spite of their
relatively small 'customer base', enterprises need to deal with a fairly large variety of choices
in the devices they support because of the specific needs of their employees, as determined by
the variety of applications that they need to employ in performing their assignments. The use of
a single type of device, or even just a few types of devices for all employees in the enterprise
is an ideal currently impossible to reach (from the end-user/employee's perspective, the situation
grows in complexity as well, since most of the time the individual ends up using a device or a
set of devices for corporate use, and a different device for her personal use). In addition to the

application variability, the employees need to interact with a large variety of external entities (e.g. suppliers, partners, customers, and other service providers). In many cases some devices are only supported by a particular operator, which translates in the enterprise's need to support relationships with multiple operators. An actor called Enterprise Chooser (for lack of a better term), considering the enterprise and employees needs, eventually decide which employees get access to what applications, through which device. Once distributed, the devices need to be continuously maintained (initially provisioned, then upgraded with new firmware and software, monitored and debugged when in trouble). The Enterprise Service Manager assumes this responsibility. But mobile devices also come with Mobile Operator's settings, and there are always settings that the enterprise user can change. Finally, in many cases, and for different reasons, enterprises allow their employees to use their personal mobile devices at work. In this case, their mobile device has now not one, not two, but three different principals that have access to device configuration and applications (the Mobile Operator, the Enterprise Service Manager, the Enterprise User), and that can create a nightmare in managing those devices (for more on this topic, see Chapter 18 on Device Management). Enterprises face challenges not only in managing devices, but also in offering access for employees to needed applications and data via those devices. Some of those challenges are as follows:

- The challenge to develop, deploy, and maintain multi-channel applications that are suitable for numerous different mobile channels (e.g. different device types, different connectivity models, different network technologies including hotspot, enterprise Session Initiation Protocol (SIP) networks, and corporate wireless network).
- The need to handle security concerns (e.g. authentication, authorization, confidentiality, access control), in particular for remote access to those applications.
- The need to integrate mobile solutions with the internal systems and database (the enterprise 'environment', including Customer Relationship Management (CRM), inventory, sales force, marketing, field service, etc.).
- The need to support collaborative applications between employees, partners, suppliers and customers, based on presence, availability, messaging, and data sharing capabilities.
- And last but not least, the challenge of doing all this, while minimizing CAPEX and OPEX.

In conclusion, there is little surprise that enterprises look to standards as a means to make their challenges and costs more controllable.

6.2   OMA Enterprise Awareness

Not all service providers are born equal, or some are more equal than others, to paraphrase George Orwell. That was a sensitive topic in the initial years of the OMA organization, and although the OMA came a long way, the theme still pops up occasionally. What is this about? It is about the fact that the interest of most service providers represented in the OMA reflects the focus on value, cost and time-to-market for the services offered to end-users. That happens to coincide with the focus of Mobile Operators, Content Providers, Application Providers, and more. It does not always coincide with the focus of some companies for which the services provided to their enterprise users are the ones critical to them. As a result, and as a show of support for focusing on aspects for employee services that may otherwise be missed in the standardization effort of service enablers, the OMA companies engaged in the Enterprise Birds of a Feather (ENTBoF) activity in late 2003, and documented its recommendations in mid-2004 in the OMA ENTBOF Technical Report [ENTBOF TR].

The [ENTBOF TR] includes a description of the enterprise needs, in particular regarding mobility aspects of services for the enterprise user, and goes on to identify very specific challenges, but also very specific benefits to the entire mobile industry chain, if those challenges could be successfully met with the support of OMA specifications. For the enterprise itself, regardless of whether offering external services (built with the OMA enablers) or not, those benefits include increased productivity, reduced cost in service development, deployment and maintenance, and increased profitability. More importantly, the report identifies benefits for all service providers. An increased customer base (through the growth of the enterprise market), increased revenue for use of bearers or through roaming of enterprise, and cost reduction because of possible delegation of issue resolution to the Enterprise Service Manager (e.g. enterprise help desk) are possible. At the end of the day, the report is actually not asking for some specific new OMA enablers, focused on the enterprise needs. Instead, it asks the OMA members to be aware of enterprise needs, and consider them when drafting use cases and requirements, and later on the technical specifications to meet them.

The ENTBOF activity had significant value because it brought to fore the Cinderella of all service providers, the enterprise. The work in ENTBOF gave the enterprise its moment in the sun. As a result, more often that before, the OMA enabler requirements include use cases that extend to enterprise users, and other actors from the Enterprise ecosystem, and their interactions. Another reason for the OMA to pay deliberate attention to the enterprise needs was not specifically captured in ENTBOF, but rather is the conclusion of the authors of the book. Service providers, in particular when they are Network Operators, because of the millions of subscribers they have to support and the effect that changes in services offered may have on global economy, take enormous precaution in introducing new architecture and technologies in support of their services. On the other hand, enterprises compete with each other, and in order to do so effectively, have to continuously reduce churn and cost of their production processes. They employ new standards and pioneer new technologies when doing so. They may take different risks than the Network Operators, since the number of users they may affect is smaller (the enterprise users), but mostly because the risk can be mitigated by trials that may involve a significant number of enterprise users to form a qualified opinion on the effects of changing a service. As an outcome, some new standards and technologies are introduced sooner in the enterprise arena than in the telecommunications arena, and lessons can be learned by paying attention to the enterprise as a service provider. For this, and the reasons listed in [ENTBOF TR], it is truly worth for the OMA members to re-visit enterprise's Cinderella story more often than just once.

6.3   Summary

Compelling applications for enterprises rely, expose or exploit features supported by a wide variety of service enablers specified by the OMA. Such enablers may be controlled by the service providers with whom the enterprise has a business relationship, by the enterprise itself, or may be done through means where one party delegates certain responsibilities to the other.

The work in the OMA has raised the awareness in finding synergies across the Mobile ecosystem and in particular for working together, across industry segments boundaries, in order to grow and exploit the opportunities of enterprise 'mobilization'. As a result, an increasingly holistic approach in the OMA is expected in the development of new enablers.

Part II

Horizontal Topics

In the first part of the book, we introduced the problem of vertical integration that the Open Mobile Alliance targets to address. We presented the OMA Service Environment, with the concepts of Interfaces, Enablers, and the Policy Enforcer as the main pillars. This sounds dandy, but will it all work? As with any novel approach, there is skepticism. Perhaps not rampant, but it is undeniably there as change is always fraught with uncertainty. So, to further cement the OSE principles in service architectures, the horizontal concepts take center stage in Part II.

The Policy Enforcer concept is detailed in Chapter 7. Chapter 8 then discusses the realization of this logical concept using an OMA enabler, the Policy Evaluation, Enforcement and Management enabler. We then continue with looking at the relation with three technology areas and how they relate to the OSE. The Utilization of IMS in OMA enabler in Chapter 9 defines how OMA enablers can make use of IMS capabilities. The Parlay in OSE enabler in Chapter 10 investigates how architectural assets from Parlay can be leveraged in the OSE. In Chapter 11, the OMA Web Services Enabler Release provides the Web Services infrastructure framework in which to deploy OMA enablers. And we conclude with addressing two enablers that offer horizontal functions for the benefit of all other OMA enablers. First, in Chapter 12, we cover the operation, administration, and management aspects in the OMA Service Provider Environment enabler, followed by the security technologies defined in the Security enabler, in Chapter 13.

The Open Mobile Alliance   M. Brenner and M. Unmehopa
© 2008 Alcatel-Lucent. All Rights Reserved

7

The Policy Enforcer Details: Model, Architecture, Realization, and Impact

This chapter is dedicated to the in-depth exploration of the Policy Enforcer (PE) entity in the OMA Service Environment (OSE), a concept introduced earlier in Section 2.3.1. The PE is a critical component of the OSE, but it holds much promise beyond what is specified in the OSE specification [OSE AD]. To do justice to this promise, this chapter will not only describe the PE's role in the OSE, but also its further reaching potential role in the Service Provider Environment.

7.1 Policy Enforcement Modeling in the OSE

Consider for starters the OSE, as described so far in the previous chapters, but without any policy enforcement function. It is essentially a layered architecture blueprint, where:

- Network, terminal, and possible Operations Support Systems/Business Support Systems (OSS/BSS) resources (e.g. rating/billing) are abstracted via adapters (I2).
- Specific functions, defined in terms agnostic to network, terminal, and possible OSS/BSS resources are made available in the OSE environment as enablers for use, through abstract I0 interfaces, by other enablers or applications.
- Some support and life-cycle management of such components are made available (via I1 interfaces).

The OSE also specifies an execution environment neutrality principle for the development of Open Mobile Alliance (OMA) enablers, which essentially allows bindings to different technology specific protocols to realize the I0 interface of the enabler using specific technologies (e.g. via Web Services (WS), Java, C++, C, etc.).

However, as illustrated in Figure 7.1, the OSE blueprint fails to address some significant aspects:

- How, in general, can enablers, applications, and resources be made available to other resources (e.g. other enabler or applications), especially when these applications are un-trusted or located in a different domain than the used resource?

The Open Mobile Alliance   M. Brenner and M. Unmehopa
© 2008 Alcatel-Lucent. All Rights Reserved

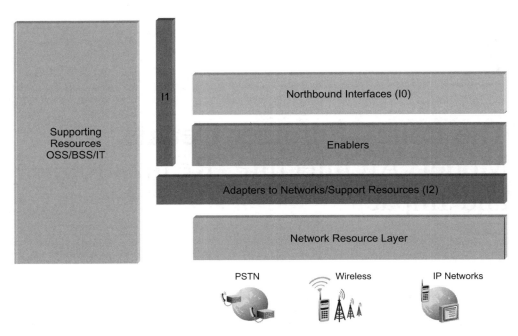

Figure 7.1   Layers introduced in the OSE, not considering policy enforcement

- How can this be achieved in a way that is viable for the service provider that exposes its assets (i.e. in a secure, billable, auditable manner, etc.)?
- How should interactions among enablers be designed? How should enablers be specified, implemented and deployed, to support such design?

The obvious answer is that the service provider must provide some mechanisms to control how each enabler, service, or resource is used by or how it interacts with other resources.

In order to re-use and share any such mechanism across the different resources, this mechanism needs to be logically separated from the resources. The resulting logically separated function is modeled in the OSE as the PE, completing the original OSE architecture picture.

The PE is a layer that logically represents components responsible for intercepting any message sent to, from, or among enablers and processing the message by executing prescribed actions. Such actions may be performed as a consequence of the output of a policy evaluation process or during a policy evaluation process. Policies are defined as any logical combination of conditions and actions. This is depicted in Figure 7.2.

The PE in the OSE aims primarily at enforcing service providers' policies, which can cover a large variety of specific service provider needs. Typically such policies can include the verification of conditions meant to protect the underlying service provider's enablers from unauthorized requests and managing the use of these requests through appropriate security measures (e.g. authentication, authorization), the triggering of charging events and/or logging events, the enforcement of Service Level Agreements (SLAs), the enforcement of user privacy (e.g. filtering of exchanged data), or the application of user and/or service provider preferences. Enforcing policies amounts to applying policy rules.

In order to satisfy the policies enforced by the PE, the requestor may have to provide additional information required by the policies and not included in the I0 interface. In the OSE these additional parameters are modeled as 'parameter P' and are logically added to the I0 interface, transforming

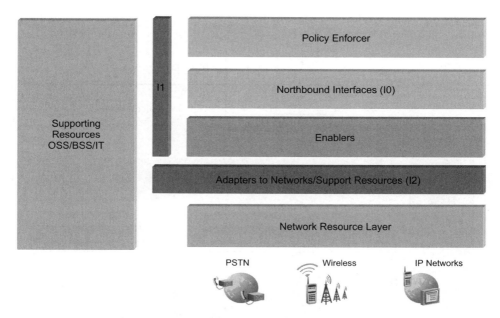

Figure 7.2 Layers introduced in the OSE, including policy enforcement

it into I0+P. In this context, P is short for policy, hence 'parameter P' are the parameters needed to satisfy the policy.

In other words, 'parameter P' is an additional set of parameters resulting from the application of policies to the I0 interface. I0+P is the transformed interface that results from the application of policies to an enabler's I0 interface. This is the category of interfaces that are really exposed to applications and enablers when policies are applied.

P and I0+P are mapped on the OSE as represented in Figure 7.3.

The PE execution model is the following:

- Whenever a request is sent by a requestor to a target enabler, it is intercepted by the PE and policies are processed, that is, conditions are evaluated and resulting actions may be executed.
- This processing (both condition evaluation, as well as action execution) may involve as much delegation to other enablers or any resources in general as prescribed by the policies. For example, charging or balance tracking is performed by delegating the processing to a charging enabler.
- Upon completion of all the processing, the policy prescribes if the request is sent to the target, or it is blocked; in the latter case, the policy also determines the response that is returned to the requestor.
- A similar execution model applies for responses to the request.
- A similar execution model applies for messages sent by an enabler to another target resource (i.e. the model is agnostic of the notion of the enabler).

7.2 Beyond the OSE: Policy Enforcement as Service Oriented Architecture Composition

When policy enforcement involves delegation to multiple enablers, it actually amounts to performing Service Oriented Architecture (SOA) composition to create new functions (i.e. SOA orchestration,

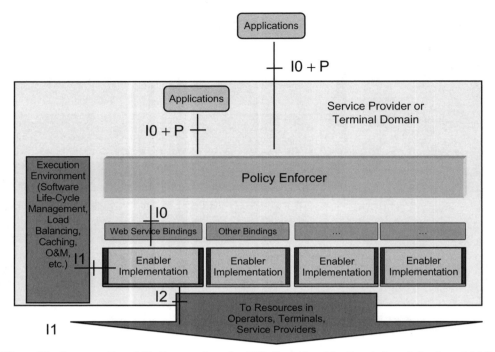

Figure 7.3 Parameter P and I0+P mapped on the OSE. Reproduced by Permission of the Open Mobile Alliance Ltd.

see [Gaur2006] for details). Albeit the definition in [W3C WS Glossary] is limited to WS, the concept is generic for any re-usable SOA component. In fact I0+P results solely from a particular case of orchestration where additional parameters are needed for the processing of the policy.

More generic policies may implement any composition of enablers as well as include in the composition any other re-usable piece of code. In particular, instead of simply processing policies to determine if a message is allowed to go through, it can be used to transform the message and therefore the interface or the binding exposed by the message target, or to modify the functions provided by this target. The result of the orchestration is in fact a new resource. The resulting northbound interface can be any transformation of I0, for which we will use the notation T(I0).

The resulting conclusion is that the PE function is in fact nothing else but an orchestrator. The OSE principles for the specification of enablers regarding northbound interfaces and de-composition into essential functions are essential to ensure that enablers are atomic SOA building blocks. With these observations, the OSE follows an SOA. When based on WS, the PE follows the Web Service Gateway (SGW) usage pattern (see [W3C WS Glossary] and [OWSEROvw]).

SOA compositions (see [Erl2005]) of enablers result in new entities that can themselves be further used, exposed, or composed.

The OSE can therefore be generalized beyond the set of OMA enablers as illustrated in Figure 7.4 where the components that can be used by applications and orchestrated by the PE are not limited to standard enablers as specified by the OMA.

The orchestration and composition is also not any more limited to policy enforcement that may require additional parameters (+P) to satisfy the policies, therefore the effect of composition can completely modify the resulting interface from I0 to T(I0).

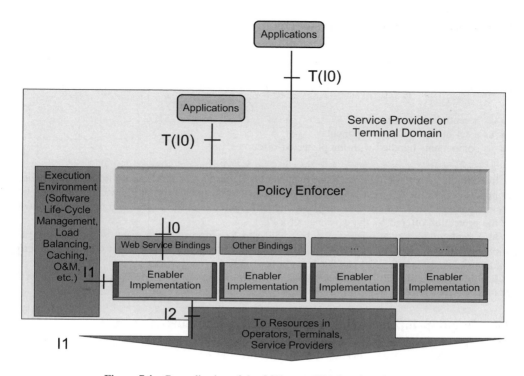

Figure 7.4 Generalization of the OSE as an SOA-based environment

In this model, enablers can be generalized beyond the OMA definition to become re-usable service layer components that provide an essential function for use by others (other enablers, applications, services or any authorized resources) through appropriately exposed northbound interfaces. They are no longer really distinguishable from applications/software components except that they provide an essential, generic, re-usable function.

In such an environment, common SOA patterns, tools and infrastructure are available and can be leveraged. Examples include the following:

- WS/Java (Java 2.0 Enterprise Edition (J2EE));
- XML;
- Web Services Business Process Execution Language (WS BPEL);
- Enterprise Service Bus (ESB);
- Universal Description, Discovery, and Integration (UDDI) (a service registry for discovery, registration and dynamic composition); and
- usage reporting.

The statement about the PE applied to interaction to, from and among enablers can also be generalized to the PE applied on any messages within the service layer, that is, to, from, and among any resources.

Following the reasoning above, it is worth noting that the OSE really provides a blueprint for an SOA architecture of the service layer.

7.3   Logical Architecture versus Deployment Considerations

It is important to keep in mind that the OSE describes a logical architecture, not deployment aspects.

The PE is a logical orchestration function and enforcer, logically present on any exchanged message, and represented as such in the OSE architecture diagram. When it comes to its implementation and deployment, the PE can however be de-composed and packaged in many ways, including:

- as a centralized component
- as a set of distributed components
- as components bundled with the protected resources.

In addition to that, the OSE does not mandate a specific way to implement the PE functionality or bundle it with the different resources it protects. It solely mandates that the PE functionality be present and specifies that enablers, applications, or resources should be designed to take advantage of the protection offered by the existence of a PE.

In a deployment model where no policy will ever be enforced when using a resource, no PE implementation is required; logically this is still modeled as policy enforcement with no policy to enforce (this case is referred to as the 'zero policy' case).

For this reason, the PE is considered as a layer or function always logically present in the OSE or in a Service Delivery Platform (SDP) deployment that complies with it.

7.4   Relationship to Parlay and IP Multimedia Subsystem (IMS)

OMA has produced reference enablers such as IP Multimedia Subsystem (IMS) in OMA [IMSinOMA AD] and Parlay in OSE [PIOSE AD] to define how the OSE relates to the IMS [3GPP TS 23.228] and respectively to the Parlay/Open Service Access (OSA) [Parlay TS] specifications.

The policy enforcement in the PE is especially important in such context because it provides horizontal service layer policy enforcement and orchestration for the IMS, at the level of the Open Service Access (OSA) Application Server (AS) and/or Session Initiation Protocol (SIP) AS. At the same time, the PE functionality complements the Parlay/OSA and Parlay X specifications by providing policy enforcement and an SOA for Parlay X.

On the basis of the generalization presented in Section 7.2 and the work in [IMSinOMA AD] and [PIOSE AD], the OSE provides a blueprint for using SOA both in the IMS and in Parlay/OSA environments.

In addition, the IMS introduces the notion of Service Capability Interaction Manager (SCIM) [3GPP TS 23.228], but under-specifies it. The SCIM is conventionally seen as either provided in the Serving-Call Session Control Function (S-CSCF), or as a stand-alone resource in the network or deployed on the SIP AS. Such implementations are typically very efficient, but unfortunately in all these cases they lack service level context and composition capability with other enablers. The OSE with the PE provides an alternative: a service level SCIM.

Within a service layer environment that follows the OSE blueprint, a service level SCIM function can be provided as follows:

1. SIP servlet composition (for SIP only) (e.g. following [JSR 116], [JSR 289]).
2. Application routing or dispatching on the SIP message. For example, a SIP server routes the SIP messages to a set of applications that process the messages in sequence or in parallel.
3. SOA composition of enablers, application building blocks or applications. For example, a SIP message results into notification at the northbound interface of an enabler or SOA software component. The notification, or a resulting action, may then be the object of SOA orchestration including responding or handling the SIP message, when appropriate.

4. Application dispatching in the service layer. For example, instead of routing or dispatching the message directly at the SIP message level, an SOA component may provide third-party call control capabilities. Examples include Parlay X Call Control or Parlay Java Realization (JR) Generic Call Control (GCC)/Multi Party Call Control (MPCC) realized on SIP (see [Parlay TS]). A dispatcher can then be implemented using call control to marshal an SIP message from application to application.

Each of the last three options can be directly implemented on an SOA infrastructure that implements the PE function. While the opportunities presented in the last two bullet items above are possibly prone to more delays, they offer the advantage of not necessarily depending on the underlying network characteristics. So, for example, SCIM as service level application dispatching and SOA composition can also be realized on legacy networks (e.g. Public Switched Telephone Network (PSTN), Intelligent Networking (IN)) and non-IMS networks.

7.5 Policy Modeling

Policies are defined as any logical combination of conditions and actions. This implies in general that a language to express policies should be Turing Complete [Brainerd1974]. Of course, under specific circumstances, it is possible to restrict the type of combinations or conditions and actions that must be processed. Examples of such restrictions led to policy languages like IETF's Common Policy [RFC 4745], OASIS' eXtensible Access Control Markup Language (XACML) [OASIS XACML] and JSR 94 [JSR 94].

Policy processing includes either only policy evaluation or both policy evaluation and enforcement, where:

- Policy enforcement is the process of executing actions, which may be performed as a consequence of the output of the policy evaluation process or during the policy evaluation process.
- Policy evaluation is the process of evaluating the policy conditions and executing the associated policy actions up to the point that the end of the policy is reached.

Evaluation may involve arbitrary computations. The conditions and actions in policy rules may require the execution of arbitrary functions that include delegation to OMA enabler implementations.

The topology of a policy is defined as a graph where each node represents a condition to be evaluated and each outbound branch has actions to be executed if the corresponding condition is true. This is illustrated in Figure 7.5.

Such a graph topology is independent of the policy language. It can support ruleset language models like those described in [RFC 3060] and [RFC 3460], workflows or business process languages like WS BPEL [OASIS WS BPEL] or other declarative or imperative/procedural languages or scripts.

Optimizing the performances of policy processing can be achieved by optimizing the graphs against a cost function (e.g. minimizing policy processing time or Central Processing Unit (CPU) requirements).

7.6 Policy Enforcer through OMA Enabler Realization

OMA is specifying the OMA Policy Evaluation, Enforcement, and Management (PEEM) (for details see Chapter 8 dedicated to PEEM). At this time the technical specification phase is still work in progress. The initial driver for the introduction of PEEM was the need to have an OMA-defined specification that can support the implementation of the PE function. It should be noted that from an OSE point of view, the use of PEEM to implement the PE function is optional. Other approaches

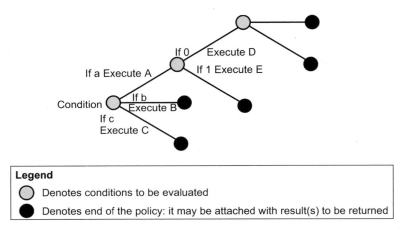

Figure 7.5   An example of a graph that describes the topology of a policy (composed of multiple policy rules)

can be used as an alternative. As the work on PEEM progressed, the PEEM enabler ended up well beyond the proxy mode that underlies the PE function.

While the details of PEEM will be explored in Chapter 8, it is nevertheless worthwhile to remind here in a generic manner how PE can be realized using some key architectural patterns, components, and interfaces. These elements are indeed provided by the PEEM enabler, and emphasizing them here will make you pay close attention to them when described in detail later on.

- The proxy usage pattern. In the proxy mode, a policy control component is implemented and deployed so that it intercepts messages to and from a target resource, processes policies and generates the resulting message possibly modified by the policy processing, blocked and returned to the originator (i.e. requester on request or target resource on response) or sends a message to a third party. Policy processing itself may involve delegation to other resources.
- The callable usage pattern. In the callable mode, a requester explicitly passes a request for policy processing to a policy control component, using a specified invocation interface. The policy control component may return a result via the invocation interface or may send such a response to another entity altogether, since policy processing itself may involve delegation to other resources, and since the policy processing is dictated by the specifics of the policy – and not by a specification. The callable pattern does not have to be used in the pure PE realization (this is a deployment choice). Examples provided toward the end of this chapter will illustrate that one may start with a pure realization of the logical PE function, and enhance it with support for the callable usage pattern, in order to create a more complex building block.
- The input to the policy control component, as well as the output from the policy control component is dictated by the specifics of the policy that is processed, including the bindings and the formats of the inputs and outputs. As such, in order to support any possible policies, the interface to the policy control component is passing input and output in terms of Binary Large Objects (BLOBs) [BLOB].
- While such open ended interface specifications are common for IT or SOA systems, they seem out of place in telecommunication systems where architectures are often specified through more rigid reference points. This challenge can be addressed by introducing the notion of templates that allow to constrain interfaces to specific sets of input and output parameters, exchanged on a particular interface binding (e.g. Simple Object Access Protocol (SOAP) or Diameter). Of course, when a template is selected in a deployment, it amounts to restricting the set of supported policies so that they result in an exchange of messages using the template. Such

a template specification also needs to include recommendations on how to encode template parameters in a BLOB (e.g. based on XML or other specifications).

- Policies processed by the policy control component need to be managed; while PE functionality is not concerning itself with this aspect, it relies on the fact that there will be a way to manage (create, modify, delete, view) those policies using well-defined mechanisms.
- It is beneficial to have policies expressed in a standardized, abstract, Policy Expression Language (PEL). Endorsement of one or more options, to support industry needs for both simple as well as more complex policies, is a desirable outcome of the specifications activity.

7.7   Relationship of Policy Enforcer to IETF PEP/PDP

A policy control component used in the realization of the PE relates to the IETF Policy Enforcement Point/Policy Decision Point (PEP/PDP) model described in [RFC 3198] as follows:

- The policy control component in the proxy usage pattern can be implemented by interceptors that play the role of PEP and query a PDP for policy decision. The interceptors then enforce the decision. Typical usage cases are often limited to gateways that provide access control. The PDP/PEP model does not account for more advanced SOA orchestration.
- The policy control component in the callable usage pattern can be modeled as a PDP called by a requester modeled as the PEP. The PDP/PEP model does not account for cases where the PDP does not send the policy results to the PEP at the end of the processing and/or interacts with other entities (e.g. if the policies launch a workflow that initiates other processes and then terminates).

In conclusion, the statement can be made that a policy control component used in one possible PE realization extends the IETF PDP/PEP model with additional SOA concepts.

7.8   Policy Assembly, Composition, and Orchestration

Policies are not specified in the OMA, even though a generic OMA PEEM enabler is specified. While the support for specifying policies will be extensively discussed in Chapter 8, it is worthwhile to take an advanced peak at policies from the perspective of the service provider, and its use of the concept of the PE. This will facilitate the understanding of decisions made in the PEEM specifications work.

7.8.1 Model and PEL Assembly

With the options described before in Section 7.6, it is possible with such a model to combine policy languages as illustrated in Figure 7.6.

In this approach, the PEL becomes a policy and orchestration expression language that can be used to model and author policies, and orchestrate services and sessions. It can be converted at authoring, uploading or execution time into an executable policy and/or orchestrated workflow.

This language may re-use options identified in the OMA PEEM PEL specifications (see Chapter 8), and could go even further by composing two (or more) individual, but complementary languages used for policy and orchestration: for example, WS BPEL and rule-based languages.

This approach allows for the following (a non-exhaustive list):

- A common PEL for interoperability and tools;
- re-use of existing engines;
- preferred policy approaches and models;
- preferred optimizations as needed and where needed;
- use each mode for what it does best;
- a common way to manage policies and rationalization of the policies;

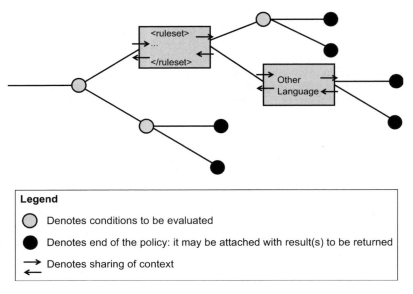

Figure 7.6 Example of policy expressed by assembling multiple policy expression languages

- a common way to exchange policies;
- a common way to delegate policy evaluation or enforcement;
- common policy expression tools;
- a single way to express OMA-specific rules.

In other words, it is now possible to have a common interface and model to rationalize, author, and manage policies in an SP domain.

As a consequence, vendors with preferred approaches or expertise would be able to continue to offer compliant products or solutions, while service providers can author and develop policies with a common set of tools.

7.8.2 Usage Considerations

In a Service Provider Environment multiple types of policies and policy requirements exist. For example, different policy types include the following:

- Network level policies that have very high performance and extremely low-latency requirements.
- Control layer policies (e.g. IMS policies) that mix low-latency requirements with the need for some expression power.
- Service level policies that have a strong need for rich and flexible expression power while remaining efficient. Those policies encompass execution environment policies and enabler/ service exposure policies.

While the requirements on policy evaluation and enforcement may differ for each policy type, consistency across these policy types is essential. As one expands the service layer for the service provider, more and more functions previously provided in the lower layer may also partially or totally be provided in the service layer (e.g. service level charging). It is therefore essential to consistently model policy rules across layers (e.g. to avoid double/multiple charging or to ensure consistent charging and charging correlation across layers, etc.).

Policy types can no longer be segregated into different domains/universes that never merge. We contend that as services become richer and network convergence continues, more and more often the policy universes overlap and merge.

A common PEL allows the same policies to drive different engines at different levels from a common source and it allows modeling them similarly for each type, therefore facilitating consistency. Without it, policy evaluation and enforcement are done in silos, something that the OMA strives to eliminate and that represents an important motivation behind the OSE.

The same is true when it comes to policy management. Ensuring common tools, interfaces and models to manage policies requires a common way to express and represent them across layers. A common PEL can achieve that. Without it, policy management is done in silos, something that the OMA strives to eliminate and that represents a main motivation behind the OSE and PEEM.

Provisioning is a major challenge for service providers. In particular, it is a necessity (albeit complex and neither sufficiently automated nor standardized) to ensure consistency between policies and OSS/BSS or to allow OSS/BSS to provision policies. Examples include supporting the need to derive policies from SLAs and other subscriptions and allowing Customer Relationship Management (CRM), Partner Management (PRM), Enterprise Resource Planning (ERP) and other OSS/BSS applications to set or derive policies from user, third-party or service provider actions or data.

OSS/BSS activation and provisioning transposes business rules into policies. Policies may then be applied in the appropriate layer with appropriate engines and technologies based on the settings and deployment choice of the service provider.

To ensure standardization of processes like the provisioning of resulting policies in the Service Provider domain by OSS/BSS, a common formalism must be in place and such formalism must be able to drive/orchestrate/translate across the different policy engines present in the Service Provider domain.

7.8.3 Policies in Service Provider Domain

Based on the previous sections, a SGW can be built on SOA principles and available advanced technologies and deployed in the service layer, where the SGW is defined as an entity that is relying on OMA-specified policy control specifications and inspired by the IETF PDP/PEP model. Such a SGW is illustrated in Figure 7.7. The SOA infrastructure also provides a service registry (e.g. UDDI v3-compliant) platform for publishing, categorizing, and discovering WS and related resources across the enterprise.

Following the OSE blueprint, the SGW is to be deployed in such a way that it enforces policies on any exchange to, from, and among resources that must be protected. In addition, following this example, the reader will observe that such a SGW is quite more than an implementation of the pure logical PE, since it has to support both the proxy usage pattern as well as the callable usage pattern.

For example, in a J2EE container with SOA support, the SGW could be implemented on an SOA suite that includes: WS, WS gateways, WS BPEL, Ruleset Engines, and J2EE security and policy enforcement.

This way, the PE evolves to a service level policy framework. It may invoke (like a PEP) or be invoked (like a PDP) by a network level policy. It is compatible with Parlay Policy Framework following [PIOSE AD] specifications.

Accordingly, it is indicated that interceptors that request policy evaluation and enforcement can take place as follows:

- within the service layer (at the edge of the Service Provider domain (at the service layer), within the Service Provider domain or called by services or enablers);
- at the edge between the service layer and the underlying network layers (including session control layer when it explicitly exists);
- within the network layer.

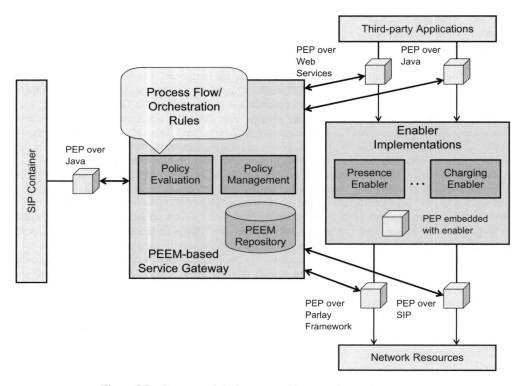

Figure 7.7 Concept and deployment architecture of a service gateway

Such an SGW can provide tools to author, manage, evaluate, and enforce all these policies if so desired by the service provider. When that is the case different scenarios may be met as follows:

- network level PEP use SGW as PDP;
- policies call network level resources for evaluation or enforcement of the policies;
- combinations of the above.

Telecommunications and Internet Services and Protocols for Advanced Networking (TISPAN) builds upon the work done by 3GPP in order to create an IMS core for both wireless and wireline networks. When deployed on TISPAN IMS [ETSI TISPAN], processing a policy may involve delegating steps that call for the services of the Resource Admission Control Subsystem (RACS) or the Policy Decision Function (PDF). Conversely, RACS deployments may be implemented such that it calls SGW for PDP steps (RACS behaving as PEP). These details illustrate, for example, the differences and advantages of using SGW with RACS/PDF. The main advantage is the possibility to consolidate in one logical location all the policy control and management functions. Note also that this is purely an optional use. If the service provider does not wish to do so, the SGW can be limited to policy evaluation and enforcement at the service layer level and at the edge of the service layer (third party and toward the network layers).

The same argument may be extended to many other network policies (when using either IMS or other network architecture – e.g. Parlay/OSA).

At the SOA level, an SDP can provide SLA enforcements, for example via SLA management and throttling on third-party requests. In general, the service layer does not drive the Quality of

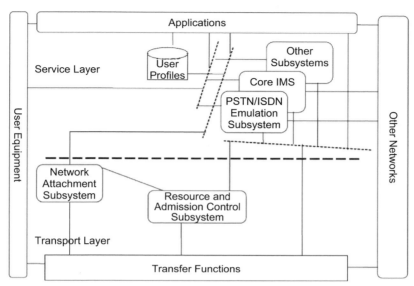

Figure 7.8 High-level TISPAN NGN architecture. © European Telecommunications Standards Institute 2006. Further use, modification, redistribution is strictly prohibited. ETSI standards are available from http://pda.etsi.org/pda/

Service (QoS) at the network level. However, an SGW can interact with elements responsible for enforcing QoS in the network, like RACS.

It should be noted that as per the TISPAN specifications RACS and policy are functions that exist at the network transport level and expose control interfaces. This is illustrated in Figure 7.8.

7.9 Summary – Next Steps

As SOA adoption increases to the point that it may become central to future service provider service layer deployments, we expect that policies, the logical PE and the OMA policy control specifications will become central notions to both other architectures and specifications development as well as to the service provider deployment environments.

We expect that vendors will provide SGW components in their service layer stacks and focus more and more on following the OSE blueprint.

At OMA, we expect that many enablers will delegate to or rely on OMA policy control specifications to provide PEEM capabilities. Already today, such work has started with Categorization Based Content Screening (CBCS) (see Chapter 23), Global Permissions Management (GPM) (see Chapter 22) and General Service Subscription Management (GSSM) (see Section 27.1). Other OMA specifications such as the Presence enabler already rely on XML Document Management (XDM) enabler specifications that encompass policy related aspects (see Chapter 14).

We also expect that OMA specifications will raise interest in other standards bodies (e.g. TISPAN), and that may lead to a policy control architecture consolidation, and a potential re-use of OMA policy control specifications. Such an expansion may also benefit OMA specifications, since it may result in refining and expanding its own policy control specifications, to accommodate specific features architected and defined outside the OMA.

Among other realization options, an SOA infrastructure on J2EE is also ready to support the PE and OMA policy control specifications implementations.

8

The Policy Evaluation, Enforcement, and Management Enabler

'IF... THEN...'. Our brain usually dictates us to behave in a logical manner, following a cause and effect pattern. Computers are driven by software programs that, for better or worse, are emulating this logical behavior of the human brain (some arguably more successful than others).

Every computer program can be reduced to sequences of 'IF... THEN...' despite the fact that such sequences could be cleverly hidden in more complex programming language constructs (e.g. 'WHILE... DO', or 'FOR... DO'). Some may say that there are computer programs that only contain unconditional execution statements. It is a mere illusion though. The fact that an 'IF' does not appear only means that the 'THEN' part is always to be executed. This is like in a case where one has no real choice. An analogy would be driving on a one-way highway with no exit, and only one final destination. Knowing that this is the case and no decision has to be made on which direction to take, or where to finally stop, you just continue driving until you reach the destination.

This goes to show that every computer program can be reduced to a sequence of condition evaluations, followed by some actions if those conditions evaluate to the Boolean value of 'TRUE'. When the conditions evaluate to the Boolean value of 'FALSE', the sequence may follow an 'ELSE' branch. In the absence of an 'ELSE' branch, the sequence may simply skip any action and just flow into a possible new condition evaluation step.

Our simple model so far has an 'IF' statement and a condition to be evaluated (the part following the 'IF' statement). The 'THEN' statement is followed by an action, which only gets executed if the condition evaluates to 'TRUE'.

Just to complicate things a bit, each condition and each action may contain mathematical and logical operations on variables, and may even themselves contain a nested 'IF ... THEN ...' construct. The good news is, that this nesting and associated interpretation stops at some point, and you will recognize the proverbial 'IF... THEN...' in its simplest form.

At this point, you may ask yourself why we just spent quite a number of sentences to explain the obvious. Well, it's simply because if you understand the notion of 'IF... THEN...', you basically understand the notion of 'policy rule'. Indeed, a policy rule is nothing more than a glorified 'IF... THEN...' statement. This may seem like introducing an entire complex theory around something that ultimately may be reduced to something very simple. But in reality, the concept of policy and the mechanisms to realize it have to emulate and react to complex business situations, while making

---

The Open Mobile Alliance   M. Brenner and M. Unmehopa
© 2008 Alcatel-Lucent. All Rights Reserved

appropriate and rapid decisions. Nevertheless, at its core, a policy rule is nothing more than an expression of a condition, with associated actions that are to be executed if the condition evaluates to the Boolean value of 'TRUE'. A policy then is a collection of policy rules, with associated criteria to determine what policy rules are to be evaluated, and in what order. A policy also usually has the implicit connotation of verification and/or obligation (e.g. 'IF you have administrative privileges AND IF the time is 12 a.m. THEN perform a full back-up of all logs').

An enterprise (in the more general sense, thus including the service providers segment) always has its own set of policies to be enforced. Such policies need to be respected and followed consistently by all those who interact with the enterprise processes, be it intra-enterprise or inter-enterprise. Examples of such policies include enterprise rules and regulations that employees, suppliers, and customers need to follow to achieve their business goals. Practically all of these policies exist in printed text or electronic form and are manually enforced. A rapidly increasing tendency is emerging though in attempting to encode such policies in a 'software interpretable' digital expression. This leads to the ability to have such policies enforced automatically as verifications and/or obligations, as part of the automated execution of enterprise business processes.

The reason for this tendency is as obvious as the 'IF... THEN...' explanation: the enterprise wants to increase revenue and bottom-line profit. Hence, it needs to ensure controlled access to and use of its own resources, offer a secure and guaranteed quality of their services, eliminate bottlenecks, increase employee productivity, and reduce Operational Expenditure (OPEX).

In the next sections we will explore how standards play in this area, and how they can help achieve the benefits that service providers and any other type of enterprise may expect from deploying these standards.

8.1   Are Those Specifications Really Needed?

The introduction may have convinced us of the obvious: business decisions follow a logical pattern, the pattern can be broken down to a sequence of granular 'IF... THEN...' steps (the essence of policy rules), and in order to achieve business benefits, an enterprise may want to include as much automation as possible in expressing and enforcing their own policy rules. But isn't each enterprise at least a little bit different from the next one? For sure, each enterprise will want to have its own, proprietary policies, based on its own, proprietary granular policy rules. This maybe either because its business is unique, or because it wants to differentiate itself from any other competitor, in particular when it comes to inter-enterprise relationships.

So why is there a need for standards for Policy Evaluation and Enforcement? Would an enterprise really care whether a vendor implementation that it assessed as meeting its needs is completely proprietary, or follows a set of standards? Furthermore, don't we already have standards for policy control and management? Yet companies are sending representatives to standards bodies to work on such specifications. In particular, the Open Mobile Alliance (OMA) wrestles with these topics in its Architecture Working Group (ARC WG), with the goal of specifying an enabler named Policy Evaluation, Enforcement, and Management (PEEM). Vendor compliance to requirements and architecture specifications is almost given regardless of topic covered, hence it is true for the PEEM enabler as well. The PEEM requirements specification reflects the market needs with respect to PEEM. Hence a vendor should reasonably expect to see at least some of those requirements in Requests for Information (RFIs) or Requests for Proposal (RFPs) issued by enterprises (e.g. service providers).

The PEEM architecture specification sets forth a logical design blueprint for the expected behavior of the enabler implementation and how it would interface with other resources in a deployment environment. A vendor should therefore always be prepared to provide a product that can interoperate with other resources, following the prescribed blueprint, regardless of whether the product is chosen to provide the complete end-to-end solution, or just to be integrated into a larger end-to-end solution. But are technical specifications of protocols, and testing specifications for PEEM also needed, given the likely proprietary nature of the policies for each enterprise? In order to start addressing some of those questions, the next section will provide a brief background on the topic of policy control and management, and an overview of existing standards covering it.

8.1.1 Policy Control and Management Overview

Every term related to policy is, unfortunately, an overloaded term and has multiple definitions and interpretations. For practical reasons, in order to understand the rest of this chapter, we will introduce some simple terms, without claiming these are formal definitions, and therefore avoid the impulse to compare or defend them against terms defined elsewhere. More formal terms, as used in the OMA, may be introduced in later sections of this chapter.

It seems natural to start with the term policy. In its simplest form, a policy is an expression of a combination of conditions, followed by actions to be executed if the conditions evaluated to a Boolean value of TRUE. Applied to telecommunication networks, policies describe conditions and actions related to network resources, behavior, such as access to and management of network resources. Networks that employ policies are referred to as policy-based networks.

Policies are usually associated with resources, or more generally with principals. A principal is an entity that has an associated identity (e.g. an end-user, a group, an organization, or any other resource). Resources include application, enablers, devices, systems, and so on.

Policy control or policy-based control is a term referring to techniques used in the control of the access to and use of network resources. Needless to say, from a technology perspective there are multiple technologies that may be used to implement policy control.

Policy Management is used in this chapter to mean the administrative aspect of managing policies, such as creating, retrieving, modifying, or deleting them.

A policy server or a policy engine is a security component of a policy-based network that provides policy-handling processing capabilities. It accepts access or usage control requests regarding network resources, processes them against a formal policy that defines how the network's resources are to be handled under given conditions and current network context, and returns access control or usage-related responses to the requesting party.

In a policy-based network, current context may include the time of day, client authorization privileges, availability of network resources, and any other factors that the network manager may specify when composing the policy, as part of expressing the conditions of the policy. With respect to the actions captured in the policy, the policy engine can allow or deny access, control the extent to which a client can use the resource, provide notifications to other resources, update different repositories, or even update parameters used by the policy in future instantiations.

A frequently asked question is where in the network does the concept of policy control apply? A major focus has been and continues to be on resource admission control and bandwidth management, in particular IP-based networks. Resource admission control and bandwidth management is practically a policy-based control of allocating IP resources, and whether IP can be compatible with guaranteed Quality of Service (QoS) seems to be everybody's question. While a complete move to IP networks is almost a foregone conclusion, operators are looking for techniques to recreate bandwidth guarantees across IP networks, to avoid degradation of high-value telecommunications services. For example, constrained resources over an air interface are a critical factor for Mobile Operators joining the IP world. Moving to IP, without a guaranteed QoS, raises the Mobile Operator's concerns with respect to the impact on high volumes of low-value ring-tone downloads or free IP voice calls, on high-value services such as mobile TV.

Standards bodies such as Internet Engineering Task Force (IETF), [3GPP, 3GPP2], European Telecommunications Standards Institute/Telecommunications and Internet Services and Protocols for Advanced Networking (ETSI/TISPAN) and others are diligently focusing on providing policy-control specifications to tackle these specific issues. Interestingly enough, none of them focus on the mechanisms to express policies, or on the policy management aspects, but they rather focus primarily on the specific policies content, and the parameters that are fed to the policy engine, or provided in response by the policy engine.

While policy control in some circles is synonymous with resource admission control for IP networks, the truth is that the nature of the telecommunications service business is changing, in the sense that service providers expect to sell and deliver a large range of complex, different services, in dire need of the more generic notion of policy control. The services offering and/or delivery may vary based on subscriber's presence and availability, the time of day, type of device used, subscriber's permissions and preferences, subscriber's identity attributes, subscriber's account, and many others.

Standards tackling generic policy handling, where it is difficult to predict the exact type of resources, requestors and network conditions that will influence the content of the policies, are also emerging, and have become the focus of additional standards bodies, such as the Organization for the Advancement of Structured Information Standards (OASIS) and the OMA. These standard bodies, in addition to focusing on generic specifications for invocation of policy processing, are tackling the topics of policy expression languages and policy management.

The focus in this chapter is on generic policy control and management, rather than on specific domains of applicability. In order to support this, the next section will summarily explore prior art that PEEM specifications rely on.

8.1.2 Standards Precursors to PEEM

Identifying all possible forums in which policy concepts have been or are being discussed is an impractical task. But using the OMA mission and principles as a general guidance, and PEEM requirements in particular, allowed us to constrain the search to a few standards development organizations, namely the IETF, the 3GPP and 3GPP2, the OASIS, the Parlay Group (Parlay) and, of course, the OMA itself.

While some of those standard bodies had numerous incursions into the field of policy, the OMA PEEM activity focused on selecting for guidance those specifications that may have an impact on PEEM for terminology and architectural concepts or be candidates for re-use or for extensions in some of the PEEM technical specifications. Rather than grouping standard precursors to PEEM by an originating standard body, we preferred to group the references by the purpose they serve for the PEEM work. Some of the precursor details will be explored in a further section, since they are directly related to specifications details, and their introduction here may be premature.

8.1.2.1 Policy Architecture Concepts and Terminology

The IETF specifications used in creating the OMA PEEM terminology and concepts and inspiring the architecture include the framework for Policy-based Admission Control [RFC 2753], the Policy Core Information Model (PCIM) – Version 1 Specification [RFC 3060], the terminology for Policy-Based Management [RFC 3198], and the PCIM extensions [RFC 3460]. In particular, specification [RFC 2753] introduces the concepts of policy, Policy Decision Point (PDP) and Policy Enforcement Point (PEP). The policy terminology is further formalized in specification [RFC 3198] with the introduction of a wealth of terms, including amongst other formal definitions for policy condition, policy action, policy rule, and refinement of the definitions for policy, PDP and PEP. Specification [RFC 3060] develops the PCIM using the earlier accepted terminology, and specification [RFC 3460] adds extensions to PCIM. There are other PCIM extensions addressed in later IETF specifications, but the OMA PEEM activity considered those too specialized (e.g. for QoS), thereby going beyond the scope of PEEM.

[RFC 2753] also introduces the conceptual architecture that uses the PEP and PDP components. Since the PEP-PDP model is a recurring theme in PEEM specifications, it may be useful to think

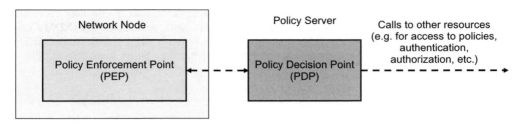

Figure 8.1   IETF PEP-PDP model

about the PDP as 'a logical component with the role making policy decisions on a request', and of PEP as 'a logical component with the role of enforcing decisions'. Figure 8.1 can be used as a representation of the relationship between the two, when deployed in a network environment.

8.1.2.2 Policy Languages

A series of IETF specifications serve as a source for the OMA Policy Expression Language (PEL) work, during architecture and technical specifications phases. The Common Policy: A Document Format for Expressing Privacy Preferences [RFC 4745] defines an extensible framework for creating authorization policies. Other IETF drafts have indeed provided extensions to the framework and schema (e.g. Presence Authorization Rules [SPRULES]).

Specifications from OASIS also contribute to the OMA PEL work. The Business Process Execution Language [BPEL] has stated its purpose to focus on specifying the common concepts for a business process execution language. The eXtensible Access Control Markup Language (XACML) [XACML] defines an extensible core XML schema for representing authorization and entitlement policies.

3GPP specifies a location policy expression [3GPP TS 22.071] and a charging policy expression [3GPP TS 23.125].

Specifications related to programming languages are important to be considered for the formalisms in defining language constructs, and expressing different variable and constant data types (e.g. programming languages – C [ISO/IEC 9899]).

Finally the OMA specifies the Push-to-talk over Cellular (PoC) user access expression language [POC-XDM-V1_0 TS] and the Presence policy expression language [Presence-V1_0 TS], which are important to consider for a smooth transition of OMA enablers, when it comes to introducing new OMA PEL specifications.

8.1.2.3 Policy Evaluation Invocation

A number of specifications serve as a source for the PEEM specification for policy processing invocation [PEM-1 TS]. The Interface Blob [J2SEBLOB] and The Java Language Specification [Java] provide support for the concept of Binary Large Object (BLOB) used in the [PEM-1 TS].

Work that originated in Parlay, the 3GPP specification, [3GPP TS 20.198-13] provided support for the concept of I/O signatures, but it stops short of defining a specific interface, and it does not support BLOB as payload.

When it comes to protocol bindings, PEEM specifications are considering Simple Object Access Protocol (SOAP) [SOAP1.2] and IETF Diameter Base Protocol [RFC3588]. More details on re-used specifications will be provided as appropriate in other sections of this chapter.

8.1.2.4 Policy Management

Policy management specifications that are considered as sources for PEEM specification for management of policies include the XML Configuration Access Protocol (XCAP) [RFC 4825]. This specification describes a protocol that can be used to manipulate XML data. To be more accurate, what is being considered is an OMA specification that handles XML documents (see [XDM Core 1.0 TS]) which is based on [RFC 4825]). The File Transfer Protocol [RFC 0959], another IETF specification, may also be given consideration as a means of handling policy management operations.

8.1.3 What Roles Are the PEEM Specifications Playing?

Having provided in previous sections a policy control and management overview on terminology, scope, and standards history, makes it easier to conclude on the purpose and scope of PEEM.

Like most OMA Work Items (WIs), PEEM WI deliverables consist of requirements, architecture, technical specifications, and testing specifications. This in itself is a good indication that the supporting companies (and the OMA as a whole, by approving the WI) believed that such detailed specifications are needed for this topic.

The goal for the PEEM WI was to standardize the management and the processing (evaluation and enforcement) of policies. Processing of policies should be possible either on-demand or transparently, on any request or response to/from a resource. Also, in line with the OMA principles, an expressed goal was that the functions exposed by PEEM should not favor any particular network layer, deployment or configuration or any particular resource that may be the target of a request. The idea behind PEEM was to give the service provider, or for that matter, any enterprise deploying a PEEM implementation, a way to expose any resources (e.g. service enablers) in a controlled and manageable manner that is separated from the actual content of the policy. At the same time, PEEM is meant to be capable of supporting the expression of policies related to any resource, and in order to be able to evaluate and enforce such a large variety of possible policies, PEEM WI explicitly asks for PEEM to support delegation to other resources. It is equally important to mention that the PEEM WI, through the absence of mentioning it, considers the definition of specific, off-the-shelf, readily deployable policies as out of scope for the PEEM specifications. Because of the large variability and differentiation between deployments, no standard or generally applicable policy can be devised, let alone mandated. When one sums up all the goals expressed in the PEEM WI, one quickly realizes that PEEM is expected to be more than 'just another enabler' with its exposed functions through its own I0 interfaces.

One of the initial drivers for PEEM was the logical concept of the Policy Enforcer (PE) in the OMA Service Environment (OSE), for which an OMA realization was desirable (see Chapter 7).

In conclusion, and answering a lingering question on the need for additional standards, PEEM specifications' intent is to formalize specifications for interfaces and language that cover generic policy control and management, a goal that none of the other standards bodies have expressed or focused on. Having said that, PEEM specifications re-use many pre-existing specifications (in some cases created for quite a different purpose), and do not introduce new specifications except where existing ones are lacking.

The next sections will start focusing on PEEM details: market requirements, architecture, and the technical specifications.

8.2   PEEM Market Needs

The PEEM Requirements Document (PEEM RD) details the PEEM WI's goals and scope, by providing a more detailed synthesis of market needs, backed up by various use cases reflecting the situations demanding PEEM technology. In addition, the PEEM RD provides to a certain degree hints about expectations to be met by the architecture specification and the subsequent technical specifications, and even hints with respect to interoperability that will be expanded in the testing specifications.

For starters, let's explore two use cases that will provide an insight into how policy evaluation and enforcement applies to most types of resources, and requests to resources.

8.2.1 Use Case for Explicit Requests to PEEM

The first use case is one in which an end-user is in the midst of using an application accessible from the end-user's mobile device. At some point the application requires interaction with a Mobile Operator's resource (e.g. a short-message system used to send a text message to another subscriber). Is the originating end-user authorized to send a text message, that is, to use the Mobile Operator's Short Message Service (SMS) system? Who will be charged for this service and in which manner will charging occur? One option is of course to have all these conditions and actions hard-coded in the application logic. Another option is to have them hard-coded in the SMS system. However, hard-coding for every possibility is not very practical – since one would have to predict all possible conditions and all possible context (or change code in either SMS system or applications or both every time a previously uncovered change in conditions or in context occurs). Then again, SMS systems need to be common resources for various applications to maximize their revenue potential, hence they should not be optimized for any particular application. And having all the policy decision making hard-coded in the application could prove to be costly from a performance perspective, as the context in which conditions need to be evaluated may have to be retrieved by repeatedly accessing other Mobile Operators' domain resources.

The conclusion one arrives at is that using policy evaluation technology, which separates the policy itself, as well as the policy evaluation logic from the resource that is faced with making complex decisions, is an appropriate alternative. Figure 8.2 shows representative steps for this use case.

In step 1, the SMS system receives a request for sending a text message to some subscriber. When using policy technology, the SMS system would at this point recognize the need for support from a policy evaluation engine, and will explicitly ask for a decision on whether the text message should be forwarded, while providing relevant information (e.g. originator's identity, target subscriber's identity) to a policy evaluation system (step 2). The policy evaluation system (realized via a PEEM enabler implementation) will evaluate a policy that expresses the conditions in which such a request should be granted (step 3), using received input information and other context information (e.g. time of day). The policy would have usually been provisioned prior to the request, or could be supplied along with the request itself. The policy would contain rules that may include verifying whether the originator is authorized to send text messages and/or ensuring that charging for the

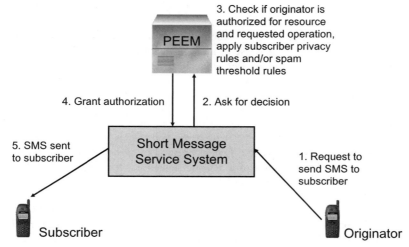

Figure 8.2 Typical use case for explicit request to PEEM. Reproduced by Permission of the Open Mobile Alliance Ltd.

service will be done appropriately. The policy could also include verification that such operation does not infringe on the target subscriber's privacy or spam threshold rules. If the policy conditions are evaluated to a Boolean value of 'TRUE', the PEEM enabler implementation would return to the SMS system a decision to 'grant authorization to send text message' (step 4). As a result, the SMS system would forward the text message to the target subscriber (step 5).

The conclusion is that the Mobile Operator can offer a very adaptable, feature-rich service, while being completely in control of its resources. This is achieved by separating the policy itself from the policy evaluation logic, and separating both from the resources that need to be controlled. A separate entity, the policy evaluation engine, is introduced, obviating the need to hard code the policy in either the SMS system or the application (or both). At the same time, the Mobile Operator is able to honor any Service Level Agreement (SLA) it may have with its subscribers (e.g. with respect to their privacy and/or any other circumstances in which they may accept text messages). The policy rules may be defined by the Mobile Operator in a supported and published high-level language, using service terms in the form of variables (hint to a specification) so that even third parties could provide policy rules consistent with their applications. The high-level language expression will be eventually mapped into an internal representation best suited for the algorithms of the PEEM enabler implementation to be efficient. The expectation is that neither the service, nor the user experience will be degraded because of the introduction of the policy technology.

8.2.2 Use Case for Intercepted Requests by PEEM

The second use case will illustrate additional aspects that the market expects the PEEM enabler to handle. One of them is the ability to intercept and verify whether a policy needs to be evaluated and enforced before allowing a particular request to reach a target resource. An additional expectation is for the PEEM enabler to have the ability to invoke other resources according to the policy rules' conditions and actions. The latter would allow for re-use of resources in the Mobile Operator's domain, and avoid the need for vertical silo-like implementations, in accordance with the principles of the OSE architecture. One may also look at this use case as performing 'enabler composition'. What we mean by this is the ability to combine the functions provided by several enablers into a more complex function that can be invoked by an application. This is achieved by combining the parameters normally needed to interface separately with multiple different enablers into a single interface, and expose this newly created interface as a composed interface to applications. This is one of the capabilities of the PE logical entity in the OSE (for more details see Chapter 7).

In this use case, an end user accesses a location-based game service offered through a third-party service provider application that makes use of multiple enablers in the Mobile Operator's domain (e.g. Location enabler, Charging enabler, PEEM enabler). The use of these resources is transparent to the end user who perceives the delivery of the game service as a single transaction. If the transaction proceeds normally, the end user receives the expected game service, and is charged by the Mobile Operator for both use of resources (operator's resources) and use of the game service (third-party provider's application). If the transaction proceeds abnormally, for example, if one of the enablers fails to respond or refuses the request, the end user is notified and, since the service was not delivered, the user is not charged. Figure 8.3 shows representative steps for this use case (note that this is only a relevant subset of a realistic sequence – for example, it does not address selecting, starting, or stopping the game service).

In step 1, the end user, using a mobile device, sends a game request that contains the desired game action (e.g. 'shoot') and choice of weapon. The Mobile Operator already knows the end-user's identity, since it is connected to its wireless network. The Mobile Operator transparently redirects such a request to its PEEM enabler implementation, since it has it deployed as a service choreography co-ordinator for most requests that need access to the Mobile Operator's resources. The PEEM enabler recognizes this as a request for the third-party service provider's game application and

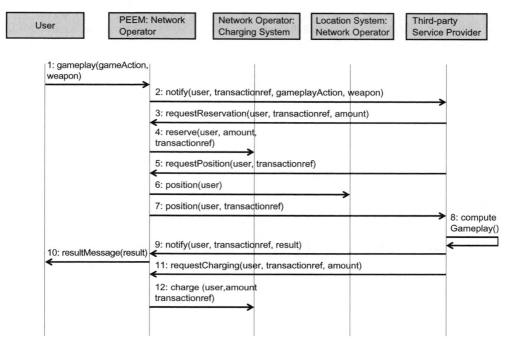

Figure 8.3 Typical use case for intercepted request by PEEM. Reproduced by Permission of the Open Mobile Alliance Ltd.

forwards the message to the third-party service provider (step 2). The third-party provider requests the Mobile Operator to reserve a certain amount of money on the user's account before executing any other operation on behalf of the end-user's request (step 3). The Mobile Operator places the indicated reserve against the end-user's account, by means of using its Charging enabler (step 4). The third-party service provider application asks for end-user's location (step 5), then the Mobile Operator determines the end-user's location using its Location enabler (step 6) and provides it to the third-party service provider (step 7). The third-party service provider application computes a result on the basis of the end-user's location (step 8) and sends the result to the Mobile Operator (step 9), which forwards the result to the originating end user (step 10). The third-party service provider requests the Mobile Operator to charge the end-user's account the fee for the game use (step 11) and the Mobile Operator does so by invoking its Charging enabler (step 12), which also removes the reserve set against the end-user's account. Steps 11–12 could have been executed at different other phases of the use case.

The end user is only interested in the service itself, and in being ensured that charges are applied only if the service is used. The Mobile Operator is interested in providing added value through its enablers, in addition to connectivity, since it will derive revenue as part of the amount charged from the game service. The third-party service provider wants to make sure that it is receiving revenue for the use of its application by any user, and it wants to focus on developing applications, rather than deploying its own enablers.

The Mobile Operator is using a PEEM enabler to intercept any application requests, and applies a selected policy that is associated with that request. The policy contains conditions and actions that invoke functions delegated to other resources in the Mobile Operator's domain (e.g. Charging enablers, Location enablers), as well as functions delegated to the third-party service provider (game service application), and responses to those functions are included in the policy processing. In case of a delegated function that results into a successful condition, the policy continues to the next rule (possibly a next invocation). Otherwise the policy handles the failed condition, which may include stopping the game and appropriately informing the end user (e.g. there is not enough money to make a reserve on the end-user's account, or location of end user cannot be obtained). The policy in effect composes multiple services (e.g. charging service, location service, interactions with a third-party service provider) into a more complex service that it offers to the application.

8.2.3 PEEM Requirements

PEEM requirements are derived from use cases such as those described in the previous section. While the PEEM WI clearly articulates the need to provide generic mechanisms and language constructs to cover any policy, and not to mandate particular policies, PEEM requirements include plenty of examples of what such policies are expected to address, as well as who may make use of them. Such requirements are a good indication of the scope of the policies. The requirements help in the definition of the PEL, and the management operations needed to handle policies. They also help define the type of resources that need policy decision support and hence set expectations on the content of the input and output policy parameters.

The market is expecting that the PEEM enabler will support any kind of policy, including but not limited to:

- end-user privacy policies, including cases that require obtaining end-user's explicit consent;
- authorization-related policies;
- charging-related policies.

Such policies may be provisioned, and later on evaluated and enforced, for a wide spectrum of requests and responses, and for various requestors and responders. PEEM should support the following:

- requests and responses from any type of resource, for any type of resource that may be individual resources or groups of multiple resources;
- requests from end-users, intending to access services of the service provider (including end-users belonging to different networks);
- requests from end users, intending to access services of a third-party Application Service Provider (ASP);
- requests from end users wanting to communicate with another end user;
- requests from another service provider (e.g. Mobile Operator);
- requests from a third-party ASP, whose application utilizes service provider's (e.g. Mobile Operator's) resources; and
- in general, requestors and responders that may be located in the same or different domains.

Some of the PEEM requirements leave little doubt on what technical specifications are needed by the industry. For example, requirements on policy expression hint toward a technical specification for a PEL. To some extent, these PEEM requirements also indicate high-level features that those specifications should cover, although they stop short of getting into architecture, design or realization details.

8.2.3.1 Policy Expression Requirements

As we have mentioned, defining specific policies is out of scope for the PEEM enabler. But knowledge of what a policy looks like is required in order to define a mechanism for policy evaluation and enforcement. Therefore there is a need for a common way to express such policies. This need is emphasized by requirements such as:

- PEEM enabler specification must be able to support delegation to one or more resource (e.g. charging, service discovery).
- PEEM enabler specification must support the evaluation of policies by delegation of the policy execution steps to enablers that may be in different security and administrative domains.
- PEEM enabler specification must be able to support the interruption of flows and rejection of requests, through enforcement of policies (e.g. failure in authentication or authorization requests, charging failure, etc.).
- PEEM enabler specification must support ways to include in a policy rule references to input data (i.e. contained in the service request/response) with the intent to be replaced by the real input parameter values during the policy enforcement.
- PEEM enabler specification must support the processing of policy rules according to their priorities.
- PEEM must specify a language based on standard schema and semantics.
- The PEL must be able to create rules that can include the use of context information such as: end-users subscriptions, market segment and/or class-of-service the end-user belongs to (e.g. platinum, gold, silver, bronze), SLAs with Mobile Operator and/or third-party service providers, end-user account status, end-user personal data, service provider variables and conditions, regulatory/legislative variables and conditions.

Note that in the requirements, the types of policies to be supported, along with types of policy variables and conditions, are often given by means of examples, rather than by an exhaustive list. This is an indication that a compliant technical specification must provide the capabilities in the form of an extensible specification. This extensible specification could be a framework, or base specification, that others are building upon, and particularize for their specific needs (see more in Section 8.5.5).

8.2.3.2 Policy Evaluation and Enforcement Requirements

Before we continue with the analysis of the PEEM requirements it may be worth clarifying a somewhat strange expression that you may encounter frequently: policy evaluation, or policy evaluation and enforcement (or variations of this expression).

The IETF has introduced the so-called PEP-PDP model. In this model, the PEP asks the PDP for a decision. The PDP evaluates the policy that was passed to it by the PEP and returns a decision. The PEP then enforces the decision that was returned to it by the PDP. In this IETF PEP-PDP model, evaluation and enforcement are separate phases, and are executed by separate actors.

In an equivalent 'PEEM world', a resource (the PEP) makes an explicit request for a decision to PEEM (the PDP). PEEM evaluates a policy and returns a decision to the resource in order to be enforced there. However, PEEM, as you will learn a bit later, needs to support other cases that are different than those supported by the IETF PEP-PDP model. And therefore PEEM not only needs to perform evaluation (as a PDP), but also needs to be able to perform both evaluation and enforcement. As a result in all cases where the nature of the request to PEEM is yet to be determined, we have to use the somewhat awkward expression 'policy evaluation, or policy evaluation and enforcement'. At some point, for simplification it was decided to replace this with 'policy processing', but the term is too bland for anybody who was not deeply involved with the work, and hence aware of its origin. So for this chapter, in most cases we made the choice of using the awkward term over the bland term, but at least now you are armed with the explanation. Now we return to the requirements analysis.

The need for a common way to express a request for either policy evaluation only, or for policy evaluation and enforcement, and to provide input context in the form of input arguments (for such policy processing) is emphasized by a number of requirements in the PEEM RD. Together, these requirements hint at an interface specification for evaluation and enforcement requests. These requirements include the following:

- Standardized interfaces must be defined for the PEEM enabler.
- PEEM enabler must support the receipt of requests for a policy evaluation (or evaluation and enforcement).
- PEEM enabler must support the identification of policies that apply to a request and response.
- PEEM enabler must support policies that allow the request to pass through without any additional policy enforcement (i.e. this allows other resources to implement their own local policies).
- PEEM enabler must support the processing of data provided as input with the processed request or response (e.g. the level of security or QoS).
- PEEM enabler must be able to determine the resource that needs to be protected and the policies associated to that resource.
- PEEM enabler specification must be able to obtain session information (e.g. for end-user identification) from the information contained in a request/response.

8.2.3.3 Policy Management Requirements

We have seen there is value in separating the policy itself from the policy evaluation logic. Requirements for the policy evaluation logic were introduced in the previous section. So now that the policies themselves are separated, and no longer hard-coded, there is a need to manage them. The need for a common way to manage policies (a hint to another interface technical specification) is emphasized by requirements such as:

- PEEM enabler specification must define interfaces for a principal to manage policies related to a resource.
- PEEM enabler must support the following functions related to policy management: create, view, modify and delete. Other functions, such as the ability to prioritize and sequence policy rules, or the ability to identify inconsistencies between policy rules, are considered optional.
- PEEM enabler specification should be able to support the override of policies (i.e. policies can be cancelled or pre-empted by other policies) due to different priority levels in different policies.
- When policies are established, the PEEM enabler should include mechanisms to facilitate detection of policies incompatible with others already established, that is, for detection of contradicting policies.
- PEEM enabler must support policy management by various actors, for example, service provider, network operator, enterprise, and end user. In addition, delegation of a right to perform policy management from one authorized principal to another also needs to be supported.

8.2.3.4 Implementation and Deployment Considerations

Detailed implementation and deployment requirements are in general outside the scope of any OMA enabler specification. However, there are PEEM requirements that provide high-level guidance relative to implementation, deployment, and operations. Predominantly, such guidance is meant to ensure that no valid deployment options are excluded, and that no resources are precluded from interacting with a PEEM enabler implementation:

- PEEM enabler must not restrict the technology and deployment options (e.g. a geographically distributed PEEM, a highly scalable PEEM).
- PEEM enabler must support the interaction with other resources to enforce the results of policy evaluation (or evaluation and execution), for example, security.

- PEEM enabler specification must support secure exchanges between requestor and responder.
- PEEM enabler must support policies that allow the request to pass through without any additional policy enforcement (i.e. this allows other resources to implement their own local policies).
- PEEM enabler specification must not preclude: charging models between different actors, establishment of SLAs, deployment of service enablers in high-availability, high-uptime, scalable environments (e.g. by requiring implementation in ways which disable the use of such pre-existing capabilities in this environment).
- PEEM enabler specification must be compatible with re-usable mechanisms defined in other enablers (e.g. for resource-related data registration and discovery), and not define its own mechanisms for this purpose.
- PEEM enabler specification must be able to simultaneously support multiple versions (i.e. multiple instances, defined according to different releases of the OMA specifications) of a target resource's interface.
- PEEM enabler must be able to create log information about the flows and events (such as error events) that the PEEM processes, and the associated policy evaluation and enforcement flows that may result (for auditing purposes).

So far we have identified the market needs for PEEM, and showcased them by referencing, with some interpretation, a subset of them, in order to facilitate the understanding of the PEEM architecture that was subsequently derived. However, one of the stated OMA goals is to re-use as much as possible, at all specification stages, before identifying the need to invent. The following sections will delve into architecture, followed by technical specifications aspects. Additional deployment considerations can be found in Section 8.5.2.1.

8.3 PEEM Architecture and Technical Specifications

PEEM architecture had to ensure that all PEEM requirements could be implemented. That includes requirements that give a good indication on what interfaces may have to be designed, requirements that give an indication on the behavior of different architectural components, and requirements that provide hints for deployment and operational aspects. There was also an implicit commitment in the PEEM WI that the PEEM enabler may provide a realization for the OSE PE. Starting with that last premise, the next section will position the PEEM enabler in the larger OSE architecture.

8.3.1 PEEM in the OSE

PEEM enabler is an interesting case when attempting to map it to the OSE. In order to introduce the concepts gradually, Figure 8.4 provides an initial mapping of the PEEM enabler to an OSE architectural diagram.

In the figure, PEEM appears in two different places in the OSE architecture. It appears in the 'Service Enabler Tier', since it is as much an OMA enabler as any other OMA enablers. As such, it exposes one or more category I0 interfaces which can be invoked by any resource.

PEEM also appears inside the PE entity defined in the OSE architecture. This is meant to indicate that the PE logical concept can be realized using the PEEM enabler. It is a distinctive feature, because the PE is the only logical entity in the OSE architecture that is distinguished by a specific name and its functionality described in detail, as opposed to other logical entities (e.g. the OMA enablers in the 'Service Enabler Tier').

Recognizing that the reader may be eager for more explanations, for the better flow of the chapter, we prefer to add further details and an updated diagram, after we have had a chance to explore some PEEM subtleties in the next sections (see Section 8.4.1 for an updated view).

The astute reader will discern that, because of these two different roles PEEM can play in the OSE, even the PE may call the PEEM enabler, using PEEM enabler category I0 interfaces. After all, the PE may invoke the category I0 interface of any other enabler in the 'Service Enabler Tier'. But

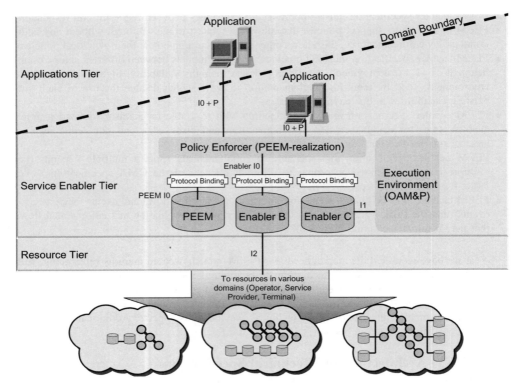

Figure 8.4 PEEM enabler in the OSE architecture – initial view

this still holds true when the PE itself is realized using a PEEM enabler implementation. Although apparently strange, this is nevertheless not only a correct and acceptable, but a very useful behavior.

As an OMA enabler in the 'Service Enabler Tier', Figure 8.4 also implies that the PEEM enabler may have to interface with other enablers using the category I0 interfaces exposed by those enablers. It may also interface with the OSE Execution Environment using a category I1 interface, and it may interface with other resources in the OSE 'Resource Tier' using category I2 interfaces exposed by those resources. Finally, the PEEM enabler will also support bindings to specific protocols, and those bindings may be different than bindings to protocols supported by other enablers.

8.3.2 PEEM Logical Architecture

PEEM logical architecture is depicted in Figure 8.5. The architecture diagram represents the agreed components and interfaces, which are sufficient in order to understand how PEEM may fit in the OSE architecture and inter-operate with other resources. But as we will later explain, some aspects (e.g. component behavior, internal architecture) are intentionally not captured by the architectural diagram in order to not make it too complex or too restrictive. Such aspects will be rather detailed in the text.

8.3.2.1 PEEM Components

In Figure 8.5, all PEEM functions are supported by a single component – the PEEM component. Further de-composition has been discussed early on, but not agreed and rather considered implementation choices (see Section 8.5.2.1). The PEEM component performs a number of functions. It

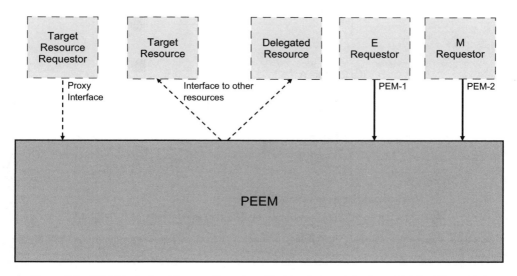

Figure 8.5   PEEM logical architecture. Reproduced by Permission of the Open Mobile Alliance Ltd.

provides the mechanisms for creating, viewing, modifying, and deleting policies. It may provide optional capabilities for prioritizing policy rules and detecting and/or preventing conflicts between policy rules. In addition, it processes requests for evaluation, or evaluation and enforcement, arriving on-demand from a requestor, or applied implicitly. Steps that PEEM may have to go through to perform such processing are as follows:

- It may first identify the appropriate policy associated with the request/requestor (a policy may contain one or more policy rules; a rule contains a condition and one or more actions).
- It evaluates the conditions in the policy using information received via requests and other context information. The component may use delegation to other resources if needed, during evaluation of conditions.
- It executes the policy actions resulting from a positive evaluation of the policy conditions. The component may use delegation to other resources if needed, during execution of actions.
- An additional effect may be that PEEM may return a policy decision to a requestor (see details for callable usage pattern) or it may allow or block a request to continue to its original target destination (see details for proxy usage pattern). If a decision is returned to the requestor, its enforcement becomes the requestor's responsibility. An alternative is that the enforcement of all actions, including such a last decision, is accomplished within PEEM itself. PEEM also supports cases in which a response is provided to other resources, instead of to the requestor.

A short explanation on how a policy is traversed during processing may provide additional insight (see Figure 8.6).

The topology of a policy is defined as a graph where each node represents a condition to be evaluated and each outbound branch has actions to be executed if the corresponding condition is true.

8.3.2.2 PEEM Interfaces

The PEM-1 interface (PEEM specified callable interface) is a category I0 interface exposed by the PEEM enabler. By callable interface, we mean that other resources explicitly use it to make a direct request for policy processing (policy evaluation, or policy evaluation and enforcement).

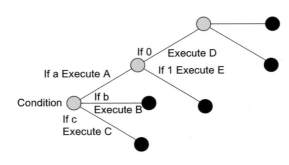

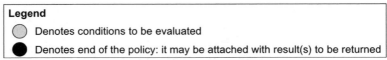

Figure 8.6 is described by the following diagram.

Legend

⬤ (gray) Denotes conditions to be evaluated

⬤ (black) Denotes end of the policy: it may be attached with result(s) to be returned

Figure 8.6 A graph that describes the topology of a policy. Reproduced by Permission of the Open Mobile Alliance Ltd.

PEEM may return a policy decision (the result of the policy evaluation) to the resource that issued the request to PEEM, using the same interface. PEM-1 is defined in a way that permits other enablers to particularize the PEM-1 interface in order to satisfy their specific requirements.

The PEM-2 interface (PEEM specified management interface) is a category I0 interface exposed by the PEEM enabler. Other resources use it to make a request for policy management. This interface is also referred to as PEEM management interface.

The Proxy interface represented in Figure 8.5 is not specified by PEEM, since it depends on the nature of the interface that it proxies for. However, it may be exposed by a PEEM implementation as a deployment choice, and used to exchange messages compliant with the interfaces to the target enablers (it is a typical proxy in that sense). More generally, it is used to exchange messages compliant to a combination of the target resource interface and the set of parameters that must be added to requests through that resource's interface as required in order to satisfying policies that are to be processed when exposing the resource. The messages exchanged through this interface may be different for each target resource. This has a direct relationship to the OSE architecture concept of I0+P, and the application of PEEM enabler as a realization for the OSE PE (see Chapter 7, specially dedicated to this topic). While all this may sound a bit nebulous at this stage, it is a concept essential to understand how the PEEM specifications are defined. This will become clearer when we go through the 'proxy usage pattern' in a later section of this chapter.

8.3.2.3 Other Non-specified Components and Interfaces

In addition to PEEM components and interfaces, there are other elements represented in Figure 8.5 for a better understanding of the architectural diagram. Like the interfaces that are not specified by PEEM, such elements are represented with dashed lines. The following is a complete list of other elements identified in Figure 8.5 that interact with PEEM.

- Target Resource Requestor is a resource that issues a request to a target resource.
- Target resource is the destination resource (e.g. application, enabler, component, etc.) for a request made by some other resource.
- Delegated Resource is a resource to which PEEM may delegate certain policy actions during the policy processing process.
- Interface to other resources is a generalization for all interfaces that may be used to exchange messages compliant to the interface of the target or delegated resources interfaces. The messages

exchanged through this interface may be different for each resource, and they are dictated by policy processing. Since policy instances are not specified in PEEM, these interfaces cannot be specified either.

- Evaluation Requestor (E Requestor) is a resource that issues a request for policy processing to PEEM.
- Management Requestor (M Requestor) is a resource that issues a request for policy management to PEEM.

8.3.3 Logical Flows for PEEM

There are several typical flows that are worth mentioning in conjunction with each of the PEEM exposed interfaces (PEM-1, Proxy, and PEM-2).

The flows involving a request using the PEM-1 callable interface are represented in Figure 8.7.

The E Requestor sends an explicit request for policy processing to PEEM (flow 1), which may make use of delegation to other resources (flows 2, 3, 4, 5) in its process of policy evaluation, or policy evaluation and enforcement. Why use the awkward term in this case, when it appears that this matches the PEP-PDP model perfectly? The answer is that the request is for policy processing, hence it could be a request to both evaluate conditions and execute some actions. Nevertheless, a decision may be returned to the E Requestor (flow 6) in either case.

The flows involving a request using the Proxy interface are represented in Figure 8.8.

Some requestor (not shown) sends a request for a target resource. The request is being transparently intercepted and redirected to PEEM in order to process an associated policy before allowing the request to reach the target resource (flow 1). During the policy processing for the request, PEEM may make use of delegation to other resources (flows 2, 3, 4, 5). Assuming a positive policy evaluation, the original request is forwarded to the target resource (flow 6), which processes the request using its own specific functions. The target resource may return a response to the original requestor. This response may again be transparently intercepted and redirected to PEEM (flow 7). PEEM applies any associated policy to this response, and during the policy processing, it may make use of delegation to other resources (flows 8, 9, 10, 11) before returning the response to the original requestor (flow 12).

The presence of PEEM as a proxy on the path to the target resource, as well as the fact that delegation may take place, is not visible to the original requester. The original requester simply issues a request to the target resource, using the target resource's I0 interface. This further illustrates the point that the PEEM Proxy interface is not specified by PEEM. Rather, the PEEM Proxy interface is used to exchange messages compliant to a combination of the target resource I0 interface and the set of parameters that must be added to requests through that I0 interface, in order to satisfy policies that are to be processed when exposing the resource.

The flows involving a request using the PEM-2 interface are represented in Figure 8.9.

The M Requestor sends a request for policy management to PEEM (flow 1). This is usually a request for creating, updating, deleting, or viewing a policy (some more esoteric, optional

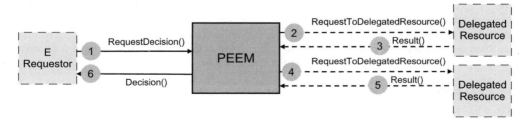

Figure 8.7   Logical flows for request via the PEM-1 interface

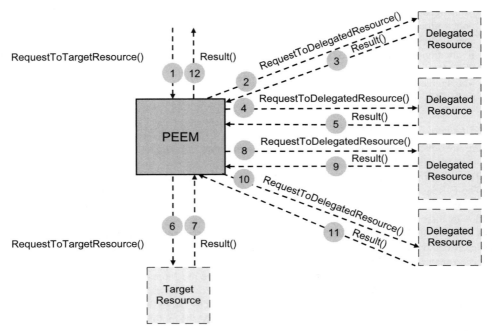

Figure 8.8 Logical flows for request via the Proxy interface. Reproduced by Permission of the Open Mobile Alliance Ltd.

Figure 8.9 Logical flows for request via the PEM-2 interface. Reproduced by Permission of the Open Mobile Alliance Ltd.

management functions such as setting policy precedence rules, are still being considered). Depending on the specific management operation, a result may be returned via flow 2. The result may be, for example, the content of the policy itself, a confirmation that the operation has succeeded, an error, or some valid combination of these options.

Using the combination of market requirements, PEEM standard precursors, and the blueprint of the architecture specification, the PEEM technical specifications materialized into a PEL technical specification, a PEM-1 (PEEM callable interface) technical specification and a PEM-2 (PEEM management interface) technical specification. All of these technical specifications are still in progress at the time of writing this chapter. However, there is sufficient content in these specifications that has been agreed, and that has been stable for quite some time, to allow us to present it as very likely to be contained in the final version of the specifications.

8.3.4 PEEM Policy Expression Language Details

The PEL technical specification defines the set of PEL constructs needed to meet the market requirements outlined in the PEEM RD. We will start with some additional detail on re-used standards.

8.3.4.1 Policy Language Standards Re-use

As we have mentioned earlier in this chapter, PEEM specifications are not developed in a vacuum, and benefit from valuable prior art. The Common Policy: A Document Format for Expressing Privacy Preferences [RFC 4745] defines an extensible framework for creating authorization policies. While it covers authorization policies for controlling access to presence and location information, the intention of this framework is to be extended by application-specific policies specified somewhere else and it provides a common policy XML [XML1.0] schema. [RFC 4745] is a very valuable source of inspiration for the PEL specification [PEL TS].

The Business Process Execution Language [BPEL] forms a foundation for multiple usage patterns and addresses both the process interface descriptions required for business protocols as well as the executable process models. [BPEL] does not include specification of bindings to specific hardware/software platforms. [BPEL] is the other very valuable source of inspiration for the PEL specification [PEL TS].

Another source of inspiration provided by OASIS is the XACML [XACML]. [XACML] specifies bindings to existing protocols (e.g. 'XML Path Language' (XPath) and 'Lightweight Directory Access Protocol' (LDAP)), and may define additional protocols for accessing and communicating the policies. One can also use [XACML] as a policy interchange format, and use other non-XACML specified protocols for accessing and communicating the policies. Although XACML is strictly an authorization policy framework, it represented a valuable source for the PEL specification, as well as for the policy evaluation and enforcement invocation interface specification.

Still related to policy expression issues, some specifications were considered as guidance for what existing policies should continue to be supported, and what kind of additional policies may need to be expressed. [IETF Draft2007a] proposes a presence authorization policy expression language. The OMA itself specifies the PoC user access expression language [POC_XDM-V1_0 TS] and the presence policy expression language [Presence-V1_0 TS]. The 3GPP specifies a location policy expression [3GPP TS 22.071] and a charging policy expression [3GPP TS 23.125]. Programming languages (e.g. programming language – C [ISO/IEC 9899]) provided some general guidance to programming constructs, expression of variables and functions, and data types.

8.3.4.2 PEL Specification

In support of the requirements, the agreed set of constructs and semantics in the PEL specification includes mechanisms for expressing policies, either as a set of separate rules, or as a workflow. The following definitions apply for PEL, and define the supportive language constructs.

- A ruleset is a collection of (policy) rules that operate as a whole to satisfy a specific policy evaluation (or evaluation and enforcement). A ruleset is identified by a name, and may have a set of variables in-scope.
- A rule is an expression that includes a rule condition, and a set of one or more rule actions.
- A condition is a Boolean expression that evaluates to a Boolean value of TRUE or FALSE.
- An action is an operation that shall be executed if the condition of a rule evaluates to TRUE.

Other PEL constructs address flow concepts, and delegation to other resources. Furthermore, PEL supports typical variable data types (e.g. bool, integer, float, string, array, and struct), constants, and mathematical and logical operators.

The consensus is that, because of the particularity of different deployment choices, different options for the PEL are needed, to cover different situations. One is needed to support a flowchart approach for orchestrating business processes, another one to support rule-based approach for handling network layers policies or subscriber's policies handling, for example, permissions and preferences.

One of the agreed options being specified is [BPEL], which is matching the need for a PEL for business processes orchestration/workflow. The other agreed option being specified is a subset of [RFC 4745], accompanied by guidelines on how it can be extended by enablers, in order to address specific needs for expressing additional types of conditions, actions and delegation to other resources. Some companies have also expressed the desire to define mechanisms that would allow combining the two options. However, it is too early to assert the final outcome in that sense.

8.3.5 PEM-1 Interface Details

The PEM-1 technical specification [PEM-1 TS] defines the callable interface for policy evaluation, or evaluation and enforcement. Since the specification relies on prior art, we will first explore existing specifications and concepts put forward there, that are leveraged by this PEEM specification.

8.3.5.1 The BLOB and the Template

The Interface Blob [J2SEBLOB] and The Java Language Specification [Java] provide support for the concept of BLOB used in the [PEM-1 TS]. The PEM-1 Template is a concept introduced by PEEM. Both concepts are critical to the understanding of the approach taken in [PEM-1 TS]. First of all, we hope not to disappoint anybody, but this is not about the 1958 motion picture 'Blob', with Steve McQueen as a protagonist (although some in ARC WG looked upon the concept with similar horror for quite a while).

The BLOB concept is defined in J2SE, but it had been in use for a while in the programming community, and never quite formally standardized. In essence, the concept was introduced to allow handling of streams of binary data, without knowing (or caring) how the data was initially structured. Think about a producer program and a consumer program. The consumer of the data obviously knows how to interpret the data; it knows the format according to which it will parse it, since in most cases the consumer is the one that dictates the format. However, the producer of the data may be told just in due time, not necessarily using a standard way (e.g. directly by the consumer, or through some intermediate service), the format in which to produce the data. In other words, the format may not a priori comply to a well-formatted pre-defined structure, well documented and known much in advance of the actual transaction between the producer and consumer. As such it does not conform to the normal expectations imposed on specifications, where one expects a well-defined input and output so that interoperability testing can be conducted between the producer product and the consumer product. But there is no other way to describe a stream of data that can be formatted in *any* possible way. Hence, for simplicity, look at the BLOB as data that can be formatted in *any* possible way. This is the way the concept is to be understood for the purpose of this chapter and the rest of the book (see also Chapter 7).

Now that the concept is explained, and hopefully at least some of the horror aspects are removed, the question remains what to do about giving advance notice to requestors about the structure of input/output data that they may need to handle, and as importantly, how to conduct interoperability testing, since the fact that we understand a concept, does not equate to solving those real issues. Well, we now know that the BLOB can support *any* format, which means *any* format can be over-imposed on the BLOB. That implies that a consumer can define any I/O data structure, convey it to the producer, and if the producer replicates it in the BLOB when making the transaction, the BLOB will carry the data to the consumer to be processed by the latter. Now think about many consumers and many producers simultaneously, all using the same protocol to communicate with each other, namely passing a BLOB, but every time it is formatted by a particular producer in the way that its consumer peer has asked for. At least some of those I/O data structures must be known in advance and could be documented, right? We refer to such pre-defined I/O data structures as Templates. Remember the BLOB concept and the Template concept, since they will come in handy in the next sections, when we will elaborate on BLOBs and how to overlay them with templates.

8.3.5.2 PEM-1 Interface Specification

[PEM-1 TS] defines as follows the use of two main concepts, as applied to PEM-1 interface:

- Support a BLOB interface [J2SEBLOB] for input and output (i.e. any input can be passed via PEM-1 by a requestor and any output may be returned via PEM-1 to the requestor). Inputs are parsed and examined and outputs are generated based on the policy processed by PEEM. Interpretation of the BLOB input data structure and generation of output data is always driven by the policy that is processed.
- Support PEM-1 Templates (which is a structured sequence of PEM-1 Parameters). The PEM-1 Templates include either policy input PEM-1 Parameters provided by the requestor for the consumption by the policy or policy output PEM-1 Parameters generated by the policy for the requestor's consumption. These parameters are technology neutral specifications of pairs of identifier and value, where the identifier also defines the data type of the accompanying value.

These PEM-1 Templates are defined to provide structure to the BLOB interface, in order to support specific pre-determined policies. Templates are also useful in creating meaningful inter-operability test cases. We already alluded to the fact that the PEEM specifications need to be extensible. To this end, PEM-1 supports the notion of Standard PEM-1 Template (i.e. defined by the OMA and included with the PEEM specifications) and Custom PEM-1 Template (e.g. defined by the service provider which deploys PEEM). Any PEM-1 Template should be designed considering the constraints of the requestor and service provider who defines the policies. The PEM-1 interface specification will contain the Standard PEM-1 Templates and PEM-1 parameters, which provide a basic subset that may be extended using the notion of Custom PEM-1 Templates defined by other OMA enablers. For the Standard PEM-1 Templates, it is likely that at least an output status (e.g. success or different errors), an internal policy reference and an external policy reference parameter, will be specified as part of the PEM-1 TS. The PEM-1 TS should at least capture those PEM-1 Parameters and PEM-1 Templates that may be re-usable (potentially including some identified as needed by other OMA enablers).

When using Templates, they will be encapsulated in the Input BLOB, respectively in the Output BLOB, which are containers transported over the PEM-1 interface. Now that we have introduced the templates to provide structure to the BLOB containers, we need to look at protocol bindings (PEM-1 Template Bindings) to transport the BLOBs across the wire.

8.3.5.3 PEM-1 Template Bindings

Supported bindings will include at least a SOAP [SOAP 1.2] binding option and a Diameter [RFC 3588] binding option. SOAP is an obvious choice when it comes to interfacing with resources that employ Web Services technology (see OMA Web Services Enabler Release (OWSER) in Chapter 11). Diameter was devised in IETF to provide an Authentication, Authorization, and Accounting (AAA) framework for applications such as network access or IP mobility, for both local and roaming situations. While initially designed to support AAA, Diameter is a fairly generic protocol, and can be used as an extensible framework for adding new applications, new Attribute Value Pair (AVP) types to be supported, and support for a variety of namespaces for its AVPs (although IETF does not necessarily endorse other uses). It is worth mentioning that Diameter is used in 3GPP specifications and other OMA specifications (e.g. Charging enabler) and considered for use in 3GPP2.

For binding PEM-1 interface messages to Diameter, a new vendor-specific Diameter [RFC 3588] application with specific command codes and a new AVP have been designed, that can be used to transfer input and output data, respectively between a PEEM Requestor and PEEM. The Diameter application implies the use of request-response pairs to conform to the Diameter state machine model. The specific vendor identification needs to still be implemented, following the IETF's Internet Assigned Numbers Authority (IANA) process.

For the SOAP binding, the model currently considered includes synchronous and asynchronous support. The synchronous model is similar to the Diameter [RFC 3588] request–response pairing. The asynchronous model supported by the SOAP binding allows the PEEM Requestor to provide a callback method in the initial request, which is paired with an acknowledgement from PEEM. Later on, when PEEM has policy processing results available, it will initiate a request toward the PEEM Requestor, in order to pass to it the policy processing results, and will wait for an acknowledgement. In addition to SOAP and Diameter, no other protocol binding options have been proposed.

Each of the PEM-1 Template Bindings requires a detailed schema definition. The schema definition for the SOAP binding is currently in progress. The schema definition for Diameter is already based on references to the Diameter Base Protocol, with Augmented Backus-Naur Form (ABNF) extensions for messages documented as part of the PEM-1 specification. Detailed schemas for syntax and transfer encoding will be provided in the technical specification once the decision on the use of XML or a different encoding is finalized.

PEM-1 Templates would be binary encoded in these containers. Currently, the use of XML encoding and some other alternatives are being considered for PEM-1 Templates transfer encoding. In order to support internationalization (i.e. multiple languages), the PEM-1 Template encoding will likely use the 8-bit UCS/Unicode Transformation Format character set [RFC 3629] for character encoding. As a positive unplanned by-product of those discussions, an Architecture Whitepaper addressing the Best Practice on recommendations for Internationalization character encoding (work in progress) has emerged.

A note of caution to the reader: a lot of details on Standard PEM-1 Templates, PEM-1 Parameters, PEM-1 Template Bindings and different protocol options are still being addressed in the technical specifications. All of them may be to some degree modulated by progress on other enablers that may depend on the PEEM enabler (see Section 8.5.5).

8.3.6 PEM-2 Interface Specification

The PEM-2 technical specification [PEM-2 TS] defines the PM interface. As such, PEM-2 needs to support all PEEM requirements for management of policies. In essence, that pertains to a set of management operations to handle policy documents, where policies have been defined using one of the PEL specification options. The set of management operations supported by PEM-2 consists of the create, modify, view, and delete policy commands.

Like it was the case for PEM-1, the PEM-2 specification provides an abstract interface definition. This definition needs to be complemented with one or more PEM-2 bindings, discussed in the next section.

8.3.6.1 PEM-2 Bindings

Some background on re-used standards is provided. [RFC 4825] describes XCAP, a protocol that can be used to manipulate XML data. It includes a set of conventions for mapping XML documents and document components into HTTP Uniform Resource Identifiers (URIs). [RFC 4825] also provides rules for how the modification of one resource affects another, as well as guidelines for data validation constraints and authorization policies associated with access to those resources. XCAP is intended to support configuration needs for a multitude of applications. The OMA specifications that handle XML documents (see [XDM Core 1.0 TS] and [XDM Shared 1.0 TS]) borrow heavily from [RFC 4825] and are considered at the current time as possible candidates for realizing the [PEM-2 TS] PEEM specification. The specification has focused so far on defining how a subset of the XDM Core [XDM Core 1.0 TS] enabler specification (in essence, the XCAP protocol) is to be re-used for the PEM-2 interface. Another proposed realization for PEM-2 consists of re-use of FTP.

Assuming the XDM Core specification subset is the only one PEM-2 binding defined, detailed message flows for PEM-2 may not be necessary, since there is nothing distinctive, at the policy management operations level, between managing policies as XML documents and managing any other generic XML documents. In [PEM-2 TS], references to existing specifications will be provided instead.

Along the same vein, assuming the XDM Core specification subset is the only one PEM-2 binding defined, detailed protocol binding schemas may not be provided, but rather references to existing specifications will be provided instead.

Another note of caution to the reader applies to PEM-2: a lot of details for PEM-2 have strong dependencies on the decisions made by the PEL technical specification, and may only be rapidly resolved once PEL resolutions are reached.

8.4   PEEM Salient Points

Having achieved a good understanding of the PEEM architecture, and the direction of PEEM technical specifications, this may be a good time to explore some peculiarities, especially since we were teasing the reader with some of them for the better part of this chapter. So let's start with the 'PEEM usage patterns' clarifications. There is no real mystery here, but, as opposed to many other enablers, PEEM may be deployed in two different usage patterns.

8.4.1 Usage Patterns

The obvious one, inspired from the IETF PEP-PDP architectural model, and one may say typical for most client-server architectures, is the pattern evident in the flow illustrated in Figure 8.7. This is known as the 'PEEM callable usage pattern' and is further explored in Figure 8.10.

An authorized principal, sometimes using an originating resource (the Requestor) will send a request to a target resource (e.g. any enabler in the Service Provider domain), using the target resource's I0 interface. The target resource runs into a situation where it cannot continue its processing without making a decision, and it may not have all the facts needed to make the decision, or the logic needed to make the decision because the way it was deliberately designed and realized. In this case, the target resource is designed to ask the PEEM enabler to provide it with a policy decision. In order to help with the evaluation of the policy that should result into the policy decision, the target resource supplies any input information needed by the policy (using the PEM-1 interface, and passing input information structured as indicated by the policy, or as pre-agreed using Standard or Custom PEM-1 Templates). The input parameters passed by the target resource to the PEEM enabler may include a reference to a PEEM internal policy, or a new policy to be evaluated and enforced may be supplied with the request to PEEM. PEEM will process the policy – evaluate conditions and execute actions – and in most cases will return a decision in its response to the target resource. The target resource will enforce the decision received and continue its processing of the original request from the requestor, and eventually return some response to the requestor. This is indeed very similar with the pattern described in [RFC2753], also referred to as the IETF PEP-PDP model.

However, there is a subtle additional twist, explicitly supported by the PEEM callable usage pattern, and possibly allowed, but not explicitly expressed in the IETF PEP-PDP model. That is the case where a decision rendered during the policy processing by the PEEM enabler is enforced in the PEEM enabler itself – hence the PEEM enabler serves as both decision and enforcement point. This allows for situations in which the target resource may continue to do processing in parallel with PEEM processing, or even situations where a response to the requestor may not come directly from PEEM. In order to understand this point, think from the perspective of the policy. The policy is a program, albeit in most cases a rudimentary one that can be implemented as sequence of 'IF... THEN...' programming statements. During the execution of some of these statements, function calls may be made to delegate functions to other resources. The policy has little control over the

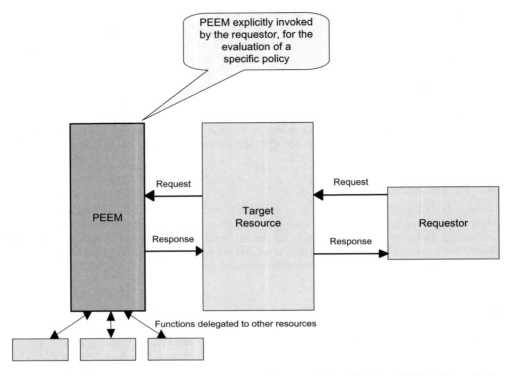

Figure 8.10   PEEM callable usage pattern. Reproduced by Permission of the Open Mobile Alliance Ltd.

delegated functions behavior; in fact it has to deal with and support such behavior. That implies, that in some cases, such functions may not return a response. This may happen by design of the delegated function. The delegated function may perform in such a way that it enforces the needed decision and/or directly communicates any decision back to the target resource. Note that in either case, a decision has not been reached within the policy, so there is nothing in return to be enforced by the target resource. In other cases, the request from the target resource may be explicitly of the nature 'evaluation and enforcement'. In this case, the policy has the obligation to both perform the evaluation of the condition and the enforcement of all the actions, while in fact the target resource may continue its processing. As an imperfect analogy, one may think about the difference between synchronous calls and asynchronous calls, although the case here is even somewhat more complex, because it involves more than two programming threads. In summary, the capability to address such situations provides for added power and flexibility to what can be achieved by the policy.

Figure 8.11 shows how the PEEM architecture diagram is impacted when PEEM is deployed in the PEEM callable usage pattern (it does not need to support the 'Proxy interface').

A perhaps less obvious usage pattern for an enabler is the one evident in the flow illustrated in Figure 8.8. This pattern is known as the 'PEEM proxy usage pattern'. It is a less obvious usage pattern, because it is not found in prior art like the IETF PEP-PDP model. And although there is nothing mystical about a proxy, it is not common for an OMA enabler at least, to support both a 'callable pattern' and a 'proxy pattern'. However, the 'PEEM proxy pattern', represented in Figure 8.12, is needed in order to support a realization by PEEM for the OSE PE logical entity (see Chapter 7).

An authorized principal, sometimes using an originating resource (the Requestor) will send a request to a target resource (e.g. any enabler in the Service Provider domain), using the target

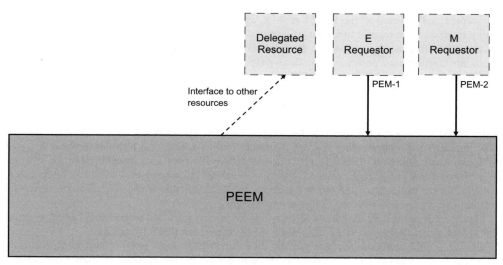

Figure 8.11 PEEM architecture in callable usage pattern. Reproduced by Permission of the Open Mobile Alliance Ltd.

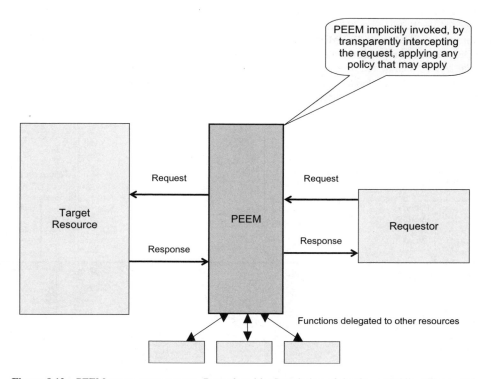

Figure 8.12 PEEM proxy usage pattern. Reproduced by Permission of the Open Mobile Alliance Ltd.

resource's I0 interface. The request is transparently (not necessarily known to the requestor) intercepted and directed to the PEEM enabler which functions as a proxy, via PEEM enabler's Proxy interface. The request to the target resource may include input information that can be used by the policy (the assumption is that the interface that was advertised to the requestor may have taken into consideration policy needs). The input parameters passed by target resource in its request may even include a reference to a PEEM policy. PEEM will process the policy – evaluate conditions and execute actions – and in most cases will forward the request (possibly stripped of certain input arguments that were to be consumed by PEEM), to the target resource which will proceed with its own processing of the request. In case of a negative evaluation of the policy, PEEM in proxy mode may reject the request, and send appropriate failure response back to the requestor – a case in which the request never reaches the target resource. The type of policies one may want to apply when deploying PEEM in proxy usage pattern are policies consistent with the concept of a 'firewall' – since it implies the possibility of blocking the request (e.g. authorization policies, without having to tie down the target resource). In summary, this is a pattern that can meet the requirements associated with the OSE PE logical entity.

Figure 8.13 shows how the PEEM architecture diagram is impacted when PEEM is deployed in the PEEM proxy usage pattern (it does not need to support the PEM-1 interface).

Having explained all the subtleties of the different PEEM usage patterns, this is a good time to revisit how PEEM fits in the OSE (see Section 8.3.1). In that section, the figure had PEEM represented both as an enabler, and as a possible realization of the PE. Let's now look at a revised diagram in Figure 8.14, that takes into consideration PEEM usage patterns, and more accurately reflects PEEM's positioning in the OSE.

The interpretation of the qualification 'in callable pattern' is consistent with the explanation given before for the PEEM callable usage pattern. One can simply interpret it as 'PEEM functions can be directly invoked using PEEM I0 interfaces'. PEEM also appears inside the PE entity defined in the OSE architecture, with the qualification 'in proxy pattern'. This is meant to indicate that the PE logical concept can be realized using the PEEM enabler, deployed in a PEEM proxy usage pattern. It can simply be interpreted as 'some PEEM functions can be transparently exercised without having to invoke those functions explicitly using PEEM I0 interfaces'.

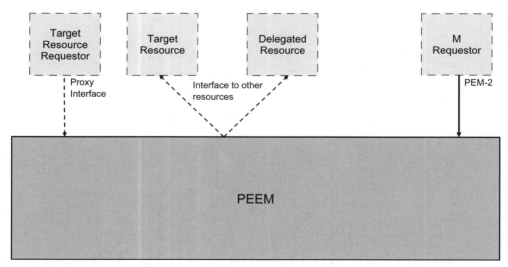

Figure 8.13 PEEM architecture in proxy usage pattern. Reproduced by Permission of the Open Mobile Alliance Ltd.

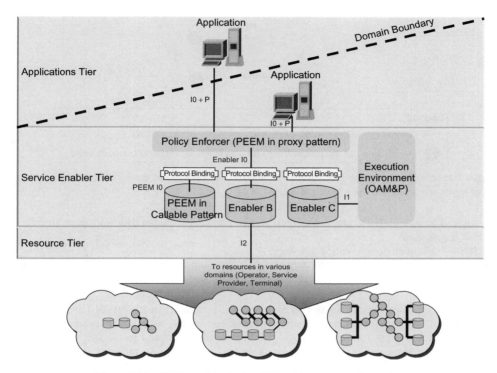

Figure 8.14   PEEM enabler in the OSE architecture – updated view

8.4.2 Expert Topics for PEL

Some interesting points can be made with respect to the policy information model in support of the PEL technical specification.

A first point is that the notion of delegation to other resources from within a policy is relatively new, at least from the perspective of giving it support in semantics and syntax in a PEL technical specification. A different point worth mentioning is the fact that just exploring one of the PEEM standard precursors, the IETF [RFC3060], we will notice that the PCIM implies that there are two execution models that may need to be supported. In the first execution model, there is a single condition to be evaluated at each node; in the second model, a 'case' statement (or 'switch' statement) programmatic model is supported at the nodes, where each case includes a priority that determines the order of evaluation of the simple conditions. PEEM enabler is covering those issues.

PEEM can also be used to perform only policy evaluation without executing any policy actions or performing any enforcement. This is the case of a simple condition as illustrated by Figure 8.15.

The topology of a policy graph can be changed in numerous ways without changing the result of its evaluation or enforcement. This may of course modify the policy conditions and actions from one graph to another equivalent graph. The reason we mention this is because different implementations may be optimized according to a certain topology, hence the PEL should not impose a single specific topology.

The following properties for an appropriate PEL were derived, and are used in assessing the progress on PEL technical specification. The expression language is as follows:

- It is capable of expressing any combination of policy conditions and actions (this includes, but may not be limited to any mathematical and/or logical operations within a condition or action,

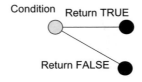

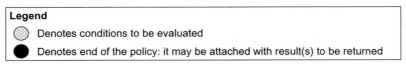

Figure 8.15 A simplified graph that describes the topology of a policy that involves only evaluation. Reproduced by Permission of the Open Mobile Alliance Ltd.

support for delegation to other resources, pattern matching on input data, and specifying format for output data).
- It does not preclude any policy topology.
- It optionally provides support for function calls, to facilitate interface transformation or generation of a new binding.

We discussed also the consideration of multiple PEL options (currently [BPEL] and [RFC 4745] are explored). Why multiple language options, when the number of optional specifications seems to be a general concern for service providers? This is simply related to the fact that the PEEM enabler may be deployed in different network layers, which impose different characteristics on the expression of policies (e.g. service orchestration/workflow policies versus network policies). In essence, the decision to support multiple PEL options was an optimization factor, to allow the use of the most appropriate technology in support of a particular network layer and deployment situation.

8.4.3 Expert Topics for PEM-1

Some aspects related to the PEM-1 specification are also worth more attention. Why did we need to support the concepts of BLOB and Standard or Custom PEM-1 Templates? Why couldn't we just do like most enablers do – that is define a single protocol, and all the input and output parameters, mandatory, optional or conditional that may be involved in a request/response message flow?
    Multiple answers apply here:

- PEEM WI and its requirements are mandating that any policy, for any type of request, and from any type of requestor needs to be supported – hence the PEEM enabler needs to provide generic mechanisms that are flexible and extensible, since the policies are unknown, and unspecified at the time of the PEEM specifications development. Since policies cannot be known at the time of writing the specifications, and should not be limited to a specific set or class, the conclusion is that the input arguments to be consumed by, and output arguments to be produced by such policies, should also not be limited during PEEM specifications development.
- A BLOB is a convenient way to practically not specify any I/O data structure (therefore not run the risk to limit such I/O data structure as applicable to only a handful of policies). At the same time, it has the disadvantage that it is difficult to prove in interoperability testing. It also has the feeling of 'not specifying anything', at least to some audience, used to a clear definition of all input/output parameters usually exchanged over a specified interface.
- PEM-1 Templates focus on the data format to be passed, with only a handful of the policy parameters being specified, but with most common data types for parameters being specified. The

PEM-1 Templates strategy allows the creation of a framework in which other OMA Working Groups (WGs) developing enabler specifications, or other organizations (standards organizations, vendors, service providers) can extend the PEM-1 specification. This can be achieved by adding new data types to be supported (if needed), and certainly adding specific policy parameters and specific PEM-1 Templates needed for their applications, for all cases in which those applications use PEEM as a starting point in their realizations.

In summary, the overlaying of PEM-1 Templates over BLOBs creates the right approach for PEM-1, given the requirements it has to fulfill.

We discussed also the consideration of multiple protocol options for PEM-1 (currently, SOAP and Diameter bindings are explored). Why were multiple optional bindings considered when the number of optional specifications seems to be a general concern for service providers? This is simply related to the fact that the PEEM enabler may be deployed in different network layers, and/or bundled with other resources into a more complex vendor implementation. In some cases, such implementations already support either SOAP interfaces or Diameter interfaces (sometimes as a consequence of the network layer where they perform, and the typical other resources they already interface with). In essence, the decision to support multiple protocol options was an optimization factor, to allow re-use of technology already available in a resource, as long as it meets the needs of the PEEM functions.

8.4.4 Divergent Views and their Resolution

This section will document a few critical, much debated issues. History often proves that rapid progress follows moments of deep division and crisis, and history has it right in all of the issues explored and debated in PEEM, which means appropriate resolution has been searched, discovered, and accepted.

One of the most divisive issues, at a critical junction in the development of the PEEM specifications (one that blocked architecture progress for a significant period of time) was the so-called Model A versus Model B approach. While neither a formal, nor informal count was ever conducted, the OMA ARC delegates seemed relatively evenly divided along the lines of either Model A or Model B. Table 8.1 illustrates an analysis that showed the agreed-to pros and cons for features in each model. Everything from BLOBs versus fully specified parameters for the interfaces, from callable versus proxy, from a programming language versus a ruleset language for PEL (and the list can go on, and on ...), was thrown into the mix. We will let the reader enjoy the comparison; any further clarifications would just spoil the effect. The good news is, that it was amazing to see that given all this controversy, common sense and goodwill in both camps prevailed, and all of the documented issues have either been resolved (as documented in this chapter) by consensus, or are on a rapid path toward a resolution at this time.

A second issue worth mentioning was a debate on the architecture components – some argued for more architectural granularity and detail, bringing the well-established IETF PEP-PDP model as an architectural established precedent, while others argued that this belongs in the realm of deployment/implementation instead. In the end, this also was settled more or less satisfactorily for both camps. The IETF PEP-PDP architectural model is fully acknowledged (and sufficiently referred) in the PEEM AD [PEEM AD], while at the same time the finer decompositions in granular components made it into an appendix describing possible implementations (we will come back to this in a later section of this chapter).

A third and final issue emphasized here is related to the PEEM terminology, and, although hard to believe, it materialized at a time when the Model A–Model B epic battle had already been settled with a truce, the PEEM architecture document was complete, and we were going through its formal review. It started with the fact that supporters of definitions for policy evaluation and policy enforcement argued that those terms are well-defined and accepted in the industry (based on IETF terminology), and overloading them with new definitions in PEEM will confuse the industry. That

Table 8.1 A feature-by-feature comparison between two alternative models for PEEM enabler

ID	Feature	Model A	Model B
1	Main characteristic	BLOB interfaces	Specified interfaces
		Expressional power of the language: 'can do everything'	Expressional power of the language: 'can do what is needed'
2	Claim support for proxy and callable usage pattern	Yes	Yes
3	Do we need a Policy Expression Language (PEL)?	Yes	Yes
4	Can you model several policies as one single policy	Yes	Yes
5	Policy loaded in advance via PEM-2 or passed as part of the request through PEM-1	Yes	No. PEM-2 only
	PEM-1 Request: 'evaluation only' vs 'evaluation + execution'	Same	Different
		There is no distinction anywhere	Distinction within PEEM engine: maybe Distinction on PEM-1 interface: yes
7	Policy enforcement (in case of: 'evaluation only') is	Running the code expressed in the PEL. No different from 'evaluation + execution'	Enforcement completes outside PEEM, based on the decision rendered by PEEM
8	What type of language is PEL?	Programming language (could be declarative or imperative)	Rule set declarative meta-language
9	How many languages do we need?	One and only one	One (optional only) or more
		PEL is general and powerful enough to express any of these policies.	Could result in • One meta-language • Multiple languages
10	There are existing OMA policy expression languages	Choose turing complete language that supports all of the semantics	• Choose a language that encompasses the expressional power of all (greatest common denominator), but not more • Or support all of them, and do not specify a single one as mandatory
11	Expressional power of the PEL	Turing complete	Derive from (1) PEEM requirements (2) Existing OMA policy expression languages (3) Any other submitted policy rules from any domain

Table 8.1 (*continued*)

ID	Feature	Model A	Model B
12	PEEM interfaces are a finite set of message types, at any given moment in time	No. Interfaces defined as BLOB to account for flexibility	Yes. Future extensions possible through interface extensibility and Change Requests (CRs)
13	Property of the PEM-1 interface	BLOB	• Specified messages/ parameters • Unspecified BLOB as optional additional parameter
14	Property of the PEM-1 interfaces: individual parameters specified?	No	Yes
15	Property of the PEM-1 interface: who/what dictates how to deal with a request	The policy	The interface (specified parameters) and the policy
16	Tagging the BLOB	Implementation choice – outside of scope for the specification. Implementations can add tags	Must be done as part of the specification. BLOB implementations can ignore the tags
17	Property of the PEM-2 interface: support for add, delete, retrieve, modify of policies and policy rules	Yes	Yes
18	Property of the PEM-3 interface: input/output specified as BLOBs?	Yes	No. PEM-3 cannot be specified by PEEM
19	Property of the PEM-4 interface: input/output specified as BLOBs?	Yes	No. PEM-4 cannot be specified by PEEM
20	Does the PEF Requestor know what policy rules should be enforced?	Yes, in case the policy is passed via the PEM-1 interface	No. All policy rules are uploaded via PEM-2 interface

was a fair argument, the problem with it is that there is no simple solution that all would agree with, to solve the argument. The more we tried to bring the definitions closer to the IETF definitions, the more additional definitions needed to be re-visited, and so on. And of course, we could not afford to loose sight of the fact that there are some wrinkles that make PEEM different from the IETF PEP-PDP model (e.g. the proxy pattern, the fact that enforcement may happen within the PEEM enabler, the fact that a decision may not always be rendered, the fact that a response may not always return to the requestor, and so on). We will happily report here that at the time we write this chapter, the differences were settled, but we will not get into further detail in explaining how.

8.5 Impact of Specifications on the Industry

PEEM work started in 2004 and is likely to be completed sometime in 2007 or early 2008, when the PEEM specifications may reach candidate enabler level. That is quite a long time. Interest was great in the beginning, it cooled down in the middle of the interval spent working on the PEEM architecture, and rose again recently when it became obvious in the industry that other OMA enablers will depend on PEEM (and will influence PEEM evolution at the same time). Policy technology plays a role at different layers in the network: it supports network elements in routing, allocating resources, and charging according to various criteria; it supports managing business decisions; it supports managing user preferences; and it supports managing administrative tasks. Services are created by involving network elements and resources at all layers in the network, and those network elements and resources rely on policy technology to perform their task easier, faster, cheaper, and with more accurate results. This leads us to conclude that policy technology will continue to play an increasing role in converged network architecture, as part of any Service Delivery Platform (SDP).

The recent decisions taken in PEEM to support both BLOBs and Templates, to create an extensible PEM-1 interface, to start to converge on PEL constructs, semantics and syntax, and the increased recent participation of delegates from all segments of the industry, are a good indication that service providers, vendors, and users are all anxious to see this work complete and address the PEEM requirements and expectations. In the meantime, the industry does not stand still. Most service providers are deploying policy technology in their network and service layers, and many vendors have policy technology implementations. The expectations are that the PEEM specifications, once approved, may be implementable in short order.

8.5.1 Impact on Service Providers

Service providers are impatiently monitoring, and in some cases nudging, the progress of PEEM specifications. For a long time, service providers listened to the different vendors' debates, and tried to dissect, digest and compare features championed by some against features advocated by others. At times, this must have appeared like comparing apples to oranges. However, as their own internal decision-making process matures, together with the better understanding of the issues involved and the solution offered, service providers seem ready now to push forward with swifter decisions, even if no perfect solution can always be found and agreed to. As opposed to some vendors specializing in providing resources for a particular network layer, service providers need all the features offered, for all network and services layers. Sometimes, service providers need those capabilities with all the bells and whistles, possibly relaxing on performance, and at other times a bare bone solution that performs at wire speed is more appropriate.

When Web Services applications are deployed, the PEEM enabler is needed there to support business process interactions, service workflows, composition, and choreography. For that, service providers need a PEEM that can deal with a variety of complex policies, and exchange requests/responses based on XML, SOAP and other Web Services protocols. But service providers also deploy converged networks, IP Multimedia System (IMS) architecture, and Core and Access networks, and there they need a PEEM that can deal with simple policies that can be processed and can yield a decision in real time, and can exchange requests/responses rapidly using lower latency protocols widely deployed in those network layers (e.g. Diameter), while asking for decisions that require less interactions between resources.

Furthermore, service providers want to reduce CAPEX and especially OPEX. They see the PEEM enabler as one of the keys to achieve this goal. Indeed, if common interfaces are defined, there is less CAPEX spent on integration-related products (e.g. mediation gateways), and there is less headaches and cost, if there is a need to replace a vendor product with another. A common PEL and PEM-2 would support the goal of reducing OPEX, by reducing the number of different PELs, tools and policy repositories that need to be purchased, mastered and supported.

The service providers also see the need to deploy PEEM in different situations and different patterns, including supporting direct revenue increase (another enabler for which they can charge any third-party service provider) and indirect revenue increase (a way to reduce cost of other services, while increasing the flexibility and extensibility of those services). There is also the expectation that the PEEM enabler may help increase customer loyalty, because of the role that it may play in protecting access to resources, including subscriber's private information. And finally there is also the promise that PEEM enabler is generic enough to allow a service provider to differentiate itself from other service providers. At times, this makes you wonder whether the pressure on the inventors of the Swiss army knife was any higher then the one facing the creators of PEEM.

8.5.2 Impact on Vendors

Since we ended up with a note on pressure in the previous section, let's start with addressing that from vendors perspective – and let's venture an educated guess that the pressure is not necessarily on the vendors. Interested vendors have likely spent their know-how and resources on building powerful, fast, well-tuned policy engine technology (i.e. the engine that cranks at evaluating conditions and executing actions). The vendors are likely going to try, most of them successfully, to reuse what they have invested in that technology, by adding support for the OMA PEEM specifications.

Vendors are the ones that contribute most to the PEEM specifications, so it is likely that they will not have to re-engineer everything in their current products, if they have any already. Yes, they will have to adapt to the to-be-approved PEEM specifications, since they will quickly learn that service providers will ask for support of PEM-1, PEM-2, and PEL in their RFIs and RFPs. Yes, some will have to develop and attach some new interfaces to their policy engines. Yes, most will have to switch from their proprietary policy language to at least one of the to-be-specified PEL options. But this process does not have to be quite sudden – compliance can be achieved in stages, PEM-1, PEM-2, and PEL are de-coupled from each other, and can be separately implemented, staged and deployed. A good product with a good proprietary language may survive for a while, as long as it supports PEM-1 first, then PEM-2. In conclusion, while PEEM enabler compliance will cause some headaches to product managers, they are of the manageable kind, at least in the near future.

Vendors can also differentiate themselves, since PEM-1 and PEL will provide plenty of opportunity for extensions, while PEM-2 may provide opportunity for optional operations.

There is also good opportunity for targeting their products where they fit best, since PEEM enablers can be applied in various deployments, and with various requirements with respect to performance, scalability, and reliability. When doing so, one may want to consider different choices of de-composition, deliberately not standardized, but provided as being informative in [PEEM AD].

8.5.2.1 PEEM Implementation De-composition Models

This is a good time and place to keep a promise made earlier. We can touch upon mapping of the logical architecture to different implementation de-compositions, a topic of interest for service providers and vendors alike.

A first possible de-composition is in separating a Policy Evaluation and Enforcement (PEF) from a Policy Management (PM) component, as depicted in Figure 8.16. Note that the interfaces are extending now to reach the appropriate components – hence they are exposed as category I0 interfaces by the newly split components.

A further de-composition splits the PEF into a Policy Evaluation (PV) component and a Policy Enforcement (PF) component, as is shown in Figure 8.17. Note that the interfaces are further extending now to reach the appropriate components – hence they are exposed as category I0 interfaces by the newly split components.

Finally, a special implementation can be provided where the PF component is not supplied at all – that is the case when only PV (in callable usage pattern), in addition to PM is needed. This implementation is illustrated in Figure 8.18.

In previous sections we have seen an architecture that only provides the PEEM proxy usage pattern as well, representing the equivalent of an implementation for the OSE PE. In addition to this, one can count that vendors will offer PEEM enabler implementations bundled with other OMA

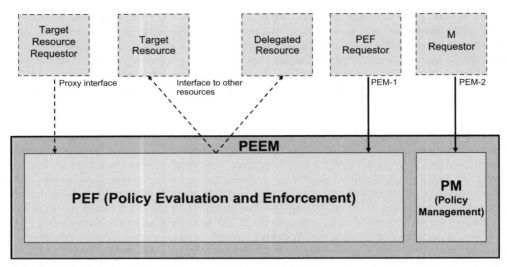

Figure 8.16 A de-composition with separate policy evaluation/enforcement and policy management components. Reproduced by Permission of the Open Mobile Alliance Ltd.

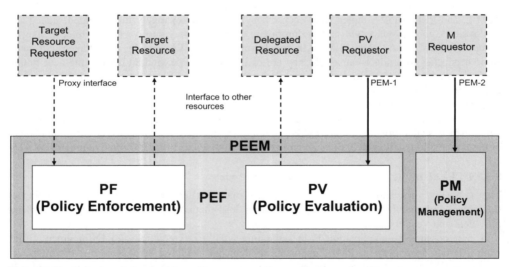

Figure 8.17 A further de-composition with separate policy evaluation and policy enforcement components.
Reproduced by Permission of the Open Mobile Alliance Ltd.

enablers, or other resources, in addition to stand-alone PEEM enabler implementations. In summary,
vendors and service providers will be provided with a wealth of options allowing plug-and-play
scenarios for the specific deployment situation.

8.5.3 Impact on Consumer Market

The end users that make up the consumer market will see a very limited number of services where
the PEEM enabler is clearly exposed in some way. They will however feel the effects of a hidden
PEEM enabler in most of the future services. For example, they will directly appreciate the effects

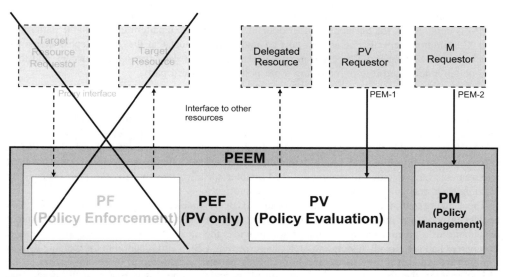

Figure 8.18 A de-composition closely matching a pure policy decision point model. Reproduced by Permission of the Open Mobile Alliance Ltd.

of a PEEM enabler when they would be allowed to create and manage the permissions rule that control the access to their private information (for release to other services). The end user will feel the effect of PEEM as subscriber to a service based on the Global Permissions Management (GPM) enabler, an enabler to be realized using PEEM enabler specifications.

Indirectly, the PEEM enabler will practically have an impact on all future services. That may manifest itself as the PEEM in proxy pattern realization of the PE in the OSE, which will imply that the interface that applications have to comply with will be impacted by some PE policy. Or alternatively, it may manifest itself as PEEM in callable pattern, which will be either bundled with other enablers, or act as stand alone to give other services the flexibility and differentiation otherwise difficult to achieve by hard-coding in one enabler all possible scenarios.

It is therefore mostly good news for the consumers. They will likely see more services, more flexibility in the services, and more security and protection for their private information. Of course, there is always some bad news, and in this case it is that somebody may have to pay more for all of that, or maybe stay loyal to a service provider longer.

8.5.4 Impact on Corporate Market

The corporations will also see a limited number of services where the PEEM enabler is clearly exposed, but they will feel the effects of a hidden PEEM enabler in most of the future services. As an internal service provider for their employees, an enterprise that deploys PEEM enabler internally may realize benefits for the corporation and their employees by providing better support to their business processes, thus increasing productivity and revenue. The same is true in services that they would expose to their suppliers and partners. At the same time, corporations and their employees also use services provided by external service providers. When using such services, the corporation and its employees will have benefits similar to those explained for the individual consumer. For example, they will similarly appreciate the effects of PEEM when they would be allowed, via a service based on the GPM enabler, to create and manage the permissions rule that control the access to their private professional information (for release to other services).

As explained in the previous section – there is a direct, positive effect on many services when PEEM is deployed in the Service Provider domain, either in proxy pattern or in callable pattern, or both. Corporations will also be able to take advantage of the fact that they may deploy their own policies in the Service Provider Environment (based on approval by the domain owner), and they may obtain a delegated role in managing those policies as a third party.

8.5.5 Impact on Other Specifications

It is worth noticing that some OMA WGs have dealt with policies before the development of the PEEM architecture even started (e.g. see [Presence-V1_0 TS], [POC_XDM-V1_0 TS]). Such OMA WGs may not look forward too enthusiastically to make changes in order to comply to PEEM specifications in future releases. At the same time, other enablers that have recently completed their requirements have decided to embrace PEEM enabler specifications and to take their chances by hitching their enabler 'wagon' to the PEEM 'locomotive'.

The Categorization Based Content Screening (CBCS) enabler is the first in this series. This enabler provides the means to decide, based on a categorization scheme, whether a certain content is suitable for a given user. In addition, it also provides the means to first categorize the content, if the content had not already undergone such categorization. CBCS can function in the callable pattern (through its exposed I0 interfaces) and in the proxy pattern. In addition to those similarities to the PEEM enabler, the content screening function of its main component is based on the processing of screening rules, which are specialized versions of PEEM policy rules. As a result, the CBCS architecture has capitalized on PEEM architecture as a precursor, and made a commitment to re-use PEEM PEM-1 and PEM-2 interfaces, while extending the PEM-1 interface with CBCS-specific Standard PEM-1 Templates and PEM-1 Parameters.

Another enabler, the GPM enabler seems to follow a similar path. Its architecture specification is currently progressing at a fast clip, building heavily on the PEEM architecture specification. GPM functions in callable pattern only, similar to PEEM in callable pattern. GPM exposes similar interfaces with PEEM (a permissions checking interface, and a permissions rule management interface), and its architectural component is processing permissions rule, which are specialized versions of PEEM policy rules. As a result, it is very likely that GPM may re-use PEEM PEM-1 and PEM-2 interfaces, while extending the PEM-1 interface with GPM-specific Standard PEM-1 Templates and PEM-1 Parameters. Success in re-using PEEM specifications for CBCS and GPM will create a valuable precedent which is expected to continue with other enablers that may have similar characteristics.

Switching our attention for a moment to other forums, there also is a distinct possibility that PEEM enabler specifications may have an effect (yet to be explored and determined) on specifications produced by other standard bodies that have policy concepts in their scope (e.g. 3GPP, 3GPP2 in particular because of the special relationship they share with the OMA).

8.6   Specifications Evolution and Future Direction

PEEM specifications are yet to be completed, so it's a bit premature to predict what may happen in a next phase. Having said that, given the emergence of other enablers dependent on PEEM (e.g. CBCS, GPM), it is not a leap of faith to assume that such enablers may actually have a reverse effect on a PEEM enabler. They may shape, to some extent at least, the outcome of the PEEM enabler specifications in their current phase. They may influence the structure of the Standard PEM-1 Templates. They may influence which PEM-1 Standard Templates and which PEM-1 Parameters are specified as part of the more generic (PEEM) enabler, versus those that may be specified as the more specialized (e.g. CBCS, GPM) enabler. Analyzing the CBCS requirements and the GPM requirements may influence the constructs, semantics and syntax for the PEEM PEL specification, and may influence some management operations as well as parameters needed to support such operations in the PEM-2 interface specification.

Looking beyond the current phase of PEEM, expectations may include extensions to the PEL in future phases, simply because PEEM specifications may have to be brought to market in this phase before all constructs and semantics have been successfully added to the PEL. Finally, one could also anticipate that, if a relationship develops between the OMA and other standard bodies (e.g. 3GPP, 3GPP2) with the explicit goal of re-using PEEM enabler specifications, then those standard bodies may indeed influence the future phases of PEEM enabler specifications, with new requirements, new templates and parameters to be supported by PEM-1, new issues for the PEL, and new operations for the PEM-2. As some may hope, and other may dread, PEEM may always be in some development 'phase'.

8.7 Summary

We hope that you are left with a good understanding of the background, market needs, standards history, architecture, and technical specifications for the PEEM enabler. Maybe you also have a feel for what worked well and what took time (and why) before it started working. Ultimately, we hope you have a handle on the PEEM impact on the different industry segments. PEEM is one of those intangibles that have the potential to quietly change a lot of things in a deployment environment, with positive effects on all segments of the industry, and the individual and corporate consumer market as well. We hope to have convinced you that the PEEM enabler really is (or at least will be) a Swiss army knife (the other famous product of Swiss origin is really not an option).

9

Utilization of IMS in OMA

The IP Multimedia Subsystem (IMS), seems to be on everyone's lips and minds as the next generation network technology that appears to be taking the communications world by storm. Network equipment vendors and market researchers alike show graphs predicting exponential revenue growth opportunities in IMS equipment sales. Initially developed by 3GPP as an IP-based overlay architecture on the packet switched domain for WCDMA mobile networks, IMS has since been embraced by other mobile standards consortia, like 3GPP2, and has even spread its wings beyond the province of mobile networks only. Epitomized by the buy-in from the ITU-T NGN (ITU-T Next Generation Network) initiative, and the ETSI TISPAN NGN and CableLabs adoption of the technology, IMS is emerging as the architecture of choice for mobile and fixed line networks. The IMS architecture creates a common core at the session control layer of both wireless and wireline networks, so connections can be setup seamlessly across these two types of networks, simplifying what is a more arduous undertaking when the networks have distinct core architectures.

While there are undeniably major cost savings to be made through convergence toward a common core network architecture, it is the strengths of IMS rapid service creation and tear-down built on reusable functional elements and standard interfaces that will bring about the biggest bang for the buck. IMS will provide service providers with the knobs, dials, and levers that will allow them to build and deliver value added services. Even new IP-based voice services, brought on by IMS, will fall prey to commodity pricing, where profit margins are slim. Voice will just be the razor. The blades are all the applications and services, and their numbers are imagined to be legion. The OMA is expected to deliver the building blocks for those applications.

This chapter introduces the 'Utilization of IMS in OMA' enabler or IMSinOMA for short. It is not the intention of the OMA or of this book for that matter, to blow the horn for IMS. There are many good books that provide an excellent coverage of the topic [Camarillo2006, Poikselka2006]. Rather, the OMA has recognized that IMS is, without a doubt, one of the predominant network and service architectures in which service enablers will be deployed and across which applications will be delivered. So, true to the spirit of re-use, the OMA has defined specifications for the utilization of IMS architecture and interfaces for the development and deployment of OMA service enablers. It is important to realize, however, that IMS is by no means the only solution for a converged SIP/IP core network. And true to the OMA principles of network neutrality, this has had an impact on how the utilization of IMS in OMA (IMSinOMA) enabler has been defined, as we will delineate in this chapter.

The Open Mobile Alliance   M. Brenner and M. Unmehopa
© 2008 Alcatel-Lucent. All Rights Reserved

9.1   Are Those Specifications Really Needed?

IMS is an architecture that will enable every device, and the people using them, to communicate with any other device, over any network with any service, in any media. It holds the promise for claiming the true mantra of any services anywhere and anytime. IMS is about bringing services and applications to users in ways that they want, through whatever device or mode they're using, and to whatever location they happen to be at.

Sounds familiar? It should, as this provides a near perfect match with the OMA objectives. IMS offers the means and the platform for service creation and delivery possibilities that are expected to lead to yet-to-be imagined innovation. Well, that is exactly the purpose of OMA enablers as well. IMS pundits expect their technology to be a dominant factor in the service creation and application delivery arena for many years to come. Indeed, OMA proponents anticipate no less of the OMA enabler specifications. While there are prominent overlaps in the objectives and scope, there is ample justification for both to co-exist and even to work in close partnership in the creation and delivery of services. There is a clear relationship that can be defined between IMS and OMA, which is exactly the scope of the IMSinOMA enabler.

IMSinOMA is one of those OMA enablers that started life in a Birds of a Feather (BoF) group, the IP Multimedia BoF (IP MM BoF). The group addressed specifically the questions regarding the scope and relationship of the IMS and the OMA. Is there a need for IMS specifications in OMA? And if there is, how does that relate to the principle of network independence? The IP MM BoF met three times over a period of 4 months in 2003 to produce a technical report on the usage of IMS service capabilities in the OMA [IMSinOMA TR]. The report concluded with a recommendation to the OMA Technical Plenary (TP) to identify the IMS service capabilities and the interfaces supporting them, with the aim to develop OMA enablers that can utilize these capabilities to their benefit, and take full advantage of the resources of the underlying IMS network infrastructure. The benefits this brings to the OMA are twofold. For starters, re-using IMS service capabilities already defined elsewhere will allow OMA to exploit these extensive standardization efforts and focus on service enabler specifications. This in turn aids and accelerates the service definition process within OMA. And, of course, it avoids duplication of work between standards bodies that might otherwise lead to the creation of an alternative architecture and alternative technical specifications.

This recommendation leads to the adoption of the work item called IMSinOMA, which would turn out to be an enabler not quite like most others standardized by OMA. Initially, the scope of IMSinOMA may seem to be in violation of one of the OMA's own principles, that of network independence. But in fact, it is in line with the principle of re-use and here is why. For those OMA enablers that are offered over IMS, and for those enablers only, IMSinOMA will tell you how to do it. As a consequence, an enabler that can utilize some capabilities from an IMS core, will not define those functions as part of its own specification set, but rather re-use according to the provisions in the IMSinOMA enabler. By now, you will have recognized this as one of the OMA Service Environment (OSE) dogmas for the avoidance of silos.

This re-use of IMS capabilities is the basis of the IMSinOMA requirements. Such a use case, however, does not take the perspective of the end user of a service, as is more commonly the case throughout the OMA requirements activities. Rather, the perspective is that of a service provider who wishes to deploy an application that makes use of a number of OMA enablers, and that will be rolled out in an IMS network. The motivation for the service provider is the desire to offer a revenue generating, value-added application to its subscriber base, whilst maximizing its return on investments in the IMS infrastructure already in place and leveraging the many IMS capabilities in an advantageous way. The high-level requirement that has led to the formation of the idea behind the 'IMSinOMA' enabler can be captured as follows. The IMSinOMA enabler shall ensure a consistent use of the IMS architecture and homogeneous access to its capabilities, by defining the functional split between the OMA functional entities and the IMS functional entities, and by determining the reference points between OMA service enabler realizations and the IMS service capabilities including the corresponding protocols to be used [IMSinOMA RD]. The upshot of this is that the IMSinOMA enabler will not produce technical specifications, but rather will define the relationship between IMS and OMA solely on an architectural plane.

9.2   Standard Precursors to IMSinOMA

The standards landscape for IMS is diverse and there is a whole host of specifications, technical reports, and support documents being developed and maintained by a number of standards organizations and interest groups. This section will only scratch the surface and will, by implication, fall way short of doing justice to the extensive work performed by all these organizations. But to understand the value that re-use brings in this particular case, we are introducing the more prominent IMS-related organizations. Probing into the vast collateral of IMS standards will be left as an exercise to the reader.

- The 3GPP can be considered the intellectual birthplace of IMS. IMS was originally established in Universal Mobile Telecommunications System (UMTS) networks as an overlay on top of the packet switched domain to provide IP multimedia services. Over time, it has evolved as an access network independent IP-based core network architecture.
- Many of the IMS interfaces, especially those pertaining to session control and service delivery, are realized using the Session Initiation Protocol (SIP) as defined by the Internet Engineering Task Force (IETF). Any enhancements to SIP as required by IMS are submitted to the IETF for inclusion in the SIP specification.
- 3GPP2, the CDMA2000 counterpart of the UMTS focused 3GPP, has adopted IMS as the realization of the MultiMedia Domain (MMD) in the 3GPP2 network architecture model. This further strengthened the value proposition of IMS as a core architecture that is neutral to any access network technology.
- ETSI has participated in the IMS effort as a Standards Development Organization (SDO) partner in 3GPP from the beginning. But the founding of TISPAN NGN and its objective to re-use the IMS, originally only created for mobile networks, in the fixed domain marked the first sign of a common architecture for fixed and mobile.
- CableLabs, a nonprofit standards-setting organization for the North American cable industry, has now also embraced the signaling core of the IMS specification in the functional architecture of its PacketCable 2.0, a program that defines requirements and develops specifications for delivering real-time multimedia services over cable networks. Again, this is adding further credibility to this approach to wireline/wireless convergence.
- The NGN activity of both the telecommunication sector of the International Telecommunication Union-Telecommunication Standardization Sector (ITU-T) as well as the Alliance for Telecommunications Industry Solutions (ATIS) has also adopted IMS as the core component of their NGN architecture supporting the provision of SIP-based multimedia services to NGN terminals.

These activities have led IMS to become a truly global common core, independent of access technology, be it fixed or wireless.

9.3   Architecture Overview

The architecture of the IMSinOMA enabler identifies a set of service capabilities within IMS that can be employed by OMA service enablers. The purpose of the architecture is to demonstrate to those enablers that are realized using IMS capabilities, how they should draw on IMS functions and how they should interface with IMS in a consistent and interoperable manner. We shall first outline a number of the IMS capabilities and functions that can be exploited by OMA enablers. The list will not be exhaustive, and the reader is referred to [IMSinOMA AD] for a complete coverage of all the features offered by IMS in this context.

At a minimum, IMS includes the support for communication services. The mechanism to perform session management, controls for session re-direction, and the ability to detect the condition of unreachable end users are basic features of the IMS architecture. Some of the functions that IMS offers over and above other SIP-based network architectures are present on account of mobile users. Provisions are in place to ensure that traffic over the radio interface is kept to a minimum. Radio bandwidth continues to be a scarce resource in cellular networks and needs to be managed sensibly. IMS has defined a specific SIP profile for communication between the IMS network and IMS mobile devices. The IMS-specific profile is interoperable with any other SIP profile. Similarly, IMS supports detection of and recovery from situations where the radio bearer is lost, either due to roaming outside of the coverage area or instabilities of the radio signal. As an important requirement for mobile networks, IMS includes support for roaming, support of service delivery when roaming, and support for splitting charges among network operators when roaming.

Other functions are provided by IMS based on network operator requirements. Support for charging, maintaining registration state, authentication of the user before the user is allowed to use network capabilities, elements that allow for network topology hiding, and Quality of Service (QoS) control to offer differentiated services are examples. Also, some regulatory bodies require support for calling line and connected line identification. The support for lawful intercept and emergency calls fall in this category as well. Yet another regulatory requirement met by IMS may be the means to allow for third-party application providers to gain controlled access to network capabilities. IMS defines the signaling provisions to support these features.

Now that we have briefly glossed over some of the more eminent IMS capabilities, we can take stock of the IMS interfaces to those capabilities. What follows is a brief description of the IMS interfaces, the use of which is defined in the IMSinOMA enabler. For additional detail on both the functionality as well as the protocol and parameter details, we suffice by referring the reader to the appropriate 3GPP technical specifications. Note that for many of the interfaces, equivalent 3GPP2 specifications exist, as well as documentation from some of the other organizations we introduced in Section 9.2.

- The SIP-based IMS interface for service control is called ISC, and provides support for SIP/SDP call control, SIP event related subscription and notification, SIP messaging, etc. [3GPP TS 23.228] ISC can be supported between an OMA enabler implementation and the IMS core.
- The Sh interface is between the enabler server implementation and the Home Subscriber Server (HSS) in the IMS core, which is the logical centralized store for IMS user data [3GPP TS 23.228]. This interface provides the OMA enabler with the data handling procedures for the user data stored in the HSS. In addition, the Sh interface can be used to register interest in receiving notifications in case user data is modified.
- In networks where more than one HSS is deployed, in order to access user data, the HSS that stores the records for that particular user has to be located first. This is the function of the Service Locator Function (SLF) in the IMS core. The SLF supports the Dh interface towards enabler server implementations [3GPP TS 23.228].
- The Ut interface resides between the enabler instance in the terminal and the enabler instance in the server [3GPP TS 23.228]. The Ut interface provides the user of the terminal with the means to securely manage and configure information related to the services, such as configuration of presence lists and location data privacy rules.
- The Ro interface provides the OMA service enabler with an event-based charging interface to the online charging system in the IMS core [3GPP TS 32.299]. Ro can be used to request credit-control information for online charging.
- The Rf interface provides the OMA service enabler with an interface to report accounting information to the off-line charging system in the IMS core [3GPP TS 32.299].
- The Gm interface is situated between the enabler implementation in the terminal and the IMS core [3GPP TS 23.228]. The Gm interface provides the OMA service enabler with the ability

to perform registration, SIP/SDP call control, and general transaction support like SIP event related subscription and notification, SIP messaging, etc.

- The Mb interface provides the OMA service enabler with the ability to support media streams for user packet data via the IMS core [3GPP TS 26.236].

Now that we have collected the piece parts from IMS that we would like to re-use, let us see how they can be assembled into a coherent OMA architecture. Chapter 2 discussed the OSE, and introduced the category of I2 interfaces as those interfaces used by OMA enablers, but defined elsewhere. The fundamental architectural concept for IMSinOMA is to define the interfaces provided by IMS as I2 interfaces. These can be used by any OMA enabler to access IMS capabilities and functions, but will not be specified (duplicated, adapted, derived, etc.) in OMA. The resulting architecture for IMSinOMA is depicted in Figure 9.1. A distinction is made between interfaces to the IMS core and interfaces to IMS terminals. Some interfaces, like the Mb interface for media streams, can terminate both in the core as well as on the device.

The architectural model in Figure 9.1 shows a clean separation between the IMS capabilities and the OMA enablers using them. But while this separation serves us well in developing the architecture for IMSinOMA based on OSE principles, reality is a bit more complicated. The standards organizations developing IMS have defined some IMS services as well, on top of their IMS core. Examples include Messaging, Conferencing, and Presence. Preferably, such IMS services should be adopted into the OMA framework of OSE. And such activities have indeed been initiated, where Presence and Messaging are now being defined as OMA enablers. But other IMS services, like

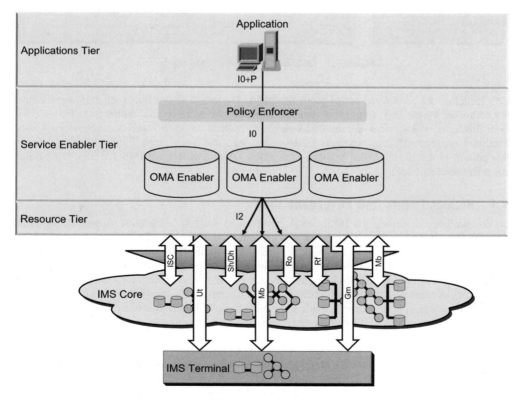

Figure 9.1 IMS interfaces in the context of OSE

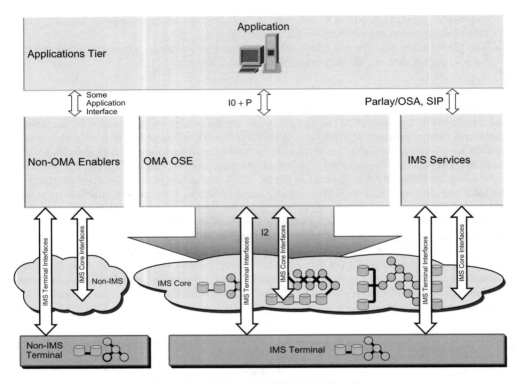

Figure 9.2   OSE and 3GPP/3GPP2 IMS services

Conferencing, are considered out of scope for OMA. Figure 9.2 shows how such IMS services are not addressed by the OSE framework, but still adhere to the same layered model as is followed by OSE. Both the IMS services and the OMA enablers reside at the same level, in the Service Enabler Tier, and consequently may serve as enablers for the same application. Figure 9.2 also extends this pattern to the model where enablers are neither OMA enablers nor IMS services, but similar considerations still apply.

9.4   Salient Points and Divergent Views

So far, we have described the IMSinOMA enabler and the role it plays in supporting the OSE mantra of avoiding the service silos. Parts of the OMA constituency with commercial interests in IMS have been contributing to the work fervently. For some, IMS will be the bread and butter securing their place in the next generation of networking. But in the introduction to this chapter we already alluded to the fact that IMS certainly may not be the only solution for a converged core. IP core networks especially have been deployed quite successfully for many years by enterprises. The Internet is one example of course, providing the most basic IP interconnectivity. More sophisticated examples are the corporate IP Intranets and managed Virtual Private Network (VPN) networks. An employee logging on to her corporate network can use all sorts of enterprise applications like corporate e-mail and access to document stores. She can use those from different office locations, and when on the road for business travel. Akin to public communication networks, corporate or enterprise networks offer a whole range of advanced features like QoS control and security, providing secure and managed access to authorized Principals. Perhaps, corporate networks only lack charging capabilities as the relationship with the end user is different. End users are employees, not subscribers. Still, some accounting, for instance, for traffic control and peak rate calculation may be performed. SIP is also making inroads in the enterprise domain, where corporate networks are increasingly embedding telecommunication abilities into business processes, improving worker productivity, and enhancing customer interactions. This shows that there are SIP/IP Core networks other than IMS that can provide many enhanced capabilities for OMA enablers to exploit.

Armed with this knowledge, and with the OMA principle of technology neutrality, a number of OMA member companies placed question marks at the necessity of specifying anything in OMA with respect to IMS. This resulted in some instances of rather heated discussions, where the gloves almost came off. These discussions truly showed the broad market participation in OMA, across the entire value chain, with a vast array of commercial interests. IMSinOMA had to tread the fine balance between the OMA principles of re-use of other standards activities, as well as independence of underlying network technology. As a result, great care was given to ensure that the IMSinOMA effort was not about finding a problem for your favorite solution, not about finding an end to a means. The focal point was on re-use and the avoidance of vertical integration. For this reason, the objective of IMSinOMA is to specify how to make use of IMS, for those enablers that want to make use of IMS. Before, this may have sounded a little contrived, but hopefully you will now have some appreciation of how this came about. The product of these efforts has proven to be a powerful instrument in the definition of other OMA enablers. In the later chapters we will see how the Presence enabler (Chapter 14), the Push-to-talk over Cellular enabler (Chapter 15), the XML Document Management enabler (Chapter 14), and the Charging enabler (Chapter 17) will draw on the IMSinOMA enabler to specify their use of IMS capabilities and functions.

We will now look at some of the implications of the way in which IMSinOMA was specified. IMS standardizes a number of functions and capabilities, and IMSinOMA defines how to exploit those if you choose to do so. The design principle of layered architecture tells us that the enabler itself does no longer have to specify these functions and capabilities as an integral part of the enabler itself. The enabler can rely on the fact that those functions and capabilities are supported

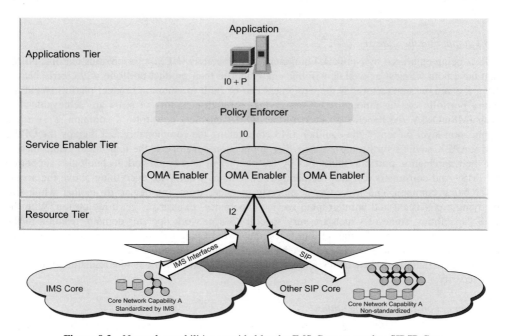

Figure 9.3 Network capabilities provided by the IMS Core or another SIP/IP Core

in the underlying core. To date, IMS is the only core that has standardized those functions and capabilities. But IP Core networks or vanilla SIP networks are equally valid solutions for use by OMA enablers. Of course, should a potential alternative SIP/IP Core emerge, the expectation is that a similar level of functional support be provided by such an alternative. That functional support, however, will typically not be standardized, and hence may introduce additional interconnectivity and interoperability considerations. Issues like roaming, cross-network charging, feature parity and regulatory considerations generally are of no or lesser concern in enterprise environments. There are different relationships with users (subscribers versus employees) and hence different expectations and requirements. That does not mean that enterprise SIP/IP core networks are less applicable. It merely means that enterprise SIP/IP core networks will need to provide support for the functions that the OMA enabler relies on, in their own way. This is illustrated in Figure 9.3.

The astute reader might ask why IMSinOMA has been subject to OMA standardization, and not others like, for instance, a potential 'SIPinOMA'. A fair question to ask, for sure. You will quickly realize, however, that work in OMA is based on member company interest, specification development is contribution driven, and any group of four member companies is welcome to submit new work item proposals. To date, no such proposal has been submitted to the OMA TP for consideration. Should that happen, OMA may choose to describe this in an enabler similar to IMSinOMA in a future enabler release. Otherwise, it would be left as an exercise to whoever deploys the enabler, in which case it will have to be proprietary realization, rather than based on an OMA specification.

9.5 Impact of Specifications

In this chapter, we have introduced the IMSinOMA enabler. We have not only looked at the requirements and architecture, but also at some of the deliberations that lead to certain decisions for the model. Discussions were often less than straightforward. This section will look at the value that IMSinOMA brings to the stakeholders that make up the OMA membership. What is the impact of IMSinOMA on the industry, who benefits and how?

9.5.1 Impact on the Industry

IMS is being embraced by Network Equipment Manufacturers (NEMs) for obvious reasons. NEMs that have both wireless as well as wireline equipment in their product portfolio will clearly benefit from a common architecture, as the equipment can be built to common product platforms and the entire portfolio can be rationalized. Cost savings through economy of scale are achievable. But with IMSinOMA, the benefits go even further. OMA enablers now form a common service and application layer on top of the common IMS core, taking the commonality and thereby the OPEX and CAPEX savings further up a notch. For application developers, the total addressable market for their application portfolio multiplies by the number of access network technologies supported by IMS. And consumers can reap tremendous benefits as well. With everything above the access layer being common, end users can seamlessly meander from one device to another while still enjoying a consistent and uninterrupted service experience. Enterprises get a leg up too. With the IMS capabilities, some of which are very specific to a network operator domain, residing in the IMS core and accessible through I2 interfaces, the OMA enablers themselves remain generic. This allows enterprises to seamlessly embed telecommunication abilities into their corporate networks, and integrate them with their own solutions for IMS equivalent functions like registration, privacy, and security.

9.5.2 Impact on Other Specifications

As explained, IMSinOMA does not produce any technical specifications itself. In fact, its main intent is to define how to use IMS capabilities and functions, for the benefit of other enablers in

OMA. These other enabler specifications are expected to be nimbler as a result. For instance, they no longer individually have to define how to request credit-control information for online charging in an IMS environment. Instead, the enabler specification can suffice by including a reference to IMSinOMA, where in turn it is described how to use the Ro interface for that purpose. In particular, the Presence enabler, the Push-to-talk over Cellular enabler (PoC), the XML Document Management enabler (XDM), and the Charging enabler have significantly benefited from the IMSinOMA enabler.

9.6   Specifications Evolution and Future Direction

Directionally, there are no changes to be expected down the line. The gist of IMSinOMA is defining how to use IMS capabilities and functions, by interworking with their specified interfaces through the concept of the OSE I2 interface classes. This essence is not likely to change. New IMS interfaces to novel core network capabilities may be specified in 3GPP, and may result in change requests to the IMSinOMA enabler. It is not unreasonable to assume, however, that the example set forth by the IMSinOMA enabler may be followed by other core network technologies. In Section 9.4 we already alluded to a possible 'SIPinOMA' enabler. Others may follow suit.

9.7   Summary

In this chapter, we have introduced the 'Utilization of IMS in OMA' enabler. An enabler that brought to bear the broad market participation in OMA, across the entire value chain. An enabler that also illustrated the strength of the OSE model for OMA specification efforts, with its I0 and I2 categories of interfaces. OMA enablers that wish to bring into play some of the IMS capabilities now have an OMA defined avenue to do so, while still marching to the tune of network technology neutrality. Later chapters in the book will outline exactly how other OMA enablers, like Presence, can take full advantage of IMSinOMA.

10

Service Architectures – Parlay and the OSE

Only in an ideal world, a hypothetical case study as part of an engineering course, do we have communication networks without any service infrastructure already present. In the world that we know, there are no greenfield deployments. Forklift upgrades are hardly ever an option. When rolling out an OMA Service Environment OSE infrastructure, one has to consider legacy systems already in place. Legacy systems have the habit of sticking around for a long time; they are not going away any time soon.

By its very nature, the OSE aims to break down the silo implementation of services, where the silos represent the installed base. Legacy systems need to be gradually phased out, as disruption of ongoing service contracts is unacceptable. However, in networks that have already made an attempt at getting rid of vertical integration of services by introducing a horizontal service architecture, putting OSE into operation will come with its share of deployment challenges. Prior investments need to be leveraged, for example, by re-deploying legacy components and transitioning embedded assets from one architecture to the other.

The OSE is not the first attempt at horizontal service architecture. One such initiative in particular that comes to mind, given the shared problem space of specifying interfaces for service capabilities that are independent of underlying network technology, is Parlay. Parlay is a service architecture for controlled, manageable, and billable third-party access to abstracted network service capabilities, and a suite of APIs to those network service capabilities.

While there are striking similarities, there are significant and palpable differences as well. As, otherwise, why bother with yet another standards initiative? The objective of the 'Parlay in OSE' enabler, therefore, is twofold. In keeping with the running theme of re-use, the first goal of the enabler is to analyze and appraise how assets from Parlay can be used advantageously in the OSE. This re-use covers both the case of re-cycling architectural attributes on a conceptual level, and re-deploying Parlay implementations in a rolled-out OSE infrastructure. The second objective, in recognition of both the similarities and the differences, is to spell out and document the relationship between these two technologies for the industry at large.

10.1   A Quick Taster of Parlay

It is not the intention to include a comprehensive coverage of Parlay in this book. However, to appreciate some of the architectural similarities, and to underpin the call for Parlay in OSE enabler in the OMA, this section will briefly run through the main concepts of Parlay. We will focus on

---

The Open Mobile Alliance   M. Brenner and M. Unmehopa
© 2008 Alcatel-Lucent. All Rights Reserved

architectural concepts, rather than details of the individual Parlay interfaces. For an in-depth study of the Parlay architecture, the reader is referred to [Unmehopa 2006].

There are many aspects to Parlay, but on the highest level, Parlay is based on two main concepts. The first concept is that of horizontal architecture, by introducing service capability features. The second notion is formed by the principles of separation, of which there are two. These two main concepts are further detailed below.

A Service Capability Feature (SCF) is the abstraction of a unit of service functionality available in a telecommunications network. It is a unit, in that an SCF has a single main functional focus, for example, Presence, Location, or Charging. As such, SCFs contribute toward the elimination of service silos. It is an abstraction, in that an SCF presents a network function at a higher level of abstraction, thereby detaching the functional definition from any particular core network or access technologies. For instance, the Call Control SCF is not specific to GSM Customized Application for Mobile Enhanced Logic (CAMEL), European Telecommunications Standards Institute Intelligent Networking (ETSI IN), or Session Initiation Protocol (SIP), because of abstracting away from any of the differentiating attributes.

Each SCF supports an Application Programming Interface (API), the so-called Parlay API for the SCF. The Parlay APIs support various bindings. The Parlay specifications contain binding definitions for CORBA Interface Definition Language (IDL), Web Services Description Language (WSDL), and Java (J2EE and J2SE). At the southbound, Parlay SCFs communicate to underlying resources in the network either through native network protocols (such as signaling protocols like SS7) or through proprietary interfaces.

The separation of service from control is the first principle of separation in Parlay. We have seen this principle before, when we introduced layered architectures in Chapter 2. The second principle of separation, that of separating access to a service from use of that service, is new and warrants some more elaboration. The access to a service represents the business relationship between the application provider and the network operator. This relationship involves the initial contact between the parties, setting up the boundaries that define the business relationship and establishing credentials for authentication and authorization. Once the confines of the business relationship have been set up, the user is provided with the means to use the service that is offered by the network, within those confines. Use of a service, of course, is realized through the Parlay APIs, in particular through the Parlay Service APIs.

The partitioning of access to a service and use of a service is codified in Parlay by the Parlay Framework component. The Parlay Framework is responsible for functions such as authentication and authorization, fault and load management, and service registration and discovery. The framework offers its own set of interfaces for the access to a service, the Parlay Framework APIs. Even though strictly speaking, the Parlay Framework APIs are of course also Parlay APIs, for our architectural comparison in the next section when referring to the Parlay APIs, we specifically mean the Parlay Service APIs.

The Parlay architecture, comprising SCFs, Parlay APIs, and the Parlay Framework, is depicted in Figure 10.1. The combination of one or more SCFs, plus the Parlay Framework, is referred to as a Parlay Gateway. This convenient way to depict the various SCFs and the Parlay Framework as a single entity will come in handy when walking through the various architecture alternatives for the Parlay in the OSE enabler. The Parlay Gateway is shown in Figure 10.2.

10.1.1 Parlay X

Parlay defines APIs to abstracted network capabilities, each supporting multiple bindings. Since the introduction of Parlay, demand has grown for even higher levels abstraction specifically for a Web Services deployment. This demand originated from the enterprise developer community that does not necessarily have any affinity with or knowledge of telecommunication protocols and their state machines. As a result, the interfaces need to be defined at a higher level of abstraction and adhere

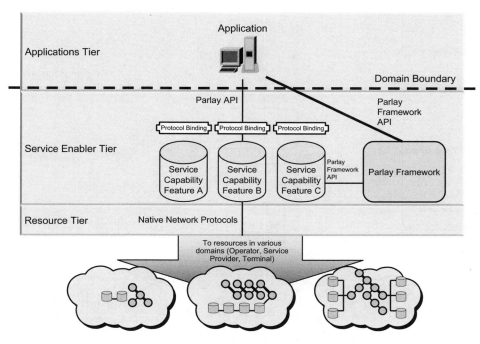

Figure 10.1   The Parlay Architecture

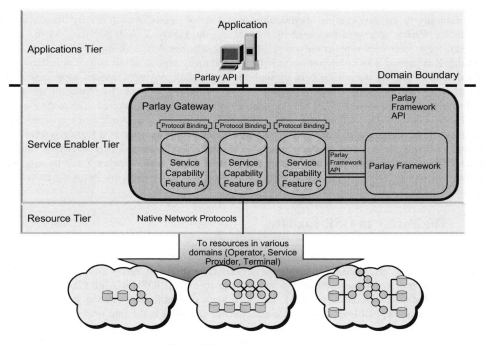

Figure 10.2   The Parlay Gateway

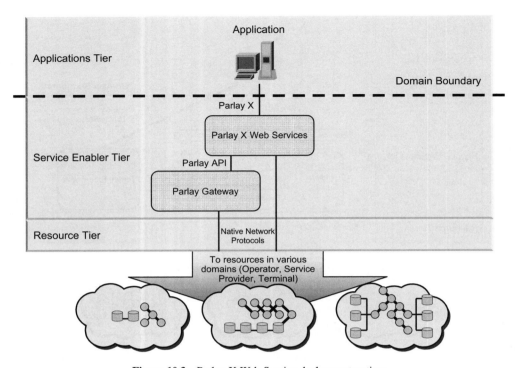

Figure 10.3   Parlay X Web Service deployment options

more naturally to the development methodologies and service paradigms in use by that developer community. Parlay addressed this need by introducing the Parlay X Web Services. As the name suggests, these interfaces support only a single binding, and are defined using WSDL.

Parlay X is gaining a lot of interest in the industry, and many aspects are worthy of note. However, for the sake of brevity we suffice here by outlining the two deployment options supported in the specifications, as our interest here is mainly on the architectural plane. By virtue of its higher level of abstraction, Parlay X Web Services can be offered through a layered architecture on top of a Parlay Gateway that serves as a proxy toward the underlying network. Such a deployment may make sense in networks where a Parlay Gateway is already present as a legacy system or in networks where both levels of abstraction are offered to application developers. However, such an intermediary is certainly not mandatory or necessary in all deployments. Parlay X can be supported without a proxy present, interfacing directly to resources in the underlying network. Both these options are depicted in Figure 10.3.

10.2   The Parlay in OSE Enabler

With a synopsis of Parlay under our belt, and the OSE concepts introduced in Chapter 2, we are now well equipped to look at how assets from Parlay can be used gainfully in the OSE. The Parlay in OSE enabler, or PIOSE for short, addresses how OSE and Parlay architectures could be integrated and how components of each paradigm can co-exist [PIOSE RD, PIOSE AD].

So let's first take a look at some of the more apparent similarities among the architectural attributes on a conceptual level. The first similarity that pops out is the one between enablers and SCFs. It is in fact the same concept by two different names, a concept derived from the notion of building blocks. Extending along this line, the following corresponding notions are the interfaces. In OSE parlance, the native network protocols at the southbound of Parlay SCFs would be termed

I2 interfaces. The northbound interfaces, or the APIs, would then match up with the I0 interfaces. If, for the time being, we leave the Parlay Framework out of consideration, and return to that concept toward the end of this chapter, you will agree that the similarities are striking. This should not come as too much of a surprise, as the objective of horizontal service architecture is shared between the two architecture approaches. In order to assess whether the two are not just similar, but really one and the same (or at the very least interchangeable), we need to look at whether both architecture approaches reside at the same layer or tier in the model we introduced in Chapter 2.

10.2.1 Parlay as Network Resource

A rather straightforward way to position both approaches is depicted in Figure 10.4, which shows the Parlay Gateway as a network resource, which is accessed by the OMA enabler A through an I2 class interface. The particular I2 interface in this configuration is, of course, the Parlay API. This architecture option chooses not to take advantage of the architectural similarities and simply regards Parlay infrastructure as any other resource that can be accessed by the enabler.

10.2.2 Parlay X Web Service as the Enabler

One of the issues with the previous architectural configuration is that it introduces service building blocks at more than one layer, that is, the Parlay SCF in the Resource Tier and the enabler in the Service Enabler Tier. In order to avoid duplication, a distinction in abstraction level would be expected. This leads to Figure 10.5, a variation of the previous architectural configuration, where again the Parlay Gateway is a network resource. The OMA enabler in this case, however, is realized

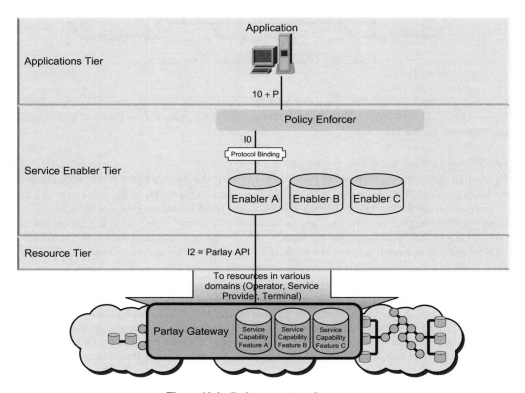

Figure 10.4   Parlay as a network resource

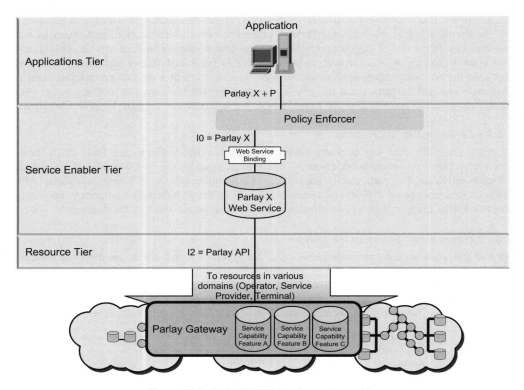

Figure 10.5   Parlay X Web Service as the enabler

by a Parlay X Web Service. The Parlay X Web Service accesses the Parlay Gateway through the
Parlay API (I2), and exposes its own functionality toward applications via the Parlay X Web Service
interface, that is, the I0.

10.2.3 Parlay Service Capability Feature as the Enabler

Figure 10.6 shows the case where the Parlay SCF resides in the Service Enabler Tier, rather than in
the Resource Tier. In this case, the OMA enabler is realized by the Parlay SCF. That means that the
I0 it exposes is the Parlay API. This configuration would result in maximum re-use of technologies.
However, the complete benefits can only be achieved in the case where all requirements for the
OMA enablers can be fully met by the Parlay APIs for the corresponding Parlay SCFs. To date,
such an analysis has not been carried out either in the OMA or in the Parlay Group.

10.2.4 Hybrid Parlay and OMA Solution

Figure 10.7 shows a scenario where Parlay SCFs and OMA Enablers co-exist in an OSE deployment. For function A, the OMA Enabler is realized by the Parlay SCF. For function B, the enabler
is provided solely by the OMA. And for function C, Parlay X provides the realization of the OMA
enabler. Any permutation of the architectural configurations outlined above is possible in a hybrid
solution. In this scenario, each OMA enabler may choose to re-use Parlay technology where appropriate, be it the Parlay APIs or the Parlay X Web Services. In case there is a mismatch between
requirements, or in case no corresponding Parlay SCF is available for the function, OMA may
decide to define the enabler and its I0 interface itself, either derived from Parlay or from scratch.

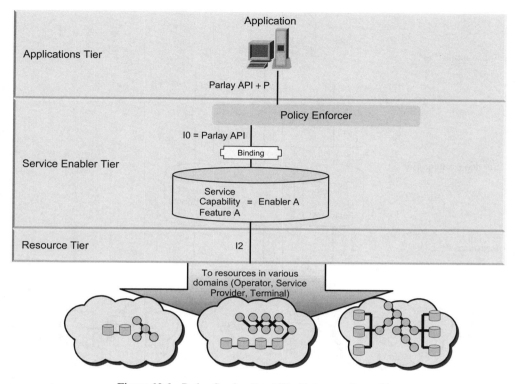

Figure 10.6   Parlay Service Capability Feature as the enabler

10.3   PIOSE Challenges

We have started this chapter by exploring a number of architectural configurations that seem to suggest that a high degree of technology re-use is achievable. But, that is only because we have put the similarities center stage. There are disparities as well, as we will go into in the following section.

When looking at the architectural configurations, the granularity took both extremes of the spectrum. Either we looked at particular SCFs individually, or at the Parlay Gateway as a whole. Two architectural concepts were deliberately left out of consideration: the framework from Parlay and the Policy Enforcer from the OSE. Both entities are the distinguishing concepts that make their respective approaches unique, and hence a mapping from one paradigm to the other will inevitably be less clear-cut.

10.3.1 Enforcing Service Provider Policies

The OSE introduces the Policy Enforcer (PE) to impose Service Provider policies on each service request. Chapter 7 discussed the PE and its function in detail, while Chapter 8 specified the OMA realization for the PE, that is, the Policy Evaluation, Enforcement, and Management (PEEM) enabler. The PE as a logical architectural concept will be present in any OSE deployment that makes use of Parlay assets. Every service request to a particular OMA enabler, which may be realized by a Parlay SCF or which may make use of Parlay resources through I2 exchanges, will be subject to policy enforcement. Parlay, however, also provides an architectural component involved in the enforcement of Service Provider policies. This component is the Parlay Framework. The Parlay

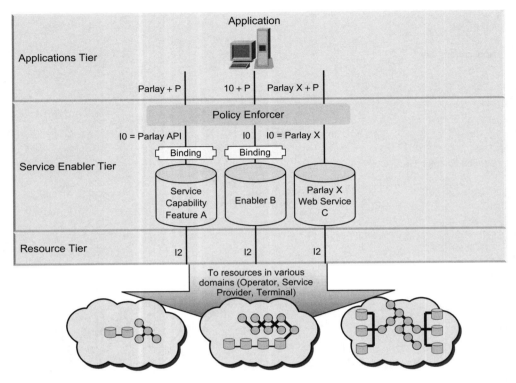

Figure 10.7   Hybrid Parlay and OMA solution

Framework is responsible for setting up the service access session, as introduced in Section 10.1, between the Application and the Enabler. Service Provider policies regarding authentication and authorization, as well as considerations with respect to the Service Level Agreement, are established through the Parlay Framework. So, one could consider the Parlay Framework as one possible technology realization of the PE logical concept, or as a different taxonomy for what the PE achieves. Such a technology realization is particularly suited in deployments where all enablers are realized through Parlay SCFs (section 10.2.3). In hybrid deployments, however, (section 10.2.4) it may not be appropriate for the Parlay Framework to enforce Service Provider policies on service requests to those enablers that are not realized through Parlay SCFs. In such deployments, a PEEM enabler implementation and the Parlay Framework may co-exist, or a PEEM enabler implementation may fulfill policy enforcement of service requests to Parlay SCFs on behalf of the Parlay Framework.

10.3.2 The Parlay Policy Management Service Capability Feature

OMA provides the PEEM enabler as a particular technology realization option for the PE logical architectural concept in the OSE. In Chapter 8 we have seen that PEEM provides the callable PEM-1 interface for enforcement of policies that may be expressed either as business processes or as rulesets. Parlay provides analogous functionality as part of the Policy Management SCF. This SCF provides an API for the enforcement of policies expressed as rulesets. The policy expression language for PEEM rulesets may not be the same as the policy expression languages that may be supported for the Parlay specification. As we have seen, the proposed ruleset language for PEEM is the IETF Common Policy [RFC 4745], whereas Parlay defines its own extended Backus–Naur form (eBNF) for the ruleset consisting of action and condition expressions.

To date, an analysis of how the Policy Enforcer relates to the Parlay Framework, or how the policy expression language for rulesets supported for Parlay compares to the PEEM policy expression language for rulesets, although interesting, has not been carried out in either the OMA or in the Parlay Group.

10.4 Impact of Specifications on the Industry

Both OSE as well as Parlay are attempts at combating vertically integrated service silos by introducing a horizontal service architecture. PIOSE documents the relationship between these two technologies as part of an architectural analysis, aimed at re-use and leveraging existing investments. This has obvious benefits for service providers who have already deployed Parlay assets as part of their services infrastructure and for equipment vendors who already offer Parlay assets as part of their services delivery and mediation portfolio.

Other specifications in OMA may be impacted as well. Based on the architectural analysis, any OMA enabler may utilize Parlay in the following ways:

- A Parlay X Web Service specification may be used as the I0 Web Services binding to some appropriate enabler.
- A Parlay X Web Service may help in defining a highly abstract, technology neutral I0 interface of some appropriate enabler (although this would result in competing APIs).
- A Parlay API specification may be used as I0 binding to some appropriate enabler.
- A Parlay API specification may help in defining a highly abstract, technology neutral I0 interface of some appropriate enabler (again, this would result in competing APIs).

The above list is not exhaustive and more scenarios can be conceived where an OMA enabler implementation may take advantage of the Parlay X Web Services and Parlay API specifications.

10.5 Specifications Evolution and Future Direction

At the time of writing this book, the OMA Architecture Working Group is preparing the PIOSE Reference Release Package (RRP) for submission to the Release Planning and Management committee for final review, and subsequently to the OMA Board of Directors for approval. The PIOSE enabler will be a reference release since for an architectural analysis, there will be neither new interface specifications nor a need for interoperability testing. In addition to the deployment options looked at in this chapter, more imaginative or sophisticated architectural configurations for the integration of components from both technologies can be explored. And Section 10.3 identified two potential areas which may be addressed in a future release of the PIOSE enabler. No such proposal to address these areas, or any other area, has been brought forward at the time that version 1.0 of the PIOSE RRP is being completed.

10.6 Summary

This chapter has explored how assets from Parlay can be used advantageously in the OSE, both on an architectural level (re-cycling architectural attributes on a conceptual level in the OSE architecture) as well as on a deployment level (re-using already deployed infrastructure in an OSE realization). For some of the more straightforward attributes (such as SCF/Enabler and API/I0) a high degree of re-use can be achieved. Consolidating the more sophisticated attributes, such as the PE and the Framework, requires further analysis which is not carried out as part of the Parlay in the OSE enabler.

11

A Web Services Technology Realization of the OSE

Chapter 3 enumerated the OMA principles set forth to allow for as wide an applicability of OMA deliverables as possible, across the entire value chain. One of these principles was independence. Independence of operating system, of execution environment, and of network access bearer. But once you start building an OMA compliant system or platform, or implementing any particular OMA service enabler specification, or planning for your OMA Service Environment (OSE) infrastructure deployment, choices have to be made regarding which technologies to use.

One such technology choice is the type of communication infrastructure and middleware. Many of these technologies come with their own set of design patterns, rules of thumb, and best practices, that help design and deploy best in class, interoperable systems. The OMA Mobile Web Services working group (OMA MWS WG) was chartered to develop specifications that define the application of Web Service technologies within the OSE architecture. The objective of the OMA MWS Working Group was to provide a Web Services infrastructure that can be used by OMA service enablers that wish to offer their capabilities as a Web Service. In the demanding global telecommunications business environment of today, service providers are rapidly expanding the scope of their services portfolio to address the needs of both consumers and enterprises. Extending Web Services capabilities into the mobile world are one way of achieving just that. The intention was not to specify individual OMA Web Service enablers themselves (the approach taken, for example, by the Parlay X Web Services specifications), but rather the goal was to provide other OMA Working Groups with an infrastructure framework and a set of best practices to develop their own Web Service enablers in an interoperable manner. This infrastructure framework is referred to as the OMA Web Services Enabler Release (OWSER). For example, if a certain OMA service enabler wishes to use a request/response message exchange pattern, or wishes to include transport security, OWSER will define how to specify this in a way that ensures interoperability in a Web Services deployment. One could qualify Web Services as one particular technology realization of the OSE, and it is OWSER that specifies how to go about.

You may have noticed we use the past tense here when describing MWS and its activities. The reason is that the working group has been closed since the successful completion and publication of two releases of OWSER. This chapter will introduce the published OWSER specifications that outline the OMA endorsed way to realize the OSE and OMA service enablers using Web Services technology. We will start with answering the question why OMA requires a framework for mobile Web Services. Then we will provide a technical account of the specifications themselves, and finally

The Open Mobile Alliance   M. Brenner and M. Unmehopa
© 2008 Alcatel-Lucent. All Rights Reserved

place them in the perspective of related industry activities and touch upon the impact they have on their environment.

11.1   Web Services Crash Course

Web Services come with their own vocabulary of defined terms, and their own alphabet soup of acronyms and abbreviations. Even a brief primer on the basics of Web Services technology is well beyond the scope of this book. And, therefore, a basic understanding of Web Services and relevant protocols is assumed as prerequisite knowledge, in order to fully appreciate this chapter. Good sources to ground yourself in this technology include [Newcomer2002, Weerawarana2005]. There are a number of definitions, however, that we will provide before delving into the wonderful world of OWSER. The first is that of a Web Service, obtained from [W3C WS Glossary]:

'A Web Service is a software system designed to support interoperable machine-to-machine inter-action over a network. It has an interface described in a machine-processable format (specifically WSDL). Other systems interact with the Web Service in a manner prescribed by its description using SOAP-messages, typically conveyed using HTTP with an XML serialization in conjunction with other Web-related standards.'

The definition above refers to other systems that interact with the Web Service. These interactions occur along distinct patterns. To complete the most basic Web Service picture, there are three roles we need to introduce. A Web Service Provider (WSP), as the name suggests, is the provider of a Web Service. This means that the WSP publishes a machine-processable interface description of the service to a lookup service. It makes available the infrastructure and execution environment such that the Web Service it provides can receive messages from Web Service Requestors (WSRs).

The Web Service descriptions are published to a lookup service, the so-called Web Service Registry. The Web Service Registry is a means of discovery for WSRs. The Web Service Registry advertises its Web Service descriptions. WSRs can find a Web Service that suits their specific need or interest, by searching or querying the registry.

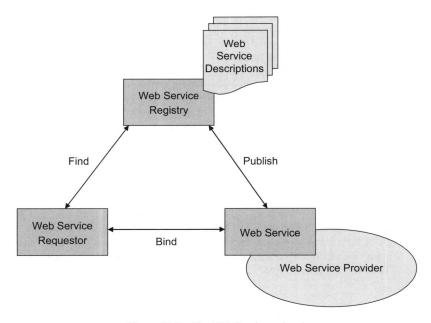

Figure 11.1   The Web Services triangle

The WSR then is the entity that consumes or invokes the Web Service in a manner prescribed by its service definition. A WSR finds the service description of interest in a Web Service Registry and uses this service description to bind to the Web Service provided by the WSP. In the previous two definitions, we already introduced WSRs. These entities are closely inter-related into the well-known Web Service triangle, as depicted in Figure 11.1.

You will find this description of Web Services, along with the triangle diagram, in just about every publication covering this topic. It explains the model at its highest level of abstraction. In fact, the model originates in the logical concept of Service Oriented Architecture (SOA), but when moving from the abstract to the concrete, Web Services is usually being assumed to be the SOA realization technology of choice. In no way, however, does the model help architects to design a Web Services infrastructure, nor does it aid the specification of individual Web Service interfaces. So now that we have stepped through this crash course in Web Services, let's quickly move to the more interesting topics.

11.2   A Web Services Infrastructure Framework

The objective of the OMA MWS Working Group is to provide a Web Services infrastructure framework that can be used by OMA enablers that wish to offer their capabilities as Web Services. Such an infrastructure framework defines the means by which OMA applications can be exposed, discovered, and consumed using Web Services technologies. OMA-defined solutions to common functions, such as security or identity management, using Web Services technologies, are provided. As 'framework' is a somewhat elusive term, but so central to what OMA MWS has produced, let's spend a few moments on what we understand a framework to be. A comprehensive Web Services infrastructure framework enables the design, implementation and deployment of a Web Service within a high performance Web Service environment. The framework provides a co-ordinated approach for the efficient engineering and design of OMA Web Services. It offers uniform methods for describing OMA Web Services as well as principles governing their design and deployment. The framework embodies interoperability profiles, best practices, rules of thumb and acknowledged wisdom, gained in commercial operational deployments. In the absence of such a framework, designers of Web Services within the OMA are more than likely to approach many of the design, implementation and deployment issues each in their own way. Such approaches may be dependent on specific domain expertise, be restricted due to unfamiliarity with Web Service technology, or simply different since no two design teams come up with the same solution. And here we are back once again at one of the central principles that oil the machinery of the OMA; avoiding vertical integration or silos. Web Services is a vast technology area, with its own domain experts. OMA wants to make technology deployment considerations as simple as possible, by providing a framework. This allows OMA specification writers to focus on salient features of their enablers, leading to less brittle architectures.

So, a framework is important for a specific technology realization. However, specifically in the area of Web Services, a framework is even more important. Web Services technology adheres to all the good qualities the OSE is built on as well, such as loose coupling and re-use. And that not only applies to the applications one can build, but also to the way the technical specifications themselves have been defined. There is no single Web Service technology specification, or even a confined set of them. Rather, there is an entire suite of inherently extensible and composable Web Service specifications. Since their names all start with 'WS-', such as WS-Addressing or WS-Security, collectively they are referred to as WS-*. Each WS-* specification is self-contained and addresses one specific function. The true value, however, is unleashed when composing more advanced infrastructures, where various WS-* specifications work in concert. [Weerawarana2005] is an excellent book addressing exactly this aspect of Web Services technology.

Much of the literature on Web Services attempts to structure the suite of WS-* specifications and Web Services base technologies by composing a so-called Web Services platform architecture. Other names in use are Web Services stack, or Web Services protocol stack or Web Services architecture stack. For example W3C [WS-Arch] and WS-I [WSI-Ovrvw] have produced their view of this problem space. Many companies active in this space have developed their own viewpoint of the Web Services stack, supported on their platforms. And there are industry fora that provide a Web Services stack based on their own survey of the market, such as [CBDI]. Each of these Web Services stacks shows a layered architecture, where each layer addresses a separate functional area. These functional areas, such as transport, messaging and so on are layered in increased order of value added to the end-user application. There is general agreement among the various Web Services stacks on what most of those layers are, especially toward the bottom half of the stack. The main differences emerge when deciding which WS-* specification should be positioned in which layer, or when deciding whether to include only approved standards or also draft or proprietary specifications, or even technical notes or recommendations. And, of course, some Web Services stacks differ in their choice of specifications among competing proposals before a dominant or unified standard has had the chance to materialize. For the purpose of this chapter on OWSER, we will use the Web Services platform architecture depicted in Figure 11.2. The specifics of how the various layers are populated with particular technologies are mostly exemplary, in particular, toward the upper layers.

An additional problem is that the arena in which Web Services specifications are created and published is very much dispersed. Dispersed not only because of their composable nature, but also in terms of the organizations creating and publishing them. Many of the WS-* specifications are defined in different standards organizations, most notably OASIS and W3C, or as company proprietary publications. Bringing all these piece parts together in a coherent way is invaluable and a necessary step toward the Web Service infrastructure framework. Architecturally, in Figure 11.2, we now have a model of how the functions relate. But it still does not give you an interoperable profile. Each function is defined in its own WS-* specification, along with its mandatory and optional features, and possibly in multiple versions. There is no single description of how to build an interoperable end-to-end system. This is where the Web Services Interoperability Organization (WS-I) comes into play.

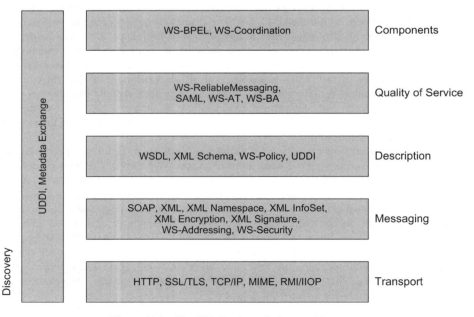

Figure 11.2 The Web Services platform architecture

The WS-I is an open industry organization chartered to promote Web Services interoperability across platforms, operating systems, and programming languages. Recognizing the need to offer clarification, resolution of ambiguities, and reduction of optionality, WS-I has created profiles for a set of base specifications that are necessary to promote interoperability. A profile consists of an agreed-upon subset and interpretation of a named group of technology specifications, at specific version levels, along with conventions and best practices about how they work together. To ensure interoperability at least at the message exchange level, the WS-I Basic Profile 1.0 [WSI BP1.0] prescribes how implementations of SOAP1.1, WSDL1.1, and UDDI2.0 may be used in unison, yielding an interoperable system. As these three base specifications have been in use for quite some time now, sufficient experience has been gained in the industry regarding the features and options that need to be restricted in a profile. The broad support and buy-in for the activities of WS-I are in large part the result of the co-operative and concerted effort of vendors of browsers and Web Service authoring tools, manufacturers of handsets and server equipment, content providers, and Mobile Operators.

The ingredients for a Web Services infrastructure framework that we have assembled so far are the Web Services platform architecture and the basic interoperability profile. So are we there yet? Well, not quite. We need to assess whether adjustments are required for the mobile domain. It is, probably, fair to say that many of the Web Service technologies seem poised to attain the same broad industry acceptance as for instance TCP/IP, HTTP and XML have achieved. The technology is certainly surrounded with a lot of buzz. But if so universal, and if so popular, then why not just apply the technology in the mobile communications domain as is? Why is there a need to do something special? There are two main reasons for this. First, there are certain restrictions in the mobile domain that are less prevalent elsewhere. Secondly, the application area for Web Services technology is incredibly extensive. The telecommunication domain is only one area, and arguably one of the smaller ones. Other areas include enterprise application integration for financial institutions, supply chain management, electronic commerce, etc. Vastly differing requirements apply for each of these domains. Furthermore, certain specification options may be ignored in one domain, whereas they are fundamental in others. So, providing a domain specific profile may make a lot of sense. The OWSER does exactly that. It is a Web Services infrastructure framework, which profiles the Web Services platform architecture for the mobile domain.

11.3   Mobile Web Services

Before we look at the technology profiles and best practices that make up the OWSER, first we take a look at what exactly we mean by Mobile Web Services. There are three aspects to Mobile Web Services that we will explore in this section.

11.3.1 The Mobile Network as Content Source for the Web Service

In the most straightforward scenario, an ordinary Web Service makes use of data obtained from a wireless network. Consider, for instance, a Web Service that uses location data obtained from the wireless network, which is in turn packaged as content in a Web Service provided to a WSR. The mobile specific data can be obtained form the network using conventional technologies (such as the Mobile Location Protocol, discussed in Chapter 25). Likewise, the Web Service can be consumed by the WSR through mainstream Web Services mechanisms. The qualification of 'mobile' in this case applies to the content.

11.3.2 The Mobile Device as Web Service Requestor

In a slightly more imaginative scenario, the mobile device consumes a Web Service available somewhere on a server in the network. The device acts as a WSR, either directly or through a proxy. The device can remain relatively lightweight where the bulk of the computing capability resides with the server.

Related activities in this field include, for example, the Web Services API for the Java 2 Platform, Micro Edition (J2ME) platform [JSR-172]. The purpose of this specification is to provide standard access from a J2ME-enabled mobile device to mobile Web Services running on a server, as well as mechanisms for parsing XML data.

11.3.3 The Mobile Device as Web Service Provider

The previous scenario involved a WSR that happened to be a mobile device. The qualification of 'mobile' applied to the requestor, not the Web Service. Extending this a bit further, consider a scenario where the mobile device acts as a WSP. Here the Web Service truly becomes a Mobile Web Service, that is, the qualification 'mobile' now applies to the Web Service itself. The Web Service offered by the mobile device can be discovered and, subsequently, consumed by any WSR, mobile or otherwise. In such a Mobile Web Service, attributes or objects on the device, such as user profile data or address book data, can be made accessible and possibly available for processing and manipulation through a Web Service interface.

We now understand what we mean by Web Service infrastructure framework, we appreciate the need for profiles, and we have a definition for Mobile Web Service. This gives us all the ingredients to start discussing the OWSER.

11.4   The OMA Web Services Enabler Release

In much the same way that Web Services rely and build on the capabilities of the web, mobile Web Services are closely tied to the capabilities of the mobile web. And this is why having a mobile domain specific effort within OMA is prudent. So let us look at some of the aspects pertinent to the mobile domain.

The concept of always-on is not yet commonplace in mobile environments. Most mobile devices are not connected all the time, which is particularly true for some of the older models still in circulation. Also, asynchronous communication patterns are quite conventional. And there are the special throughput considerations and delay and latency characteristics of the radio bearer. Specific to the mobile device, there are challenges and restrictions as well. Compared to client platforms in the wired web, mobile devices are constrained in terms of processing power, memory footprint, battery life, and user interface capabilities. Since SOAP and WSDL, two of the base technologies for Web Services, are both XML-based, the verbose XML messages have to be parsed on both the server and the client. The physical and performance limitations of mobile devices to date have meant that true mobile Web Services have been unwieldy at best. The OMA MWS Working Group has, therefore, looked for an approach that provides as complete a set as possible of Web Services capabilities to ensure that mobile end users have access to the broadest range of available Web Services.

OMA MWS has adopted the Direct Model, as depicted in Figure 11.3, where both the server as well as the client support a full Web Services stack. Or, in other words, the WSR runs on the client. In the Indirect Model, the WSR acts as a proxy for a mobile device with a limited capability stack. The Indirect Model is out of scope of OWSER.

Figure 11.4 shows the same Web Services platform architecture as before, but identifies the technologies at all layers that are addressed by OWSER. Basically, OWSER addresses the jagged triangle identified on the left side of the figure, from the top left to the bottom right. The decision on which technologies to include and which ones to consider out of scope was made when OMA MWS compiled their own list of functional requirements necessary for a service architecture in a Web Services environment. These requirements were divided into phases, based on the maturity and industry acceptance of the available external specifications in the Web Services arena. It is immediately apparent that OWSER covers more ground than the WS-I Basic Profile 1.0 [WSI BP1.0].

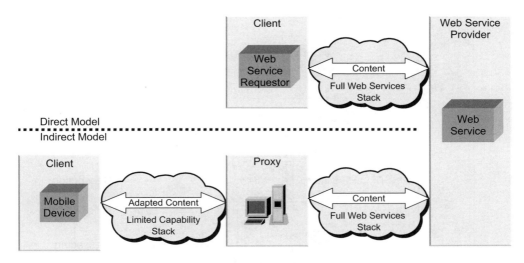

Figure 11.3   Direct and Indirect Architecture Model

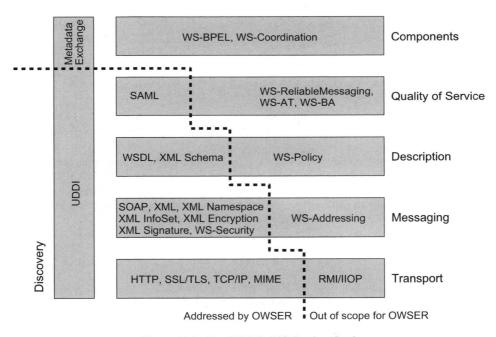

Figure 11.4   The OWSER Web Services Stack

The idea is to elevate the level and scope of interoperability beyond basic message exchange functionality. This entails support for interoperability on higher-level infrastructure services in the Web Services platform architecture.

Figure 11.5 once more shows the OWSER Web Services stack, this time highlighting the various external standards organizations specifying and publishing the many technologies that make up the stack.

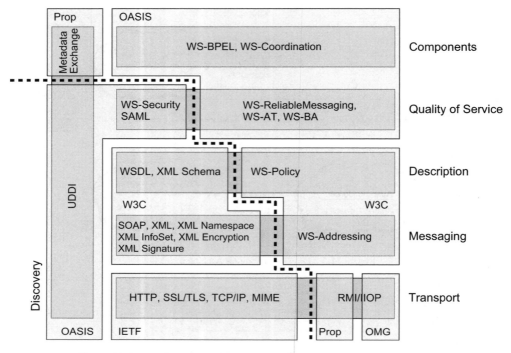

Figure 11.5 The OWSER Web Services Stack. Prop, proprietary specification

What follows is a quick overview of the set of documents (all part of the latest available release OMA Web Services V1.1) that together describe and specify components of the OWSER.

- OMA Web Services Enabler: *Requirements* – provides the market-driven requirements for the use of Web Services technology in OMA, derived from a set of use cases [OWSERReq].
- OMA Web Services Enabler: *Overview* – provides the rationale for using Web Services as well as an overview of the technologies to implement a set of identified common functions that are expected to be available to all OMA applications [OWSEROvw].
- OMA Web Services Enabler: *Core Specifications* – provides the specifications of the components needed to realize the capabilities of the OWSER as identified in [OWSEROvw], in particular, the normative use of Web Service technologies to implement such capabilities [OWSERCore].
- OMA Web Services Enabler Best Practices: *WSDL Style Guide* – provides non-normative information on the use of WSDL that may be used by OMA-defined Web Services [OWSERWSDL].

11.5   The Technologies Specified by OWSER

We will now outline the profiled technologies of the OWSER specification by using the functional layers defined in the Web Service platform architecture, that is Transport, Messaging, Description, Quality of Service, Components, and Discovery. All the technologies are summarized in Table 11.1.

11.5.1 Transport

As the transport mechanism in the stack of Web Services platform architecture, OWSER has selected the Transmission Control Protocol/Internet Protocol (TCP/IP) suite. Due to the ubiquitous

Table 11.1 Technologies making up OWSER

Function		Technology	Profiled
	Transport	TCP/IP	
	Enveloping	MIME	
	Message transfer	HTTP/1.0, HTTP/1.1	WS-I BP1.0
	Transport level security	SSL1.0/TLS3.0	WS-I BP1.0, SAML Conf
Messaging	Messaging	XML1.0	WS-I BP1.0
	Messaging	SOAP1.1	WS-I BP1.0
	Message attachments	SOAPwAtt	
	Message level security	XML SIG	
	Message level security	XML ENC	
	Message level security	XKMS	
	Message lvel security	OCSP	OCSP MP
	Message level security	XML Canon	
	Message level security	XML XCanon	
Description	Service description	WSDL1.1	WS-I BP1.0
	Service description	XML Schema Part 1 structures	WS-I BP1.0
	Service description	XML Schema Part 2 datatypes	WS-I BP1.0
QoS	Application level security	WS-SEC	
	Application level security	SAML	SAML Conf
Discovery	Service registration	UDDI 2.03 Data structures schema	WS-I BP1.0
	Service registration	UDDI 2.04 Publishing API	WS-I BP1.0
	Service discovery	UDDI 2.04 Inquiry API	WS-I BP1.0

and universal deployment of TCP/IP, interoperability of the transport layer is an established and well-understood area, obviating the need for any profiling. The Web Services messages across this transport layer will be enveloped using Multipurpose Internet Mail Extensions (MIME) [RFC 2045] and transferred using HTTP. [WSI BP1.0] requires either HTTP/1.0 [RFC 1945] or HTTP/1.1 [RFC 2616], but recommends the latter for its improved performance characteristics.

For security at the transport layer, the cryptography protocol suite Secure Sockets Layer/Transport Layer Security (SSL/TLS) is used to provide privacy and data integrity between two end points. Two profiles are applicable for SSL/TLS. [WSI BP1.0] requires the use of SSL 3.0 [SSL3.0] and TLS 1.0 [RFC 2246]. The Conformance Program Specification for the OASIS Security Assertions Markup Language [SAMLConf], the SAML interoperability profile by OASIS, has defined the list of cryptographic algorithms or cipher suites for use with HTTP over SSL/TLS.

11.5.2 Messaging

The Web Services paradigm is based on the exchange of messages between a Web Service and a WSR. The basic message format is provided by SOAP [SOAP1.1], defining the structure of an overall envelope, containing an optional message header and a mandatory message body. Serialization of the message, for transport across the network, is done using XML [XML1.0]. Both the use of SOAP as well as that of XML is profiled by [WSI BP1.0]. Embedded in the use of XML are two other W3C recommendations, XML Information Set (Infoset) [XMLInfoset] and XML Namespaces [XMLNS]. XML Infoset provides a consistent set of definitions of the common data objects that may be found in a well-formed XML document. XML namespaces provide a mechanism to incorporate external XML vocabularies identified by a URI reference.

Messages that carry attachments can be formatted using SOAP Messages with Attachments [SOAPwAtt]. It is important that SOAP messages and their attachments are encapsulated such that the correct processing of the message, when delivered to the destination, is preserved. For example, the WSR needs to be able to associate the attachment in its native format with the SOAP message it was originally attached to. [SOAPwAtt] defines a binding for a [SOAP1.1] message to be carried within an MIME multipart message.

In addition to the basic message format (including attachments) and message serialization mechanisms, OWSER defines a host of message level security mechanisms as well as some technologies required for their support. One of the more basic needs is the ability to ensure message integrity using cryptographic checksums. SSL/TLS provide for data integrity at the transport level. XML Encryption [XML-ENC] and XML Digital Signature [XML-SIG] provide support for data integrity at the message level. In order to validate a digitally signed XML document, the serialization of the content is important. Note that differences in serialization, such as the order of attributes or the use of spacing or indentation in an XML document do not change the information content, but do change the cryptographic checksums. Because of these permissible changes in serialization, there is a need for a canonical form of XML documents for encryption and digital signing technologies to be successful. The XML Canonicalization [XML-Canon] and Exclusive XML Canonicalization [XML-XCanon] recommendations from W3C define the canonical form of an XML document that accounts for the permissible changes in XML.

When using digital signature or encryption technologies, you need protocols for the distribution and registration of public keys and digital certificates. OWSER defines two mechanisms for key management. The Online Certificate Status Protocol (OCSP) is used to query a central server about the revocation status of an X.509 digital certificate, that is whether a certificate is still valid or has been revoked. Since generating, signing, receiving, and validating certificate status messages may require extensive processing resources, a mobile profile of OCSP tuned for the mobile environment has been defined by OMA, as the Online Certificate Status Protocol Mobile Profile [OCSPMP TS]. If OCSP is used, OWSER mandates the use of OCSPMP. The second mechanism supported by OWSER is the XML Key Management Specification [XKMS]. [XKMS] defines a protocol that can delegate all the tasks required to process an XML Signature to an XKMS service, minimizing the complexity of applications using XML Signatures.

11.5.3 Description

Web Services are defined by their interface, which is described in a machine-processable format. This format is provided by the WSDL, which is an XML format for describing Web Services as a set of endpoints operating on messages. The operations and messages are described abstractly, and then bound to a concrete network protocol and message format to define an endpoint [WSDL1.1]. [WSI BP1.0] places a number of constraints on the use of [WSDL1.1]. For example, only the SOAP binding is allowed as concrete network protocol and message format specification for a compliant Web Service. [WSDL 1.1] uses XML Schema (Structures [XMLSchema1] and Datatypes [XMLSchema2]) as one of its possible type systems. [WSI BP1.0], however, mandates the use of XML Schema as the type system for WSDL descriptions of Web Services.

Although WSDL allows you to provide an extensive description, not all of the information needed to fully describe a Web Service can be expressed. For example, the service provider policies governing the interactions between a WSR and a Web Service (such as which security mechanism to use in an enterprise environment) cannot be described using WSDL. W3C specifications like [WS-Policy] play in this space. Once such specifications gain broad industry acceptance, or become the subject of profiling activity, their use may be incorporated in future releases of OWSER. The higher we climb in the stack for the Web Services platform architecture, the more examples we will find of functional areas that are not yet incorporated in any interoperability profiling efforts. And this is especially true for the next layer in the Web Services stack, Quality of Service.

11.5.4 Quality of Service

Many aspects may be considered under Quality of Service. Performance characteristics can be enhanced by adding support for reliability, scalability and additional security. As most of these aspects are out of scope for OWSER, as depicted in Figure 11.4, and also out of scope of the profiling activities in the industry, this section will only succinctly touch upon one of the many facets of Quality of Service, that is transactions.

Transactions are an important notion in any computing technology. Operations in a distributed environment depend on a reliable outcome, and each participant in the operation will require access to that same, undisputed outcome. In the event of errors, operations will have to be corrected in order to return to a stable state. Corrections can be made using a simple rollback, in the case of atomic operations, or via a compensation mechanism in the event of an operation made up of multi-faceted, parallel steps. The OASIS specification WS-AtomicTransaction, or WS-AT, provides a set of protocols for the support of atomic transactions (a task that only succeeds if all component sub-tasks complete successfully) [WS-AT]. If one component fails, the entire set of component services is rolled back. WS-AT is predominantly used for short-lived tasks. The task either succeeds in its entirety, in which case the result is published and made permanent, or the task fails completely. Its counterpart WS-Business Activity (WS-BA), provides a set of protocols to implement long-running business processes [WS-BA]. Since intermediate results are made visible throughout the typically long-running business process, failed components are not rolled back for the simple reason that those intermediate results have already been made visible to other components and further processing may have occurred based on those results. To address this situation, such erroneous intermediate results are compensated to reverse the results of those sub-tasks that have already been performed.

11.5.5 Components

The top layer in the Web Services stack is Components. Web Services are loosely coupled, self-contained software components, capable of performing a specific function or activity. This opens the possibility to combine individual Web Services into more complex ones. Web Service components can be strung together into a single application workflow. They can achieve that, only if such Web Services are designed and architected in an application agnostic manner, prepared for unanticipated use, without making any unnecessary or restricting assumptions, as we have argued in Chapter 2 when introducing the principles of OSE. Service composition refers to the technique of composing arbitrarily complex services from relatively simpler ones. With loosely coupled, message-based services, composing a well-behaved, aggregated service with deterministic behavior is a significant challenge. Service composition becomes an issue.

OWSER does not include any provisions in the area of service composition, mainly as at the time of completing the OWSER specifications, no dominant technology choice had emerged in the industry. The OMA Policy Evaluation, Enforcement and Management enabler (PEEM, described in Chapter 8) however, at the time of writing this book, is in the process of adopting the Business Process Execution Language for Web Services [WS-BPEL] as a technology choice for the PEEM Policy Expression Language (PEL) to express service provider policies. WS-BPEL may be used for Web Services composition.

11.5.6 Discovery

There are various ways to perform registration and discovery. Some use cases, not further detailed in OWSER, include off-line means such as developer community websites, promotional collateral (e.g. a CD), or e-mail. In an online scenario though, Web Services are published, or registered, by their WSPs, in a Web Services Registry, for discovery and use by WSRs. When there is a need for automated and distributed registration and discovery, OWSER prescribes Universal Description, Discovery and Integration (UDDI) as the technology to use.

A UDDI Registry is a distributed and searchable repository or catalog where WSPs publish their Web Service descriptions. In addition to a description of the capabilities of the Web Services it provides, the WSP may include information about itself as a business entity, and the information required to bind to the Web Service. Registries may be browsed or navigated by prospective WSRs to select from a set of registered Web Services entries those that support the interface and capabilities that the requestor is compatible with. On selecting the preferred Web Service, the requestor may retrieve the connection information.

To register a Web Service, OWSER prescribes WSPs to use the UDDI 2.04 Publishing API [UDDI]. Similarly for service discovery, WSRs are to use the UDDI 2.04 Inquiry API [UDDI]. Each entry in the Web Service Registry needs to be described using the UDDI 2.03 Data Structures Schema [UDDI Data].

11.6 Network Identity

The initial OWSER (OMA Web Services V1.0 release), superseded by the OMA Web Services V1.1 release referred to throughout this chapter, included an OWSER Network Identity specification. The latter was a result of fulfilling OMA MWS Network Identity requirements derived to conform to the Identity Federation Framework (ID-FF) specification, version V1.1, created by the Liberty Alliance Project organization. That initial work in Identity Management focused on single sign-on and identity data federation. A later release, separated from OWSER, and including exclusively OMA Web Services Network Identity (OWSERNI) specifications, will be the focus of our attention in this section, since it covers not only Identity Federation and Single Sign-on, but also Attribute Sharing and other identity management capabilities. While no longer part of the core OWSER release, we will cover the OWSER Network Identity specification in this chapter, since its realization is based, by and large on Web Services technology, and therefore it represents an example of applying OWSER.

But before launching into some details of the OWSERNI technologies, a brief overview of the terminology and concepts that Liberty Alliance Project specifications (and as a consequence the OWSERNI specifications as well) rely on, and how they relate to Web Services may prove useful.

11.6.1 Identity Management Concepts Overview

Identity Management is a broad concept that can hardly be confined to a section in a chapter. While some of the concepts outlined are generic, the goal of this section is to pragmatically focus on network identity, which is the term describing the basic functionality that is used with a variety of network services to provide a coherent use of state or data related to a Principal. We also want to project such functionality in an environment conformant to the principles of Web Services architecture discussed in this chapter as a whole. Figure 11.6 illustrates the main concepts, roles, and interactions that support an Identity Management model, and it will serve as anchoring point for the rest of the Network Identity section.

A Principal using an access device (e.g. a mobile phone) may intend to access several services that it may be aware of, or finds out through browsing the Internet. This begs the immediate question of what is a Principal, and why we refer to this notion with 'it'?

Principal is a convenient way to capture a more generic entity that may use services, than an end user (usually identified with a human being). It is an entity that has an identity, and is capable

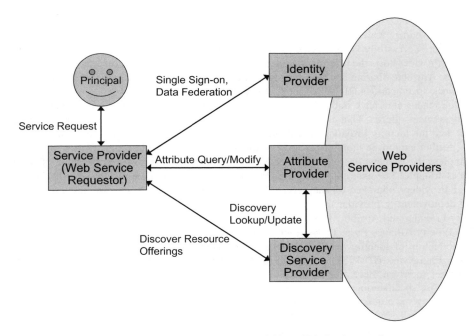

Figure 11.6 An Identity Management model in a Web Services environment

of providing consent and other data, and to which authenticated actions are done on its behalf. Examples include, but are not limited to individual users, groups of individuals, corporations, service enablers/applications, system entities, and other legal entities. Services accessed by the Principal may not all belong to the trust domain of a network operator with which the Principal may have a subscriber account. To facilitate a valuable Principal experience, the concepts of Identity Federation and Attribute Sharing have been introduced.

Identity Federation is a process of associating identity data about a Principal that exists in two or more entities. An immediate useful result is the ability to provide a service called single sign-on, which allows a Principal to authenticate itself once (at a trusted Identity Provider), rather than every time it accesses services at other Service Providers, within an active authentication session. In order to support Identity Federation, three roles are identified: the Principal (previously defined), the Identity Provider and the Service Provider (a role well understood). The Identity Provider is an entity that creates, maintains and manages identity information for Principals and may provide authentication assertions to other service providers, after a relationship of trust is established with them. Usually, the Principal authenticates in an Identity Provider. When subsequently the Principal tries to access services at some other Service Providers, the latter can ask the Identity Provider then for data federation and single sign-on for that Principal. Identity Federation has been the focus of a set of Liberty Alliance Project ID-FF specifications, now at release 1.2.

Attribute Sharing is a process by which a Principal's identity attributes may be queried and/or modified, by Service Providers that may use such attributes for providing other valuable services. In order to support Attribute Sharing, four roles are identified: the Principal (previously defined), the Attribute Provider, the Discovery Service Provider, and the Service Provider (a role well understood). The Attribute Provider is an entity that provides attribute information (in particular, it is a Web Service that hosts Principal's attributes). The Discovery Service Provider is an entity that provides an identity service that allows requestors to discover resources (in particular, it is a Web Service that hosts information about how to find and access Attribute Providers). Usually, the use of Identity Federation is already subsumed. A Principal may try to use a service offered by a Service Provider, which requires identity attributes (for this, or for another Principal) in order to complete successfully. The Service Provider will use the Discovery Service to find out which Attribute Provider hosts the information, then access the Attribute Provider and query for the needed attributes. Attribute Sharing has been the focus of a set of the Liberty Alliance Project Web Services Framework specifications (ID-WSF), now at version 2.0.

As the reader may have noticed, the roles described have been devised from the perspective of identity services offered. That also allowed us to characterize in Figure 11.6 the Service Providers as WSRs, and the Identity Providers, Attribute Providers and Discovery Services Providers as WSPs. As we further explore in more detail some of the technologies, it will become evident that in order to complete the framework, roles may occasionally switch sides from the perspective of the Web Services triangle. For example, Attribute Providers may also become WSRs (for the Discovery Service Providers, and even for the Service Providers). Finally, it may be worth mentioning that in a real deployment, a provider may play multiple roles (e.g. a provider may subsume the roles of Identity Provider and Attribute Provider, or Identity Provider and Discovery Service Provider, etc).

The Liberty Alliance Project also progressed on specifications for additional capabilities, including a collection of Identity Services Interface Specifications, as well as a draft for Identity Web Services Framework (ID-WSF) Advanced Client specifications, both at release 1.0. However, we will neither focus on these, nor on the latest available release for ID-FF and ID-WSF, but rather only on those specifications that are in-scope for OWSERNI.

What follows is a quick overview of the set of documents (all part of the latest available release OMA Web Services Network Identity V1.0) that together describe and specify components of the OMA Web Services Network Identity enabler.

- MWS Identity Management (OWSERNI) Requirements – provides the market-driven requirements for Network Identity, covering identity data federation and management, single sign-on and attribute sharing and transfer, derived the use of Web Services derived from a set of use cases [OWSERNIReq].
- OMA Web Services Network Identity Architecture – provides the architecture for technical solution to the requirements listed above, based on the Liberty Alliance Identity Federation Framework ID-FF and Identity Web Services Frameworks (ID-WSF) [OWSERNIArc]
- OMA Network Identity Federation Framework – provides the specifications of the components needed to realize the requirements of the OWSERNI regarding identity data federation and management [OWSERNI-FF].
- OMA Network Identity Web Services Framework – provides the specifications of the components needed to realize the requirements of the OWSERNI regarding accessing user-related attributes (e.g. user location, presence status etc.) in a privacy-protected manner in a Liberty-enabled Web Services Environment [OWSERNI-WSF].

We will now outline the technologies used by the OWSERNI specifications to meet the OWSERNI requirements, as summarized in Table 11.2.

11.6.2 Identity Provider Introduction

In order to support Identity-based services, Service Providers supporting the ID-FF need to know the Identity Provider associated with a Principal. One solution is provided by the Liberty Bindings and Profiles Specification [Liberty-BindProf], which defines an introduction profile on the basis of the use of a common domain cookie, and a mechanism with which implementations must comply if they use this profile. Alternatively, a Service Provider may use other means to obtain knowledge about the Identity Provider that a Principal is using, for example using a Liberty enabled Client/Proxy, and including an appropriate header as specified in [Liberty-BindProf], in the message sent to the Service Provider.

Table 11.2 Technologies making up OWSERNI

Function	Technology
Identity provider introduction	Liberty-BindProf
Identity Federation and Single Sign-On	Liberty-ProtSchema, Liberty-BindProf
Name registration	Liberty-ProtSchema, Liberty-BindProf
Authentication context	Liberty-AuthnContext
Single Sign-Out	Liberty-ProtSchema, Liberty-BindProf
Federation Termination Notification	Liberty-ProtSchema, Liberty-BindProf
Attribute query and/or modification	Liberty-IDWSF-DST
Usage directives	Liberty-IDWSF-SOAP-Binding
Interaction service	Liberty-IDWSF-Interaction-Svc
Bootstrapping Identity based Web Services Framework	Liberty-IDWSF-Disco, Liberty-IDWSF-AuthnSSO
Discovery service	Liberty-IDWSF-Disco
Liberty enabled User Agent	Liberty-IDWSF-Client-Profiles
Security	Liberty-BindProf, Liberty-ProtSchema, Liberty-IDWSF-security-mechanisms, Liberty-IDWSF-SOAP-binding

11.6.3 Identity Federation and Single Sign-On

An Identity Provider facilitates Single Sign-on and Identity Federation by processing incoming requests from Service Providers, on behalf of Principals that want access to services, and generating authentication assertions. The Service Provider requests the Identity Provider to provide an authentication assertion for the Principal, and optionally may ask for the Principal's local identities (at the Service Provider and Identity Provider) to be federated. In normal conditions (assuming the Principal has authenticated with the Identity Provider, and an active sessions exists), the Identity Provider will fulfill the request. The Identity Federation and Single Sign-on Protocol have to conform to the specifications in the Liberty Protocols and Schema Specification [Liberty-ProtSchema]. The establishment of an authentication session by the Principal at the Identity Provider is out of scope for the functionality provided by single sign-on. [Liberty-ProtSchema] defines three profiles for the Identity Federation and Single Sign-on Protocol, in order to support to different capabilities exercised on behalf of a Principal, where each of these profiles must follow the common interaction and processing rules specified in [Liberty-BindProf]. The three profiles are as follows:

- browser artifact profile
- browser POST profile
- liberty-enabled Client/Proxy profile.

11.6.4 Name Registration

Upon engaging in Identity Federation, the Identity Provider generates an opaque handle that serves as initial name identifier for the Principal, for the use of the Service Provider's communications. After a successful Identity Federation, either the Service Provider or the Identity Provider may register a new name for the Principal, which then must be used in all communications. For the name registration process, both Service Provider and Identity Provider must comply with the procedures specified in [Liberty-ProtSchema], which specifies two profiles for Name Registration:

- SOAP/HTTP-based. This profile is mandatory for both Service Providers and Identity Providers.
- HTTP redirect-based. This profile is optional for both Service Providers and Identity Providers.

The profiles described in [Liberty-ProtSchema] must be implemented as specified in [Liberty-BindProf].

11.6.5 Authentication Context

Authentication context is additional information (e.g. authentication mechanism, methods for storing and protecting credentials, etc) that the Service Provider may require, together with the authentication assertion itself, in order to render a decision regarding what services the subject of the authentication assertion should be allowed to access. Liberty Authentication Context Specification [Liberty-AuthnContext] defines authentication context classes that are representative of current technologies and practices, to facilitate the handling of authentication assertions, in combination with the additional information available. Both Identity Providers and Service Providers must comply respectively with a request or response that includes authentication context information, in conformance with the provisions of [Liberty-AuthnContext], which specifies the mandatory syntax for the definition of authentication context statements and an initial list of authentication context classes.

11.6.6 Single Sign-Out

Within the Identity Federation Framework, single sign-out occurs either when a Principal logs out at the Identity Provider, or when the Principal invokes a single logout process at one of the Service Providers where the Principal is currently signed-in, thus triggering a sign-out request from the Service Provider to the Identity Provider. Upon receiving such a request, the Identity Provider will inform all Service Providers to which it previously provided authentication assertions in the current session for the Principal, and this will be followed by each of them acknowledging the request for sign-out. Finally, the Identity Provider must terminate the Principal's current session, and refuse to release further authentication assertions for the Principal, until the latter authenticates in a new session. The single sign-out mechanism must comply with the procedures specified in [Liberty-ProtSchema], which specifies the following three profiles:

- SOAP/HTTP-based. This profile is mandatory for initiation at both Service Providers and Identity Providers.
- HTTP redirect-based. This profile is optional for initiation at both Service Providers and Identity Providers.
- HTTP GET-based. This profile is optional for initiation at Identity Providers.

The profiles defined in this specification must be implemented as specified in [Liberty-BindProf].

11.6.7 Federation Termination Notification

A Federation Termination Notification interaction can be initiated by either Identity Provider or Service Provider, in response to a Principal terminating an Identity Federation, and the protocol specified in [Liberty-ProtSchema] must be used. Both Service Providers and Identity Providers must support the SOAP/HTTP-based profile, and may optionally support the HTTP redirect-based profile. All interactions must be implemented as specified in [Liberty-BindProf].

11.6.8 Attribute Query and/or Modification

A Service Provider may query and/or modify a Principal's identity attributes stored at an Attribute Provider. ID-WSF provides optional mechanisms specified to support such a case in the Liberty Data Service Template [Liberty-IDWSF-DST]. The elements specified in [Liberty-IDWSF-DST] are provided in the form of an XML template which may be used to implement query/modify semantics. When using this template, schema and usage for both query and response, and the processing rules for those messages must comply with [Liberty-IDWSF-DST].

11.6.9 Usage Directive

A Service Provider that makes attribute queries may accompany them with Usage Directives, indicating the mode for handling the Principal's to-be-obtained attributes (i.e. the policies governing the use of the attribute). At its turn, when receiving such a request, the Attribute Provider may respond by providing its own Usage Directives associated with that Principal's attribute. If used, Usage Directive headers and procedures used by both Service Providers and Attribute Providers must comply with the specifications provided in Liberty ID-WSF SOAP Binding Specification [Liberty-IDWSF-SOAP-Binding].

11.6.10 Interaction Service

An Attribute Provider may query a Principal, using an Interaction Service. This may be the case when a Service Provider queries an Attribute Provider for a Principal's attribute, and the Usage Directives associated with that attribute require the Attribute Provider to contact the Principal. The Interaction Service requests and responses must comply with the procedures defined in Liberty ID-WSF Interaction Service Specification [Liberty-IDWSF-Interaction-Svc]. While typically the Service Provider is playing the role of a WSR, with the Attribute Provider playing the role of a WSP, the Interaction Service also supports a role reversal, a good example of the dynamic nature of Web Services. While performing the Interaction Service, the Attribute Provider may request the Service Provider to redirect the Principal to a URL at the Attribute Provider, using mechanisms specified in [Liberty-IDWSF-Interaction-Svc]. In this case, after obtaining the necessary information from the Principal, the Attribute Provider redirects the Principal back to the Service Provider to complete the sequence.

11.6.11 Bootstrapping Identity based Web Services Framework

Two mechanisms are provided for accessing the ID-WSF:

- The Discovery Service bootstrap leverages the ID-FF, to allow an Identity Provider to offer a Service Provider the resources offerings (associations resource and service instances) needed for the Service Provider in order to contact a Discovery Service. When this access procedure is supported, it has to conform to the mechanisms specified in the Liberty ID-WSF Discovery Service Specification [Liberty-IDWSF-Disco].
- The Authentication Service and Single Sign-On Service is a mechanism by which an Identity Provider can provide a Service Provider with resources offerings needed to contact other Service Providers, including those that may provide a Discovery Service. When this access procedure is supported, it has to conform to the mechanisms specified in the Liberty ID-WSF Authentication Service and Single Sign-On Service Specification [Liberty-IDWSF-AuthnSSO].

11.6.12 Discovery Service

In order for a Service Provider to query an Attribute Provider for a Principal's attribute, the Service Provider needs to first identify the appropriate Attribute Provider. The Discovery Service may be used by Service Providers to meet this goal, by helping them discover resource offerings. In addition, the Discovery Service may also provide the requesting Service Provider with necessary credentials needed to access the Attribute Provider.

An Attribute Provider would use a Discovery Update procedure in order to insert, delete, or modify resource offerings at a Discovery Service. A Service Provider would use a Discovery

Lookup procedure to obtain resource offerings from a Discovery Service. The Discovery Update and Discovery Lookup procedures are defined in [Liberty-IDWSF-Disco], and must be adhered to by the Attribute Provider and Service Provider when using the Discovery Service.

11.6.13 Liberty enabled User Agent

In ID-WSF terminology, user agents and/or devices that support WSR or WSPs that serve a limited number of users are referred to as Liberty enabled User Agents and Devices (LUAD). Interactions involving LUADs, acting either as WSR or as WSP must adhere to the specifications defined in Liberty ID-WSF Profiles for Liberty enabled User Agents and Devices [Liberty-IDWSF-Client-Profiles].

11.6.14 Security

When using ID-FF specifications, the security considerations described in [Liberty-BindProf] apply. The use of SSL/TLS, SOAP messages, XML Signatures and XML Encryption must comply with the specifications provided in [OWSERCore]. Use of XML Signatures also must conform to the specifications in [Liberty-ProtSchema].

When using ID-WSF specifications, the enforcement of authentication, confidentiality, privacy, authorization, and message correlation must adhere to the specifications defined in Liberty ID-WSF Security Mechanisms [Liberty-IDWSF-Security-Mechanisms].

- For authentication, [Liberty-IDWSF-Security-Mechanisms] defines procedures for both peer entity authentication and message authentication.
- For confidentiality [Liberty-IDWSF-Security-Mechanisms] mandates the use of appropriate SSL/TLS cipher suites for transport layer channel protection, while also providing optional alternative recommendations based on Kerberos and Internet Protocol Security (IPSec). For integrity and confidentiality of message exchanges between communicating Providers, the specification defines encryption of the child elements of the SOAP body. It also specifies encryption of the Principals' name identifier and/or the Uniform Resource Identifier (URI) mechanism for ensuring identifier privacy.
- For authorization information generation, transmission and consumption, [Liberty-IDWSF-Security-Mechanisms] defines procedures that rely upon XML Schema support, such as proxy schema for conveying the identity of a proxy, session context to convey session status between entities, and resource access to convey information regarding the accessing entity and the resource for which access is being attempted.
- Finally, for message correlation support, [Liberty-IDWSF-Soap-Binding] defines an optional element in the request message header, which indicates the need for a correlation response.

11.6.15 Network Identity Conclusions

This concludes the tangent into the topic of Identity Management, exploring an OMA enabler realized through Web Services technologies (given the rift that it created, we would not at all be surprised if this statement in itself is debatable). What is undisputable is that it follows the SOA principles, and uses many of the technologies endorsed by OWSER. What also is indisputable is the fact that it is a topic of great interest to network operators and service providers. Following such interest, a later OMA activity emerged to create an Identity Management Framework neutral to realization technology, meant to serve as a top-down approach to engineer specifications, rather than reverse-engineer the Liberty Alliance Specifications (which basically was the case with OWSERNI). The activity started in neutral *ad hoc* requirements group (not in MWS) and the resulting approved requirements document [IMF RD] practically doubled the Network Identity pre-existing requirements from MWS. Unfortunately, after starting to work on the subsequent architecture phase, the interest of advancing this work decreased significantly and eventually it was stopped. While this may be partially explained by the lack of resources from the handful of contributing companies, the reality may be that the timing of producing this work was not ideal: it coincided with the effort of the same companies to propose new identity management specifications to OASIS. Since the latter have now either been approved (e.g. WS-Secure Conversation [WS-Secure Conversation], WS-Trust [WS-Trust]), or are progressing well (WS-Federation [WS-Federation]), there is hope that the Identity Management Framework architecture work may be revived at some point. Ideally, it would then cover how to leverage and combine all the different models and capabilities created in different standards organizations and industry forums.

11.7 OWSER and the OSE

The introduction to this chapter positioned Web Services as one possible technology realization of the OSE. So let us project the Web Services SOA triangle from Figure 11.1 onto the OSE logical architecture, as defined in Chapter 2. The first, rather obvious trait is, of course, that all protocol bindings are Web Service bindings, defined as per OWSER. All I0 interfaces are Web Service interfaces. And of course, this means that the enabler itself is a Web Service. The application invoking the Web Service, through its I0 Web Service interface, acts in the role of a WSR. The Service Provider operating the Service Enabler Tier then is the WSP. To complete the triangle, a Web Service Registry is added to the picture. This role can be fulfilled by an OMA Registration and Discovery enabler. Although the need for such an enabler, not only in a Web Services realization, has been identified almost at the onset of OSE discussions, no such work item has ever been approved by OMA. For our discussion here though, we assume there is an OMA Registration and

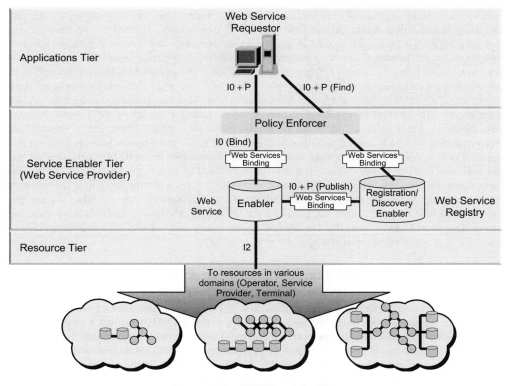

Figure 11.7 OWSER and the OSE

Discovery enabler present, where the registration and publication I0 interface is formed by the UDDI APIs defined by OASIS. Note that the Policy Enforcer is logically involved in every I0 exchange, adding P parameters where appropriate according to the service provider policies (this includes the publish flow, although not shown in the figure for reasons of simplicity). Figure 11.7 depicts an OWSER realization of the OSE.

A central concept of the OSE is the notion of Policy Enforcement. And although OWSER does not provide specific guidance on how to apply that notion in an OWSER deployment, we will briefly explore how this can be achieved. The concept of adding P parameters is realized in different ways across technologies. For a Web Services binding to SOAP, adding of P parameters can be accomplished by including particular SOAP headers in the SOAP envelope defined by the enabler. For example, take a look at security. Even while OWSER does not specifically identify the area of security as subject to service provider policies, it does specify the inclusion of WS-Security headers in the SOAP message, when using certain token profiles (which may be required by a service provider). The WS-Security headers could be considered P parameters in this example realization.

11.8   Divergent Views and their Resolution

While the initial goals of MWS to work on OWSER were enthusiastically supported by almost all companies, some subsequent decisions created a heated debate, and eventually led to suspending the activities of the group, hopefully only a temporary measure. What happened? A number of companies proposed and supported the idea of covering in the first OWSER release Web Services capabilities related to Identity Management (also referred to as Network Identity). Those capabilities included identity data federation and single sign-on using Web Services technologies, and conforming to Liberty Alliance Project's Identity Federation specifications. The inclusion of those specifications in the initial OWSER V1.0 release caused a significant rift between companies participating in the MWS group. At the time, some OMA companies were either not members, or not very supportive of the Liberty Alliance Project organization, and/or were supportive of other specifications for handling Identity Management. A subset of opposing companies perceived the inclusion of the Liberty Alliance Framework specification in the generic OWSER framework as an attempt toward endorsing those specifications by OMA, at a time when they were considering starting to socialize a different set of Identity Management specifications, mentioned earlier, in OASIS. Despite the rift, the first OWSER release ended up including a subset of the Liberty Alliance Specifications. Irrespective of which set of specifications for Identity Management should have been endorsed by OMA, a valid argument was eventually made that Identity Management is not a generic Web Services framework core topic, but rather an enabler in itself. MWS recognized that it could have handled matters differently, and corrected itself by re-releasing an update of OWSER stripped of the Network Identity specifications, and instead focused on the latter in a new separate enabler release. The result was the OWSERNI set of specifications that we described earlier. The rift between the companies, over the solutions for Identity Management, subsided somewhat, but never disappeared, and eventually contributed to the diminished interest of some companies to continue to contribute, and eventually to the closure of MWS.

11.9   Specifications Evolution and Future Direction

The following are some of the areas that were discussed within OMA MWS as potential areas for future work. As we pointed out in the introduction to this chapter, the work of OMA MWS has ceased after the successful completion and publication of the OWSER version 1.1 enabler release. OMA member company interest, however, may rekindle based on two developments. First, as more OMA Working Groups start to define a Web Service interface to their enabler, new requirements for a Web Services infrastructure framework may be identified. Moreover, profiling is in large part based on experiences gained through commercial deployment. As more WS-* specifications enter the mainstream of Web Services technology, the profiles may move upwards in the Web Services stack.

There is another important aspect though in looking at the next steps, even if those steps are never taken in reality in OMA. And that is, that it is good to understand where OWSER stops short. The Web Services infrastructure framework defined by OWSER demarcates a minimum common ground for interoperability. It provides you assurances on what aspects you may comfortably rely on, but also which functionality you would need to settle in addition, for example using bilateral agreements between requestor and provider, or by defining additional domain specific, or proprietary profiles.

11.9.1 Web Services on Devices

OWSER V1 focused on the so-called direct architecture model where each entity supports a full Web Services stack. Such a direct architecture model specifically excludes small footprint, less capable mobile devices. To complete the picture, brief discussions in the OMA ensued around the possibility to develop the indirect architecture model as well. Technological developments have since surpassed these discussions though, resulting in significantly reduced member interest in this work area. Device capabilities in terms of processing power and memory footprint have ramped up radically. Battery life is becoming less of a limiting factor. Device manufacturers are now offering full Web Service stacks along with development tool kits and run-time environments on the latest generation mobile devices, making it easier to put web-enabled desktop-like functionality in the end-users' hands. A good coverage on mobile Web Services platform on the device, and the platform APIs that come with it, can be found in [Hirsch2006].

11.9.2 XML Usage Guide

The XML Usage Guide was planned as the second document in the set of OWSER Best Practices, the first being the WSDL Style Guide. The intent was to provide informative guidelines on the use of XML and XML Schema within OMA Web Services. Such best practices would be based on user experiences with tool support and programming language bindings. An example of one of the best practices considered at the time is to advise against the use of the XML any type, as this type cannot be mapped predictably, requiring the application to do XML parsing and to have knowledge of what is being parsed. Interest in this activity dwindled mainly because of two reasons. When OWSER V1 was published, no OMA enabler had defined a Web Services interface and hence there were no user experiences specific to OMA to draw upon. Furthermore, XML has firmly established itself as mainstream technology and hence the necessity to provide guidance on its use for people new to the technology has been largely superseded.

11.9.3 Common XML Dictionary

As OMA Enabler Working Groups start working on a Web Services interface for their enabler, it is the expectation that these efforts will identify data types for common attributes, for example *address* or *time and date*. In order to avoid overlap and duplication, OMA MWS may define a Common XML Data Dictionary, capturing these common XML data definitions. Such a dictionary would serve as a controlled collection of XML data types for common use across Web Service interfaces for OMA enablers. Data type commonality and re-use greatly facilitates developmental efforts when stringing together multiple enabler implementations into a single application workflow. Developing a Common XML Data Dictionary could be undertaken jointly with the OMA Developers Interest Group (DIG). The Common XML Dictionary may be extended even further, for instance, with common fault definitions. Applications can then provide common exception handling routines for the entire suite of OMA enabler implementations.

11.9.4 Additional WS-I Profiles

As tool and platform vendors start incorporating support for more of the WS-* specifications in their products, *de facto* profiles will emerge. This in turn will contribute toward the maturity and broad industry acceptance of these technologies. The WS-I responds to this development by extending their existing profiles and introducing new profiles addressing functionality higher up in the Web Services stack. This section briefly glosses over these extended and new profiles by WS-I.

The WS-I Basic Profile Version 1.2 is the latest derivation of the Basic Profile published by the WS-I. It incorporates solutions to problems found to date and includes support for requirements on the serialization of envelopes and their representation in SOAP messages. WS-I BP V1.2 includes support for WS-Addressing (for the exchange of Web Service endpoint references) and Message Transmission Optimization Mechanism (MTOM) (for the exchange of binary data).

The WS-I Basic Security Profile Version 1.0 covers security aspects including transport security, SOAP messaging security and other security considerations. OWSER V1.1 was written in anticipation of the WS-I Basic Security Profile, as the latter was not yet completed at the time the OMA MWS Working Group conducted their work. The profile provides guidance on the use of WS-Security, developed by OASIS, which addresses message integrity, confidentiality, and authentication of the message sender by using security tokens, for the various types of encryption and authentication that are available. The profile further outlines interoperability considerations on the formats of these security tokens.

The WS-I Reliable Secure Profile Working Group is the most recent addition to the WS-I organization, and has to date not published a profile deliverable. The aim is to provide interoperability guidance for the OASIS specifications WS-Reliable Messaging [WS-RM] and WS-Secure Conversation [WS-Secure Conversation]. Where the WS-I Basic Security Profile is focused on the secure exchange of individual messages, the WS-I Reliable Secure Profile is focused around the enablement of shared security contexts that can be used for an entire session or conversation within which related messages are exchanged.

11.9.5 Other Industry Profiles

While the WS-I aims to promote interoperability for the entire Web Services community, there are also initiatives deployed by industry verticals, developing profiles for a particular domain. This section will list only a few examples, where a more detailed survey is left as an exercise to the reader.

As an example of a domain-specific profile, the ACORD Web Services Profile (AWSP) provides a recommended way of applying Web Service standards to use cases specific to the insurance industry and related financial services industries [Acord]. In addition to Web Services interoperability guidance, AWSP gives guidance on how insurance business processes specific to the industry should be related to Web Service operations. Another example of a domain- specific profile is the General Web Services Base Profile developed by the IMS Global Learning Community (not to be confused with IMS as in IP Multimedia Subsystem) [IMS GLC]. IMS GLC develops and promotes the adoption of distributed online learning and training technologies for the education sector. Both these domain-specific profiles address an immediate need for a particular industry vertical. There are large overlaps in functionality though, with the various profiles developed by WS-I; hence it is not improbable that these will be superseded by WS-I going forward.

Section 11.9.1 introduced the potential future work area of Web Services on devices. There have been profiling activities in this space elsewhere in the industry. The Devices Profile for Web Services (DPWS) has been developed by a group of companies as a set of implementation constraints with a focus on lightweight implementations in embedded devices like office peripheral equipment and consumer electronics [DPWS]. Controllable appliances in office locations (such as printers, copiers and scanners, conference room projectors, and the like) or home automation environments (e.g. lighting, audio and video entertainment systems, thermostats, etc.) can use the Devices Profile for Web Services to communicate using a Web Services infrastructure.

Considerations on the Mobile Web Best Practices [W3C MWBP], a proposed recommendation by the W3C, are included in Chapter 26 on the Mobile Application Environment.

11.10   Impact of the Specifications

This section explores the impact of the OWSER specifications. The OWSER specifications are unlike other enabler specifications developed in OMA. Rather than defining an enabler, in terms of a piece of functionality that can be invoked through its I0 interface, OWSER defines an infrastructure framework. Hence the impact of OWSER on the industry and on other OMA specifications holds a somewhat different view.

11.10.1 Impact on the Industry

The profile defined by OWSER is a snapshot in time. As Web Services technology matures, more WS-* specs will be profiled as they enter the mainstream and reach universal or at least sufficiently wide industry adoption. And even more aspects will fall prey to detailed specification (the Web Services platform architecture in Figure 11.4 will be extended upwards) and all these will likely have to be profiled as well. Whether such further profiling activities will be carried out in OMA as a future release of OWSER, or whether indeed profiles specific to the telecommunication domain are even needed, is anyone's guess. But even though Web Services technology is making its indistinguishable mark in IT, and has definitively entered the telecommunications space, it is not yet the lingua franca in the latter. And until that happens, OWSER may serve as the profile service providers, network operators, and network equipment manufacturers can comfortably rely upon. OWSER may serve as their entry level guide into this exciting and promising technology. Web Services will be a main factor in their business in the years to come, and OWSER charts part of the path forward.

OWSERNI is already making a distinct impact in the industry. Implementations of Identity Management Frameworks based on Liberty Alliance Project specifications are capturing mindshare and market share, and OWSERNI represents a very good snapshot in time of those specifications, as applied to the mobile market. What remains to be seen is how the industry landscape will evolve to support different approaches (e.g. Liberty Alliance Project specifications, WS-* identity management specifications, open source OpenID specification, etc.) and combine them to offer the most suitable capabilities to use Principal's identities, while protecting them at the same time.

11.10.2 Impact on Other Specifications

OWSER is specifically targeted at other OMA enabler specifications. OWSER defines the means by which OMA enablers can be registered and discovered, exposed, and consumed using Web Service technologies. OWSERNI is specifically targeted to address single sign-on and attribute sharing in the OSE, when using Web Services realizations, and the assessment of its impact on other enablers may have to wait till other enablers start developing Web Services realizations. The Web Services infrastructure framework defined by OWSER provides specification writers in OMA with a single solution to common problems, for deployment in a Web Services realization. If, for example, the Presence and Availability Group (PAG) in OMA chooses to define a Web Services realization of the interface to subscribe for presence updates, OWSER will define how secure exchanges across that interface can be ensured. The WSDL Style Guide [OWSERWSDL] will aid the presence subject matter experts in PAG to specify a normative description of the interface in a language technology in which they are not necessarily fluent. If it weren't for the OWSER Web Services infrastructure framework, OMA enabler specification writers are bound to conceive solutions and designs on their own. Such solutions may not adhere to the best practices or design patterns used by those skilled and proficient in Web Services technology. And beyond any reasonable doubt, individual solutions will diverge significantly.

11.11   Summary

In the OWSER specifications, MWS describes a toolkit for secure Web Service interfaces to OMA enablers based on industry standards This is achieved by referencing the WS-I basic profile for basic networking infrastructure and by anticipating the content of the WS-I Basic Security Profile for secure Web Services. Further additions, to elevate interoperability above merely the message exchange level are also introduced. For network identity, OWSERNI makes reference to the specifications of the Liberty Alliance project. So a fair question would be 'what value does OMA MWS add' above and beyond other industry activities? One answer might be 'very little, in terms of specified functionality'. However, there is certain significance in that the OWSER is the first industry attempt to provide a broad range service environment view in the mobile space for Web Services. The WS-I approach stems mainly from the point of view of tool vendors and Web Services stack vendors, in their attempt to build interoperable products. OWSER assumes the point of view of architecting a service environment. OWSER provides a Web Services infrastructure framework for the mobile domain. This framework allows OMA specification writers to design and architect OMA Web Service enablers suitable for deployment in a Web Service environment in an interoperable way. The fact that the arena in which Web Services specifications are created and published is very much dispersed, gives way to a role for OMA MWS to bring all these together in a coherent way in defining this Web Services infrastructure framework for the mobile realm. Since the successful publication of two versions of the OWSER specifications, the OMA MWS group has closed down and its responsibilities have been subsumed by the Technical Plenary. As more enablers, however, develop Web Service interfaces, the work may be resumed, with some of the activities alluded to in Section 11.9 of this chapter.

12

The OMA Service Provider Environment Enabler

Most service providers plan to provide a continuously increasing set of diverse services to their users, individual consumers, and/or corporations. Being able to do so increases customer loyalty and attracts new customers. At the same time, with the addition of new and diverse services, there are always heightened concerns about the issues related to engaging in new deployments. Amongst these, two stand out: time-to-market and Operational Expenditure (OPEX). In the good old times of fixed telephony, all new services were implemented and deployed as new capabilities of the same circuit switching technology. Hence, one only needed to worry about some small incremental complexities specific to the added features, but not about major changes related to significant architectural or technological changes, as long as they were adding to the existing deployed network equipment, rather than replacing it. For example, service providers needed to be able to provision for new configuration parameters, monitor new events, and understand new log messages, but this was done in a way already handled by their deployed Operations Support System (OSS). This not only facilitated relatively painless upgrades, but also ensured quicker time-to-market, lower expenses on incremental training for their operational staff, lower expenses on incremental capabilities maintenance, and ultimately the ability of backing-off the new capabilities without major network changes, in case they did not perform to the service provider's satisfaction. In fact, till not very long ago, even when replacing technology, service providers were mostly doing so in order to improve performance and reduce OPEX, while providing the same or very similar services as the older technology, simply in order to provide higher-quality service to the end users, at eventually lower cost and higher profit.

Today, the situation has changed. The emergence of Next Generation Networks (NGN) is driven by both introduction of new technology (e.g. technology able to handle converged network services such as IP Multimedia Subsystem (IMS) technology) and the continuous business transformation of the individual consumer and corporate markets. Both markets are thirsty for diverse and complex new services; the new services may be often combined and blended into even more complex services, and it is difficult to predict all the patterns in which such services may be combined over time. The diversity of the new services brings with it diverse technology that needs to be absorbed from a multitude of different vendors.

The so-called triple-play (the ability to blend voice, Internet access, and IP Television (IPTV)) is an excellent example of what service providers are looking for: a one-stop-shop offer, a package of services that will induce customer loyalty, and a way to compete effectively with other service

The Open Mobile Alliance   M. Brenner and M. Unmehopa
© 2008 Alcatel-Lucent. All Rights Reserved

providers that specialize in one service only. At the same time, the introduction of triple-play requires significant changes that the service provider needs to cope with, primarily the introduction of new network infrastructure and the organizational restructuring, with the multitude of changes the latter usually brings about. In most service providers' operations, different departments usually deploy and maintain their own OSSs, fine-tuned to the need of the specific separate services, and the technology upon which those services are built. The relative independence of services offered required reduced connectivity or sharing between those networks, and almost none between the OSSs that supported them. In contrast, a service like triple-play needs to appear as a single coherent service to the end user. This is impossible to achieve without achieving smooth communication, data sharing, and consistency in data provisioning and monitoring between all components involved in delivering the blended service, in order to reduce time-to-market and OPEX.

The challenge of continuous business transformation of the communications services and the markets they serve needs to be addressed with improved means of ensuring stability, consistency, and the handling of the variability in services and in the ways they may blend with each other. The vendors are rising to the challenge: they are doing a good job in providing tools and OSS to support the deployment of the services that their products offer, sometimes including excellent support for provisioning and monitoring potential blended services. But in the absence of following the same standards in provisioning and monitoring services, the service providers are left with the choice of signing up with a single vendor for all their OSS needs, or engaging in complex integration projects. The latter is obviously not the best recipe for reducing time-to-market and ongoing OPEX.

As recognition of the described challenges driven by continuous business transformation, the Open Mobile Alliance (OMA) engaged in the OMA Service Provider Environment (OSPE) work. While other standards bodies have immersed themselves in detailed analysis of the complexity of the processes and interactions between them, that needed to be put in place in order to support what is being called Service Fulfillment, Service Assurance, and Service Billing, OSPE is pragmatically focusing initially on supporting Life Cycle Management (LCM) of services and the ability to trace their activity, in a top-down fashion. The next sections will guide the reader through the evolution of OSPE and set expectations on what this enabler may achieve.

12.1   Are Those Specifications Really Needed?

In the introductory section, we presented the case that new service introduction carries the potential of delayed time-to-market and increased OPEX, and that both require a better solution for the Operation, Administration, Maintenance, and Provisioning (OAM&P) of complex services, from potentially different sources, and with the potential of being blended into combined services offered via a single logical pipe to the customers. While many solutions in support of new services deployment and activation exist today, we noted that in order to address multi-vendor sourcing as well as to ensure consistency over time in each vendor's approach, it becomes increasingly necessary to adhere not only to best practices and guidelines, but to re-use a set of procedures and tools across the board. Since service providers want to continue to have the choice of vendors, a set of *de facto* or *de jure* standards need to be followed. New converged services are assembled using telecommunications and IT components and technologies, which in itself is a paradigm that standards bodies have yet to fully absorb.

In the telecommunications world, many specifications have been developed to deal with low-level granularity provisioning of specific network equipment configuration parameters or monitoring of events related to those fine-granularity network objects that represent a network element (e.g. Simple Network Management Protocol (SNMP) and other management protocols, see Section 12.4). Those specifications have been successfully implemented and entire networks are currently managed using OSSs that facilitate provisioning and monitoring based on those specifications.

In the IT world, despite attempts to expand such an approach to handle IT entities such as servers and databases as network objects, the use of specifications that emerged in the telecommunications world never quite caught on. Other standards emerged from the IT world, but never really penetrated into the telecommunications world (e.g. Distributed Management Task Force/Common Information Model (DMTF/CIM), also discussed in Section 12.4). At the same time, with the exception of detailed specifications for information models, best practices, and guidelines (such as those from the TM Forum), standards for the most basic life cycle management of services are still inexplicably missing.

How can a service provider ensure that a new service can be easily (fast time-to-market, low OPEX) added, removed, started, or stopped if those basic functions are supported with different tools for each of the services they want to deploy, coming from different sources? Imagine yourself operating a VCR, and watching movies released by different production companies. True, you are most likely annoyed that you can't consistently see the same options offered, and offered in the same consistent way, and can't consistently skip previews or deliberately see them, and may have to look for minutes to find and set the subtitles and audio according to your needs. This is, of course, because of lack of standards at the lower granularity level. But at least the industry has approached this the right way, first dealing with standardizing the larger granularity operations: you can consistently count on the fact that pressing play, stop, fast forward, rewind, next chapter, and previous chapter will always get you the expected result, no matter if you are watching a video produced in another region of the world. Similarly, it is this relatively simple layer that this first phase of OSPE is trying to address, and clearly trying to fill a gap or rather lapse in focus by other standard bodies. We could not find an explanation for the current lack of such standards, other than the fact that those topics seem so simple and obvious ('life cycle management for dummies'), to the point that they are deemed uninteresting to sophisticated standards fora, and therefore easily overlooked. This is not necessarily true from an information modeling perspective, but it is almost for sure from the perspective of support in interface specifications. Just as well, those specifications are badly missing, and hence needed, and therefore the OMA initiative to tackle this topic is both very timely and welcome.

As we will explore in more detail in the next sections, OSPE specifications are focused on the deployment, integration and life cycle management of services and service components with the goals of reducing time-to-market and OPEX, allowing service component interchangeability and providing means to improve service level diagnostics. All these properties will ultimately result in improved Quality of Experience (QoE) for the users of the services.

12.2 OSPE Use Cases

This section and the next will give the reader an idea about what void OSPE work is trying to address. OSPE's main goal is to provide a service provider with standard means of deploying and maintaining applications in the Service Provider's Environment. In particular, OSPE is concerned with the following aspects:

- Life Cycle Management (LCM), defined as the sequence of steps of deployment (including download, installation, configuration, activation, and publishing), update (including download, installation, and activation), and removal/withdrawal of components and services.
- Service Level Tracing (SLT), defined as the ability to capture and log all relevant information at each component participating in the service execution of a specific service that is initiated either by an end user or a component.

In order to facilitate support of service deployment and service maintenance in a generic way, services must conform to a certain information model. While this topic will be further explored in the later logical architecture section of this chapter, it is useful to note that this information model assumes that services can be de-composed into finer, more granular (preferably re-usable) components. Also, it is assumed that multiple services (in particular, when they share re-usable components) can be combined in a larger entity referred to as a service package. Service Model

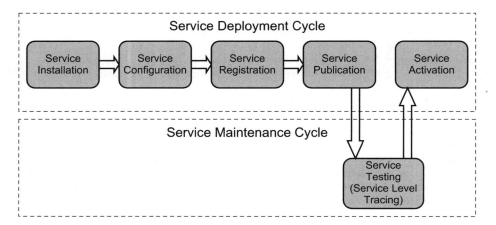

Figure 12.1   Deploying a new application in the Service Provider Environment

Management (SMM) is defined as the ability to manage information about services, and resources, as well as their relations and versions.

Figure 12.1 illustrates the Service Deployment cycle, and shows how it inter-relates with the Service Maintenance cycle in the particular use case of deploying a new application in the Service Provider Environment. Only aspects that are in scope for OSPE (LCM, SLT) are shown in the figure.

The figure is helpful in explaining a typical use case scenario in which the service provider wants to deploy a 'Restaurant Finder' application, as part of a larger 'Consumer Entertainment Services' package. The new application may re-use pre-existing service components in that package (e.g. a Charging component), but requires new components to be deployed (e.g. a 'User's location' component). Once the service is activated and in use, effective tools must exist for troubleshooting in case of problems reported by the customers.

For this example, the following assumptions are made:

- The service provider has previously completed analysis and planning and as a result has determined the customer segment to which the new application will be offered as a service, the service package that it will become part of, and the correspondent charging and billing plan.
- Using application requirements provided by the application developer, the service provider has also identified existing service components in its environment that the new application may re-use, and has acquired and integrated the new service component 'User's location' into the target service package.
- The interface definitions of all the needed service components have then been made available to the application developer.
- Policies with respect to access to the different service provider resources as well as privacy rules for the end user have been put in place.
- The service provider maintains all the details about services, service components, and relationship between them in a service catalog (a central services data repository that supports the Service Management model).
- The new service is discoverable by the target customer segment, and/or promoted to the target customer segment.

Now let's follow what happens in the Service Deployment cycle in Figure 12.1. The service provider uses its OSPE-based enabler implementation to perform several deployment steps. It installs the new application 'Restaurant Finder' in the Service Provider Environment, as part of the 'Consumer Entertainment Services' package. It then installs the new 'User's Location' component in the Service Provider Environment, and installs the configuration logic that determines how the new application runs in its environment. It then upgrades, if needed, existing re-usable service components that may be needed by the new application. It updates the service catalog with details for the new application, and for the new 'User's Location' component, details about the relationship between them, and details about the relationship between the new application and component with the other services and components existing in the service package. It provisions the new application and components for maintenance. It associates the new application with its service package. A series of pre-live tests are performed – this is where the Service Deployment cycle relies on capabilities offered in the Service Maintenance cycle. For example, the service provider may emulate the situation in which a customer using the new service is calling to report an issue with the service. The service provider then enables all service components for tracing and marks the testing device. It then replicates the user's scenario; as a result of device marking, during the service sequence execution, a token is passed from the device to the next service component in the service, and in a chaining sequence, to any other service components reached by the service. The components enabled for tracing and reached by the token will produce traces. The analysis of the traces is used to isolate and detect a potential problem that can then be addressed. Once the pre-live tests get completed successfully, the service provider publishes the new application as part of the 'Consumer Entertainment Services' package and makes it available to the targeted consumer segment. While not explicitly shown, during this cycle, notifications to appropriate resources may also be sent.

There are benefits resulting from using a standard way to deploy and maintain a new application. The application developer will be able to re-use service components that he/she may have become familiar with, and for which they already have developed access APIs. The end user will receive new and improved services, with a similar, or better, QoE as in the past. The service provider will be able to introduce the new service rapidly, with minimal integration efforts and OPEX, while re-using deployed service components and maintaining service continuity for existing services and will also have the ability to independently troubleshoot the new service.

12.3   OSPE Requirements

OSPE requirements related to service LCM focus on mechanisms needed by the service provider in order to provision and retrieve information related to applications, services, service components, and relationships between them, while supporting service continuity for ongoing service sessions and transactions (see [OSPE RD] for details). The requirements identify the need for a standard-ized interface that would allow a service component to be installed, removed, started, stopped, upgraded, downgraded, activated, and de-activated and the service catalog refreshed to reflect the changes. Since some of the operations mentioned may trigger post conditions or actions, OSPE also needs to support mechanisms to perform corresponding updates to service catalog entries and send notifications for updates to back-end systems, policy management systems, and authorization systems.

In order to support service maintenance, OSPE's initial focus is on providing mechanisms that would allow a service provider to trace in real time the execution of a service, at any or all components that the service traverses. In order to do so, OSPE requires any service component, including client devices, to support marking (a process allowing triggering SLT by the marked component by means of a tracing token, to all components that the service may traverse, at the time the service is instantiated). It also details how a marked component can identify the other components in the service chain and how components receiving the tracing token have to react.

OSPE requirements further detail the minimal information that needs to be included in a trace (e.g. the specific tracing instance, service component and/or enabler identification, supported protocol and version, key performance indicators, IP address, port, hostname, destination address, any end-user visible events, etc.). Traces are to be retrieved through a standardized interface from all applicable service components.

Some requirements are more directed toward the implementation, than to the OSPE specification – unless we are to interpret them as hints that other phases may follow; for example, there is one generic high-level requirement referring to the need of every service component to support FCAPS model (Fault, Configuration, Accounting, Performance, Security) through a standardized management interface, but there are no further detailed requirements on the topic. Overall, the OSPE requirements provide a pretty good indication of what the OSPE architecture needs to accomplish. But OSPE architecture also needs to keep in mind currently existing and deployed management specifications and architectural frameworks. In the next section we will explore the management standards landscape that preceded OSPE development.

12.4   Standard Precursors to OSPE

The operation, administration, and maintenance standards history is quite extensive; the problem, of course, is that OAM&P standards are most of the time focused on trying to catch up and adapt with the evolution of technology and networks, instead of imposing a top-down behavior, from management perspective, on new implementations. OPEX reduction has no prayer when we continue to march along with this predicament.

It is worthwhile however to present a summary of the OAM&P standards landscape, in order to understand where the focus of OSPE is, and more so, where it is not.

The telecommunications industry and the IT industry have approached OAM&P standardization efforts differently, and it is therefore worthwhile to summarize the history of those efforts. Although OSPE in its first phase is focused on a manageable set of objectives, it may evolve later to cover more OAM&P areas. To understand the broader standards landscape, and be in a better position to assess why OSPE selected particular topics to tackle, the next sections will provide the reader with an overview of standards in this space.

12.4.1 OAM&P Standards in the Telecommunications Industry

The general approach that the telecommunications standards dealing with OAM&P took initially was to separate operations from implementation technology by defining an OSI-compliant management architecture common to multiple technologies and services, with capabilities grouped into Fault (F), Configuration (C), Accounting (A), Performance (P) and Security (S) – summarized by the acronym FCAPS. Later on, with the management starting to focus on the service layer, rather than purely on the network layers, three other dimensions were added, Service Fulfillment (F), Service Assurance (A) and Service Billing (B) – summarized by the acronym FAB. FCAPS and FAB are till today the prevalent management paradigms in the communications industry, and the FAB paradigm encompasses the FCAPS paradigm, with many of the FCAPS capabilities being mapped into each of the FAB dimensions.

Protocol specifications in support of those concepts were developed in the Internet Engineering Task Force (IETF), the International Standards Organization (ISO), the DMTF, and the TM Forum.

The SNMP [RFC 1157] is an application layer protocol that facilitates the exchange of management information between a Network Management System (NMS) and managed network elements. Network elements are represented by an information model called Management Information Base (MIB), and SNMP agents are fronting the managed network elements providing an interface between the NMS and the different MIBs. SNMP was targeted for both provisioning and monitoring at the finest granularity level (each manageable network object represented in the MIB can be accessed for 'set' or 'get' operations). SNMP uses User Datagram Protocol (UDP) to reduce the overhead. While SNMP is still widely used for fault management at the network element level, and network level, provisioning using SNMP has proven effective only when trying to surgically set a specific parameter, but not for massive provisioning; that is not only because of the relative unreliability, but mainly because of the unwieldiness of going through a complete provisioning transaction round trip for every single detailed parameter. It also failed to gain significant adoption rate in the IT world – hence MIBs for managing servers, application features, or databases, never really made it into standards extensions, although attempts were made by different vendors in that direction.

The Common Management Information Protocol (CMIP) [ISO/IEC 9595] is an ISO Open Systems Interconnection (OSI) protocol used with the Common Management Information Service Element (CMISE), supporting an information exchange between Network Management (NM) applications and management agents (a model similar at high level with the SNMP model). CMISE defines a system of NM information services. CMIP supplies an interface that provides functions that may be used to support both ISO and user-defined management protocols. CMIP/CMISE protocols were proposed as an alternative to SNMP. CMIP uses an ISO reliable connection-oriented transport mechanism and has built-in security that supports access control, authorization, and security logs. The management information is exchanged between the NM application and management agents through managed objects. Managed objects are a characteristic of a managed network element that can be monitored, modified, or controlled and used to perform tasks (in the OMA there is some resemblance to this approach in the Device Management Managed Objects, see Chapter 18 for details). CMIP does not specify the functionality of the NM application, but it only defines the information exchange mechanism of the managed objects and not how the information is to be used or interpreted. The major advantages of CMIP over SNMP consist in the fact that CMIP variables are in fact objects that can be used to perform tasks; also CMIP is a highly reliable specification and also ensures a safer implementation, having built-in support for authorization, access control, and security logs. The attempt to overcome all the shortcomings of SNMP and the high ambitions of the CMIP/CMISE set of specifications to address all management aspects comprehensibly also resulted in mixed results in its acceptance. While S in SNMP stands for Simple, C in CMIP might as well stand for Complex. It was however widely adopted in managing the optical and transport layers, in particular when it comes to provisioning aspects, though a full deployment of the entire set of specifications across multiple technology services and network proved to be too heavy and complex. Today, a mixture of implementations of CMIP/CMISE (mainly for provisioning) and SNMP (mainly for fault management) co-exist, along with other standard-based and/or proprietary implementations for the different FCAPS capabilities in the FAB paradigm.

12.4.2 OAM&P Standards in the IT Industry

In the IT industry, many advances in technology and business models led to vertically integrated end-to-end solutions that were initially introduced sporadically, on an as-needed basis. As a result, corporations now have a large variety of deployed networks, systems, and applications, including management applications. The DMTF was formed as a standards organization with the mission to develop a consistent set of management standards and guidelines for desktop and Internet environments in the enterprise. One of the standards created by DMTF is the CIM, which includes the CIM Infrastructure specification [DMTF CIM] and the CIM Schema [DMTF CIM Schema]. The CIM Infrastructure specification provides a language and methodology for defining management data, without prescribing specific CIM implementations. The CIM Schema provides a Core model, Common models, and Extension Schema. The Core model captures a set of classes (e.g. Managed Element, System, Service, Component, etc.) and related associations, properties, and methods that provide a basic vocabulary for describing managed systems. The Common models use the Core model as a starting point, and extend it by capturing notions that are particular to specific management areas, while still independent of technology realization (e.g. systems, applications, networks, and devices). Extension schemas are technology-specific extensions of the common models (e.g. applicable in particular environments, such as specific operating systems). DMTF also developed a set of management and Internet-standard technologies, known as Web-Based Enterprise Management (WBEM), with the goal of unifying the management of distributed environment. WBEM supports the exchange of CIM information, and includes protocols, query languages, discovery mechanisms, and mappings. The primary WBEM specifications are a set known as WBEM-CIM-XML. This set defines all the interactions between management clients and management infrastructure as CIM messages. The WBEM-CIM-XML set also includes an encoding specification that defines XML elements written in Document Type Definition (DTD), the CIM Operations over HTTP Specification, to allow retrieving and manipulating CIM data ([DMTF CIM HTTP]), and the CIM Representation in XML ([DMTF CIM XML]). Another WBEM set is represented by Web Services (WS) specifications, referred to as WBEM-WS. Amongst the WBEM-WS specifications, WS Management [DMTF WS Management] describes a Simple Object Access Protocol (SOAP)-based protocol for managing desktops, servers, devices, etc. CIM and WBEM specifications have enjoyed varied levels of adoption in the enterprise, especially through the introduction of initiatives designed to deliver a solution to a specific vertical area. Examples of such initiatives include the Systems Management Architecture for Server Hardware (SMASH) Initiative for managing servers, and the Storage Management Initiative (SMI). So far, CIM and WBEM have not made significant incursions in the management of telecommunications networks and services, but DMTF has recently added a new subgroup chartered to extend CIM models to cover Telecommunications Systems and Services.

Finally, the landscape is completed by the TM Forum, which is focused on providing leadership, strategic guidance, and practical solutions to improve the management and operation of information and communications services; it is also the forum that coined and developed the FAB paradigm. The TM Forum started as the OSI/NM forum, and released a set of specifications based on CMIP/CMISE. It later released the Telecommunications Operations Map (TOM), followed by the Enhanced Telecom Operations Map (eTOM), which addresses business process automation and was adopted as an International Telecommunication Union (ITU) standard in 2004 [ITU M.3050]. The eTOM is part of TM Forum's Next Generation Operations Support System (NGOSS) initiative – a comprehensive, integrated framework for developing, procuring, and deploying OSS/BSS. In addition to eTOM, NGOSS includes a systems analysis and design feature delivered as the Shared Information/Data (SID) model, a solution design and integration feature delivered as the Contract Interface and Technology Neutral Architecture (TNA), conformance testing delivered in the NGOSS Compliance Tests, and procurement and implementation delivered in Return on Investment (ROI) model, Request for Information (RFI) template, and Implementation Guide documents.

With this management standards landscape in mind, the question is, where will OSPE fit? At the time of writing this book, OSPE has completed its requirements and architecture specifications, but has yet to progress in the detailed technical specifications for protocols. One thing is sure, based on its professed goals: OSPE will not try to resolve all the OAM&P problems, not even at the highest level, so it will most definitely not engage in defining a comprehensive framework of specifications to cover FCAPS or FAB as a whole, at the service layer. OSPE will be focused, at least immediately, solely on specifications for protocols, and possibly on information model for SLT. In pragmatic fashion, the Architecture Working Group that is working on the OSPE topic has recently decided to defer handling the service LCM requirements to a later phase. In not so many words, that pretty much excludes endorsing immediately either the SNMP suite, or the CMIP/CMISE suite, or the CIM suite as a whole. However, we can't exclude, although chances are small, the possibility that the specifications may end up being particular extensions of any of those more complete frameworks. With respect to the information model, the TM Forum's SID was looked into early on, and the OSPE architecture work has drawn inspiration from that source, and still includes it as an informative reference. Furthermore, recognizing this possibility, the OMA has initiated a cooperation agreement with TM Forum, and, in the preparation of the OSPE architecture specification, the OSPE activity has liaised with TM Forum, which shared a number of SID documents under the cooperation agreement. Given the OMA's principles of re-use, all we can say at this point is that every effort is being made to re-use existing specifications, should they meet the OSPE requirements, before engaging in creating yet a new set of specifications.

12.5   OSPE Architecture and Technical Specifications

The OSPE architecture focuses on the three aspects that have been introduced earlier: LCM for service components and services, SLT, and SMM.

Before we start detailing those architectural aspects, the next section will illustrate the OSPE mapping to the OMA Service Environment (OSE), setting the stage for understanding OSPE's overall role in the Service Provider Environment, relative to the other resources (e.g. enablers). For a complete understanding of the OSPE architecture, see [OSPE AD].

12.5.1 OSPE Enabler in the OSE

OSPE requirements have some peculiarities, when compared to other OMA enablers, although not necessarily from a management's perspective. Like in the case of most management paradigms, in order to achieve OSPE goals, other enabler implementations need to be compliant with OSPE approach. The OMA enablers' implementations may routinely use interfaces exposed by other enablers, in compliance with the OSE architecture. However, in the case of OSPE, other enabler implementations must incorporate OSPE functionality in order for OSPE to successfully execute a management dialog with these enablers. Figure 12.2 provides a mapping of the OSPE enabler to an OSE architectural diagram.

While the figure provides a glimpse into the OSPE detailed architecture, the intent here is to make the reader realize the relationship between OSPE and most of the other OMA enablers. For sure, an OSPE implementer will provide an OSPE implementation (OSPE server) that exposes interfaces through which a principal can issue provisioning and tracing related commands. Note however that

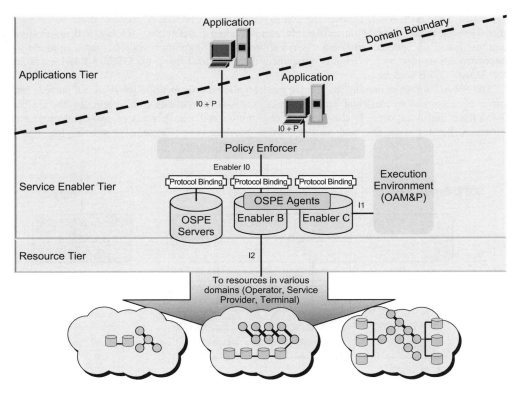

Figure 12.2   OSPE enabler in the OSE architecture

those high-level deployment commands cannot terminate in a black hole; they need to convey information to or retrieve information from other enablers and resources. As hinted in previous section, a service catalog contains information describing all relationships between services, enablers, and components. Post conditions or actions resulting from service deployment or SLT operations may have a subsequent provisioning or tracing impact on other enablers, and mechanisms to support them have to be standardized (OSPE agents). Depending on specific vendor implementation, such mechanisms will be integrated with other resources (e.g. enablers), or integrated with the main OSPE functionality. The integration of OSPE agents with other resources is not in scope for OSPE, but the integration of OSPE with the Execution Environment is in scope for the OSE. Since we had to make a choice for the diagram, we represented OSPE in a certain way, to indicate its origin as an OMA enabler. In a deployed architecture, one may represent the OSPE enabler as part of the Execution Environment as well, where at least some of the OSPE interface may be considered as being part of the I1 category of interfaces, and being commonly used for some aspects of the service LCM of all other enablers.

12.5.2 OSPE Logical Architecture

The logical architecture has five components, grouped in two layers, that can be referred to as the OSPE server layer and the OSPE agent layer. Each of the layers expose I0 interfaces. An OSPE application (a management application) would usually invoke the I0 interfaces exposed by the OSPE server layer, and the OSPE server layer components would usually invoke the I0 interfaces exposed by the OSPE agent layer. The OSPE architecture is illustrated in Figure 12.3.

The OSPE server layer includes the OSPE server and the Service Model and Catalog (SMAC). The OSPE server is the central point of execution, co-ordination, and distribution of LCM and SLT processes. The OSPE server exposes the OSPE-1 and OSPE-2 interfaces; requests received through those interfaces are mapped internally into corresponding provisioning, tracing, and notification actions, based on specific proprietary service provider configuration choices, and compliant to dependencies defined by service and component data, obtained using the OSPE-3 interface, from the SMAC OSPE component.

The SMAC server maintains the service models, allowing them to be provisioned, parsed, and traversed according to particular search criteria expressed in requests coming through the OSPE-3 interface that it exposes. It also supports registration and management of service deployment instances, service packages, and partner service provider data. Elements of the service model

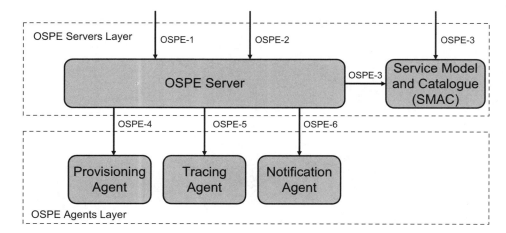

Figure 12.3   OSPE enabler architecture. Reproduced by Permission of the Open Mobile Alliance Ltd.

maintain inherent attributes such as the service life cycle state, version, and location, as well as service specific attributes such as the maximum number of concurrent users. The SMAC understands and manages the syntax of the service attributes, but not their semantics. The latter is the prerogative of the SMAC Requestors.

Finally, the OSPE agent layer includes a Provisioning Agent, a Tracing Agent, and a Notification Agent, which respectively expose OSPE-4, OSPE-5, and OSPE-6, used by the OSPE server to send provisioning actions, and/or tracing actions, and/or notification actions resulting from the OSPE processing of incoming requests for LCM or SLT. The OSPE Provisioning Agent receives and processes LCM operations and data configurations for target resources. The Tracing Agent receives and processes SLT-related actions and reports tracing data from target resources. The Notification Agent receives notification requests for the target resources, with updates about status and/or configuration changes to the service and/or service components. OSPE Agents can be embedded in the target resources, or stand alone, or be combined with the OSPE server. In either case, they interact with target resources via interfaces that are not in scope for OSPE (most likely I2 interfaces, although if appropriate I0 interfaces exist, they should be of course re-used).

OSPE architecture includes six interfaces:

- OSPE-1 (also referred to as OSPE LCM requests interface) supports service and component LCM requests (e.g. installing, activating/deactivating, modifying, packaging, or withdrawing a service and/or component of a service), service and/or component data configuration requests, and service and/or component data retrieving requests.
- OSPE-2 (also referred to as OSPE SLT requests interface) supports service tracing requests (e.g. activate/de-activate service tracing), service tracing data reporting (i.e. push from a service component, which uses callback information obtained at provisioning time via OSPE-5), and service tracing data retrieving requests (i.e. pull).
- OSPE-3 (also referred to as Data Management interface for SMAC) supports requests for service and/or component registration/un-registration and requests for management of other service and component related data (e.g. creation/updating/deletion/retrieval of catalog data).
- OSPE-4 (also referred to as OSPE provisioning interface) supports LCM configuration requests for target resources, and requests for retrieval of configuration data from the target resources.
- OSPE-5 (also referred to as OSPE tracing interface) supports tracing initiation and/or termination requests for target resources, and marking commands for target resources.
- OSPE-6 (also referred to as OSPE notification interface) supports requests for notifications for target resources. The notifications indicate status or configurations changes for a target resources, resulting from an LCM operation performed on a service or component that contains that target resource.

12.5.3 OSPE Logical Flows

A typical deployment flow is shown in Figure 12.4. An OSPE Requestor (a management application) issues a request for modifying a service component, using the OSPE-1 interface (1). The OSPE server parses the request and relies on the SMAC server to provide it with component dependency information, through the OSPE-3 interface (2, 3). Based on the initial request and the dependency information, the OSPE server determines the affected target resources and communicates the modification request(s) to the appropriate Provisioning Agent(s) using the OSPE-4 interface (4). Upon receiving confirmation that the modifications have been taken care of by all impacted Provisioning Agents (5), OSPE server will update Notification Agent(s) that are responsible for issuing additional notifications to other back-end systems, using OSPE-6 interface to send the notifications and receive the confirmations (6, 7), so that any interested back-end systems may be informed of the status or configuration changes that had occurred. Once all target resources provisioning and notification of back-end systems are completed, the OSPE server will update the component dependency

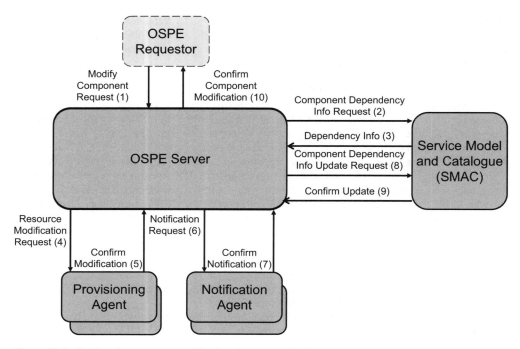

Figure 12.4   Deployed component modification. Reproduced by Permission of the Open Mobile Alliance Ltd.

information in the SMAC, using the OSPE-3 interface (8). SMAC will confirm the update (9), and the OSPE server will send confirmation to the OSPE Requestor that the process of upgrading the component has completed, via the OSPE-1 interface (10).

Other deployment flows follow a similar pattern. An OSPE Requestor will issue in sequence, granular requests to the SMAC server for registration (using OSPE-3) and to the OSPE server for service deployment using OSPE-1; the latter will result in a cycle of interactions with different Provisioning Agents via the OSPE-4, and then with Notification Agents via the OSPE-6. When the Provisioning cycle gets completed successfully, as the last deployment step for a service, the OSPE server will issue an activation request via OSPE-3, updating the service data in the service catalog. Once the service is activated, it is ready to be published and made available to its users.

Two typical SLT flows are shown in Figures 12.5 and 12.6.

In Figure 12.5, an OSPE Requestor issues a request for turning on SLT, using the OSPE-2 interface (1). The OSPE server parses the request and relies on the SMAC server to provide it with information on the components of the service, and their interdependency (e.g. sequence in which they may be used), though the OSPE-3 interface (2, 3). OSPE service identifies all Tracing Agents impacted, and sends to each of them a request to turn on component tracing, using the OSPE-5 interface (4). Once confirmations are received from all Tracing Agents (5), the OSPE server concludes that SLT is enabled, and confirms it to the OSPE Requestor, using the OSPE-2 interface (6).

Once SLT is enabled across the service, one can proceed to instantiate an SLT session, represented by the next flow. In Figure 12.6, an OSPE Requestor, using the OSPE-2 interface, issues a request for creating a new instance of an SLT session (multiple SLT sessions may exist in parallel for the same service), to be initiated from a given service component (1). The OSPE server parses

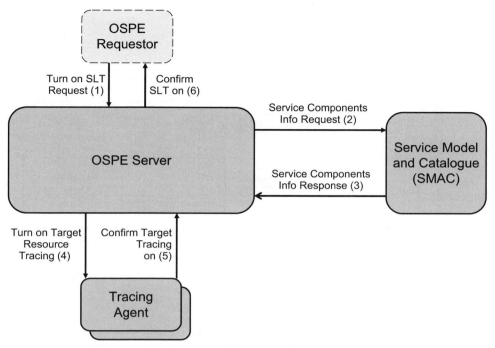

Figure 12.5 Turning on Service Level Tracing (SLT). Reproduced by Permission of the Open Mobile Alliance Ltd.

the request, and by means of OSPE-5 exposed by the Tracing Agent of the indicated component, marks the component (e.g. a client device) where the service will be initiated with an SLT session (2). The Tracing Agent will construct a tracing token and confirm marking (3) via OSPE-5 back to the OSPE server. The OSPE server will then request the Tracing Agent, via OSPE-5, to trigger the start of the SLT session (4). At this time, the OSPE server may also provide a callback mechanism, to allow the Tracing Agent to report the traces to the OSPE server later on. The Tracing Agent will initiate the SLT start by passing the token to its attached component (either by initiating the service, or simply continuing to execute the service), using internal implementation, out-of-scope for OSPE specifications (5). Upon receiving the tracing token, the component starts tracing the service by posting appropriate log messages. When the service switches to use of the next component in the sequence, the token is being passed along as part of the message payload, and the tracing session continues at the next component. Since the communication between the Tracing Agent and its attached component as well as the specifics of each service chaining are out-of-scope for the OSPE specifications, there may, or may not be a mechanism through which each component confirms the starting of an SLT session, but it is not represented in the flow by a separate arrow. However, it is assumed that there is a way for each Tracing Agent to acknowledge that SLT has started, and each Tracing Agent will confirm it back to the OSPE server, using the OSPE-5 interface (6). It is also assumed that the OSPE server knows the entire sequence of service components from the SMAC (this part is not illustrated in the figure); once the OSPE server has obtained confirmation on SLT start across the service, it will confirm back to the OSPE Requestor via the OSPE-2 interface that the SLT session has been created and is now active (7). In the meantime, different components in the service are producing traces, and reporting their availability to the respective Trace Agent (8),

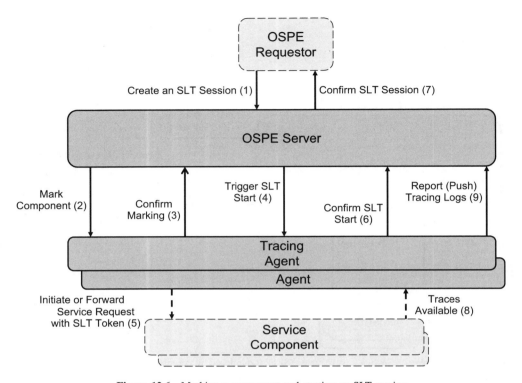

Figure 12.6   Marking a component and starting an SLT session

through some internal mechanism, out-of-scope for OSPE specifications. Once tracing is completed at a given component, the Tracing Agent for that component will report the traces to the OSPE server (9), pushing them using the callback mechanism provided in flow (4). The traces from all Tracing Agents are collected by the OSPE server, which will make them available for a later request from an OSPE Requestor (this is part of a different flow, and therefore not illustrated here).

12.6   OSPE Salient Points

There are a few noticeable characteristics to the OSPE architecture. If one looks at the overall approach, OSPE has definitely taken cues from some of the existing management paradigms described earlier. First, it has taken the approach of breaking down larger issues into more manageable issues, and as a result has proposed a two-layer architecture (a layer of servers, and a layer of agents – which in fact are servers for the first layer). Secondly, the two main capabilities that OSPE is focusing on (LCM and SLT) fit neatly into the FAB paradigm: LCM is clearly a Fulfillment (F from FAB) feature, while SLT is clearly an Assurance (A from FAB) feature. We also note that, while OSPE's requirements mandate support for automated deployment, the OSPE architecture's interpretation is that automation will be provided only for the individual steps of the Service Deployment cycle (e.g. registration, provisioning, activation, etc.) but not at the highest level. In other words, the OSPE server will have the knowledge, using the SMAC component for a source of relationship data, to break down the individual steps mentioned, but will not take on the task of breaking down the entire life cycle. In doing so, OSPE is relinquishing the responsibility of creating and managing end-to-end workflows for the LCM of the service provider services to the OSPE Requestor applications (e.g. service provider's OSS/BSSs). This is consistent with the general OMA enablers' philosophy to find and specify critical aspects of an end-to-end service or systems, but stopping short of specifying the functionality of the entire system. On the other hand, an OSPE server implementation will include support for breaking down individual tasks all the way down to a task that can be executed using a single component, and in most cases, a single interface, and will specify those interfaces and the behavior of the components that expose them. But one may ask, why did OSPE not allow for a three-layer architecture, where the first layer accepts commands like 'deploy service X' (currently missing) and breaks the command down into registration, provisioning, activation for a second layer, and the second provisioning layer breaks the provisioning command down into configuration commands toward specific provisioning agents. We are not sure we have the answers, since the needed service status data seems to be maintained in the SMAC (e.g. whether a service is deployed or not, registered or not, configured or not, activated or not). Of course the order of these operations, and whether all of them are needed, or whether other additional operations are needed, may be specific to a service provider, but then again, a way could have been devised, via an existing or additional interface, to feed such relationship (order of the deployment steps) into the SMAC. The value of this is that it would further simplify the interactions between a high-level OSS, and each of the services it deals with, getting closer to the notion of 'objectizing' a service. Maybe this will be considered in a future phase.

Let's also take a quick look at the interfaces exposed by the agents layer. According to the OSE principles, an interface is exposed in such a way that it can be invoked by any requesting resource conforming to the interface specification. But in the case of OSPE-4, OSPE-5, and OSPE-6, the OSPE architecture shows that only the OSPE server uses those interfaces to exchange messages with the OSPE agents. There is indeed nothing preventing an OSPE Requestor, other than the OSPE server, to exchange messages with the OSPE Agents, so while not evident from the figure, this should not be considered a deliberate limitation.

Finally, OSPE has chosen to analyze what is needed to support LCM and SLT, from a service model perspective, but is not specifying a service information model. This proves to be a little bit tricky, but nevertheless, again, is consistent with OMA philosophy. OSPE defines what its components do, but does not specify how they are to do it. Instead, OSPE uses hypothetical service package and service information models to derive from it the data templates, and the actions on data templates that such informational models need to support – which will be specified in the form of the OSPE-3 interface messages. This allows for a multitude of service information models to be implemented and maintained through the use of OSPE-3. Our expectation is that extensibility will also be provided in the OSPE-3 interface itself, to allow new types of service and relationship data to be managed, as service models evolve beyond the hypothetical model on which OSPE will base its OSPE-3 initial interface specification.

OSPE has a relatively high number of interfaces (6) and components (5) to specify. Architecture specifications in OMA usually address high-level architecture, and OSPE architecture specification (OSPE AD) makes no exception. A number of questions may be raised when going through the logical flows, and in some cases one cannot find the expected explanations in the AD; because of this, our view is that a number of architectural issues may be uncovered during the technical specifications phase (just starting at the time of writing of this book), and some fine-tuning of the architecture may be necessary as an outcome.

12.7 Impact of Specifications on the Industry

Specifications of interfaces for LCM and SLT of services are long overdue in the market. As we have described in earlier sections, most existing and used specifications focus on lower level of granularity (lower layers of management) in order to support the wealth of data that needs to be provisioned and reported at network element levels. The proliferation of network elements and IT elements had to be mirrored by management mechanisms simply because having different tools of configuring and monitoring every single element was not even an option. Now that we have ways, albeit not perfect, and not universally adopted, to handle elements, and even networks of elements in a bottom-up manner, the effort of looking top-down, from an end-user and/or service provider executive perspective, on how to control an entire service, has become as critical. The number of services that can be devised through blending will continue to grow, and may soon equal (and hopefully outgrow) the number of types of elements involved. This is not unconceivable anymore, especially when the emphasis now is on re-use of elements for multiple services. In summary, service scalability starts making demands for appropriate standards, and the purpose of OSPE specifications is to fill some of those demands.

12.7.1 Impact on Service Providers

Service providers will be the main beneficiary of the OSPE specifications. Both time-to-market and OPEX should be positively impacted, when products based on OSPE specifications emerge.

A service provider OSS will only need to support the OSPE-1, OSPE-2 (and maybe OSPE-3) interfaces, in order to manage the life cycle and tracing of *all* their services. The only difference between the services managed will be the data associated with those services, but any service data will be passed through well-defined exchanges between an OSS and the OSPE server (and maybe between an OSS and the SMAC) using the OSPE-specified interfaces. This may be a considerable improvement over today's situation, where there are no equivalent specifications; hence a service provider OSS needs to interface through proprietary mechanisms, in most cases multiple, to the different tools for deployment and activation and tracing acquired from different vendors. Introducing a new service will therefore be much facilitated and will require much more reduced integration efforts, and hence will improve time-to-market. The fact that only one set of management tools (the ones integrated in the OSS to exchange messages with OSPE) will be needed will reduce the need for personnel, and for personnel training – which is the main source of OPEX (40% according to industry sources).

Last but not least, service providers will also be able to maintain or increase customer loyalty, by decreasing the time-to-market for new services and by having the ability to offer improved Service Level Agreements (SLAs) for upgrade, availability, and troubleshooting of those services. They will also be able to better support branding, as well as accommodate and offer third-party services, since deployment, isolating, and troubleshooting, and removal if necessary, are facilitated though the OSPE specifications.

12.7.2 Impact on Vendors

OSPE specifications will likely be welcomed by vendors that specialize in management tools, which will jump at the opportunity to provide OSPE server, SMAC, and Provisioning, Tracing, and Notification Agents, as well as tools to facilitate migration. It may also be welcomed by vendors who provide multiple other resources (e.g. enablers), and who normally incorporate functionality similar to the agents embedded in their offerings. This is because with a standard approach, they can focus on their main competency (their enablers), and integrate with a re-usable type of agent template, which should facilitate both integration and testing. Vendors specialized in service provider integration services may have to re-focus their efforts once software implementation based on the OSPE specifications emerge and are embraced by service providers. Professional services are a complex business, and they are used to constant change and adaptation, so this should not take them by surprise; there will certainly be a transition time where integration services will initially increase, before they level off again. But this may be a welcome signal of change for vendors that offer both products (e.g. enablers) and integration services, since the integration efforts around OSPE will require narrower, rather than broader, integration expertise.

12.7.3 Impact on Consumer Market

The deployment of OSPE-compliant implementations should also spell good news for the users. The individual consumers should see much-waited-for new services come to market more rapidly, and will see noticeable improvement in mechanisms that facilitate service discovery, subscription, upgrade, and troubleshooting. There are also additional side effects to the end user, should the service provider decide to offer them. For example, the ease of including a service component into a service and a service into a package may be expanded to allow user service preferences and user privacy settings to follow the model and be inherited and re-used.

12.7.4 Impact on Corporate Market

The arrival of solutions based on OSPE specifications should provide multiple benefits to corporations. Like in the consumer market, corporations will welcome the quicker offering of new services by service providers, when new technological advances emerge. Corporations rely on increased availability of services, and will welcome an offer of improved SLAs from service providers; ultimately services that they use directly affect their revenues. But corporations are also service providers to their own employees – they usually OAM&P their corporate networks and services. In that role, corporations face similar OPEX issues and time-to-market issues as any service provider, so at least to some extent, OSPE standardization may also bring a positive effect on future OPEX and time-to-market for internal enterprise services.

12.7.5 Impact on Other Specifications

It may be too early to assess whether and how OSPE specifications will impact other enablers' specifications. Other enablers' specifications may be considered for re-use for some of OSPE interfaces; should that be the case, they may have to undergo some changes to accommodate OSPE needs. The reverse is also possible – once OSPE interface specifications become available, they may become dependencies for some enablers – in particular if those enablers recognize a need for such dependencies to be documented, because they may play a part in a more complex flow than their enabler needs to support. The OSPE-in-OSE picture we presented earlier implies a symbiotic relationship between OSPE and other Service Provider Environment resources (via I2 interfaces) on one hand, and OSPE and other OMA enablers, on the other hand. The conclusion is that the OMA enablers' activities need to recognize and pay attention to this relationship, and specifically address it as appropriate to their particular tasks.

12.8   Specifications Evolution and Future Direction

The first question to resolve is the direction that the OSPE technical specifications will take, in order to fulfill OSPE requirements. Will they draw upon existing specifications (and which ones), or will the contributors feel compelled to create new protocols and messages, or will they limit themselves at creating profiles of existing specifications? As we alluded to earlier, additional layers of management specifications could be envisioned, and certainly new OSPE capabilities could be defined (e.g. much more could be done in the Service Assurance area, particularly with respect to Quality of Service (QoS) and SLAs).

12.9   Summary

OSPE did not raise a lot of enthusiasm in the OMA initially, but it does hold a lot of promise, and it has received a lot of attention during its architecture phase. OSPE requirements and architecture focus on some aspects not currently on the central radar screen of other standard bodies. Should the current service providers' and vendors' attention and allocation of resources continue during the technical specifications phase, then OSPE outcome has a good chance of legitimately becoming one of the OMA achievements stories.

13

The Security Enablers

The use of the Internet and other information and networking technologies has become an integral part of corporations' business strategy and individual consumers' lifestyles. This means that many companies are using the Internet to communicate and advertise, exchange information, and conduct electronic commerce. For individual consumers this means anything from just searching for information online and exchanging information via e-mail, instant messaging, and text messaging to ordering online goods, and using digital services such as managing, storing and accessing personal information, music, videos, photos, and all the way to online banking, paying bills or participating in online gambling or auctions. And most corporations and individual consumers consider the security of their online data to be of great importance – in fact, in many cases, security is quoted as one of the reasons why e-commerce and online digital services do not take off even faster. The main reason for this is the concern about misuse or loss of sensitive information. How were we accomplishing all these services years ago, before the development of the Internet craze, and do we seem to be so much more concerned now than ever before?

Of course, the number of available services and our appetite for them increases over time. But many, if not most, of modern day services had their equivalent in the past. We were and are continuing to give out information such as name, address, age, gender, ethnicity, identity or social security numbers, credit card account numbers, bank account numbers, driver licenses numbers, passport numbers, and much more to governmental institutions, financial institutions, and a whole lot of other categories of institutions, including companies that offer free or for-pay services. However, in most cases in the past, this information was pervasively shared in a manner perceived more private and secure (e.g. in a direct face-to-face or phone conversation, or written exchange) and predominantly stored as a paper hardcopy. Re-distribution of one's private information was more work-intensive, and each such operation exposed the information to just one more entity and was done with human intervention. Today, the same information is predominantly shared over the Internet and stored in an electronic repository. Different techniques of sharing, distributing, and storing are used, which leads to quite a different risk scale. Since the distribution is electronic, it requires only little more work to e-mail to millions of people rather than just one person. That also makes it harder to track where the information was distributed, since there is no single human contact that one can inquire. Therein lies the huge difference, and this is a story of numbers and technology. Numbers are not everything, and it is probably healthy not to think about them every time we get online and share some of our private information (rest assured, you are guaranteed to share some of it in every instance, even if you are unaware). What numbers? Your pick, but let's start with over 1 billion Internet users. This includes those users who choose to use online digital services, suggesting that they, knowingly and willingly, give out private information to access

The Open Mobile Alliance M. Brenner and M. Unmehopa
© 2008 Alcatel-Lucent. All Rights Reserved

such services, as well as all those who just browse the Internet in search of information, which usually implies that they give out at least their IP addresses. In increasingly more regions of the globe, the number of users that access online digital services keeps growing and reaching staggering proportions – so the conclusion is that we are rapidly reaching a point where most Internet users are knowingly and willingly sharing private information with entities that offer them online services. Such sharing occurs not only once, but repeatedly, possibly with every new online transaction they are conducting. In essence, we are really talking about hundreds of billions of pieces of private information, distributed over probably hundreds of thousands of systems worldwide. While in the past, sharing information was mainly a matter of establishing trust (with the entity you gave out your information to), the much larger issue now is how likely is it for the information to fall maliciously or inadvertently into the wrong hands? Unfortunately, the answer to the latter question is 'very likely'. In the past, in order to steal private information, one needed to physically break into a cabinet file located in some building, and it was relatively easy to make this a very difficult proposition, and certainly one easy to detect and pursue. Today, preventing break-ins or even detecting intrusion to electronic information has become non-trivial. Malicious users do not have to be physically close to the information. Also, once tapped into, information today can be shared with other malicious users almost instantaneously. So yes, numbers and technology does matter.

But what exactly are the concerns related to security and how are they to be handled? In the prevalent security terminology, the concerns are related to the following characteristics:

- Confidentiality – Sensitive information sent over the Internet needs to be kept confidential, and only made available to the person the information was intended for; using encryption is an effective way to keep information confidential.
- Authenticity – Those conducting transactions over the Internet must be able to authenticate themselves; in other words, prove they are who they claim to be; using passwords, digital certificates, digital signatures, or shared secrets are some of the ways to authenticate principals.
- Non-repudiation – Participants in a transaction cannot complete a transaction over the Internet and later deny it happened, since there is technology to prove that the transaction took place; digital signatures can be used to support non-repudiation.
- Integrity – Integrity means that information sent over the Internet or accessible on the Internet cannot be altered (in particular for a message sent over the Internet, the content of the message received must be the same as the content of the message sent); digital signatures can prove data integrity by detecting changes, while encryption can be used to protect the generated signatures.
- Access Control – Enforcing access control implies that only authorized principals can access the controlled service, resource or information; tools to control access include firewalls, access rights, passwords, and authorization certificates.
- Availability – Finally, availability means that when a service, resource or information is needed, it can be accessed reliably; information, software, and hardware must be physically and logically protected and made reliably available to authorized principals, using techniques and methodologies such as monitoring, data back-ups, anti-virus software, and adequate computer resources.

As you can see, security specifications have their work cut out. Given that technologies meant to deal with security concerns work almost equally well for both well-behaved and malicious users, secure handling of the sheer volume of information shared and transactions used to share it are all daunting issues for security experts. Security concerns are handled at many different layers in the network with many different techniques and appropriate specifications, depending on specific critical detectable threats at such layers. One needs to constantly look at the issues both top-down and bottom-up, since none of the security measures offers a 100% fail-proof warranty. The layering is also meant to address issues that are possibly not completely understood or solved yet at a single layer. In principle, Open Mobile Alliance (OMA) security is working on several angles, which will be detailed in the sections that follow. One of those angles is to profile existing security specifications from other standards fora for the benefit of use with OMA enablers. Another angle is to ensure that a number of common techniques, technologies, guidelines, and methodologies are re-used by OMA enablers, to ensure consistency in expectations and deter OMA enablers from re-inventing the proverbial wheel. Finally, another very important angle to the advancement of applications and converged services is the ability to isolate and expose a number of security functions via interfaces that can be invoked whenever needed by other OMA enablers or resources in the Service Provider (SP)'s environment. This will ultimately allow SP's policies to determine the level of security needed, the type of security mechanisms applied, and the extent to which such measures are applied (e.g. inter-domain versus intra-domain exchanges), rather than having the security implementations tightly integrated with all enablers, irrespective of how those are used. Of course, both the tight integration of security functions, and the off-loading of security functions to re-usable resources have to be made available as provisionable capabilities, with the choice of which ones to use or to what extent to combine such usage, remaining an SP's decision.

13.1   Are Those Specifications Really Needed?

As we learned from the introductory section on security, the security concerns are not going away easily – despite the fact that for every identified threat, a number of proposed solutions exist. While not everything can be turned into a specification, a number of frequently used techniques need to be standardized, regardless of whether a vertical integration of security technologies or an isolation and specialization of a security enabler as a separate entity is advocated and deployed. In either case, interoperability between vendor products is a must. In the first approach, clients and servers may come from different vendors or built in-house, hence the security functions integrated into those resources need to be able to inter-operate when brought together to form an end-to-end solution. Likewise, and even more so, in the second approach, all security functions ever to be invoked by some other resource (e.g. an OMA enabler) in the SP environment needs to be standardized, so that such resources coming from different vendors can, indeed, integrate with the security functions provided by some other vendor. The real question is, therefore, not whether specifications are really needed (they clearly are), but rather which specifications have more impact than the others, in terms of market criticality. The OMA Security Group has decided that ensuring that an enabler has all the functions needed to ensure its security at its disposal and, therefore, knowing how to integrate into such a security framework, is of highest priority. As we get into discussing specific security enabler aspects, we will quickly realize that the approach of exposing to other enablers interfaces for security functions is something that may be considered only later. This may quite possibly be a result of a difference in approaching information security issues, between network security architects and IT security architects. However, the expectation is that the approach of opening up interfaces through which any resource can invoke a needed security function will take off as more pressure is applied on standards fora like the OMA, to address application needs. One conceivable specific example that may lead to such an outcome is the applications push for enablers to adopt a Service Oriented Architecture (SOA) realized through Web Services Technology.

Approaching the needed specifications in a pragmatic manner, the Security Working Group (SEC WG) has been working so far on several security activities, some related to documenting the inherited WAP Forum security specifications, others introducing some changes to those specifications, and yet others focusing on Security Common Functions (SEC-CF) for all OMA enablers. The last activity will be detailed in the following sections, since it has the most relevance to the OSE and the most impact on interactions with other resources (e.g. OMA enablers), and it raised interesting debates in the OMA (some of which are not completely resolved at the time of writing). But before we dive into describing that activity in more detail, we will shortly mention the other OMA security specifications published so far.

13.1.1 Wireless Public Key Infrastructure

The OMA Wireless Public Key Infrastructure (WPKI) enabler was created as part of the WAP Forum and adopted by the OMA. It provides the means to establish public key security exchanges between clients and servers in either the transport layer, or the application layer, or both. Such features include authentication, confidentiality, and integrity of exchanged messages. For more details, see [WPKI DF].

13.1.2 On-board Key Generation (OBKG)

The On-board key generation (OBKG) and key enrollment (OBKG) enabler is an enabler initiated in the WAP Forum, and completed in the OMA when WAP Forum was folded into the OMA. It is aimed at supporting OBKG (see [OBKG RD]) in the device rather than a network-based server, by defining European Computer Manufacturer Association (ECMA) scripts and added functions in the Wireless Identity Module (WIM) [WIM TS]. WIM is used to store and process information for user identification/authentication (e.g. a Smart card). Changes in the ECMA script to support an object for cryptographic functionality of the ECMA Script Mobile Profile (ESMP) have been included in [ESMP CR]. The OBKG enabler also includes a new release of the WPKI definition [WPKI DF]. See more on the use of the ECMA Script Mobile Profile in Chapter 26, on Mobile Application Environment.

13.1.3 Online Certificate Status Protocol Mobile Profile

This specification also originated in the WAP Forum. The specification defines a profile of the Online Certificate Status Protocol (OCSP) [RFC 2560] for mobile environments. OCSP specifies a protocol used to determine the current status of a digital certificate instead of using standard Certificate Revocation Lists (CRLs). The scope of OCSP Mobile Profile Technical Specification (OCSPMP TS) is to provide an OCSP subset that permits efficient implementation by constrained wireless devices and supports interoperability with OCSP responders available in the market. For more details, see [OCSPMP TS]. Recall that OCSPMP is one of the two key management mechanisms as part of the Web Services infrastructure framework defined in OMA Web Services Enabler Release (OWSER), described in Chapter 11.

13.1.4 Smart Card Web Server (SCWS)

The Smart Card Web Server (SCWS) specification [SCWS TS] defines the interfaces exposed by a HTTP server in a smart card embedded in a mobile device (e.g. SIM, USIM, UICC, RUIM, CSIM). The specification defines the URL to access the SCWS, the transport protocol between HTTP applications in the device and SWCS, the HTTP profile that the SCWS needs to implement, a secure remote administration protocol for the SCWS, and how a principal authenticates with the SCWS. For more details, see [SCWS TS].

13.2 Security Common Functions Enabler

Having looked briefly at other OMA security specifications published so far, let us now shift gears and introduce the main body of work by the OMA SEC WG, that is the SEC-CF enabler. OMA enablers typically expose protocols invoked by resources (e.g. applications or other enablers), such as the Device Management Protocol, the Location Privacy Checking Protocol, and the XML Document Management Protocol. The use of these protocols varies; hence the protocols are diverse. However, they share some critical common features, such as security features (e.g. authentication, confidentiality, integrity), for which the same security protocols can and should be re-used. The goal of SEC-CF is to provide common security functions (not specific to any particular enabler) for use by any OMA enabler.

13.2.1 SEC-CF Use Case

One typical use case is where a client establishes in a mobile device a secure connection to several enablers in its home network – through an authentication proxy (AP). Alternatively, the client could establish a secure connection to individual enablers, but such a use case is simpler, and in fact a degenerate case of the one we are illustrating here. In the case where the mobile device is in its home network, it has pre-established credentials based on a shared key mechanism. The connection is either protected with Pre-Shared Key Transport Layer Security (PSK-TLS) [RFC 4279], using a shared key for mutual authentication of the endpoints or TLS [RFC 2246] with server certificates for server authentication and a shared key HTTP Digest [RFC 2617] for client authentication. The assumption is that the mobile device has established Transmission Control Protocol (TCP) connections to the Key Management Centre (KMC) and the AP and that the AP is authorized to use the KMC (in general, the SPs will regulate such usage via authorization policies).

A variation of this use case is when the mobile device is in a visited network. In this case, since the Visited Network operator is passive and only ensures connectivity between the visited and the home network, the diagram and flows are similar. Flows supporting both the instantiation from the home network and from a visiting network are represented in Figure 13.1.

The mobile device connects to the KMC (1, 1′) and obtains a shared key. The mobile device connects to a target enabler in the SP domain, and the connection is intercepted by the AP. The mobile device uses a PSK-TLS session to indicate what shared key (2, 2′) will be used. The AP retrieves the indicated shared key (3), as well as end-user identity information. The role of the shared key is to provide payload data protection (confidentiality) between the mobile device and the AP. All subsequent traffic to/from mobile device to enablers (4, 4′) is proxied by the AP, before it reaches the enablers (5). The result is a protected connection between the mobile device and any enabler accessed, where the endpoints have been mutually authenticated, and with the added benefit, in the case of using an AP, to provide additional information about the user to the enablers (e.g. end-user identity information that the AP obtained from the KMC).

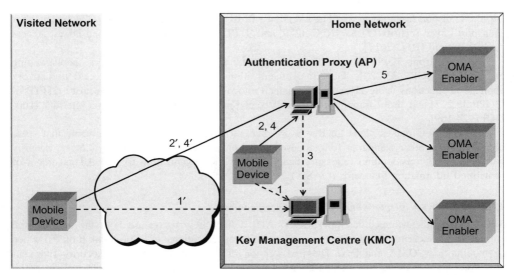

Figure 13.1 Authentication using authentication proxy. Reproduced by Permission of the Open Mobile Alliance Ltd.

13.2.2 Security Common Functions Requirements

The SEC-CF requirements have been derived from a combination of use cases such as the one described in the previous section, which is only a representative example. The set of use cases as a whole illustrates requirements with respect to handling the secret data that is used in the process of protecting user data, authentication, data integrity, confidentiality and privacy, key management, and security data administration and configuration. Requirements covering integrity mandate protection against accidental or intentional changes to transferred data, regardless of whether the transmission originated and terminated in different networks, and encryption is mandatory for confidentiality. All or almost all requirements implicitly mandate some sort of access control or authorization mechanism, to ensure that any of the functions may be performed only by authorized principals. Authentication credentials, selected from those that are supported by the SEC-CF, will have to be presented by any requestor to the resource that makes use of such SEC-CF. Mutually, the resource that uses SEC-CF must be able to authenticate itself toward the requestor if required – therefore, the SEC-CF enabler must also provide for such mechanisms. Authentication must be supported directly between a resource and an enabler using the SEC-CF, optionally through the use of an AP. Replay protection mechanisms and authentication of the data origin, including authentication of the source of broadcast or streaming data must be supported. Given the possibility that an enabler is implemented in a distributed architecture, including the possibility of having some capabilities deployed in the home network, while others in a visited network, the SEC-CF must support authentication between peer components residing in different networks. Requirements also exist for how to share keys, in a secure way, for any resources in either home or visited networks.

13.2.3 Standards Precursors to Security Common Functions

OMA security specifications are not developed in a vacuum. They rely heavily on the guidance and specifications from other standards fora, such as the Internet Engineering Task Force (IETF), 3GPP and 3GPP2.

OMA security specifications use terminology documented in the 'Internet Security Glossary' [RFC 2828]. OMA SEC-CF specifications build heavily on IETF specifications such as 'Security Architecture for the Internet Protocol' [RFC 2401], 'IP Encapsulating Security Payload (ESP)' [RFC 2406], 'Transport Layer Security (TLS) Version 1.0' [RFC 2246], 'Pre-shared Key Ciphersuites for Transport Layer Security (TLS)' [RFC 4279] and 'HTTP Authentication: Basic and Digest Access Authentication' [RFC 2617].

Precursors from 3GPP include 'Generic Authentication Architecture; Generic bootstrapping architecture' [3GPP 33.220], 'Generic Authentication Architecture (GAA); Access to network application functions using Hypertext Transfer Protocol over Transport Layer Security (HTTPS)' [3GPP 33.222] and 'Bootstrapping interface (Ub) and network application function interface (Ua)' [3GPP 24.109].

As OMA SEC makes plans for the future phases of this enabler, it is conceivable that specifications from other standards fora, focused more on services and applications layers security will come into consideration (e.g. specifications from the Organization for the Advancement of Structured Information Standards (OASIS)).

13.2.4 SEC-CF Architecture and Technical Specifications

SEC-CF Architecture specification [SECCF AD] defines how to (re)use both the architectural entities (e.g. Security Gateways, etc.) and security specifications (e.g. protocol profiles) when developing new OMA enablers. The first version of the SEC-CF specifies security functionality for OMA enablers that are based on a client-server operational model. The client entity is generally implemented in some resource (e.g. application, the OMA enabler, etc.) that can reside in the network or on a mobile terminal. The server entity is likely to be the part of an

OMA enabler such as location servers, charging servers, etc. which resides somewhere in the network. The architecture in the current phase of the work does not cover operational models other than client-server operational model (e.g. does not cover a peer-to-peer operational model).

13.2.4.1 SEC-CF in the OMA Service Environment

SEC-CF Architecture provides a common set of security mechanisms that support multiple deployment options for OMA enablers in the OSE. The rationale behind this security architecture is to avoid, where possible, duplication of security efforts for each OMA enabler that requires security functionality. Figure 13.2 provides a mapping of the SEC-CF enabler to an OSE architectural diagram.

This conceptual diagram is agreeable at this stage to most directly contributing to, or closely monitoring the work on SEC-CF in OMA SEC. This is mainly the case because it allows multiple interpretations, at a time where the final architecture is still work in progress and needs significant ongoing efforts and collaboration from all parties. As you notice in Figure 13.2, one interpretation could be that an application issues a request via its I0+P interface to one of the enablers, which in turn may (in some cases must) use some of the SEC-CF capabilities, through tight integration. However, another possible interpretation is that SEC-CF should expose I0 interfaces that an application (or any other resource) can invoke, like any other OMA enabler. Some in OMA think this is how far we need to advance. This would then allow de-coupling of some security functions from a tight integration with other enablers, and provide support for an architectural model consistent

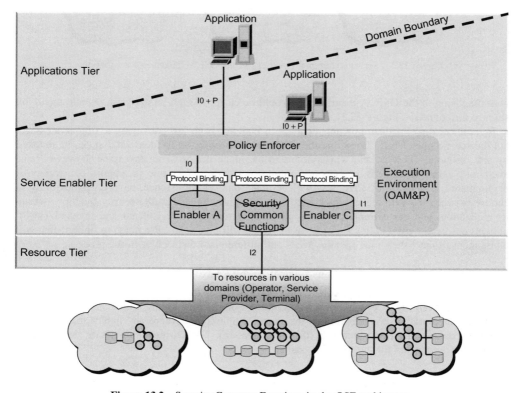

Figure 13.2   Security Common Functions in the OSE architecture

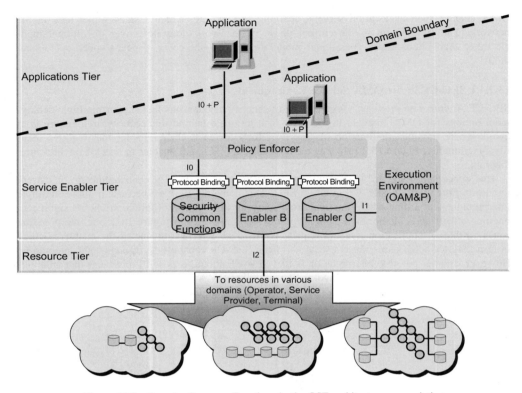

Figure 13.3   Security Common Functions in the OSE architecture – a variation

with the vision of the OSE. A diagram that would be closer to such interpretation would then look slightly different (see Figure 13.3).

In essence, the two diagrams are identical in content. Both are conveying a similar message, but the second one clearly shows that the SEC enabler exposes an I0 interface that can be invoked by any resource. There is, and will continue to be, much debate about this issue; however, once everybody agrees that this is a conceptual architectural view, which allows supporting a variety of deployments, it is likely that progress will be made quicker. In essence, having the flexibility to choose between the extreme in which each enabler tightly integrates all security functions within its realization, and the extreme in which all security functions are isolated and invoked via SP policies enforced by the Policy Enforcer in the OSE, will give each SP a range of options that will allow them to meet their own specific needs and differentiate themselves in the process.

13.2.4.2 Security Common Functions Logical Architecture

SEC-CF consists of architectural components and interfaces to such SEC-CF components, and/or interfaces between SEC-CF components and other resources (see Figure 13.4).

The architectural diagram represents the more complex case where an enabler may be either within or outside the home network (the SP's domain). The current architecture defines three functional components for the SEC-CF enabler:

- The Security Agent (SECA): This component must be included in an application, enabler, or other resource that wants to interact with an OMA enabler. In many cases, SECA is integrated

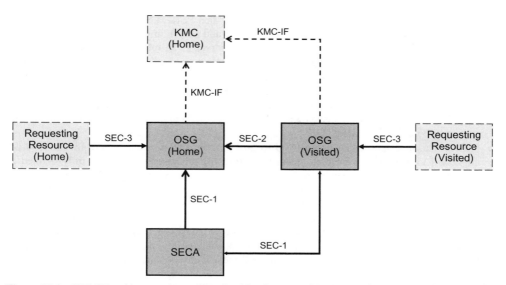

Figure 13.4 SEC-CF architecture for enablers in either home or visited network. Reproduced by Permission of the Open Mobile Alliance Ltd.

into a device that includes a removable security container such as (USIM/RUIM), but it could also be integrated into an application server that invokes other application servers, if security credentials can be stored in a secure manner. In general, the SECA acts on behalf of the user and all identifiers in the SECA are bound to the user (subscriber) identities. In cases where SECA is implemented on application servers, SECA can represent either the subscriber (on behalf of the user) or the application server itself. Device identifiers are not used within the security context of this version of the SEC-CF.

- The OMA Security Gateway (OSG): This component provides security services such as authentication, encryption, and integrity protection for OMA enablers that make use of the SEC-CF. The OSG can be fully integrated into the enabler itself or it can be deployed as a separate standalone component (AP) that can provide services to a number of enablers that can be reached via an OSG.
- The KMC: This component provides the necessary security keys to the OSG. KMC can also be integrated into the OSG. This version of SEC-CF only defines a KMC based on 3GPP (Generic Bootstrapping Architecture (GBA)) if it is not integrated into the OSG.

The following interfaces are defined between the SEC-CF components and other resources:

- SEC-1: This interface is exposed by the OSG, supporting the SECA-OSG client-server operational model. In this phase, SEC-1 interface will only provide support for the TCP/IP transport protocol. When OSG is integrated in an enabler, the enabler may choose to use a higher level application specific protocol to be implemented over TCP in a Client-Server model for communications with the SECA, but the protocol selected will be secured using the security mechanisms implemented by SEC-1; security services for this interface are implemented at the transport and application layers. This interface is an I0 interface in the OSE [OSE AD] architecture. This interface must support at least TLS for transport layer security to provide authentication of the OSG to the SECA. In case the OMA enabler protocol uses HTTP, then HTTP Digest must also be used to provide authentication of the SECA to the OSG. If the OMA Enabler does not use

HTTP as the application protocol for this interface, then PSK-TLS must be supported in order to provide mutual authentication between the OSG and SECA in the transport layer.

- SEC-2: This interface is exposed by the OSG and serves as an interface to another OSG. This interface can be used for distributed enabler deployments when the SECA wants to communicate to an OMA enabler in a visited network via the home OSG. Alternatively, SEC-2 can be used to secure communications between both application servers that have integrated OSGs. This interface is an I0 interface in the OSE architecture. This interface must support at least TLS [RFC 2246] and should also support IPSec [RFC 2401] in tunnel mode with confidentiality and integrity protection [RFC 2406].
- SEC-3: This interface connects an OSG to an OMA enabler in cases where the OSG is not integrated into the OMA enabler. Security features of this interface are not fully defined as part of the SEC-CF architecture as each OMA enabler can implement SEC-3 based on the enabler-specific protocols. This interface appears as an I0 interface in the OSE architecture, and is named as though it is a SEC-CF interface, but in fact it is not defined in this version of SEC-CF, and each OMA enabler can use its own specific protocol or APIs (if OSG is integrated to the enabler) in order to interface with the OSG. The use of SEC-3 may be a naming glitch, or an indication that there is hope for it to be specified at some point. Since the SEC-CF Architecture Document is yet to be approved, this issue will most likely be addressed at some point.

In addition to the interfaces described above, the architecture also relies on the Key Management Centre Interface (KMC-IF) interface. This interface is exposed by the KMC component, and supports OSG communications to the KMC in cases where the OSG is not fully integrated with a KMC. This interface is an I2 interface in the OSE architecture, not specified as part of this enabler. For 3GPP-based implementations this interface corresponds to the Zn interface defined in GBA defined in 3GPP and 3GPP2 specifications.

13.2.4.3 Logical Flows for SEC-CF

The typical flow is the one represented in Figure 13.5. A request toward an enabler will require authentication, which is performed via an AP function implemented in the OSG. The authentication function could also be integrated with the targeted OMA enabler, but logically it is a separate function.

A SECA client is sending a request to an OMA enabler (flow 1). The request is intercepted by the OSG, who, using the SECA resource identifier recognized in the request, is requesting and obtaining authentication credentials from the KMC (flow 2, 3), then issues an authentication challenge to SECA (flow 4). SECA provides its authentication credentials (flow 5), which the OSG validates against those previously obtained from the KMC. If they match, authentication succeeds (flow 6), and the OSG will bind the requestor ID to the channel, and ensure the integrity of the channel by using encryption. The SECA will re-issue its request toward the OMA target enabler (flow 7). Having authenticated the requestor, OSG will forward this request to the OMA target enabler (flow 8) potentially including additional information about the identified requestor (e.g. additional identity information obtained in flows 2, 3). Upon receiving a request from an authenticated source, the OMA target enabler processes the request and returns the processing results (flow 9) to the OSG, which in turn forwards the response to the SECA (flow 10).

A variation of this flow (not represented in a figure) supports the case where the OMA target enabler notifies the SECA (through a secure trigger request initiated by the OMA target enabler) that SECA needs to send an OMA target enabler request. Once the secure trigger notification is delivered to the SECA client, the flows are similar with the ones described.

13.2.5 SEC-CF Technical Specifications

Now that we have defined the architectural elements and the interfaces they support, we can take it to the next level and introduce the SEC-CF technical specifications.

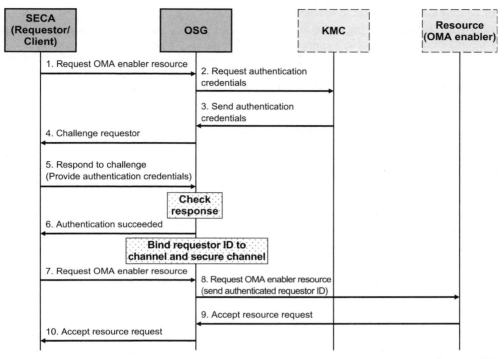

Figure 13.5 SECA initiated authentication via OSG. Reproduced by Permission of the Open Mobile Alliance Ltd.

13.2.5.1 OMA TLS Profile

TLS [RFC 2246] provides confidentiality and integrity protection at the transport layer, via a secure and reliable transport mechanism between two communicating parties. TLS provides multiple optional features.

In order to avoid potential interoperability issues caused by the selection of different options from the features supported by the TLS Protocol, an OMA TLS Profile specification is provided. Since the OMA TLS Profile is a specified subset of TLS 1.0 [RFC 2246] specifications, all OMA TLS Profile compliant implementations must also conform to TLS 1.0 specifications. This specification profiles a particular implementation of TLS 1.0 and other relevant specifications that can be used with TLS 1.0 such as PSK-TLS.

The OMA TLS Profile specifies the following:

- Supported Cipher Suites for TLS and for PSK-TLS are available for both client and server.
- 'Session Resume' must be supported by both client and server.
- 'Server Authentication' must be supported by both client and server.
- 'Client Authentication' should be (is recommended to be) supported by the server. For this situation, OMA TLS Profile specifies the certificate type supported.
- 'Client Authentication' may be (is optionally) supported by the client. For this situation, OMA TLS Profile specifies the certificate type supported.
- TLS tunneling [RFC 2817] via HTTP proxies is supported, and profiles the TLS tunneling for OMA Enablers.

For complete details, see [TLS Profile TS].

13.2.5.2 SEC-CF Technical Specification: OMA GBA Profile

The GBA [3GPP TS 33.220][3GPP2 S.S0109] provides a secure and reliable method to bootstrap a security association between a client and a server, using long-term security associations that are stored in a tamper resistant module (typically a smart card or a Universal Integrated Circuit Card (UICC)) in the client, and in a central network element (e.g. a Home Location Registry (HLR)) or in the Home Subscriber System (HSS) of a mobile network operator (MNO). Based on long-term security associations, short-term GBA credentials are created during a bootstrapping procedure. Those credentials can then be used between the client and the server.

The OMA GBA Profile specification [GBA Profile TS] provides a common profile of GBA that can be used by all OMA enablers, in order to avoid potential interoperability issues, and the need to re-define such profiles for each individual enabler's use. OMA GBA Profile is based on the 3GPP GBA [3GPP TS 33.220] and [3GPP2 S.S0109] specifications. Since the OMA GBA Profile is a specified subset of the 3GPP GBA, all OMA compliant implementations specification must also conform to the 3GPP GBA specification set. OMA GBA Profile specifies a particular implementation of 3GPP GBA and other relevant specifications that can be used with GBA such as Digest authentication [RFC 2617] and PSK-TLS [RFC 4279].

The OMA GBA Profile specifies the following:

- The mandatory list of supported bootstrapping mechanisms by the client.
- The server must be able to use GBA credentials established using any of the mandatory list of bootstrapping mechanisms.
- How to support inter-operator Generic Authentication Architecture (GAA), utilizing 3GPP GBA, respectively 3GPP2 GBA. Inter-operator GAA ensures that if the Network Application Function (NAF) operates in a different network than a subscriber's home network, the 'foreign' NAF is able to request GBA credentials from subscriber's home Bootstrapping Server Function (BSF) across operator boundaries.
- If the client and the server use GBA in Digest authentication [RFC 2617], the client and the server must comply with the procedures defined in [3GPP TS 33.220] and [3GPP TS 24.109].
- If the client and the server use GBA in HTTPS over TLS with Digest authentication, the client and the server must comply with the procedures defined in [3GPP TS 33.222] and [3GPP TS 24.109].
- If the client and the server use GBA in PSK-TLS, the client and the server *must* comply with the procedures defined in [3GPP TS 33.222] and [3GPP TS 24.109].

13.3   SEC-CF Salient Points

As was mentioned in previous sections, the SEC-CF specifications have their roots in IETF and 3GPP, hence they are very consistent with the 3GPP security architecture. In most cases, this also translates into a similar statement that can be made to be consistent with 3GPP2 security architecture (in particular, the 3GPP security architecture supports the 3GPP IP Multimedia Subsystem (IMS) capabilities, and the 3GPP2 security architecture supports the Multimedia Domain (MMD) capabilities).

SECA is a component whose realization resides in a device or an application server, and interfaces with the OSG, while also communicating with removable security tokens. The SECA ensures that unique identities are bound to the subscriber, and while it may also support a unique device identity, the SEC-CF does not mandate the latter. While not being part of the specifications, it is also expected that the SECA can access secure non-volatile memory for security credentials (e.g. keys) and can perform authentication, authorization, confidentiality, integrity protection functions, as well as optionally denial of service (DoS) protection function. As discussed earlier, it communicates with OSG in the home network or in a visited network. In the case of 3GPP deployments, the

SECA interfaces with removable security tokens such as the USIM in the case of supporting 3GPP deployments, and the RUIM in the case of supporting 3GPP2 deployments.

Another slight difference is evident through the existence of the OMA GBA Profile, indicating OMA specification support for the 3GPP GBA set of specifications. There is no equivalent OMA security profile in support of the 3GPP2 domain. That implies that the KMC has a well-specified way in OMA to support key management to the SECA in the case of SECA realizations in 3GPP, but an equivalent specified support of key management for SECA realizations in 3GPP2 does not exist yet.

13.3.1 Divergent Views and their Resolution

There are not many divergent views amongst the security experts in OMA SEC. However, as discussed in the earlier sections, there seems to be different expectations on the set of SEC-CF functions, and in particular the I0 exposed interfaces to access those functions. It is truly too early to tell whether this is just a matter of evolution, need for additional resources and contributions, and a meeting of the minds of security conscious principals from different segments of the industry, or if this is rather a sign of a serious impasse. In principle, SEC-CF has defined I0 interfaces, but likely not at the granularity and expected convenience for applications, which should be able to interface at a higher layer than protocols such as TLS. There is clearly a disconnection here that will be addressed sooner or later as the pressure of building applications that securely use SP enablers starts to build up. While OMA does not favor any particular realization, it has started and will continue to face the reality that many applications that are being developed today are realized using Web Services technology (see OWSER, Chapter 11), and may soon be partly conforming to newer paradigms (e.g. the impact of Web 2.0 is yet to be fully understood), and that implies being sensitive to security models that are synergistic with newer realization technologies. Security models as well as security-related specifications that support Web Services realizations are in many respects different from those supported by the current OMA SEC-CF. The resolution of this issue is somewhere in OMA's future, and unfortunately, unlikely to be fully understood, let alone settled, before this book will be published.

13.4   Impact of Specifications on the Industry

The current SEC-CF specifications will have a positive, but not dramatic effect on the industry, since no new protocols or security models are being specified as of yet. OMA SEC-CF are proving that the OMA security experts are taking a pragmatic approach of first creating a basic framework in which OMA enablers can inter-operate with a consistent level of security amongst themselves and with external resources. The OMA TLS and OMA GBA profiles specifications, as well as the other SEC-CF technical specifications, planned to be delivered, will help avoid interoperability issues between different realizations of OMA enablers and other resources and should, in general, reduce the amount of work in deciding on choices for OMA enablers and their realizations. The real question, however, remains about what the future phases of SEC-CF may bring in terms of resolving the different views regarding what other SEC-CF interfaces are needed and how to expose them. That may be addressed as part of solving yet a much larger issue – the need for a more complete and complex security model that addresses the security issues in converged networks and the security issues in services and applications that need to run over such converged networks, across heterogeneous environments, platforms from different vendors, and across corporate boundaries and network operator domains. It is yet questionable if such over-arching issues will be addressed in organizations such as the IETF, 3GPP or 3GPP2, or OASIS. OMA seems to be one of the few standards fora with an explicit mission of ensuring that specifications are neutral with respect to underlying networks and realization technologies, and as such the forum where specifications from other standards fora find a home where they can be looked at in concert, profiled appropriately and made available as a more encompassing framework.

13.4.1 Impact on Service Providers

SP requirements are driven, at least partly, by their customers: the individual consumers and the corporations that use SP services. Those requirements include the need to continuously improve security measures to combat malicious traffic, viruses, worms, or attempts to 'phish' or 'pharm'. The constant threats for services that have been deployed need monitoring and require maintenance, as the type and level of security threats seem to increase with every new service deployed (and the customers have indeed a voracious appetite for new services). That requires SPs to be increasingly more responsible for the endpoint behavior, and it is part of the responsibilities of being in this market. On the other hand, SPs (in particular those that are network operators) are painfully aware of the costs involved with constantly deploying new solutions, in particular, if that requires new customer premises dedicated equipment or network topologies to be massively reworked, but even if those costs are only involving less drastic changes such as encryption algorithms, key management mechanisms, or support for new authentication credentials. The promise of openness that the Internet has brought, and the initial promise of implicit trust in digital technologies has changed to an impression of massive distrust of the Internet, arbitrated by security policies at every step, and inspections of every packet. From this angle, today's reality on the ground seems to imply that security aspects have to be pervasive, and cannot be delegated to a single network appliance. This is consistent with the approach that 3GPP and 3GPP2 standards fora are taking in their security model, and is confirmed by the overall endorsement that OMA security experts gave to those security models through the SEC-CF specifications. The current approach in those security models is that an SP cannot take any chances. At the same time, given the costs involved, many SPs are considering switching to a model with a single security appliance. In reality, lots of chances are taken, since it is only a question of how much one wants to spend to offset the risk.

Looking purely from the OMA security specifications perspective, SPs should welcome the profiling of IETF and 3GPP specifications as a productivity improvement for OMA specifications writers, for vendors, and ultimately for themselves, since they help streamline the Request for Proposals (RFPs) that they issue to different vendors. The current specifications have the calming effect that they are not introducing turmoil, at a time when SPs may not be convinced that significant changes can be absorbed, be it for lack of proof of validity, or lack of proof of cost effectiveness, or both. However, we would not be totally surprised to see the SPs being the ones starting to push for new security models that can offer similar or better security than the overall security available through today's security models, if significant Capital Expenditure (CAPEX) and Operational Expenditure (OPEX) savings can be derived.

The SCWS specifications are certainly a nice addition for the SPs allowing network operators to improve the user experience when using network operator services in the smart card (e.g. allowing for Internet browsing-like experience when using services offered by network operators via smart cards for their mobile subscribers). Without taking anything away from the benefits offered by implementing the SWCS specification, this could rather be considered a quality-of-experience improvement, rather than a security improvement.

13.4.2 Impact on Vendors

Since the OMA security specifications do not introduce any new security specifications, but rather clarify expectations of use of existing specifications for interactions involving OMA enablers, the vendors that incorporate security functions in their products or interface with such security functions in other vendors' products, should be pleased with the current status quo. Vendors that are pushing the envelope in terms of new security specifications are not likely to do so in the OMA standards forum, but in IETF, or 3GPP or 3GPP2.

That said, we may see a category of vendors with increased interest in resolving application-level security issues in interfacing with networks while avoiding awareness of specific network protocols, and embracing security models that better fit new paradigms in the development of services and applications. Nobody denies that different (apparently conflicting, in reality complementing) views exist in the industry with respect to security models, and it is only a matter of time before those will be reconciled. An honest high-level look at the security specifications landscape will, however, conclude that there is, indeed, a stringent need for a security framework that combines the best of security specifications developed in standards bodies focused on Web Services (e.g. OASIS, Liberty Alliance Project, and W3C) with those developed in standard bodies focused on telecommunication networks (e.g. IETF, 3GPP, 3GPP2).

13.4.3 Impact on Consumer Market

Unlike as in the case of other enablers related to user information security (see Global Permissions Management, Chapter 22), the individual consumers won't directly feel the impact of the OMA SEC-CF specifications in their current rendition, since the SEC-CF specifications do not change the way the consumers access or use the services they subscribe to. Since access to those services is via some application, the most change an individual consumer would experience is the need to download a new application, when the latter may have changed because of adapting to one of the OMA security profiles. A significant impact in terms of blending services may have to wait until a more dramatic change in the security model and the security specifications occurs. When it comes to the SCWS specifications, these are nice additions in terms of improving the quality-of-experience for the individual consumers. The SCWS specifications allow the consumers that use WAP Browsers to capitalize on the WAP Browser's rich features when accessing smart-card-based operator services (e.g. access to network operators FAQ, whether online or off-line) or security-oriented services requiring keys that are stored in the smart card.

13.4.4 Impact on Corporate Market

The corporate market won't feel the impact of the OMA SEC-CF specifications in their current rendition, since they do not challenge or improve the way the corporations currently access and use their services. As OMA enablers start aligning with those specifications, using the guidelines and profiles offered, and as vendors start providing compliant implementations, the impact will be the usual impact of deployment and/or use of any new enabler. The use of such enablers beyond the corporate boundaries is likely to be completely hidden by applications. As corporations are increasingly looking forward to deploy improved collaboration applications and services, they are starting to pay more attention to Web Services as a technology for realization of such projects. This seems to point to a future where we focus not only on connecting applications in a pre-agreed sequence, but rather count on an environment in which a completely new service configuration may be instantiated at any point in time. For such a future to become a reality, security issues need to be identified and resolved before any corporation would venture into such architectures beyond their own boundaries. Pressure for new security models and security specifications to support this paradigm is building up very gradually, since the SOA paradigm has to be first proven within easier-to-secure corporate boundaries, where all security aspects are under a single entity's control, before even considering extending it beyond them. That said, it is only a matter of time until the OMA SEC WG, along with other standards fora will increase efforts in that direction.

As in the consumer market, the SCWS specifications are a nice addition for corporate users as well, since ultimately they are individual consumers of services to which they have access. It will be perceived as an improved quality-of-experience, rather than better security protection.

13.4.5 Impact on Other Specifications

The net effect of the current OMA security specifications (in particular, OMA TLS and OMA GBA profiles) is that it clarifies what other OMA enablers should use when conducting secure exchanges with other resources (e.g. OWSER, Chapter 11). What is less clear is whether this is a temporary, or long-lasting approach, or whether the short-term decisions may be complemented with other long-lasting decisions from OMA security. This will be further explored in the next section.

13.5   Specifications Evolution and Future Direction

The current SEC-CF specifications endorse the letter of the OSE (they have identified some I0 interfaces), but at least some would say they have a long way to go to endorse the spirit of the OSE – which is to encourage avoidance of vertical integrations to the largest extent possible. What is that largest extent, and what is possible, remain as some of the questions. Can all security mechanisms be logically isolated, grouped, and exposed in such a manner that vertical integration in each OMA enabler is no longer necessary, let alone mandated? This is likely to evolve gradually, and possibly moving toward that extreme, but only as proof is obtained that the vertical integration of secure functions in each OMA enabler is replaceable with a completely equivalent singe re-usable protection component offering protection mechanisms (ideally offering better protection) that is more cost effective to deploy and maintain. While such an approach has been proven to work on a smaller scale in enterprises, to make it work in the OSE would certainly imply some changes to the security model. Projecting changes that will resolve the current differences of opinions with respect to the I0 interfaces that should be exposed by security functions is a difficult and risky proposition. Yet, even when that is addressed, it is still likely to be considered less than what the industry expects, when faced with a variety of security problems and an almost equal range of different solutions to those problems, some of them proprietary, not completely compliant to standards, and offered by a single vendor. Single sign-on specifications based on Radio-Frequency Identification (RFID), and retinas, and fingerprints are still not in the mainstream, and not because the technology does not exist, but rather because we would like to see such solutions brought to market by a multitude of companies, before embracing them. While the industry is also working on standards for federated trust (see also Chapter 11), there are still multiple competing standards that propose different federation schemas. Another aspect of security specifications that still has a long way to go is how to address issues that come to fore by the emergence of new applications and services realized through Web Services or Web 2.0 technologies. Security is usually driven by a company's architecture and business model, so a realization through Web Services in itself should not be equated to a drastic need for change in the existing security model, if all that is desired is a replacement of existing technology realization. The real issue lies, however, in the fact that SOA and its contemporary realization through Web Services technology bring upon a new level of openness, possibilities for collaboration and creation of new services. Openness to new services, however, comes with the inherent risk of opening new security holes. In order for the promise of Web Services to become a reality, more complete security models and security specifications will have to resolve thorny issues, such as authentication, identity management, trust, confidentiality, and integrity that applications face when working across heterogeneous platforms from different vendors and across different network domains. Tracing, diagnosing, and responding to attacks across different web servers, applications, services, and network domains is a very complex issue, without complete support in specifications so far. The conclusion is that there is a long and not easy to travel road ahead for OMA security, more resources need to be applied in working those issues, and expectations have to be constantly managed.

13.6   Summary

This chapter provides an overview of the OMA security specifications; it explains the rationale for the approach taken by OMA SEC WG, as well as what additional work may lie ahead of the group. Security-related specifications in other standards continue to evolve, in particular those related to Web Services technology. As a response to existing and new security threats, new industry solutions for security protection emerge all the time. The need to deploy more new services and applications that work across company boundaries and network domains will be a main catalyst for overall changes, but in particular to security-related changes. All these factors will eventually determine the need and timing for addressing such changes and improvements in the OMA security specifications; like for any other enabler, the market will dictate when that time has arrived.

Part III

Selected OMA Service Enablers

We started this book by articulating the overall approach and laying some of the ground work by focusing on the horizontal topics. We are now going to shift gears, bump it up a level. This part of the book will provide detailed descriptions of a selection of OMA enablers, so prepare for more technospeak. We have carefully selected a range of OMA service enablers, however there is no bulletproof strategy to guide such a selection. Ultimately, the market will decide on the winners, each of these enablers is given a chance to thrive. They will either win their place or die of neglect.

In Chapter 14 the Presence and Group Management enablers are discussed. The Push-to-talk over Cellular enabler will be the topic of Chapter 15. Mobile e-mail is covered in Chapter 16. Chapter 17 describes the Charging enabler. Chapter 18 provides a perspective on Device Management enablers. Chapter 19 addresses the Digital Rights Management enabler. Chapter 20 focuses on Mobile Broadcast, the first of the Browser and Content enablers described in the book, while the Dynamic Content Delivery enabler is covered in Chapter 21. Global Permissions Management enabler is the focus of Chapter 22, and Categorization Based Content Screening takes center stage in Chapter 23. The Game Services enabler is the subject of Chapter 24. Chapter 25 deals with the Location enabler. Remaining BAC topics are accumulated in Chapter 26 on the Mobile Application Environment. And finally, tackled in different OMA Working Groups, a few selected topics that are still very much work-in-progress at the time we wrote the book, have been grouped together in Chapter 27. These 'Recent Topics' cover General Service Subscription Management, Device Profile Evolution, Converged IP Messaging, and Mobile Advertising.

The Open Mobile Alliance   M. Brenner and M. Unmehopa
© 2008 Alcatel-Lucent. All Rights Reserved

Part III

Selected OMA
Service Enablers

14

The Presence and List Management Enablers

Alice loved to use Instant Messaging (IM). After signing up with Freedom Wireless, her cellular communications provider, she discovered that now she had the same capability from her handset as well. She could manage multiple lists of contacts (aka buddies) and keep this 'buddy list' synchronized across her handset and desktop clients. And she would be notified whenever her friends connected or disconnected from the network. Rich media support over IM meant she could send one or more of her 'buddies' not just plain text, but also voice clips, pictures, etc. 'I'm really getting hooked on Presence', she told herself, 'it all started with IM as an application that I used every day, and now, I find myself using buddy presence and availability information to do all kinds of things – whether to call someone or leave them a voicemail instead or just to check if Charlie wants to play chess with me if he's free.'

14.1 Presence – What is it?

The term presence means different things to different people. But in this book, when we talk of presence, we refer to the 'connectedness' of the user or, more specifically, of one or more of the user's devices to the network.

Presence has several applications, and as such, is considered and marketed as a powerful technology enabler, more so than as an independent technology in its own right. Alice's experience in the above vignette underscores this point. Today she uses presence as an enabler for IM, but the service provider seems to be tagging on more applications she can invoke from within a presence context, and this 'stickiness' is not easy for users to resist. And the stickier the experience, the easier it is for service providers to attract new subscribers, and the more reluctant existing subscribers would be to change carriers.

In this chapter, we start out by exploring what presence is and what some of its applications are, then briefly agree on the vocabulary we will need for further elaboration, discuss the standards relating to this field, reference architectures, a simple deployment configuration, and finally some advanced topics for interested readers. Since this is a book about Open Mobile Alliance (OMA) enablers, the primary focus of discussion will be OMA specifications, though we will first introduce building blocks that the OMA specifications rely on, to present a more complete picture.

Presence and Availability are two distinct but related notions. As previously stated, the former indicates whether a user is connected to the network, while the latter states her preferences for being contacted, and her interest in engaging in communication with others over particular channels. For

The Open Mobile Alliance   M. Brenner and M. Unmehopa
© 2008 Alcatel-Lucent. All Rights Reserved

example, Alice may be 'present' in that she is connected with her mobile phone network, and she may indicate availability for communication with Bob (her friend from work) via IM or 'texting', Carol (her neighbor) via voice, Doug (her husband) via any mode available, and be unreachable to Ed (her boss) after 5 PM on weekdays and on weekends. These two complementary notions play an important role in the use of this enabler, as we shall see in what follows.

14.2   A Constructionist View of Presence Architectures

IETF's 'A Model for Presence and Instant Messaging' [RFC 2778] and 'Instant Messaging/Presence Protocol Requirements' [RFC 2779] provide a description of some of the requirements typical presence standards attempt to fulfill as they define reference architectures and protocols. Different standards bodies (e.g. the Internet Engineering Task Force (IETF) [IETF][find_RFCs], 3GPP [3GPP][3GPP_specs], Parlay [Parlay], etc.) sometimes use different terms for the same entities. In some cases, standards bodies support liaisons with other standards bodies to ensure a compatibility of direction, or co-evolution of working documents. A generic way of how this is achieved between the IETF and OMA standards bodies is outlined in RFC 3975 [RFC 3975]. Here, we study simpler protocol-independent definitions with a view to utilizing the defined terms in the sections that follow. Familiarity with these terms would enable the reader to effortlessly pick up the details of various specifications even if there are slight differences in the meanings associated with these in the various standards bodies.

14.2.1 Basic Elements

A *presentity* is an entity whose presence is of interest to other entities (presence + entity = presentity). From the definition it follows that the network can either derive the presence of the presentity by some means, or that the presentity is able to register its changes of presence or availability information with the network. The former is called 'implicit presence' and the latter is 'explicit presence'. In the example above, Alice, or rather her device, would be a presentity. The act of a user or device providing explicit presence information to the system is referred to as 'presence state publication' and the user/device is said to have published her/its presence status.

Presence could include various kinds of information (called 'presence aspects'):

1. Whether a terminal or agent is connected to the network at a particular time.
2. Whether the terminal is involved in a call or session at that time.
3. The availability of a particular capability at the terminal, or the ability or willingness of the user to engage in communication via that capability, and user information such as mood or place-type (e.g. 'at home', 'in the office', 'on the way to work', etc.).
4. The location of the terminal either in terms of coarse granularity location such as cell-ID, cell sector etc., or in terms of geographical co-ordinates, etc.

The astute reader will note that in the above we refer to terminals when we talk about presence. With cellular technology, where a cell-phone is a very personal thing, presence of a cell-phone equates with the presence of the associated user. The degree of association may vary in other networks. For example, in wired networks, the status of a terminal might represent whether the phone is in use in an apartment for example, and doesn't necessarily represent which of the people who live there might be using it.

Some standards refer to Alice as a 'principal' that is represented by her device in the network. Others refer to Alice as an 'identity' and to her device as an 'agent'. Standards vocabulary in use in the various standards bodies tends to have overlapped meaning for terms in many cases, so we will use the simple terminology we define here, which we hope will enable the user to understand enough to be able to pick up and associate terminology from specific standards of interest, to the concepts that we cover in this section.

A *watcher* is an entity that is interested in the presence of presentities. A more generic definition of watchers might indicate that these are entities that watch 'a resource of interest'. This is because, in the broader sense, watchers may watch presentities, watchers watching them (e.g. Alice wants to know who is watching her at any time, and receives updates when new watchers sign-on to or off from the system), or documents they have access to (i.e. be notified of changes to these documents). These scenarios are supported over different 'event packages', described later in the chapter. So, for example, if Bob were 'watching' for updates or status changes to Alice's presence, then Bob would be a watcher of Alice. Watchers can be other users in the system or simply programs that gather up presence update information in order to be able to provide value. For instance, Alice may have signed up with a weather application that would download a weather forecast to her phone every morning at 8 a.m., Central European Time. Such an application may watch for Alice's presence (or more specifically, her location), and push a relevant forecast of her current area to her handset.

Another important point to note is that Alice may watch Bob's presence if Bob is a contact in her buddy list and has authorized Alice access to his presence status. Simultaneously, Bob may also watch Alice if similar conditions hold in the other direction. Thus, in this scenario, Alice is a watcher and Bob is a presentity in the first case, whereas their roles are reversed in the second. In other words, entities in the system may be presentities, or watchers, or both, or neither, at any given point in time.

The standards define various types of watchers:

1. A *fetcher* is a watcher that performs a simple fetch of presentity status information through a query. The response contains the information being sought.
2. A *poller* is a watcher that issues fetch requests at periodic intervals. Polling may be implemented either through a poll request followed by multiple reports till the request is revoked by the initiator (server-side polling) or by having the initiator issue periodic fetch requests (client-side polling). Different standards support different capabilities – e.g. Parlay explicitly supports periodic location reports through server-side polling, while any standard that supports fetching can be made to support polling from a client perspective with changes to client service logic. The astute reader will note that server-side polling tends to be somewhat more efficient than the other kind.
3. A *subscribed watcher* is the most sophisticated kind of watcher and works by subscribing to status updates pertaining to presentities of interest. Whenever a presentity's status changes, all authorized watchers that have registered an interest in that presentity are provided with updates in terms of asynchronous notifications.

14.2.2 Presence Service Interfaces and the Resource List Server

A Presence Server (PS) is a network entity that gathers presence from various presentities and makes it available to authorized and interested watchers. Thus, it carries out two operations – those of collection and dissemination of presence information. The interfaces over which presentity status updates are received (e.g. user publishes the update, or implicit presence is derived from a network element) are typically called 'presentity interfaces', while those over which interactions with watchers take place (e.g. watcher subscriptions are received and processed, watcher performs fetch or receives a notification event) are referred to as 'watcher interfaces'.

PSs may be able to support watcher subscriptions on either a simple contact identity (i.e. an address that uniquely identifies a presentity within a network context, e.g. alice_kr@freedomwireless .net), or on a unique list identity where this binds to a document that contains multiple unique contact identities (alice_friend_list007@freedomwireless.net, where this list contains bob_k@freedomwireless.net, charlie_c@freedomwireless.net, and dan_e@freedomwireless.net, each a unique handle within the freedomwireless.net domain). Addresses of the form username@domain are typically referred to as Uniform Resource Identifiers (URIs). Typically, these are preceded by a protocol

ID and a ':' as in sip:alice@freedomwireless.net. In the latter case, the URI is called a 'Session Initiation Protocol (SIP) URI'. Many other types of protocol-specific URIs also exist.

In the latter case, where the PS is able to process presence subscriptions on a list identifier, it is sometimes called a Resource List Server (RLS) (in IETF standards), or a Presence List Server (PLS) (in 3GPP/2 standards), and in this text we shall use those terms interchangeably. Henceforth, when we refer to a PS, we speak of the logical function capable of only the basic contact-level presence reporting capability.

Support for list-based subscriptions offer several advantages, including the following:

1. Improvement of the end-user experience: Alice, or her terminal to be more exact, in the scenario above doesn't have to issue several distinct requests for subscription of the presence states of each of her buddies. A simple subscription on her buddy list suffices.
2. Reduction in messaging between the client and server: This could be critical, particularly, in low bit-rate wireless environments.

However, RLS support also imposes new requirements on the solution context. Now, the watcher entity would also need to maintain and manage the lists of contacts (collectively referred to as 'list management operations'). To facilitate this, another logical function, called the Group List Management Server (GLMS) is defined.

Whenever presence information is distributed to interested, authorized watchers, it is typically encoded in a standards-defined XML-based format. The most widely used document format for this is called Presence Information Data Format (PIDF) and is defined in the IETF. The presentity is able to specify rules or policies to indicate which watchers might be permitted access to which aspects of its total presence information, and under what conditions. When Alice from our example decides to let her boss only have access to her presence information between 9 am and 5 am on weekdays, this is what she is doing. In addition, watchers may also decide what subset of the presentity's presence they want to receive updates on. They do this by setting limits when they subscribe using a construct called 'presence filters'.

14.2.3 Presence Authorization Policies

The standards also define authorization policies. For instance, Alice may decide to allow a certain list of people (or watchers, more generally) to subscribe to her presence information. She does this by adding unique addresses identifying these entities into her 'allow list'. All such parties are considered authorized to access her presence information and are provided with presence updates as they occur. Similarly, if Alice wants to prevent someone from receiving her presence information, she may add them to her 'deny list' and effectively block them from receiving presence updates. Any subscription requests for Alice's presence from people on her deny list would be rejected by the PS.

Two advanced authorization policies are defined – 'polite block' and 'confirm'. 'Polite block' is used when Alice wants to indicate to watchers that request her presence information that she has accepted their request (so as to appear polite), but in reality doesn't want to share any presence updates with them. Presence systems typically indicate Alice as always off-line to watchers she has 'polite blocked', though more advanced PSs might allow Alice to customize her presence appearance to 'polite blocked' watchers.

The 'confirm' disposition is used to support what is also called 'reactive authorization'. In this mode, whenever a watcher on Alice's 'confirm list' makes a subscription request, Alice is notified of this request, at which point she may either approve the request (thereby moving the watcher into her 'allow list'), or deny the request (moving the watcher to her 'deny list'), or, in more advanced implementations, even approve the request for her presence status just that one time (and retain that watcher in her 'confirm list').

One of these dispositions may be marked as a default disposition, in which case this is applied to all new subscription requests if a watcher-specific policy is not already specified. For example, if Alice has a 'confirm' default disposition but has Bob already in her blacklist, Bob's subscription request for Alice's presence is automatically rejected. However, if Charlie subscribes to her presence, and Charlie's identity is not explicitly specified in any of Alice's lists, Alice receives a confirmation request (since her default policy is confirm) and can decide whether to 'allow', 'deny', or 'polite block' Charlie.

All these lists are managed using the List Management protocol that is defined within the standards suite. For IETF standards, this protocol is 'The Extensible Mark-up Language (XML) Configuration Access Protocol (XCAP)' [RFC 4825].

14.2.4 Presence-related Event Packages

In the foregoing, we have discussed how the Presence protocols can be leveraged to support subscriptions to various kinds of events and receive asynchronous notifications from the network on those events. However, we have also described scenarios where different kinds of events are needed. For example, to deliver presence updates to watchers, one needs to permit watchers to subscribe to presence events. Similarly, to enable presentities to receive notifications when new watchers are added, or come online, watcher information (sometimes abbreviated as winfo) event subscriptions need to be supported. And finally, to notify users of list change updates (e.g. Alice calls a customer service representative and has her lists updated, and these later need to propagate to her handset device), a third event set that tracks document changes is needed.

Each of these event sets is called an event package. Standards typically define separate event packages for each function: (contact) presence, list presence, watcher information, and list update notifications (see Section 14.2.9 for details).

14.2.5 Presence Optimizations

Oftentimes, presence-enabled services are deployed in error-prone, low bit-rate network environments such as cell networks. In such cases, shipping large XML documents or using chatty protocols for handset to network interactions can be problematic. To help resolve some of these issues, standards tend to provide for mechanisms that allow for the distribution of partial presence updates and list fragments (e.g. change logs that the client can apply to a local copy to end up with the same document version as that at the server).

Similarly, some protocols (e.g. XML Configuration Access Protocol (XCAP)) re-use the concept of e-tags on documents that serve as markers of the document version. If these are used in conjunction with conditional headers (as in 'get this document from the server only if the entity tags (e-tags) is different from my local copy'), end-to-end traffic could be greatly reduced. These constructs could also be utilized to prevent concurrent list writers from compromising the integrity of the document – to support this, the writer would indicate the update to be made along with the e-tags of the local copy of the document. If the server-side e-tag matches with this, the update would be applied. Otherwise, the update request would be rejected, and the client could download the server version of the document with the latest e-tag and try again.

Other optimizations deal with reducing the frequency or the message size of the presence notifications. This is achieved by throttling or rate-limiting the presence notifications at the server, throttling the publication sources, or by aggregating presence updates in 'discretized' time intervals and zeroing out conflicting updates (e.g. if updates are provided every five minutes, and Alice was online at the beginning of the interval, but then took a call – status busy – and resumed being online at the end of the interval, the net of these events is no change in her status, so watchers need not be notified).

While we have addressed some of the optimizations discussed in standards, various others are also possible, and many tend to be closely guarded secrets that enable vendors to differentiate their products against those of competitors. Since optimizations can be made in processing logic without affecting external interfaces, carefully conceived and implemented optimization mechanisms do not generally negatively impact interoperability.

To sum up, all standards bodies agree on these most basic and generic definitions (though they may be phrased slightly differently in different documents) and functions. Interfaces supported, or required to be supported, by network elements such as the PS may, however, vary widely from one standard to another, or even from one deployment to another (even if the two deployments actually support the same standard). There is a great deal of flexibility offered by the standards when it comes to implementation, especially in terms of the number and type of interfaces supported, which makes it all the more important to ensure seamless interoperability of implementations as well as the inter-connectedness between the PS and other network elements it may communicate with to obtain network-specific presence information tied to various entities.

14.2.6 Presence Standards

By now, it should be apparent to the reader that several Presence standards are extant. Vocabularies and terminology vary from one standards body to another and from one model of the Presence architecture to another. In particular, there are striking differences in the terms used in the 3GPP and IETF views of the world, and terms from both these models shall be explored in upcoming sections. These models are widely used by other standards bodies in their own work – e.g. 3GPP2 specifications [3GPP2][3GPP2_specs] follow the IETF terminology, while the Open Service Access (OSA) [OSA] draws from and uses the base 3GPP vocabulary set. Other specifications like OMA Wireless Village (WV) use their own generic terms and remain model neutral from an architectural standpoint. Since this is a book on OMA specifications, we shall focus mostly on those and only make passing mention of the other standards as required in support of the narrative.

14.2.7 The 'Three-Layer Brick' Model

In order to reconcile the differences between various standards, and to show how the standards relate to one another, the OMA specifications define a reference model informally called the 'Three-Layer Brick' model – this shows how many of the leading standards relate to each other and to the OMA reference model.

Figure 14.1 depicts this reference model. At the lowest layer, there is a single 'brick', namely the IETF, which defines the protocols, how these can be used to support presence information collection and dissemination, list management operations, and the logical components such as the RLS, the GLMS, and the PS. While IETF work is carried out in several working groups including the SIP, the Session Initiation Protocol (SIP) for Instant Messaging and Presence Leveraging Extensions (SIMPLE), and the Extensible Messaging and Presence Protocol (XMPP) (now concluded) Working Groups (WGs), our focus shall be mostly on the SIP/SIMPLE WGs since we are looking at standards through an OMA lens. The IETF also indicates how the end-to-end routing aspects are addressed within a typical SIP-capable network. Some of these aspects are modified slightly in more 'specialized' environments such as IP Multimedia Subsystem (IMS) (see [Camarillo2006], [Poikselka2006]). These are discussed in a later section.

The second layer consists of two 'bricks' – the 3GPP and 3GPP2 standards and reference models that define how the standards are to be used within the Global System for Mobile Communication (GSM) and the GSM-evolved (to Universal Mobile Telecommunications System (UMTS)) environments, and within the Code Division Multiple Access (CDMA) and the CDMA 3G evolution environments, respectively.

The topmost layer is the OMA layer that defines the application-level semantics and guidelines for the use of the various standards. The OMA specifications also define usage scenarios and refinements to the underlying specifications to ensure that different vendor implementations would remain compatible from an end-to-end call flow standpoint.

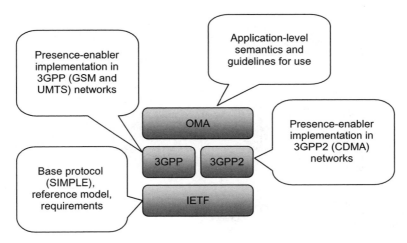

Figure 14.1   The three-layer brick model. Reproduced by Permission of the Open Mobile Alliance Ltd.

Thus, the Three-Layer Brick model defines an overarching structure that relates the most important standards to one other. The upper layers build upon or leverage the lower ones. Now, we look at each of these standards in little more detail. Since a large number of standards form the basis of this topic, as a general rule we will provide highlights in the text, and more details in the tables in Annex A.

14.2.8 The IETF Presence Model and Standards

In the IETF, generic work in presence was first done in the Instant Messaging and Presence Protocol (IMPP) WG, now defunct. IMPP [IMPP] defined the basic IETF model for presence, and generated the two RFCs mentioned earlier, RFC 2778 and RFC 2779, that form the basis for all other protocol-specific presence-related work in the IETF. These RFCs also cover some aspects of the Common Profile for Instant Messaging (CPIM) and the Common Presence Profile (CPP) Framework – the basic capability set defined by the IMPP WG.

Currently, IETF presence work is carried on in two other WGs – SIMPLE [SIMPLE], where the focus is on the use of SIP-based mechanisms in support of presence and IM, and XMPP [XMPP], whose focus is on the use of an XML-based protocol for near real-time messaging and presence.

Both WGs deal with presence and a single application, namely, IM (perhaps the most important and widely used application). However, neither standard requires that compliant servers support both capabilities, but merely that at least one of the two functional sets be implemented in order to be considered compliant.

Both WGs provide support for page mode (disconnected message sets) and session mode (all messages within a session context) IM. SIMPLE does it through the definition of a separate protocol (Message Session Relay Protocol (MSRP)), and XMPP through support for the group-chat and thread mechanisms to track IM sessions. Both support the publishing of presence information, its retrieval either on request or through asynchronous notifications succeeding a subscription (i.e. with subscribed watchers), and group list management (called 'roster management' in XMPP), so they are largely comparable in functionality (see Figure 14.2). Since this is a book on OMA specifications, and the OMA work is more closely tied to IETF SIMPLE standard, we ignore XMPP from this point on in the document, and focus on work efforts within the SIMPLE WG.

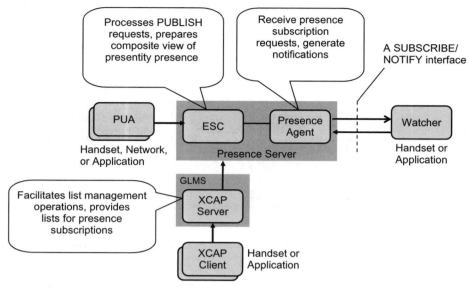

Figure 14.2 XCAP usage for manipulating presence document contents. ESC, Event State Compositor; PUA, Presence User Agent

14.2.9 A Summary of IETF Presence Standards

Presence work is mainly based on IETF standards. A brief summary of the standards defined within the IETF for presence is presented in tables in Annex A. We split this discussion into three parts:

1. In Table 14.1, we summarize base-level specifications from other working groups that are leveraged by IETF SIMPLE as building blocks. This includes such specifications as the SIP protocol, SIP extensions for SUBSCRIBE/NOTIFY, PUBLISH and MESSAGE, and SIP support for content indirection.
2. Next, in Table 14.2, we present the SIMPLE RFCs or proposed standards that outline various currently accepted aspects of how the Presence service may be supported in SIP/SIMPLE.
3. Last, in Table 14.3, we briefly highlight the work-in-progress drafts that are being defined in the SIMPLE working group as of this writing.

It is to be emphasized that this is the view as of this writing. Drafts in the IETF are work-in-progress, and many new ones are introduced, and old ones either moved forward into the RFC track or discarded, from one IETF meeting to the next. There are several IETF meetings each calendar year, so the 'current' view at any time can perhaps be best computed by looking at the appropriate WG page. For SIMPLE, this is located at [SIMPLE].

14.2.10 The 3GPP2 Presence Model and Standards

The 3GPP2 body of standards generally accepts and utilizes the work completed in 3GPP, and then applies these to the CDMA network environment. Presence is one notable exception to the above general rule, for here, 3GPP2 derives its Presence model not from 3GPP (which derived an IMS view of its requirements from the general model specified by the IETF), but instead, directly from the IETF (the 3GPP section explains how the 3GPP standards relate to the IETF ones).

3GPP2 standards for the Presence model and for IM support in mobile network contexts are specified in documents S.R0062-0 v1.0 [3GPP2 S.R0062-0] and S.R0061-0 v1.0 [3GPP2 S.R0061-0], respectively. The Presence model is heavily based on IETF RFCs 2778 and 2779, and lists requirements for privacy, security, accounting, user and operator views of Presence services, etc. The differences between the IETF model and the derived 3GPP2 form are not very pronounced (see Table 14.4 annexed at the end of the book).

14.2.11 The 3GPP Presence Model and Standards

The 3GPP standards define a Presence model in the documents summarized in Table 14.5, annexed at the end of the book. The 3GPP specifications borrow heavily, as do the 3GPP2 specifications, from the IETF standards. Only here, they specify the application of the IETF model to the context defined by the IMS architecture. Thus, the overall architecture picture looks slightly different from that described in the IETF documentation, but conceptually, this can be viewed as one implementation of the concepts outlined in the IETF standards body.

The 3GPP Presence model is depicted in Figure 14.3. This architecture is adapted from 3GPP TS 23.141 [3GPP TS 23.141], which also describes each reference point referred to in the picture. The Presence Network Agent (PNA) aggregates network presence information from network entities. Network presence is actually inferred from the signaling message generated by the network nodes, for example, when a mobile user 'attaches' to a mobile network, Mobile Application Part (MAP) messages are generated to indicate such an event. The Ph, Pi, Pc, Pl, etc. are reference

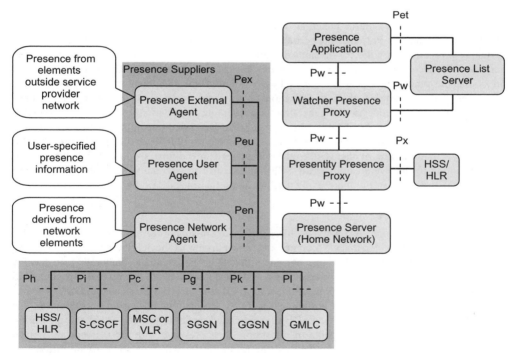

Figure 14.3 3GPP reference architecture to support a Presence service in an IMS environment. 3GPP(tm) TSs and TRs are the property of ARIB, ATIS, ETSI, CCSA, TTA and TTC who jointly own the copyright in them. They are subject to modifications and are therefore provided to you "as is" for information purposes only. Further use is strictly prohibited

points to all network entities from which the PS is able to collect any network-related event that can be translated to a presence event.

The 3GPP standards have not standardized the Pen interface between the PNA and the PS, leaving this open to interpretation. This is why some wireless service providers choose to consider the PNA as being collocated with their network entity, thereby giving them greater flexibility in the interfaces they can demand to be supported via Pen, to the PS. This also explains how service providers can, for instance, demand that a SIP-based protocol be supported between their Authentication, Authorization and Accounting (AAA) server and the vendor's PS implementation. This is still being discussed in standards.

The Peu interface between the Presence User Agent (PUA) and the PS is defined by 3GPP to be a SIP-based protocol, though at the same time, the standard permits the use of multiple other protocols to meet other needs along this interface that SIP may not have accounted for through basic primitives already available within that protocol. PUAs may be network hosted or collocated within the terminals themselves.

The Pex reference point is not constrained to use any specific or single protocol. Standards guidance is that a combination of multiple protocols can be used, but Pex is typically not supported in systems today, and its use will likely only become more prevalent once more PS implementations are deployed and there is a need to share presence information between them.

The Pw reference point is intended to support watcher interfaces and provides for both an active fetch and an asynchronous subscribe/notify model of operation. Information may be filtered appropriately along its path from the PS to the ultimate watcher of this presence information.

The Presentity Presence proxy maps to the Interrogating Call State Control Function (I-CSCF) and the Serving-Call State Control Function (S-CSCF), while the Watcher Presence proxy maps to the Proxy Call State Control Function (P-CSCF) and the Serving-Call State Control Function (S-CSCF). The former Presence proxy helps determine the identity of a PS associated with a particular presentity, provides for the authentication of Watcher Presence proxies, and supports the generation of accounting information for updates to presence information. The Watcher Presence proxy, on the other hand, provides for address resolution and identification of target networks associated with presentities, the authentication of watchers themselves, inter-working Presence protocols for watcher requests, and generation of accounting information for the watcher requests.

The OSA Presence and Availability Management (PAM) Service Capability Feature Application Programming Interface (SCF API) specified in 3GPP TS 29.198-14 [3GPP TS 29.198-14] also comes under the purview of the 3GPP, but as explained in the next section, it is better viewed as contributing to the overall OSA PAM SCF model, since it essentially elaborates the interface reference point defined in Pw more explicitly, but along the lines of a programmatic API.

14.2.12 The OSA PAM SCF Model

The OSA PAM SCF defines its own vocabulary and model in support of presence capabilities. This may be a bit surprising given that OSA comes under the purview of the 3GPP umbrella of standards, but seems to fall into place when one considers that OSA is essentially elaborating on the Pw reference point already defined to be part of the 3GPP IMS architecture. To be more specific, IMS defines support for two kinds of Application Server (AS) entities – a SIP AS and an OSA Gateway that supports OSA API interfaces northbound to OSA applications hosted on an OSA AS. The latter gateway and AS utilize the PAM SCF and associated model to provide presence capabilities.

In the PAM model, devices capable of registering their presence with the network are termed *Agents*, and the people that own the devices (the astute reader will note some subtle differences here with the IETF definition of Principals), are called *Identities*. *Aliases* (pseudonyms) for identity addressing, as well as *Groups* (group addressing) mechanisms are also built in. In addition, PAM client applications are supported by the model, and these are comparable to watchers from the IETF context.

Bindings between agents and identities may be provisioned and modified on the fly through the API. The API also provides applications various capabilities to set and retrieve presence information, including asynchronous notifications on presence status changes, and is roughly analogous in terms of capabilities to those supported by the IETF model. Since the OSA standards are not closely related to the OMA standards, OSA PAM is not covered in detail in this book. The interested reader is referred to [Unmehopa 2006].

Other Parlay-related, but independent, Presence standards also exist. An example of these is Parlay X – which defines Web Services style interfaces to presence and list management capabilities. Readers interested in Parlay X are referred to [Parlay X].

14.3   The OMA Presence Model and Specifications

The OMA work in the presence area is focused primarily in the group management, SIMPLE-based presence for the support of other enablers such as Push-to-Talk-over-cellular (PoC) and SIP/SIMPLE IM. This work takes place in the OMA Presence and Availability (PAG) WG. Most of the examples presented in the OMA specification documents in the presence arena tend to use PoC as the basis for their scenarios and call flows. OMA Presence activity started with Instant Messaging and Presence Service (IMPS), originally the WV activity. With the emergence of SIP-based enablers such as PoC, the OMA Presence-related activity progressed to SIP-based presence and supporting group management. The group management capability is provided through an enabler referred to as XML Document Management (XDM). The OMA IMPS, OMA Presence SIMPLE (Presence), and OMA XDM enablers are described in turn, starting with their mapping to the OSE architecture.

14.3.1 Presence, XDM, and IMPS Enablers in the OSE

Presence, XDM, and IMPS are enablers with well-defined I0 interfaces, some of them already broadly re-used by other enablers. Figure 14.4 provides their mapping in the OSE. All of them rely heavily on the Resource Tier, in particular, on what is referred to as the SIP/IP Core, described later in the chapter.

14.3.2 Wireless Village and OMA Instant Messaging and Presence Service

When OMA was created, one of the original aims was to consolidate the micro-fora that were created in the late nineties to progress in service-related standards. One such organization was WV, which was created specifically to build a community around new and innovative messaging and presence. While this community was primarily aimed at the mobile environment, it specifically extended the capabilities to fixed-line clients and included inter-working with other proprietary IM systems. When WV as an organization was affiliated with OMA, the specifications were adopted as the IMPS, or OMA IMPS, where they went through several updates, the last approved version being IMPS version 1.3 [IMPS AD]. The specifications will be maintained in OMA (i.e. any necessary corrections) but there are currently no plans to create further new releases within OMA primarily due to transition to SIP-based presence and messaging. WV/IMPS has been commercially deployed by several carriers and currently enjoys a great deal of success.

The IMPS framework is built around a client-server system, where the IMPS server acts as the central point for interactions between IMPS clients. Clients may be deployed in mobile devices or in fixed-line PC clients as well as other services or applications. The IMPS architecture is shown in Figure 14.5.

The IMPS Server contains four 'service elements': Presence, Instant Messaging, Groups, and Shared Content. In addition, the server defines three Service Access Points: Client-Server Protocol (CSP) Access, which addresses authentication and authorization, Server to Mobile Core Network

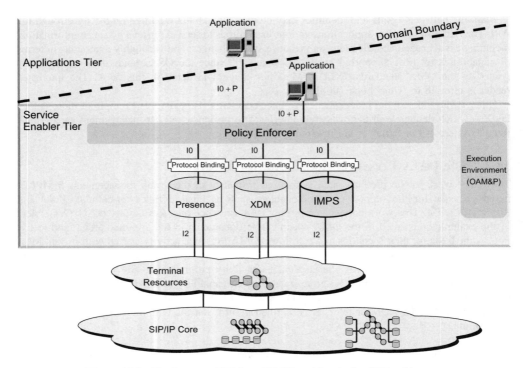

Figure 14.4   The Presence, XDM, and IMPS enablers in the OSE architecture

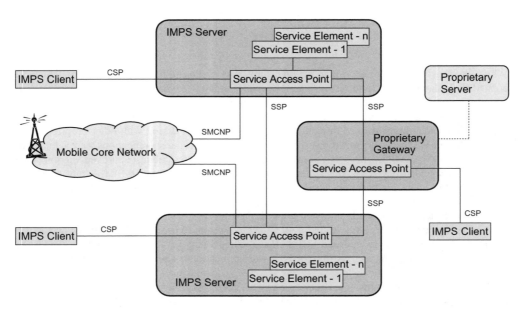

Figure 14.5   OMA IMPS architecture. Reproduced by Permission of the Open Mobile Alliance Ltd.

Protocol (SMCNP) Access, which addresses user profile management and Server to Server Protocol (SSP) Access, which provides the ability for server-server interaction, primarily for access of clients from outside a provider's network either via other IMPS Servers or through proprietary gateways.

- The Presence Service Element, as the name implies, provides the presence information management, which allows either explicit user-defined presence (such as mood or user status) or implicit server-derived presence (e.g. phone switched off).
- The Instant Messaging Service Element provides the capability for end points to exchange near-instantaneous messages either as plain text, sound, pictures, or videos.
- The Group Service Element provides the ability to define 'groups' to enable services such as chat.
- The Content Service Element provides the ability for users to share content such as images or documents with our IMPS users. This is achieved by sharing Uniform Resource Locators (URLs) and the specifications do not provide any details as to how the content is uploaded or downloaded.

Of primary relevance to this chapter is the Presence Service Element. In IMPS presence information is standardized as a set of attributes using XML. This presence information is classified as either *client status attributes* or *user status attributes*. The client status attributes describe the status of the client embedded in a device. For example, one of these attributes is registration. This attribute indicates whether the client is registered with the server, implying online capability. The user status attributes describe the status of the user associated with the device. An example of this is the emotional state of the user such as his/her mood. These attributes are defined to ensure interoperability between manufactures. However, in addition to the client status and user status attributes, the specifications allow for 'extended presence information', which are either vendor specific or service provided, non-standard attributes that serve as extensions to the defined set of attributes. This allows for potential differentiation between service providers and vendors. A list of the OMA IMPS specifications can be found in Table 14.6 in Annex A.

14.3.3 OMA Presence SIMPLE

Figure 14.6 depicts the OMA specifications view of the Presence architecture. The components and interfaces that are intrinsic to OMA Presence SIMPLE architecture [Presence AD] and specified by this enabler are depicted with solid lines, while those that are dependencies defined elsewhere, are represented with dashed lines. Although still in draft status at the time of writing this book, the Presence SIMPLE architecture has been recently completed, and the expectation is that the enabler will move to candidate status soon – hence we chose to focus on this more recent version instead of the approved one.

Being the top layer of the Three-Layer Brick Model, the OMA Presence model utilizes the IETF, 3GPP, and 3GPP2 models in supporting end-to-end presence scenarios. There are no significant differences here from standards already published by those respective bodies though, as previously indicated, the OMA standards tend to refine aspects already covered in the other standards. Some of the OMA refinements include the definition of elements such as the aggregation proxy, various XML Document Management Servers (XDMSs) as XML document repositories, presence document schema extensions, usage scenarios, etc., some of which are described in the sections that follow.

The OMA Presence architecture includes components specified by this enabler, as well as others that the enabler is dependent upon:

- Presence Server: This component collects both dynamic network presence information of an implicit nature based on devices' connectivity to the core network, obtaining this information from various network elements, as well as the user-specified presence information of an explicit

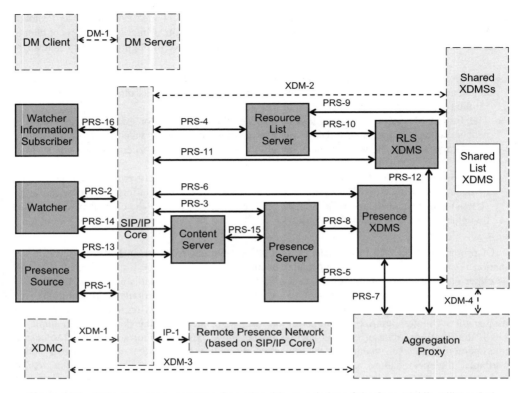

Figure 14.6 OMA Presence architecture. Reproduced by Permission of the Open Mobile Alliance Ltd.

nature gathered via user-initiated publications (via SIP PUBLISH message, for example). It also processes subscription requests from various watchers, and delivers presence updates to them as they occur.

- Presence Source: A Presence source could be any element that provides either 'implicit' or 'explicit' presence information to the PS. Implicit presence or network-determined presence information, for example, update notifications every time Alice turns on or off her cell-phone, can be obtained by the PS from the Home Location Registry (HLR) in the cellular network. Explicit presence, on the other hand, is the user set presence and availability information, for example, what Alice sets as her presence from her handset 'busy', 'out to lunch', 'gone fishing' etc. In the latter case, the handset becomes the Presence source.
- Watchers: These elements could be of various types (apart from falling into one of the three categories already described in IETF section). For instance, users that act as presentities in one scenario may also be watchers in others. As an example, Alice, who publishes her presence information to the PS, may be watched by Bob, and Bob, another presentity, might be on Alice's contact list, making Alice his watcher. So it is possible for an entity to participate in multiple roles concurrently. Presence-enabled network hosted applications may also function as watchers.
- Watcher Information Subscriber: These elements subscribe to the Watcher for information about a presentity.
- Resource List Server: The RLS function defined in IETF (and called the PLS in 3GPP TS 23.141) defines the capability whereby the end-user is able to request list subscriptions and receive list notifications on presence updates.

- XDM Client (XDMC): This component is contained within the client software on the handset and enables the client to interact with various XDM servers in the network through the aggregation proxy by issuing XCAP (defined by the IETF) transactions. Operations such as XCAP GET, PUT and DELETE need to be supported to enable the client to retrieve contacts or lists and insert/add and remove/delete contacts from server hosted lists.
- Presence XDMS: This component supports the definition of presence authorization rules – namely the 'allow', 'deny', 'polite block', and 'confirm' dispositions. This function is subsumed in the IETF GLMS.
- Resource List Server XDMS: This component enables management of and access to lists of contacts that could be utilized for presence subscriptions.
- Content Server: This component gets involved when there is a large amount of data (e.g. updates relating to list presence for large lists, or other such situations) that needs to be transmitted from a server in the network to the client application on the handset. In this case, alternative mechanisms supported by protocols such as SIP involving content indirection could be used whereby the server sends the client a URL with a pointer to the hosted content on the server. The client then fetches this content using established mechanisms such as Hypertext Transfer Protocol (HTTP).
- SIP/IP Core: This represents the logical core network that is capable of supporting SIP and XCAP operations. This could be either a generic SIP network environment or an IMS core network environment.
- Shared XDMS: This component enables management of, and access to, shared lists of contacts. These sets of contacts are tied to a name, which enables this list to be re-used in various application scenarios.
- Aggregation Proxy: This component provides routing (between the XDMC and one of many XDMSs), transaction charging, flow security, and other related operations within the XCAP context.
- Device Management Server (DM Server or DMS) and Device Management Client (DM Client or DMC): These components support the initialization and updating of all the configuration parameters necessary for the presence functional entities within the terminals (e.g. Watcher, Presence source, etc.)
- Remote Presence Network (based on SIP/IP Core): This logical element within the OMA reference architecture refers to support scenarios for wider proliferation of presence solutions, when operators might want to share presence information across network boundaries. This is sometimes referred to as 'inter-carrier presence'.

14.3.4 OMA XML Document Management

This chapter describes the OMA document management architecture based on OMA XDM Architecture version 2.0 [XDM AD], a candidate release at the time of writing this book.

Enablers like Presence require a certain amount of user-specific service-related information to fulfill their task. This information can be either specific to an enabler or common to multiple enablers. Generally, such information is expected to be stored within the service provider's network, i.e. not in the terminal, but it can be accessed and manipulated by end-users as well as applications or enabler. By way of example, in the Presence enabler we have already discussed the need for users to include authorization rules for disseminating presence information. These user-created rules are utilized by the PS to determine which portions of the presence information watchers are authorized to receive. Another example is the group list URI, where a single URI can be used to represent a group of other URIs. This group list can be used by several enablers or applications, for example a user can subscribe to the presence of a group of presentities or can establish a PoC session with the same group.

OMA decided to adopt XML as the technology of choice for storing this user-specific service-related data, mainly due to its flexibility and extensibility, although in a wireless bandwidth restricted

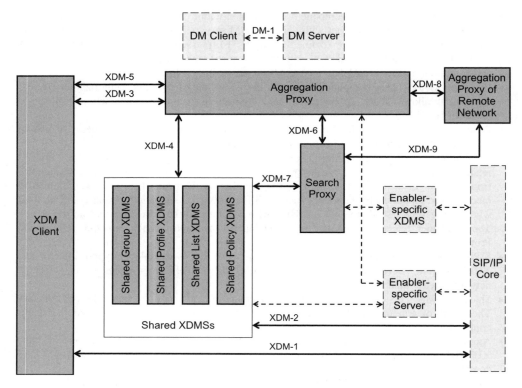

Figure 14.7   OMA XDM Architecture. Reproduced by Permission of the Open Mobile Alliance Ltd.

environment it does have disadvantages, due to its inherent verboseness. In order to be able to create, modify, delete, and access this data, the enabler XDM was created. This enabler was, in fact, originally named the group management enabler, but as new data that was unrelated to the management of group URIs was needed, a new name was sought. Given that all the data was XML based, the most appropriate term was XDM.

The XDM specifications define how information is structured in XML documents, how these documents are accessed/manipulated and how consumers of the documents are notified of changes made to the documents. The specifications use the IETF XCAP framework for document manipulation and the IETF SIP and SIP Event package framework to keep consumers of the data updated with any changes made.

From an OMA specifications perspective, the logical architecture that forms the XDM enabler is shown in Figure 14.7. The components and interfaces that are intrinsic to OMA XDM architecture and specified by this enabler are depicted with solid lines, while those that are dependencies defined elsewhere, are represented with dashed lines.

Functions performed by some of the XDM enabler components have already been explained when describing the OMA Presence architecture (e.g. XDMC, aggregation proxy, SIP/IP core). Documents forming part of the XDM enabler are stored in logical repositories, referred to generically as XDMSs. Enabler-specific XDMS will generally have an enabler-specific name, such as the Presence XDMS that stores the presence authorization rules. XDMSs that are accessed by more than one enabler generally have a name that describes the type of document it stores. The Shared XDMS is a convenient way to group together several of those components:

- Shared List XDMS: This component maintains and manages the content of URI List and Group Usage List XML documents and notifies subscribers of changes in managed XML documents.
- Shared Group XDMS: This component maintains and manages the content of Group XML documents, provides search results, and notifies subscribers of changes in managed XML documents.
- Shared Profile XDMS: This component maintains and manages the content of User Profile XML documents, provides search results, and notifies subscribers of changes in managed XML documents.
- Shared Policy XDMS: This component maintains and manages the content of user access policy XML documents and notifies subscribers of changes in managed XML documents.

Other components included in the XDM architecture are as follows:

- Search Proxy: This component manages search access from XDM clients to different XDMSs.
- Aggregation Proxy of Remote Network: This component is the contact point for a trusted network to access XML documents stored in XDMSs of the remote network.
- Enabler-specific XDMS: This component maintains and manages XML documents that are specific to a selected service enabler that needs such support, in addition to the pre-defined Shared XDMSs. The interfaces that this component may define or use can only be described once the specific XDMS role is defined by the enabler needing it.
- Enabler-specific server: This component represents the functionality of an enabler that uses the XDM functions. The interfaces that this component may expose or use can only be described once the new enabler is defined.

Users of XDM data are referred to as XDMCs, where such clients could either be end-user clients in user's device or could be server-based applications or other enablers. Purists might object to the mention of application server-based watchers indicating that standards do not explicitly support these flows. However, in real-world deployments, many a time support for such flows becomes a requirement.

The clients, irrespective of their type, use a common protocol, XCAP, to manage this data stored in the XDMS and this is represented by the reference point XDM-3 in Figure 14.7. XDM-1 is a SIP-based reference point, which allows a client to receive notifications of updates of XML document. An XDM client thus needs to support two protocols: XDM and SIP.

In order to safeguard the integrity of XML documents, authentication of XDM clients is necessary before any client is able to access any of the XDM capabilities. OMA only specifies how an end-user-based client is authenticated, where the aggregation proxy in Figure 14.7 performs this functionality. This aggregation proxy is, in fact, the main entry point for end-user-based clients into the XDM enabler. In addition to authentication, the aggregation proxy performs the important function of routing XCAP messages to the appropriate XDMS. The way this is achieved is through the Application Usage Identity (AUID). Each enabler using XDM defines detailed information on the interaction of the enabler with an XCAP server, which includes defining a particular usage identity, XML schema, authorization policies, etc. This AUID allows the aggregation proxy to route the XCAP messages to the appropriate XDMS.

XDM does not specify how the SIP messages are routed between the XDMS and XDM clients and defers this task to the SIP/IP Core. In many situations, this would be supported by a 3GPP/3GPP2 IMS, but in essence only requires SIP proxies to ensure appropriate routing.

The OMA Device Management (DM) enabler is used to provision the XDMC resident on a terminal device, depicted in Figure 14.7 by the DMC, residing on the same device as the XDMC and the DMS. This provisioning is archived through a defined XDM Management Object (MO), which provides the necessary service configurations. The interested reader is referred to Chapter 18 for more details of the OMA Device Management enablers.

14.3.4.1 XML Document Management Functions

The main document management functions, defined in the first XDM release, include the following:

- Creation of a new XML document, element or attribute
- Deletion of an XML document, element or attribute
- Modification of an XML document, element or attribute.
- Retrieval of an XML document, element or attribute.

In the XCAP framework, the XML documents and attributers get mapped to HTTP URIs, which allows the XCAP to use the HTTP commands of GET, DELETE, and PUT to, in effect, allow the retrieval, deletion, and creation or modification/addition of an XML document, element, or attribute.

XDMCs may store local copies of the XML documents – this may be particularly true for user-based terminal XDMC, since not only would it be time consuming to retrieve the XML document every time it is needed for an application, but it would also be wasteful of bandwidth, a resource that is precious in a mobile environment. Local copies in XDMS raises the issue of synchronization of XML documents, especially when one considers that an XML document may be modified by multiple clients.

One mechanism to ensure that an XDMC has the most up-to-date version of an XML document is through the use of the SIP Event package framework [RFC 3265]. This allows an XDMC to use the SIP subscribe feature, so that it receives notifications of changes to the XML document (or fragments thereof). The XDMC specifies the XML document it wishes to be notified about changes in a Subscribe message; when the document changes, the Notify message will contain the updated XML document. However, race conditions can arise where an XDMC client attempts to modify an XML document, where its local copy is out of date as a different XDMC has just modified the document. This particular situation is avoided through the use of XCAP's entity tag, or e-tag, which is effectively a version number associated with an XML document. An XDMC attempting to modify an XML document in an XDMS will include the e-tag of its local copy, where the XDMS checks the e-tag value before changes are made to the XML document. If the XDMC receives a failure response indicating a mismatch in e-tag, then the XDMC knows that it has a stale copy of the XML document and fetches the latest copy of the document form the XDMS before attempting to modify the document.

14.3.4.2 XDM Client Authorization

As previously indicated, the aggregation proxy authenticates an XDMC prior to accessing the XML documents. OMA recognizes that 3GPP and 3GPP2 have existing frameworks within their respective IMS specifications that deal with authentication and hence does not provide specific details of how this is actually achieved in practice. It leaves this aspect open where it recommends the 3GPP/3GPP2 solutions if they exist or suggests an HTTP proxy acting as a reverse proxy to be used in absence of a 3GPP/3GPP2 environment.

The work on XDM continues, where the first version, XDM1.0 has been through several OMA TestFests to the extent that it became an approved enabler in the fall of 2006.

This implies relative stability of the specifications and expected full-scale commercial deployment in 2007. XDM 2.0 has added the optional ability to search for data in XML documents using Limited XQuery over HTTP, as well as optional support for compression by content encoding in the aggregation proxy. If compression is used, it would normatively follow the provisions of RFC 2616 [RFC2616]. These features were requirements driven from the needs of the PoC2.0 and SIMPLE Instant Messaging 1.0 enablers.

14.4 A Deployment Example – Deploying Presence and XDM Enablers in an IMS or MMD environment

One of the questions that gets asked repeatedly is how an OMA Presence architecture is deployed together with the 3GPP or 3GPP2 Presence service. There is a perception that the Presence service defined in 3GPP/3GPP2 competes with the OMA Presence service. This could not be further from the truth; they do in fact complement each other very well, and although there are overlapping functionalities all it means is that the entities are one and the same thing.

Figure 14.8 shows a deployment scenario that includes the mapping between the 3GPP/3GPP2 Presence service/IMS entities and the OMA Presence/XDM entitles. As we have seen in previous chapters, in a 3GPP/3GPP2 environment, the SIP/IP core is realized through the IMS functionality. The IMS reference points discussed in the Utilization of IMS in OMA (IMSinOMA) reference release (e.g. ISC, Gm, etc. – see Chapter 9) are at the disposal of the Presence and XDM enablers. For the sake of keeping the diagram simple, we place the watchers and presentities in the same service provider's domain although this is not necessarily always the case. Table 14.7 provides a summary of the mapping between the architectural entities.

Mobile end-user presentities publish presence information over the OMA PRS-1, or the equivalent 3GPP Pep reference point, where in IMS, this is the Gm reference point, which through the access network (which in reality is represented through the complexities of a Packet Data Serving Node (PDSN) via CDMA 2000 or GPRS via UMTS, GSM or EDGE) provides access to the presentity Presence proxy, which is realized by the combination of the P-CSCF and the S-CSCF associated with the user. Once the user's presence information reaches the assigned S-CSCF, filter criteria

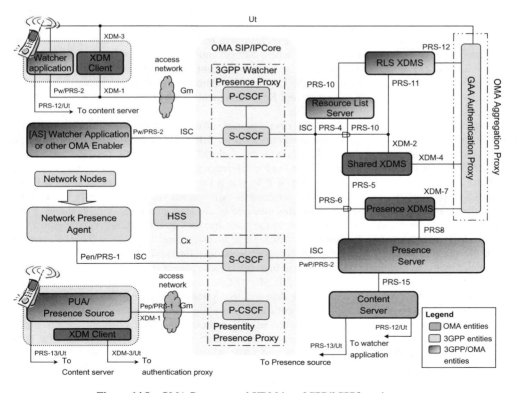

Figure 14.8 OMA Presence and XDM in a 3GPP/3GPP2 environment

Table 14.7 Mapping of architectural entities

OMA entity	Equivalent 3GPP/3GPP entity
Presence server	Presence server
SIP/IP Core	IMS network entities of P-CSCF, S-CSCF, I-CSCF and HSS, which are the key elements in routing SIP messages to and from end-users and the presence server, as well as between the presence elements, such as between the Presence server and the resource list server
Presence server	Presence server
Aggregation proxy	GAA authentication proxy
Resource list server	Resource list server
Presence source	Network Presence Agent, Presence User Agent

provide the necessary routing information to determine the PS associated with the presentity. In Figure 14.8 we notionally attach the PS to the S-CSCF of the presentity, but this does not necessarily need to be the case.

If the associated presence information requires content to be indirectly uploaded, the PS provides the user with a URL at which the content is uploaded via HTTP, which in OMA is represented by PRS-13 and in IMS by the Ut reference point. As previously seen, there are authorization rules associated with the user's presence information that dictate who is authorized to view this presence information. These rules, stored in the Presence XDMS, are managed through XCAP over HTTP (carried over the IMS Ut reference point).

The OMA aggregation proxy provides authentication of the XCAP clients. In IMS, authentication is carried through an authentication proxy where authentication of the subscriber and server takes place. 3GPP does not mandate a particular subscriber mechanism. One of the options is the Generic Authentication Architecture (GAA) [3GPP TS 33.220], where server/subscriber mutual authentication takes place using the Authentication and Key Agreement (AKA) protocol and agreed sessions keys.

Watcher applications resident on a subscriber's device subscribe to a presence information either by directly subscribing to a particular presentity (via its SIP URI) or by subscribing to a group URI, which is an alias for multiple URIs. In both cases, the SIP SUBSCRIBE messages are carried over the PRS-2 interface, which in 3GPP is the Pw reference point, which map to the Gm interface, as these are routed via a P-CSCF. The P-CSCF forwards the subscribe message to either a PS or the RLS depending on the presentity the message is destined for. In reality, it may be possible that other CSCFs are involved in routing this message to the appropriate PS – for example, if the SUBSCRIBE is for an end-user that resides in the same network as the watcher as in Figure 14.8, the S-CSCF associated with the watcher sends the SIP message directly to the S-CSCF associated with the presentity. If the presentity and watcher were in different IMS networks, the S-CSCF associated with the watcher would recognize that this is to be routed outside the service provider's domain and is forwarded to an Interrogating-ICSCF (I-CSCF) of the destination network. Watchers using XCAP to access and manage XDM data use the XDM-3 reference point, which is the Ut reference point and undergo a similar authentication process as previously described.

Watcher applications that are server based usually representing other enablers such as PoC, access the PS through the ISC reference point, where the IMS will route the SIP messages for both presence and XDM document updates back and forth. XDM data is managed through an XCAP interface that also requires authentication via the GAA Authentication proxy, but for the sake of clarity it is not shown on the mapping diagram.

Table 14.8 Mapping of reference points

3GPP Presence Service reference point	OMA reference point	3GPP/3GPP2 IMS reference point
Pep	PRS-1	ISC
Pen	PRS-1	Gm + ISC
Pw	PRS-2	Gm in the case the watcher is a mobile terminal and ISC in the case where the watcher is an application/enabler
Pwp	PRS-3	
	XDM-3, PRS-13, PRS-14	Ut
	PRS-3, PRS-4, PRS-6, PRS-11	ISC
	XDM-1	Gm+ISC

Table 14.8 provides a mapping of 3GPP Presence service reference points to OMA reference points and to 3GPP/3GPP2 IMS reference points.

14.5   Impact of Specifications on the Industry

Services based on XDM and Presence are already being deployed by service providers, and use some of the specifications described. Re-use of resources based on specifications such as OMA Presence, Shared XDMSs, etc. can only be welcomed by service providers looking to gain most of the already deployed capabilities.

Vendors enjoy re-use of specifications, since it allows broadening of their portfolios, with only incremental development costs.

OMA itself is benefiting tremendously from re-use of specifications – in this case, in particular, the collection of XDM specifications.

Last, but not least, the consumer and corporate market have most to benefit, since features offered by Presence and XDM will support rapid proliferation of new applications – because of the exposure of these enablers' functions through well-defined I0 interfaces.

14.6   Specifications Evolution and Future Direction

XDM and Presence are key supporting enablers to broader enablers such as PoC. Other potentially needed capabilities, such as the ability to delegate the ownership of an XML document and a history capability that allows a user to view a history of the changes applied to an XML document, are yet to be addressed. The evolution of XDM continues as we write, where at the time of writing XDM2.0 has reached candidate status.

As the need for XDM increases, more enablers will be relying on the capabilities offered by XDM. With client applications already supporting the necessary protocols, the impact on the end-user clients is minimal. At the time of writing, another enabler, in addition to the ones mentioned, planning to (re)use the XDM and Presence enablers is SIMPLE IM.

14.7   Summary

To sum up, the OMA specifications leverage specifications defined by other related standards bodies to outline a comprehensive end-to-end view of a framework that enables one to build and deploy a presence solution capable of presence data management and list management operations, as well as support a plethora of applications that leverage the Presence enabler. In this chapter, we have merely scratched the surface of the technical aspects of the Presence enabler, with our focus being mainly OMA specifications for presence. We hope to have whetted readers' appetites enough so they will use their new found knowledge and understanding from this discussion to explore this rich area in more detail (starting out with the helpful references provided here) on their own.

15

The Push-to-talk over Cellular Enabler

Of all the enablers being developed and published by the Open Mobile Alliance (OMA), Push-to-talk over Cellular (PoC) has certainly managed to capture its share of media attention. This is a service that could change the way we use our mobile phones today.

Traditional mobile phone networks and devices utilize full-duplex communications, allowing users to call each other and be able to simultaneously talk and hear the other party. For that, a connection is initiated by dialing a phone number and the other party needs to answer the call. The connection remains active until either party ends the call or the connection is dropped in some other way. Any transmission to be sent to other parties on the network without first dialing them up, a feature available when using two-way radios, is not supported. Mobile Push-to-talk (PTT) service – popularly described as 'walkie-talkie for the mobile phone' – provides functionality for individual half-duplex transmissions to be sent to another party on the system without needing an existing connection to be already established. It allows users to engage in immediate communication with one or more receivers. The PoC service allows you to select a contact from your phone's address book, push and hold a button, and begin talking. There is no need for dialing and ringing, and you are more or less instantly connected. Releasing the button allows the other party to speak. Since the system is half duplex (utilizing a single frequency), only one user can transmit at a time; the other party has to wait until the transmitting user finishes.

Instant 'walkie-talkie'-style communication has been known for a while, mainly among worker communities like police officers, taxi drivers, truckers, and construction workers. This blue-collar population needs to communicate efficiently and promptly, and the traditional mobile phone system simply does not allow for those types of casual transmissions without first dialing the other person up. Offering a PoC service on mobile phones allows such users to achieve the same, while carrying one device less. Also, it is certainly no wild stretch of imagination that communities other than business users will quickly embrace the service. There is expected to be high interest from the consumer market as well, when the service is offered in an attractive way. Communication savvy teens arranging to meet in the mall, parents keeping track of their kids in an amusement park, friends driving to the football stadium in separate cars – basically any circle of interest can benefit from instant casual communication.

The half-duplex nature of the communication channel means that at most one person can speak at any given time. It however does not imply that PoC is limited to one-to-one sessions. Indeed, one-to-many communication is one of the salient features of PoC, bolstering the appeal to circles

The Open Mobile Alliance   M. Brenner and M. Unmehopa
© 2008 Alcatel-Lucent. All Rights Reserved

of interest. This means that in addition to the signaling required to support the set-up, maintenance, and tear-down of PoC sessions, features like group list management and floor control need to be provided. Another aspect of PoC is the instant nature of communication. To guarantee some level of success in reaching the other party as well as to limit the intrusiveness of the service, aspects of presence, availability, and privacy are of prime importance. If I am an end-user, I would like the ability to limit my availability for receiving instant talk bursts when I am in a meeting or engaged in some other activity that does not allow for interrupts. Therefore, it would be useful to have the option to control how to be notified or to limit my involvement in instant talks with others. Conversely, before initiating any communication, I might be interested to know whether my buddies are online and free to chat.

This chapter will provide an overview of the PoC enabler, the market requirements that drive the service, the architecture describing the main entities and their relationships, and the service enabler's functionalities.

15.1   Are Those Specifications Really Needed?

The PoC service offers a different communication style with its nature of a 'walkie-talkie' experience known from various different business fields. Some proprietary PTT services are already being offered by a number of service providers today. Success of today's new services however can only be ensured if the services offered can cross network boundaries, remove carrier barriers, and provide flexibility in the user's choice for devices and networks. With an inter-operable standard in place, it will become feasible to have PoC sessions that span across networks and carriers. A PoC standard would significantly contribute toward avoiding further market fragmentation and enable wide industry interoperability. Otherwise, the experience of instant and casual interaction is limited to subscribers of the same carrier, using compatible equipment, rendering the experience dramatically less instant and casual.

15.2   Standard Precursors to OMA Push-to-talk over Cellular

Several years ago, Nextel Communications introduced the first PTT service, starting from the early versions for construction workers in their own special environment and evolving to the extension of the service from coast-to-coast for the mobile consumer market.

A pre-standard for a PTT service had been defined by a specific industry consortium with the aim of creating a commercial offering enabling interoperability between vendors. While completing this pre-standard, the involved companies entered the OMA and actively participated in a joint open standard activity contributed by more companies. In the meantime, several pre-standard solutions are already available. This leads to the unsatisfying market situation that terminal vendors have several variations of software installed on mobile terminals, so there is no interoperability available among them. The diversity of the deployments can only be given with examples: the US market is the main market where PTT services are deployed and offered to the mass market. Those however are not inter-operable and are based on different packet- and circuit-switched technologies.

Operators in other countries, like Thailand and Australia also launched their first PTT services. In Germany, the offered PTT solution is a managed service for enterprises. In Japan, PTT services have been introduced in late 2005 with the introduction of new special series handsets. In Canada too, the service is provided by several carriers. The overview above serves as an example to illustrate the pre-standard landscape for PTT solutions showing the urge for an inter-operable solution to cross carrier and country boundaries.

While most of the solutions are based on a variety of technologies, a common industry standard allows users to benefit from the potential of instant communication. OMA strives not only to provide a common basic specification, but also addresses the challenge to provide interoperability functions to allow proprietary solutions to link toward standardized inter-working between the existing solutions in the market. In this sense, OMA not only provides a new specification but also actively targets inter-working of the different approaches in the market over the common OMA specification.

15.3   Architecture and Technical Specifications Overview

PoC is a form of voice communication providing the users with the possibility to engage in immediate communication with one or more users. While the first release focuses on pure voice communication, the subsequent release still under development at the time of writing, extends this communication style beyond voice, including other media like video streams and discrete media-like images, video clips, and text messages.

From the user's perspective, the service offered is easy to use. Implementations following the OMA enabler specification provide users the ability to connect to other PoC users from different operators (inter-carrier support). The service concept integrates low-latency indications to speak, coupled with the well-known experience of using a walkie-talkie service. The PoC service applies to one-to-one as well as different group communication styles, and can therefore be applied in any kind of voice communication environment.

OMA members have invested significant effort to develop enabler specifications for the PTT service, inheriting experiences and concepts from pre-standard solutions in the industry, starting with the first standardized PoC V1.0 release, over many extensive TestFests leading to the approved PoC V1.0 specifications in June 2006, up to the new concepts for enhancing the basic version into the PoC V2.0 reaching the Candidate status in 2007, and into the PoC V2.1 release (expected in 2008). The following section will describe the first standardized PoC V1.0 enabler in its architecture and functionality, and will thereafter give you a view of the enhancement functions included in PoC V2.0, and others potentially expected in subsequent releases, as far as they are known today.

15.3.1 PoC V1.0 Architecture and Functional Description

The PoC enabler interacts with a number of external entities. Figure 15.1 illustrates the enabler relations in the context of the OMA Service Environment (OSE).

The PoC enabler is relying on a Session Initiation Protocol/Internet Protocol (SIP/IP) core for its session and media control. The SIP/IP core is considered as an infrastructure that includes a number of SIP proxies and SIP registrars, and supports the PoC enabler by performing functions like the SIP signaling between client and servers, discovery and address resolution services, SIP compression, authentication, and authorization of the user at the client based on the user's service profile, maintaining of the registration state, support for identity privacy on the PoC signaling control layer, support for charging information, as well as capabilities to perform lawful interception [POC-V1_0 RD], [POC-V1_0 RD]. The PoC enabler defines functionalities which utilize the standardized SIP/IP core based on the 3GPP IP Multimedia Subsystem (IMS)/3GPP2 Multimedia Domain (MMD) as specified in [3GPP TS 22.228] or [3GPP2 X.S0013.4]. A detailed description of the Utilization of IMS in OMA (IMSinOMA) enabler which provides the link between the IMS and the OMA enablers in the context of the OSE is given in Chapter 9.

The major partner enabler of PoC is the XML Document Management (XDM) enabler. The XDM enabler manages XML documents stored in the network. It provides a specific repository for PoC-specific documents in the PoC XDM server, as well as a common repository, for example, for contact and group lists for PoC and other enablers in the Shared XDM server. The XDM enabler is described in Chapter 14. The Presence enabler is often understood as an important trigger for communications. The PoC enabler does not mandate the use of presence information to initiate a PoC communication, but presence can be used by the PoC server in the role of a Presence source as well as a Watcher. The Presence enabler is described in more detail in Chapter 14 as well. The provisioning enablers are supporting enablers in order to provide the PoC client

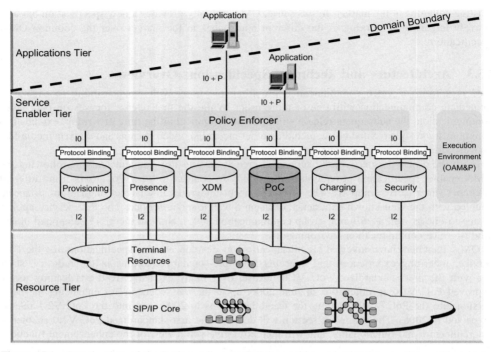

Figure 15.1 Generic view of the Push-to-talk over Cellular enabler and related supporting enablers in the OSE representation

with the initial and updated configuration parameters needed for PoC service sent by the service provider through provisioning mechanisms specified in Chapter 18. The provisioning server might also provide possibilities to retrieve software updates for application upgradeable handsets. The PoC enabler allows on-line as well as off-line charging in correlation with the underlying SIP/IP core, and is supporting subscription-based charging as well as traffic-based charging as specified in [3GPP TS 32.272]. Chapter 17 provides more details on this topic.

The PoC enabler does not provide special I0+P interfaces toward the application domain. Support for specific interfaces for value added services and third-party services has been considered in later releases (for PoC V2.1 and beyond).

15.3.1.1 Architecture and Protocols

While the previous section gives a simplified approach for the interaction of the whole PoC enabler with its supporting OMA enablers and Resource Tier functionalities, this section will look at the PoC V1.0 architecture in more detail, and will describe its major concepts. The PoC architecture is built upon a client-server architecture approach. Figure 15.2 provides the logical connection of the PoC components to the supporting enablers applied over the OSE view.

The PoC enabler specifications define the functionalities and protocols between the three major PoC entities: PoC client, PoC server, and PoC XDM server. While the PoC client and server are the actual entities for the PoC communication handling, the PoC XDM server is a vital part of the data management. The PoC server uses the Shared XDM server as well as the PoC XDM server for the data handling. While the Shared XDM server contains data accessible for PoC as well as for other enablers, the PoC XDM server is a PoC-specific entity holding PoC-specific parameters, for example, PoC session policies or PoC-specific user preferences.

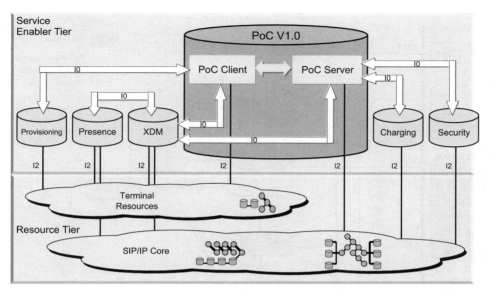

Figure 15.2 Logical high-level Push-to-talk over Cellular V1.0 architecture illustrating relationship to supporting enablers in the OSE view

Figure 15.3, taken from [POC-V1_0 AD], outlines the details of the PoC architecture including the protocols between PoC internal as well as external components. The main protocols involved are the SIP Protocol for session control and management [RFC 3261], the XML Configuration Access Protocol (XCAP) for communication with the XDM service entities [RFC 4825], and the Real Time Protocol/Real time control Protocol (RTP/RTCP) for the media handling [RFC 3550], [RFC 3605]. These protocols are defined by the Internet Engineering Task Force (IETF) [IETF]. The OMA PoC working group has a strong interest to evaluate these protocols, and develop the needed extensions. OMA supports this by maintaining a liaison relationship with the IETF for discussing the dependencies of OMA enablers on IETF protocols.

The session control between PoC client and PoC server is established using the POC-1 and POC-2 interfaces via the SIP/IP core, while the media transport and control is performed via the POC-3 interface. In order to retrieve needed data information stored in shared or PoC-specific XDM data stores, the PoC server communicates via POC-5 and POC-8 with the Shared XDM server and the PoC XDM server respectively. Using the interfaces POC-2/XDM-2 and POC-2/XDM-6, the PoC server can subscribe to and be informed about modifications of XDM documents needed for the PoC session management. The involved protocols in these interfaces with their related entities are tabulated below in Table 15.1.

15.3.1.2 Functional Description of the PoC V1.0 Enabler

PoC Server and its Roles – The PoC server, representing the PoC service's network functionality, is responsible for all actions involved in order to set up, maintain, and delete PoC sessions. It performs its tasks in two different roles: the Participating PoC Function (PF) and the Controlling PoC function (CF). Both functions are very distinct in their role for the session and media. While the server performing the PF is dedicated to serve a specific client, the server performing the CF is rather dedicated to serve a specific call. Figure 15.4, taken from [POC-V1_0 AD], visually describes the different roles of the PoC server and its relations with each other, shown with multiple networks involved.

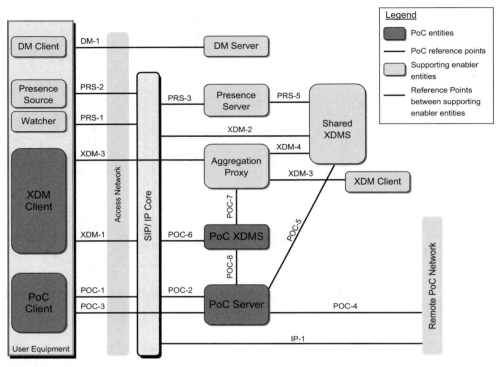

Figure 15.3 Detailed Push-to-talk over Cellular V1.0 architecture. Reproduced by Permission of the Open Mobile Alliance Ltd.

Table 15.1 PoC V1.0 reference point and associated protocol assignment

Reference Point	Involved entities	Protocol
POC-1	PoC client – SIP/IP core	SIP
POC-2	SIP/IP Core – PoC server	SIP
POC-3	PoC client – PoC server	RTP/RTCP
POC-4	PoC server – Remote PoC server	RTP/RTCP
POC-5	PoC server – Shared XDM server	XCAP
POC-6	PoC XDM server – SIP/IP core	SIP
POC-7	PoC XDM server – Aggregation proxy	XCAP
POC-8	PoC server – PoC XDM server	XCAP
XDM-1 to XDM-4	XDM enabler defined entities	See Chapter 14
PRS-1 to PRS-5	Presence enabler defined entities	See Chapter 14
DM-1	DM enabler defined entities	See Chapter 18
IP-1	IP connection interface between local and remote networks	IP protocols

The two different roles are outlined below:

- The relation between PoC client and PoC server performing the PF is defined as one server per client. This server is always in the home network and therefore responsible for its home network accounting. It is aimed at the PoC session set-up for this particular client, and can also

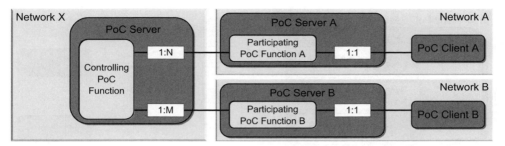

Figure 15.4 PoC server roles of participating and controlling PoC functions illustrated in different networks. Reproduced by Permission of the Open Mobile Alliance Ltd.

perform media relay functions if it is kept in the media path. As a client can optionally hold more than one PoC session at a time, there is however always only one PoC server performing the Participating Function for this client regardless of how many simultaneous PoC calls exist for the same mobile device.
- The PoC server performing the CF is assigned as one server per PoC session. It is responsible for the PoC session–specific tasks, for example, the call control and media-floor arbitration, media duplication to all participants, participant notifications, or the centralized call accounting.

PoC Session Establishment Models – In order to establish any type of PoC communication, the PoC enabler utilizes the session-based concept. In general, a PoC session gets established by sending an invitation to one or more users, and the communication will be established when the invitation and its negotiated media and session parameters are accepted. The OMA specification for the PoC enabler provides a variety of modes to handle a PoC session establishment request as follows:

- pre-established versus on-demand mode – given as different options for the PoC client;
- manual answer, automatic answer, or manual answer overwrite mode – given as different options for the invited or inviting PoC user; and
- confirmed or unconfirmed indication of session acceptance – given as different options for the PoC server.

Before sending or receiving an invitation for a PoC session, two modes can be considered for the PoC client configuration: the pre-established session mode and the on-demand session mode. Figure 15.5 illustrates the differences between the two models. The pre-established session model – given as an optional feature – is based on static SIP sessions between the PoC client and its specific PoC server performing the PF. These kinds of 'half' SIP sessions remain continuously during the valid registration to the PoC service. The PoC server uses these 'half' static SIP sessions and brings them together to a full PoC session during session establishment time, whereby the 'half' SIP sessions persist beyond a given PoC session. The on-demand session model however, does not maintain any persistent SIP session states either before or beyond a PoC session. The SIP sessions are established 'on demand' at the start of the PoC session. These two models work seamlessly with each other, and the interactions between the two models are handled by the PoC servers. The pre-established model has been introduced with the mindset to decrease the session establishment time.

When sending or receiving a PoC session invitation the user can also be given several possibilities to react on or influence a PoC session establishment. What options are available to a user depends on the options the PoC client really offers on the user's handset. PoC clients receiving session invitations can either request the PoC user to *answer manually* over the client user interface, or can

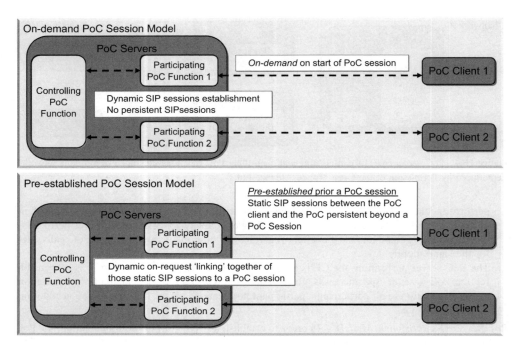

Figure 15.5 Illustration of the pre-established and on-demand session models

answer a call *automatically*. The manual-answer mode is mandatory and therefore given for all PoC clients. The automatic-answer mode can optionally be supported. The automatic-answer mode has the effect that PoC sessions get established without the direct involvement of the user. If offered with both modes, PoC users have the possibility to configure their PoC clients to apply any of those two modes based on their preferences and context. Additionally, the inviting user could also request to override the user's configuration by, for example, enforcing the automatic answer of the call. This is an optional feature called *manual-answer-override* mode. These optional features are useful in particular professional situations, where an automatic-answer mode for example, supports a hands-free instant response of the invited user, or an enforcement of the manual overwrite is suitable, for example, when providing a priority call enforcement.

Further, the PoC server also provides options on how to handle invitations and the possible reactions of the invited users. In the normal mode, the PoC server expects a confirmation for session acceptance from the invited user, where the session set-up is on hold on the server prior to receiving confirmation from the receiving user. This mode is called the *confirmed* indication and is mandatory. The server can also optionally set up the session in an *unconfirmed* mode, which means that it does not wait for the active session acceptance of the invited PoC user. The unconfirmed mode provides the opportunity to complete the session set up on the inviting party's side, grant the right-to-speak to the inviting user, and to store the receiving talk burst coming from the inviting user already on the server while waiting for confirmation of the invited party. Especially in large group sessions, this mode makes sense to decrease the latency for the media delivery.

As an example to illustrate the case of a PoC session establishment with manual-answer mode of the invited PoC user, the session set-up flow with confirmed indication is shown in Figure 15.6 (taken from [POC-V2_0 ControlPlane TS]). The flow is initiated in step 1 when a session invitation has been received at the PoC server performing the CF in the network (network X), which will host the PoC session. In the sequential order of steps 2, 3, and 4, the received invitation as SIP INVITE

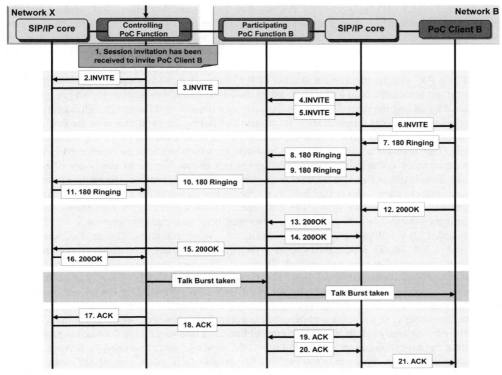

Figure 15.6 PoC session establishment with confirmed indication. Reproduced by Permission of the Open Mobile Alliance Ltd.

request is sent by the PoC server in network X over the SIP/IP cores to the PoC server of the network of the receiving client (network B). The PF in network B sends the invitation request over its SIP/IP core to the PoC client B (step 5 and 6). The client in this example flow is assumed to be set to manual-answer mode. The client indicates the invitation request to the user and waits for the user's action. Meanwhile, the client sends a 180 'ringing' response back to the originating client (given by sequentially following step 7 to 11 back to the PoC server in network X). When the user is accepting the call, the client instantly sends an SIP 200 OK response from the PoC client B back to the originator, sequentially from step 12 through 16. After completion, the PoC client B will be informed (by the 'Talk burst taken' message sent over the media plane) that the right-to-speak is granted to another user in the PoC session. The acknowledgment message SIP ACK sent from the inviting user to the receiving user is shown in steps 17 to 21 sequentially, and completes the session establishment procedure. The flow shown in Figure 15.6 illustrates the path from the CF to the receiving client. It is applicable for a one-to-one as well as a one-to-many session.

Group Communication Styles – The PoC enabler supports different styles of group communication. In order to have group communication among a defined list of participants, the user has two possibilities to set up such PoC groups, either as a *pre-arranged PoC group* or as a *PoC chat group*. These are created and managed using the XDM enabler entities. The differences between both group types are determined by the establishment of PoC sessions.

A pre-arranged PoC group session is identified by a persistent PoC session identity that has an associated set of individual PoC users. While establishing a PoC session for this type of group, all group members are invited. The chat PoC group is also a type of a persistent group in which each member however, individually joins the PoC session. This means that when a PoC session for such a chat group is established, it does not involve the invitation of all group members. In order to learn about the existence of persistent groups and who belongs to them, a group advertisement function is available to inform the group members about operational group-related information. In contrast to the two group communication styles discussed above, the concept of an *ad hoc PoC group* is defined as a PoC session involving a number of PoC users, that is temporarily supported in a PoC server and not associated with a persistent PoC session identifier. The session for *ad hoc* groups is established by adding the participant list to the invitation request, and the server individually invites all listed users and creates a temporary session identifier lasting for the duration of the PoC session.

Discussions in a group environment are affected by diverse cultures, purposes, and participant behaviors. This involves a variety of user's preferences, which needs to be considered in order to participate in group communications. As elaborated in Chapter 22, one of the issues often raised is privacy. People either like to hide their own identity in certain communications (e.g. public chat rooms), or want to know who is involved in a specific conversation prior to joining or expressing their opinions on a discussion topic. The PoC enabler allows users to use nicknames, hide their participant information, or also subscribe to other members' participant information.

Half-duplex Style ('Who has the Right to Speak?') – Voice communication in PoC sessions is performed in half-duplex mode. Half-duplex style enforces that any user listens to the speech of the talking user until that user has finished. Therefore, there is a need to control the right-to-speak in a session with a standardized solution. The right-to-speak (also called *floor*) can be requested by pressing a dedicated right-to-speak button at the user's PoC client. This button can be realized by a hardware as well as a software button depending on the user's client and handset. The voice communication between the session participants is controlled by the PoC server performing the CF. While the server already fulfills the session control functions like negotiating the session parameters, controlling the invitation acceptance of the users, the user's joining, re-joining or leaving actions, and managing the participant information, this server also fully takes care of all media control functions like granting the right-to-speak and the distribution of the media to all participants. This server can be hosted either in the home or remote network.

Media Control – Besides the session control mechanisms, additional media control features like media negotiation, quality feedback for the voice transmission, user-controlled media on-/off support as well as media buffering are provided. During session establishment, the media codec as well as the media parameters are negotiated between the PoC clients and PoC servers performing CF. Voice transmission is performed via RTP/RTCP according to [RFC 3550] where the PoC client is established as an RTP endpoint, and the PoC servers performing either the PF or the CF act as translator of the RTP/RTCP flow. Quality feedback can be provided by sending and receiving reports. During an ongoing session, a re-negotiation of the media codec and parameter might be triggered by either the PoC client (e.g. roaming conditions) or by the PoC server (e.g. when a PoC client with lower media parameters enters the PoC session).

In order to give the user control over the received media in a session, the functionalities for putting media on or off hold are provided. These are triggered by the PoC client resulting from a user interaction. Additionally, the PoC servers performing the CF may offer a media buffering functionality that allows for smaller latency in media transmission during session set-up time. After forwarding the media from the buffer, it is not kept on the server, so that PoC clients answering later in a session do not retain those early buffered media packets, but will be provided with those media only available after joining.

Media Codecs – Aligning with the media requirements of underlying SIP/IP core infrastructure as defined for [3GPP TS 22.228] and [3GPP2 X.S0013.4], the PoC server supports the following codec as default speech codec:

- Enhanced Variable Rate Codec (EVRC) speech codec [3GPP2 S.R0100-0],
- Adaptive Multi-rate (AMR) narrow band speech codec [3GPP TS 26.235], and

- Adaptive Multi-rate Wide Band (AMR-WB) speech codec, if the terminal on which the PoC client is implemented uses 16 KHz sampling frequency for speech.

The media parameters for the AMR narrow band speech codec and the AMR-WB speech codec are described together with the RTP payload format for the speech codecs in [RFC 3267]. The AMR and AMR-WB RTP payload formats offer a number of options that can be used for the RTP Media transport. The options that should be used in PoC are specified in [3GPP TS 26.236] as well as in the User Plane specification document of the PoC enabler specifications [POC-V1_0 UserPlane TS].

Simultaneous PoC Communication – While enjoying the walkie-talkie concept of voice communication, the user however is not restricted to a single PoC session only. PoC client and PoC server can optionally support a user's involvement in several simultaneous PoC sessions. Besides the tendency that humans in general have, to try to do several things in parallel with a more or less satisfying quality, the human perception of parallel voice communications in an unfiltered environment, however can be considered unsatisfactory. Therefore, the standard of the concept of simultaneous sessions involves a media filtering function to manage individually how a user wants to receive the talk bursts delivered in different sessions. The primary function is voice filtering on the client's PoC server. The PoC server performing the PF is the prime entity to fulfill the client's session control and management task. Via the PoC client, the users can be offered specific user-controlled functions to define a priority to each of their active sessions and to lock oneself temporary in a specific session without terminating the other ongoing sessions. This gives the user full flexibility to decide which session to listen to and participate in at a given time. The talk bursts in the parallel sessions, which are not received while listening to the one specific session, are filtered out by the PoC server. If there are no priorities given, the current active session is always served with ongoing speech delivery from server to client. If no speech traffic is available on that session anymore, another session can be served. The server filters accordingly so that only the voice transmission in a single session is delivered to the client.

Barring, Alerts, and Other Supporting Service Control Options – The acceptance of the PoC communication concept is much influenced by the user's environment the service is offered to. The enabler therefore provides additional features outside the direct communication in order to control the service, prepare communication, or manage the client's behavior.

One of the issues already mentioned is the configuration for client's answering modes. Another function is a feature offered to the user for so-called incoming session barring. The users can set a barring option in order to block all incoming session invitations to be forwarded to them. The PoC server will then reject those invitations without interaction with the user. This user appears to any inviting party as busy.

In certain contexts, the culture of communicating between humans might consider the direct active session invitation as too intrusive or not appropriate at a certain time. In such cultures, a request to inform about the desire to communicate is preferred. The inviting user might ask for a later option to talk with the other user, but wants to leave it to the invited party to decide upon a convenient time for the conversation. In such situations, the feature of sending a personal alert to the targeted person might be used in order to express the desire. This feature is called Instant Personal Alert. In this case, an alert in the style of an instant message is sent. Similar to the option to avoid receiving PoC session requests, there is also an optional support for an Incoming Personal Alert Barring, which avoids receiving alerts for communication wishes.

15.3.2 Enhancements for PoC V2.0 in Architecture and Functionality

The PoC V1.0 enabler provides the basic infrastructure and functionalities to offer PoC services. Approaching the end of the development of the first version, many ideas for needed enhancements have been discussed. While starting the extensive interoperability tests with implementations based on PoC V1.0, in autumn 2004 the OMA initiated the further development of the enabler. The

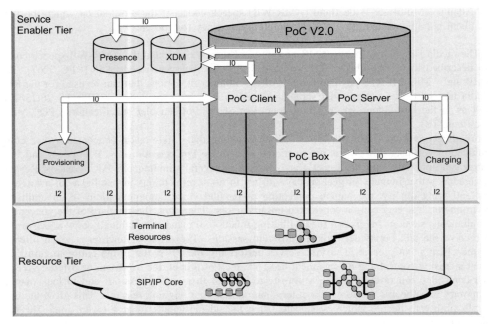

Figure 15.7 Logical high-level Push-to-talk over Cellular V2.0 architecture with relation to supporting enablers in the OSE view

PoC V2.0 enabler is expected to deliver new functionalities to enhance session establishment and control, to provide new PoC communication styles, PoC session control and storage functions, and inter-working support with non-PoC enabled networks. PoC V2.0 specifications also target to provide increased performance objectives and interoperability with PoC V1.0 implementations. The main new concepts are explained below.

15.3.2.1 The PoC V2.0 Architecture

On the architecture level only few extensions are visible in the appearance of new entities. The major enhancements however are coming in the functionalities. As shown in Figure 15.7, the architecture is extended by an entity called PoC Box. This PoC Box is a repository entity to store missed communications. Figure 15.7 provides the logical connection of the PoC components to the supporting enablers using the OSE context.

As visible by the I2 interface connections of the PoC Box entity, there are two options provided for such repository realizations, a user equipment-based storage (the so-called UE PoC box) and a network-based storage (the so-called NW PoC Box). The detailed architecture view for PoC V2.0 is shown in Figure 15.8, where the new logical entities for the PoC Box are highlighted in bold [POC-V2_0 AD]. Compared to PoC V1.0 shown in Figure 15.3, modifications to the XDM enabler are also shown. An explanation for the differences can be found in Chapter 14.

15.3.2.2 Enhanced Functionalities

As indicated above, the main differences between PoC V1.0 and PoC V2.0 are not apparent at the architecture level, rather they are visible in the list of functional enhancements introduced in PoC V2.0.

- extensions for session establishment procedures

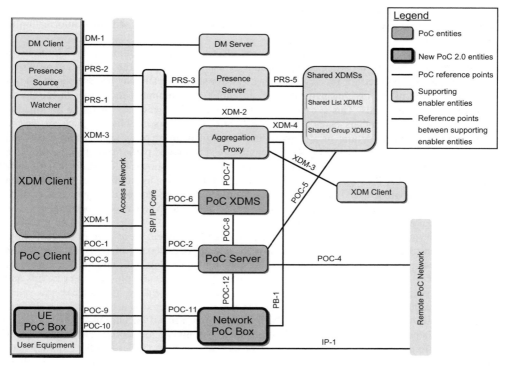

Figure 15.8 Detailed Push-to-talk over Cellular V2.0 architecture. Reproduced by Permission of the Open Mobile Alliance Ltd.

- session handling
- media control handling
- PoC box
- control different user experiences
- inter-working capabilities
- new support functions.

The following sections will elaborate these functional enhancements.

Session Establishment – The establishment of sessions has been extended with the following functionalities:

- session establishment with more media types: for example, video, images, text, and files;
- session invitations enriched with media content;
- rejection of session establishment due to hidden identity of an inviting PoC user;
- PoC sessions with multiple PoC groups; and
- browser-based PoC client invocation.

Though the PoC enabler was originally aimed at offering a new style of voice communication, users have the desire to share other types of media during a communication. The Version 2.0 introduces the half-duplex communication for media types other than voice to be sent and received during PoC communications. The supported media types are either continuous like the voice and video, or they might be discrete in nature like images, text, video clips, and files. Version 2.0 also developed an option wherein communication invitation requests can be enriched by adding media, in order to, for example, personalize the user's invitations, or to provide additional information to the PoC session.

Privacy is an ever raised concern involved in any electronic communication. In PoC V1.0, users have the ability to hide their participant information or especially request the information of others. Besides respecting the need for privacy of other users, for some users it may be essential to always know the identity of the inviting party prior to accepting any communication from them, and to not accept anonymous calls. This is especially relevant for *ad hoc* sessions, where the information of the invited group members cannot be known beforehand. Users establishing such an *ad hoc* session can include the identity of all invited users and of themselves as the inviting party, and make this information available during session invitation. The invited parties can decide if they like to participate or not, based on this information. In addition, an optional PoC server functionality is offered to allow the PoC server – based on his service policies – to enforce the rejection of an invitation if the inviting user hides his identity. This allows users to set their preferences such that they only receive PoC session invitations for which they can always make a personal decision based on the known originator and participants.

Humans are social beings living in environments formed by different groups, for example, family, friends, and colleagues. In normal life, groups of people are occasionally brought together. While the first release puts in place the basic handling for communicating with another participant or with a specific group of participants, the new version offers to join multiple persistent groups and individual users into a single session. While users can manage different groups, they can now select to bring for example, two pre-arranged groups temporarily together into a single session without creating a kind of persistent super-group, which might not be needed for later use.

The PoC client might be the commonly used approach to invoke the service. However, there is also the need to allow the automatic invocation of the PoC client via different client applications. Therefore, the basic PoC enabler has been enhanced with the option to invoke the PoC client from a browser. The use case of browser-based PoC service invocation has an interesting meaning in providing content to mobile users with embedded PoC communication means, for example, customer service center and chat groups in mobile social networks. By watching the content, the user can easily trigger a PoC session communication via the browser-based links that invokes the user's PoC client in the same mobile device.

Session Handling – The functionality for session handling has been extended with the following capabilities:

- dispatcher function
- full-duplex call follow-on proceed.

The options for different communication modes have been extended with the capability to create one-many-one Dispatcher group session. This new possibility allows the set up of group communication in the one-many-one configuration. While this was already mentioned as a specific configuration option of a pre-arranged group, in Version 2.0 a dedicated dispatch PoC group has been assigned. In this group, one participant is given the role of the dispatcher, and the others are assigned the role as kind of fleet members. In a one-many-one communication, the media from the dispatcher is distributed to all participants in the session, while the media of a fleet member is only send to the dispatcher. In order to keep the half-duplex mode of the communication, the media-floor control is distributed to all fleet members and the dispatcher itself.

While the PoC enabler provides a new way to enter into the PoC client via the browser-based client invocation, there is now also an optional way out of a PoC communication into another voice-call service. There might be situations, where the half-duplex style of the PoC communication is no longer sufficient as the session progresses and the users want to leave the PoC session and continue their conversation in a full-duplex mode. Version 2.0 provides the capability to allow a user to send an indication for a full-duplex follow-on call containing the call identifiers to the participants in the call. The users receiving this indication are able to use the information to initiate a call using a full-duplex voice client located on the same mobile device. Those clients can be, for example, for voice over IP calls as well as for circuit-switched voice communication.

Media Control Handling – Introducing new media to the PoC enabler certainly leads to the need to add new functionalities for media handling. The following capabilities have been added:

- capability for independent media control for each media in a PoC session;
- capability for single media control for multiple media in a PoC session (synchronized media);
- queuing;
- media traffic optimization; and
- advanced revocation alert functions.

Besides enhancements to the session set-up capabilities, the media-floor control handling had to be developed to cover different aspects to control multiple media in a single session. When providing the option to permit more than one media per session, the media control can be synchronized for the different media or the control is realized independently for each media. This allows that for example, voice can be sent synchronized with the video, while in another situation the user can distribute a video file independent from the ongoing voice communication. During a PoC session establishment, the PoC server performing CF can apply specific media burst control scheme in the PoC session. These specific media burst control schemes provide some policy for how the PoC server grants permissions for sending media to participants.

In certain human communications (e.g. exciting topics in OMA meetings), the desire to queue the right-to-speak requests of participants might arise to ensure a good communication style among the participants. Such a feature allows the user to react on a certain topic and be allowed to speak in the order of request received, without having to permanently vie for the 'right time to press the button' with other participants. For PoC V2.0, the PoC client and PoC server can negotiate support of queuing for a PoC session media-floor control entity during session set-up. In this case, the PoC server performing the CF will place the right-to-speak in a session queue, and will provide the PoC client with a notification of its status in the queue.

In order to increase the optimization of the PoC media traffic, the PoC servers can support the negotiation of unidirectional media stream transmission. In these cases, the PoC server performing the PF forwards media streams from the PoC server performing the CF to PoC clients or PoC Boxes with unidirectional media stream transmission and media stream set off hold. The PoC server performing the PF re-negotiates directions of media stream transmissions when PoC clients or PoC Boxes served by the PoC server performing the PF leave the PoC session or when PoC clients set their media stream on hold.

Aiming to increase the user experience, the media control handling has been extended with the functionality to provide an advanced revocation alert to the user who is granted the right-of-speak. With this new alert feature, a client is giving the user an early indication when the time for sending speech or other media is about to finish and the granted right is revoked by the server. This time window determining the maximum transmission time granted to the user will be informed by the PoC server (CF) which is in charge of the media control.

PoC Box – The architecture has been extended with the PoC Box entities. These entities are repositories to store PoC sessions on behalf of a PoC user, containing exchanged media and related information. The stored information includes the media and other relevant session data like participant information or times (e.g. date and time, sender identity, participant information). While the concept itself appears like the 'brother' of the voice mail services existing today, it involves quite some consideration in case of group communications. As the usage of a PoC Box might bring convenience to its owning user, it might bring headaches to the users confronted with this tool in the case of any group communication style, as it also functions as a recording tool automatically when involved in these sessions. Therefore, there are functions developed for the PoC Box feature, which allow the inviting user, the user owning the PoC Box as well as the members of a PoC group session to control their involvement in sessions in which a PoC Box has been joined in and is recording the conversation.

Control Different User Experiences – Enhancing the voice-based PoC communication with any kind of discrete and continuous media naturally triggers questions about the availability of network resources to guarantee certain performance and Quality of Service (QoS) expectations. This problem has been tackled with the introduction of the concepts of Quality of Experience (QoE) profiles and the function of prioritization and pre-emption of PoC sessions. The QoE profiles are used to map the QoS expectations of the users at the application level with performance criteria which are realized at the underlying network. These criteria consider the QoS per PoC session and per media in the session, as well as the priority of this PoC session. The QoE profiles are assigned to individual users as part of their PoC service subscription, to pre-arranged PoC groups and to the PoC sessions at session establishment time. Users can select their QoE profile on a per-session basis. The participation in pre-arranged groups might be restricted to users with a defined QoE profile at session establishment time. As per the standard, QoE profiles called 'Basic', 'Premium', 'Professional', and 'Official Governmental Use' are defined. While the 'Basic' profile provides best effort QoS experience, the 'Premium' profile user has higher QoS needs and expectations, for example, for streaming communications. The 'Professional' profile applies to service contract with professionals aiming for yet higher QoS needs for application purpose, streaming, etc. 'Official Government Use QoE' profiles require priority access to the PoC service and are intended for national security and emergency preparedness purposes and are therefore subject to applicable regulations. It is assumed that those profiles take precedence over all other QoE profiles. The PoC server determines the QoE profile of a PoC session during session establishment. If the PoC servers support those profile evaluations and the subsequent function for session prioritization and pre-emption, the PoC server can manage the resources available for the given PoC sessions based on their QoE session profile. This allows providing the limited network resources to the high-prioritized users. For example, in the case of a natural disaster, the network can provide high-performance PoC service to the crisis handling personnel, while private PoC service usage is limited to the best effort delivery.

Inter-working Capabilities – As seen from the history of the PTT service, several proprietary solutions are deployed in the market already. In order for the PoC service to be successful, a standardized solution as developed with these specifications was needed. However, further attention to the existing solutions needs to be considered in providing a flexible inter-working solution to non-standard PTT infrastructures. In PoC V2.0, functionalities to support the following have been provided:

- External PTT Networks to inter-work with PoC service infrastructure; and
- Capability to support PoC remote access.

The focus of the inter-working service is set to inter-working with external networks by providing PoC interaction experiences between PoC users and users of the external PTT networks. Additionally, the functionalities are designed such that, PoC users who are not directly connected to a PoC network, can also be provided with remote access to the PoC network.

New Support Features – Last but not least, there are also new support capabilities integrated in service invocation and session handling like the following:

- operator-specified warning messages
- lawful interception.

Using the PoC service, the user can be confronted with certain situations, in which the service cannot provide the desired options or needs to inform about specific service contexts. For those situations, the enabler has been enhanced with specifically defined operator-specific warning messages. These messages are text messages sent from the PoC server to the clients to present miscellaneous information given by the service provider. As these messages are operator-specific and with this also language-specific, the enabler allows support of any kind of language applicable in the service provider's network.

Another requirement dependent on the service provider's context is the lawful interception functionality. The capability to intercept any telecommunication traffic and related information may be required from the service providers according to national (e.g. US) or regional (e.g. European Union) laws and regulations. The PoC V2.0 service does not contain specific functions to ensure lawful interception techniques, but is specified in such manner, that deployed functionalities of the underlying service infrastructure are guaranteed to be applicable for the PoC service.

15.4 Salient Points

While PoC V1.0 enabler has been seen as the establishment of a first standard to realize the basic PTT services, it already gained sufficient market attraction. The specifications have been developed with broad industry participation in finding wider industry consensus for the provided features. In February 2005, OMA has approved PoC Version 1.0 enabler as Candidate enabler. Since May 2005, the PoC V1.0 enabler has already been tested in several OMA Interoperability (IOP) TestFests. This is not just a requirement for OMA's enabler approval process, but it is also an opportunity for the industry to participate in such TestFests to test the developed specifications and prove the compliance of their products to specification. In June 2006, the OMA released the PoC V1.0 approved enabler specification.

Comparing it with pre-standards and proprietary solutions, the OMA specifications helped to provide a standardized basis to develop this technology further to realize attractive service offerings. In the development of PoC V2.0, we find enhanced functionalities which go far beyond those given in current proprietary deployments and have been defined within the scope of urgent market demands in various regions. Examples to address the urgent feature needs are the introduction of the QoE profiles to provide selective user experience (European market), the inter-working function solution for non-PoC solutions (American market), or the introduction of a browser-based PoC service invocation (Japanese market) – just to name some market-specific features.

15.5 Impact of Specifications on the Industry

In this chapter we have introduced the PoC enabler, with all its functions and capabilities. While looking at the architecture and technical details, we also provided justification for the existence and use of optional features. This section will look at the value that PoC brings to the stakeholders that make up the OMA membership. What is the impact of PoC on the industry, who benefits, and how?

15.5.1 Impact on Service Providers, Vendors, Consumer, and Corporate Market

As we already have emphasized, the development of the PoC enabler has been undertaken with broad attention to all involved stakeholders. Not only did the OMA consortium define the requirements for different markets, it also tackled the challenge to prioritize those and to select a new feature set for the PoC V2.0 release driven by the most urgent market needs identified in the beginning of 2006.

Depending on the nature of the service offered using this technology, the impact of the cultural environment on the success of this communication style can certainly not be underestimated. Instant communication is arranged within the context of social life and might therefore be selective with regards to media choice and interaction patterns. While PoC V1.0 embraced a system consisting of the main mandatory functionality set with few optional functions, the PoC V2.0 feature set selection demonstrates exemplarily how flexible an enabler technology can be developed in order to address the different market needs sensitively. The diversity of optional functions offers vendors as well as service providers the possibility to provide PoC solutions adaptable to consumer and corporate markets and to offer distinct and competitive end-user solutions while still ensuring interoperability.

15.5.2 Impact on Other Specifications

While developing the PoC enabler, it impacted the standardization work in OMA, 3GPP, 3GPP2, and IETF significantly. During the technical development phase, the liaison with ongoing work in 3GPP and 3GPP2, as well as with IETF has been improved, which strongly increases the value of the work performed in these consortia as well. Within the OMA, the PoC enabler development has been closely carried out with the XDM and Presence enablers activities. Several concepts for the XDM enabler have been developed with strong need for PoC as well as Instant Messaging (IM). Also, the importance of the Presence enabler has to be strengthened. Even if the usage of presence information is an optional supported feature, not only does the availability of presence information impact the way of communication, it also ensures a certain sense of 'instant' communication as aimed for with the PoC enabler technology. When introducing other media beyond voice for the PoC enabler in V2.0, the IM enabler technology has been utilized in order to handle the delivery of discrete text-styled media.

The future PoC enabler versions might impact those enablers further while addressing more enhanced features to enrich the PoC functionalities. The just upcoming communication services convergence as currently under discussion in the OMA for the Converged IP Messaging (CPM) enabler will also play a major role in the evolution of PoC as well as related enablers.

15.6 Specifications Evolution and Future Direction

There are many other different service enhancement ideas for an upcoming PoC V2.1, that have been discussed in the OMA already. A large amount of new features have been already collected, but given the need for certain features to be available earlier in the market than others, the feature set has been divided in PoC V2.0 (released for candidacy in summer 2007) and later releases. OMA already has a set of features for the planned V2.1 scheduled for 2008.

In the meantime, new service ideas were brought forward in OMA. One of them is a new enabler called Converged IP Messaging (see also Section 27.3). This enabler aims to provide an environment which converges functionalities and user experiences across different communications enablers like IM, Short Message Service (SMS), Multimedia Messaging Service (MMS), PoC and provides a new enhanced enabler technology offering flexibility to create communication services with any media (like text, voice, images, video) and with any communication style (full duplex, half duplex, presence enabled). While adding functionalities like a converged network-based address book or multiple device environments, this service also looks for the interoperability with existing solutions. The PoC enabler and its feature set is certainly a major part of this new enabler's inter-working functionality, as a pool for standardized functionalities as well as in the scope of inter-working with other non-OMA services.

15.7 Summary

In this chapter, we have introduced the 'Push-to-talk over Cellular' enabler. We hope to have given you a view of the most talked about mobile application of 2004 – an application which turns a normal mobile phone into a fancy walkie-talkie. The biggest obstacles back then have been the questions on the revenue potential and the ability to ensure standardization and interoperability. Since PTT is primarily a group activity and since it is quite realistic to find the group members as subscribers in different networks, PTT equipment has to be able to work together. This chapter has shown how the OMA pushed for an exciting standard solution ever since. Besides voice-only, walkie-talkie fun, the excitement for an enriched multimedia experience over that service is about to emerge. Did we trigger your curiosity regarding this exciting communication style? That's exactly what we aimed to achieve.

16

Mobile E-mail

In a survey by the Yankee Group [Yankee2006b], consumers were asked to rank mobile data services that appealed to them the most. Mobile e-mail came second (54%) to the Short Message Service (SMS) which polled 59%. This survey reveals a latent demand for non-corporate mobile e-mail, which could translate into a significant revenue potential for Mobile Operators from their existing consumer subscriber base.

As an important forum for the standardization of service enablers that enable services in converged networks, the OMA has recognized the above potential by specifying a service enabler for mobile e-mail (hereafter referred to as OMA Mobile E-Mail (OMA MEM)). OMA MEM is considered a globally accepted end-to-end interoperable and secure standard for mobile e-mail that supports the widest possible deployment and usage. To this end, the OMA MEM Requirements Document [MEM RD] represents a market-driven study based on both consumer and enterprise user experiences (such as the need to support both push and pull types of e-mail interactions), while the OMA MEM Architecture Document [MEM AD] describes a logical architecture that is consistent with Internet Engineering Task Force (IETF) protocols and architectural models. This strategy is designed to meet both user expectations and time-to-market, ensuring that any existing and on-going developments to existing Internet e-mail protocols would lead to the widest possible benefit, and thus lead to successful deployment in the mobile domain.

16.1 Background

Mobile e-mail could be described as e-mail optimized when an e-mail client is deployed in a mobile device allowing over-the-air inter-working with traditional e-mail systems via a mobile network operator, enterprise, or third-party application provider. Although the OMA already has a track record for addressing the messaging needs of service providers by maintaining legacy standards for mobile messaging protocols including those with significant traction toward e-mail applications (e.g. Multimedia Messaging Service (MMS), Wireless Application Protocol (WAP)/E-Mail Notification (EMN), Synchronization Markup Language (SyncML)), a single globally accepted standard for mobile e-mail has hitherto been unspecified. OMA started work on its specifications for a Mobile E-mail enabler (OMA MEM) in June 2004 and has been focusing on the application layer aspects specific to its charter for mobile e-mail messaging service interoperability.

Given that much of the recent advancements for mobile e-mail, or e-mail for constrained devices have been developed in the IETF, a co-ordinated activity between the OMA and the IETF has been adopted to maintain a good level of co-operation between industry stakeholders and to ensure a pragmatic way forward for maximum interoperability in converged networks.

The Open Mobile Alliance   M. Brenner and M. Unmehopa
© 2008 Alcatel-Lucent. All Rights Reserved

In order to achieve these market-driven goals, the OMA MEM specifications activity has concentrated on the following:

- identifying early, the requirements of using e-mail protocols over mobile networks from all value chain stakeholders and ensuring that the solutions are addressed in the appropriate place to avoid the proliferation of multiple competing standards;
- ensuring that the OMA MEM logical architecture maintains good compatibility with IETF License to Enhance Messaging Oriented Network Access for Diverse Endpoints (LEMONADE) [RFC 4550] protocols and architectural models, for example, separation of mailbox and message submission functions;
- specifying a logical architecture that allows multiple technical realizations; and
- remaining consistent with the concepts of horizontal services architecture of OMA, that is, the OMA Service Environment or OSE [OSE AD].

The standardization of the Mobile E-mail enabler by the OMA is seen as an opportunity for the industry to put an end to the proliferation of the many proprietary solutions such as those that offer Internet Message Access Protocol (IMAP) derived, mobile-optimized implementations as illustrated in Figure 16.1, where both e-mail clients and servers implement both standards-based and standards-derived protocols (see Section 16.1.2 below for more about these protocols). What is not shown in Figure 16.1 and may also be implemented, for example, on some smart phones, is a proprietary e-mail solution requiring separate non-standard protocol stacks on the client. The classic example in widespread usage today is the Blackberry™ [RIM] operating with the Microsoft Exchange Server [Exchange].

While some service providers have extended web-based e-mail (e.g. Yahoo® Mail) to the WAP client with text-based alerts [YahooMail], most continue to indicate a strong desire to have e-mail

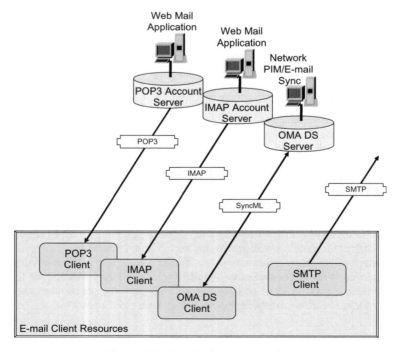

Figure 16.1   E-mail client/server options

solutions based on one globally accepted standard for mobile e-mail that scales well and provides maximum interoperability between fixed and mobile domains.

16.1.1 Market Drivers

Much of the market drive for standardizing mobile e-mail has come from the needs of the enterprise, where mobile device capabilities vary widely from small mobile phones (with storage and user interface not intended primarily for e-mail), to laptops connected via medium to high bandwidth bearers (e.g. General Packet Radio Service (GPRS), Universal Mobile Telecommunications System (UMTS), 1 times Radio Transmission Technology (1xRTT)). Unfortunately, many of the e-mail applications available today use different, often proprietary technologies. The multitude of solutions represents a significant burden on the enterprise IT infrastructure which is faced with extending important productivity related applications like Personal Information Manager (PIM) and e-mail to the mobile workforce while maintaining corporate security/IT policies.

From an enterprise mobilization perspective in particular, what is required is the secure interaction between the e-mail client and the server to ensure:

- EMN:
  - near-instantaneous notification of e-mail to the online client when it arrives at the server.
- E-mail reception:
  - new e-mail or portions of it, are downloaded to the client securely and with minimum delay;
  - any attachments are downloaded and viewed in a way adapted to the device characteristics;
  - if e-mail cannot be successfully sent to the client, user experiences a graceful degradation of the service.
- E-mail composition and sending:
  - The user composes a new e-mail or a reply to an existing e-mail message.
  - The client connects securely and with minimum delay to the e-mail server.
  - The e-mail is sent from the e-mail server.
- Event-driven bi-directional synchronization of client- and server-side changes such as:
  - e-mail store changes
  - address changes
  - calendar changes
  - folder changes.
- Off-line usage:
  - Client updates the mobile e-mail server with changes made off-line.
  - Client obtains/acts on the changes that took place on the mobile e-mail server.
- Filtering:
  - server-side filtering to decide which messages will be accessible by the client;
  - local, client-side filtering (e.g. deletion of e-mails or attachments that may be retained on the server).

In addition, there are other important requirements to consider in the mobile-worker usage pattern (that are extremely important in the mobile environment) such as:

- message viewing without download;
- support of intermittent connectivity inherent to the mobile network;
- forwarding a mail (and its attachments) to another account without downloading it to the mobile device;

- attachment conversion and compression;
- search folders without download;
- compatibility with firewalls;
- synchronizing e-mail over the air via another device (e.g. another Personal Computer (PC), Personal Digital Assistant (PDA)) or Local Area Network (LAN);
- billing models to support various deployments.

16.1.2 The Standards Landscape

Post Office Protocol (POP), IMAP, and Simple Mail Transfer Protocol (SMTP) are the three *de facto* Internet-standard mail protocols that virtually all mail systems support, to guarantee interoperability. The following section describes these and other established and on-going OMA MEM related standards and activities.

16.1.2.1 The Post Office Protocol (POP)

The POP represents a set of text-based instructions that allows an e-mail client to retrieve e-mails from an e-mail server. The POP3 protocol is specified in [RFC 1939]. It offers a comparatively simple mail drop type of service, which usually results in e-mail being downloaded and deleted from the server and is therefore typically used in web mail applications or where access to the mail is from a single workstation. POP has generally not been defined with good mobile usage in mind and assumes abundant bandwidth availability and device storage capability.

16.1.2.2 Simple Mail Transfer Protocol (SMTP)

SMTP-Submit, represents a set of text-based instructions (MAIL, DATA, RCPT, SEND...) that allows an e-mail client to submit e-mail to an e-mail server. Enhancements (called Enhanced SMTP or ESMTP), have been added in [RFC 2821] to reduce bandwidth and improve performance especially when larger files are sent or in bandwidth constrained devices.

16.1.2.3 Internet Mail Access Protocol (IMAP)

Like the POP protocol, the IMAP represents a set of instructions that allows an e-mail client to interact with the e-mail server to handle the sending of mail. Unlike POP, IMAP allows access to e-mails without deleting them from the server making it easier to access e-mail from several different workstations. IMAP4rev1 is the latest version of this protocol, defined in [RFC 3501]. Other features supported include the manipulation of mailboxes (folder management) and the use of metadata, for example, to keep track of messages that have not been read or have been forwarded. IMAP4rev1 provides support for an off-line client to re-synchronize with the server.

There have been several IMAP-derived implementations, some of which have been standardized such as:

- P-IMAP [IETF P-IMAP]: an IETF draft extending IMAP and IETF LEMONADE to support a mobile push deployment model. One of the key features of P-IMAP is that unlike an IMAPv4Rev1 server, which relies on the client to constantly initiate contact to ask for state changes, the P-IMAP server can push crucial changes to a client. There are also specific transport bindings to HTTP/HTTPS to defeat firewalls.
- M-IMAP [3GPP2 X.S0016.31]: created as an alternative message submission and retrieval protocol used in the MMS MM1 interface, now adopted by 3GPP2 (see Section 16.1.2.4). Notification is not covered by M-IMAP. Instead, the 3GPP2 specifications reference existing mechanisms such as SMS or OMA Push. M-IMAP retains the benefits of IMAP4rev1 such as the rich message retrieval functions but uses an MMS/Push-based messaging model with built-in triggers for billing.

In addition to the above standardized variants of IMAP, there are numerous examples of non-standard, mobile-oriented IMAP or IMAP-derived implementations already deployed in the market.

16.1.2.4 The Third Generation Partnership Projects, 3GPP/3GPP2

The 3GPP and 3GPP2 standards organizations have well-established architectures for MMS from which mobile e-mail applications have been deployed. The MMS/e-mail architecture based on [3GPP TS 23.140] is illustrated in Figure 16.2.

The 3GPP specifications reference the OMA/WAP standard [MMS-V1_2 ERELD] for the MM1 interface as does 3GPP2 but the latter leaves the specifications open to other protocols as well, such as the M-IMAP, as mentioned above.

OMA chose not to evolve the MMS specifications specifically for OMA MEM for a variety of reasons. The underlying market-driven requirement for OMA MEM is that typical deployment patterns are driven by the enterprise. Such environments have well-established scalability, security, and application requirements, which may have precluded the MMS standard from evolving to meet the requirements of OMA MEM. Another factor, which affects both consumers and enterprises, is user experience, in particular client-side/inbox message storage and manipulation.

Another goal of OMA MEM is to achieve maximum interoperability between fixed and mobile networks. A limiting factor for the MMS standard has been the lack of interoperability between MMS servers and e-mail servers across the MM3 interface (e.g. because of incompatibility of header types and the complexity of mapping of delivery reports). Indeed the standardization of MMS and its general inter-working (GSM-GSM, GSM-CDMA) has only recently been addressed by the standards bodies. Despite this, the re-use of MMS messages for example for out-band notification of events in OMA MEM is not precluded.

16.1.2.5 The Open Mobile Alliance (OMA)

The OMA has already successfully delivered interoperable specifications for e-mail related technologies, through its inheritance of the Multimedia Messaging Service Interoperability (MMS-IOP)

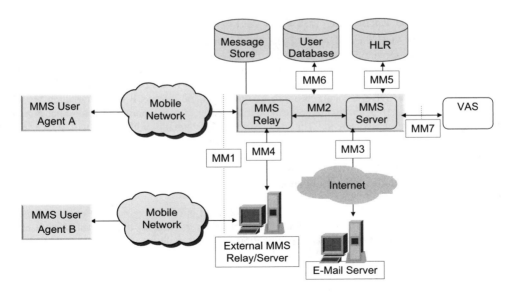

Figure 16.2   MMS architecture elements

process, the WAP Forum, and (perhaps most significantly for the OMA MEM architecture) the SyncML Initiative. These standards include:

- MMS 1.3 [MMS-V1_3 ERELD]: The OMA MMS 1.3 enabler defines application layer protocols for the MMS system. MMS payload interactions between the MMS client and MMS Proxy-Relay are defined according to either of two configurations; one using the traditional WAP methods for transport WSP [WSP TS] via a WAP proxy and the other using HTTP to carry the MMS payload. In the latter case a WAP PUSH proxy may be used for notification. MMS inter-working with traditional e-mail servers is also supported via support of SMTP and POP or IMAP at the MMS Proxy-Relay.
- OMA Push (PUSH) [PushOTA TS]: The WAP 2.0 specifications already specify a push mechanism over either of the above configurations (WSP or HTTP). OMA Push specifies the push functionality as a separate enabler either to allow (originally Wireless Markup Language (WML)) content to be delivered to a mobile device without prior authorization. OMA has extended this capability to use the Session Initiation Protocol (SIP) as the delivery protocol for event-based notifications. This variant of OMA Push will use the IETF SIP configuration framework as the underlying technology [PushSIP TS].
- OMA EMN [PushEMN TS]: OMA EMN enables e-mail servers to invoke the e-mail client residing on the mobile device using the OMA Push framework, that is, in an interoperable way. OMA EMN distinguishes EMNs as a separate content type to be pushed. OMA EMN is already supported today (typically using SMS or WSP) on many mobile handsets supporting personal e-mail applications.
- OMA Data Synchronization (DS) [DS-V1_1_2 ERP]: Originally defined by the SyncML Initiative, the SyncML protocol (now OMA DS) was originally designed for PIM data such as calendar and contacts, but e-mail has now been added. It is not a true push protocol but can be implemented to give an experience similar to push e-mail, that is, e-mail is treated as a data object subject to synchronization updates of XML data between client(s) and server. Section 16.2.2 below gives more detail about OMA DS as a candidate technology for OMA MEM.

16.1.2.6 The Internet Engineering Task Force (IETF) LEMONADE

The IETF LEMONADE Work Group of the IETF, (originally an abbreviation of License to Enhance Messaging Oriented Network Access for Diverse Endpoints) [LEMONADE], is chartered to enhance Internet e-mail standards to support diverse service environments, with mobile type applications (bandwidth limited/high latency, low power devices) being the main drivers.

The IETF LEMONADE specifications are based on the general Internet E-mail Messaging Model summarized in Figure 16.3. In this diagram the e-mail server must support both traditional e-mail clients as well as web-based clients. The User Agent (UA) interacts with the e-mail server that comprises the Message Transfer Agent (MTA) for e-mail submission, and with the Mail Store (MS) for retrieval.

The challenge for IETF LEMONADE is to provide a viable open standard for mobile e-mail. This does not just include protocol implementation considerations but user experience and other ergonomic factors for mobile devices.

The first phase of the IETF LEMONADE profile (i.e. a set of extensions, restrictions, and usage modes) covers addressing, message routing, and formatting, as well as access (submission and retrieval) and notification protocols. The specifications will also include:

- forward without download;
- quick mailbox resynchronization; and
- several IMAP and SMTP extensions that allow bandwidth savings.

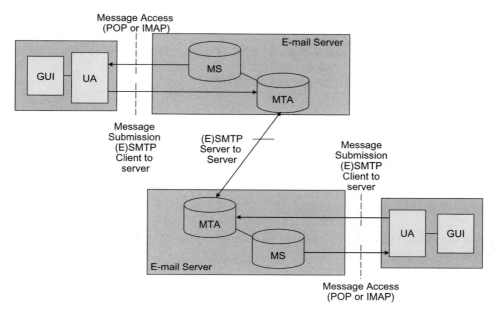

Figure 16.3 Simplified Internet messaging model

The next section describes in more detail the salient aspects of the IETF LEMONADE profile and additional IETF extensions required to satisfy the OMA requirements for OMA MEM (IETF LEMONADE Phase 2 or LEMONADE profile bis [LEMONADE bis]).

16.2 MEM Architecture

The OMA MEM logical architecture and interfaces between the MEM client and MEM server are depicted in Figure 16.4.

- ME-1: OMA MEM client I0 interface to interact via the OMA MEM protocol with the OMA MEM server.
- ME-2: Corresponding I0 interface of the OMA MEM server.
- ME-3: Out-band OMA MEM server I0 interfaces (e.g. to support generation of server to client notifications).
- ME-4: Out-band OMA MEM client I0 interfaces (e.g. to receive server to client notifications).

Other interfaces in the logical architecture include an interface for the management of OMA MEM enabler server settings, user preferences and filters in addition to interfaces for device management [DM-V1.2 ERP] (see also Chapter 18) and for the transcoding of e-mail message bodies and attachments [STI ERP].

The OMA MEM logical architecture is defined to support several deployment models, including a proxy mode in which an OMA MEM proxy function channels I0: ME-1/ME-2 protocol exchanges in the presence of firewalls. Other deployment options can be found in [MEM AD].

16.2.1 Analysis

The following section describes the essential functionality of the OMA MEM enabler, as defined in [MEM AD] followed by further elaboration on the two candidate technologies being specified.

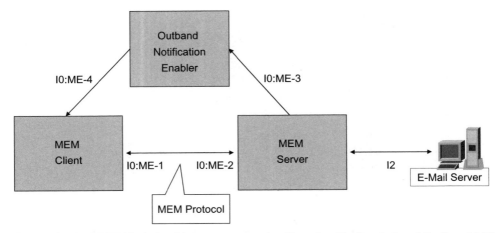

Figure 16.4 OMA MEM logical architecture representation. Reproduced by Permission of the Open Mobile Alliance Ltd.

The OMA MEM server:

(1) identifies the client;
(2) supports server-side filters to determine what e-mails/events are to be sent/notified to the client;
(3) supports forward without download;
(4) supports reply without download;
(5) supports mutual authentication with the e-mail server of the client;
(6) maintains integrity of session state with client's e-mail server;
(7) supports administration functions;
(8) supports transcoding/adaptation of message content;
(9) supports the ability to have multiple clients associated with the same e-mail account;
(10) applies user preferences; and
(11) supports charging for e-mail.

The OMA MEM client:

(1) operates in off-line mode (storing the e-mail and data to be sent to the OMA MEM server when not connected;
(2) determines when network connection is available and re-synchronizes with the OMA MEM server if necessary;
(3) encrypts e-mail data stored in the device;
(4) supports client-side filtering;
(5) requests media conversion or transcoding of a body part or attachment;
(6) processes events sent to it by the OMA MEM server; and
(7) requests e-mail body conversion from the server.

The OMA MEM protocol:

(1) supports secure exchanges between OMA MEM client and OMA MEM server;
(2) inter-operates and inter-works with Internet e-mail;

(3) supports secure server to client notifications (in band);
(4) supports the identification of the e-mail account;
(5) supports optimized bandwidth limited channels;
(6) mitigates the effects of intermittent connectivity;
(7) supports the communication of changes to filters/preferences/settings;
(8) allows the client to determine information from the content of e-mails without having to first download the e-mails;
(9) supports the subsequent reaction by the client to a particular event; and
(10) allows the client to forward/reply e-mails without having to download them first.

16.2.2 Data Synchronization (DS) Realization

The OMA DS specification [DS-V1_1_2 ERP] (represented by OMA approved release version OMA DS 1.1.2), provides a synchronization enabler for data in both clients and servers (i.e. to establish and maintain changes between multiple copies of equivalent data). One pertinent example is the synchronization between the Microsoft Outlook™address book and the mobile local address book. The original SyncML standard was released in 2000, and now OMA DS is considered the *de facto* synchronization enabler for mobile devices. OMA DS is data type agnostic and will support any Multipurpose Internet Mail Extensions (MIME) type for example, RFC822 Internet e-mail text message type [RFC 822] as well as OMA DS defined e-mail object. The enabler is also transport-agnostic but has specified bindings to HTTP [RFC 2616], OBject EXchange (OBEX) [OBEX] and WSP/WAP [WSP TS]. In OMA DS, protocol messages are encoded in eXtensible Markup Language [XML1.0].

OMA DS 1.1.2 is now being deployed in the market to deliver optimized and interoperable 'push' e-mail and PIM synchronization solutions on mobile devices. OMA DS 1.2 [DS-V1_2 ERP] improves on this, and provides:

(1) Server Alerted Synchronization (SAS) which is a bearer-independent notification mechanism (with a binding to WAP Push in OMA DS 1.2) to start a synchronization session;
(2) filtering to synchronize only the parts of data that have changed;
(3) Suspend and Resume, without loss of data during intermittent operation; and
(4) hierarchical synchronization (for child/parent data items).

In an OMA DS representation of the OMA MEM architecture, SyncML is used as a common transport layer protocol for the synchronization of any mailbox object supported at the back end. The DS server implementation would support the various interfaces toward the e-mail servers. Figure 16.5 illustrates this principle.

In the OMA MEM client, the DS logic (i.e. which implements the client-side OMA MEM protocol) is separated from the DS user interface layer (i.e. which handles the operations to be performed on the local e-mail messages such as view, compose, manage etc.). The DS logic realizes the transport protocols to deliver and retrieve e-mails. Another component is the storage component holding local messages being composed, such as drafts for pending delivery.

The DS server is essentially split into two components, namely, the DS protocol layer and the e-mail server-side layer. The former function includes message filtering, notification signaling, content adaptation and termination of the ME-2 interface. The MEM server side terminates the I2 interface with back-end mail servers for message storage and submission.

OMA DS uses an XML-based data format to exchange information about the data objects and changes to those data objects. The OMA DS protocol [DS-V1_1_2 ERP] supports different types of synchronization for e-mail objects, summarized in Table 16.1.

The OMA DS realization of OMA MEM will use the OMA DS defined e-mail data object [ObjEmail TS] (which encompasses the RFC 822 message format), file [ObjFile TS], and folder

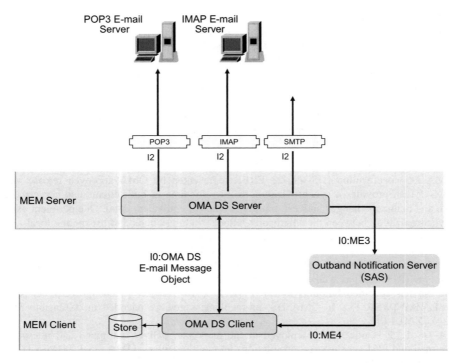

Figure 16.5   OMA DS realization of OMA MEM

Table 16.1   OMA DS methods

	One-way (Either the client or server only sends its modification data)	Two-way (Both client and server exchange information about any modifications to the data)
Full (All the items in the client database are compared with all the items in the server database on a field-by-field basis)	–	Full (slow) sync is requested by the client which sends all its data to the server
Incremental (Each client and server is connected to a database, which contains analogous data that needs to be synchronized)	• Export sync involves the client sending its modifications to the server, but the server does not send its modifications back to the client • Import sync is where the client gets all modifications from the server but the client does not send its modification to the server	The two-way process involves the client sending its data modifications to the server to update its database. The server sends its own data modifications to the client device, which updates its database accordingly. A mapping between the modified data is created to maintain synchronization

Table 16.1 (*continued*)

	One-way (Either the client or server only sends its modification data)	Two-way (Both client and server exchange information about any modifications to the data)
Refresh	• Back-up of the server database in which the server replaces all its data with the data sent by the client • Restore of the client database with the data sent by the server	–

[ObjFolder TS] objects uniquely defined as a MIME media type (e.g. application/vnd.omads-e-mail). The objects are either represented by or encapsulated in a mark-up language defined by XML. Meta or state data is included in the representation (e.g. Read/Unread, Creation Date, and Last Modified Date).

16.2.3 LEMONADE Realization

The IETF LEMONADE profile is a set of extensions to the IMAP and ESMTP protocols to improve the overall user experience of e-mail messaging [LEMONADE] where optimizations are required due to the constrained environment, that is, by ensuring less protocol 'chattiness' in bandwidth limited networks and to enable graceful degradation when connections are intermittent. Note, that POP is not being optimized by the LEMONADE profile.

The entire list of LEMONADE extensions is given in Table 16.2. Also included in this table are the extensions being created as the LEMONADE profile bis [LEMONADE bis], a set of extensions that fulfill the protocol requirements of the OMA MEM architecture.

In addition to the above, there are several other extensions being drafted by the IETF as part of the LEMONADE Profile-bis. These include COMPRESSION, CONTENT TRANSFORMATION (using OMA STI), Firewall Traversal, and encryption. More information can be obtained from the LEMONADE WG [LEMONADE].

Figure 16.6 shows the OMA MEM architecture realized using LEMONADE (SUBMIT and STORE) servers and protocols.

Figure 16.6 shows the OMA MEM server and e-mail server functional components as one logical entity realized by the LEMONADE IMAP store and submit servers. As described earlier, the OMA architecture [MEM AD] for OMA MEM identifies several deployment models that require the use of an OMA MEM proxy in case the e-mail server is behind a firewall. The architecture also allows non-LEMONADE compliant stores/servers to be used permitting migration from old mail systems to new ones. For example, a mobile service provider deploys LEMONADE server and an enterprise has non-LEMONADE server.

Not shown in Figure 16.6 are mechanisms for server to client notifications of e-mail events and filtering such as:

- Administrative Filters – Set up by an e-mail service provider as policies for content filtering, virus protection, spam filtering, and usually not configured by the user.
- Deposit Filters – Filters that are executed upon the deposit of new e-mail messages, for example, on vacation notices.
- View Filters – Filters that define which e-mails are visible to the mobile e-mail client and which would use the SIEVE protocol to manage these filters (SIEVE is a language script

Table 16.2 IETF LEMONADE Profile and Profile-bis extensions

LEMONADE profile extensions to IMAP 4 Rev1 [RFC 3501]

Feature	Description
CATENATE (RFC 4669)	Realizes 'Forward without Download' by allowing the client to create messages on the IMAP server that may contain a combination of new data along with parts of (or entire) messages already on the server. The client can forward a message by editing it without having to first download the data and then upload it back to the server.
URLAUTH (RFC 4467)	Together with other extensions (CATENATE, BURL) offers strategies to enable 'Forward without Download'. URLAUTH is a component of a URL that conveys authorization to access stored data addressed by that URL. This simplifies the trust relationship between the IMAP and SUBMIT servers.
UIDPLUS (RFC 2359)	Extensions to IMAP to help reduce the amount of time and resources used by some client operations. UIDPLUS adds the UID EXPUNGE command allowing a client that has been disconnected to ensure that it does not inadvertently remove messages marked by other clients, while the former was disconnected.
LITERAL+ (RFC 2088)	A literal is a general form of a string (zero or more octets). Normally, IMAP4 requires the client to wait for the server to send a command continuation request between sending the octet count and the string data. LITERAL+ are non-synchronizing literals. This extension allows clients to save a round-trip each time a non-synchronizing literal is sent.
CONDSTORE (RFC 4551)	This extension allows efficient resynchronization of mailbox flag changes, an update mechanism for message state changes and conflict resolution between multiple mail clients.
IDLE (RFC 2177)	In order for the client to see new mail immediately, the server must transmit updates in real time. The IDLE command is a message that is used by the client to inform the server that it is ready for such real-time updates.
POSTADDRESS	This extension permits a client to discover an e-mail address that can be used to send messages to an IMAP mailbox.

LEMONADE Profile Extensions to SMTP [RFC 2821]

Feature	Description
AUTH (RFC 2554)	An SMTP service extension whereby a client may indicate an authentication mechanism to the server, perform an authentication protocol exchange, and optionally negotiate a security layer for subsequent protocol interactions.
START TLS (RFC 3207)	This extension allows the SMTP server and client to use Transport Layer Security (TLS) to provide authenticated communication over the Internet.
BURL (RFC 4468)	Adds a new command to SMTP to fetch data from an IMAP server and inject it into the submit server without downloading it to the client and uploading it back to the server.

Table 16.2   (*continued*)

Feature	Description
PIPELINING (RFC 2197)	SMTP's intrinsic one command-one response structure is significantly penalized by high latency links. This extension allows an SMTP server to declare that it is capable of handling pipelined commands that is, the receiving server to accept new commands before issuing a response to the previous command. Pipelining commands dramatically improves performance by reducing the number of round-trip packet exchanges and makes it possible to validate all recipient addresses in one operation.
SIZE (RFC 1870)	This extension provides a mechanism by which the SMTP server can indicate the maximum size message supported.
DSN (RFC 3461)	This extension allows the SMTP server to accept explicit delivery status notification requests. Delivery Status Notifications (DSNs) allow user agents to keep track of the delivery status of messages sent.
CHUNKING (RFC 3030)	This service extension permits the support of a high-performance binary transport mode by allowing client and server to negotiate the sending of large MIME messages in chunks (using the BDAT – command). The BDAT command provides a higher efficiency alternative to the DATA command, especially for voice. The BDAT command provides for native binary transport of messages.
BINARYMIME (RFC 3030)	ESMTP servers can accept binary encoded MIME messages to optimize bandwidth.
8BITMIME (RFC 1652)	An alternative to BINARYMIME using octets allowing optimization for non- seven-bit ASCII messages.
ENHANCEDSTATUSCODES (RFC 2034)	These codes can then be used to provide more informative explanations of error conditions, especially in the context of the delivery status notifications format defined in DSN.

LEMONADE Profile-bis extensions to IMAP 4 Rev1 [RFC 3501]

Feature	Description
CONVERT	Server to client conversion (adaptation) of e-mail content, for example, HTML to text or attachment conversions. Client may request conversion or server may determine conversion format based on capability of device.
Notifications & Filters	SIEVE, SEARCH WITHIN, VFOLDER, ESEARCH, MSGEVENTS
RECONNECT	Provides quick reconnection facilities in case the transport layer is cut, whether accidentally or as part of a change in network.
BINARY APPEND	The BINARY extension extends the IMAP4 protocol to allow clients and servers to exchange data in a binary (unencoded) format. This extension allows the client to append binary data.
ANNOTATEMORE	This extension permits clients and servers to maintain 'metadata' on IMAP4 servers. It is possible to store data on a per-mailbox basis or on the server as a whole.

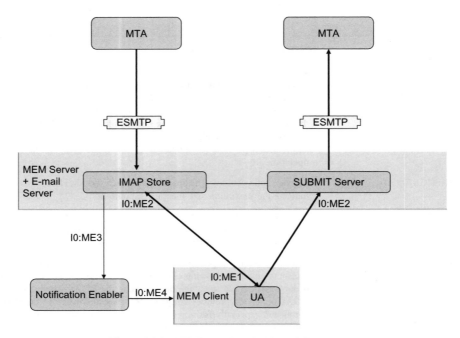

Figure 16.6 LEMONADE realization of OMA MEM

that implements server-side filtering mechanisms that allows the user to apply rules to e-mail, e.g. by looking at headers).

- Notification Filters – Filters that define for what e-mail server event an out-band notification is sent to the client.

16.3 Summary

Mobile e-mail, defined as access to e-mail from a mobile device, could turn into a revenue generator for Mobile Operators. This chapter has introduced the OMA MEM enabler as a globally accepted end-to-end interoperable and secure standard for mobile e-mail that supports the widest possible deployment and usage. Two technology realizations for OMA MEM can be supported by the same logical MEM architecture, and both realizations have been discussed in detail.

17

The Charging Enabler

Charging – the least glamorous of the standards topics and traditionally treated as an afterthought in standards development. Yet, it is the most critical component of any application when it comes to deployment. From a business perspective, the most exciting new telephony feature is irrelevant if consumers aren't willing to pay for it or if the appropriate call details aren't recorded to allow for appropriate billing. The Charging enabler provides just that call detail recording for applications and services that allows the service provider to generate revenue and remain in business.

One key common attribute of charging standards across all forums has been the need to differentiate charging from billing. While these terms are often used interchangeably in a conversational mode, they have very specific meanings in the industry, with potential for legal repercussions for the misuse of a term. This distinction has been maintained since the early days of circuit-based wireline telephony and has carried over into wireless and IP-based standards. In the industry, charging refers to the capture and transmission of call details that may be used to generate a charge to the customer. These include, but are not limited to, call details such as start and end time, calling and called-party identifiers, and indication of services invoked (e.g., call forwarding, call waiting, call barring). Billing, on the other hand, refers specifically to the process of setting a price on a service and collecting payment from the end-user for that service. Owing to the sensitive nature of the subject, discussions of billing are forbidden in standards setting organizations to prevent any appearance of anti-competitive behavior on the part of participants or member companies.

With that distinction, the actual description of charging has varied over time and across standards bodies. Historically, in circuit-based wireline and wireless standards, the call attributes that could be recorded were pretty straightforward (e.g. the call-party identifiers, the services invoked, the duration of the call). In all those cases, the charging data indicates the use of resources, and does not reflect the value to the user or outcome of the service delivered. As services became more advanced with the advent of intelligent networking in the 1980s, charging also became more complex and additional types of call details became available for recording. Intelligent networking allowed the use of additional network capabilities such as a voice mail system, subscriber-specific announcements, and subscriber-specific ring tones. Charging was extended to include recording data associated with the usage of these functions. Another significant change came with the introduction of prepaid charging, which required a means of monitoring a subscriber's account, debiting that account as services were consumed, and taking action when the account balance fell below a pre-set threshold.

The introduction of IP telephony in the 1990s brought even more changes for charging. Now, a 'call' could be an IP session, using an entirely different set of network elements, extending over multiple parties, and lasting very long periods of time. To address these changes, charging has

The Open Mobile Alliance   M. Brenner and M. Unmehopa
© 2008 Alcatel-Lucent. All Rights Reserved

been extended beyond simple pre- and post-paid scenarios to offline and online scenarios. Offline charging may encompass both traditional pre- and post-paid charging where data is collected in real time and the billing may occur in real time or may be deferred until a later time. Online charging supports real-time interaction with the charging infrastructure for charging data collection and account management. Applications may use online charging capabilities to determine the extent of the service to be provided (e.g. allow one hour of game playing), or to refund bonus points earned back to the user's account. As IP telephony services expand beyond the traditional voice services to video, downloading ring tones, online game playing, and text messaging, charging functionality has had to expand to support charging for these new types of services as well.

Building on these new IP-based capabilities is the concept of Mobile Commerce: using a mobile phone to effect a funds transfer from a customer's account to a provider of goods and services. Mobile Commerce then brings a whole new set of requirements for conveying charging data. Mechanisms are needed to carry pricing information for the purchased good or service, and new secure transactions are needed to support the funds transfer. Additionally, a new set of entities becomes involved in the charging data transaction – entities more familiar to the financial industry than to the telephony industry. The customer account may now be outside the telephony domain, for example, it may in fact be a checking account at a bank. The provider of goods and services is also outside the telephony domain, perhaps being a vending machine or an Internet-based merchant.

So with that understanding, what does the Open Mobile Alliance (OMA) Charging enabler focus on? In its first release, it focused primarily on support for IP telephony applications, specifically those defined in OMA, while also being positioned to support Mobile Commerce in future releases. A great deal of effort went into defining Charging enabler requirements to support both the IP-based services and Mobile Commerce transactions. On the basis of those requirements, the Charging enabler was then designed to support the various types of interfaces and functions that would be needed. As the work progressed, the scope of the first release became more tightly focused for various reasons, not the least of which was the need to identify another OMA enabler for testing purposes. The Broadcast (BCAST) enabler (see Chapter 20) was selected as a test case for interoperability, and as a result, the messaging and parameter development in the first release focused more on the specific needs of BCAST and less on Mobile Commerce.

17.1   Are Those Specifications Really Needed?

This interesting question was quite literally discussed during the development of the Charging enabler. Various participants argued that specifications for the 3GPP's Online Charging System (OCS) and, in particular, the interfaces and protocols for charging information exchange could be re-used by the OMA Charging enabler. Other participants, sensitive to the fact that the OCS is used in conjunction with a 3GPP IP Multimedia Subsystem (IMS) infrastructure, have argued that OMA enablers would not always be used in conjunction with the 3GPP IMS infrastructure. Additionally, IMS charging information is based on monitoring signaling related to resource usage (the external observer's point of view), and it cannot possibly provide any information related to the actual content of the service delivery. This information needs to be provided by application servers, even when they may make exchanges using an IMS infrastructure. Fortunately, the latter arguments prevailed and the Charging enabler was developed to support OMA enablers independent of the underlying network.

Without the call detail records generated by the Charging enabler, service providers would be greatly disadvantaged. Charging records not only provide information to the service provider in support of a profitable billing structure but also provide information supporting network maintenance and engineering. Call detail records indicate what resources are being used, at what times, and for what duration over an entire customer base and over time. This information may be used to establish billing practices for the service provider as well as indicate network congestion or other engineering concerns. In North America, where typical telephony billing structures are based on flat rates over a period of time, the call detail records provide sufficient information for service providers to set the flat rates at a profitable level. In other markets, there may be a more direct correlation between the charging details recorded and the bill generated for the end-user.

Additionally, the Charging enabler support for Mobile Commerce is a critical component in the usability of various other OMA enablers such as the Gaming enabler. The user may have an account that is separate from their telephony service provider that can be charged/credited/debited for the user's access to a game played over the Internet. Although limited Mobile Commerce support is provided in the first release of the Charging enabler, it is envisioned that this could be extended to support charging for a complete Mobile Commerce online shopping experience.

17.2   Standards Precursors to Charging

Although typically an afterthought, charging standards have always played a key role in telephony. After all, charging is the cornerstone of the telephony business. The perception of charging varies in different business segments, and this has resulted in different approaches to charging across the industry. As OMA brought people from a wide range of backgrounds together, those perspectives have had to converge in the Charging enabler.

Initially, membership in the Mobile Commerce and Charging (MCC) Working Group included representatives of not only the wireless telephony industry but also the finance and IT industries. These once disparate arenas began to converge with the introduction of IP telephony. The representatives of these industries brought with them the understanding of charging as it had already been implemented in their respective fields. One of the first documents generated by the MCC was the MCommerce Landscape white paper [MCOM WP] describing the various charging and mobile commerce standardization efforts across the different industries.

17.2.1 Mobile Commerce Four Party Model

In addition to the [MCOM WP], MCC also went through an exercise of modeling Mobile Commerce transactions to aid in the Charging enabler design. The model illustrated in Figure 17.1 is a very generic model applicable to the selection, order, payment, and delivery of goods and/or services, whether they are physical or digital in nature.

In this model, four related parties are involved:

- The Customer, who is paying for the goods/services and is usually the one receiving them.
- The Merchant, who is the provider of the goods/services to the Customer.
- The Acquirer, who is an enabling party for the Merchant (e.g. hosts goods/services).
- The Issuer, who is the party that manages the Customer's account and payment credentials.

The Customer is an end-user with a chargeable account managed by an Issuer (e.g. the Mobile Operator, a bank, a credit card), the Merchant is a content provider selling content, and the Acquirer is a service provider hosting the service the Customer is interested in. A single party could, of course, fulfill several roles (e.g. the Mobile Operator could also be both Issuer and Acquirer). There are two assumptions in the model:

- the Merchant has a business relationship with the Acquirer, and
- the Acquirer has a relationship of trust with the Issuer.

The following scenario illustrates the transactions between the parties in the model when a Customer purchases a service. In order to pay for the service, the Customer needs to obtain payment credentials from the Issuer. The Customer uses the payment credentials, potentially supplemented by information (e.g. transaction details, Customer authentication) to generate Transaction

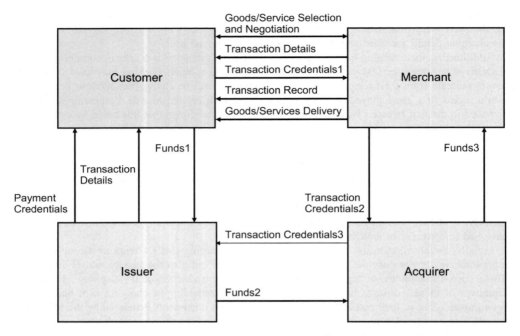

Figure 17.1 Mobile commerce reference model. Reproduced by Permission of the Open Mobile Alliance Ltd.

Credentials1 for the Merchant. The credentials provided by the Customer, while going through additional transformations when passed further from Merchant to Acquirer, and from Acquirer to Issuer, are meant to convince the Issuer that the Customer was, indeed, entitled to make use of the payment credentials, and that the Customer authorized the purchase of the service. If this is the case, the Issuer will authorize the purchase and as a result the Acquirer will authorize the Merchant to deliver the service to the Customer. The Customer receives the service purchased. At some point, on the basis of the agreed purchase, and depending on the specific agreements, the Issuer obtains Funds1 from the Customer (e.g. by debiting the Customer's account), and then releases Funds2 to the Acquirer, who in turn releases Funds3 to the Merchant. The difference in Funds released (Funds1 vs Funds2 vs Funds3) is based on pre-agreements between the different parties.

As a result of this modeling exercise, the Charging Enabler design includes support for the Merchant-Acquirer interface. The Charging enabler may be used to generate the Transaction Credentials2 as well as convey information identifying the requested service from the Merchant to the Acquirer. The Customer-Merchant Mobile Commerce processes have been identified as another potential area where the Charging enabler may be of use; however, these are not in scope for the current OMA Charging enabler release, and work on this would need to be explored in a future release.

17.2.2 Convergence of Financial, IT, and Telephony Aspects of the Charging Enabler

As the Charging enabler requirements [CHG RD] were developed, it became evident that the focus of financial and IT industries was different from that of the telephony industry. The financial and IT industries were mostly interested in the so-called real Point-of-Service (POS) use case, where the mobile terminal is used to exchange information on user identity, payment instruments, and possible service selection, but the actual delivery takes place on a physical counter or, for example, from a vending machine. At the same time, the telecommunications industry was mainly interested in the so-called virtual POS use case, where the actual service (any kind of content) is delivered digitally to the terminal, and the mobile commerce transaction has no link to a particular physical point of sale. What is worthwhile noticing is that the need to cover charging information exchanges between the Merchant's and the Acquirer's systems (see previous section for the M-Commerce reference model) is essentially the same in all use cases. The differences between the real POS and virtual POS use cases are related to the Customer-Merchant interactions, which are currently not covered in OMA Charging enabler, or anywhere else in OMA.

The bottom-line in terms of what functionality was included in the first release of the Charging enabler finally came down to who continued to participate in the Working Group. Over time, many of the representatives from the financial and IT industries reduced their participation and eventually dropped out altogether. As a result, the first release focused more on interoperability with the existing wireless telephony charging infrastructures defined in 3GPP and 3GPP2.

17.2.3 Influence from Other Standards

With the focus of the Charging enabler on 3GPP and 3GPP2 infrastructures, MCC was able to take advantage of charging protocol work already in existence. 3GPP and 3GPP2 both base their charging functionality on Internet Engineering Task Force (IETF) standards, most significantly, IETF's Diameter Base Protocol [RFC 3588], Diameter Network Access Server Application [RFC 4005], and Diameter Credit-Control Application [RFC 4006]. Additional Diameter enhancements specific to 3GPP and 3GPP2 are also found in Diameter Charging Applications [3GPP TS 32.299], IP Multimedia Subsystem – Accounting Information Flows and Protocol [3GPP2 X.S0013-008], and IP Multimedia Subsystem – Online Charging System [3GPP2 X.S0013-015]. Accordingly, for each of the generic capability descriptions of the Charging enabler, a mapping is provided to the Diameter protocol as defined in those specifications.

Interest in alternate protocols has been expressed from other OMA enabler development groups. While the first release provides mappings only to Diameter, future releases may introduce mappings to other protocols, such as Simple Object Access Protocol (SOAP)/eXtensible Markup Language (XML), based on the requirements from those other enablers. In such cases, the existing standards would be used with enhancements for OMA specific support as needed.

17.3   Charging Requirements

The MCC Working Group's requirements for the Charging enabler were driven by a need to provide a functional framework for charging across a wide spectrum of OMA enablers. The Charging Requirements Document [CHG RD] includes requirements supporting various charging data recording options such as selection of charging models, charging criteria, charging events, and whether charging should be performed pre-service delivery, post-service delivery, or during service delivery. In addition to this basic framework, the initial release supports charging capabilities that are relatively common across and re-usable by various enablers concurrently in development in OMA.

As work on the Charging enabler matured and other enablers began to take advantage of the functionality offered, a few enhancements were made specifically in support of those enablers. As new enablers providing new kinds of functionality are developed in OMA, it is quite likely that additional enabler-specific enhancements will be needed to support charging information recording for these new functions. However, the group was well pleased to discover that their initial effort to provide a broad base of re-usable charging components was quite successful.

17.4   Charging Architecture and Technical Specifications

The following sections will explore the mapping of the Charging enabler to the OMA Service Environment (OSE) architecture and its relationship to other OMA enablers, and will take a closer look at the Charging enabler logical architecture and technical specifications.

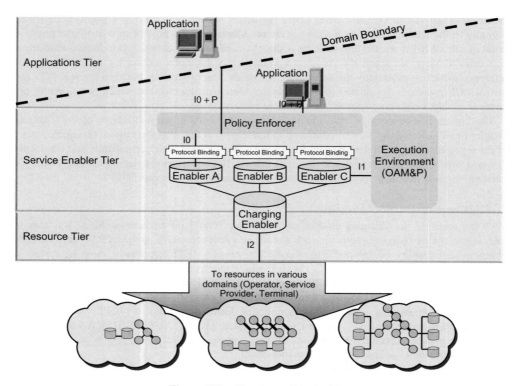

Figure 17.2   Charging enabler in OSE

17.4.1 The Charging Enabler in the OSE

The Charging enabler has an orthogonal position in the OSE relative to other OMA enablers, as shown in Figure 17.2. That is, the Charging enabler would not be implemented as a standalone enabler, rather it works in conjunction with other enablers to support transmission of charging information related to use of those enablers to an underlying charging infrastructure. As noted earlier, charging infrastructures for IP networks already exist and are in use independent of OMA applications and enablers. Simply put, the Charging enabler provides a standardized interface to be used by OMA enablers for charging information exchange, and maps that interface to existing charging infrastructures.

17.4.2 Charging Logical Architecture

The Charging enabler provides more than a simple relay function for the charging information. Figure 17.3 shows that the Charging enabler supports flows for both online and offline charging. A third function, that of determining whether offline or online charging should be used, was initially considered for the Charging enabler. As the work matured, it became clearer that the choice between online and offline charging is not necessarily dynamic, but may be a configuration choice dependent on the nature of the service provided by the application server. The Charging Enabler User can then determine the correct usage by inspecting the configuration. In order to ensure a fallback mechanism in case an explicit configuration is not selected, in this first release online charging may be invoked as the default if the Charging Enabler User is otherwise uncertain of which method to use. The Charging Enabler User may be any entity (e.g., OMA enabler, application) that invokes or interacts with the Charging enabler. Additional details are provided in [CHG AD].

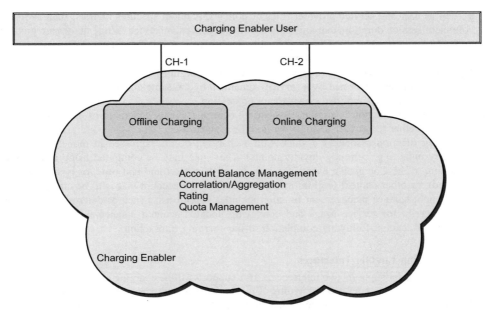

Figure 17.3 Charging enabler functional architecture. Reproduced by Permission of the Open Mobile Alliance Ltd.

Offline charging supports non-real-time charging, in that charging data elements may be conveyed from a Charging Enabler User to the underlying infrastructure during or after a charging event has occurred. There is no real-time interaction with the charging infrastructure. The Charging enabler may perform correlation/aggregation functions on the data elements it received before sending them on. Offline charging is described in detail in [CHG OFFLINE TS].

Online charging supports real-time charging, in that charging information may be exchanged through the Charging enabler before, during, and after a charging event occurs in a Charging Enabler User. When online charging is used, the Charging enabler may interact with the underlying charging infrastructure to perform a credit check before a charging event occurs. It may retrieve a quota from the user's account to allow the Charging Enabler User to gauge the extent to which service may be provided. It may retrieve rating or coordinate refunding of unused quota. It may also perform correlation/aggregation functions on the data elements it received before sending them on. Online charging is described in detail in [CHG ONLINE TS].

The determination of whether to use online or offline charging is left to the Charging Enabler User in the first release of the Charging enabler. Specifying the criteria for making such determination is out of scope for the Charging enabler specification, but examples include querying an external entity for the information (e.g., Authentication, Authorization, and Accounting (AAA) server or Home Subscriber Server (HSS)) or attempting the default invocation of an online charging session and upon failure, invoking offline charging.

17.4.2.1 Charging Enabler Functions

While the architecture diagram does not further decompose the Charging enabler into finer components, it does define the functions performed by the enabler.

- The quota management function allocates and grants quotas of service usage. Quotas are determined by the charging information available (e.g., rate, type of service, account status) as well as user and service provider rules or policies. A quota specifies metrics, such as usage volume or session duration, that are applicable to the particular service. While quotas are granted by the Charging enabler, the Charging Enabler User is responsible for not exceeding the granted quota, or requesting additional quotas when the original allocation is exhausted.

- The aggregation function provides an association of charging events (indications of particular chargeable actions performed by a service) generated by the same entity for the same user over a period of time for simplified downstream processing.
- The correlation function is similar, associating charging events generated by different entities working together to provide a single service for a given user.
- The rating function associates a value with a charging event, expressed in monetary or non-monetary units (e.g. currency, loyalty points). The value may be computed using information pertaining to the Chargeable event (e.g. volume of data, start and end time, or type of service accessed), or other context (e.g. information related to the account that is to be charged).
- The account balance management function includes several tasks such as determining whether to grant credit for service usage and conveying updated account balance information to the subscriber's account following completion of the charging transaction.

17.4.2.2 Charging Enabler Interfaces

The Charging enabler supports two interfaces. CH-1 supports offline charging event reporting, where charging information is generated at the time of resource usage and where charging information has no real-time impact on the service being invoked. CH-2 supports online charging event reporting, where the charging information can impact the invoked service in real time.

17.4.3 Charging Logical Flows

Orthogonal to online and offline charging, the Charging enabler supports two charging models. In the event-based charging model, the Charging Enabler User sends a single charging request for a service usage. In the session-based charging model, the Charging Enabler User sends a start charging request, one or more interim charging requests, and a stop charging request. Both online and offline charging support each charging model.

The various combinations are illustrated in the following Figures 17.4–17.7. Variations of the session-based flows could include operations that only ask for reserving units or only ask for debiting the subscriber's account. The interactions between a user agent and the Charging Enabler User are out of scope for the Charging enabler specifications, and are only shown for a better understanding of the charging model. In each scenario below, the charging transaction occurs between the Charging Enabler User and the Charging enabler and is transparent to the user agent.

Figure 17.4 illustrates the flows in the event-based charging model, when using offline charging. A user agent invokes a service (flow 1). On the basis of configuration and/or current policies, the Charging Enabler User sends a Charging event request toward the Charging enabler (flow 2). The Charging enabler processes the request and returns a response to the Charging Enabler User (flow 3). The Charging Enabler User may notify the user agent that the Charging data recording task has completed.

Figure 17.5 illustrates the flows in the session-based charging model, when using offline charging. A user agent invokes a service (flow 1). The Charging Enabler User sends a start session request, indicating to the Charging enabler to start a logical session associated with the service interaction. In this flow, additional information such as service description and subscriber identification may also be passed on. The Charging enabler processes the request by starting a charging session and recording the event and responds with an acknowledgment or with an error to the Charging Enabler User (flow 3). The service interaction (flow 4) provides charging information to the Charging Enabler User for recording purposes. The Charging Enabler User sends an interim request conveying the charging data collected (flow 5). The Charging enabler processes the received data, records the

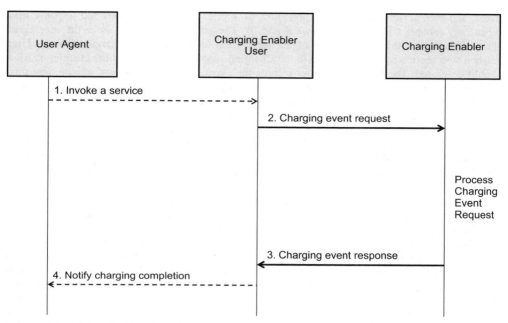

Figure 17.4 Offline charging flows in the event-based charging model. Reproduced by Permission of the Open Mobile Alliance Ltd.

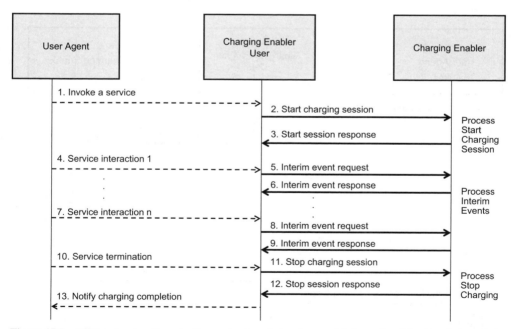

Figure 17.5 Offline charging flows in the session-based charging model. Reproduced by Permission of the Open Mobile Alliance Ltd.

event, and then acknowledges completion (flow 6). Cycles of interim requests and response may repeat any number of times (e.g. flows 8 and 9). The service termination from the user agent (flow 10) indicates that this instance of the service has terminated. The Charging Enabler User sends a stop session request (flow 11) to the Charging enabler indicating that the charging session should be closed. The Charging enabler records the event, closes the charging session, and then informs the Charging Enabler User of the outcome (flow 12). The Charging Enabler User may notify the user agent that the charging data recording task has completed.

Figure 17.6 illustrates the flows in the event-based charging model, when using online charging. A user agent initiates a service request for charging for service usage (flow 1). The Charging Enabler User sends a direct debit request toward the Charging enabler (flow 2). The Charging enabler debits the subscriber's account and returns a response to the Charging Enabler User (flow 3). The Charging Enabler User informs the user agent that the account was debited, and as a result the service can be delivered.

Figure 17.7 illustrates flows in the session-based charging model, when using online charging. A user agent invokes a service (flow 1). The Charging Enabler User sends a start session request to the Charging enabler to start a logical session associated with the service interaction. In this flow, the Charging enabler also receives charging units reservation information. The Charging enabler processes the request by starting a charging session, reserving the requested charging units, and responding with an acknowledgment or with an error to the Charging Enabler User (flow 3). The Charging Enabler User begins supervising the reserved units in this session. Every time a service delivery interaction request is sent to the Charging Enabler User (see flows 4 and 7) during the established session, the Charging Enabler User sends a debit units and reserve units request (see flows 5 and 8) towards the Charging enabler. The Charging enabler will debit the subscriber's account, reserve new units if necessary, and then send an acknowledgment to the Charging Enabler User (see flows 6 and 9). Multiple debit and reservation cycles may happen within a charging

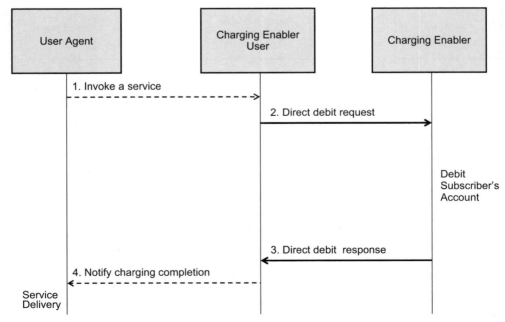

Figure 17.6 Online charging flows in the event-based charging model. Reproduced by Permission of the Open Mobile Alliance Ltd.

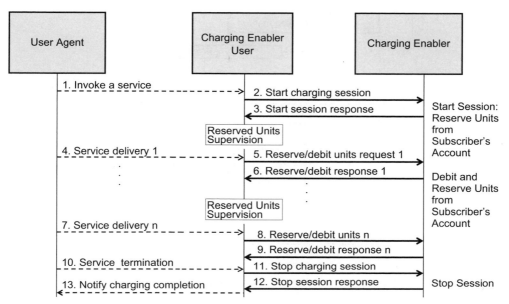

Figure 17.7 Online charging flows in the session-based charging model. Reproduced by Permission of the Open Mobile Alliance Ltd.

session. The session termination from the user agent (flow 10) indicates this instance of the service has terminated. The Charging Enabler User sends a stop session request (flow 11) to the Charging enabler indicating that the charging session should be closed. The Charging enabler records the charging data received, closes the charging session, and informs the Charging Enabler User of the outcome (flow 12). The Charging Enabler User may inform the user agent that the charging data recording task has completed.

17.4.4 Charging Enabler Technical Specifications

The charging specifications define the event- and session-based charging models, the message types applicable to the CH-1 and CH-2 interfaces, and the message bindings to Diameter. Additional message bindings may be defined in future releases of the Charging enabler.

The messages over CH-1 and CH-2 are pairs of requests and responses. A request message may represent the report of an aggregated one-time event (in the event-based charging model) or a report in a series of events corresponding to a session (in the session-based charging model).

17.4.4.1 Offline Charging Interface (CH-1) Technical Specification

Figure 17.8 illustrates the hierarchy of messages applicable in the two charging models.

The two charging models require the support of four different types of request messages, where the type of offline charging request is indicated using a 'Request Type' parameter:

- EventRecord is used to convey charging information for a single event that is to be recorded independent of any other charging event.
- StartRecord is used to indicate the start of a charging session. Charging information for an initial event may be included as part of the start request.
- InterimRecord is used to convey charging information related to subsequent events following the initiation of a charging session. The InterimRecord may be sent at regular intervals or triggered

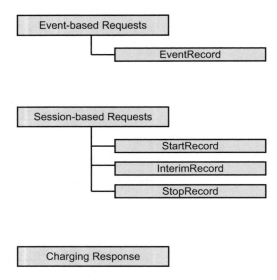

Figure 17.8   Charging messages hierarchy for offline charging

as needed. There are no limits, either minimum or maximum, on how many InterimRecords may be sent within a given session.

- StopRecord is used to convey the final charging information from a session, and request the offline charging system to terminate the session recording.

In response to each of the preceding charging request message types, a charging response is returned, with the value of the parameter 'Request Type' set to indicate the corresponding request message. A 'Result Code' parameter in the response indicates the result of processing the particular request.

17.4.4.2 Online Charging Interface (CH-2) Technical Specification

Figure 17.9 illustrates the hierarchy of messages applicable in the two charging models.

The two charging models require support of seven different types of request messages, where the type of online charging request is indicated using a 'Request Type' parameter. The event-based model uses four of these request message types:

- Debit Request is used to debit an account prior to service delivery. A failure response may be returned if there are not adequate units in the account to cover the requested debit amount. Some precaution is needed in using this message rather than the session-based credit reservation, as once the account is debited it is assumed the service will be provided. Should there be some service delivery failure, there is no automatic means of crediting the account.
- Balance Check Request is used to retrieve the current account balance. The Charging Enabler User may use this information to determine if adequate funds are available for a service prior to delivery.
- Refund Request is used to refund units to an account. This may be applicable for services where the user 'wins back' units, such as a gaming service, or to credit an account if there is a service delivery failure.
- Price Inquiry Request is used to determine the cost of an anticipated service usage. The Charging Enabler User may use this request to get a cost estimate for its own internal use or may use it

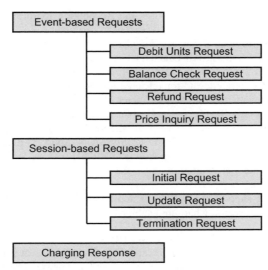

Figure 17.9 Charging messages hierarchy for online charging. Reproduced by Permission of the Open Mobile Alliance Ltd.

in an interactive scenario with a user to allow the user to decide if he/she wants the service at the indicated price.

The session-based model uses three request message types:

- Initial Request is used to convey the initial Charging event information, reserve units for the service, and initiate a charging session.
- Update Request is used to report used quota, request additional quota if previous quota has depleted, and record charging event information, during a charging session. There are no maximum or minimum limits on how many Update Requests may be sent in a given charging session.
- Termination Request is used to convey any final charging event information and terminate the charging session.

In response to each of the preceding charging request message types, a charging response is returned with the value of the parameter 'Request Type' set to indicate the corresponding request message. A 'Result Code' parameter in the response indicates the result of processing the particular request.

17.4.4.3 Binding Charging Interface Messages to Diameter

[CHG OFFLINE TS] provides a binding for CH-1 messages to Diameter Accounting defined in IETF [RFC3588]. All Diameter Base Protocol mandatory elements are supported. For the CH-1 interface, the Charging Enabler User implements the role of a Diameter client that monitors the service usage, generates charging data, and sends charging requests to the Charging enabler. The latter implements the role of a Diameter server that receives, processes, stores Charging records, and acknowledges Charging requests. The Charging Enabler User implements the client accounting state machine, while the Charging enabler implements the server accounting state machine 'SERVER, STATELESS ACCOUNTING' (see [RFC3588]).

For charging events, the CH-1 interface uses the Accounting Request (ACR) and Accounting Answer (ACA) messages.

[CHG ONLINE TS] provides a binding for CH-2 messages to the Diameter Credit-Control Application defined in [RFC4006]. All Diameter Credit-Control Application mandatory elements are supported. For the CH-2 interface, the Charging Enabler User implements the role of a Diameter credit-control client that sends requests for resource allocation and credit control to the Charging enabler. The latter implements the role of a Diameter credit-control server that authorizes and allocates credit for resource usage. The Charging Enabler User implements the state machine described for 'CLIENT, EVENT BASED' and/or 'CLIENT, SESSION BASED', while the Charging enabler implements the state machine for the 'SERVER, SESSION AND EVENT BASED' in order to support event charging and session charging (see [RFC4006]).

For charging events, the CH-2 interface uses the Credit-Control Request (CCR) and Credit-Control Answer messages.

Both CH-1 and CH-2 support the following additional Diameter Base Protocol messages as specified in [RFC3588] between a Charging enabler User and a Charging enabler:

- Re-Auth-Request (RAR) and Re-Auth-Answer (RAA)
- Capability-Exchange-Request (CER) and Capability-Exchange-Answer (CEA)
- Device-Watchdog-Request (DWR) and Device-Watchdog-Answer (DWA)
- Abort-Session-Request (ASR) and Abort-Session-Answer (ASA)
- Disconnect-Peer-Request (DPR) and Disconnect-Peer-Answer (DPA)

OMA charging data elements are mapped to the Diameter Attribute Value Pairs (AVPs), which are re-used from [RFC3588], [RFC4005], [RFC4006], or [3GPP TS 32.299]. Additionally, mapping of OMA charging data elements to AVPs defined by OMA can be found at the Open Mobile Naming Authority (OMNA) [OMNA].

The Charging enabler specifications include a generic part that is re-usable across OMA enablers. However, the Charging Enabler User behavior as well as the requests issued may vary between enablers. Figure 17.10 represents the protocol layers architecture.

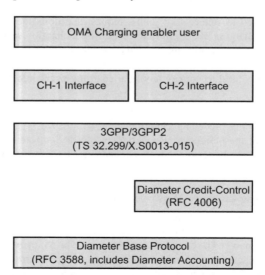

Figure 17.10 Charging interfaces protocol layers. Reproduced by Permission of the Open Mobile Alliance Ltd.

Each protocol layer specifies the use of optional protocol elements of the underlying layer. Layers may also extend an underlying protocol by adding AVPs.

17.5   Divergent Views and Their Resolution

During the course of developing the Charging enabler, there were many opportunities for expressing divergent views. This began right from the start with writing the Requirements Document. The initial discussions attempted to capture every conceivable charging detail for each and every aspect of any call or session. As time passed and the group became more aware of the charging needs of other OMA enablers, the discussions became less detail oriented and focused on those requirements of most use across a range of enablers. This new focus brought cohesion to the requirements that had been lacking initially and resulted in a solid, if not comprehensive, set of requirements that could be met in a reasonable amount of time and that would satisfy the majority of the charging needs for other enablers. Future work will include addressing new, perhaps enabler-specific, requirements as they arise.

Once past the requirements phase, maintaining consistency with the Requirements Document and acknowledging the need for future enhancements could resolve most issues. One significant exception arose during the stage 3 development period. OMA states that its mission is to develop access agnostic specifications for use on a variety of base core networks, including IMS, credit card networks, and cable networks. With that in mind, it was agreed that, for the first release of the Charging enabler, a protocol mapping to Diameter would be included in the specification. This decision was made on the basis of the ongoing high level of interest and participation from the wireless telephony industry as opposed to other industries. For practical purposes, the group agreed to re-use existing (i.e. already defined in IETF, 3GPP, 3GPP2) Diameter AVPs whenever possible. The Diameter protocol supports such re-use across applications and this would eliminate duplicate work within the industry. As the specification matured and other OMA Working Groups were consulted for specific usage of the Charging enabler, it became apparent that new Diameter AVPs would be needed to address specific needs.

The controversy then arose over where these new AVPs would be developed. Many preferred to outsource the AVP development to 3GPP, to simplify their implementations. Others preferred to have OMA develop the AVPs, to minimize reliance on an outside organization and maintain the purported access independence of OMA. A compromise of sorts was reached with an agreement that these new OMA-specific AVPs would be defined in OMA and described on the OMNA web page, but that 3GPP would provide AVP code administration – meaning that the AVPs would be given AVP codes under the 3GPP vendor ID and this code would be maintained in the 3GPP charging specifications rather than in the OMA Charging enabler. This compromise allowed the Charging enabler to move forward through the OMA publication process.

17.6   Impact of Specifications on the Industry

Now things become interesting. Not being one of the glamorous marketable features, charging does not hold a place of high visibility in the industry. However, it has great significance to service providers, without which, they would not be able to stay in business. Charging data recording contributes to network maintenance, as well as allowing appropriate billing, but service providers cannot directly pass along the cost of charging to end-users who would just as soon do without it, and the ensuing bills. Charging is more of an infrastructure staple than a revenue generating capability. Mobile commerce has a similar status. It is a capability that supports other marketable ventures, but is not revenue generating in and of itself. With that, let's look at what impact the Charging enabler does have.

17.6.1 Impact on Service Providers

The Charging enabler has the most significant benefit for service providers. That is, it enables service providers to develop applications using OMA enablers that can then be deployed on a variety of network infrastructures. By providing a framework for information exchange between the Charging Enabler User and the underlying infrastructure, the Charging enabler provides a degree of portability when applications are deployed in different environments. For the first release, this is somewhat limited to the 3GPP and 3GPP2 IMS networks, although there is some re-usability for other Diameter-based infrastructures. Future enhancements adding mappings to other I2 protocols will extend portability to other network types as well.

17.6.2 Impact on Vendors

The Charging enabler has minimal impact on traditional telephony vendors. Since the first release was carefully crafted to be compatible with deployment over a 3GPP/3GPP2 compliant charging system that provides direct support for Diameter, it will readily integrate into a network product line that supports the 3GPP/3GPP2 charging infrastructure (e.g. based on IMS architecture).

For vendors in other industries, such as finance or IT, the Charging enabler will again have minimal impact in the first release because the realization based on Diameter will not likely be implemented in those industries. Hence, enhancements to the Charging enabler (e.g. other protocol mappings) are needed to support the specific needs and protocols of other industry uses. These enhancements will come about only when other industry representatives again take an active role in the MCC deliberations. However, it is worth mentioning that the white paper on Charging Deployment Scenarios [CHG WP] discusses a charging agent deployment scenario, to support use of alternative protocols.

17.6.3 Impact on Other Specifications

The Charging enabler is already being used by other OMA enablers such as Broadcast and Messaging. The Working Groups developing these enablers have worked with MCC to define the common and the enabler-specific AVPs needed to support their Charging requirements. By using the Charging enabler, these other enablers are building in transparent migration to other network infrastructures when the market needs lead to the necessary Charging Enabler enhancements.

Other OMA enablers such as Push-to-talk Over Cellular (PoC) are relying strictly on the 3GPP IMS infrastructure to support charging and are bypassing use of the Charging enabler. This provides a near term gain in efficiency for deployments in that network architecture, but will lead to portability problems in the future if service providers attempt to deploy the same applications on a different infrastructure.

In order to encourage and facilitate the use of the Charging enabler by other enablers, the MCC Working Group developed the Charging Specifications Best Practices white paper [CHG BP]. The white paper provides an overview of the requirements, architecture and charging models, and most importantly, pointed guidelines about how to select the use of specific commands and parameters supporting other enablers' specific needs. In particular, the white paper underscores the need for other OMA Working Groups to identify specific charging requirements early on. The MCC Working Group can then extend the Charging enabler to support those requirements, if needed, and provide the mapping to protocol commands and AVPs needed in the later technical specification stages.

17.7 Specifications Evolution and Future Direction

As the first release of the Charging enabler has progressed through candidate status and prepared for Interoperability (IOP) testing, interest in a second release has heated up. The first release supports a generic set of charging requirements intended to meet a high percentage of the common charging needs across OMA enablers. As development on other enablers has matured and those enablers have begun to look at how they can integrate use of the Charging enabler, additional requirements have now been identified. In addition to enhancements to the Requirements Document, these may become enabler-specific extensions to the messages and information elements in the next Charging enabler release.

Other OMA Working Groups have expressed interest in alternative charging protocols for future releases. Specific interest exists in a SOAP/XML-based binding for interaction with the mobile device, in addition to the current approach based on a 3GPP/3GPP2 charging infrastructure. With a simpler infrastructure on the mobile device, SOAP/XML offers advantages over Diameter by streamlining the charging implementation. At the time of this writing, support for SOAP/XML-based binding is being planned for the second release of the Charging enabler.

17.8   Summary

As we can see, the value of the Charging enabler comes in the portability provided for accessing different underlying charging infrastructures. It enables service providers to develop specific applications deployable in a variety of environments, thus increasing their revenue-generating opportunities. The Charging enabler is now a valuable tool supporting the current trend among service providers to offer subscribers a single, common service package across multiple access technologies and multiple service infrastructures.

18

The Device Management Enablers

It is becoming harder (and for the many young adults, impossible) to remember a time when we did not have access to a personal computer. It will soon be as hard to remember a time when the Internet was not at our fingertips. And with the emergence of smart phones we are no longer limited to very simple mobile communications, but instead are increasingly able to combine the powers of a personal computer, with the wealth of information available on the Internet, while no longer being tethered to the home or the office. Individual consumers use mobile devices not only to talk to each other, but also to exchange text and multimedia messages, browse the Internet, listen to music, download and play games, and download or upload video clips and photos. Smart phones are becoming the social organization tools for this new class of highly-connected citizens. New service applications offer seemingly endless new ways to interact with friends, family, and colleagues, to organize one's work and social life, and for personal enjoyment and relaxation. However, as always, everything comes at a price.

- *Individual consumers* often don't appreciate or don't care (nor should they, really), that the differences between mobile device brands, perceived by consumers as a wealth of market choice, create fragmentation for service providers.
- *Small business owners* enjoy the benefits of novel collaborative communication applications such as Push-to-talk over Cellular (PoC) and Instant Messaging (IM), allowing their employees and project managers to stay in touch no matter where they are dispatched. However, these applications require ongoing management as new employees join and others leave the company. Small businesses often don't have the in-house expertise to manage these types of applications, nor the financial incentive to host the service themselves. Outsourcing to mobile network operators or to third-party application service providers requires a trade-off between the employee choice of the phone they carry and interoperability of devices with the application and management services.
- *Enterprise employees* are using smart mobile devices for real-time collaboration, access to corporate digital assets and services such as product catalogs, line-of-business applications, and Customer Relationship Management (CRM) systems, and co-ordination with their colleagues through shared calendars, corporate e-mail accounts, and a centralized corporate address book that requires ongoing management of authentication, authorization, and access.

And while Chief Information Officers (CIOs) openly admit, that they would like nothing more than to specify a single type of device for all employees, this is far easier for fixed, inside the office,

The Open Mobile Alliance   M. Brenner and M. Unmehopa
© 2008 Alcatel-Lucent. All Rights Reserved

personal computers, and wired phones. It is impractical when it comes to the highly-personal mobile devices such as smart phones and Personal Digital Assistants (PDAs) – employees demand diversity of choice in the devices they carry with them.

Corporate IT departments must then face the reality that no single device will handle every application while appealing universally to their employees. Collaboration with external partners, suppliers, and customers further eliminates this reductive approach – the many different technologies adopted by these *extranet* users will imply support for a multitude of disparate devices (at least to some extent).

In short, electronic services used are numerous, complex, and diverse. They require sophisticated and sometimes specialized devices. And these devices are manufactured by vendors who want to differentiate themselves from each other in order to gain market share, leading to proprietary features that make these devices both more user friendly and better equipped for a particular set of specialized applications. However, given the sheer number of users, it is safe to assume that if there is one differentiated device, there will soon be dozens or hundreds – it is estimated that the number of mobile subscribers in the world in 2007 may be close to 2 billion.

While it is a huge (if classical) challenge to distribute new smart devices to the hands of millions of consumers (or thousands of employees) and enable access to new services, ensuring that those devices are managed once distributed is an equally large challenge. Couple that with the desire for extended service life for mobile devices – as a tool to reduce churn and lower Capital Expenditure (CAPEX) – and serviceability, as distinct from initial provisioning, becomes a cost-management imperative for both enterprise and mobile network operators. Device Management (DM) in this context then includes not just initial provisioning but full life-cycle management, which is not only installing new service client software, but also troubleshooting and repairing, updating firmware and software with new versions, applying preventive security features in response to discovered software defects or malware, performing backup and restore services, and monitoring how devices are used to avoid inappropriate handling that may cause later problems.

With the number of devices in a typical enterprise or mobile network operator's deployment, it is an impractical and expensive proposition to have them physically brought to a location where such management services could be performed. Remote management services, using Over-the-air (OTA) facilities to distribute data, programs, and firmware updates to mobile devices, and to collect usage information and configure device options and software are becoming the norm.

OTA facilities certainly help with the scalability issue, but still leave the variability and complexity issues not completely resolved for the entire industry segment: there are many vertical solutions which address one segment of the management problem while not offering general DM facilities. And there are more general DM solutions that unfortunately target only a single (or a narrow set of) device brand(s). This may be sufficient for a particular device manufacturer, assuming all the devices they manufacture can be submitted to the same management processes, using the same solutions (even that is a stretch).

However, devices are distributed to individual consumers and enterprises by Mobile Network Operators who provide the end-to-end access and communication services. And in the case of enterprises, the enterprise IT departments further distribute the devices to their employees (we call these *front-door devices*). Operators are offering a variety of devices, to meet the needs of a subset, or all of their services, or a specialized service. Individual consumers can choose an operator, and then a device offered by the operator out of a range of devices supported. An enterprise does the same, but could also work with multiple operators simultaneously, in particular when operating in different geographical locations, and they may even allow employees to use their personal devices (we call these *back-door devices*). That adds yet another dimension to the diversity of devices in the enterprise domain.

In order to solve the issues of device variability and complexity, remotely available OTA services need to be based on uniform, consistent, re-usable, and interoperable protocols and message formats. Those protocols and message formats are to a large extent standardized, or in the course of being standardized. They include standards for supporting access to networks and access to specific services – and both categories imply the need for provisioning firmware, software, and supporting material such as certificates, as well as configuring settings on the device. And since operators, enterprise administrators and vendors need to interact with those devices for various reasons, standards will also have to meet the challenge of allowing multiple authorized principals to access, co-exist, share and ideally collaborate with each other when using those management services.

DM in Open Mobile Alliance (OMA) refers to the collection of protocols, Management Objects (MOs), and best practices used to manage the installation, provisioning, retrieving, maintaining, monitoring and diagnosing of the firmware, software, and hardware capabilities of a mobile device. MOs define configuration options, operating parameters, firmware/software versioning, application settings, and user preferences residing on the mobile device (and in some cases on the Subscriber Identity Module (SIM) card) that are the target of those protocols. These standards also frequently prescribe the behavior of client and server – beyond the requirements of the base DM protocols – to ensure interoperability between devices and servers of independent manufacture. This need for interoperability must, however, be balanced against the vendor's need to innovate. The OMA Device Management (OMA DM) specifications strike a careful balance between standardization of interfaces and protocols while leaving most (but not all) behavior and perimeter interfaces to implementers.

18.1 Device Management Requirements

Development of the OMA DM enabler was driven by both market and technical requirements collected from stakeholders. Among these was the requirement to balance the needs of Mobile Network Operators with their carrier-class demands and wide device portfolios, with those of enterprises with their need for tight security and flexible, device-specific configuration policies. This balancing act brought forward several technical challenges that could not have been faced by either constituency alone. The result is a more robust specification, informed by cross-domain requirements and strong business needs.

Among the technical requirements for OMA DM was the need to leverage existing data communication infrastructure in both network and enterprise domains. This is evidenced by the choice of an XML-based message-passing protocol, based on Internet infrastructure, transport, integrity, and security standards such as TCP/IP, HTTP, Secure Socket Layer/Transport Layer Security (SSL/TLS), Message-digest Algorithm 5 (MD5), Uniform Resource Identifiers (URIs), and common Internet content types and encoding.

The choice to begin with Synchronization Markup Language (SyncML) is both historic (the work began in the SyncML Initiative, a precursor organization to OMA) and pragmatic (the SyncML message format and metadata schema were largely complete by the time the DM work began). So, basing the protocol on SyncML was less of a requirement than it was a pragmatic starting point.

18.2 Device Management Architecture

This section explores DM architecture approach. References to precursor standards are provided throughout both the architecture and the following technical specifications sections. While more details will be provided in the following sub-sections, it is important to understand that the DM architecture is following a client-server architecture pattern, where a DM client and a DM server exchange information using well-defined interfaces. With this in mind, let's proceed to see how DM fits in the OMA Service Environment (OSE).

18.2.1 DM in the OMA Service Environment

The DM enablers are an integral part of a deployment that follows the OSE blueprint. Like most enablers, DM enabler exposes category I0 interfaces. While, in principle, such well-defined interfaces can be used by any other resource, the DM enablers provide both endpoints of a client-server

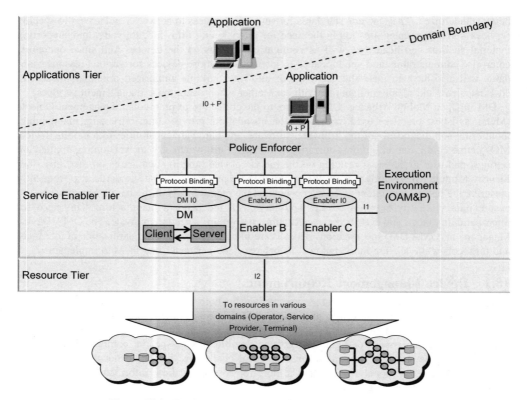

Figure 18.1 Device management in the OMA service environment

architecture, which may not be the case with many other OMA enablers. Nevertheless, exchanges over the interfaces exposed by a DM client and a DM server can be subject to policies controlled by the Policy Enforcer (PE), hence DM is in compliance with the OSE and can be mapped to it. Figure 18.1 attempts to illustrate both points.

DM client exposes an I0 interface to the DM server, and DM server exposes an I0 interface to the DM client. In addition, both the DM client and the DM server may interact with other resources, whose functionality, and the way they interface with the DM components is described in sufficient detail, although not specified by DM specifications. The direct arrows between DM client and DM server should be interpreted as the use of their respective I0 interfaces, and was shown here like this for simplification. The logical PE can always intercept such requests (based on service provider's deployment model) and apply policies before allowing the requests to reach the components of the DM enabler. In other words, the logical paths of communication between a DM client and a DM server are similar to any application's path. Like other enablers, a DM may also interface with other resources using I2 interfaces exposed by them.

18.2.2 Generic DM Architecture – Components and Interfaces

When thinking about mobile DM architecture in a commercial context, it is useful to identify the replaceable system elements. The interfaces between the replaceable elements will cause the greatest pressure on interoperability while offering the greatest opportunity for cost optimization. Figure 18.2 shows a high-altitude view of a mobile DM architecture.

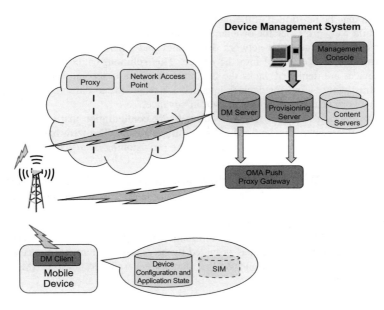

Figure 18.2   Mobile device management generic system elements

The mobile DM domain is divided into three realms:

- The DM System. This is the realm of the management authority. Provisioning, content, and DM servers are organized into an interoperating system controlled by a management console. The system elements may be sourced from a single vendor and they may even be deployed in a single physical server element (for small-scale systems). Alternatively various system elements may be multi-sourced from several vendors and assembled by IT staff into a cohesive system. Large-scale and carrier-class installations often have geographically diverse server installations that are interlinked and managed remotely as a single DM system.
- The Network. This realm is a combination of private and public network resources. The servers may use a combination of IP networking and mobile-specific protocols such as binary Short Message Service (SMS)/Wireless Application Protocol (WAP) Push to communicate with the mobile devices under management. The network may include DM system elements such as dedicated Network Access Points (NAPs) and proxies, and an OMA Push Proxy Gateway may be dedicated to the DM system for session triggering and initial provisioning of DM credentials over the air.
- The Mobile Device. This realm includes the device firmware, DM client software, any layered software agents that may be configured and managed through the DM protocols, a persistent configuration store, and Mobile Operator assets such as the SIM and radio firmware that are used or managed by the DM system.

18.2.3 Initial Provisioning

A fresh-from-the-package network-capable mobile device, however fully featured, is unable to connect to any network-based resources or services until it is configured. End-users often lack the technical skill (or for that matter, patience or even basic interest) in learning to perform this necessary function for themselves. *Initial provisioning* is the function of configuring the device for basic data connectivity and for access to network services including basic network data bearers.

This function may be performed at the factory when a device is manufactured under contract for a specific Mobile Network Operator or enterprise customer. In that case, the Original Equipment Manufacturer (OEM) includes the network data bearer and other access configuration as part of the factory firmware image loaded into the device. This solution, while inexpensive when large numbers of devices are deployed, lacks the flexibility required to account for regional differences in network infrastructure. And for devices intended for retail sale to consumers without a service contract, the network settings cannot be known in advance.

To provision generic devices, post-retail, with network configuration that is necessarily specific to a particular network, two standardized solutions are available. The term bootstrap refers to the initial network provisioning step but also includes the provisioning of management server access:

- Bootstrap from the SIM – includes the core network configuration in a file on the SIM and provides a means for the mobile device to read and apply this information whenever a new SIM is inserted.
- Bootstrap OTA – provides a configuration file via the SMS or other direct data push function. In this case, the SIM need not include information that may become stale weeks or months after it leaves the factory before it is provided to the consumer. Further, devices without SIM capability (for example, CDMA and Wi-Fi® devices generally do not use SIMs) may still be provisioned directly.

The essential purpose of initial provisioning is to configure a device to connect to the data network and to the management resources. Once this has been done, OTA management is possible, and further configuration of device capabilities (such as access to e-mail or corporate resources) can be performed using the DM system.

Note also that initial provisioning in both its flavors – from a file on the SIM card or over the air – is a one-way process without the possibility of direct feedback at the time of provisioning. The term *bootstrap* is intended to convey this limitation and the minimal and reductive nature of what is configured during this first step.

In early 2001, the WAP Forum published WAP Client Provisioning (CP) as a means to configure a mobile device with the necessary settings and credentials enabling access to WAP infrastructure and applications. The OMA Client Provisioning (OMA CP) enabler (a follow-up published by OMA shortly after its assumption of the work of the WAP Forum) provides a means to support this initial configuration function in a way consistent with legacy WAP infrastructure and practices. It also provides a means to bootstrap an OMA DM infrastructure to enable OTA full life-cycle management of devices.

OMA CP and OMA DM are designed to work together in hybrid devices, which require both sets of capabilities – legacy WAP infrastructure provisioning (see [Prov AD]) and active DM. In hybrid devices supporting both OMA CP and OM DM, the OMA DM enabler provides for the use of OMA CP to bootstrap the DM client. However, it does not rely exclusively on OMA CP for this purpose. Many devices do not support OMA CP but rather choose to implement only OMA DM. For these devices, the OMA DM enabler provides for both SIM and OTA bootstrap without the use of OMA CP.

18.2.4 OMA Device Management Architecture

The capability to remotely monitor the digital health of mobile devices, diagnose aberrant conditions, update firmware, patch software, and re-configure device functions is collectively referred to as *device management*. Figure 18.3 provides a view of the OMA DM system architecture including the system elements involved in bootstrapping. Components and interfaces represented with dashed lines are not specified in OMA, and only shown here for better relating to the generic DM architecture diagram.

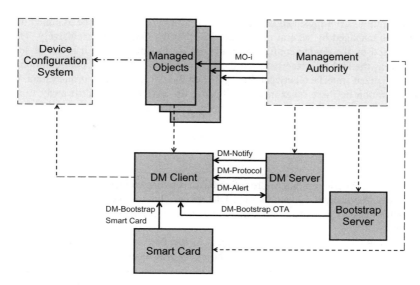

Figure 18.3 OMA DM architecture

In the OMA DM architecture, the Bootstrap server and smart card serve as delivery agents for initial provisioning of the DM account credentials. This action of provisioning client and server credentials on behalf of a management authority is referred to commonly as DM client Bootstrap and may also be seen as *enrollment* into the management program. Credentials may be delivered over the air using the DM-bootstrap OTA interface – exposed by the device using OMA Push [Push ERP] – or they may be delivered in a file stored on the smart card (for GSM or Universal Mobile Telecommunications System (UMTS) devices) and read during startup (or when changed). Credentials may also be factory provisioned to avoid any post-retail bootstrap requirement, but that procedure is not specified by the OMA DM enabler.

The management authority interacts with enrolled devices through a set of management objects (MOs). These management objects are tree-structured collections of data and function points exposed by the device through the DM protocol. Some common MOs are shared by many device types (such as the standard objects, DevInfo, DevDetail, and DMAcc, documented in the DM protocol specifications and others described later in this chapter). Other MOs are vendor- and device-specific.

A management authority uses the DM-Notify interface to provoke a previously enrolled device to begin a DM session. The session between the DM client and DM server is carried out according to the DM protocol. The DM client may send asynchronous notifications to the management authority by using the DM-Alert interface exposed by the DM server and expressed through the DM protocol.

It is typical for a management authority to pre-provision its servers with knowledge of the MOs schemas for the various device types it expects to enroll in the management program. This pre-knowledge of device types simplifies enrollment and allows for smoother integration of new device models. It is also typical for the DM server vendors to deliver a set of MOs schemas for common device types as part of the initial server installation. However, the ability of a DM server to adapt to new device types is an essential feature.

One key characteristic of the OMA DM architecture is the assumption of device-side state management. That is, servers need to keep very little state for each enrolled device (typically just client and server credentials used to support the protocols). As the device configuration system typically exposes a common API for use by different internal software agents (e.g. OMA CP, signed configuration script files, and user interface control panels), it must be assumed that a device configuration is managed by several means, not just through OMA DM exclusively. The common interface exposed by the device configuration system is un-named (since it is out of scope) and it is shown both as the real interface between the DM client and the device configuration system, as well as a 'virtualized' interface between the MOs and the device configuration system. Changes to device configuration by these other means will cause the device state to drift away from any state that might be assumed by the management authority for that device. For this reason it is common for management actions to begin by querying the device for its current configuration state before any commands are issued to change the device configuration.

18.2.5 Bootstrapping

Bootstrapping the DM client includes providing basic network connectivity, a local device address, and the address and access credentials of a DM server. Just as mentioned previously, there are several popular means for bootstrapping including factory provisioning, SIM bootstrap, and OTA bootstrap.

After it is configured, the DM client connects to the DM server over the configured network bearer, and once authenticated by the server, the client will receive management commands from the server. OMA DM is a server-as-master protocol, but sessions are always client-initiated. This means that the server is responsible for queuing management actions, notifying the client when management actions are required, and utilizing the query, replace, add, delete, and execute functions to carry out the management actions on the device. However, if all sessions are client-initiated, how does a management server, which has queued actions for a device, cause that device to connect in the first place?

Just as the SMS is used by OMA CP to push provisioning content to a WAP device, SMS (in the form of OMA Push [Push ERP]) may also be used by DM infrastructure to notify a DM client of pending management actions. The Notification Initiated Session procedure is initiated by a binary SMS message pushed to a previously bootstrapped DM client. These notification messages are digitally signed to ensure the authenticity of the source and the integrity of the message.

However, unlike OMA CP messages, these DM notification messages do not include any management actions. When received, the notifications are treated by the client as though it was passed a note reading, 'Now would be a good time to connect to your management server.' It is assumed that the client will connect as soon as it is practically possible, but not necessarily immediately upon receipt. Voice-call activity, low battery, or limited network connectivity may make an immediate connection to the server impractical or impossible.

18.2.6 The DM Protocol

The DM protocol utilizes a half-duplex, message-passing strategy – once a session is established, the DM server alternately sends commands to the client and receives responses and alerts from the client. This protocol is suitable for carriage by a variety of transport technologies over a variety of network bearers. The OMA SyncML and DM specifications include transport bindings for HTTP [SyncML-HTTP TS], HTTPS [SyncML-HTTP TS] (using SSL 3.0 or TLS 1.0 [DM-Security TS]), and OBject EXchange (OBEX) [SyncML-OBEX TS] (over Infrared Data Association (IrDA) or Bluetooth) but do not preclude the use of other network transports. There are widely deployed bindings for these network transports to both Internet Protocol (TCP/IP) and non-Internet network bearers.

At the time of this writing, the majority of implementations of the OMA DM enablers are hosted on HTTP/HTTPS for use over the public Internet and over existing private or commercial mobile networks. This choice is a natural one that leverages the vast array of network component offerings and best practices established over the last two decades in the development of the public Internet. It further allows an enterprise to add mobile DM facilities to its existing, fire-walled corporate network without deep cuts into the infrastructure. And it brings the scalability of the Internet, supported by a TCP/IP infrastructure, to handle growth of the facility over time.

OMA DM messages are based on the SyncML Representation Protocol [SyncML-RepPro TS], as defined by the SyncML Initiative and as also used in the OMA Data Sync [DS-V1_2 ERP] enabler. These basic message formats, data representation, meta-information, and transport bindings are common with SyncML. Indeed, OMA DM normatively references the same SyncML Common Protocol [SyncML ERP] enabler that is referenced by OMA Data Sync. However, DM goes further by adding conventions in the use of the SyncML message facilities and in the formal contents of the messages.

At its simplest, SyncML is a message-passing structured data exchange protocol. And not unlike many other contemporary protocols, it uses an XML-based markup language to describe the messages. The unit of exchange in the DM protocol is the *package*. Each package may consist of multiple messages, each sent and replied to individually. Each package flows either from client to server or from server to client, and each message in the package has a *header* and a *body*. The body introduces new material for consideration by the receiving protocol endpoint, while the header carries status and responses to the previous message sent by the other side.

The first several packages are used to exchange credentials and basic device and server capability, and following packages carry management actions and responses. Each package sent by the server may contain several (many) commands. Likewise, each package sent by the client may include several responses as well as new client-generated alerts. The management session continues as long as the server continues to send commands to the client. When a package with no commands is received by the client or a specific abort alert is sent by the client to the server, the session ends.

Since most commercial implementations utilize HTTP, a peek into the HTTP/HTTPS binding for SyncML is worthwhile at this point. It is notable that the DM protocol is always client-initiated. This implies that a session opens with the DM client issuing an HTTP POST to the DM server. The payload is quite logically Package 1. It contains the client credentials and a challenge to the server for its credentials. The server returns Package 2 in the HTTP response. Package 2 contains the server credentials and may include a new challenge to the client (if the credentials are invalid).

Further packages are exchanged in a strictly turn-taking and inter-leaved fashion with each odd numbered package flowing in a POST to the server and each even numbered package flowing in the response back to the client.

While there are hundreds of additional details in any actual SyncML protocol implementation, this high-level view should give the reader a feeling for the half-duplex, command-and-response strategy sufficient to understand the DM enabler capabilities at a functional level.

Let's look now more closely at the management interface itself as hosted on the DM protocol. The DM interface can be divided into three main parts:

(1) the schematic configuration structure exposed by the client and targeted by the server (called the *management tree*);
(2) the management commands a server can issue; and
(3) the responses and alerts a client can issue.

18.2.7 The Management Tree

The DM client exposes to DM servers a tree-structured, file system like schematic interface to its device configuration subsystem. This *management tree* may be formally described using the OMA DM Device Description Framework (DDF), an XML language defined as part of the OMA DM enabler. Each management command issued by the server targets one or more nodes in the client's management tree. Each of these nodes is either an *interior* node – that is, a parent of other nodes – or a *leaf* node, which represents some configurable element of the device's functionality, such as a home screen background color or the address of a mail server.

Each node in the management tree has a set of properties – meta-information about the type, representation, name, access limits, and a value. Interior nodes have no explicit value as their purpose is to provide the branches that define the structure of the tree. Leaf nodes define the configurable parameters and provide access to the current value of these parameters.

Collections of interior nodes and leaf nodes form clusters or sub-trees with cohesive meaning (e.g. settings for a single e-mail account). The parent-most interior node of each functionally cohesive sub-tree defines the top of what is termed a *Management Object* (MO).

The interior node that defines an MO carries a *Management Object ID* (MO ID) as its *type* property value. Standardized MOs all specify the MO ID (or type value) that must be used to identify the parent-most interior node. These types most frequently take the form of URIs, though other syntactic forms are allowed. OMA maintains a type registry for MOs defined by OMA as part of the Open Mobile Naming Authority (OMNA). Vendors are also encouraged to expose proprietary MOs and assign their own MO ID values as URIs.

The path through the management tree to any particular node is given in the DM commands as a URI reference (e.g. './email/Personal/ServerID'). The reference context for resolving the provided target URI (see [RFC3986] for a formal definition of URIs and URI references) is the management context established when the server account was bootstrapped to the client. The management context may be the same for all servers, in simple implementations, or, the management context, and hence the tree exposed to each server, may be distinct and isolated from the management contexts of other servers.

Each device type has its own unique collection of capabilities and configuration parameters, and so each device type will also have its own distinct management tree. While this variability is certainly thrillingly flexible, it may also at first reading appear chaotic and hard to manage. Yet, best practices and limited standardization of the shapes of certain MOs do bring order and interoperability where it is needed without stifling innovation where it is otherwise appropriate and encouraged.

Finally, while this interface appears to resemble a file system or configuration registry, that is merely an abstraction. Devices may synthesize parts of their management tree interface using active code, may represent MOs as rows in a database table, or may simply offer a file system or configuration registry with little structural or behavioral limitations or boundaries. The OMA DM enabler supports any of these configuration strategies.

18.2.8 Management Commands

OMA DM defines commands to manage the structure of the management tree (for those clients that support the capability of a server to alter the shape of their management tree) and to query and set the values of leaf nodes. It also defines commands to support interaction with the device user and to form aggregate operations that guarantee the order or atomicity of executed operations. There is also a facility to allow the server to start long-running operations in the client and for the client to alert the server upon completion of those *asynchronous* operations. Let's look at the core management commands first:

- The *Get* command is used to query either the structure of the tree or to retrieve values of leaf nodes.
- The *Replace* command is used to replace the value of a leaf node.
- The *Add* and *Delete* commands are used to add and remove nodes (and complete sub-trees) from dynamic areas of a client's management tree.

These operations can be applied node-by-node, with the server adding or deleting individual leaf and interior nodes one-by-one. Alternatively, OMA DM defines aggregate operations that allow complete sub-trees to be added or removed with a single management action. We cover these aggregate operations later in this chapter.

Given this query and action command language, servers do not need to maintain extensive state knowledge for individual devices. Beyond access credentials and server-side transaction state for complex, long-running operations, device state is maintained in the device and exposed by the DM client through its DM tree only as the tree is queried by the DM server.

18.2.9 Client Responses and Alerts

After each set of commands issued by the server is carried out by the client, the client sends a response message back to the server with the status or outcome of each command. This send/reply tennis match continues until the server has no further commands to issue, at which point the session ends.

As noted previously, the server may target an operational node in the client's management tree. This is done using an *Exec* command, which informs the client that it should start the operation represented by the target node. Only certain nodes, by vendor specification or by standard specification, are permitted to be targeted by *Exec* commands. Such nodes have the *Exec AccessType* among their property values.

The operations initiated by the *Exec* command are complex client behavior that may require indeterminate time to complete. Examples include the downloading of content from a network server, the application of software updates or patches, or restarting a device. In these cases, the client will likely queue these operations, and when the management session ends, perform them at the earliest practical opportunity. Once complete, the client will establish a new session with the server and issue an alert to provide the results of the long-running operation.

18.2.10 Aggregate Management Operations

The following aggregate management operations are available to simplify some management tasks or reduce client-server network traffic:

- *Structural Query*
- *Implicit-Add*
- *Inbox*
- *Tree-pruning*
- *Serialized MOs*.

The first of these aggregate management operations is the *Structural Query*. A *Get* command may target an interior node and specify that the structure of the tree with or without values for each leaf node is to be returned. This optimization allows an account object, such as e-mail account settings, to be retrieved from the device in a single query operation. All clients support the Structural Query operations.

When adding a node to a management tree but specifying a path through the tree that crosses non-existent nodes, those interior nodes are added automatically. The *Implicit-Add* feature allows the fast creation of deep sub-tree structure without issuing first a myriad of *Add* commands to construct the parent nodes. Not all clients support this facility.

A specialized interior node in every management tree is the *Inbox*. This is a virtual 'drop-box' into which MO instances may be added by the server but applied and repositioned by the client. This concept allows new application account settings to be provisioned directly without knowing in advance where in the tree these settings reside. The inbox concept then decouples the account provisioning function from the specific shape of an individual DM tree allowing standardized MOs to be used to represent the account settings for a variety of device types. It also reduces the 'chatty' message shower that would otherwise result from having to query, add, and replace individual nodes in the tree to configure an account. Which MOs may be added through the inbox is left to implementers and to other specifications outside the scope of the DM enabler.

Finally, a *Tree-pruning* aggregate operation is specified when an interior node is the target of a *Delete* command. In this case, not only the targeted node but the entire sub-tree rooted at that node is removed from the management tree.

OMA DM V1.2 [DM-V1.2 ERP] introduced the Tree and Description Serialization (TNDS) format [DM TNDS TS]. This format is an extension of the DDF language, mentioned earlier as the XML language used to describe a device's management tree. TNDS allows the serialization of self-described MO instances (called *Serialized MOs*) for storing in persistent media (e.g. storage cards). It allows the wholesale exchange of MO instances, both structure and data, both inside and outside an OMA DM session. Serialized MOs are particularly useful when combined with the inbox to provision service accounts in a variety of device types.

18.2.11 Configuration Data Storage Models

The DM enabler offers facilities to accommodate a spectrum of device complexity from the very simple, fixed-function device, to the most flexible smart phones and PDAs. There have emerged, however, three predominate configuration data storage models in commercial DM implementations:

- *Fixed*
- *Database-like*
- *Fully Dynamic*

As noted previously, not all devices support the addition or removal of nodes from their management trees. These simple fixed-tree devices can still be managed using the *Fixed* configuration data storage model, but the structure of their trees is fixed at the factory.

Other devices may support the addition and removal of application accounts (e.g. e-mail or Multimedia Messaging Service (MMS)) but may not support the addition or removal of individual leaf nodes. Clients of this type generally expose a *Database-like* storage model to maintain account settings where each account object (or sub-tree) is represented conceptually as a row in a database table. An account is added by the server targeting a non-existent interior node at the proper place in the tree with an Add command. The device responds by automatically creating a sub-tree rooted at the interior node with the proper shape and initial values for all leaf nodes. Likewise when deleting an account, the server targets the interior node that represents that account object and the device responds by removing the entire account sub-tree rooted at that interior node.

In the *Fully Dynamic* model, a file system-like or configuration registry-like interface is exposed. The fully dynamic tree has no preset shape or constraints beyond the base data types and complexity limits imposed by the implementation. Servers must create the MO structure in the correct position in the management tree by issuing Add commands. Each interior and leaf node is created and its value set appropriately. The position in the tree and shape of the individual MOs in this model is established solely by convention and documentation – the DM client does not enforce any constraints.

It should be noted that devices may implement a single or more than one of these data storage models in a single management tree, depending on the domain-specific requirements and constraints of the underlying configuration subsystem. There are idiomatic expressions in the vendor's DDF identifying areas of the management tree which support fixed, database-like, and fully dynamic node structures and hence which areas may be the target of (or require the use of) Add and Delete commands.

18.3   Device Management Enabler Specifications

The OMA Device Management Working Group (OMA DM WG) has published several enablers and is working on several new dependent enablers in parallel, with the explicit goal of supporting transparency, large participation, and time-to-market. By and large, in addition to specifications addressing requirements and architecture, one may place OMA DM enabler specifications in two categories: specifications for protocols and specifications for MOs. Each of the enablers evolves, if needed, by adding subsequent releases – while care is being taken to ensure that at any given time, a set of approved specifications can work well in concert. In the next sections we will focus on some of these different DM enablers, with the main focus on enablers that have reached stability and maturity at the time of the publishing of the book.

18.3.1 History

DM activities in OMA did not start with a clean slate. OMA inherited a set of specifications from the WAP Forum and SyncML Initiative as those organizations were merged to form the OMA. The specifications begun in these ancestor organizations served as the foundation for the DM enablers published by the OMA.

As evidence of the urgency to solve the mobile DM dilemma, even in 2002 when OMA was formed, the first work item approved by the nascent OMA was for Mobile DM – Work Item Document (WID) 001. And while OMA is not the only industry consortium pursuing DM and provisioning standards, by virtue of its cross-industry participation and balanced governance model, OMA is perhaps uniquely positioned to enable market progress and reduce friction in this important area.

The core or foundational DM specification suites that were folded into OMA when it was formed, are WAP CP and SyncML DM. These specifications were revised and improved and subsequently published as OMA CP and OMA DM.

18.3.2 OMA Client Provisioning

As mentioned in Section 18.2.3, WAP CP was introduced as a means to configure a mobile device with the necessary settings and credentials enabling access to WAP infrastructure and applications. The WAP infrastructure includes access points that devices use to connect between the wireless and wireline networks. WAP also defines in-network proxies to simplify the design of mobile devices by pushing certain functions into the network. Examples include the Wireless Session Protocol (WSP) proxy, Wireless Telephony Application (WTA) proxy, and traditional Domain Name Service (DNS). Each of these network elements require access through a specific network address and port and may further require credentials to authorize access.

The OMA CP enabler provides a means to support this initial configuration function in a way consistent with legacy WAP infrastructure and practices. It also provides a means to bootstrap an OMA DM infrastructure to enable OTA full life-cycle management of devices.

The OMA CP specifications allow operators to send device and application settings over-the-air to end-users, who can save them onto the mobile device and use services relying on the new settings. Higher usage rates, new revenue streams, and reduced customer helpline costs are amongst the main net benefits to operators.

OMA CP V1.1 [CP ERP] is an OMA release of a suite of specifications that initially reached OMA candidate status in the fall of 2002, and is a backward compatible extension of the CP functionality included in WAP 2.0. The inherited WAP specification has been enhanced by OMA DM work in that it has added support for direct access (and WAP Proxy support), as well as application access provisioning. The candidate OMA CP V1.1 enabler includes specifications for CP architecture, provisioning bootstrap, provisioning content, provisioning smart card, and provisioning user agent behavior.

Yet, despite some initial deployments, the OMA CP enabler had not yet achieved OMA approved status at the time of this writing. Lack of sufficient interoperability evidence is often cited as the procedural roadblock to approval. However, while that might be the proximate cause, the root cause is more certainly vendor apathy. OMA has no active Work Items to prepare follow-on releases to OMA CP.

18.3.3 OMA Device Management

DM is a process that supports the full mobile device life cycle and encompasses procedures for provisioning, configuring, and servicing mobile devices on behalf of end-users. These procedures would be typically used by third parties (e.g. wireless operators, service providers, or corporate information management departments) that serve in the role of management authority.

Using DM specifications, a management authority can perform any number of remote operations, including initial provisioning and configuration of application software, ongoing management of operational settings such as connectivity configuration and service access credentials, the installation of firmware updates, and monitoring and diagnosing the behavior of installed firmware or software.

OMA DM V1.1.2 [DM-V1.1.2 ERP] is an OMA release of a suite of specifications that reached OMA approved status in January 2004. The set of specifications build upon the inherited SyncML Initiative specifications. The approved OMA DM enabler suite V1.1.2 includes specifications for DM Bootstrap, Notification Initiated Sessions, DM protocol, a SyncML representation protocol, security, a set of standardized DM Objects, DM Tree and Description, DM DDF, and Conformance Requirements.

The more recent OMA DM V1.2 [DM-V1.2 ERP] is an OMA release of a suite of specifications that reached OMA approved status in February 2007. This new release of the OMA DM enabler was a substantial undertaking and includes important clarifications to improve interoperability between clients and servers of differing design and implementation. It also includes significant improvements to security, bootstrapping, data representation, and the core protocols. Among these notable improvements are the support for TLS using SSL 3.0 or TLS 1.0 and the ability of clients to generate asynchronous alerts to notify servers of the completion of long-running operations. An XML serialization format for persisting and exchanging MOs, the TNDS format, was also introduced along with the *Inbox* concept. Backward compatibility with the prior version is directly addressed in this release.

18.3.4 Domain-specific Device Management Enablers

The layered architecture of the OMA DM enabler permits a careful separation of domain-specific functionality from the horizontally applicable protocols and message formats. As evidence of this, consider first the three standard objects that are bundled with the DM enabler specification suite, DevInfo, DevDetail, and DMAcc (DM account object). These are used specifically in support of the DM protocols. While they may prove useful to applications outside of the DM system itself, that is not their primary function. OMA might have taken the approach of bundling all MOs into the core specifications suite, but this would become logistically unsupportable over time.

In unbundling the MOs from the protocol specifications, the OMA followed the example given by Simple Network Management Protocol (SNMP). Management Information Bases (MIBs) serve a similar purpose in SNMP as MOs do in OMA DM – they separate the application-specific data schema from the core protocol specifications. So the OMA DM specifications define how to describe MOs and configuration settings, but do not specify what those objects and settings should be or how they should be used.

Following are some of the DM specifications that include their own MO definitions for use in concert with the OMA DM enabler. Some, like Connectivity Management Objects (ConnMO), are just schematic in nature – they define only MOs intended for configuration. Others, like Firmware Update Management Object (FUMO) and Software Component Management Object (SCOMO), include application-specific behavioral guarantees in addition to MOs.

18.3.4.1 ConnMO – Connectivity Management Objects

When introducing OMA DM in this chapter, we discussed the need to provision a new device with basic data network connectivity as part of the DM-Bootstrap operation. This essential first step in the management life cycle has until recently relied either on factory provisioning, or on OMA CP, or on the indulgence of a patient end-user or retail store clerk. And as not all devices support OMA CP, proprietary remote provisioning facilities have also emerged.

These factors have complicated the initial data access experience for mobile device users. Consider that a factory-fresh generic GSM mobile phone is ready to make and receive voice calls as soon as the SIM is inserted and the power is turned on. It is ironic that for the more capable devices with faster processors and extensive Read-Only Memory (ROM) and Random Access Memory (RAM), such as smart phones and PDAs, initial access to data services is not as straight-forward as placing the first voice call.

The ConnMO enabler specifications [ConnMO TS] constitute a suite of specifications that define a set of MOs intended for the provisioning and management of basic data network connectivity in a standardized way. The specifications define settings for *Network Access Points (NAPs)* and *network proxies* of various types.

The variability in-network technologies deployed makes a universal set of NAP and proxy definitions challenging. To affirm the OMA principle of *network neutrality*, the specifications are partitioned into *bearer-neutral* parts and bearer and proxy *type-specific* parts. This partitioning strategy was intended to alleviate the release churning that can occur when new network technology standards are issued. It is anticipated that the NAP and proxy neutral parts will remain relatively stable even as new NAP and proxy types are defined independently in the future.

The partitioning of technology-specific parameters also simplifies implementation as only the parameters relevant to a particular device type need be exposed through the DM client. This could of course have been done by simply dropping parameters one-by-one from a monolithic NAP or proxy specification. However, by organizing the technology-specific parts together into a cohesive set, the base specifications need not be revised and irrelevant technology concepts can be ignored by implementers. It is anticipated that this simplification will improve interoperability.

The *NAP* is the element in the mobile data network that serves as an entry point for the mobile device. Each network and NAP has an address, though the syntax for NAP addresses depends on the network technology (e.g. an *access point name* in dotted notation for 3GPP packet switched access or an IPV4 address for a Wi-Fi® access point). There are also other common data elements such as a local IPV4 or IPV6 address assigned to the mobile device, a gateway address, network mask, and authentication credentials. This common data set is captured in the NAP MO.

However, each network technology also has its own unique configuration requirements. Every Wireless Local Area Network (WLAN) has a *Service Set Identifier* (SSID); circuit-switched data access (using a modem) requires a phone number and a modulation type; 3GPP and CDMA networks often require specific settings to utilize their quality-of-service guarantees. These network-specific parameters are defined separately, one specification for each of the major network technologies. There are bearer parameter specifications for 3GPP (both packet-switched access and circuit-switched access, including GPRS and W-CDMA), CDMA (including Evolution-Data Optimized (EVDO)), and WLAN (including both enterprise and personal Wi-Fi networks).

Network proxies are an additional challenge to configure. The ConnMO Proxy specification factors out the configuration elements common to all network proxies. Examples of this generic configuration are the proxy address, the active service ports (e.g. 80 for HTTP, 25 for Simple Mail Transfer Protocol (SMTP), etc.), and authentication credentials.

And just as the NAP definitions are partitioned into neutral and technology-specific parts, so too are the proxy definitions. There are separate specifications that define the technology-specific aspects of WAP proxies and HTTP proxies. Other proxy types may be defined in the future and vendors may offer their own proprietary definitions. The ConnMO enabler also fully anticipates vendor extensions to the base specifications but these extensions are limited to reserved areas of the MO definitions to preserve interoperability.

18.3.4.2 FUMO – Firmware Update Management Object

The FUMO V1.0 enabler specifications [FUMO TS] describe the MO(s), and behavior(s) they expose to manage the downloading and installation of firmware updates in mobile devices. The choice of OMA DM as the service tier was a simplifying notion that enables the re-use of management infrastructure and processes. Direct provisioning of binary images to devices using the OMA DM protocols is supported, while alternate download mechanisms (such as HTTP, FTP, OMA download [DLOTA ERP], or proprietary download protocols) are also supported and their use is described.

FUMO V1.0 as implemented by a device vendor, and exposed by the vendor's DM client as an MO, is the transaction management layer representing the firmware update capabilities of the device to the management infrastructure used by the management authority to download and update firmware. Specification of this transaction management layer is the scope and province of the FUMO enabler – implementation details regarding firmware update package creation and formats, digital integrity guarantees, guarantees of authenticity or suitability of a firmware package, and the means by which a package is applied to update a device's firmware are left to the vendors and the market. We believe this balanced combination of standardized formal interface and incentive for vendor innovation in the internal details will lead to a thriving, multi-tiered set of interoperable market solutions. Indeed, evidence of this healthy market is already emerging.

OMA FUMO V1.0 is an OMA release of a suite of specifications that reached OMA approved status in February 2007. The OMA FUMO V1.0 enabler suite includes FUMO Architecture and technical specifications. A FUMO DDF template is also provided, which describes the required, recommended, and optional elements of the FUMO interface. Device vendors adapt this DDF template to describe their own specific implementations of FUMO. The vendor's DDF is then used by server vendors and management authorities, along with vendor-specific documentation, to configure a server to manage the firmware update process for that vendor's devices.

18.3.4.3 SCOMO – Software Component Management Object

The SCOMO enabler [SCOMO TS] is intended to support the remote management of software catalogs. The enabler is modeled on FUMO and focuses on transaction management rather than on deep protocol and format details. At first reading, the SCOMO architecture may demonstrate a passing resemblance to the one defined by the Open System Gateway Initiative (OSGi), but there is no formal relationship between the specifications.

SCOMO defines three main states that software components move through during their life cycle, and there is a corresponding sub-catalog for components in each of these three states – the Download, the Delivered, and the Deployed sub-trees of a SCOMO software catalog MO.

The Download sub-tree holds a collection of descriptions of available software packages. Each of the elements in this catalog describes the name, Uniform Resource Locator (URL), and other vital information relating to a package of software components that may be downloaded from a content server. There are operational nodes that may be targeted by an *Exec* command to cause the download and optional installation steps to be carried out asynchronously.

The Delivered sub-tree holds a collection of descriptions of packages that have been delivered to the terminal. Direct binary delivery of the packages is possible, using the DM Large Objects facility. However, download of the packages described in the Download catalog using alternative protocols will also result in new delivered package entries in the Delivered catalog. These delivered packages may be thought of as data archives containing one or more software components, resources, scripts, and other collateral such as installation wizards. There are operational nodes for each delivered package that may be targeted by an *Exec* command to cause the installation of the components contained in the delivered package.

The Deployed sub-tree holds a collection of descriptions of individually managed software components after they are installed. Deployed components may be Active or Inactive – a platform-neutral notion that suggests whether a component is visible to the end-user or to its execution environment or whether it is isolated for management reasons. One might think of the addition of a short-cut onto a program menu as Activation of a software program. Likewise, removal of that short-cut does not remove the software component, but does make it for most purposes Inactive – it is not possible for the end-user to run the program. Components other than software programs, such as home-screen themes and wallpaper, may also support activation and deactivation, though using different means.

It is a simple matter of using the query facilities of OMA DM to acquire an inventory of delivered or installed packages and software components. For this reason it is generally not necessary for the SCOMO server to maintain extensive state information for each device – when needed, the information may be queried from the device.

And finally, it is possible to remove delivered packages before they are installed or to remove software components from the device after installation by targeting a *Remove* node on the specific package or component entry in its catalog.

As in FUMO, only the formal interface between the client and server, with some abstract behavioral requirements such as state transitions, are specified in the SCOMO enabler. The details of package creation and their formats, digital integrity guarantees, guarantees of authenticity or suitability of a package to a particular device type or execution environment are left to implementers and the market. Likewise, the details of internal catalog management details in the device such as cleanup of installation packages, script language support, activation and deactivation logic, and execution environment issues are left to vendors.

One final point about scope: SCOMO is not an execution management subsystem. It does not address the launching, monitoring, prioritization, or aborting of software applications. Its function is to serve as a remote interface between software providers and their software catalogs on the device.

18.3.4.4 Application-specific Management Objects

Many OMA enablers which include client and server infrastructure elements require configuration. The OMA has adopted a strategy of including MO definitions in these enablers as either an appendix or separate specification. It has also become a best practice to include a DDF template for use by implementers. Examples of enablers that include MO definitions in their suite of specifications include, OMA PoC, OMA Push [Push ERP], and 3GPP's IP Multimedia Subsystem (IMS) [3GPP TS 24.167]. OMA maintains a registry of these MO IDs, the OMNA [OMNA].

18.3.4.5 Vendor-defined Management Objects

Vendors are encouraged not only to implement the standardized MOs defined by the OMA and other standards developing organizations, but to expose the unique characteristics of their devices for management using the same protocols. The flexibility of the OMA DM protocol permits servers to adapt to these uniquely proprietary features while not requiring wholesale replacement or re-programming of the server infrastructure. It is anticipated that, as a result of this balance between standardization and vendor innovation, new and novel management solutions will emerge both through the process of pre-market standardization and through market forces.

18.3.4.6 OMA Work-in-progress – New DM Specifications

In addition to the previously described MOs, OMA has a number of ongoing Work Items in various stages of draft. Following is a representative list of the work with the widest likely impact on the DM infrastructure:

- Device Capability Management Object (DCMO) – intended for management of mainly hardware capabilities such as camera, Infrared (IR), Bluetooth, Universal Serial Bus (USB), etc.
- Web Services Interface for Device Management (DM-WSI) – intended to provide access to an existing DM infrastructure for re-use by other (possibly external) applications. It is anticipated that a management authority would provide access for its business partners and service vendors using this Web Services (WS) interface and may use the interface to link its DM system to its own internal service and application infrastructure.
- DM Scheduling – intended to support execution of management actions, according to a time-based or event-driven schedule, outside of a DM client-server session;
- Diagnostics and Monitoring (DiagMon) – intended to enable detection and troubleshooting of device problems to reduce customer care costs;
- Device Management Smart Card (DM-SC) – intended to address specific smart card capabilities, in addition to bootstrapping from the SIM (as described in OMA DM V1.2). This enabler is intended to address MOs on smart cards, secure dynamic provisioning of MOs on smart cards, and other security extensions for DM enablers using smart cards.

18.4   Impact of DM Specifications on the Industry

While it is still in development in the OMA, DM has received broad support from OMA members, including service providers, mobile device vendors, service provider equipment vendors, and content providers. Wide-scale deployments by mobile network operators and new client and server product offerings are being announced frequently. It is now common to find OMA DM among the requirements that mobile network operators issue in their Requests for Proposals (RFPs) to terminal manufacturers.

With the initial success and uptake of OMA DM, other parts of the IT industry are taking notice: enterprises and fixed data network operators are beginning to look at OMA DM as part of the solution to their respective DM problems. We will look at the future potential for a converged management solution a bit later in this chapter.

18.4.1 Impact on Service Providers

When a new client-server technology rolls through an industry segment, interoperability problems are usually on top among the complaints of early adopters. The first public release of OMA DM V1.1.2 contained enough ambiguity that early implementers often read different meanings from the specifications. These differences in interpretation lead to some significant problems when connecting one vendor's client to another vendor's server. And these problems were inevitably discovered by the network service providers as they began trials and moved into wider deployments.

OMA DM V1.2 incorporates many significant improvements to the language of the specifications. And as is often said of government regulations, each of these changes was caused by a public disagreement over the meaning of the specifications. As each interoperability problem was discovered, problem reports were prepared and alternatives discussed within the OMA until an agreeable solution could be documented in the specifications. This process of successive refinement was reinforced by OMA TestFests – events during which servers and clients are randomly paired and caused to perform a set of standardized tests.

The impact of this process was to reduce the number of significant interoperability problems that service providers discovered as they moved to wide deployment. This is evidenced by the improved results in recent TestFests and in the anecdotal reports of the mobile network operators and enterprises.

As the OMA DM begins to see wide deployment, it is expected that customer satisfaction for first-line support calls will improve. The ability of the network operator call center to remotely adjust the configuration of the subscriber's mobile device should bring noticeably improved outcomes to problems caused by account mis-configuration and out-of-date firmware.

18.4.2 Impact on Vendors

OMA DM and FUMO have most directly affected terminal and server vendors by raising the level of interoperability between different vendors' management products. This has created a network effect that has improved the ability of vendors to respond to Mobile Operator requirements for remote DM and remote firmware updating with the greatest reach. It is expected that as remote firmware updating becomes more widely deployed by operators, device churn may be reduced as firmware is remotely updated to include new functionality, improved security, and critical bug fixes.

18.4.3 Impact on Consumer Market

Imagine calling your mobile network operator customer care center, frustrated that you cannot get your mobile e-mail to sync with your Internet mail account. The customer care representatives use their management console to retrieve your e-mail account settings, correct the spelling of the server name, and adjust the sync schedule and then send these changes seamlessly back to your device.

Contrast this scenario with the present game of '20-questions' that must be played to try to uncover the problem. If the problem cannot be solved or if patience simply runs out, the consumer is left to switch devices, switch networks, or both. Most consumers would likely stay put if any problems they encounter can be quickly and efficiently handled.

So the largest impact on the consumer is expected to be a more efficient problem diagnosis and resolution cycle – nothing will drive loyalty more strongly than the satisfaction of a problem well solved.

18.4.4 Impact on Corporate Market

As mobile devices enter corporations through the back door, their use may become wide-spread even without the support of IT departments. However, as these devices are embraced by corporate culture, adherence to corporate policy and public regulations may become problematic. Corporate management may then require centralized IT support if devices are to contain corporate communications or work product. And in high-minded enterprises, IT may even source devices for use by information workers for these applications.

As these devices begin to adopt OMA DM, IT departments may target their configuration, maintenance, and upgrading using enterprise-class DM servers. This is expected to bring relief to the IT crisis caused by grass-roots adoption of back-door mobile devices or the desire to deploy pallet-loads of front-door devices to information workers.

18.4.5 Impact on Other Specifications

Nearly any service application with a client component that runs in a mobile device is likely to face the problems of initial provisioning and ongoing configuration and management. As OMA publishes enabler specifications such as PoC, Secure User-Plane Location (SUPL), or other client-server enablers, standardized configuration schema, in the form of MOs will also be specified.

18.5 Specifications Evolution and Future Direction

SyncML has matured into a widely used messaging technology. As the basis for OMA DM, it offers a competent, secure, remote management interface to a variety of device types from a broad set of suppliers. Server vendors likewise have embraced it as the core technology for a variety of management functions that they offer to their mobile network operator and enterprise customers. However, as with any maturing technology, some of the early simplifying notions that enabled early adoption and ease of implementation may become brittle with age.

During the past 5 years, a new form of service architecture has emerged based on the eXtensible Markup Language (XML) and the technologies of the World Wide Web – XML Web Services (WS). A suite of specifications has since been standardized to provide a generic infrastructure for a service architecture that is both rich and factored into functionally cohesive modules. It is now possible, using the WS suite of specifications known as WS-*, to develop both simple and complex architectures for the interconnection of mobile devices and service offerings from a standardized, *composable*, and interoperable set of architectural components.

In April 2006, the Distributed Management Task Force (DMTF) published WS-Management [DMTF WS Management], a Web Services-based architecture for the management of enterprise devices (mobile and non-mobile). An exploration is underway in OMA at the time of this writing to evaluate WS-Management as the possible basis for the next technology cycle in mobile DM.

The benefits of moving to WS architecture are strong, but it will not be a smoothly paved path. Much work has gone into the existing suite of DM enablers and deployments are beginning to take hold in the market. It is important for vendors and service providers to split their focus between active deployments of the strong DM offerings already available while studying and preparing for the future. The authors expect the OMA DM enablers to remain an important component of both enterprise and mobile network provider infrastructures for years to come.

However, as we prepare for the next technology cycle, the good news is that WS uses the same Internet technologies in its infrastructure as does the OMA DM. So the design center for a WS-Management adaptation to mobile devices will be to establish a transition from the SyncML foundations to WS while not completely invalidating the technical infrastructure that underlies OMA DM nor the layered management enablers like FUMO and SCOMO.

18.6 Summary

Coming to grips with the enormity of the task of managing a portfolio of millions of end-user mobile devices requires a fortitude that will be constantly tested in the fires of operational experience. Scalable systems built of replaceable and interoperable elements but with a pragmatic view of the balance between standardization and vendor innovation are the path to fulfilling this business need.

Deploying a remote DM infrastructure that deals with genuine market realities is a tall challenge, but one that will be repaid by longer device service life, lower service deployment costs, and ultimately a contribution to profit margin for all market stakeholders.

19

The Digital Rights Management Enabler

This would be a good time to let you know that, in general, Open Mobile Alliance (OMA) delegates are sticklers for definitions for the terms they use in their specifications – and that is a good thing, especially when one decides to write a book about the OMA specifications. Surprisingly enough – we didn't find the term 'Digital Rights' defined in any of the OMA Digital Rights Management (DRM) specification documents, or those referenced by them (e.g. the specifications of the Open Digital Rights Language (ODRL) [ODRL] initiative).

The term 'Digital Rights Management' isn't defined either ... but it can be inferred by studying the DRM specifications. Wondering for an explanation, we assumed that the terms are so common that OMA DRM did not consider a need to define them – but that is not good enough for a book that is supposed to make things a bit easier. To our surprise, a couple of hours of google-ing came up almost empty – you cannot find a straightforward definition for 'Digital Rights', although you can find plenty for 'Digital Rights Management' – which makes you wonder how one goes by explaining extensively how to manage an undefined object.

Rest assured that this is not for lack of effort in the industry – we found several organizations and fora that are dedicated to exploring this topic, and at least one that has posted a glossary under the title 'digital rights glossary'. Guess what though – 'digital rights' itself is not one of those terms defined there! A recent news article on the topic quotes that organization as acknowledging that the term is difficult to define, and it will only become more obvious with emergence of abuses and technologies to defend against such abuses.

Well, this is not good enough for us. For the scope of this book, we will assume that 'Digital Right' is defined as the digital expression of a relationship between some digital content and the intellectual property associated with that content (as a side effect, one may also consider entering change requests to the appropriate OMA documents). That leads to a possible definition for 'Digital Rights Management' as the mechanisms used to control access to and usage of content (e.g. software, music, movies) and hardware, handling usage restrictions associated with a specific instance of a digital work. Such mechanisms must support the production, preview, consumption, transfer, distribution of digital content, and its associated digital rights. That is, DRM must address the management of the life cycle of digital content as well as aspects related to security, certification, and trust.

DRM is a controversial topic in an industry that is fragmented over rights issues. It is certainly necessary to prevent unauthorized duplication of a copyright holder's work to protect fair

The Open Mobile Alliance   M. Brenner and M. Unmehopa
© 2008 Alcatel-Lucent. All Rights Reserved

revenue; however, some 'open source' supporters claim that the more proper term would be 'Digital Restrictions Management'. Of course, one cannot help but ask oneself whether there is any conceptual difference between 'digital rights' and their management, and traditional copyrights and their handling – issues that have been addressed a long time ago. But then one also quickly realizes that, while the concepts can be emulated, it is so much easier to copy, distribute, and/or even broadcast digital content at minimal cost to multiple users and diverse devices, than it was to do so for more traditional content – and, therefore, new concepts backed by new technologies need to be introduced to protect the copyright owners from content piracy.

Regardless of terms, there's little doubt that this is a very important topic and that specifications to be followed by different technologies are much needed by the industry. There's certainly more to it than meets the eye in the OMA DRM specifications: in addition to specifying how digital rights operations are to be performed, these specifications handle issues related to digital rights security, streaming, user privacy, implications on devices and smart cards.

19.1   What Were the Drivers for Those Specifications?

It comes as no surprise to see that today's landscape for rights protection has been driven mainly by the entertainment industry and no one has been more vociferous in its battle against copyright theft than the music industry (represented in particular by the major record labels and their artists). This has been due to the explosion in the demand for digital music, the high value associated to it as a product, and the availability of a number of new enabling technologies that were a fillip to its success.

In the 1980s, the UK music industry ran an anti-piracy campaign called *'Home Taping is Killing Music'*, which became a major initiative, specifically designed to remind consumers that transferring original and copyrighted music content by any means, (in those days typically from vinyl or CD formats to audio tape or other media) was a crime. A picture of a skull and crossbones was plastered on almost every CD being sold to remind us that the music industry was united in enforcing its rights to prevent illegal copying. This campaign was quickly followed by others related to the use of VCRs and video taping. However, consumers continued to copy. Why? Probably because they wanted to play the songs they knew and loved on other devices that belonged to them. The increasing availability of new digital media players at that time offered to make those songs even more portable and, in effect, available by definition for sharing with friends and family in even more convenient ways. This may have been the perception, but in fact these consumers were still crossing the boundaries of their rights. What we had (and still have today to some extent) was a deadlock between the content providers and its consumers in an industry faced with more stringent policing and higher prices.

In today's digital media age, the stakes are pretty much the same as they were decades ago, when the entertainment industry was burgeoning with the growth of mass communication. Content creators still want their intellectual property respected while consumers still want to consume products and services. However, today's requirements have shifted slightly in a highly competitive and thriving market where consumers are beginning to expect even more sophisticated ways of consuming services. As a result, content creators and providers are able to enforce rules for the consumption of their products and services in digital format.

The age of the Internet, digital media, and mobile communications has not only given the consumer more choices, but more consuming power too. The standardization of SIP/IP core technologies for more diverse environments like mobile networks coupled with enhancements to end-user devices have helped change the way consumers access and store content as well as how they consume it. The demand for content has soared together with the increasing availability (and affordability) of digital camera technology, media players, and personal computers. These media players have not only become the de facto way that users play their music, store images, and perform their work, but they have opened up new creative and enterprising possibilities for content production and distribution by the end-users themselves. Users are not only able to download content, but they can create their own work by using a combination of resources and media objects available from several devices or applications.

With use, of course, comes the potential for abuse, so governments, institutions, and the industries have had to keep abreast of technology to tackle piracy in the digital age. A content provider could just encrypt its content with a digital 'key' to protect illegal copying and rely on the courts to deal with any miscreants, or take a step back and look more carefully on what is at stake and whose copyright is being protected. There has to be a balance between what's legitimate, what allows for a good user experience, and what makes good commercial sense. Should an amateur band using the Internet to promote itself be restricted by the same rights as an established band on a major record label? Surely, the commercial value of content varies with the stakeholder.

What one expects to see is a service model that encourages content creation and where creators are able to attach flexible rules according to the value of the content being distributed or to the consumer's needs. If a consumer is willing to pay for content, then the rights that come with it should at least be clearly defined to them. By associating usage rules (i.e. the Rights Object (RO)) with digital content, only devices having those rights can access that content. Furthermore, by separating the RO from the encrypted content itself, consumers can enjoy more flexible distribution options and purchase rights independently of the content. DRM, therefore, becomes an enabling technology, not a restricting technology (and as we mentioned in the introduction), facilitating the life cycle of digital content in the world of rich media and blended services.

19.2   Are Those Specifications Really Necessary?

In mobile networks, devices are increasingly being required in both IT and consumer domains and often have to cater for both. More and more copyrighted content is finding its way into mobile devices, either via push mechanisms [PushOTA TS], or browsing, or via memory card. Content providers are, therefore, naturally demanding that content destined for mobile devices is adequately protected.

The benefits of applying standards to DRM are manifold. An approach that encourages a trusted end-to-end interoperable standard would create a secure environment for service provisioning and encourage content provisioning across network domains. End-user experience is critical to the take-up of digital services and users will expect usage rights to be applied proportionately according to the value of the content. Service providers want to ensure that their investments in services are protected across multiple device platforms and ensure time-to-market for their services. Vendors can ensure interoperability with each other's products and content providers can continue to create content using standard technologies and interfaces.

A universal ('one size fits all') approach to standardized DRM is difficult, if not impossible, to achieve. Stakeholders in different value chains have different requirements, not only from a technology perspective but from a business level. When we think of all the different DRM technologies out there, it is easy to wonder if much attention has been paid to the real requirements of all the stakeholders in the value chain.

The work of OMA DRM began in the Wireless Application Protocol (WAP) Forum and 3GPP, where Mobile Operators wanted simple and inexpensive solutions for protecting the free distribution of downloadable applications like ring tones and screensavers. The goal was to create a truly interoperable DRM standard for the mobile industry based on market demand and convergence with the consumer electronics world.

The OMA DRM version 1.0 Enabler Release specification provides a limited solution for the mobile phone industry. It includes a mechanism for protecting user-created content ('Forward Lock') and is now widely deployed. Its appeal lies in its simplicity and lightweight design for

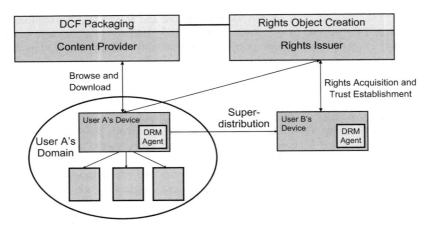

Figure 19.1 OMA DRM logical model

protecting limited content like screensavers and ring tones. OMA quickly saw the potential for more sophisticated rights protection with the increasing use of richer and higher value applications on mobile handsets.

Along with the additional security, trust models and new peer-to-peer distribution options standardized in OMA DRM version 2.0, the mobile industry has an end-to-end interoperable mechanism for content providers to distribute protected content and for devices to acquire the RO from a Rights Issuer (RI) independent of underlying media formats and execution environments.

From the logical model shown in Figure 19.1, a number of use cases have been derived that are used as the basis of high-level requirements on OMA DRM 2.0 system entities. Protected content is packaged in a secure container known as the DRM Content Format (DCF) using symmetrical encryption keys. The DRM agent is the trusted entity in the device that decrypts the protected DRM content.

What follows are a number of these use cases.

19.2.1 Basic Download

User A browses the portal of the content provider and agrees to the terms and conditions of usage of the selected content, a rich media (.rmf) file. The permissions allow for metered usage. The protected content together with the RO is delivered together to User A's device (combined delivery). In the case of separate delivery, the RO is pushed to User A's device.

User A's rights expire after a period of time, but User A's device automatically requests renewal of the RO for the purchased content and User A is informed ('silent rights renewal').

Later, User A buys a new set of rights for the same content which allows User B to receive and consume the content from User A.

19.2.2 Multiple Device Usage

This section contains use cases that deal with multiple device usage.

19.2.2.1 Domain Model

User A has access to a number of other devices either belonging to him or his friends. User A creates a usage 'domain' on his service provider's portal where he is informed of the terms and conditions for domain usage including which types of devices are allowed, according to available domain profiles. User A registers a number of devices to his domain, one of which is a media player which has no network connectivity. Being an unconnected device, the media player is unable to contact the RI and render the content. The principal device is a mobile handset that downloads DRM protected content in MP3 format and a domain RO. User A transfers the content embedded within the domain RO to the media player.

19.2.2.2 Rights binding

One of User A's devices is another mobile device. The RI issues an RO that allows User A to consume Advanced Audio Coding (AAC) encoded content on either device, as long as the SIM card belonging to User A is present in the device.

19.2.3 Super-distribution (Peer-to-Peer Sharing)

The RI provides a type of RO that allows User A to copy an Over The Air Activation (OTA) ring tone without a bundled RO to User B's device. User B separately purchases the RO for the content, allowing User B to receive and consume the content from User A.

19.2.4 Preview

For high-value content such as soccer or video clips in MPEG4 format, the content provider can offer a preview service in which User A can acquire the rights to view only a short version of the full original content, or even the full original with time limitations.

19.2.5 Buying the Rights Object for another User

User A wants to share with User B, the content he has purchased from the content provider. The content provider offers User A options to buy the rights for playback on User B's device. This feature allows additional 'gifting' options where the User B can consume the content without separately purchasing the RO.

19.2.6 Streaming Content

This section contains use cases that deal with streaming content.

19.2.6.1 Basic Streaming

User A purchases the RO to view real-time streamed media content. The content is encrypted while streaming. As part of the permissions contained in the RO, User A is prevented from storing the content on his device for forwarding, or replay at a later stage.

19.2.6.2 Multicast

User A subscribes to a number of real-time content channels provided by his content provider. As part of the subscription management, User A purchases the RO for each channel.

19.2.7 Backup and Restore

In order to manage the storage memory in his device, User A is able to create backups of the RO and content in an off-line storage area offered by his content provider. Alternatively, User A can backup the RO and content to a removable memory card.

19.2.8 Export of Rights Object

User A obtains permission for the RI to transfer content he has already purchased together with the RO to User B's device which uses a non-OMA DRM system.

19.3   OMA DRM Requirements

Now that we have looked at a number of use cases, we introduce the high-level requirements on OMA DRM 2.0 system entities that have been derived from these use cases. The [DRM RD] contains high-level market expectations and functional requirements related to security, streaming, distribution, storage and backup of RO's, smart card and media storage as well as on user privacy.

19.3.1 Types of Content

OMA DRM has to protect a wide variety of content, ranging from simple ring tones to adult material. Content is cryptographically protected both in transit and storage and unusable without the associated RO obtained for a particular device, but the standard remains flexible to permit a range of key strengths.

19.3.2 Rights Objects

OMA DRM will offer content providers and RIs a broad variety of flexible usage rights for content. The following permissions (or a combination thereof) may be granted: play, display, execute, print, and export.

A number of different rules-based constraints can be expressed based on time/date or metering options, for example, to create stateful ROs:

- Based on a count, restricting the number of times a permission to execute the protected content is granted.
- A countdown that specifies the number of times permission may be granted for the protected content with timers, for example, permission to watch a video clip up to 5 times within 10 minutes.
- 'Date and time' based, specifying a validity period within which the content can be executed.
- 'Interval' based, specifying a period of time during which the associated protected object can be used.

Of course, permission may be set to 'Unlimited' grants, that is, no constraints.

19.3.3 Content and Rights Object Delivery

OMA has made sure that delivery of protected content and the RO is not tied to any specific transport mechanism, so the standard allows for any mechanism to be used. The following are examples of what could typically be used. Note that these include both online and offline mechanisms:

- HTTP/WSP (Wireless Session Protocol)
- Push [PushOTA TS]
- MMS Delivery [MMS-V1_3 ERELD]
- LAN
- Via Memory Card.

19.3.4 Streaming

Although continuous media clips like audio or video may be accessed by either downloading or streaming, more applications are becoming available that require support for real-time streaming of media. The OMA DRM 2.0 standard supports both broadcast and multicast modes of delivery of streamed media, which makes the availability of high-value real-time streamed content to mobile devices more compelling.

19.3.5 Enhanced Security

The market is expecting OMA DRM 2.0 to facilitate the governance of much higher value content delivered over mobile service provider networks. This places more emphasis on security and protection and thus assumes a trust model that is commensurate with such content. OMA DRM 2.0, therefore, has to ensure that devices are authorized and authenticated before receiving content and provide a robust content protection environment (including protection against replay attacks), authentication and revocation of any device whose security is compromised. It also has to support security mechanisms that allow for flexible usage rights, for example, where usage rights vary for different components of content. Those different components may require different levels of encryption or none at all (multipart DCF).

OMA DRM 2.0 includes the cryptographic binding of the device, that is a secure association between the DRM user agent and a unique key pair. This enables authentication based on Public Key Infrastructures (PKI). A PKI-based trust model is assumed in OMA DRM, but its realization is not specified by the enabler. PKI ensures that certificates and private keys are distributed to both the device and RI thus making the system secure and easier to administer. It also allows for authentication of the RI by the device. For more information about PKI, see the Chapter 13.

OMA DRM 2.0 does not specify the implementation of the trust model. Service providers could implement their infrastructure based on a different model but this would create interoperability issues.

19.3.6 Export of Rights Object

The export of OMA DRM RO into other systems (e.g. copy-protected media) would greatly enhance user experience and even though this is partly addressed in OMA DRM 2.0, it is assumed that the exact conversion mechanisms will be addressed by other DRM systems. The OMA DRM set of permissions for ROs include an 'export' permission which, when granted by the RI, allows the export of RO to take place.

19.3.7 Super-distribution

The requirements for super-distribution allows for content to be shared in a transport-independent manner. Those devices receiving the content must be able to obtain the RO in a user-friendly way. By that we mean that the user can find out if his terminal can first render the content before acquiring the RO and have the RO available to download using the same transport method as that used for downloading the RO and protected content together.

19.3.8 Backup and Storage

In the old days, if you lost your music, you lost your rights to use it. The beauty of backup and storage in DRM is that since your usage rights are physically separate from the content, they can be separately stored and reinstated if the content is lost. OMA DRM 2.0 supports backup and re-storage of stateless RO's in line with many content provider offerings, but stateful ROs may have restrictions imposed.

19.4 Architecture and Technical Specifications Overview

The logical architecture for OMA DRM 2.0 is shown in Figure 19.2. The architecture is described in terms of three functional entities: the DRM Agent which is usually an application installed in the device and two server-side logical entities called the Content Issuer (CI) and the Rights Issuer (RI). Of course, being logical entities, they should not be necessarily viewed as physical network entities.

The CI and RI portals are considered user interfaces to the DRM governed content system. DCF media content files are accessed via the CI portal. Usually, the device's browser will be directed to the URL of the RI portal when trying to access and download that protected content.

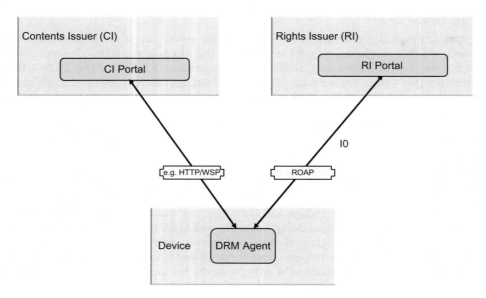

Figure 19.2 OMA DRM logical architecture

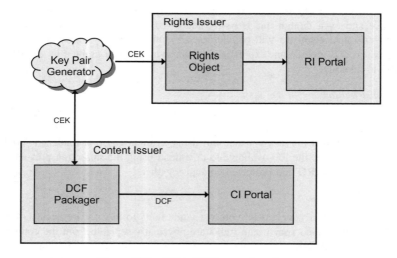

Figure 19.3 OMA DRM protection element

As well as being the content server, the CI is associated with other functions, the main one being protection of content. Digital media objects are made available as protected digital media objects using symmetric Content Encryption Keys (CEK). This protection element is not shown in the logical architecture picture but can be viewed as the source of DCF protected media objects and ROs. Neither the interface between the Content Issuer and the Rights Issuers nor the interface between the DRM Agent and the Content Issuer is specified in the OMA DRM.

A closer look at the CI protection element is shown in Figure 19.3.

Although shown as separate entities, the process of creating DRM governed content requires a close association between the CI and RI. Unprotected content is encrypted using a CEK and packaged into a DCF together with a Content Identifier and the URL for the RI portal. The CEK used for each DCF and made available to the CI has to be contained in the corresponding RO stored by the RI. This ensures that the DCF cannot be used without an associated RO. In addition, the CEK is protected by the RI using a Rights Encryption Key (REK).

The RI is responsible for the authentication of DRM agents and the generation and secure storage of ROs, that is provide a secure environment for RO generation and distribution. The storage of ROs in a database is an important aspect, since DRM agents may need to be authorized to perform functions over the governed content, which would require a check against this database to see if permission is granted. OMA ROs are written in a profile of a language called ODRL [ODRL], see below. If an RI supports ROs written in other formats, the RI may support the tools to translate them, although this functionality is not currently supported in OMA.

The DRM Agent is provisioned with a key pair and certificate that validates the key pair to that particular DRM agent. This allows the DRM agent to be authenticated as a trusted entity in the OMA DRM system. The DRM agent must recognize and enforce the permissions and usage constraints contained in the RO as well as ensuring that those sensitive parts are not tampered with or used without authorization.

In OMA DRM 1.0, the ROs are received using [PushOTA TS]. For DRM 2.0, mutual authentication between the DRM agent and RI is established using the Rights Object Acquisition Protocol (ROAP).

ROAP is broken down into two main aspects: a protocol for registering a device with the RI and two delivery protocols, one that allows the DRM agent to accept delivery of a RO by using the PUSH Protocol (2-pass) and another one that allows the DRM agent to request and deliver the RO (4-pass). ROAP also allows for a device to join and leave a domain. A ROAP sequence is initiated when the device receives an ROAP trigger, which is basically an XML document containing a URL to identify the RI hence obtaining the permissions and constraints of content usage.

The 4-pass protocol includes mechanisms for the negotiation of protocol parameters, exchange of certificate information, the negotiation of cryptographic key information, and mutual authentication. The 2-pass protocol is a lightweight version, which assumes that the device has a pre-established context at the RI.

Finally, this section briefly discusses about the ODRL. [ODRL] is the Open Digital Rights Language of which OMA specifies a lightweight mobile profile. The function of any Rights Expression Language (REL) is to enable metadata and identify content as well as specify the permissions and constraints of content usage. ODRL is adopted by the OMA with specific goals in mind, namely to reduce the complexity for value chain players to adopt DRM and to specify flexible permissions and constraints independent of the content type or transport mechanism. To this end, the syntax of ODRL includes rights models that group the rights elements and attributes for simple specification. Examples of elements include <rights>, <context> or metadata, <version>, and <permission>. Further information can be found in the [DRM REL].

19.5   Salient Points

OMA DRM gives content providers and service providers the tools for specifying the content formats, REL, authentication/authorization protocols, and protection mechanisms for digital media. The following looks more closely at the issues and benefits for some of the key stakeholders.

19.5.1 Divergent Views and Their Resolution

OMA DRM 2.0 is a fully open specification that provides the enabling functionality for the management of copyrighted content. Ironically, the implementation of the OMA DRM specification itself is bound with Intellectual Property Rights (IPR) under which device manufacturers and service providers have to obtain appropriate licenses. Like some other standardized technologies, OMA DRM licensing is handled by a patent pool that is responsible for setting a licensing model and pricing schemes for essential IPR contained in the specification. The [MPEG-LA] is the patent pool for OMA DRM.

The divergent views in the industry over licensing of DRM technologies and the need to break the stalemate have been well documented. What exists in the market now is a general reluctance to take-up OMA DRM that threatens to stifle end-to-end interoperability and open competition. As a result, service providers have started to look with even greater interest in point solutions. There is obviously broad agreement between stakeholders to achieve pragmatic solutions that are vital in such a nascent market for high-value governed content. How and when these concerns are addressed is still subject to scrutiny and anticipation. So, in April 2005, the [MPEG-LA] announced that the patent holders of OMA DRM had revised its terms for licensing the OMA specification following high profile statements of consternation at the original terms and conditions from some trade bodies and researchers. Despite this, discord still persists and further fragmentation threatens the industry, which could move toward alternative DRM solutions unless more flexible licensing models are supported.

At the time of writing this book, the final license agreement from [MPEG-LA] has been subject to much speculation in the industry and the market response was eagerly anticipated. The fact is that patent holders are unlikely to meet all the demands of the implementers and the implementers themselves are faced with market pressures to avoid further fragmentation in the industry. The resolution of this matter has to be investment in solutions that offer incentives for the implementation of OMA DRM in products and services and not those that disenfranchise its implementers. In the meantime, solution providers will continue to seek ways to interoperate between different solutions so that multi-DRM technology devices may be possible. Recent examples include OMA DRM plug-ins for the Windows Media Player®.

19.6   Impact of Specifications on the Industry

OMA DRM was created using the combined efforts of mobile handset vendors, mobile service providers, content providers, and other value chain players and has enabled the mobile industry to distribute more compelling content to mobile device users and maximize the interoperability between value chain stakeholders. To this end, OMA DRM 1.0 has undergone, probably, the most substantial interoperability testing amongst all of the OMA service enablers.

As device capabilities continue to be enhanced and services architectures converge, the secure and trusted distribution of multimedia content remains a key issue as even more potentially lucrative services are being considered (e.g. IP Television (IP TV)). OMA DRM 2.0, which is designed to extend the mobile device capabilities to the IT and consumer electronics domain, is also undergoing rigorous testing at OMA TestFests, but its take-up is being tempered by legacy and proprietary DRM solutions that are still in use. However, OMA DRM 2.0 should not be accused of not being sufficiently featured. For widespread deployment, the challenges, as mentioned above are business and legal and not really technical or regulatory.

19.6.1 Impact on Service Providers

OMA DRM enables mobile devices to access more value added services, allows their users to try out and buy new products and allows service providers to maximize their revenue with branded and partnered services. The introduction of the technology into service provider networks will impact several existing system components, including download and delivery servers, databases, security, and trust systems. The content provider or RI, that is any entity responsible for the delivery of the service, will have to integrate with billing and customer care systems and possible re-use notification mechanisms such as those offered by existing messaging platforms (SMS/MMS). The RIs themselves may want to integrate with several third-party content providers.

The use of an open interoperable DRM technology will provide opportunities to lower the CAPEX and eventually the OPEX, by the use of common interfaces and common functions compared to having to support different proprietary solutions from different vendors. Indeed, there are many different solutions with different approaches to rights management. For a service provider, trying to determine the best one will be challenging. In terms of functionality, OMA DRM 1.0 uses simple technologies (forward lock) that are relatively fast to deploy over existing technologies and will enable quick and simple solutions.

As a standard-based solution, OMA DRM, by definition, creates an open playing field and competitive environment. It is designed to integrate with existing service-enabling technologies like [PushOTA TS], OMA Broadcast [BCAST ERELD] (see also Chapter 20), and Dynamic Content Delivery (DCD) [DCD RD] (see also Chapter 21) for download and billing of content to users and thus quickly establish a critical mass for profitable service provision. The enhanced features offered by OMA DRM 2.0 will keep customers interested and engaged with free previews, super-distribution, and loyalty schemes for example and help push the boundaries for service provider differentiation using content personalization.

19.6.2 Impact on Vendors

Before OMA DRM was specified, there was no rights management technology being deployed *en masse* in mobile devices. The fact is that OMA DRM is a thoroughly tested specification that enables devices to become a trusted endpoint in the distribution of governed content, significantly enhancing its potential market reach in terms of connectivity and interoperability in the value chain. This has helped increase the competition between device vendors, making OMA DRM a basic feature of all devices.

Devices must be able to download and render content and support several usage models such as metered-time, gifting and content bundles. Support of file formats as basic as those supported by [MMS-V1_3 ERELD] to more complex streamed content in [3GPP TS 23.246] transport standards are expected as well as additional memory and storage capabilities for rights backup. Security is enabled by the presence of public keys on the device that cryptographically bind the ROs to the device.

System and service delivery vendors will keep abreast of market requirements from service providers by offering a standards-based DRM solution. Their products will be interoperable with both connected and unconnected devices in converged network architectures increasing the value of the content supported on those platforms. As expected, several wireless vendors have already started to partner with OMA DRM software solution providers and strengthen their multimedia delivery platforms by future proofing its services portfolio.

19.6.3 Impact on Consumer Market

You might be thinking from the above that DRM is a panacea for all the ills related to the content distribution and copyright theft. The fact is that the benefits of DRM have been the subject of intense debate. Many who are unconvinced cite the impact on the consumer market (the bread and butter of OMA DRM) as the reason. As mentioned above, before OMA DRM there was no other enabling technology like it on mobile devices. Consumers, with the right technology, could download and consume the plethora of unmanaged open source content out on the Internet. Even with DRM enabled on the device, this of course is still possible, but one of the goals of DRM is to make the risks associated with this practice unnecessary and, instead, offer reasonable incentives for using appealing content within a realistic permissions framework.

The expectations from a user perspective are high and the people responsible for the OMA specification know that. Although OMA does not directly specify user interface or performance requirements, a certain quality of experience is expected from OMA DRM. For instance, the DRM Agent will have to distinguish between protected and unprotected content in a multipart DCF. Devices will have to render the content in an unambiguous way. A clear example of a multipart DCF is a stream that is preceded by a free preview where options, instructions, and guidelines will be presented to the user. In reality, the operator's guidelines will shape how we experience DRM managed content in terms of performance and usability.

But many consumers won't care about the technology. They will want the user experience to be as transparent as possible and hide all the complexities of the underlying system. In reality, there will of course be some challenges for the complete novice. She can now move content from one device to another (perhaps using [Bluetooth]), share the content with other users, backup the content, and buy extended rights. OMA DRM has the potential of enabling the content management of almost all multimedia content being delivered. In turn, content that was previously difficult to deliver in a controlled manner due to fears of copyright theft can be enjoyed on compatible and trusted devices.

The consumer angle requires continual attention for consistency and usability reasons. Whether this actually happens or not remains to be seen. What might be an equally important factor is if and how the consumers themselves start creating and distributing their own digital content and using OMA DRM-enabled handsets for instance. This brings us on to the types of consumers who might be a bit more savvy when it comes to technology – who might buy a device specifically for the purpose of creating and applying their own rights for its usage. This is not just about being able to forward lock an MMS message, but the ability to download the tools to enable users to protect and apply their own RO, metadata, etc. to user-generated content. This may be the value-add that consumers are looking for from OMA DRM, and which could really benefit the user in more creative ways.

19.6.4 Impact on Corporate Market

DRM is growing in the enterprise domain. Although all the use cases described here have been taken from the consumer perspective, there has been growth in the corporate sector for managing sensitive resources, data, and other corporate assets, and protecting them from intellectual property theft. Examples include financial reports, specifications, contacts, etc.

The mobilization of the corporate environment has in turn seen a rise in demand for enterprise applications. One of the most pertinent examples is document control and the application of rules-based control of documentation, for example, edit but not delete contents. OMA DRM could come part way to meeting the demands of the enterprise but in reality only provides 'lightweight' DRM opportunities for enterprise security systems that employ strict business processes. The fact is that OMA DRM was designed chiefly with consumer devices in mind. Only until OMA can fully appreciate how underlying policy management and security schemes of the enterprise can integrate and leverage its DRM specification, can the needs of the enterprise be met by the specification.

19.6.5 Impact on other Specifications

Any service enabler enabling content delivery will have an interest in the OMA DRM specification. OMA [BCAST ERELD] and [DCD RD] are two examples of specifications that may require DRM. Ever since broadcast TV started to enjoy a growth in demand, service providers have had to implement adequate security without any restriction to the content or its quality. In OMA, a broadcast DRM extension profile has been created for streamed broadcast media because OMA DRM 2.0 did not fully meet all the requirements for BCAST. The specification is known as [DRM XBS] and includes additional usage models such as pay-per-view, record and edit, and DRM enhanced service provisioning. There have to be changes to ROAP as well to meet the unidirectional channel requirements for broadcast and the specification of a leaner RO that scales well in point-to-multipoint channels.

DCD [DCD RD] specifies enabling functions for the asynchronous distribution of personalized content to the device. In richer media applications, content providers may need to use DRM to provide a secure mechanism for content management. It is thought that the entity issuing DCD content is likely to be the same entity as the DRM CI. On the device side, the DCD client may have to interact with the DRM agent.

In addition to the above, OMA's Download DRM specifications experts have set to work on additional technologies that make OMA DRM a step closer toward being fully functioned. Interoperability between DRM technologies, or rather the lack of it, is an area that is gathering closer scrutiny with the purpose of creating more practical solutions for DRM interoperability. OMA's work on Secure Content Exchange (SCE) [SCE RD] represents a leap forward in functionality related to content exchange between OMA enabled environments and other technologies. As mentioned earlier, OMA DRM 2.0 so far only allows the export of ROs, SCE specifies a method for importing non-OMA DRM protected content into OMA DRM-enabled devices. The [SCE RD] specification also enhances OMA DRM 2.0 to addresses more flexible rights transfer, bound by time (borrowing) or location and on an ad hoc basis. More flexible rules for moving ROs are intended to appeal to those who have enjoyed content exchange in the pre-DRM days of open sharing, or just want more fun ways of distributing content. With the SCE import function, content sharing is no longer bound to the same protection technology. A user can, for example, give a friend using an OMA DRM-enabled device one or more counts of his right to play a piece of video.

With ad hoc sharing there is the need to have a less restrictive domain environment. In OMA DRM 2.0, domains are created by the RI, which places a requirement on each device in the domain for network connectivity. SCE introduces the concept of a user domain in which users can create a group of devices and share rights with them without the need to involve a RI. This allows the inclusion of unconnected devices in the domain. As a consequence, OMA DRM architecture will include two new elements: the Domain Authority and the Domain Enforcement Agent to manage the trust in this enhanced sharing environment. SCE also involves enhancements to ROAP.

By enhancing OMA DRM 2.0 with SCE, OMA has taken an important step closer to creating a more homogeneous protection environment and will receive broad encouragement especially from those companies behind MARLIN, (from [INTERTRUST]) which represents another certificate based trust management DRM solution fostering interoperable DRM for the consumer market and media player industry. Others taking a similar approach include Sun Lab's [DReaM] and [CoreMedia], the latter being responsible for plug-ins for Windows Media Player for the rendering of OMA DRM protected content.

Another limitation of OMA DRM 2.0 is the user's inability to transfer ROs between compliant devices without the creation of a domain. OMA's Secure Removable Media [SRM RD] specification represents a significant step toward enabling more flexible portability of ROs via trusted removable media and hence user experience.

19.7 Specifications Evolution and Future Direction

It is not easy to predict the future of direction of OMA DRM. OMA DRM 2.0 is a well-defined and interoperable specification for content protection which is being deployed in the market. So much is the appeal for one interoperable standard that more content providers seem to be moving away from closed solutions in favor of OMA DRM 2.0, especially in the area of mobile music.

In specifying SRM and SCE, OMA has begun to address other important gaps in the specification, that have threatened to limit the user's experience of DRM in the market and proved the specification's ability to adapt to the demands of technology outside of OMA's remit.

Some other DRM bodies (e.g. [DMP]) have painstakingly analyzed usage rights that they think should be prioritized for DRM because of their existence in the days of analog media. Examples include the ability to edit and annotate or make copies with lower quality. Maybe OMA will revise its permissions and constraints framework as a result of this analysis by outside bodies.

Consistent user experience for new media formats will be critical for the success of converged services. Inside OMA, new service enablers in the area of messaging and push-to-talk are themselves evolving and converging toward common IP-based platforms. OMA may need to quickly update or create additional DRM profiles for these new service enablers if required. The truth is, however, that OMA DRM is yet to get a firm footing in North American carrier markets where proprietary solutions predominate. Notwithstanding this disappointing market take-up, OMA DRM 2.0 has begun to show a lead in the industry by building in the hooks for interoperability with other DRM solutions. Trade associations and analysts may continue to encourage the standards organizations in this direction but since DRM casts a wider net than the wireless industry, it is not an area that a single organization alone can solve. The mobile industry is in a good position to take a lead on the issue. As a leading forum for converged service environments, maybe OMA can be the focal point for a more proactive role in the drive toward interoperability.

19.8 Summary

OMA DRM 2.0 brings much needed enhancements to the elementary capabilities of the OMA DRM 1.0 Enabler Release, which is now considered as a basic feature by some mobile vendors. OMA DRM 2.0 has captured the requirements of the consumer, mobile, and IT worlds and is capable of new media support (audio/video streaming) and new usage models enabling attractive marketing opportunities for service involving premium content.

The OMA DRM 2.0 Enabler Release Specification Baseline has five documents. The Requirements Document [DRM RD] provides use cases that describe the market drivers for the technical requirements for enhanced security and functional requirements. The Architecture Document [DRM AD] uses the requirements to expand on the essential functional elements and their interfaces which expose the intrinsic functionality of OMA DRM. The DRM Specification, [DRM TS] defines the semantics of the protocols and messages, the ROAP messages, the domains functionality, binding rights to user identities and is a starting point for developing the tools required to export OMA DRM protected content to other DRM solutions.

The DRM REL [DRM REL] specifies a mobile profile of the Open Digital Rights Language (ODRL) XML-based REL, which describes the permissions and constraints for protected content. Finally, the DCF specification, [DRM DCF] defines the content format for DRM protected media objects. In addition, OMA has created XML schemes for the ROAP protocol and the OMA DRM REL.

20

The Broadcast Enabler

Imagine it is 24 August 2008. You are in Las Vegas, USA. You are winning, and winning, and winning. But suddenly LeBron James and the US basketball team are back on your mind. What happens in Vegas, stays in Vegas. But what about what is happening in Beijing right at that time? The United States plays Spain for the gold medal, you certainly can't miss that. Do you have to make a tough decision, like abandoning your winning streak at the Blackjack table and run to the closest TV screen, in the hope it is tuned to the event? You are just about to make a move, when you sense the silent notification coming from your mobile device. You take a look at it, and all you have to do to see LeBron in action is push a single key (your mobile device is truly smart). Far fetched? Not at all, since according to the Chinese press mobile users, at least in China, will be able to watch the basketball final, and a wide selection of other Olympic Games TV broadcasts. And not only on mobile phones, but also on big-screen Personal Digital Assistants (PDAs) and MEPG-4 Advanced Video Coding (MP4) players, that will also be able to receive TV signals. There are over 400 million mobile subscribers in China, and many of them probably hope to be in possession of the appropriately enabled mobile device. There are also about 350 million basketball fans in China, so between the two statistics, even if Yao Ming does not make the final, there will be a substantial audience for this event, using mobile devices, just in China alone. And what about the hundreds of millions of other basketball fans around the world who may not be next to a TV when that happens? It is not unreasonable to assume that efforts are on the way, and if it does not happen by the 2008 Olympics, there is surely a better chance it will be in time for the London Olympics. And since LeBron is quite young, he may still be around for the 2012 final game.

Something else though, much more important has to happen: broadcast standards, technology, service providers' business models, and regulatory laws have to progress in unison, and have to progress fast. That represents a whole lot of things that have to go right; this chapter's intention is to shed some light only the first of them – the broadcast standards.

Mobile Broadcast (BCAST) has seen increasing interest, evidenced through the implementation of field trials throughout the world, using recent developments in terminal technologies, mobile network systems, and digital broadcast systems that enable broadcast services in the mobile environment. Such technology will enable distribution of rich, interactive, and bandwidth consuming media content to large mobile audiences. What exactly are broadcast services? These are services that distribute content packages simultaneously to many recipients, without necessarily knowing each individual recipient. Examples of broadcast services include mobile TV, mobile newspapers, mobile file downloading (text, audio, video), broadcast interactive voting/auctioning/betting/trading, etc. The assumption is that each recipient has a similar receiving device, or that the content package includes information, which allows terminal clients to process the content according to their current

The Open Mobile Alliance   M. Brenner and M. Unmehopa
© 2008 Alcatel-Lucent. All Rights Reserved

conditions. The term Mobile Broadcast services refers to a broad range of broadcast services, and a large number of competing and occasionally complementing standards for broadcast exist to support unidirectional one-to-many broadcast services and bi-directional unicast services paradigm in a mobile environment, where such services can be consumed, among other things, on mobile handheld devices. This may open up significant new business for media companies, network operators, content and service providers as well as for terminal and network equipment vendors. But in order to watch any worldwide event, while being in Vegas or anywhere for that matter, BCAST services will also require seamless interoperation of diverse infrastructure components and new functionality. And in turn, that implies additional work on standard specifications.

A broadcast framework, which is the stated goal of the Open Mobile Alliance (OMA) BCAST services enabler, is a very complex topic, and to cover it in detail may require an entirely dedicated book in itself. Instead, what we propose to do in this chapter is to provide an overview of the BCAST market requirements, then focus mostly on presenting the architecture of the BCAST enabler, in order to give the readers a chance to later navigate on their own through the detailed specifications (the BCAST Architecture Document alone has over 180 pages).

20.1 Are Those Specifications Really Needed?

Broadcast is certainly not a 'greenfield' by any stretch of imagination. Pre-existing, diverse and heterogeneous infrastructures, such as underlying Broadcast Distribution Systems (BDSs) must be supported in the BCAST framework. A BDS is defined as a system that provides the capability to transmit the same IP flow to multiple terminal devices simultaneously. A BDS typically uses techniques that achieve efficient use of radio resources. Since the BCAST enabler addresses BCAST services, and BDS typically assumes the presence of air interfaces, BCAST will work over cellular networks for which an IP-broadcast/multicast system is defined, and also needs to work over any cellular network. The cellular network is also used to support the so-called interaction network – a system supporting the ability of a terminal device to exchange IP flows, Short Message Service (SMS), Multimedia Messaging Service (MMS) with a BCAST Service Application (BSA).

The BCAST enabler achieves this by recognizing, and re-using the concepts of a broadcast channel and an interaction channel as part of its framework.

- The broadcast channel is provided by a specific BDS to be used as a generic broadcast link for the BCAST enabler.
- The service interaction channel enables a specific interaction system (e.g. a cellular network) to be used as a generic interaction link for the BCAST enabler. This channel is sometimes an alternative to the broadcast channel, for BCAST delivery (e.g. in case a BDS is not present). In other cases, as we will see later in the chapter, the interaction channel is the only architectural alternative (e.g. for the Service Interaction (SI) functional area).

So, the OMA BCAST enabler will make use of existing bearers, or BDSs. At the same time, true to the OMA principles, the BCAST enabler has to achieve the goal of bearer independence. Therefore, the focus is on functional areas that are generic and common across many BCAST services that can be abstracted in a bearer-independent way. The BCAST Requirements Document [BCAST RD] defines the following functional areas:

- Service Guide (SG), which enables a principal to discover and access BCAST services. This functional area covers the data model, network-agnostic transport, and external interfaces for service providers.
- File Distribution (FD), which enables support for the distribution of content in the form of (a set of) files in BCAST services. This functional area covers coding and transport of files, and related signaling.

- Stream Distribution (SD), which enables support for the distribution of continuous or intermittent content streams in BCAST services. This functional area covers coding and transport of streams, and related signaling.
- Service Protection (SP) and Content Protection (CP), which provides the mechanisms by which BCAST services and content can be protected to enable various purchasing and charging models, usage tracking, and usage rights enforcement. The SP covers access control for any kind of IP-based service, whereas CP covers application-level end-to-end security for file- and stream-based services.
- Service Provisioning (SPR), which enables a service provider to provision BCAST services for a principal. This functional area covers subscriptions to services and related payments.
- Terminal Provisioning (TP), which provides mechanisms for terminal settings needed to support BCAST services.
- Notification (NT), which supports:

  - A principal in specifying a set of rules that help BCAST services determine when broadcast content exists which is of interest to the principal; and
  - The sending of notifications to the principal to raise awareness of the broadcast content of interest.

20.2   Standards Precursors to BCAST Enabler

As mentioned in the previous section, the BCAST enabler is bearer independent, while ensuring it can support any specified underlying BDS. Standards specifying the underlying infrastructure are relevant for the BCAST enabler, because the BCAST enabler functions may need to consider services provided by the BDSs. While BCAST specifications do not exclude support for other underlying BDSs, they specifically call out normative compliance with the specifications dictated by 3GPP Multimedia Broadcast/Multicast Service (MBMS), 3GPP2 Broadcast/Multicast Services (BCMCS) and the Digital Video Broadcasting IP Datacast (DVB IPDC). The relevant standards from these three organizations are summarized below.

- 3GPP – The 3GPP TS 23.246 specification [3GPP TS 23.246] describes the architecture for the MBMS bearer service, as well as considerations on the manner in which MBMS user services should make use of the MBMS bearer service. [3GPP TS 23.246] defines the MBMS bearer service as the service provided to MBMS user service for delivery of IP multicast datagrams to multiple receivers, using minimum network and radio resources; it defines the MBMS user service as the service provided to the end-user by means of the MBMS bearer service and possibly other capabilities. The 3GPP TS 26.346 specification [3GPP TS 26.346] defines a set of media codecs, formats and transport/application protocols to enable the deployment of MBMS user services over the MBMS bearer service within the 3GPP system. The 3GPP TS 33.246 specification [3GPP TS 33.246] provides the security architecture for point-to-multipoint service in a 3GPP system, addressing in particular how to handle authentication, key distribution, and data protection when securely transmitting data to a given set of users as part of a MBMS service.
- 3GPP2 – The 3GPP2 X.S0022-A specification [3GPP2 X.S0022-A] defines the service architecture and core network protocols and procedures for support of BCMCS in CDMA 2000 networks. The 3GPP2 S.S0083-A specification [3GPP2 S.S0083-A] defines the security framework (authentication, key management, data protection) needed to support BCMCS in 3GPP2.
- DVB – The European Telecommunications Standards Institute (ETSI) EN 300 468 specification [ETSI EN 300 468] specifies Service Information data included in the DVB bitstreams, in order to support a user in the selection of services and/or events within the bitstreams. The ETSI TS 102 005 specification [ETSI TS 102 005] defines the use of video and audio coding

in DVB services delivered over IP protocols, without involving an MPEG-2 transport stream (hence using a toolbox approach of delivering DVB applications over IP). IP datacast over Digital Video Broadcasting – Handhelds (DVB-H) is an end-to-end broadcast system for delivery of any type of digital content and services optimized for devices with computational or battery life constraints (e.g. handhelds). The ETSI TS 102 470 specification [ETSI TS 102 470] describes the usage of Program Specific Information/Service Information within the constraints of DVB-H. The ETSI TS 102 471 specification [ETSI TS 102 471] describes the Electronic Service Guide (ESG) which helps the user in selection of services and defines the data model, representation format, encapsulation and transport of the ESG for DVB-H. The ETSI TS 102 472 specification [ETSI TS 102 472] defines Content Delivery Protocols for file delivery and streaming in IP datacast over DVB-H, with the goal of harmonization with 3GPP MBMS. ETSI TS 102 474 specification [ETSI TS 102 474] defines two Service Purchase and Protection profiles (18Crypt and Open Security Framework) applicable for the provisioning and protection of IP datacast services over DVB-H.

The specifications summarized above are the standards precursors, in that they define the BDSs that must be supported by the BCAST enabler to provide the BCAST services. In addition to these standards precursors, the BCAST enabler also relies on other OMA enablers. Since content delivery is relevant to some BCAST enabler functional areas, some OMA Digital Rights Management (DRM) specifications are worth mentioning here (read more about DRM in Chapter 19). The OMA DRM specification 2.0 [DRM DRM] defines an end-to-end system for DRM content distribution. The OMA DRM Content Format (DCF) specification [DRM DCF] defines the DCF used to encrypt and package media objects. The OMA DRM Rights Expression Language specification [DRM REL] defines the grammar and vocabulary used to define the rights for DRM content. Finally, the OMA DRM Working Group working jointly with OMA BCAST Working Group also produced the OMA DRM 2.0 Extensions for Broadcast Support specification [DRM XBS]. The BCAST enabler extensions in [DRM XBS] are in the areas of the Rights Object Acquisition Protocol (ROAP), rights expression language, subscription group addressing, authentication of broadcast rights object, broadcast service support, and token management. For its Terminal Provisioning function, the BCAST enabler relies on Device Management (DM) enablers (read more about DM in Chapter 18).

The BCAST enabler also relies on a broad range of Internet Engineering Task Force (IETF) standards, in particular when it comes to the BCAST enabler security functional area. However, these are not further detailed in this section.

In summary, all proposed technologies upon which the BCAST enabler is specified are based on public specifications or drafts that may soon become public specifications. Thus the functions further described in the section on architecture fully comply with the notion of 'openness' and 're-use' promoted by the OMA initiative.

20.3   BCAST Architecture

The BCAST Architecture Document [BCAST AD] defines the overall BCAST Architecture, its logical entities, and reference points. There are two purposes to the top-level BCAST Architecture.

To begin with, as we have seen, the BCAST service is defined in terms of functional areas common across the various BDSs. The top-level BCAST Architecture places the enabler in the context of the underlying BDSs, service operation, and content provisioning. Section 20.2 introduced the BDSs specified by 3GPP MBMS, 3GPP2 BCMCS, IPDC over DVB-H. The top-level BCAST Architecture however does not preclude any other BDS.

Secondly, in addition to defining the context, the top-level BCAST Architecture defines the logical entities and their relations. Each logical entity provides a function that is exposed through an interface. These interfaces in turn will be the basis for further technical specifications. The latter specifications however are not the focal points of this BCAST chapter.

20.3.1 BCAST Logical Architecture (Reference Points)

The BCAST framework makes an architectural distinction between a broadcast channel (provided by a BDS) and an interaction channel (e.g. provided by a cellular network). While availability of both is generally assumed, either channel may also be temporarily unavailable (e.g. because of lack of radio coverage). Also, while devices that do not support an interaction channel are not specifically excluded, features needed by such devices are left outside the BCAST specifications (we will see this in some of the functional areas explored in the next sections).

Intrinsic functions (i.e. functions specified in the BCAST enabler) match the functional areas identified in the [BCAST RD] and discussed in an earlier section of this chapter. The architecture work uncovered one separate additional functional area referred to as Service Interaction. The role of this additional functional area and in general more details on how functions in different functional areas are exposed will become more evident in dedicated following sections. With so many functional areas to cover, each involving multiple components and interfaces, an initial top-down approach of presenting an architecture diagram employing reference points is used in the Broadcast Architecture Document [BCAST AD], as well as in this section. This approach will prove to be useful when pursuing in more detail the architecture for each functional area, since it would make the architecture truly easier to follow.

Figure 20.1 represents the BCAST overall logical architecture diagram, containing the main BCAST enabler specified components and reference points, as well as some non-BCAST entities that help in the completeness of the framework (see legend for representation conventions).

The main BCAST enabler components are identified as those components that perform the functionality needed to support one or more of the identified functional areas. Each such main BCAST component may be further de-composed into functions that are easier to map into functional

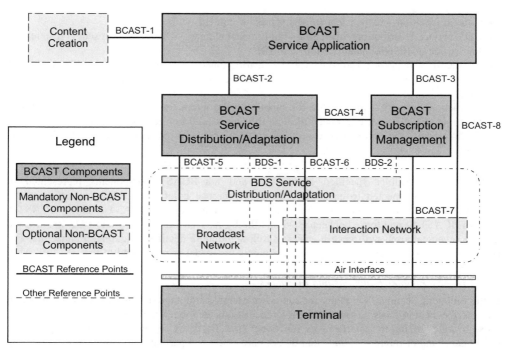

Figure 20.1 BCAST logical architecture (reference points). Reproduced by Permission of the Open Mobile Alliance Ltd.

areas. This will be emphasized in more detailed diagrams per functional area in the next sections. At the logical architecture level which uses reference points, the following BCAST components are defined:

- BSA supports the SG, FD, SD, SP, CP, SI, and NT functional areas. It provides the functions of media encoding and interaction (e.g. streaming audio/video or movie file download) related to the BCAST service, as well as forwarding service attributes to other BCAST components, such as the BCAST Service Distribution/Adaptation (BSD/A) and BCAST Subscription Management (BSM).
- BSD/A supports the SG, FD, SD, SP, CP, and NT functional areas. It provides the functions needed for file and stream distribution, service aggregation, service and content protection, service guide generation and delivery, notification delivery, and the adaptation to the underlying BDS.
- BSM supports the SG, SP, CP, SPR, Terminal Provisioning, and NT functional areas. It provides the functions needed for notification, service and content protection management, service guide generation support, terminal provisioning, exchanges with charging systems, and interaction with the BDS Service Distribution/Adaptation for subscription management information exchanges (in our opinion and in retrospect, based on the functionality included, and as we will see in the more detailed sections, a BCAST management name may have been more appropriate).
- Terminal supports all BCAST enabler functional areas. It provides all the client functions needed in the user device to handle reception of broadcast content and service-related information (e.g. service guide, content protection information).

Entities that are outside the scope of the BCAST specification include:

- Content Creation – responsible for the source of content
- BDS Service Distribution/Adaptation – an optional element, which when present is responsible for service distribution/adaptation to the BDS
- Broadcast Network – responsible for the distribution of content over the broadcast channel (which may involve the same or different radio network than the one used by the interaction channel)
- Interaction Network – responsible for supporting the interaction channel (which may involve the same or a different radio network than the one is used by the broadcast channel)
- Air Interface – the radio-based communication link between the terminal and the cellular network.

The BCAST enabler specified components and non-BCAST components represented in Figure 20.1 are connected to each other through reference points. For simplification purposes, we have chosen to name only the reference points specified by the BCAST enabler (BCAST-1 through BCAST-8) and those between BDS and the BCAST enabler (BDS-1 and BDS-2) since the naming scheme chosen will make it easier to follow the more detailed functional architecture. For additional names and details on the reference points the reader is referenced to the [BCAST AD].

20.3.2 BCAST Enabler Functions and Interfaces

In the following sections, following the top-down architectural approach at a lower level of detail, we describe the interfaces that realize the reference points mentioned in the previous section, and we do so by categorizing the interfaces by functional area. By doing so, we have deliberately left out components and/or reference points that do not play a role in a particular functional area definition, in order to present an easier way to follow the diagram and help focus on the main message each diagram needs to convey to the reader. For example, we have consistently left out the air interface, because since the topic is BCAST service, it is self-evident that a cellular network with an air interface to the terminal is supposed to be present. That is a departure from the diagrams the reader may find in the [BCAST AD], which usually show all components, interfaces and reference points, whether they are essential or not in a specific functional area. However, the interface numbers are following the respective reference point numbering scheme, so you should not be surprised to see interface numbers out of sequence. The reader should rather interpret the absence of a number in an interface name as an indication that, for the reference point that carries that number, there is no corresponding interface for the particular functional area described.

In general, interfaces are shown as uni-directional arrows, following the OMA Architecture Best Practices conventions [ARC BP]. However, in some of the diagrams we have used bi-directional arrows to make the point that similar interfaces may need to be exposed by either component linked through a reference point. This is purely a simplification to avoid cluttering of the diagram. The bi-directional representation implies that each component may expose such an interface; the interfaces may be realized in different ways, but complement each other in achieving the functions that are exposed through those interfaces for the specific functional area described.

20.3.2.1 Service Guide Functional Architecture

Figure 20.2 illustrates the SG Functional Architecture. The SG provides the BCAST services users with information on broadcast content available in their region, delivered to the user's terminal either via IP datacast or as a BDS-specific message or both, depending on the underlying BDS capabilities. The SG promotes programmed or on-demand content for users to order, watch, and consume. The SG Generation/Adaptation can be done either in the BSD/A component or in the BDS Service Distribution/Adaptation (if one exists).

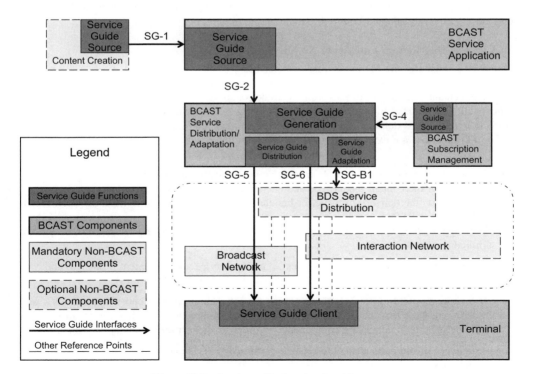

Figure 20.2 Service guide functional architecture

The SG functions are exposed through the following interfaces:

- SG-1 supports the delivery of content attributes (e.g. description information, location information, target terminal profile, target user profile) from a Service Guide Content Creation (SGCC)
  source to the BSA, in the form of BCAST service guide fragments, or in proprietary format.
- SG-2 supports the delivery of content attributes from the BSA to the BSD/A in the form of
  BCAST service guide fragments.
- SG-4 supports the delivery of service and/or terminal provisioning information, subscription
  information, promotional information, etc. from the BSM to the BSA, in the form of BCAST
  service guide fragments.
- SG-5 supports the delivery of the SG from the BSD/A to the terminal, through the broadcast
  channel (over the underlying BDS). This may include traversing the BDS Service Distribu-
  tion/Adaptation, if one exists.
- SG-6 supports the delivery of the SG from the BSD/A to the terminal, through the interaction
  channel.
- SG-B1 is an interface that can be exposed by one or both of the connecting components, to
  support the delivery of BDS-specific attributes to BCAST SG Adaptation function to assist in the
  adaptation, or the delivery of BCAST SG attributes to BDS for the SG distribution. This interface
  is used in MBMS or BCMCS implementations where the BDS Service Distribution/Adaptation
  for the SG is not integrated in the BSD/A.

As one can see from the diagram and the interfaces description, SG sources are distributed in
different components (a recipient of SG attributes may become a source for the next component).

The SG generation function assembles the BCAST SG fragments and generates the SG, which
may be subsequently adapted before distribution.

20.3.2.2 File Distribution Functional Architecture

Figure 20.3 illustrates the FD Functional Architecture.

The FD supports the distribution of files to terminals, either over the broadcast channel or the
interaction channel. Examples of files would include sound files, images, video clips, etc. Additional
functionality is provided through other functional areas (e.g. SP and CP functions). Forward error
correction and/or post-delivery file repair is also supported.

The FD functions are exposed through the following interfaces:

- FD-1 supports the delivery of a file from a Content Creation Source to the BSA. The interface
  is agnostic of the content media type and encoding scheme.
- FD-2 supports the delivery of a file, or bundle of files, which may be content protected, from
  the BSA to the BSD/A.
- FD-5 supports the following deliveries using the broadcast channel between the BSD/A and the
  terminal:

  - Distribution of file (or bundle of files), possibly service and/or content protected; and
  - Delivery of in-band signaling to accompany the file (or bundle of files).

- FD-6 supports point-to-point deliveries using the interaction channel between the BSD/A and
  the terminal. Note that the interface is represented as bi-directional, which implies that it may
  be exposed by both connected components, in order to support the following exchanges:

  - delivery of file parts needed to repair a previously distributed file over the broadcast chan-
    nel; and
  - delivery of a file repair request or a reception report from the terminal.

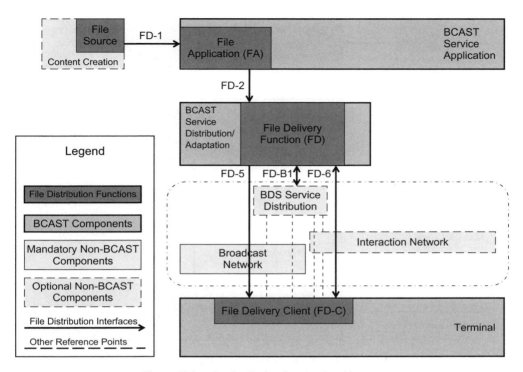

Figure 20.3   File distribution functional architecture

- FD-B1 is an interface that can be exposed by one or both of the connecting components, as needed in order to support exchanges between BSD/A and the underlying BDS. This interface is used in MBMS or BCMCS implementations where the BDS Service Distribution/Adaptation for the FD is not integrated in the BSD/A. The following deliveries are supported by this interface:
  - delivery of a file (or bundle of files), optionally with service and/or CP to BDS;
  - delivery of signaling information and/or bearer information from BDS, to be taken into account by a file or a bundle of files to be distributed; and
  - signaling of content priority to an underlying BDS.

File delivery can be achieved in several ways, including a BDS transparent mode, in which the file delivery function negotiates the bearers with BDS through FD-B1, or a BDS-assisted mode (the latter is out-of-scope for BCAST).

20.3.2.3 Stream Distribution Functional Architecture

Figure 20.4 illustrates the SD Functional Architecture. Contrary to FD, a stream is a continuous string of content, which is delivered and represented (buffering may be used) at a constant rate. The SD supports the distribution of streams to terminals, predominantly using the broadcast channel, while the interaction channel remains a possible alternative. Codecs supported in the BCAST enabler are those defined by underlying BDS. For a given BDS, the terminal must support the BDS's mandatory codecs, should support BDS's highly recommended codecs, and may support BDS's optional codecs.

Additional functions, usually provided through other functional areas (e.g. SP and CP functions) may be performed here instead. Forward error correction may also be supported.

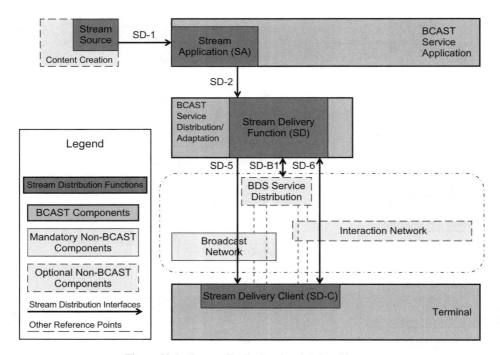

Figure 20.4   Stream distribution functional architecture

The SD functions are exposed through the following interfaces:

- SD-1 supports the delivery of a stream from a Content Creation Source to the BSA. The stream's media type and codec have to be among those supported by the BCAST enabler.
- SD-2 supports the delivery of a stream, with media type and codec supported by the BCAST enabler, from the BSA to the BSD/A.
- SD-5 supports the delivery of streams using the broadcast channel between the BSD/A and the terminal, and this delivery may include traversing the BDS Service Distribution/Adaptation.
- SD-6 supports deliveries using the interaction channel between the BSD/A and the terminal. Note that the interface is represented as bi-directional, which implies that it may be exposed by both connected components, in order to support the following exchanges:
  - Delivery of a stream to the terminal
  - Delivery of a request for stream retransmission, or a report from the terminal to the BSD/A.
- SD-B1 is an interface that can be exposed by one or both of the connecting components, as needed in order to support exchanges between BSD/A and the underlying BDS. This interface is used in MBMS or BCMCS implementations where the BDS Service Distribution/Adaptation for the SD is not integrated in the BSD/A. The following deliveries are supported by this interface:
  - delivery of a stream, optionally protected, from BSD/A to BDS;
  - delivery of a stream attribute from BSD/A to BDS to help the BDS in determining the bearers used for stream distribution;
  - delivery of bearer information from BDS to BSD/A, to be used for stream distribution;
  - delivery of BDS-specific profile for stream adaptation, from BDS to BSD/A; and
  - signaling of stream priority to the underlying BDS.

Stream delivery can be achieved in several ways, including a BDS transparent mode, in which the Stream Delivery function negotiates the bearers with BDS through SD-B1, or a BDS-assisted mode (the latter is out-of-scope for the BCAST enabler).

20.3.2.4 Service and Content Protection Functional Architecture

In the OMA BCAST Architecture, SP and CP are applied in a way that is agnostic to the presence or type of underlying BDS. SP and CP could also be completely realized by the underlying technology, but this is out-of-scope for BCAST enabler. Also, BCAST SP and BCAST CP only cover the delivery channel itself, and do not explicitly cover the content after its delivery to the terminal.

The same layered key hierarchy applies for both SP and CP:

(1) Layer 1 supports subscriber/device registration. Data generated in this layer is referred to as Subscriber Management Key (SMK) or Rights Encryption Key (REK) depending on the key management profile, and is used to protect the delivery of the long-term key generated in Layer 2.
(2) Layer 2 supports the delivery of the Long-term Key Message (LTKM) over the delivery channel (broadcast or interaction). This layer generates an intermediate key (either a Service Encryption Key (SEK) or a Programme Encryption Key (PEK)). The role of the intermediate key is to protect the delivery of the key generated at the next layer.
(3) Layer 3 supports the delivery of the Short-term Key Message (STKM) for the delivery channel (broadcast or interaction). This layer generates the Traffic Encryption Key (TEK), or generates data that can be used to derive the TEK. The TEK is being distributed together with content identifiers, using the SEK or PEK encryption from Layer 2, as part of the STKM delivery.
(4) Layer 4 supports the delivery of encrypted content using the TEK (or a derivation of the TEK) generated by Layer 3 (this encryption is possible at network layer, transport layer, session layer or presentation/content layer).

In essence, the functional architecture for SP and for CP is the same. In the BCAST Architecture they have been represented separately since components that implement the respective functions may indeed be separated to focus on the main difference: namely, focus on protection for the end-to-end service in the case of SP, versus focus on protection of individual pieces of content in the case of CP. The diagrams used to represent SP and CP Architecture focus on the mapping of interfaces to those functional areas, along the lines defined by the BCAST enabler reference points, rather than mapping the four-layers key-hierarchy model described before. The mapping of the functions to those layers will instead be described in the text that describes the functions.

Figure 20.5 illustrates the SP Functional Architecture. The SP supports access to a broadcast service (i.e. a pre-defined set of audio/visual data) for a specified amount of time, and is in-scope only for the delivery channel between the endpoints that implement the protection (e.g. SP does not cover the content after it reached the terminal). In addition, SP also covers Subscription Management. In the BCAST Architecture, the assumption is that the entire SP is realized by the BCAST enabler. SP could also be completely realized by the underlying technology, but this is out-of-scope for the BCAST enabler.

The SP functions are exposed through the following interfaces:

- SP-2 supports the delivery of an encrypted file or stream from the BSA to the BSD/A.
- SP-4 supports exchanges of key-related information between the BSA and the BSM. The following exchanges are supported:
  - exchange of information related to STKM generation between the BSD/A and the BSM, supporting the Layer 3 definition;

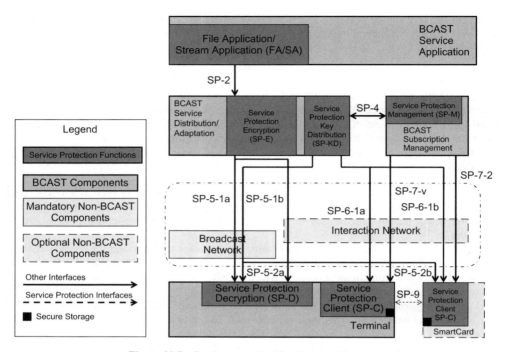

Figure 20.5 Service protection functional architecture

- delivery of STKM generated by BSM, for STKM delivery over the broadcast channel, supporting the Layer 3 definition; and
- delivery of LTKM by BSM to BSD/A, for delivery only over the broadcast channel to the terminal, supporting the Layer 2 definition.

- SP-5-1* supports the implementation of Layer 4 in the key-hierarchy model (alternatively, the content may also be delivered unencrypted). BSD/A may use either the broadcast channel (SP-5-1a) or the interaction channel (SP-5-1b) for delivery to the terminal. This delivery may include traversing the BDS Service Distribution/Adaptation.
- SP-5-2* supports the exchange of key-related information between BSD/A and terminal or BSD/A and smart card, when using the broadcast channel. Key-related material is maintained in secure storage in the terminal or the smart card. Deliveries over the broadcast channel may include traversing the BDS Service Distribution/Adaptation. The following exchanges are supported:

  - delivery of STKM to terminal, supporting the Layer 3 definition (SP-5-2a);
  - delivery of STKM to smart card, supporting the Layer 3 definition (SP-5-2b);
  - delivery of LTKM to terminals, supporting the Layer 2 definition (SP-5-2a); and
  - delivery of information to terminals, supporting the Layer 1 definition (SP-5-2a).

- SP-6-1* supports the exchange of key-related information between BSD/A and terminal or BSD/A and smart card, when using the interaction channel. Key-related material is maintained in secure storage in the terminal or the smart card. The following exchanges are supported:

  - delivery of STKM to terminal for DRM Profile, supporting the Layer 3 definition (SP-6-1a); and
  - delivery of STKM to smart card Profile, supporting the Layer 3 definition (SP-6-1b).

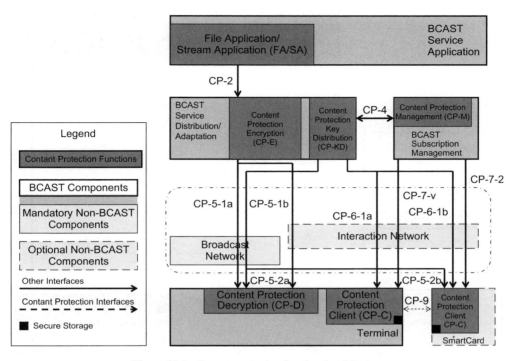

Figure 20.6   Content protection functional architecture

- SP-7* supports the signaling exchanges for Layer 1 in the key-hierarchy model, as well as delivery of LTKM by BSD/A to terminal (SP-7-1) or to the smart card (SP-7-2), supporting the Layer 2 definition.
- SP-9 supports the interface between BSM and the smart card, and is only present for terminals that support smart cards. This interface is shown for completeness only, and is not specified by OMA BCAST enabler.

Figure 20.6 illustrates the CP Functional Architecture. The CP supports the securing of individual pieces of content within a service. Content may also have post-delivery usage rights associated with it. CP is agnostic to the content itself.

The functional architecture for CP is practically identical with the one shown in Figure 20.5, with the exception of the fact that each interface name starts with CP instead of SP. The CP functions are exposed through the CP-2 through CP-9 interfaces, providing support for delivery of encrypted content, or key information, and bear a one-to-one equivalence to the interfaces described for the SP.

20.3.2.5 Service Interaction Functional Architecture

Figure 20.7 illustrates the SI Functional Architecture. The SI supports the point-to-point communications between the BSA and the terminal, when BCAST services require user interaction (e.g. real-time voting, real-time betting, or real-time request for additional services). This function is usually supported by a cellular mobile network and services such as SMS, MMS, downloads, e-mail, and/or links to additional sites or operator portals.

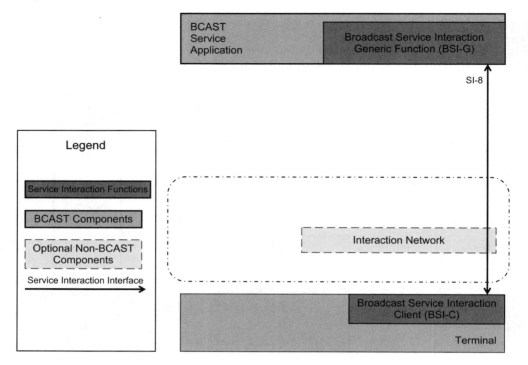

Figure 20.7   Service interaction functional architecture

The SI functions are exposed through the following interface:

- SI-8 supports the delivery of an end-user request from the terminal to the BSA or, in the reverse direction, a response for the user, from the BSA to the terminal. The interface is shown as a bi-directional arrow, since in fact a separate realization of the SI-8 interface may be needed to be exposed by both BSA and terminal, to support asynchronous communications of request/responses between user and the BCAST enabler.

20.3.2.6 Service Provisioning Functional Architecture

Figure 20.8 illustrates the SPR Functional Architecture. The SPR supports user subscription to and/or ordering of BCAST services, pay-per-view services, and related payment exchanges. The general assumption is that this function is supported through the capabilities of the interaction network.

The SPR functions are exposed through the following interfaces:

- SPR-7 supports the delivery of user requests for BCAST services (subscription, ordering, etc.) from the terminal, to the BSM, and responses from BSM to the user, via the terminal. SPR-7 also supports inquiries for account status and payment. The interface is shown as a bi-directional arrow, since in fact a separate realization of the SPR-7 interface may be needed to be exposed by both BSM and terminal, to support asynchronous communications of request/responses between user and the BCAST enabler.

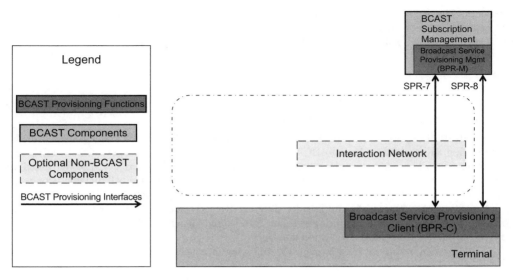

Figure 20.8 Service provisioning functional architecture

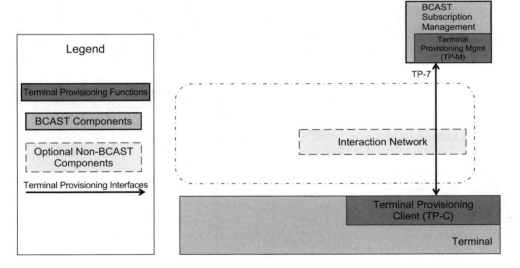

Figure 20.9 Terminal provisioning functional architecture

- SPR-8 is a placeholder for out-of-band handling of subscription and purchases of BCAST services. This interface may not need support of a cellular network. It is not specified in the BCAST enabler.

20.3.2.7 Terminal Provisioning Functional Architecture

Figure 20.9 illustrates the Terminal Provisioning Functional Architecture. The Terminal Provisioning supports the maintenance of terminal configuration parameters needed to support the BCAST services. The BCAST enabler is dependent on DM enablers for providing this function (see Chapter 18 for details on DM).

The Terminal Provisioning functions are exposed through the following interface:

- TP-7 supports the delivery of terminal provisioning messages from BSM to the terminal over the interaction channel.

20.3.2.8 Notification Functional Architecture

Figure 20.10 illustrates the NT Functional Architecture. The NT Function delivers to the terminals information about events related to BCAST (e.g. changes in the SG, changes in the user's sub-scription, promotions or notifications on events based on a subscribed service). The SG function remains the primary way for the delivery of changes in the SG though; the NT function is only an additional way to notify the user of such changes, rather than a replacement.

A notification event can be initiated by different BCAST enabler components, by creating a notice about the event, and delivering it to the Notification Generation Component in BSM, who is responsible for generating notification messages.

The NT functions are exposed through the following interfaces:

- NT-1 supports the delivery of a notification message, and/or notification attributes from the Content Creation Source to the BSA.

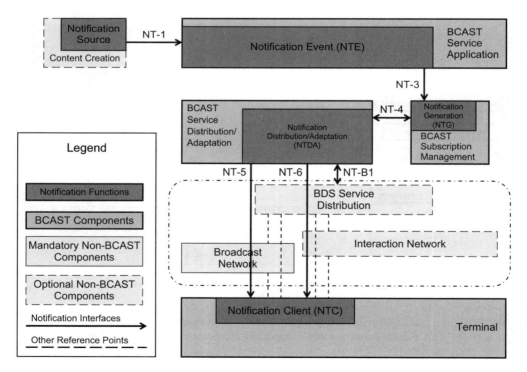

Figure 20.10   Notification functional architecture

- NT-3 supports the delivery of attributes needed for the generation of a notification specific to SG changes, as well as delivery of notices about notification event from a Content Creation Source.
- NT-4 supports the delivery of notification messages between BSM and BSD/A, including:
  - notification messages from BSM to BSD/A;
  - notices from BSD/A to BSM about notification events received from underlying BDS; and
  - notices from BSD/A to BSM about notification events in the BSD/A.
- NT-5 supports the delivery of notification messages from the BSD/A to the terminal, through the broadcast channel (over the underlying BDS). This may include traversing the BDS Service Distribution/Adaptation, if one exists.
- NT-6 supports the delivery of notification messages from the BSD/A to the terminals using the interaction channel.
- NT-B1 is an interface that can be exposed by one or both of the connecting components, to support the delivery of a notice about a notification event, the delivery of a notification message to BDS or the interaction network, and signaling of notification message priority to the underlying BDS. This interface is used in MBMS or BCMCS implementations where the BDS Service Distribution/Adaptation for the NT is not integrated in the BSD/A.

In the previous sections, we have followed the top-down architectural approach and described all functional entities, reference points, and the interfaces that realize them. And to maintain sight of the overall picture, we have done so by categorizing the interfaces by their functional area. Now that we have a good comprehension of the BCAST Architecture, let us take a look at what the potential impact of these specifications on the various industry segments may be, and what the future may hold for the enabler.

20.4   Impact of Specifications

The primary role of the BCAST enabler is to ensure a uniform approach to BCAST services, while leveraging standardized components of BCAST technologies (e.g. BDS) and/or available interaction channels. While seeing LeBron handle the basketball in the last seconds of the championship, made possible via broadcasting streaming content that millions of subscribers worldwide would like to enjoy during the Beijing 2008 Olympic Games may be quite within reach, BCAST services have larger obstacles than the broadcasting of any single event. BCAST services need to support at the same time broadcasting of contents of wide variety to a large number of subscribers, using different types of mobile devices in a global manner (hence supporting a large variety of broadcast channels and interaction channels). The BCAST enabler may not solve all the issues, but it is a good step forward in specifying clearly distinguished functional areas, and components and interfaces to implement those functions in a uniform, consistent manner that can leverage existing underlying infrastructure and terminals. As an example, the use of smart card profile for SP, based on 3GPP MBMS security, and binding subscription to a Subscriber Identity Module (3GPP (U)SIM or 3GPP2 (R)UIM/CSIM), is a valuable accomplishment of BCAST enabler release 1.0.

The BCAST framework is therefore clearly of importance to all service providers. The approach also creates a clearer landscape for vendors, which can focus on specific functional areas, and identify re-use of products from their portfolio that can perform well in a specific BCAST enabler functional area (e.g. SP and CP, SPR, Terminal Provisioning, NT). End-users will see the benefits through their Quality of Experience in using broadcast services, in particular when BCAST services are made available on a variety of terminals, and when the event selection and interaction becomes more uniform regardless of the service provider offering the broadcast service.

As far as other specifications are concerned, the BCAST enabler already spawned extensions to DRM specifications, and the creation of BCAST Management Object, while re-using DM specifications. Other services, such as those supported by the Dynamic Content Delivery enabler (see Chapter 21) may depend on the BCAST specifications.

20.5   Specifications Evolution and Future Direction

At a time when the BCAST enabler is just wrapping up its first release, the focus is still very much on making sure that it stabilizes and undergoes appropriate scrutiny through TestFests, leading to the approval of BCAST 1.0. The BCAST enabler specifications have been worked on for an extensive period of time, and resulted in a very complex architecture, and even more complex specifications. Over 2700 comments were entered and addressed during the BCAST enabler consistency review process, which speaks volumes about the complexity of the work. One of the lingering issues may be the surviving as part of the technical specifications of a very large number of options, which is a potential trap for interoperability between vendors. If anything, some streamlining of the number of options remains a desirable goal. For example, eliminating the need for multiple options for the same function, and the amount of interactions between different functions just to accommodate support of those multiple options should be an achievable goal.

Furthermore, while support for diverse IP-based broadcast/multicast bearers is already provided in BCAST release 1.0 (e.g. 3GPP MBMS, 3GPP BCMCS and DVB-H IPDC) an evolution of BCAST enabler could extend this by possibly supporting WiMAX Multicast and Broadcast Service (WiMAX MBS). Other potential areas of work could include more comprehensive standardization of MobileTV server and terminal components (e.g. interactivity, back-end interfaces).

20.6   Summary

OMA BCAST enabler specifications leverage specifications defined by other related standards bodies (3GPP, 3GPP2, IETF, ETSI) to create a comprehensive end-to-end framework for broadcast services. The BCAST chapter has touched upon the background of broadcast services standards and the functional areas needed to focus on to ensure uniformity, and re-use of existing infrastructures, and presented the BCAST architectural approach. We hope to have achieved the goal of giving the readers a solid overview, and raised their interest in further exploring the detailed BCAST specifications.

21

The Dynamic Content Delivery Enabler

Dynamic Content Delivery (DCD) is intended to simplify user access to content services by providing automated delivery of personalized content direct to users' devices. Current browser-based services require users to be constantly clicking to find content on the Internet, remember or bookmark websites, hitting a refresh menu option to update the current page, or navigate forward/backward to find something they were just looking at. In contrast, users of DCD-enabled services will have simple means to discover available services and select the services they want to receive, after which the content will be automatically delivered directly to the users' devices, without further user actions.

How is this possible? The answer is by using syndication, which is a general approach to delivering Internet content. 'Syndication' means the collection and delivery of content on behalf of content providers. Syndication simplifies the effort required by content providers to deliver content to users, and similarly users' effort to get the content. Syndication is the idea behind Really Simple Syndication (RSS) [RSS], which is used by many Internet sites to provide users with easy access to regularly updated news, blogs, images/music/video, and, in general, to any content that changes over time. Through syndication, collections of content are delivered in channels (also called 'feeds'), a familiar service delivery concept. Users know, for example, that they can access specific services or related content through channels, and that the channels can be subscribed to, and may have a subscription cost. Newer syndication services use customized RSS and the Atom Syndication Format (an updated version of RSS, see [RFC 4287]) to deliver many services users are very familiar with, for example from iTunes, podcasts, and Google.

Users typically don't know (or need to know) that RSS/Atom are being used to deliver their services. Users typically just start a program, and optionally login to a service and select the services that they want to use. The program then communicates with content servers using the syndication methods, and the user enjoys the automatically delivered content. The content delivery service may be provided by an 'aggregator' (a service provider through which content is syndicated), or by content providers directly.

DCD is being developed in a content services market environment under which various general changes as follows are occurring:

- Broadband service growth is resulting in availability of an always-on Internet service environment.

The Open Mobile Alliance   M. Brenner and M. Unmehopa

- Service providers are taking advantage of this by providing applications that are becoming more autonomous, dynamically interacting with Internet-based services for automated content retrieval.
- As a result, content delivery models are changing on the Internet, as seen by the rise of:
  - content syndication and technologies that support it, for example, RSS, Atom;
  - approaches toward 'behind the scenes' transfer of data to applications, for example, the web design technique known as AJAX (Asynchronous JavaScript and XML).
- Users are becoming familiar with automated delivery of personalized content to their devices (e.g. computers, iPod, etc.), leading to a service environment in which much of their content experience is based upon local consumption of pre-delivered content, for example:
  - via established tools (e.g. iTunes/Microsoft Network (MSN)/America Online (AOL)/Yahoo/ Google desktop clients);
  - via new tools (e.g. Apple Dashboard, Yahoo Widgets, Microsoft Gadgets).

21.1   Why Do We Need New Specifications for DCD?

As users become more familiar with syndicated services delivered to their desktop computers and connected devices, they will come to expect the same ease of use for services accessed via their mobile devices. In order for service providers (e.g. Mobile Network Operators) to successfully support the same user experience in a mobile environment, various mobility-related enhancements are needed:

- The cost of providing content delivery in the mobile environment must be manageable. Mobile networks provide much less overall bandwidth compared to wired networks. As a result, both users and Mobile Network Operators are sensitive to the cost of providing services. The automated nature of syndicated services has the potential to create a lot of network traffic, and the cost of supporting this traffic must be balanced with the richness and responsiveness of the services. DCD will enable cost management through the following features:
  - Content delivery can be pre-arranged to use various networks and protocols (e.g. IP, SMS, broadcast), allowing the service provider to optimize use of limited network resources.
  - Different delivery methods, for example, Pull (client-initiated) and Push (server-initiated), can be chosen to best support the type of DCD-enabled service being delivered.
  - Flexible content scheduling and packaging enables delivery of just what needs to be delivered, how it needs to be delivered, and when it needs to be delivered.
  - Efficient, reliable methods of subscriber identification/authentication can enable personalized services, while minimizing the impact upon network systems that provide the subscriber identification/authentication.
- The impact upon limited mobile device resources must be manageable. Mobile devices generally provide limited content storage space compared to other devices. Syndicated services have the potential to deliver very significant amounts of content. The combined storage needs of multiple applications that may be running on a device will further complicate storage management. DCD will address these needs through storage management features:
  - Content storage space can be reserved on the device, for each application. DCD will manage this content storage on behalf of the applications, resulting in more consistent/reliable memory management, with the additional benefit that application developers can spend less effort on storage management design.
  - Content delivery can be intelligently adapted to the available storage. The DCD server will be aware of the amount of storage available for each application. This will allow service providers to select an optimum mix of local (pre-loaded by DCD) and remote content, enabling services to be deployed across a wide range of devices.

- It must be easier for application developers to create applications that can be integrated with underlying content delivery enablers for operation across a variety of networks, and executing on a wide variety of terminals. DCD will address these needs as follows:
  - DCD will provide a simple, standardized set of device-internal interfaces for application connection to content delivery services, and interaction with those services. Developers can then focus most of their effort on content presentation and user interaction.
  - Beyond the application interface, DCD will directly manage all subscriber identification/ authentication, content delivery, and storage management functions on behalf of the applications.

- It must be easier to get content providers and users together, overcoming the inherent limitations of mobile devices for service discovery and subscription. In the PC world, with large screens and easy input options, users can discover more easily and subscribe to services. With mobile devices, this can be frustrating, turning away potential subscribers or significantly limiting their efforts to use mobile services, and limiting the number of content providers that make the effort to reach out to mobile users. DCD will address these needs by simplifying both ends of the content provider and subscriber relationship as follows:
  - Content providers will be able to announce service changes, for example, publish the availability of new services, through DCD service providers.
  - Subscribers and their applications will be able to discover the available services automatically. DCD will only enable the automatic publication of the service changes. Applications will present the service options to the user in the manner that best suits the application.
  - In the process of service selection and subscription, content providers and DCD-enabled applications will be able to exchange information about each other, so the service can be tailored for the subscriber.

The nature of mobility also provides opportunities for service providers to offer value added services for mobile users:

- 'Mobility' means, in general, the ability of users to access services from different locations involving different types of networks and connections. It is not limited to public wireless networks, but also applies to private wireless networks (e.g. Wireless Fidelity (WiFi®)) and even wired networks. Thus, depending upon the type of connections available to devices, users may be able to access services in many different environments and even on multiple devices at the same time (e.g. mobile phone, WiFi-enabled device, broadcast-enabled device, PC, cable set-top box). DCD will provide the ability for service providers to deliver services to users in a consistent manner in multiple environments, across various networks and connection types. Thus, DCD-enabled services will be truly 'mobile'.
- Mobile networks and mobile devices also can provide service-enhancing information about users, their applications, location, and devices. This information can be used to dynamically adapt services, providing a more personalized and relevant (e.g. by location) user experience.

21.1.1 DCD Use Cases

DCD is not an end-user service by itself. It is intended as an enabler of services based upon content produced from sources, and consumed by applications, that are themselves external to the enabler. For users, the term 'Applications' typically means the program that they use on their devices, but in a larger sense also includes the handling of the interaction of content providers and the device-based programs, which are called the 'client applications' here. Applications provide the end-user services, and DCD only facilitates interaction of content providers and client applications.

DCD is a complementary mechanism for other content delivery methods, for example, Browsing, Wireless Application Protocol (WAP) Push, SMS, and MMS. It is not intended to replace these enablers but will allow evolution of some services that are currently supported by them, for example:

- Browsing can evolve from a request/response experience requiring transactions across the mobile network, to a much more responsive experience based on an 'On-Device Portal' (ODP) concept. Normal browser behavior will not be limited, that is, users can still browse Internet sites; however, large amounts of dynamically updated and personalized content can be pre-loaded by DCD for direct consumption by the user. As a result, the ODP experience will be much more effective, allowing users to get to the content they want much faster, and browse content of personal interest even when outside network coverage.
- Information services can evolve from a user experience in which a variety of delivery methods and inbox clients (e.g. SMS, MMS, WAP Push) present an inconsistent set of features and user interfaces, to an experience in which the variety is in the types of content that can be supported by a single client with consistent features and user interface.

DCD is primarily a network-to-user content delivery enabler, but will also facilitate peer-to-peer services:

- Client applications will have the ability to upload content, which can be delivered to other users in various application-specific ways. DCD will not limit those options, but only enables the upload of the content and if required by the application, the delivery of the content to other users.

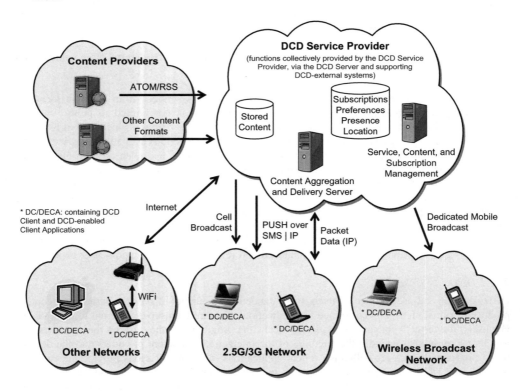

Figure 21.1 Dynamic content delivery in a ubiquitous service environment

- Since applications can deliver any arbitrary content to client applications, this could include social-networking information such as personal status (e.g. presence, location), conversations (e.g. blogs, message boards), and media (e.g. photos, audio, video).

DCD will also enable Internet-style news feed applications (typical RSS/Atom-type services) and any similar service based on content syndication.

Beyond enhancing/complementing legacy services and supporting typical syndication services in a mobile environment, DCD will enable entirely new types of services. This is primarily because DCD makes no assumption about the content type that is delivered, for example, its organization or purpose, beyond being a collection of delivered content objects. DCD's role is limited to managing the delivery and storage of a set of content objects, per limited set of delivery options specified by the content provider and/or application user. An example of a new service that can leverage DCD capabilities is mobile advertising (see Section 27.4).

The goal for DCD is to provide a service enabler that has long-term usefulness in a variety of markets and service contexts. Figure 21.1 illustrates the potential applicability of DCD in a ubiquitous service environment in which the user is rarely out-of-coverage of some type. However, when out-of-coverage events do occur, DCD will have provided an opportunity for a significant amount of content to have been pre-loaded on the user's device, which the user can then enjoy off-line.

21.2   Standards Precursors to DCD

As described above, DCD has been 'inspired' by the growth of content syndication services on the Internet. The related standards are also expected to be represented in DCD-specified interfaces, or at least, similarly inspire the general approach to development of the interfaces. The 'standards' include the de facto standard [RSS] and the Internet Engineering Task Force (IETF) proposed standard Atom Syndication Format [RFC 4287]. Both of these specifications define content 'channelization' mechanisms employing an XML-based content enveloping structure with embedded content metadata. The developing suite of Atom specifications includes both content delivery to clients (see [RFC 4287]) and from clients (see An Atom Publishing Protocol [IETF Draft2007b]).

Published examples of using XML namespaces to extend RSS and Atom (see e.g. http://rss-extensions.org/wiki/Main_Page) provide a good baseline for the methods likely to be used in DCD.

21.3   DCD Architecture and Technical Specifications

This section is focusing on DCD specification aspects that are still very much work in progress. Due to the market drivers for DCD, its architecture looks like more than a simple granular OMA enabler, but stops short of specifying a complete end-user consumable service. Such an approach is justified by the need to ensure that the various DCD-based services (features offered by the DCD enabler) offer more than just technical feasibility support, and address real deployment issues such as spectral efficiency and mobile device constraints.

21.3.1 DCD in the OMA Service Environment

As any other OMA enabler, DCD deployment can include access control management of its interfaces through inclusion within an OMA Service Environment (OSE) enabled deployment.

Like most enablers, DCD enabler exposes category I0 interfaces. In principle, such well-defined interfaces can be used by any other resource, and usually the use of such interfaces would follow a client-server pattern, where the server is the one exposing interfaces to be used by the client. Figure 21.2 symbolically outlines some peculiarities with respect to the DCD architecture relative to the overall OSE architecture.

The DCD architecture includes both a DCD client and a DCD server, and each of them exposes an I0 interface used by the other component. In addition, both the DCD client and the DCD server interact with other external entities (e.g. other OMA enablers), whose functionality, and the way

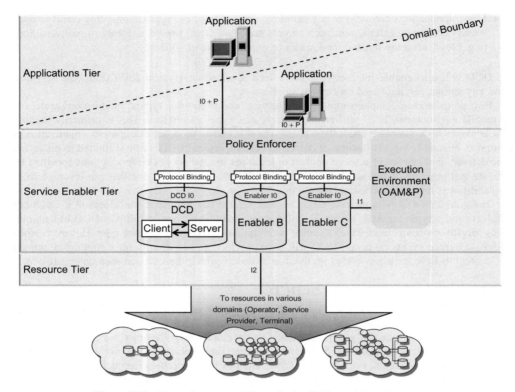

Figure 21.2   Dynamic content delivery in the OMA service environment

they interface with the DCD components is described in sufficient detail, although not specified by DCD. The direct arrows between DCD client and DCD server should be interpreted as the use of I0 interfaces, and has been shown here like this for simplification. The logical Policy Enforcer (PE) can always intercept such requests (based on service provider's deployment model) and apply policies before allowing the requests to reach the components of the DCD enabler. In other words, the logical paths of communication between a DCD client and a DCD server are similar to any application's path. Like other enablers, DCD may also interface with other resources using I2 interfaces exposed by them.

21.3.2 DCD Logical Architecture

The architecture of the DCD enabler depicted in Figure 21.3 (see [DCD AD]) includes the following elements:

- Actors: the individuals and organizations that use the DCD enabler to provide or access services, for example, content providers, subscribers, and users. Note: the term 'subscriber' is often used to mean the same thing as 'user' (a service consumer), with the exception that being a subscriber also means having the role of selecting and subscribing to services. As a subscriber, a person has a relationship to service providers; as a user, a person is a service consumer.
- External entities: application servers that originate content, client applications that present it to users, or other entities that enhance the operation of the DCD enabler. External entities are not

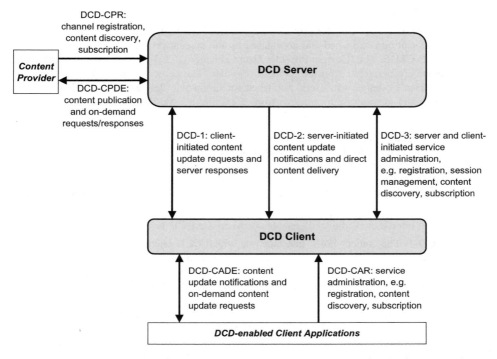

Figure 21.3 DCD architecture. Reproduced by Permission of the Open Mobile Alliance Ltd.

impacted by the DCD enabler unless they choose to implement and use an interface provided by the DCD Enabler. These entities include:

- Content provider: while also used as an actor, the term content provider is also used to refer to the systems that provide content to the DCD enabler.
- Client applications: mobile-terminal-based software clients that use the DCD enabler to access content. The client application may present the content to users or use it for any arbitrary purpose.
- Other Enabler Entities: as specified by OMA, these are entities that provide specific interfaces via which the DCD enabler can add value to its operation for specific services.

- DCD Entities: servers and clients that provide DCD interfaces, interact with other enablers, and implement other specific DCD requirements. The interfaces and functions of these entities are defined as part of the DCD enabler. They include the following:

  - DCD Server: generally serves as the network-side endpoint of the DCD enabler, providing a variety of functions such as channel aggregation/adaptation and delivery to the DCD client. In the process, the DCD server may apply for personalization.
  - DCD Client: generally serves as the device-side endpoint of the DCD enabler, providing a variety of functions such as channel reception/storage and delivery to the client application. In the process, the DCD client may apply for personalization.

- DCD Interfaces: points of interaction between two entities, defined as a set of transaction types and related data formats. The interfaces may be used over a variety of transports and bearer networks. They include:

- External facing interfaces of the DCD server.
  - DCD-CPR: The 'Content Provider Registration' (CPR) interface, via which content services can be established and configured by the content provider.
  - DCD-CPDE: The 'Content Provider Data Exchange' (CPDE) interface, via which content items are delivered from the content provider. The content items may be published in advance of delivery to users, published for immediate delivery, or provided by content providers in response to requests from users through the DCD enabler.
- External facing interfaces of the DCD client
  - DCD-CAR: The 'Client Application Registration' (CAR) interface, via which client applications connect to the DCD enabler. Once connected, client applications can begin data exchange via the DCD enabler.
  - DCD-CADE: The 'Client Application Data Exchange' (CADE) interface, via which client applications receive content, and interact with content services, including content uploading.
- Internal interfaces of the DCD enabler between the DCD server and DCD client
  - DCD-1: The content 'Pull' interface, via which DCD clients initiate content delivery.
  - DCD-2: The content 'Push' interface, via which DCD servers initiate content delivery.
  - DCD-3: The 'administration' interface, via which DCD clients establish access to DCD servers, and DCD servers and clients manage the operation of the DCD enabler.

The DCD architecture also references externally defined functions and interfaces that are usable by DCD entities in fulfilling specific DCD requirements. The architecture only clarifies how the DCD entities should support interaction with them (i.e. via which interfaces) and for what purpose (i.e. the specific requirements that are related to their use). They include the following:

- The 'Other Enabler Entities' mentioned above, for example, those of the OMA enablers supporting access to information or other functions related to Presence, Location, Digital Rights Management, Device Profile, Charging.
- Entities and functions not yet released as enablers by OMA but which are related to active work items, for example, Content Screening, Subscriber Profile, and Subscription Management.

21.3.3 DCD Technical Specifications

DCD technical specifications were still under development. They are expected to cover the DCD 'semantics' (behavior of entities and use of interfaces), DCD 'syntax' (detailed formats for interface data), and data flows.

21.4 DCD Deployment Options

DCD is specifically intended to support a variety of service deployment approaches and enabling various business models. The approach selected for use by a particular content provider will depend upon the types of value added DCD capabilities that the content provider seeks to leverage. These may include the following:

- ability to deliver content over a variety of networks, transport bearers, and using different delivery methods;
- ability to integrate services such as Location and Presence for personalization of content delivery;
- ability to integrate services such as Charging for flexibility in the cost of data transport usage;

- ability to integrate services such as Content Screening for malicious or inappropriate content blocking;
- ability to aggregate content and information from diverse sources into new and personalized content services.

Leveraging these capabilities for specific user communities may require content providers to deploy DCD-based services via a DCD service provider. The DCD service provider may be a Mobile Network Operator, or another service provider, which is engaged in this role with one or more Mobile Network Operator. The DCD service provider operates the DCD server and may additionally support one or more of the capabilities described above. Content providers may also operate DCD servers directly, and support some of the capabilities described above, depending upon their relationship with providers of the value added capabilities. In this case, the content provider must support the DCD internal interfaces that it intends to leverage.

21.4.1 A DCD Deployment Example

Figure 21.4 illustrates a high-level view of an example deployment leveraging both broadcast and point-to-point networks.

The DCD server, via 2.5G/3G networks, can send notifications and deliver content directly to DCD clients using WAP Push and IP-based transport (e.g. HTTP and HTTPS). Through these networks, the DCD server and client also directly interact for DCD administration actions, for example, registration and session management.

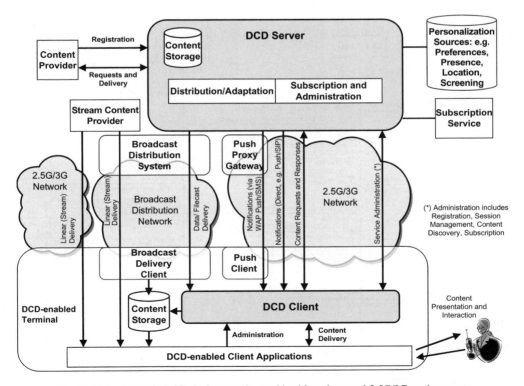

Figure 21.4 Example DCD deployment in combined broadcast and 2.5G/3G environments

In this example, the DCD server may also send notifications and deliver content to a broadcast-supporting community of devices, using filecast services of a Broadcast Distribution System which delivers the filecasted objects to Broadcast Delivery clients in devices. The Broadcast Delivery clients deliver the notifications or content to the DCD client in the device. The objects may be placed into the device content storage directly by the Broadcast Delivery client or by the DCD client.

Linear (streamed) content may also be delivered to client applications via broadcast or point-to-point methods. In this example, the linear content is not delivered via the DCD server (another deployment option). The linear content can be integrated by reference in the content (e.g. application language) delivered via DCD, with the client application using other clients to access/render the linear content when selected by the user.

It is also possible that one or more of the delivery methods (e.g. push or pull), or transport bearers (broadcast, SMS, or 2.5G/3G) may not be applicable to a specific device, user (by subscription, preference, or dynamic attribute), service, or client application. In that case, the DCD server will select an available/compatible delivery method and transport bearer. In some cases, such limitations may prevent the use of some DCD interfaces, for example DCD-3, and the limitation must be overcome by other methods (e.g. pre-configuration).

21.4.2 A DCD Service Example

The Figure 21.5 illustrates a high-level view of part of a service life cycle, for example, a DCD-enabled service. Note that this example only shows a few of the functions of DCD, and a specific case for subscription (delivery of default or pre-subscribed channels).

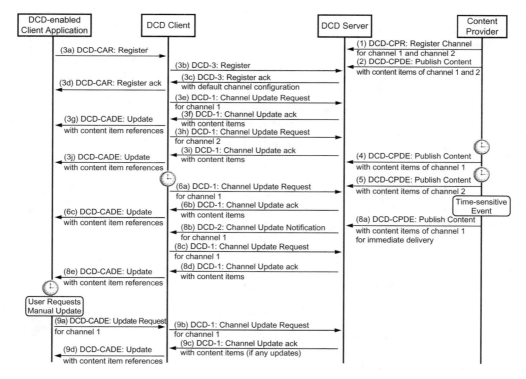

Figure 21.5   Example DCD-enabled service data flow

Notes on the operations in the data flow:

(1) The content provider establishes a service for delivery via a DCD service provider, and defines the delivery options for two channels related to the service. The DCD service provider assigns channel IDs for the new channels.
(2) The content provider delivers content for the channels that the content provider has previously established. This step may refer to many content publication actions over time, for example, the user in this case is new to the service, but the service has been in operation for a while.
(3) The DCD-enabled client application starts up. It attaches to the DCD enabler by registering with the DCD client, and retrieves initial content for subscribed channels.

    (a) The DCD-enabled client application sends a register operation, and includes its application characteristics, and optionally channel configuration data for services to which it seeks to establish access.
    (b) The DCD client forwards the register operation to the DCD server (either a default DCD server or as specified by the DCD-enabled client application). As part of this operation, the DCD client is authenticated, if required by DCD service provider policy.
    (c) The DCD server responds with an assigned session ID and optionally a channel configuration for default or pre-subscribed channels. The session ID, which is present in all subsequent operations over the DCD interfaces, enables optimized transaction routing and authentication for subsequent requests.
    (d) The DCD client confirms registration success.
    (e) The DCD client initiates a channel update request to retrieve initial content for the first channel.
    (f) The DCD server responds with the currently available content.
    (g) The DCD client saves the content in its storage, and sends a notification to the DCD-enabled client application. The notification includes a reference to the content in the local storage.
    (h) The DCD client initiates a channel update request to retrieve initial content for the second channel.
    (i) The DCD server responds with the currently available content.
    (j) The DCD client saves the content in its storage, and sends a notification to the DCD-enabled client application. The notification includes a reference to the content in the local storage.

(4) Sometime later, the content provider publishes content for the first channel. Note that various publication methods (e.g. pull, push) may be used for each channel.
(5) Sometime later (perhaps on a different schedule), the content provider publishes content for the second channel.
(6) At a scheduled time as defined in the channel configuration, the DCD client requests a channel update for the first channel.

    (a) The DCD client initiates a channel update request to retrieve new content for the channel.
    (b) The DCD server responds with the newly available content. Various synchronization methods can be used by the DCD service providers, to avoid re-delivery of content already received by the DCD client.
    (c) The DCD client saves the content in its storage, and sends a notification to the DCD-enabled client application. The notification includes a reference to the content in the local storage.

(7) At a scheduled time as defined in the channel configuration, the DCD client requests a channel update for the second channel. The process is the same as in (6a–6c).

(8) Sometime later, the content provider publishes content for the first channel, for immediate delivery. This may be related, for example, to some time-sensitive event, such as a breaking news story, sports game event, or forum update. An update notification is pushed to the DCD client, which immediately retrieves the content.

  (a) The content provider publishes the content to the DCD server, and indicates that immediate delivery is required.
  (b) The DCD server pushes a channel update notification to the DCD client. Note that since many subscribers may get the same notification, the DCD server may spread the notifications over a period of time.
  (c) The DCD client initiates a channel update request to retrieve the new content for the channel.
  (d) The DCD server responds with the newly available content.
  (e) The DCD client saves the content in its storage, and sends a notification to the DCD-enabled client application. The notification includes a reference to the content in the local storage.

(9) Sometime later (perhaps in response to the previous pushed update notification), the user requests a manual update of the channel content. Note this operation can also deliver application-specific data from the DCD-enabled client application to the DCD server, by which the user can interact with a DCD-enabled service (e.g. a forum viewer/update application).

  (a) The DCD-enabled client application requests an update of the channel, optionally providing application-related data in the request.
  (b) The DCD client forwards the update request to the DCD server.
  (c) The DCD server responds with content, which may be specifically related to what the DCD-enabled client application included in the update request.
  (d) The DCD client saves the content in its storage, and sends a notification to the DCD-enabled client application. The notification includes a reference to the content in the local storage.

Note that while this description includes references to application-specific handling, such functions are outside the scope of the DCD enabler itself, and are included here only to help clarify the service-enabling features of DCD, for example, opaque delivery of arbitrary content between content providers and DCD-enabled client applications. DCD servers may implement or integrate with content provider functions for arbitrary applications, but those aspects are not directly the functions of DCD.

21.5 DCD Salient Points

Most of the key differentiators of DCD, as compared to current content delivery approaches and standards, can be distilled from the objectives, architecture description, and examples above. They are repeated here in summary.

- Current content delivery approaches and standards do not address the cost of providing syndicated content delivery in the mobile environment. DCD will provide the ability to optimize what, when, and how content is delivered.
- Current content delivery approaches and standards do not address the impact of syndicated content delivery upon limited mobile device resources. DCD will provide the ability to optimize content delivery for specific users and devices, and simplify application developer effort for content storage management.
- Current content delivery approaches and standards do not address the cost and complexity of designing applications for syndicated content delivery in a variety of devices, across various

networks, and using various transport protocols. DCD will simplify content provider and application developer effort by providing a simple set of interfaces for service administration and content delivery, beyond which the specific delivery methods and transport network issues are completely or largely transparent.

- Current content delivery approaches and standards do not address the complexity of getting content providers and users together, by overcoming the inherent limitations (e.g. in supporting user interaction) of mobile devices for service discovery and subscription. DCD will facilitate content providers in announcing service changes, users and their applications in discovery of available services, and exchange of information between content providers and users in the subscription process.
- Current content delivery approaches and standards do not consider the nature of mobility and mobile network enablers, and the opportunities they provide for service providers to offer value added services for mobile users. DCD will specifically leverage these aspects to facilitate true service mobility (ubiquitous service access) and adaptive content delivery.
- Current content delivery approaches and standards do not consider how to provide personalized services, and especially not personalization based upon the characteristics of mobile service environments. DCD will specifically leverage these aspects to facilitate service personalization based on, for example, serving network, the device in use, user location, and, in general, information about the user and their preferences for content delivery.

21.6 Impact of Specifications on the Industry

While it is still under development in OMA, DCD has received broad support from OMA members, including service providers, mobile device vendors, service provider equipment vendors, and content providers.

There have been deployments of services using similar content delivery approaches (although proprietary, and narrower in scope as compared to DCD). Some of these deployments have contributed to the lessons learned, and resulted in specific interest and new requirements as represented in DCD.

21.6.1 Impact on Service Providers

Service providers, for example, Mobile Network Operators and Value Added Service Providers (VASP), will gain significantly from availability of DCD in the market. DCD will enable their service users to more easily access personally relevant content, as well as address key aspects of scalable service delivery for syndicated content services. This is likely to increase service usage, and facilitate development of innovative services that further attracts users.

Service providers will have a range of options in deployment of DCD-enabled services, which will result in significant differentiation opportunities. Mobile Network Operators, for example, will be able to leverage OMA enablers within their domain for personalization of DCD-enabled services. VASPs will be able to specialize on integration of various application types into a DCD-enabled service delivery framework, and can specialize in service delivery over various network types.

Service providers can take on various roles in a DCD-enabled service delivery environment, including content provider, content aggregator, subscription management, and personalized/adaptive content delivery. The roles may vary with the specific service, for example, for some large content providers the service provider may provide only content delivery, whereas for smaller content providers the service provider may fulfill a variety of additional roles.

21.6.2 Impact on Content Providers

In addition to the option of being supported by the service provider-fulfilled functions described above, content providers will find that services can be more effectively delivered to users, with less content server infrastructure. This is because the content providers are not impacted for every service request from users. Instead, they can periodically publish content for delivery by the service provider to all subscribed users.

Content providers can also use a variety of options for personalizing content for specific users, including direct personalization (by serving individual channel update requests forwarded by the DCD server), and personalization through channel configuration (e.g. establishment of personalization rules that the DCD server executes upon each channel update request). This enables a high degree of service logic to be pre-defined, and then implemented by the service provider in the actual service delivery. The content provider in that case can focus on the core role of providing the interesting content that users want.

21.6.3 Impact on Application Developers

A key objective of DCD is to simplify the effort of application developers in creating mobile data applications. With DCD, application developers need not worry about detailed content delivery protocols that may vary between content providers and Service Provider Environments (e.g. bearer networks), or storage management for the content that is delivered. Instead, two simple interfaces (for administration and content delivery) provide everything that the application developers need to enable their applications to attach to content services, and receive content from them. The DCD client-provided storage management functions avoid any need of the application developer to deal with content caching or garbage collection. DCD-provided storage management, and the consistency of DCD interfaces regardless of the service environment, enables application developers to focus on the core role of providing content presentation and interaction to users.

Application developers can extend the basic service provided by automated content delivery with application-specific operations that execute over the DCD content delivery interface. This facilitates specialized and interactive application deployment, while leveraging the simplicity of the core content delivery functions.

Overall, these capabilities should reduce the cost of application development and reduce application time-to-market, while still enabling application differentiation and allowing the application developers to focus on the best user experience.

21.6.4 Impact on Vendors

As the basic methods of syndication as an approach to content delivery are well understood by the marketplace and are based upon conventional Internet technology, infrastructure vendors should easily be able to adapt current content delivery systems to support DCD, especially existing ones with somewhat similar capabilities. Vendors may also find it straightforward to augment current delivery systems (e.g. caching WAP Gateways, Push Proxy Gateways, and content download servers) with the functions of the DCD server, extending the lifetime of the current products.

Because the standardized functions of the DCD server are limited in scope, and focused mainly on providing adaptive content delivery based on pre-defined channel configurations, significant room remains for DCD server vendors to augment the DCD functions with differentiating capabilities, for example, specialized support for various functions or networks.

Also, because the DCD-defined administration and content delivery interfaces between content providers will be kept simple and flexible, content server vendors can use them for basic content delivery, while also being able to use them for specialized application-specific purposes. This will enable content server vendors to grow their markets with innovative services based on a simple/flexible content delivery framework.

21.6.5 Impact on Consumer Market

The cost, market availability, and capabilities of consumer services should be improved through the overall benefits that DCD will provide to the industry. Since the consumer will not need to work so hard to use DCD-enabled content services, and can receive highly personalized services, overall service subscription and usage levels should increase, which will further drive down per-user costs.

21.6.6 Impact on Corporate Market

DCD will support various key objectives of corporate markets, including increased security, reliability, and reduced cost of application development and operation. Many current corporate-focused applications could benefit from DCD enablement, for example, Customer Relationship Management (CRM), workforce management, collaboration, as well as corporate-specialized information services. The current complexity, design variability, and resulting high cost of deploying such services to mobile devices have inhibited development of this rich market opportunity. DCD should eliminate much of these inhibiting factors, and significantly improving the corporate market for mobile services.

21.6.7 Impact on Other Specifications

DCD is currently a work item specific to OMA, and has no impact on other OMA specifications. Beyond OMA, it is envisioned that incorporation of key DCD innovations into IETF and W3C specifications, where applicable, is a likely step in the future, which will benefit the overall convergence of standards.

21.7   Specifications Evolution and Future Direction

Currently, only one release of DCD is specifically planned, although some functions and adaptation/enhancements for some environments and transport networks may be deferred to future releases. These may include:

- IP Multimedia Subsystem (IMS)/Session Initiation Protocol (SIP) networks, including utilization of the OMA Push over SIP enabler.
- Dedicated broadcast networks, for example, as defined by OMA Broadcast (BCAST) (see Chapter 20 for details).
- Service Discovery: currently DCD will support the delivery of channel configuration/description information (as a 'channel guide') for unspecified use by the DCD-enabled client applications, and for specified uses by the DCD client (e.g. to setup channel access). These functions may be expanded and/or aligned with other enablers in future releases, for example, the OMA BCAST Service Guide (see Chapter 20).
- Service Subscription: the level of explicit subscription process support, beyond the establishment of channel delivery for a particular user, is to be defined in the current DCD release. Similar to service discovery, these functions may be expanded and/or aligned with other enablers in future releases, for example, as defined for OMA BCAST (see Chapter 20).

21.8   Summary

This brief overview of the DCD enabler has touched on a few of the key objectives, characteristics, and market impacts of this enabler. It is hoped that the reader has gained a basic understanding of these aspects, and the relationship of DCD with current content delivery approaches and standards. Readers are encouraged to seek out the public documents of the OMA Content Delivery Working Group for further information.

22

The Global Permissions Management Enabler

You have already trusted someone with some information you would not like to share with just anyone else. For example, your wife or husband may know your credit card's pin number and your kids may know that there is a key under the second flower pot by the door should they get locked out someday. You wouldn't want that information to become publicly available even though the risks in most real-life situations are relatively limited. Your son may tell a friend about the hidden key, but the information won't be shown on TV during prime time.

In your 'digital life', however, you are much more exposed to potentially risky situations. Indeed, the global nature of the Internet makes your sensitive information vulnerable to theft, hypothetically by anyone, anywhere in the world. Nowadays, spamming, 'phishing', identity theft are unfortunately becoming familiar terms.

However, at the same time, the Internet is a wonderful tool to communicate and deliver services, which makes our life easier and more enjoyable. The potential of the Internet seems almost unlimited, and more and more people are online using new innovative services. So, eventually, you will feel compelled to share some of your sensitive information through the Internet in order to enjoy some of those services. You may possibly have purchased a plane ticket on an airline's website already and you may have had to share with them important data, such as your mailing address, your credit card number, your cell phone number, etc.

Appropriate security systems can be used to prevent data theft; therefore, the airline website may use strong encryption methods and other techniques to protect your data. However, what happens next? Your data is kept by the airline in case you come back in the future and purchase another plane ticket. You won't have to enter your profile information all over again, which is great because it will make your user experience much better. But, the airline may want to have a much more complete view about you and ask you about your flying habits, your hobbies, your household composition, your income level ... and you may even be eligible for a discount in your next purchase or other promotion in exchange for completing your user profile with all kinds of detail.

Of course, you know that they use that information to 'improve their service and adapt it to your preferences', but also to better target the advertisements they display when you are browsing their website. You may have noticed that often there is some small print and a check box reading 'I authorize XYZ Airlines to share my profile information with selected partners'. Don't be surprised when you may be reached by e-mail by suitcase makers or by a resort in the Maldives with offers especially tailored for you as a privileged client of XYZ Airlines.

The Open Mobile Alliance   M. Brenner and M. Unmehopa
© 2008 Alcatel-Lucent. All Rights Reserved

If you check that box (actually it may need unchecking, since more likely than not, it is usually checked by default) you are 'giving permission' to XYZ Airlines to do something else with your personal data than the original reason why you gave them the information in the first place (which was to buy a plane ticket of course).

But actually, checking that box does not give you a lot of control about who gets which piece of information, you basically rely on XYZ Airlines' due diligence to select trustworthy partners who will provide you with offers you are really interested in so that you won't perceive them as spam.

Also, if in addition to that, you also bought a second hand barbecue on an online auction using an instant messaging system, and were invited to one of those social network websites and accepted the invitation, you have personal, potentially sensitive information spread a bit all over the place. Each of those services will have their own methods and policies to share that information with other users or third parties. Some of them may provide you with more sophisticated input options than the check box example, but at the end of the day most people, including ourselves, are really lost and don't have a very accurate idea about who knows what about them in the digital world.

For some people, this does not seem to be a major concern, and they are increasingly using online services in spite of their potential risks. However, for some others, often depending on age and cultural background, keeping control of their private information is of utmost importance and, therefore, they may feel a lot of reluctance, for example, to purchase plane tickets, or use an instant messaging service over the Internet. Fear of spam, credit card fraud, identity theft, to give but some examples, are concerns that prevent many people from using online services from a service provider.

This is exactly what Open Mobile Alliance (OMA) Global Permissions Management (GPM) is all about. OMA GPM's intention is to give the user full control of how their private information is used by their service provider so that they can know at anytime who knows what about themselves, therefore increasing trust and removing fears about using advanced online services.

22.1 Are Those Specifications Really Needed?

The OMA GPM work item was initiated based on the realization that inside the OMA, individual enablers were already addressing user permissions in their own ways, focusing on their specific contexts. The two most significant enablers in this situation are OMA Location and OMA Presence, both of which have developed their own solutions.

Therefore a need ensued, according to the OMA Service Environment (OSE) basic principle of separating intrinsic functions from generic functions, to develop a generic way of handling user permissions in OMA which would avoid future enablers to develop once again their own permissions management mechanisms.

However, the most important driver for the work item was, as explained in the introduction, the need to put users back at the center of permissions control, in order to restore their trust in online services. Indeed, without a generic way of handling permissions, users need to provision those permissions in different places, with different methods, different user interfaces, etc. The potential complexity behind it without OMA GPM may make mainstream users completely lose control and trust and patience in using online services.

Therefore, OMA GPM goes beyond the technical exercise of rationalizing the way permissions are managed within the OSE (which is a very valuable target per se) and provides real benefits for end-users by increasing their trust and confidence in service providers and, thereby, the adoption of their online services.

To sum up, market requirements for OMA GPM are twofold, and targeted toward:

(1) Developing a generic way of handling user permissions in the Service Provider Environment, where:

(a) The introduction of generic, re-usable mechanisms will reduce costs and time-to-market of new services.
(b) Additionally, it will reduce standardization time of future enablers as they won't have to define their own system for permissions control.

(2) Providing the user with a consolidated view of their permissions and a single way of managing them from a central point, so that it will increase trust in the service provider and thus increase service adoption and revenue.

One may wonder whether there is a real need to standardize OMA GPM, or whether the same benefits could be obtained by using proprietary developments. While we do not claim that such proprietary developments are not feasible, the fact that information to be protected is distributed in different entities of the Service Provider domain makes OMA GPM or its equivalent proprietary system interact potentially with every other enabler implementation or other resource. Without a standardized Permissions Checking interface (see later sections for more details) it would be impractical, if not impossible, to integrate all present and future service enablers in a Service Provider's Environment with a centralized permissions management system.

Furthermore, some of the discussions during the development of the OMA GPM Requirements Document showed that in some cases the information to be protected was to be found directly on a handset side resource. In that case, handsets might also have to interact with OMA GPM to check permissions. Because there is such a large variety of makes and models of handsets, the service provider can only rely on standards in order to introduce new functionality. A specific proprietary development would really be impossible if it needed to be deployed in tens of millions of handsets. Therefore, the need for standards is very straightforward.

22.1.1 GPM Actors and Main Concepts in the Requirements Document

The generic nature of OMA GPM has led to defining actors and their interactions in a very general way, so that the enabler is applicable in a large variety of environments including, of course, enterprise applications. Figure 22.1 is the GPM requirements' representation of actors and their interactions. We will try to summarize the main concepts behind the GPM requirements in the following paragraphs (see [GPM RD] for details).

A piece of sensitive information that is subject to permissions rule is called Target Information in OMA GPM terminology. This information pertains to an individual, who we call Permissions Target. Target Information is usually present or can be obtained from some Service Provider resource which can include OMA enablers (e.g. Presence or Location) or other non-OMA defined entities such as an application (e.g. a photo album, an electronic wallet) or entities within the service provider's IT system, for example, a billing system.

The individual or third party who would like to access the Target Information is called a Target Attribute Consumer. This will be the one actually using that piece of information and is, in most cases, a human end-user. However, in many cases, the Target Attribute Consumer does not query a Service Provider resource directly but uses another service enabler or application as an intermediary. This intermediary application or service enabler will often provide some value added service functionality for the Target Attribute Consumer (e.g. if the Target Information consumed is location information, the geographical co-ordinates that are provided by the location system may be transformed into a map, a ZIP code, or a street address, which are more meaningful to humans than raw location information expressed in latitude and longitude co-ordinates). The service enabler or application that acts as an intermediary between the Target Attribute Consumer and the Service Provider resources is referred to as Target Attribute Requestor in OMA GPM vocabulary.

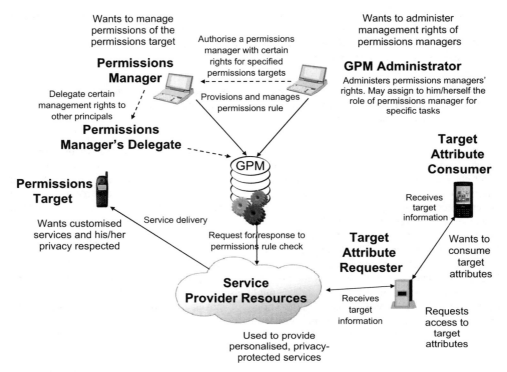

Figure 22.1 Global Permissions Management actor chain. Reproduced by Permission of the Open Mobile Alliance Ltd.

22.1.2 A Typical GPM Flow

Figure 22.2 illustrates the following sequence of events. Whenever a Target Attribute Requestor tries to access Target Information, it will send a Target Request to the Service Provider resource. Before releasing the information, since it is recognized as being subject to user permissions, the Service Provider resource will perform a Permissions Checking Request with the OMA GPM enabler. This request will contain information about the Target Information, the Target Attribute Consumer, the Target Attribute Requestor, and maybe some additional information like the intended use of the attribute. The information contained in the Permissions Checking Request allows OMA GPM to determine which Permissions Rule should apply among those rules that have been previously provisioned for the Permissions Target.

A Permissions Rule is an expression of a set of conditions and a returned result if the set of conditions are met. The results that can be expressed in a Permissions Rule include 'grant', 'deny', and 'ask'. The 'grant' and 'deny' results are self-descriptive, and they indicate to the Service Provider resource the further actions that need to be taken.

The 'grant' result may optionally include further granularity, for example, to provide partial access to information (some parts of the information are not to be given out) or to restrict the accuracy of the information provided (especially relevant in the case of location information, for example, only provide ZIP code, but not accurate position). OMA GPM requirements describe different types of Permissions Rule and what they may contain.

The 'ask' result is a special case which means that OMA GPM is not able to make a decision based on the existing provisioned rules, and a special actor (most likely a human) needs to be

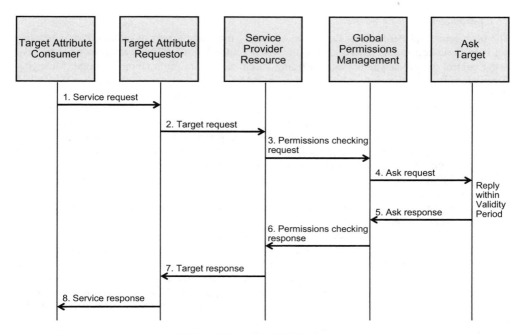

Figure 22.2 Typical GPM use case

queried via an Ask Request. This actor is called Ask Target. The Ask Target, among others, will be able to 'grant this time only', 'deny this time only', 'grant always', and 'deny always'.

OMA GPM requirements include a section on Ask Management, describing the interactions between the OMA GPM enabler and Ask Targets, and dealing with validity periods, Ask Target preferences, etc.

Once the Permissions Rule has been evaluated (with or without the intervention of the Ask Target), a Permissions Checking Response (i.e. deny, grant, grant with some limitations, etc) is sent to the Service Provider resource which will, in turn, craft an appropriate response to the Target Request according to the returned response.

In many instances, the same individual may be playing the role of several actors, thereby simplifying the picture. A typical case is one in which you use a mapping application for your mobile phone that requests your own location information to display a map of your whereabouts (and optionally traffic information, businesses within the area, etc.), and the Permissions Rule provisioned in OMA GPM for this case include the need to 'ask' the person being located (i.e. yourself in this case) then the roles in OMA GPM would be mapped as follows:

- Target Attribute Consumer: you
- Target Attribute Requestor: mapping application
- Service Provider Resource: location server
- Ask Target: you.

This would reduce the number of actors in this use case to only three, thereby greatly simplifying the picture. However, OMA GPM concepts were defined to be as flexible and adaptable as possible, so that they would apply in most situations, hence the relative complexity and large number of actors.

22.1.3 Management of Permissions Rule

The management of Permissions Rule is an extremely important aspect of OMA GPM, which has not been described so far. Indeed, one of the stated goals of OMA GPM is to allow users to have better control over their permissions regarding how their private information is shared. Managing Permissions Rule is, therefore, a key function in OMA GPM and as a consequence the OMA GPM Requirements Document is quite thorough in describing every aspect of it.

By managing Permissions Rule we understand the typical management operations one can imagine such as create, edit, delete, copy, activate/de-activate, list, sort, etc. OMA GPM defines provisioning interfaces that allow these operations to be performed on Permissions Rule.

An essential actor called Permissions Manager is tasked with the responsibility of managing the Permissions Rule for one Permission Target or an identified set of Permissions Targets. It is the role of the GPM Administrator to assign management rights to individual Permissions Managers, and in case there are several Permissions Managers who have rights to manage permissions for the same Permissions Target, it is also the role of the GPM Administrator to define relative priorities for Permissions Managers.

Finally, there is the notion of delegation, by which a Permissions Manager can delegate all or part of their management rights to a Delegate who will then be able to act on their behalf.

In the typical mass market context, the GPM Administrator's role will be assumed by the service provider, who will subsequently assign management rights to its subscribers. In many cases, subscribers will be managing Permissions Rule for themselves (i.e. subscribers play the role of Permissions Targets and Permissions Managers at the same time). However, in some other occasions, the GPM Administrator may designate a different Permissions Manager than the Permissions Target. An example of this situation could be an underage subscriber (the Permissions Target) whose Permissions Rule are managed by his or her parent or guardian (the Permissions Manager). The parent or guardian may allow the child to manage part of their permissions, and they would therefore delegate part of their management rights to the child, who would then become a Delegate in addition to being a Permissions Target.

In the enterprise context, the GPM Administrator may be the Enterprise's IT Administrator, who would assign management rights to team leaders (Permissions Managers). Team leaders may delegate parts of their rights to team members (Delegates) or may even delegate their rights completely to a particular team member who is tasked with managing permissions for the whole team.

As you can see the introduction of these three actors makes GPM's Permissions Rule management very flexible and adaptable to different contexts, but can also be simplified when several roles are played by the same individual.

22.2   Standards Precursors to GPM

GPM was not the first work item in OMA dealing with privacy protection. Indeed, OMA produced a reference release including generic OMA Privacy Requirements [Privacy RD] to be used across future OMA work. The document is referenced quite often by other OMA enablers including GPM itself, however the work item on Privacy did not have the goal of producing any technical work beyond the requirements document and this was another reason why GPM was initiated.

OMA Policy Evaluation, Enforcement and Management (PEEM) could also be considered a precursor of OMA GPM, as part of the concepts and models developed for OMA PEEM are largely being re-used by OMA GPM at the architecture level (see Chapter 8 for more details).

Also as mentioned previously in this chapter, the OMA Location and the OMA Presence enablers have defined their own methods to check permissions.

In the OMA Location Architecture (see Chapter 25 for details), privacy management is provided by the Privacy Profile Register (PPR). Before requesting the Serving Mobile Location Center

(SMLC) to locate a user, the Gateway Mobile Location Center (GMLC) issues a privacy request to the PPR to check whether the requesting application or third party is authorized to locate the end-user or not.

The OMA Privacy Checking Protocol (PCP) is used between the GMLC and the PPR to check the end-user's privacy settings before the location can be computed and provided to the requesting application. OMA Privacy Checking Protocol (PCP) is part of OMA Mobile Location Services (MLS) V1.1 which was approved as a Candidate enabler in October 2006.

In the OMA Presence, Availability and Group Management Working Group (PAG), privacy management is extensively inspired from the Internet Engineering Task Force (IETF) work. The most relevant specification is the Common Policy: A Document Format for Expressing Privacy Preferences [RFC 4745]. It defines a framework for authorization policies controlling access to application-specific data, written with Location and Presence information in mind. This specification supports the representation of rules useful in expressing the willingness of a principal to communicate a piece of information to another principal, in an eXtensible Markup Language (XML) format made of three basic elements: condition, action, and transformation. Specific extensions to [RFC 4745] in support of Presence rules, are the subject of the Presence Authorization Rules [IETF Draft 2007a]. The rules would be stored in a server using another IETF specification, the XML Configuration Access Protocol (XCAP) [RFC 4825]. OMA is referring to such a server as the XML Document Management System (XDMS). XCAP is used to put modified rules in the server, or retrieve them from the server, while Session Initiation Protocol (SIP)/SIP for Instant Messaging and Presence Leveraging Extensions (SIMPLE) methods (publish, subscribe, notify) are used to handle the interactions between the XDMS storing the rules and the application server (usually the Presence server) which is the one releasing information to 'watchers'. For more details on Presence, use of SIP/SIMPLE, XDMS, and XCAP see Chapter 14.

As you can see, both Location and Presence enablers have developed concepts similar to those in GPM and one of the challenges will be to establish a convergence path between the GPM enabler and the Presence and Location enablers' capabilities that handle privacy. This is an issue that needs critical attention and management, as these enablers continue to evolve and add new functionality, potentially overlapping with GPM.

22.3 GPM Architecture and Technical Specifications

GPM's role in the OSE is to protect access to user's information, which may be attempted by other resources (e.g. other OMA enablers). While it is possible that applications themselves may also directly invoke the GPM enabler, the emphasis is on the invocation of GPM by other OMA enablers.

22.3.1 GPM in the OSE

OMA enablers will use the GPM's I0 interface to verify whether they are granted permission to access user's information, and provide it to requesting applications. Figure 22.3 provides a mapping of the GPM enabler to an OSE architectural diagram.

To avoid some awkwardness in Figure 22.3, we have shown other OMA enablers directly invoking GPM. However, it should be understood that the logical Policy Enforcer can always intercept such requests (based on service provider's deployment model) and apply policies before allowing the requests to reach the GPM enabler. In other words, the logical path of an OMA enabler call to GPM is similar to the applications' path. Like other enablers, GPM may interface with other resources using I2 interfaces exposed by them. In particular, GPM would do so in order to get access to additional information about the user, regulatory policies, and preferences, when needed to include them in the evaluation process of the Permissions Rule.

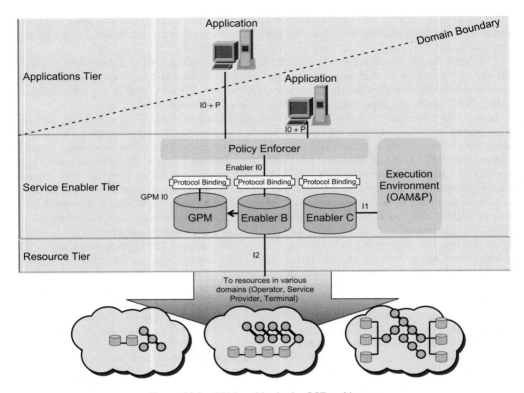

Figure 22.3   GPM enabler in the OSE architecture

22.3.2 GPM Logical Architecture

GPM logical architecture (see [GPM AD] for details) is depicted in Figure 22.4. If you have read Chapter 8 on PEEM, you will recognize interfaces and patterns. The architecture diagram represents the agreed components and interfaces, which are sufficient in order to understand how GPM interacts with other resources.

It may be useful to explain the similarities and differences between GPM and PEEM. In essence, GPM is a specialized version of PEEM, with the focus on processing Permissions Rule, which are policy rules geared toward assessing whether target user attributes can be accessed and released to other entities, considering pre-established user and service provider preferences, and/or by obtaining explicit permission from the target user. The rules would usually indicate that permissions to access and release such attributes may be either granted or denied. You will remember that PEEM supported two patterns: a proxy pattern and a callable pattern. GPM supports only the callable pattern (a proxy pattern is a matter of deployment, and can always be realized if so desired, by using the Policy Enforcer), and that's why the Proxy interface represented in PEEM Architecture is no longer shown here.

PEEM specified callable interface (PEM-1) and PEEM specified management interface (PEM-2) are the PEEM interfaces, which GPM is re-using, and the interface description will emphasize any fine differences. Finally, 'Other Resources' are similar to the 'Delegated Resources' in the PEEM architecture; they are used by GPM to obtain information needed in the processing of Permissions Rule.

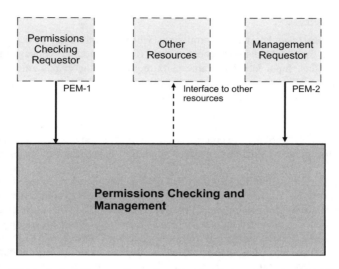

Figure 22.4   GPM logical architecture. Reproduced by Permission of the Open Mobile Alliance Ltd.

22.3.2.1 Permissions Checking and Management Component

All the following GPM functions are supported by the Permissions Checking and Management:

- Processing of the Permissions Rule, going through the following typical steps:
  - Identification of the Permissions Rule associated with the Permissions Checking Request.
  - Evaluation of the Permissions Rule using input arguments received from a Permissions Checking Requestor (a resource that issues a Permissions Checking Request to GPM enabler) and using other GPM context information (e.g. GPM user attribute's release preferences).
  - Reaching a decision to GRANT permission to release target user attributes, or a decision to DENY permission to release target user attributes, and returning the decision to the Permissions Checking Requestor. Optionally, the Permissions Rule may indicate that an Ask for consent from an authorized principal is also needed, before returning the decision.
- Providing the Permissions Rule management functions to a Management Requestor (a resource that issues a management request) such as:
  - Creating, reading, deleting, modifying, listing, suspending, resuming, and prioritizing of Permissions Rule, overwriting priorities of Permissions Rule;
  - Associating/disassociating permissions rule with attributes, application feature sets, and permissions targets.
- Notifying authorized principals when changes occur, including changes in Permissions Rule, changes in protected target user attributes, or changes in management roles/responsibilities.
- Notifying authorized principals and/or asking them for consent on permissions and checking decisions (e.g. send Ask Request to Ask Target). Such operations may be modeled via policy processing associated with management (e.g. when a particular change occurs, policy processing results in sending notifications or outbound Ask Requests and in the latter case possibly awaiting confirmation before finalizing the change).

22.3.2.2 GPM Interfaces

The PEM-1 interface (also known as Permissions Checking interface) is derived from PEM-1 [PEEM AD], using the PEEM defined process for re-using and adding Standard PEM-1 templates and PEM-1 parameters. Input identifier-value pairs required in the evaluation of the Permissions Rule (e.g. Permissions Target identity, Target Attributes, Target Attribute Requester identity and other information), respectively output identifier-value pairs (e.g. decision rendered by the evaluation of Permissions Rule) are passed over this interface.

The PEM-2 interface is derived from PEM-2 [PEEM AD]. It enables authorized principals to manage Permissions Rule. Some specific GPM requirements may require additional arguments to be specified and passed using this interface (e.g. for suspending and resuming Permissions Rule).

Other interfaces, used by, but not specified by GPM include notification interfaces, interfaces to carry the 'Ask for consent' request and response, as well as interfaces to administer and manage roles and responsibilities needed for a complete GPM system. Since GPM will re-use existing messaging and notification interfaces provided by other OMA enablers (e.g. Short Messaging Service (SMS), Multimedia Messaging Service (MMS), Wireless Application Protocol (WAP) Push and SIP Push) and/or other proprietary interfaces, these will not be further explored in this chapter. For more details on PEM-1, PEM-2, and Policy Expression Language (used by GPM to define permissions checking rules) see Chapter 8.

22.3.3 Logical Flows for GPM

The typical GPM permissions checking flow, similar to PEEM flow in callable pattern is illustrated in Figure 22.5. In this flow, the Permissions Checking Requestor uses the GPM PEM-1 interface to request GPM to perform permissions checking for specified attributes that the requestor wants to release to some application (flow 1). GPM identifies the relevant Permissions Rule and starts the process of evaluating them. The Permissions Rule, in fact, dictate the behavior of GPM during policy processing, for example, they may require GPM to interact with other resources, using the 'interface to other resources' for that purpose (see flow 2 and flow 3). On completion of the processing of Permissions Rule, a decision indicating what actions should be executed (Grant, Deny, or Ask) is reached. The GPM enabler will always return a Permissions Checking response (flow 6) of Grant or Deny to the Permissions Checking Requester. If the Permissions Rule require it, the

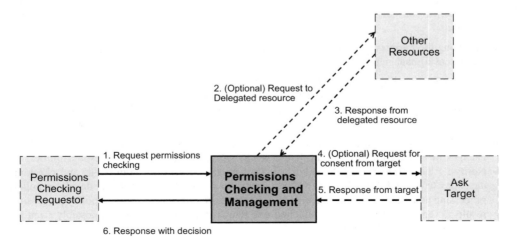

Figure 22.5   Typical GPM permissions checking flow

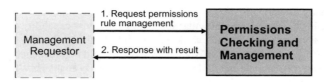

Figure 22.6   Permissions Rule management flow

GPM enabler may have to perform an Ask Request (flow 4 and flow 5), and obtain target user's consent, using an unspecified GPM interface, before returning the Permissions Rule' decision to the Permissions Checking Requestor. The response from the Ask Target (flow 5) may change the decision to be returned. An additional option is to include supplemental information in the response (e.g. a conditional grant, indicating some usage limitations). The expectation on the Permissions Checking Requestor is that it will comply with and enforce the decision obtained from GPM.

A typical GPM Permissions Rule management flow, depicted in Figure 22.6, is practically identical with the PEEM management flow. In this flow, a Management Requestor issues a request for Permissions Rule Management (flow 1 in Figure 22.6) to the GPM enabler, using the PEM-2 interface (e.g. a request to create, modify, delete, or retrieve a permissions rule). The GPM enabler identifies the management operation, performs the appropriate function, and returns the results to the Management Requester (flow 2). The processing of a management operation may also involve notifying principals or asking authorized principals for confirmation that the management operation is authorized, before completing its execution.

22.3.4 GPM Technical Specifications

GPM technical specifications work cannot realistically progress much before the PEEM specifications are stable, because of dependencies on PEEM interfaces and Policy Expression Language.

GPM may add GPM-specific standard PEM-1 templates with new parameters, while relying on the overall PEM-1 interface structure and protocol bindings. The work on PEM-2 may also raise some challenges, since the GPM management operations for Permissions Rule have added requirements. When completed, the Policy Expression Language (in particular, the ruleset-based version currently discussed in Chapter 8 on PEEM) should provide a good framework for expressing the Permissions Rule. However, supporting or facilitating migration of Permissions Rule currently used in existing OMA enablers (e.g. Location, Presence) may prove a non-trivial challenge.

22.4   GPM Salient Points

Where should we start? Since its inception, the GPM Work Item created quite a bit of controversy and vigorous debate. The supporters of the work argued that protecting user's information privacy is a stringent market need, and pointed to the proliferation of "silo" implementations to address the issue as the incentive to start work on this horizontal enabler that could benefit many other enablers. The opponents argued that permissions checking to protect user's privacy are a mere subset of a larger need to create a general authorization enabler. The opponents also went further in arguing that such an authorization enabler should be developed under the auspices of the OMA Security Working Group, in the context of the Security Common Functions (SEC-CF) Work Item (see Chapter 13). While these were interesting arguments, the real issue was that the SEC-CF had no intentions to produce an authorization enabler, as envisioned by the GPM opponents, at least in the initial phase of SEC-CF. From the OSE perspective, it would indeed be useful to have a general authorization enabler that exposes I0 interfaces (e.g. an interface that allows a resource to certify whether the access to and use of a resource is authorized or not, including optional exchange of usability clauses). Indeed, if a more generic authorization enabler would have existed, the GPM permissions checking functionality that covers verification of access to and use of a user's attributes could indeed have been covered as a particular subset of the broader capability of authorizing access to resources and services. Since no such work was in sight from the Security Working Group, the opponents of GPM argued that the GPM Work Item scope should be broadened to cover all generic authorization aspects (i.e. become the OMA generic authorization enabler). While from a technical perspective this was not unreasonable, the market needs to cover the privacy aspects with a sense of urgency requiring more immediate action. Developing a generic authorization enabler in the Security Working Group may indeed take longer, since it is a more complex topic. In retrospect, this is indeed true, since the work on the generic authorization enabler in OMA Security Working Group is yet to get initiated.

So, market forces had the upper hand, and the GPM work finally got started in 2006 with the initial scope of only addressing the management of Permissions Rule, and checking of permissions for access to and use of user's private information. However, the issues related to the controversy did not cease, they rather morphed and continued to accompany GPM development phases. A relatively large number of issues had to be resolved during requirements review, and an equally large number of issues (in some cases still related to scope of work) were still debated and addressed as part of the development phase of the GPM Architecture. GPM Architecture Document (AD) has finally undergone review, after having to resolve quite a number of issues, many still reminiscing of the original scope issue.

There are also a number of technical issues, for which requirements exist, but for which standardization may not be achieved within the confines of GPM work.

For starters, GPM requirements address in quite a bit of detail the need for notifying principals on a variety of events in GPM, while a subset of the requirements also require notification confirmation or consent to be obtained in response to queries. During architecture development, the agreed conclusion was that such functions would have to rely on capabilities out of scope of GPM specifications, but we would not be surprised at all if this subject would require re-visiting during the GPM specifications phase, especially if it ends up affecting GPM interoperability. Furthermore, a number of requirements in GPM Requirements Document [GPM RD] point to the need for GPM to identify and manage associations of data describing Permissions Rule, permissions targets, permissions managers, applications, features of applications, and target attributes. Other requirements focus on the permissions data and Permissions Rule management roles and responsibilities for a given user (e.g. assigning, retrieving, modifying, revoking, delegating management responsibilities on a permissions target basis). However, specifying all of that may amount to specifying a complete service, and some aspects seem to point to the need for developing additional tools/scripts. In addition, GPM architects assessed that all of these ancillary requirements are not quite specific to GPM, since many services could re-use such functions, hence they may be better addressed by a separate enabler. If that would be the case, GPM would re-use such functions when available. However, any aspects of these requirements that may have an impact on GPM interoperability will be analyzed and decided upon in the GPM technical specifications phase.

While handling notifications and obtaining consent may indeed rely on use of interfaces outside the scope of GPM, how events are triggered that would cause such notifications is something that GPM cannot ignore as its own responsibility. Our expectation is that some of these issues may find their resolution in the PEM-2 interface. In some cases, the management operations itself (e.g. create, update, or delete a Permissions Rule) may be a sufficient trigger for notifications, while in other cases more specific processing indications may have to be passed either via the XML documents representing permissions checking rules, or through some yet-to-be-defined different mechanism. Therefore, extensions to PEM-2, or even to the PEEM Policy Expression Language, to support GPM additional requirements, cannot be counted out yet.

In conclusion, many of the technical issues still await resolution in the GPM technical specification phase. Let's conclude this section by reminding you what GPM will not include for sure: it will not include complete ready-to-deploy Permissions Rule. The process of creating the

Permissions Rules will be performed by using the GPM permissions rule expression language, but the actual content of those rules, as well as the publishing of the related input and output parameters, are responsibilities of the service providers, with support from their future GPM capabilities suppliers.

22.5 Impact of Specifications on the Industry

The appearance of OMA GPM in the marketplace may change the way service providers design their services, especially considering how their infrastructure interacts with and uses OMA GPM functions. Service providers are very likely to require in their future Request for Proposals (RFPs) for service enablers or application servers the support for a standardized Permissions Checking interface compliant to OMA GPM specifications. We will also see impact on devices, maybe at a later stage, due to the need to support the Ask Request. Also, some requirements suggest that in some occasions the Permissions Checking interface may be implemented by a device, for example, as in OMA Secure User Plane Location (SUPL).

22.5.1 Impact on Service Providers

OMA GPM may allow service providers that use it to increase the trust their customers have in their services thanks to the greatly improved control they gain over their privacy. This results in increased service adoption, strengthening of service provider's brand values, increased customer loyalty and revenues in general.

The introduction of OMA GPM in the Service Provider Environment may allow it to reduce complexity and overall costs (compared to having individual services that implement their individual, proprietary permissions management systems and which require user interface development to hide the underlying complexity). If a solid, unique framework emerges, supporting the creation of all Permissions Rule in a similar, straightforward fashion, this would be a very positive achievement, with long-lasting impact on lowering current Operational Expenditure (OPEX). In addition, OMA GPM may ease administration tasks and increase the efficiency of customer care responses to questions or complaints about privacy.

Differentiation between service providers and OMA GPM will come mainly from management tools. Indeed, although basic provisioning interfaces will be standardized in GPM, management tools themselves are vendor specific. Service providers will probably choose and tailor their management tools in order to offer better service than their competitors.

22.5.2 Impact on Vendors

From a vendor perspective, GPM should be seen as an opportunity to address a market need clearly expressed by service providers. The adaptation of legacy Service Provider Environment to GPM concepts, however, is not trivial as existing enablers or resources will need to evolve to incorporate the Permissions Checking interface and some additional logic to enforce the results. Vendors will differentiate themselves in their ability to provide management tools according to their customer's needs and through the flexibility provided to facilitate integration of GPM in an existing environment.

22.5.3 Impact on Consumer Market

Consumers will certainly benefit from GPM deployments as they will have greatly improved control over their privacy, probably by means of service provider specific tools that will offer high levels of usability for sometimes conceptually difficult operations by means of default configurations, templates, etc. It is worth noting, however, that even if the technology does not prevent it, it is likely that due to the context of the market, GPM's reach may remain confined to each Service Provider's domain and including their partners (third-party application or content providers), hence limiting somewhat the consumer's freedom to mix and match services from different service providers.

22.5.4 Impact on Corporate Market

During the GPM Requirements' definition phase in OMA, several enterprise use cases were discussed. It is clear that the complexity of GPM's conceptual model for the enterprise is requiring specific deployments. This is particularly true in situations where target principals may have shared attributes used in their private services, as well as in their services used as enterprise employees. Many of the particularities may be resolved by introducing target attributes that would allow for differentiating between the private persona and the enterprise employee persona of the same target principal. In this case, such attributes may be used when writing the Permissions Rule to differentiate between handling one situation versus the other. Another deployment alternative is to build a hierarchy of GPM enablers that can delegate to each others responsibilities, while each focusing on processing permissions rule in their own domain of responsibility (e.g. Service Provider domain vs Corporate domain). Either way, use of GPM seems to be of even higher relevance when it comes to corporate services.

22.5.5 Impact on Other Specifications

Presence and Location will need to contemplate how to use GPM in future versions of their enablers. For each of these enablers it may be more or less difficult to address changes, depending on the direction OMA GPM technical specifications take, but also depending on the timeliness of GPM specifications availability. However, in some other cases where there is no legacy to deal with (new enablers in the requirements definition phase, or enablers that decided to leave permissions management out of their scope but are in need of such a solution), GPM has been mentioned several times as a piece of useful functionality which may be re-used. Concrete examples are OMA Device Profile Evolution and OMA Games Services. It is expected that when GPM is finalized and becomes a concrete enabler, more OMA enablers will take it into account.

22.6   Specifications Evolution and Future Direction

GPM specifications are yet to gel and, therefore, it is much too early to make any predictions. However, it is appropriate to pose some questions to ourselves. Will this work be embraced and used by other enablers? If yes, then one can expect that future phases will have to handle specific requirements from such 'early adopters'. Requests for new input/output parameters to be supported in PEM-1, additional management operations in PEM-2, additional data to be provisioned, either via PEM-2 or some new interface, additional permissions rule language constructs, variable data types, constants, are all a potential target for future GPM requirements.

Will GPM work be expanded in a later phase to become the sought after OMA authorization enabler?

The answer is, probably, no since developing a new enabler in a bottom-up approach may not be optimal.

22.7   Summary

Hopefully, after reading this chapter you are left with a clear idea about OMA GPM: what it does, what for, which benefits, how it works, its main past and future challenges in standardization and in the marketplace, as well as what it does not address (it is not a generic authorization enabler!). Now you should be able to tell right away whether your service provider is 'GPM enabled' or not, and get a sense on the level of protection of your private information that your service provider is managing.

23

The Categorization Based Content Screening Enabler

Having un-tethered access to knowledge and the ability to share it is undoubtedly one of the cornerstones of education, at all stages. The Internet, with the wealth of information it makes readily available is an extraordinary tool handed to our generation, leveraging the technological advances in electronics, telecommunications, and computer science with incredible benefits. More often than not, disruptive technologies, such as the Internet, bring upon progress in quantum leaps. But like with any progress, there is a price to pay. Since freedom of expression is something that is being universally cherished and the Internet is pretty much a self-regulating ecosystem, the proliferation of content that may be controversial, objectionable, and even harmful to society cannot be easily denied. As a consequence, digital content promoting pornography, violence, drug addictions, hate messages, or abuse is not only tolerated (be it consciously or connivingly) on the Internet, but is taking aggressive advantage of the free delivery system that the Internet provides. Objectionable content is not only made available to everybody, including children and unsuspecting adults, but in many cases such undesired explicit content finds its way through messages, pictures, and sound into our homes, schools, and offices, without being directly or even indirectly invited.

In essence, the problem is more generic in nature: while it is relatively easy to assess what type of content is undesirable to reach a specific audience (such as young Internet users), any content can be objectionable to one or another, and sometimes it depends on the location one finds oneself at, the time of day or the function that one finds oneself involved in at that time. For example, employers would like to limit employees' access to content that bears no relationship to their work activities, during working hours. An adult who is shopping online for electronic accessories, may not want to find, or even worse, be forced to (at least temporarily) deal with pushed content related to home mortgage refinancing, although that is something he may consider of interest at other times. Where there's a problem, there is also an opportunity, and so it is not surprising that a number of web content filtering solutions have been developed, many of them being commercially available. One of the issues with such solutions is that most of them handle only English-language text, while the Internet has no boundaries along language-drawn lines. Another issue is how to handle images. Should an entire website be filtered and maybe blocked in some cases, based on some identifiable piece of text, or is there a need for employing image pattern recognition software and scan each of the images presented? And would the pattern recognition algorithms be good enough to distinguish between a nude depicted in a work of art (not objectionable to most) and a pornographic image (frowned upon or objectionable to many)? Assuming perfect algorithms and software implementing

The Open Mobile Alliance   M. Brenner and M. Unmehopa
© 2008 Alcatel-Lucent. All Rights Reserved

these are provided, is such solution scalable (can we realistically think that every piece of content, every text, video image, or audio soundtrack available on the Internet will be scanned, bit-by-bit to determine what it represents)? Are legal concerns to be taken into consideration (censorship versus privacy)?

In looking for answers, one needs to start with some undeniable facts on the ground, one of them being the international nature of the Internet, which implies that any solutions need to rise to that challenge, and will likely have to be a combined result of mechanisms provided by various governments and private sector initiatives. Another fact is the need to distinguish between illegal content and inappropriate, controversial, or otherwise objectionable content. Illegal content and/or its use is specifically identified by (objective) existing laws (albeit the specifics may be somewhat different from country to country), and it is applicable usually to both the physical world and cyberspace. Typical examples of illegal content include child pornography, solicitation of children for sexual acts, sexual harassment, violent threats, and hate propaganda. Other content may be deemed inappropriate or objectionable on social, religious, cultural, ethnic, or other grounds to some individuals or some communities, but it may not be illegal (although it may be harmful if accessible to or delivered to those individuals or communities) This may include, but is not limited to adult pornography, content rich in use of violence, drugs, alcohol. Hence, depending on specific country legislature, proliferation of illegal content on the Internet is punishable by law, while proliferation of other legal content, though objectionable, is not, and therefore needs to be prevented to become harmful by other means.

While it is reassuring that at least there is a legal remedy for promoting illegal content even on the Internet, applying a country's laws in the cyberspace is easier said than done. From a technical perspective, content screening techniques can be applied to any content before delivering it to its intended destination; that can be done either when a user tries to pull content, or when a user is being pushed content. The content screening task consists of determining whether content should be made accessible and/or should be delivered to its intended audience, and it takes into account a combination of government regulations that address privacy concerns, local policies (e.g. school policies, corporate policies, parental policies), and/or individual user preferences. While not a trivial process, content screening is a manageable task, if the content to be screened has been pre-categorized. That brings us to the notion of content categorization, or content rating – the process through which a well-defined category can be associated to a given content. The notion of content categorization implies that there are agreed categories, as well as objective criteria to categorize content in one of the agreed categories. It also assumes that there are effective mechanisms by which those criteria can be applied against any given content. If that can be achieved, then any content, or at least any content suspect of being objectionable, can be pre-categorized before screening (to speed up the actual screening process) or categorization can be performed during the actual screening process. Content categorization allows the screening process to simply focus on how to handle content, based on its identified category and policies affecting its delivery. Objectionable content, whether illegal or not, can be stopped from being harmful if a category can be assigned to it prior to delivery. In addition to that, detecting illegal content delivery or even mere availability may result in legal procedures and consequences. There is no doubt that content categorization is the more difficult aspect of the overall problem, especially given the sheer amount of content available on the Internet. While matching content in any kind of media to a category is a challenging technical prospect, requiring sophisticated pattern searching and matching algorithms, the larger issues to confront are related to how to establish objective criteria, who is responsible for establishing them, and last but not least, how to deal with the sheer volume of content available, and who has the responsibility to perform content categorization.

Voluntary rating is seen as a possible response to the responsibility and scale issues, and it is consistent with the self-regulating nature of the Internet. Rating results in associating a pre-defined 'label' (category) to content, which allows the screening process to check the 'label' (almost like the cigarettes pack labels informing consumers that use of the product is endangering their health). A new organization called the Internet Content Rating Association (ICRA) has picked up the work of its predecessor, known as the Recreational Software Advisory Council (RSAC) and is developing several projects and guidelines supporting an international system based on voluntary rating of Internet content by website and other content providers (more on ICRA's initiatives in a later section in this chapter). Some say that voluntary mechanisms are more likely to gain support when pitched against the specter of government regulations and censorship, but in practical terms voluntary schemes are yet no match against the resources of actors in the industry intent on delivering their content, objectionable or not. It is like comparing not-for-profit organizations with for-profit organizations (the latter will always be better equipped financially, with all the secondary implications). As a result, a voluntary rating system is still slow to gain universal acceptance and it may take a long time until it is accepted as the norm on the Internet. Then there is of course the issue of criteria (what is offensive where), since this may differ from culture to culture, or depend on circumstance. Now that may not be a problem during screening, since a service provider could apply local policies to the content being screened, but it is a problem for rating, and it compounds the scalability issue, since multiple rating labels may have to be associated to each piece of content. And then there's still the issue of who is authorized to perform the rating, and how?

Looking at rating labels (or what is behind the label) as content metadata, there are currently three approaches to deal with the issue of creating it: professional creation, author creation, and user-creation. Professional creation of content metadata is in the form of catalog records and is usually performed by trained dedicated professionals such as librarians, using well-documented criteria; such metadata is considered of high quality, but it is costly to produce. Author creation of content metadata was facilitated by the Standard Generalized Markup Language (SGML), but it is shadowed by inaccuracies and abuses. User-created content metadata consists of metadata created by content users, maybe initially for their own consumption, but later shared with a community of interest, and is seen increasingly as a grass-roots categorization initiative. The latter is certainly not as rigorous as the classification provided by trained professionals, but it is free of cost. It does not provide a taxonomy, but instead it provides what some may call a 'folksonomy', in which there are no necessarily clear relationships between the terms used.

The inevitable conclusion is that content categorization and screening is a difficult problem to solve, and it will continue to be an unstable issue for a period to come. At the same time, one must recognize the fact that the Internet itself has not been around for that long, and that the technology of the web is constantly evolving, to the point that objectionable content will no longer be harmful. In that sense, initiatives such as those conducted by ICRA, emergence of labeling systems, access control technologies and standards that are just starting to emerge are all encouraging signs that the problem has now gotten the attention of society and industry. The Open Mobile Alliance (OMA) is currently engaged in specifying an enabler having in its scope both aspects of the problem examined in this introduction: content categorization and content screening. Other standards bodies have focused on support of rating systems by focusing, for example, on metadata that can describe the nature of the content. The OMA Categorization Based Content Screening (CBCS) enabler is instead focusing on defining mechanisms of communicating relevant information in this multi-step process. For example, for the content categorization issue, CBCS defines how to communicate that a category is to be associated to a given content and how to retrieve a category that was previously associated with a given content, while keeping out of scope the pattern searching and matching algorithms, or the criteria by which a category is associated to content. For the content screening issue, CBCS is focusing on mechanisms to request and obtain a decision on whether content may be delivered, as well as on mechanisms to encode how decisions are to be made – again without providing cookie-cutter recipes as part of the specification. The next sections will explore in more detail the CBCS requirements, architecture and technical specifications, and their impact on the industry.

23.1   Are Those Specifications Really Needed?

The CBCS work in OMA started because service providers realized that undesirable content reaches their end-users, in some cases without the knowledge and/or consent of the subscriber (end-user is not necessarily the same as the subscriber, who is responsible for the account and the relationship with the service provider). Such undesirable content may include illegal content, unsolicited content, malicious content, and inappropriate content. Despite the fact that efforts are taking place to stem this trend, partly through regulations and partly through industry voluntary initiatives, there will unfortunately, always be rogue parties, or parties not aware of or not concerned with such norms, that will disregard them. As was already mentioned earlier (see Chapter 5) the end-users ultimately hold the Operator (in particular a Mobile Operator) responsible for all the services they receive through the communication channels they have subscribed to even when such services have not been subscribed for. As such, the Operators have to take measures to filter, limit and in some cases block the delivery of undesirable content to their subscribers, through mechanisms that are within their own control. Currently there are no industry specifications to deal with content screening, nor do specifications exist to support a programmatic way to set and/or retrieve a category (rating) associated to a particular content. The CBCS work is intended to address these gaps, and is focused on the following:

- the process of screening (filtering or blocking) content targeted to an end-user, when such content is deemed for example, illegal, unsolicited, malicious and/or inappropriate;
- providing advanced customer warnings associated with content that may be delivered;
- screening scenarios, which include but are not limited to: content provider-to-user and user-to-other principals (e.g. other users, or other resources, or service providers); and
- the process of content categorization (content submitted to screening may or may not be pre-categorized).

While the need for service providers to have such mechanisms is probably obvious by now, it may not be as clear why a proprietary implementation may not be sufficient. In order to under-stand the need for specifications, and vendor compliance to them, it may be useful to explore the different actors involved in the handling of content. Figure 23.1 illustrates a simplified actor chain, viewed from the perspective of the service provider that offers a CBCS service to its subscribers. Figure 23.1 is the CBCS representation of actors and their interactions. The main concepts behind the CBCS requirements [CBCS RD], and implicitly the need for standardization, are summarized in the description of interactions.

The main actors are the CBCS service provider (represented by the CBCS solution and the different Rules Managers), the Content Source, the Content Categorization Provider, the Regulatory Body, other Resources, and of course the Subscriber to the CBCS service. For simplification, the figure shows a single Mobile Operator's domain, but roaming scenarios can also be supported.

- Subscriber – The Subscriber has a relationship with the CBCS service provider. The Subscriber has an account with this provider, who could also be at the same time its Mobile Operator, and/or provides the Subscriber with other services. The subscription to the CBCS service provider service allows the Subscriber to describe the type of content that is undesirable to be delivered to any end-user covered by the subscription, and in what circumstances. Such information is usually stored in a user profile at the service provider (in this case it could be a special CBCS user profile).
- CBCS Service Provider – The CBCS solution consists of programming logic to handle Content Categorization and Content Screening, and data stored in different repositories. The solution employs Content Categorization Rules and Content Screening Rules, which are administered by the CBCS service provider. The Content Screening Rules are logical expressions that

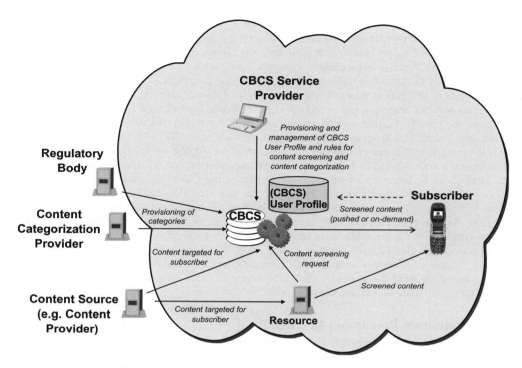

Figure 23.1 Categorization-based content screening actor chain

allow evaluation of different conditions, including information pre-provisioned on behalf of the Subscriber in the CBCS user profile.

- Content Categorization Provider – Is an authoritative source of content categories (for the purpose of CBCS understanding, 'categories' has the same meaning as 'ratings'). This actor associates categories to content, and the CBCS service provider may use such services to cache such associations in its own repository.
- Regulatory Body – Is an actor that may determine association of categories to illegal content, and therefore the CBCS service provider would provide means to provision such associations for the CBCS repositories.
- Content Source – Is any source of content (where content has a more generic connotation, for example, could be text, image, audio, video, and any kind of messages exchanged between resources).
- Resource – Can be any system, application, or enabler in the Service Provider domain or from a different domain.

Content from a Content Source is being pushed to, or is requested by the Subscriber. Content could also be pushed to or requested by a Resource on the Subscriber's behalf, as part of interactions of the Subscriber with some other service. Content targeted to the Subscriber may be intercepted and directed to the CBCS solution, where it undergoes Content Screening. In this process, Content Screening Rules are being applied, and evaluate the pre-provisioned Subscriber information and the content category, and a decision is reached on whether the content is appropriate or not as a whole, or partially. Based on the decision, the screened content is blocked or forwarded to the Subscriber. Similarly, content may arrive to a Resource, which will request the CBCS solution to evaluate whether the content is appropriate for the particular Subscriber (the Content Screening process is similar to the previous interaction described). The decision of the screening process goes back to the Resource, which then decides whether to deliver the content to the Subscriber.

The question still is, are standards needed, and why? Some of the answers require getting more familiar with the detailed requirements. However, one obvious need for standardization lies in the fact that any resource may issue a request for Content Screening. Since resources may come from a range of different vendors in any given Service Provider domain, there is a need to have a standard way for any of them to request content screening, and receive a response with the results of the process. Furthermore, we mentioned rules that need repositories where they may be stored, and interactions between third parties and repositories of CBCS Solutions. Rules are truly logical expressions that are completely independent of underlying resources. The content of the rules should not be affected by how the repositories are implemented, by how the rules themselves are handled, or by what vendor provides which part of the CBCS solution. It means that there needs to be a known, specified way to express the rules (a rules expression language), which needs to be vendor independent, which in turn implies the need for a standard rules expression language. Since service providers may use different vendors for the tools to manage the rules, and for the repositories for the rules, there also needs to be a standard way to manage rules, which would provide the glue between the two. Finally, the CBCS service provider's solution may need to have electronic exchanges with multiple Content Categorization Providers and/or Regulatory Bodies, hence the need for a standard interface to support such exchanges. But surely, standard specifications to handle those issues already exist, or don't they?

23.2   Standards Precursors to CBCS

Prior art in Content Categorization is best represented by the Resource Description Framework (RDF) [W3C RDF], a family of specifications created in the World Wide Web Consortium (W3C) with the goal to model metadata. Content labeling systems, in particular ICRA, use RDF to encode content labels.

Conceived between 1960 and 1970, the SGML [W3C SGML OVW] was a predecessor to the better known XML [XML1.0], initially published as a W3C recommendation in 1998. Both SGML and XML are 'meta' languages and therefore useful in tooling for content metadata description (SGML is more customizable, obviously at a cost).

CBCS is the first work item in the OMA dealing with content screening, but not the first initiative that advocates using rules evaluation, enforcement, and management as part of the process. Screening Rules and Categorization Rules are in fact policy rules specialized in a well-defined domain, but they are based on the work conducted under the OMA Policy Evaluation Enforcement and Management (PEEM), described earlier in Chapter 8. All of the PEEM specifications are re-used by CBCS, including the Policy Expression Language (PEL) (see [PEL TS]), the policy invocation interface (see [PEM-1 TS]), and the policy management interface (see [PEM-2 TS]). As detailed in Chapter 8, there is a rich history of specifications that preceded PEEM, and since PEEM work builds on it, so does CBCS.

23.3   CBCS Architecture and Technical Specifications

CBCS plays the unique role of protecting principals from receiving undesirable content. In the absence of a deployed CBCS enabler, illegal, malicious, or inappropriate content may be delivered to any end-user or resource. The CBCS architecture is defining the components and the interfaces needed to provide a CBCS solution that meets the CBCS requirements at the logical level. The CBCS technical specifications detail the protocols for the interfaces, the format and flows of the messages and the parameters that are exchanged using CBCS interfaces, and may further detail the behavior of the components. As discussed in the introduction, content may be screened by CBCS when content carrying requests are intercepted, or when content screening is explicitly requested. That implies certain interactions between entities in the OMA Service Environment (OSE), a topic for the next section.

23.3.1 CBCS Enabler in the OSE

CBCS is an OMA enabler hence it maps into the enabler layer in the OSE blueprint as illustrated in Figure 23.2. Any message (carrying explicit content, or just being considered content in itself) first traverses the logical Policy Enforcer (PE) layer. If a policy exists at that level, it may also contain delegation to CBCS, in which case it would use the I0 interface exposed by CBCS. When doing so, the PE acts like other resources that invoke CBCS. For simplification, requests between a resource invoking content screening and CBCS have been shown in addition to the layered approach (e.g. Enabler B may invoke CBCS directly for Content Screening). As any request, such a request may also be submitted to PE scrutiny. In addition, CBCS can also act like a proxy by intercepting messages and processing content carried by those messages. In that sense it acts like a specialized PE. CBCS may use I2 interfaces (not specified in OMA) to obtain information helpful in evaluating the screening rules, in the processing of content submitted to it. An example of such an interface is one through which CBCS may obtain information from a CBCS user profile. While this could at some point be an OMA-specified interface, it is not at this time, and therefore not addressed in the CBCS work. The following section will describe the architectural components and interfaces offered by CBCS.

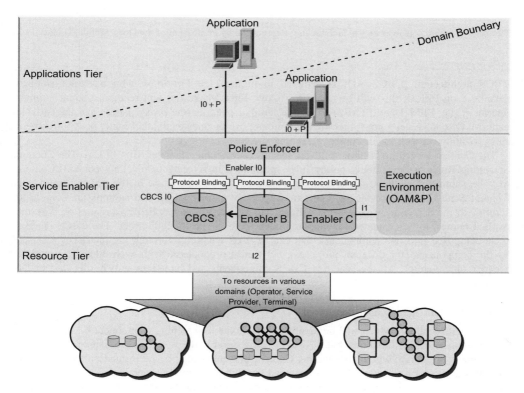

Figure 23.2   CBCS enabler in the OSE

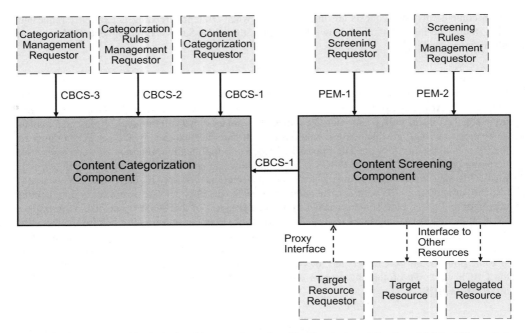

Figure 23.3 CBCS enabler logical architecture. Reproduced by Permission of the Open Mobile Alliance Ltd.

23.3.2 CBCS Logical Architecture

CBCS architecture [CBCS AD] is depicted in Figure 23.3. For those who have not skipped Chapter 8 on PEEM, this will be easier to follow. First, the reader will recognize some familiar interfaces (i.e. PEM-1 and PEM-2) and some familiar patterns (the proxy pattern and the callable pattern). Of course, let's not forget the predominant use of rules evaluation logic, both for content categorization, as well as for content screening.

The Content Screening portion of the architecture is evidently modeled after PEEM. The Content Screening Rules are essentially policy rules specialized in filtering or blocking content. Content may be submitted to the Content Screening process via two patterns. In the proxy pattern, the Content Screening component intercepts messages that carry content, and submits the content to scrutiny of the Screening Rules. In the callable pattern, content is supplied by a requestor, with the explicit request to be evaluated for inappropriateness for a specific subscriber. The CBCS enabler is de-composed into two components, that can be used separately through the interfaces exposed by the components (for different purposes), but can also cooperate with each other to provide a broader functionality. All the specified CBCS components and interfaces will be detailed in the following sections.

23.3.2.1 Content Screening Component

With some exceptions, which will be identified, the Content Screening Component performs functions similar to PEEM functions, but instead of being generic, the functions are tuned and/or added for Content Screening, where appropriate. Content Screening may be performed either as a result of a message carrying content being intercepted through the Proxy interface (proxy usage pattern, see Chapter 8), or as a result of an explicit request through the PEM-1 interface (callable usage pattern, see Chapter 8). The Content Screening consists of Screening Rules processing, which is characterized by the following functions:

- Identification of the Screening Rules associated with the incoming request for screening (regardless of whether through the proxy interface or an explicit request).
- Identification of the submitted Content and any other parameters that may relate additional information in the screening process (e.g. identification of the sending resource, identification of the Content Category).
- Obtaining a Content Category, if one (or more) did not accompany the submitted content, or if the source that performed the categorization cannot be trusted or verified. In this case, the Content Screening Component will attempt to obtain the Content Category through other means. One such means is to use the other component of the enabler, through the CBCS-1 interface it exposes (see next sections for details).
- Processing of the Screening Rules. These are logical expressions that evaluate the Content Category, the Content itself (if the category cannot be obtained or cannot be trusted), the source of the content, the source of the request, and any other actual values of parameters passed via the request, or obtained using those parameters, against settings representing the Subscriber's private information and indications for content treatment. Subscriber's data may consist of subscriber and/or dependent end-users' identification, date of birth, location, indication of type of content appropriate for delivery, willingness to accept content and/or need to ask for consent in real time, etc. This data may reside in the CBCS user profile or in other repositories to which CBCS has access. During processing of the Screening Rules, CBCS may need to delegate functionality to other resources, which may not be specified by CBCS or in OMA. Examples of such functions are pattern matching functions, needed in screening the content, if a trustworthy category cannot be obtained otherwise. Other examples are functions that need to be invoked in order to access the CBCS user profile. Simply put, since the Screening Rules themselves are not specified in CBCS, interfaces needed to resolve those rules may not be anticipated and specified in advance, or restricted to a handful of cases that could be anticipated. Leaving those functions out of scope for CBCS also supports CBCS service differentiation.
- Decision making, dependent on the result of the Screening Rules evaluation. The decision could be that the content is appropriate for delivery, inappropriate, or only partially appropriate. In either case, what the Content Screening Component does, depends on the CBCS usage pattern:
  - In the proxy usage pattern, the Content Screening Component will implement a decision of forwarding the content (partial or complete) to the Subscriber, or alternatively, a decision to block the content, and instead return an error to the CBCS Target Resource Requestor.
  - In the callable usage pattern, the Content Screening Component will return the decision to the Content Screening Requestor, which is supposed to process the decision.

The Content Screening Component also provides the management functions of creating, deleting, modifying, and viewing of Screening Rules, which can be invoked through the PEM-2 interface.

Roaming scenarios can also be supported, but the manner in which they are supported depends on the business agreements between the different service providers, the deployed CBCS enablers in each domain, and the extent of co-operation between them. If only one of the service providers involved has deployed a CBCS solution, then the service provider may authorize other service providers to enter their own Screening Rules, in addition to their own. Screening Rules are modeled using a PEL that supports delegation (see Chapter 8 for details). If both service providers have deployed CBCS enablers, then, in addition there is also the possibility for keeping the Screening Rules for the two domains separate, but writing the Screening Rules in such a way that delegation to the other CBCS enabler is an option. In this case, given that each Content Screening Component acts similar to a policy engine specialized in Content Screening, one of them can invoke the other using the PEM-1 interface exposed by the other.

23.3.2.2 Content Categorization Component

The Content Categorization Component includes the following functions:

- Mapping of content (or reference to content) to a set of categories (zero or more). The Content Categorization Component may use Content Categorization Rules for this purpose, and as part of the processing may involve other non-specified functions (e.g. pattern recognition). In the simplest case, the Content Categorization component may find that the Content submitted for categorization was already categorized (e.g. an association between the content and some categories has already been provisioned in a repository that the component can access via a non-specified interface). This function can be invoked through the CBCS-1 interface.
- Providing the management functions of creating, deleting, modifying and viewing of Content Categorization Rules. These functions can be invoked through the CBCS-2 interface.
- Providing the management functions of creating, deleting, modifying and viewing associations between Content References (e.g. Uniform Resource Identifiers (URIs)) and Content Categories. These functions can be invoked through the CBCS-3 interface.

As with any enabler, the interfaces exposed by CBCS components can be used by any other resource. In the case of CBCS-1, a generic resource that may use the interface is designated as Content Categorization Requestor. But as we have seen in the description of the Content Screening Component, it itself may need to invoke CBCS-1 in an attempt to obtain the categories associated with the content being screened. That explains why the CBCS-1 interface is shown twice in the figure, although it is one and the same interface, used by two different requestors. As two CBCS-1 arrows are represented in Figure 23.3, this component can be used either by the Content Screening Component or another requestor. Like the Screening Rules, the Categorization Rules are also expressed as PEEM Rules (see Chapter 8 for details).

23.3.2.3 PEM-1 Interface

PEM-1 interface is used to request Content Screening. While the structure, message flow and protocols are the same as those defined for this interface in PEEM (see Chapter 8), it is possible that additional parameters, specific for Content Screening may need to be supported over the interface. For that reason, and since the interface details will be captured in the technical specifications work, the PEM-1 interface used in CBCS is said to be 'derived from' PEEM's PEM-1 interface, while keeping the name by convention, since the nature of the interface does not change. The reason for re-use is obvious: since the CBCS Screening Rules are nothing more than specific PEEM policy rules, then invoking their evaluation and enforcement can be done using the same interface.

The request sent over this interface includes the content itself, or a reference to the content. It may include the following non-exhaustive list of additional parameters (to be defined during the specification phase):

- Identification of the Content target
- Identification of the Content source
- Content or a Content reference (e.g. URI)
- Content metadata (if not included with the Content).

The response sent over this interface may include the following non-exhaustive list of parameters:

- the decision resulting from the processing of the Screening Rules; and

- additional information related to the decision (e.g. type of content identified, or justification of a decision to not allow access to Content).

23.3.2.4 PEM-2 Interface

PEM-2 interface is used to request management of Screening Rules (i.e. create, delete, modify, and view Screening Rules). While the structure, message flow and protocols are the same as those defined for this interface in PEEM (see Chapter 8), it is possible that additional management operations, or additional parameters in existing management operations, may need to be supported over the interface. For that reason, and since the interface details will be captured in the technical specifications work, the PEM-2 interface used in CBCS is said to be 'derived from' PEEM's PEM-2 interface, while keeping the name.

23.3.2.5 CBCS-1 Interface

CBCS-1 interface is used to obtain the Content Categories associated with a given Content. A non-exhaustive list of input parameters in the request may include:

- the Content itself or a reference to the Content (e.g. URI)
- Content metadata and categorization information
- Content Source.

A non-exhaustive list of output parameters in the response may include:

- a set of Content Categories (i.e. zero or more); and
- metadata associated with the Content Categories (e.g. for a music category: genre of music, artist).

23.3.2.6 CBCS-2 Interface

CBCS-2 interface is used to create, delete, modify, and view Content Categorization Rules. While the structure, message flow and protocols are the same as those defined for PEM-2 (see Chapter 8), this interface was renamed because the component that exposes it in this case (the Content Categorization Component) is not modeled after PEEM. It just happens to include an identical function (the rules management function), and hence the management operations supported by those functions will probably be supported using the same protocols.

This is an interesting approach, since it underlines the point that PEEM could have been further de-composed to present a separate 'Policy Management Component' (see discussion on deployment models in Chapter 8, for details), which could have then also caused a different de-composition of the CBCS enabler (e.g. to have a separate CBCS Rules Management component). However, re-use in OMA is a key principle, hence CBCS re-uses PEEM as specified in its current release.

23.3.2.7 CBCS-3 Interface

CBCS-3 interface is used to manage (create, delete, modify, and view) associations between Content References (e.g. URIs) with a set of categories (i.e. zero or more). CBCS-3 may be used by authorized principals (e.g. authorized third parties) to provision such associations, or to retrieve such associations for review.

23.3.2.8 Non-specified Interfaces

As any typical enabler, CBCS may use other interfaces in its content screening and/or categorization processing, but the interfaces described so far are the only ones specified in CBCS. In order to fulfill its requirements of being able to be deployed in a proxy usage pattern, a CBCS realization may have to implement proxy interfaces for specific types of requests to be intercepted. To capture this concept, the Proxy interface is shown in the architecture diagram. Similarly, when deployed in this pattern, CBCS needs to be able to forward appropriate content to the target resource, and the Interface to Other Resources is shown to capture this capability. Both Proxy interface and interface to Other Resources are however not specified in CBCS.

Finally, during the Screening Rules processing, the expression of the rules may indicate the need to delegate some functions to other resources. An example of interaction between Screening Rules and other resources is the sending of a notification or issuing of a query for consent to the Subscriber, before delivering content. Such functions may be performed using existing mechanisms (e.g. Short Messaging Service (SMS), Multimedia Messaging Service (MMS), WAP Push and Session Initiation Protocol (SIP) Push) but the protocols for these deliveries are not specified in CBCS. The same is true for functions that would allow resources acting on behalf of the Subscriber, to subscribe for such notifications (e.g. SIP SUBSCRIBE).

In short, one cannot anticipate the functions that will be invoked by the Screening Rules, since specific Screening Rules instances are not part of the CBCS specification. As a result, none of the interface to Other Resources cannot be specified in CBCS.

23.3.3 Logical Flows for CBCS

In general, the CBCS flows over the PEM-1 and PEM-2 interfaces involving the Content Screening Component are very similar with the PEEM flows over those interfaces (see Chapter 8). It is therefore more interesting to explore here some expanded flows that illustrate the use of CBCS-1 interface, in the context of processing of Screening Rules. Figure 23.4 represents the flows when CBCS is deployed in a proxy usage pattern.

In Figure 23.4, the components represented with dotted-line borders, and interfaces exposed by them are not specified in CBCS. In particular, the CBCS Proxy function is neither specified in the

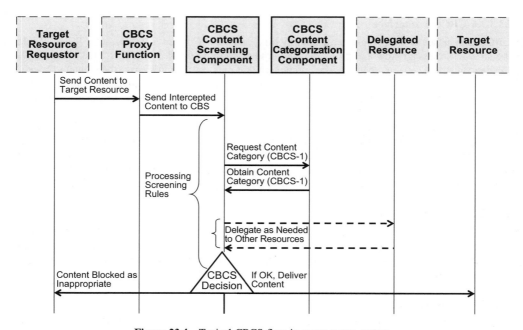

Figure 23.4   Typical CBCS flow in proxy usage pattern

CBCS architecture, nor will the CBCS Technical Specification address it. However, since the CBCS enabler has to support a proxy usage pattern, such a function is normative in a deployment where messages carrying content need to be intercepted. In the proxy usage pattern, content sent to a target resource is intercepted by a CBCS proxy capability, and re-directed to the CBCS Content Screening Component. The target resource is assumed to be a resource that the Subscriber interacts with for content presentation. There, the message is inspected for content, and other context information to help in the identification and processing of the applicable Screening Rules. During the Screening Rules evaluation, if content categories were not identifiable in the message (or the source cannot be trusted), the Content Screening Component will use interface CBCS-1 to obtain categories. The CBCS Content Categorization Component is the one that specializes in obtaining categories, and exposes the CBCS-1 interface for such requests. During the Screening Rules processing, other functions (not specified) involving Delegated Resources, may be invoked as needed to help the Screening Rules processing completion. At the end of the Screening Rules processing, a decision is made whether content can be delivered (possibly filtered) or needs to be completely blocked.

In the callable usage pattern (see Figure 23.5), the content is sent to some target resource, without being intercepted by the CBCS enabler (although of course the logical PE component in the OSE might intercept it to apply service provider policies). The target resource is assumed to be a resource that the Subscriber interacts with for content presentation. However, as opposed to the proxy usage pattern, in this case the resource may be configured to request the CBCS enabler to screen content that the resource submits. At the end of the processing of the Screening Rules a conclusion about the content indicating what decision the target resource should take, is returned to the target resource. Armed with knowledge about the appropriateness of the content with respect to the targeted Subscriber, the target resource will act accordingly, either delivering or blocking the content.

The Screening Rules management and the Categorization Rules management typical flows are practically identical with the PEEM flows for policy management (see Chapter 8). We also chose not to represent the use of the CBCS-3 interface in a figure. Although the use of the interface is

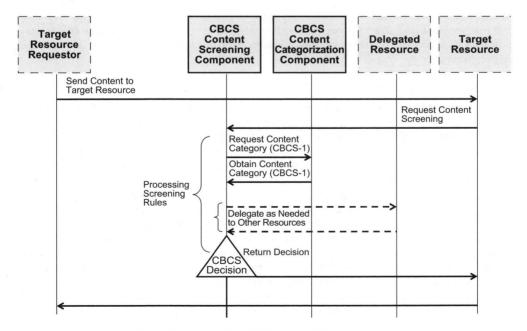

Figure 23.5 Typical CBCS flow in callable usage pattern

important, such a flow is not very interesting, consisting of a simple request/response pair, where the request is to create, modify, delete, or view the association between a Content Reference (e.g. URI) and a set of categories, and the response is in most cases an acknowledgement, an error, or retrieved information (depending the nature of the requested operation).

23.3.4 CBCS Technical Specifications

At the time of writing this book, the CBCS technical specifications were not complete. It is clear though what will be specified, and that includes all the interfaces described in the previous section. CBCS will produce a specification for PEM-1 (a re-use of PEEM PEM-1 specification, probably with added PEM-1 Standard Templates and I/O Parameters) to reflect the specific parameters that characterize content. CBCS will produce a specification for PEM-2, and chances are it may be identical with the PEEM PEM-2 specification, so that the same specification could be re-used to satisfy the CBCS-2 interface. The novel interfaces specified in CBCS are CBCS-1 and CBCS-3.

Apart from interfaces, it is expected that CBCS will also re-use PEEM PEL. It is too early to tell whether a workflow-based PEL option or a ruleset-based PEL option may be more appropriate, but chances are that each may be applicable. For example, Screening Rules that would involve a lot of interactions with other resources (e.g. pattern searching on submitted content, because the categories have not been made available) may benefit from the use of the workflow-based option. When it comes to simple evaluation of pre-configured conditions against submitted actual parameter values, the ruleset-based option may prove to be a more efficient approach.

23.4   Impact of Specifications on the Industry

Introduction of CBCS solutions in the marketplace may mark the beginning of a shift in strategy and tactics to handle the growing threat of proliferation of inappropriate content via the Internet. While any measure of stemming such proliferation will be welcomed by the marketplace, there will certainly be exceptions (see specific market sections). The more interesting question is, to what extent standards-based, controllable, manageable, and responsible services dealing with content categorization and screening can handle the unparalleled creativity of those that intentionally distribute such content. In OMA, enthusiastic support of this work has raised the stakes in this ongoing struggle.

23.4.1 Impact on Service Providers

With the availability of CBCS-compliant implementations, service providers will practically have at their fingertips a toolkit dealing with Content Categorization and Screening, which will support a broad variety of deployment choices. The Content Screening Component and the Content Categorization Component can be deployed independently, or in co-operation. Each of them expose several interfaces, allowing for several ways to manage data required by the rules logic, and allowing to build a CBCS solution as simple or as complex as one may need to put in place. The Content Screening Component can be deployed in different usage patterns not only to accommodate the service provider's architectural philosophy, but also to provide the flexibility in supporting a variety of resources available in the market. Powerful PELs are made available to express rules as simple, or as sophisticated as needed, and support complex scenarios involving functions in other resources, as well as roaming across Service Provider domains. The task on the hands of the service providers is to have an analysis of their own services and resources, in order to determine the best configuration, and most appropriate deployment pattern for a CBCS-based service. That would lead to an optimized complex solution, while reducing the need for one-off, proprietary solutions put in place in the absence of specifications. With a solid CBCS solution deployed, service providers will enjoy differentiation, increased customer satisfaction and loyalty, and may derive additional revenue from the CBCS service itself.

23.4.2 Impact on Vendors

There is probably nothing a vendor would like to hear more often, then a market need for a new solution, that can be provided with significant re-use of existing capabilities. CBCS-compliant products will emerge as soon as a realistic opportunity is presented by the service providers. Most challenges will lie in the integration of a new range of products in the Service Provider's Environment. A gradual deployment is likely, where well-behaved resources built to use the CBCS exposed interfaces will benefit first. There is a great opportunity for smart proxies, and an equally great opportunity for extending the PEL with constructs that facilitate integration with a large variety of (delegated) resources. There is also a significant opportunity for tools that are efficient in pattern searching, as well as in any other algorithms that can help in determining content categories on the fly.

23.4.3 Impact on Consumer Market

A large percentage of the consumers will react very positively (concerned parents and educators, any subscribers with particular privacy concerns, governmental agencies etc.) to the introduction of CBCS, assuming results are palpable. Other segments however may not like, agree, or co-operate with CBCS-based solutions. A particular end-user that may deliberately want to get access to content deemed inappropriate by others (the reason behind the desire is irrelevant from the CBCS perspective) will be at least disappointed, and maybe frustrated. Those that are in this category and happen to be authorized to set their preferences, will likely set their CBCS user profile preferences in such a way that would defeat the CBCS purpose (except for the cases where Screening Rules may be in place by regulators, and may take precedence over those set by minors, for example). On the other hand, these types of users are not the users we are concerned with anyway. They do not want or need protection from inappropriate content now, so they will find ways to avoid it. It is by far more important to focus on the market segment that has previously not been exposed to inappropriate content, and ensure it is protected from such exposure. Protecting the innocent, in addition to protecting the unwilling from exposure to inappropriate content is what we can hope CBCS can realistically achieve.

23.4.4 Impact on Corporate Market

CBCS is very relevant for the corporate market, where it is quite probable to find wide support, from all actors involved. The problem with inappropriate content getting to the enterprise Intranet has multiple dimensions, regardless of whether such content arrived unsolicited or as a result of some unruly employee query. First of all, most enterprises have clear rules, restricting employees from accessing such content during work hours, while using company's resources. The employees see the enterprise as mainly responsible for the services (or lack thereof) they receive while at work (see Chapter 6), and companies face the risk of being sued by their employees, when the companies fail to do their best to protect them from inappropriate content. Proliferation of inappropriate content in the enterprise also contributes to reduced productivity, and wasted resources in handling removal of such content from the company's Intranet, after delivery. Finally, most employees themselves are concerned with receiving unsolicited inappropriate content, since it is difficult to prove how it arrived, at a time where companies are introducing fines, and sometimes drastic measures (e.g. firing) to stem access of their employees to such content.

23.4.5 Impact on Other Specifications

CBCS may have some impact on PEEM specifications. Since work on CBCS technical specifications has started before the completion of the PEEM specifications to be re-used (PEM-1, PEM-2 and PEL, see Chapter 8), there is a slight possibility that CBCS may require some last minute changes to PEEM. More realistically though is the scenario where CBCS may define new PEM-1 Standard

Templates and new PEM-1 I/O Parameters, that would not necessarily require a new PEEM release (it depends whether those extensions may be considered generic and applicable to other enablers, or just specific to CBCS). There is also a possibility that extensions to the PEL ruleset-based option may be crafted to support CBCS needs. Finally, additional optional rules management operations may prove necessary. All these cases are hypothetical, but there is a realistic possibility that PEEM will have to absorb some Change Requests (CRs), if not undergo work for a new release altogether. Other specifications are unlikely to be affected by a CBCS release.

23.5   Specifications Evolution and Future Direction

It is hard to predict what a future phase of CBCS may include, but one possible impact on such plans may come from additional work on user profile. Discussions have taken place concerning the fact that user information regarding preferences, subscription information, user personal data, and characteristics is spread in different repositories, and each enabler comes up with local optimizations and solutions to model, provision, or access such information. Screening Rules need access to data in what we called the CBCS user profile, a loosely defined collection of information in an undefined repository, accessible through undefined functions. Aside from the common work on such user profile that all enablers can take advantage of, information modeling would leave room for specificity provided by different enablers. Therefore, requirements and more architecture work seems likely for CBCS, and additional technical specifications for extensions of a general user profile enabler seem to be a possible option, if CBCS user profile is perceived as critical to be specified.

Looking from a different perspective, CBCS will probably face new, unpredictable challenges in the future. The industry will also find new ways to come up with content categorization. Those are trends that ask for periodic re-evaluation of the validity and effectiveness of approved specifications.

23.6   Summary

The CBCS enabler is a good example of what OMA promises to deliver. It offers creative, useful building blocks, yet allows for significant differentiation and stops well short of defining a complete service. CBCS also delivers on the OMA mission to re-use other enablers, and to facilitate its own re-use by others. Hopefully, this is what the reader comes away with from reading this chapter. Of course, the proof is in the detailed technical specifications, and the way they get realized and deployed.

24

The Game Services Enabler

With the unprecedented proliferation of mobile devices, we are witnessing a relentless push to provide attractive services for end-users. Service providers are reaching beyond traditional voice or even data communication services. As people carry their devices everywhere and are almost always connected, new services are being designed to appeal to people during their down time – a few minutes to kill waiting for a plane at the airport or between appointments. The aim is to provide non-stop rich media content for the mobile device, to entice end-users to fully use, and of course pay for, the high-speed data networks that have been and are being deployed globally.

In the past 10 years there has been a remarkable evolution in game software, gaming consoles, mobile gaming devices, game hosting, game communities, and game networking. Connected games is a strongly emerging market component, making mobile gaming more interactive than ever. A 2006 survey of worldwide gaming habits [Nokia 2006] indicated that, among gamers, multiplayer gaming is a regular part of the mobile gaming lifestyle. 45% of the 1800 gamers interviewed play a multiplayer game at least once a month and 22% play a multiplayer game at least once a week.

A 2007 International Data Corporation (IDC) study [TelecomTV 2007] estimates the number of mobile game purchasers to grow 16% annually, reaching nearly 50 million customers by 2010, and a 2006 Informa study [Informa 2006] predicts that global revenue from mobile games will increase from US$2.4 billion in 2005 to US$7.2 billion by 2010. Community and multiplayer games are expected to reach approximately 40% of the gaming market by 2009 [IDC 2006a]. The very nature of competitive and role-playing games fosters the growth of gaming communities. While multiplayer gaming is still in its infancy, it is a popular and growing phenomenon. In one major survey [Nokia 2006], 62% of gamers indicated they would share game demos with friends. It is likely that service providers and game hosting environments will support global gaming communities and continue to contribute to the growth of the market.

In Japan, the world's largest gaming market, the increasing numbers of mobile phone gamers has been enabled by the convergence of:

(1) a highly games-literate user base (roughly 25% of the total Japanese population are game players);
(2) advanced handset technologies which allow for a richer user experience and allow developers to design more sophisticated games; and
(3) a more harmonious relationship between game developers and service providers, allowing them to focus on the product and user experience rather than protracted negotiations over revenue sharing [Ovum 2007].

Mobile gaming is a nascent market that is set to claim a large piece of that mobile content space. As phones and mobile devices are growing up to support the kind of rich content that's

The Open Mobile Alliance   M. Brenner and M. Unmehopa
© 2008 Alcatel-Lucent. All Rights Reserved

developing on the Internet, with more powerful operation systems, extensive browsing capabilities and impressive color screens, it is easy to see how you can turn your phone into a gaming console. Mobile games can be built into the mobile device, downloaded to the device, or accessed online. Many mobile devices now support a run-time environment for executable games. Various business models for mobile gaming exist, including a walled-garden approach where the service provider hosts a third-party game and collects a slice of revenue from the content, or where the service provider allows the end-user to connect to any gaming platform and generate revenue from increased network usage.

24.1   Are Those Specifications Really Needed?

There are currently over 100 models of game-capable phones on the market and a myriad of development platforms. Game-enabled phones have become more powerful and today include color displays, large memory, as well as download and execution environments making game applications more fun and easier to access. Due to enhanced device capabilities of regular mobile handsets and newly emerging devices, specifically for gaming, the market for mobile gaming is growing rapidly.

In the wireless data services segment, mobile gaming is emerging as a mass market, and often used as a time killer. A significant trend is that connected mobile gaming consoles are moving from the traditional games industry into mobile networks. This segment, targeted to passionate gamers, is setting new standards for mobile game play. Broadband networking allows games on mobile devices to contain the rich graphics previously confined to PCs or game consoles and enables them to function in a distributed multiplayer environment [Yankee 2004].

Mobile games are the fastest growing type of applications for mobile devices. Good game applications can create high service provider/brand loyalty and user involvement, as well as stimulate a significant amount of network traffic and end-user consumption of high-value content. Also, as high-end mobile devices include some of the best graphics and networking capabilities, the gaming community demographic is shifting to include business professionals as well as the large base of younger users [BusinessWeek2007].

The diversity of gaming devices, game platforms, and game types can benefit from some taxonomy and some standardization. Mobile games fall into a number of categories based on architecture, game type, and game experience [Game Services AD]. It is useful to distinguish between the following categories of games:

- *Externally delivered games*, which are distributed physically, through various media (e.g. memory cards) and are executing on the mobile device in conjunction with a game server that is accessed over a wireless network.
- *Downloadable online games*, where game logic is downloaded and executed on the device, but here in conjunction with a game server that can be accessed over a wireless network.
- *Downloadable offline games*, where game logic is downloaded on the mobile device and is executing on the mobile device only.
- *Mobile browser-based games*, using, for example, a Wireless Application Protocol (WAP) or i-Mode browser.
- *Messaging-based games*, which are games using Short Message Service (SMS) or Multimedia Messaging Service (MMS) messaging protocols, and have their game logic purely on the server. Such games can only be played when users are connected to the mobile network.

Additionally, one can identify the following game types [Game Services CSI TS]:

- Soloplay
  - Highscore Game – does not require network-based game; communication is not critical;
  - Shadow Game – multiplayer game 'feel', but it is a single-player challenge.

- Turn based
  - Round Robin – Board Games (e.g. Chess, Backgammon, etc.); defined turn order;
  - Simultaneous Movement – Strategy games (2–n players); data sent to all players after each turn is complete;
  - Custom Turn – Strategy games (2–n players); turns decided by game client.
- Act Whenever – 'Virtual World' games (1–n players); user's representation within the game (e.g. character) is unavailable when the user is offline.
- Slow update – Long-term strategy games, Virtual Pets; user's representation within the game (e.g. character) stays available, executes commands or acts independently even when the user is offline.
- Real Time – Racing games, 3D Shooter games; users are connected directly and can compete against each other without latency time.

There is a need in the games industry to standardize around some basic platform principles that enables greater integration with communication networks, greater portability across devices, and greater utilization of intrinsic network capabilities. The Open Mobile Alliance (OMA) Game Services enabler was created for this purpose. Development of these specifications has the real potential to expand the gaming market and significantly reduce the development cost and integration efforts for game developers and service providers.

24.2   Standards Precursors to Game Services

In July 2001, several vendors founded the Mobile Games Interoperability Forum (MGIF) to define a mobile games interoperability specification and Application Programming Interfaces (APIs) in an effort to allow game developers to produce and deploy mobile games that could be distributed across multiple game servers and wireless networks, and played over many different mobile devices. The aim of the initiative was to specify a global standard and to develop certification procedures to encourage wide adoption of the standard. By November 2002, MGIF was absorbed into the OMA.

Following the successful integration of the MGIF, OMA established the Game Services Working Group (WG). OMA Game Services built on the specifications developed in MGIF to define interoperability specifications, APIs, and protocols for network-enabled gaming. The specifications developed by this WG enable the development and deployment of mobile games that can interoperate more efficiently with OMA compliant platforms and networks. The ultimate goal is to reduce costs for game developers, game platform owners, and service providers and stimulate the growth of this new revenue stream for all mobile business stakeholders.

24.3   Game Services Specifications

The goal of the OMA Game Services effort is to define specifications, generic APIs, and protocols for network-enabled gaming. The Game Services specifications will allow game developers to develop and deploy mobile games that can interoperate more efficiently with OMA compliant platforms and networks. The intent is to produce significant cost reduction for game developers, game platform owners, and service providers. OMA does not intend to develop new competing specifications where recognized standards exist, but to leverage existing standards where applicable to achieve the OMA goal of convergence. The Game Services WG was created and chartered to:

- develop interface specifications and protocols of game-related services with bearer and device layers as well as with service providers or third-party backend systems;
- drive the specification of the mobile game platform architecture toward a common set of standards;

- define and evolve a Gaming Platform, a Game Services Architecture and a Game Services Client/Server specification;
- document the OMA enablers used by games to offer specific functionality and services to ensure that OMA technologies are available to game developers on mobile devices;
- develop a common terminology for mobile gaming, and document performance and functional characteristics needed by mobile games.

In accordance with these directives, the Game Services WG has developed and published a Gaming Platform Specification, an Architecture Document (AD), and a Client/Server Interface (CSI) Specification. These documents were developed within the context of Game Services requirements as described by a set of use cases to be supported by the specifications. A high-level overview of these documents follows.

24.3.1 The Gaming Platform

The Gaming Platform [Gaming Platform], completed in 2003, introduced the basic entities comprising the mobile gaming platform architecture, described requirements for communication between those entities, and specified APIs for implementation. This platform enabler is an extension of work originated in the MGIF.

The approach taken within the Gaming Platform Specification allows game developers to create games that can more easily be ported between gaming platforms and networks and played on a variety of mobile devices.

The Gaming Platform Specification is an event-based specification, since most application environments are event-driven. As the gaming application detects actions and occurrences, responses and information transactions are communicated over the gaming platform interfaces. The Session Management API defines the core of the event model. Session Management describes the framework for the applications executing within the gaming platform, facilitates the management of player actions and provides access to other interfaces and APIs necessary to create the application (e.g. Connectivity, Metering, Scoring). The Gaming Platform also introduced and defined the relationships among the set of gaming entities to provide context and a framework for a games session. Session entities of the gaming platform are defined as follows:

- User: an object representing the actual end-user connected to the system by a mobile device. The user places requests to the system to play a particular game. Each user has a unique user ID on the gaming platform.
- Application: the installed code or logic of a game. The Application is used for creating specific running instances (i.e. game boards). Application defines shared information for all Application Instances.
- Master Application Instance: an object representing the deployed, static parts of the application (game).
- Application Instance: an object representing an instance of an application. It can have any number of Actors.
- Actor Session: the actual representation of a User Session in a game (Application Instance). One user can have many Actors.
- Actor: represents the persistent data for the Actor Session.

The Gaming Platform is shown schematically in Figure 24.1. APIs specified in the Gaming Platform include:

- Connectivity API – provides high-level access to network communication layers. It includes client messaging/browsing and synchronous/asynchronous message transfer.

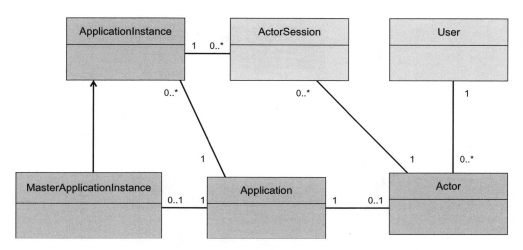

Figure 24.1 Relations among session entities. Reproduced by Permission of the Open Mobile Alliance Ltd.

- Metering API – provides a standard mechanism for communicating billable events to the gaming platform. It includes traffic-based events (e.g. data transfer, game duration) and game-specific events.
- Scores and Competition Management API – provides mechanisms for reporting and retrieving scores from the gaming platform which serves to support multiplayer gaming communities.
- Logging API – provides a standard mechanism for reporting game status to the gaming platform. This information is useful for application management and troubleshooting.
- Timers API – provides the mechanism by which a game schedules and delays activities, as well as provides unified access to time-based event triggers.

24.3.2 Game Services Architecture

The first release of the OMA Game Services Architecture specification [Game Services AD] was completed in March 2006. It describes a client-server game architecture for the Game Services enabler with functionality based on the variety of game types already defined in the industry and on a number of specific use cases. The scope of the Game Services Architecture is limited to the game functionality itself and the relationship with other OMA enablers that may enhance the game experience for the end-user (see Figure 24.2).

The Game CSI describes the interface between the game client and the game server in the Game Service enabler domain, and will be discussed in a later section of this chapter. The I0 in Figure 24.2 indicates that interactions with other enablers are achieved through interfaces defined by other OMA enablers and used by the Game Service enabler.

It is recognized that game applications and game servers may be part of a larger network and service platform architecture, relying on functionalities from other network elements and components. As depicted in Figure 24.3, users may access games via multiple networks and network gateways. Game services are usually accessed by means of a service delivery platform (that may also be shared among service providers), providing generic functionality to many applications. The game applications themselves may reside on a game server or may be provided by a third party. The specifics of these network and service elements are out of scope for the OMA Gaming Service, which can be regarded as a generic infrastructure on the server side providing common services to a range of game applications.

Collaboration among enablers is a key objective within OMA. Game Services may utilize other OMA enablers not only to perform some of the basic gaming functions (e.g. Charging), but may also

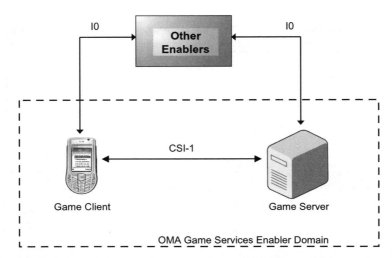

Figure 24.2   Game services enabler architecture. Reproduced by Permission of the Open Mobile Alliance Ltd.

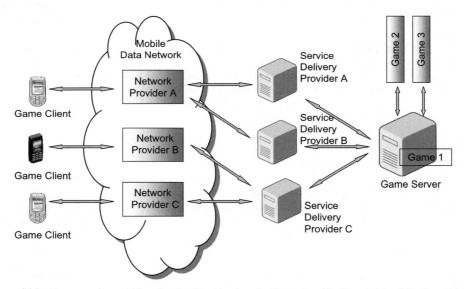

Figure 24.3   Game services within a Service Provider domain. Reproduced by Permission of the Open Mobile Alliance Ltd.

use other OMA enablers to support new and innovative use cases that enhance the user experience (e.g. Presence, Messaging). An example of this context collaboration is shown in Figure 24.4. The game server provides the Game Services functionality, communicating with the game players via the CSI. Other enablers may interact with the game client and game server to add functionality.

24.3.3 Game Services – Client/Server Interface Enabler

The first release of the OMA Game Services CSI enabler [Game Services CSI TS] was completed in 2006. Game Services CSI 1.0 specifies the communication between a game client on a mobile

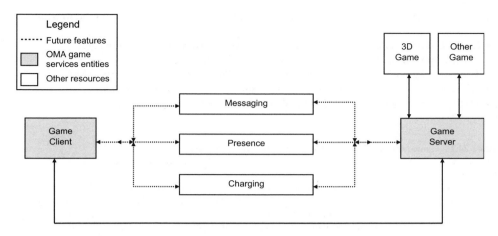

Figure 24.4 Example of game services context model

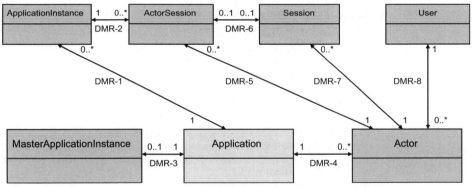

Figure 24.5 Domain model relationships for game services CSI 1.0. Reproduced by Permission of the Open Mobile Alliance Ltd.

device and a game server, but not the mobile client or game server themselves. The mobile client requests operations from the server and events generated on the server side are communicated to the client. Depending on the underlying network, the Game Services CSI can run on top of various transport layers, such as HTTP, Simple Object Access Protocol (SOAP), or User Datagram Protocol (UDP). The Game Services CSI specification defines operations, events, sequence diagrams, and eXtended Markup Language (XML) schema-defined data types.

It should be noted that the Game Services CSI 1.0 enabler is different from and not completely aligned with the Gaming Platform described in Section 24.3.1. CSI 1.0 is an evolution of the event-based specification and is described by a new domain model. In particular, a new 'Session' entity has been introduced in the CSI 1.0 domain (see Figure 24.5). Figure 24.5 shows the Domain Model Relationships (DMRs) for Game Services CSI 1.0.

The following DMRs are identified:

- DMR-1: relationship between Application and Application Instance (one-to-many relationship).
- DMR-2: relationship between Application Instance and Actor Session (one-to-many relationship).

- DMR-3: relationship between Application and Master Application Instance (one-to-many relationship).
- DMR-4: relationship between Application and Actor (one-to-many relationship).
- DMR-5: relationship between Actor and Actor Session (one-to-many relationship).
- DMR-6: relationship between Actor Session and Session (one-to-one relationship).
- DMR-7: relationship between Actor and Session (one-to-many relationship).
- DMR-8: relationship between User and Actor (one-to-many relationship).

Table 24.1 Game services CSI 1.0 operations (called from the client)

Operation	Description
Registration, login, logout	Registration registers a new user. This user can use any application on the server. Login logs in a user for a specific application. Logout invalidates the session for the user.
Game persistence	*GetAS* retrieves detailed information about all assigned Actor Sessions of an Actor. *GetInv* all invitations of an Actor. An Invitation is a special kind of Actor Session. *Activate* activates a specific Actor Session. *Deactivate* deactivates a specific Actor Session. *Name* assigns a name to an Actor Session
Game creation and matchmaking	*CreateAI* creates a new AI for the Actor. *CreateAIPrivate* creates a private AI. ASs for the calling Actor and all invited Actors are created. *ForceAIRnd* allows an Actor to randomly join an open public AI. An EvJoinAIRnd is sent to all Actors attached to the AI.
Game play	*Start* starts the AI. An EvStart is sent to all connected Actors. *End* ends the AI. An EvEnd is sent to all connected Actors. *Quit* quits the ASs. The AI is *not ended.* *HandoverTurn* signals the handover of the turn to all connected Actors. An EvTurn is sent to all connected Actors. *SendData* sends data to all connected Actors.
Messaging	*SendTxtMsg* sends a text message to all connected Actors.
Highscore	*SetScore* sends a score to the server. *GetScorePos* gets the position of a score with the ScoreID. *GetScoresByPos* retrieves a certain number of scores from a specific position. *GetScoresByID* retrieves a certain number of scores for a specific ID. *GetScoresByUser* retrieves a certain number of scores for a specific username.
Shadows (Ghost Players)	*SetShadow* sends a Shadow and Score to the platform. *GetShadow* retrieves a score from the platform.
Event queue operations	*GetEvents* retrieves events from the event queue in the *AS specified by the Actor Session ID (ASID)*. *GetEventHistory* retrieves a (maximum) number of events from the event queue in the AS *specified by the ASID* that have been retrieved before, beginning with most recent events. *RaiseEvent* raises a custom event in the AS.
Miscellaneous operations	*Ping* instantly returns to measure the Ping time. *DateTime* gets the current server time and date (Coordinated Universal Time (UTC)).

Table 24.2 Game services CSI 1.0 events (generated by the server)

Event	Description
EvDeactivate	An AS has been deactivated. The corresponding ActorNr of the Actor that deactivated its AS is specified.
EvActivate	An AS has been activated. The corresponding ActorNr of the Actor that activated its AS is specified.
EvJoin	Notifies all Actors connected to a specific AI that another Actor has joined the AI. Actor number and username are given as part of the event parameters.
EvStart	This event is sent to all players when the team leader uses the Start operation.
EvEnd	This event is sent to all players when the Application Instance Master uses the End operation.
EvQuit	This event is sent to all players when a player quits the game.
EvTurn	Notifies a particular player to make a move.
EvData	Notifies all players connected to a specific Application Instance about new data.
EvTxtMsg	Notifies all players connected to a specific Application Instance about a new text message.
EvStatus	Notifies all players connected to a specific Application Instance about a login/logoff operation.

Although there are many types of networked games (see Section 24.1), Game Services CSI 1.0 focuses on single player (i.e. soloplay) games. The use cases and sequence diagrams of the specification, therefore, reflect a single instance of a game client. Additional game types may be supported in future releases of OMA Game Services specifications. Table 24.1 lists the CSI 1.0 specified operations. Table 24.2 lists the CSI 1.0 specified events.

24.4 Impact of Specifications on the Industry

The convergence of telecommunications, media, and information technology enables the development of new kinds of games that can be played anywhere, anytime, and with any device. Games will be a key revenue generator for all stakeholders in the mobile business. However, the current wireless game market is heterogeneous and fragmented because of existing technology barriers and missing standardization. This is preventing all of the stakeholders in the mobile business to fully benefit from this new revenue stream.

Mobile gaming was included as one of the top 10 telecommunications industry trends in a 2006 IDC report [IDC2006b]. Multiplayer mobile online gaming is attracting users from the currently larger market segment of PC-based online gamers who want continued online connectivity. A key challenge, noted in the report, is the need for a ubiquitous mobile gaming platform like the PC in order to successfully bridge the gap between online and mobile gaming. The Game Services AD and CSI provide a framework and standard set of operations to initiate game play, interact with the game application, and facilitate communication among players. Adoption of standardized models, operations, and message flows by operators, developers, and mobile device vendors serves to increase interoperability and portability of mobile games. Guidelines for fundamental architectural and platform considerations that significantly impact application performance in the Game Services white paper on Mobile Gaming Evolution [Game Services WP] can be used by content providers,

Mobile Network Operators, and handset manufacturers to create appropriate devices, content, and services for the mobile gaming market that better gaming consumer expectations.

The Game Services specifications, supporting the mobile gaming business drivers, provide a means to facilitate co-operation and inter-working among all parties involved in the value chain. The end-to-end value chain for interactive games includes many entities – operators, publishers, game developers, handset vendors, application hosting facilities, and users. The goals of OMA Game Services include meeting new user and market requirements in the standardization process to encourage wide adoption of the standards for mobile gaming.

24.4.1 Impact on Service Providers

Service providers may be the primary beneficiaries of a significant expansion of the mobile gaming space, as collaborative games will create new occasions for communication, drive service consumption, increase revenue, and reduce customer churn [Motorola2006]. Network operators view gaming as a family of applications, which significantly drives up network traffic, offers opportunities to sell more high-value content, and increases user loyalty. By adopting the OMA Game Services Framework for networked gaming, service providers can provide a standardized platform for developers to create games and a vehicle for enhancing the game player's experience through the inter-working with other OMA enablers.

Combined with mobile advertising and content delivery, service providers will be able to create and build mobile gaming communities, while increasing interactive play, building the market, and building brand loyalty. Mobile Operators benefit from revenue sharing with developers/publishers on higher margin games, consumer attraction and retention, and increased utilization of 3G networks. Mobile Operators are also branding mobile handsets with performance parameters optimized to their specific offerings in order to create their own gaming communities and marginalize independent portals.

24.4.2 Impact on Vendors

The OMA Game Services enabler focuses on mobile games that access a game server during play. The enabler allows game developers to produce mobile games that can be played on a broad range of mobile devices and deployed on various game platforms and mobile networks. This will significantly reduce the development cost and integration efforts for game developers and game server owners.

For game publishers and developers, a mass market is emerging because their products are becoming accessible by an increasing variety of games-capable devices. Mobile gaming is a complement, not a replacement, for console gaming. Wireless connectivity will add value through an additional mass-market delivery channel. The proliferation of mobile devices has often required game developers to create different versions of a game for different mobile devices. Porting from one device to another is a reality, but there are efforts underway to minimize the impacts of re-design by creating guidelines relative to mobile device and game performance parameters. The OMA white paper on Mobile Gaming Evolution [Game Services WP] provides just such guidelines. For a similar set of parameters, the focus is on the consistency of user experience as a game is played on different devices.

Enabling mobile gamers to access Massively Multiplayer Online Games (MMOGs) and other multiplayer games and interact with gamers is key to the developers', publishers', and handset manufacturers' success. Game publishers benefit from higher return on investment due to reduced porting effort and higher average unit price for premium games. For multiplayer games to become popular and mainstream, they must be easily accessible. Handset manufacturers benefit from increased phone replacement rate driven by graphics technology evolution that induces consumers to upgrade their handsets to improve their gaming experience.

24.4.3 Impact on Consumer Market

For the user, the impact of the OMA Game Services enabler is dependent on the adoption and implementation of the specifications by the rest of the gaming industry value chain, but user satisfaction is, of course, a major focus of the rest of the value chain. The real potential in utilizing the Game Services enabler is the ability to enhance the user's game experience through a standardized framework that provides access to other OMA enablers (e.g. Presence, Location, Messaging) and the focus on particular use case categories such as social networking, advertising, and distribution of game content. Also, since the Game Services enabler allows game developers to produce mobile games that can be played on a broad range of mobile devices and deployed on various game platforms and mobile networks, consumers benefit from a broader library of premium quality games, including mobile versions of leading console titles, and a consistent user experience across handsets.

The Game Services enabler may also have an impact beyond the immediate context of the game itself. Massively Multiplayer Online Role Playing Games (MMORPGs) is one large game category that fosters player communities. The MMORPG notion of a persistent game universe plays a strong role in community interaction and cross-marketing opportunities. Standardized support of use cases for social networking and advertising will directly serve the interests of the user community and help assist service providers to better serve their market. For example, studies have shown that gamers tend to recall advertisements in games and that in-game advertisements do influence purchase decisions [Yankee 2006a].

24.4.4 Impact on Other Specifications

For the collaborative gaming community, interaction with other enablers is extremely useful. Game Services may make use of a number of other OMA enablers such as the enablers addressed by the Browser Technology Working Group, the Digital Rights Management enabler, and the Push enabler. The Presence enabler is key for the initiation of game play and for establishing communication. The PEEM enabler is critical for game establishment and for assessing user profiles. Other key enablers include Charging, Location, DCD, and communication enablers such as Instant Messaging (IM).

24.5 Specifications Evolution and Future Direction

Work on OMA Game Services has continued since the publication of the Game Services AD and Game Services CSI 1.0. Emphasis of the published Game Services enabler has been on *game portability* (running a game application on a number of server side game platforms) and *game interoperability* (enabling game applications, executing in different environments, to exchange information and share common services) of the server-side game logic. Use cases described in the Game Services Requirements 1.0 [Game Services RD] were limited to basic game functionalities such as obtaining a game, initiating match play, sharing data, and chat, along with high-level functionalities such as security, charging, privacy, and interoperability. And, ultimately, Game Services CSI 1.0 was limited in its scope to network-based soloplay games.

Work continues on new use cases for a variety of Game Services scenarios that expand the relevance and applicability of Game Services to new game categories and more widespread applications. A few of the recent use cases describe scenarios for game discovery, charging for and distribution of game content, social networking, and advertising. One of the more complex use cases (and one of the most interesting and practical) is the real-time multiplayer gaming use case, shown in Figure 24.6.

Future Game Services enhancements are also expected to leverage on the developments of the IP Multimedia Subsystem (IMS) [IMSinOMA AD] and additional OMA enablers as they are developed. The context model shown in Figure 24.7 was introduced in the Game Services AD.

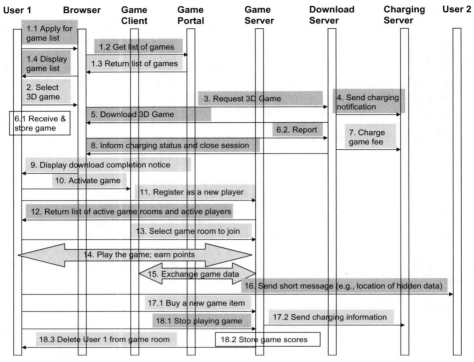

Figure 24.6   Example flows for real-time multiplayer gaming. Reproduced by Permission of the Open Mobile Alliance Ltd.

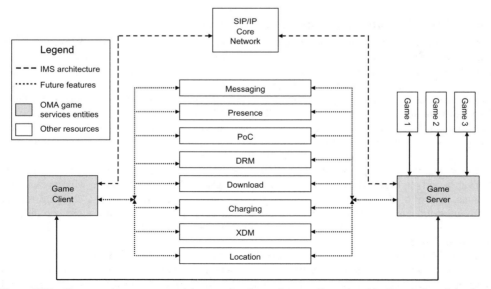

Figure 24.7   Game services context model supporting future features. Reproduced by Permission of the Open Mobile Alliance Ltd.

It is outside the scope of Game Services to define IMS service capabilities, but it is noted that IMS provides a framework for providing multimedia services. The IMS Session Initiation Protocol (SIP)/IP Core provides functionality for Security, Discovery/Registry, Authorization/Authentication, and Charging. The Game Services enabler may access these resources via the interfaces of class I2, which are not specified in OMA.

Additional work can also be done to further explore game portability issues. The Mobile Gaming Evolution Whitepaper [Game Services WP] highlighted a number of parameters in game software and mobile device hardware that can be used to provide a more uniform user experience and aid developers in porting games to various devices. The games industry is moving rapidly to not only port games among different mobile handsets, but to develop converged gaming or multiple screen gaming, where a single game can be played on all major multimedia platforms – mobile devices, PCs, game consoles, and TV.

Mobile gaming innovation requires core technologies to enable a collaborative mobile gaming platform and game concepts that leverage the communication and peripheral platform capabilities of advanced mobile devices [Motorola 2006]. It is anticipated that new gaming requirements, based on new, realistic and innovative game-centric scenarios will lead to inter-working of the Game Services enabler with additional OMA enablers. Guidelines described in the Mobile Gaming Evolution [Game Services WP] can provide useful insights into the relationships among game application parameters, mobile device capabilities, and user experience. Future discussions of these guidelines could lead to additional Game Services use cases and evolution of the architecture.

Increased engagement with the service provider and developer communities is already generating discussions that will almost certainly lead to new Game Services Requirements and an evolution of the existing Game Services Architecture. For example, Peer-to-Peer (P2P) Architectures have yet to be explored in detail. In the greater OMA context, P2P gaming is not much more interesting than soloplay gaming, since functionalities residing in the network are not necessarily involved. But the extension of the existing CSI Architecture to include P2P communication, creating a Personal Area Network (PAN) for gaming, would utilize the standardized benefits of the OMA Game Services enabler and other OMA enablers, while at the same time defining more realistic and popular use cases for gaming.

24.6 Summary

Mobile gaming has significantly gained in popularity and sophistication due to simultaneous technology advances in gaming software, mobile device design with increased computing power and graphics capabilities, and mobile broadband networking. This has led to the proliferation of scores of mobile devices supporting different platforms and game software targeted for a particular platform that is not readily portable to other platforms or even other mobile devices. There is a need in the games industry to standardize around some basic platform principles that enable greater integration with communication networks, greater portability across devices, and greater utilization of intrinsic network capabilities. The OMA Game Services enabler was created for this purpose. The enabler allows game developers to produce mobile games that can be played on a broad range of mobile devices and deployed on various game platforms and mobile networks. This promises the realization of significant reductions in development costs for game developers and increased networked gaming integration for service providers.

Collaboration among enablers is a key objective within OMA and especially for Game Services. Game Services may utilize other OMA enablers not only to perform some of the basic gaming functions, but may also use other OMA enablers to support new and innovative use cases that enhance the user's gaming experience (e.g. Presence, Messaging). The Game Services enabler focuses on mobile games that access a game server during play. The game server provides the Game Services functionality, communicating with the game players via the CSI. Other enablers may interact with the game client and game server to add functionality.

The Game Services AD and CSI provide a framework and standard set of operations to initiate game play, interact with the game application, and facilitate communication among players. Adoption of standardized models, operations, and message flows by operators, developers, and mobile device vendors serves to increase interoperability and portability of mobile games. Extension of this framework to include P2P networking, to include real-time multiplayer gaming, and to include portability or convergence of games across mobile devices, PCs, consoles, and TV is the future of the games industry and the future of the Games Service enabler.

25

The Location Enabler

This chapter will provide an overview of the Mobile Location Service (MLS) and Secure User Plane Location (SUPL) enablers defined by the Open Mobile Alliance (OMA) Location Working Group (LOC WG). The chapter will cover the market requirements and architecture considerations for Control Plane and User Plane solutions, and provide an overview of the technical specifications for both of these solutions. The relationship with other industry initiatives will also be addressed.

End-users of mobile devices move around; they do not stick to one place. How is that for a blinding flash of the obvious? But as evident as that may be, this one characteristic has brought about a whole slew of complex technologies for mobile phone systems. It is not sufficient to simply deploy radio towers at the peripheral of the traditional fixed-line networks, and offer mobile service. Procedures like moving around temporary copies of subscriber data to the switch currently serving the subscriber, paging mobile phones before completing a call, and handing off voice channels when the subscriber roams from one coverage area to the next, need to be in place. The collection of these procedures is called mobility management.

However, in addition to the normal operation of mobile networks, such as call routing and delivery, the information required for mobility management can also be gainfully deployed for value-added applications. Context sensitive data, like knowing where someone is, can enrich applications and enhance the end-user experience. The OMA is of course not the first organization to make this observation. Location Services (LCS) have been in operation in virtually every mobile network for quite a while now. Organizations like the Parlay Group, and the now affiliated Location Interoperability Forum (LIF), provide interfaces to obtain location information from the network.

But the network is not the only source of location information. Who better to ask where the mobile device is located than the mobile device itself? Many mobile phones in use today integrate support for Global Positioning System (GPS) technology, a satellite-based navigation system providing a granular level of accuracy for the device's geographical position.

The OMA LOC WG provides specifications for obtaining location data from both the network as well as the device. The MLS enabler defines support for a Control Plane Location service, that is, the network locates the phone. The SUPL enabler, as the name suggest, defines support for a User Plane Location service, where the device (possibly with assistance from the network) calculates the position and deploys User Plane data bearers to communicate the location information.

Privacy considerations are critical for personal data, such as user location. Permissions to access information about a person's whereabouts should be strictly safeguarded. Many regional or national regulatory factors apply, protecting privacy information from unlawful, unsolicited, or inappropriate access.

The Open Mobile Alliance   M. Brenner and M. Unmehopa

25.1   What is Location?

For reasons of mobility management, mobile networks must continuously keep track of the cell in which any particular mobile device is currently located. Each cell has a unique physical location (identified by the cell identifier, or cell ID), and its coverage can be delimited with some precision, based on the range of the cellular base station. Depending on radio bearer technology and signal frequency, cell site size can vary anywhere from a few hundreds of meters to several kilometers. And as the location of a device can only be expressed in terms of cell tower range, cell ID location offers rather wide accuracy margins. This imprecision excludes Location Based Services (LBS) that require pinpoint accuracy, but provides sufficient information for the typical 'where is the nearest X?'-style services that lead the user to nearby points of interest. As the number of cell sites per area increases, for example to serve densely populated neighborhoods, the accuracy also increases. Since cell ID location relies on information that is inherent to the mobile network, the most significant advantage of this technology is that it is readily and ubiquitously available to all users.

To further enhance the accuracy, technologies like Time Distance of Arrival (TDOA), which is a triangulation method based on radio signal strength, have been developed. TDOA measures the time difference of arrival of radio signals from a mobile device at different cellular base stations, and uses that data to triangulate the location of the device. The accuracy range improves as the number of cell sites that receive a mobile device's radio signal increases. This technology enables accurate location readings within a matter of meters.

The GPS is also a triangulation technique, but use radio signals received from multiple satellites orbiting the earth, rather than from cellular base stations. GPS yields location readings with pinpoint accuracy, enabling highly location-sensitive applications such as turn-by-turn driving directions or pedestrian directions from point A to point B. The GPS satellite constellation is operated and deployed separately from the mobile network and as such may not be universally available to all mobile subscribers. However, as advancements in component technology continue to result in reduced size and cost for GPS chipsets and receivers, GPS-enabled mobile devices will increasingly become a widespread and established phenomenon. And along with this trend, the availability of detailed GPS-compatible maps along with points-of-interest overlays is growing as well. This makes GPS exceedingly suitable for LBS.

The high degree of accuracy obtained with GPS does come with some drawbacks though. To be able to operate, the GPS-enabled device needs to maintain a line of sight with the satellites in orbit. In highly populated areas with a lot of high-rise development, this may result in so-called urban canyons. In addition, GPS suffers from low in-building penetration, resulting in poor indoor operation. An additional problem with GPS is the amount of time it takes for the mobile device to lock on to the orbiting satellites after turning on the device (or, for instance, having temporarily lost the GPS signals in a tunnel). This is called the Time to First Fix (TTFF). To combat these downsides of GPS, where short response times are a requirement or where line of sight is hampered by buildings, thick foliage, or simply by being indoors, a hybrid approach has been developed called Assisted GPS (A-GPS).

A-GPS is a technology where the GPS-enabled mobile device uses other resources, such as an assistance server, to assist the GPS receiver in reducing the TTFF. One of the reasons that the time it takes to obtain the first fix on the satellites can be long, is the fact that several pieces of data need to be obtained, whereas the mobile device may have limited processing capabilities or indeed reduced line of sight. The assistance server, which is a dedicated, high-performance server, has the ability to obtain GPS information on behalf of the mobile device. It can obtain data on the orbit of individual satellites (ephemeris data) as well as data on the entire constellation of available satellites (almanac data) and communicate this to the mobile device across the normal terrestrial channels, obviating the need for the device to download this information from the satellites themselves. With this assistance data, the GPS-enabled device can now more easily and hence more quickly, obtain a fix to several satellites.

With the spread of location technologies and (A-)GPS-enabled devices, an entire class of LBS is unlocked. Especially as real-time, contextual information is co-ordinated with the positioning data (after all, the novelty of knowing your latitude-longitude co-ordinates quickly wears off, and I would rather know my position relative to a certain point of interest). Map and direction-based applications, like turn-by-turn driving directions, local traffic information, and map display on mobile devices become a reality. Enterprise applications like asset monitoring and tracking (of valuable goods), fleet tracking (of vehicle and driver), colleague finder tools, and location-enabled directory assistance can be realized using this technology. The 'first responder' community, such as law enforcement officers, firefighters, and emergency medical professionals, can draw tremendous benefits from adding location awareness to their communications means.

As an example of the new value-added applications a Location enabler may yield, we take a look at geo-fencing. A geo-fence is a virtual boundary delimiting a geographic area. Based on positioning information, the Location enabler can recognize the event when a mobile device is entering or leaving the area. Such events can be subscribed to in the form of notifications, alerting subscribers with respect to which mobile device has entered or left the area and where the mobile device is located at that point in time. One could foresee many possible uses for this type of information. For example, a law enforcement agency can use geo-fencing to oversee a convict's home confinement as an alternative to using ankle monitors. Car rental agencies can ensure that hired cars do not cross state boundaries (e.g. violating insurance policies), and boat owners who rent their vessels can ensure that pastime captains do not stray from their stated travel plans. Fleet managers can quickly pinpoint vehicles that venture into unauthorized areas, and parents can monitor whether their children stray from safe playing areas.

25.2 Location Architectures

We have seen how the location of a mobile device can be either calculated or derived, and how it can be expressed, with varying levels of accuracy. We have seen a glimpse of the applications that can be enabled by adding location awareness. Now let us look at various architecture options for how location information can be obtained and disseminated. In the introduction to this chapter we made a brief mention of User Plane and Control Plane solutions. The difference is rather fundamental, leading to completely different architectures, as we will outline in the following sections. We will start with explaining Control Plane solutions.

25.2.1 Control Plane Location

One could argue about what initially triggered the development of mobile location technology, but it is fair to say that wireless Enhanced 911 (E911), a regulatory requirement in the United States by the Federal Communications Commission (FCC), played a large part. E911 aims to improve the effectiveness and reliability of the wireless emergency service by providing emergency dispatchers with additional information on incoming emergency calls. With E911, the FCC mandates Mobile Network Operators to provide the phone number and location of the person calling the emergency number. This will help the first responder community to expediently travel to the site of the emergency in cases where the caller does not know her location or is otherwise incapable of providing this information. E911 has counterparts in other markets as well, where national or international regulatory bodies impose similar requirements on network operators for the support of emergency calls. As such E911 in large part prompted the definition of a new location architecture.

As the requirement was to provide a location estimate within the context of an emergency call, the approach chosen was to re-use the control plane already in place in circuit-switched networks for voice-call processing such as call detection, routing, delivery, and handoff. The Signaling System number 7 (SS7)-based signaling system, an inherent part of a Mobile Operator's voice-call distribution system, performs the positioning-related activities on the control channels in the background of the voice call. The Control Plane Location solution is controlled and managed as part of the overall Core Network (CN) of the operator. This highly reliable and secure infrastructure makes Control Plane Location very appropriate for emergency services. In addition, by exploiting the SS7-based signaling infrastructure, the location functionality is available to every device connected to the network, which is another regulatory requirement for emergency calls. Control Plane Location provides for support of network-initiated location queries. Such queries do not require any initiative or intervention by the mobile device (or the end-user using it), while they work irrespective of a device's operating system or other device capabilities and have no significant impact on device battery power consumption. Network-initiated location queries can be issued based on one-time requests or periodic time intervals. Notifications can be triggered in case the network detects that the device is moving in or out of a pre-defined geographical area.

With the Control Plane Architecture, the idea is to provide device location to the infrastructure. This design is ideally suited for emergency services. Other applications that make use of location information to enhance communication features for the device, for instance, a location-aware call center application, can also readily be supported using Control Plane Architecture solutions. Furthermore, the technology is aptly suited for applications like asset monitoring and tracking, where location information is queried for large volumes of devices out in the field and subsequently processed on a back-office server for use in some automated enterprise process.

Location architectures for the control plane quite naturally have been developed by the standards organizations responsible for defining those control planes. For example, the Control Plane Location Architecture for GSM/Universal Mobile Telecommunications System (UMTS) has been developed by 3GPP whereas 3GPP2 has specified the Control Plane Location Architecture for CDMA2000 systems. Figure 25.1 depicts the Control Plane Location Architecture defined by 3GPP for GSM/UMTS networks.

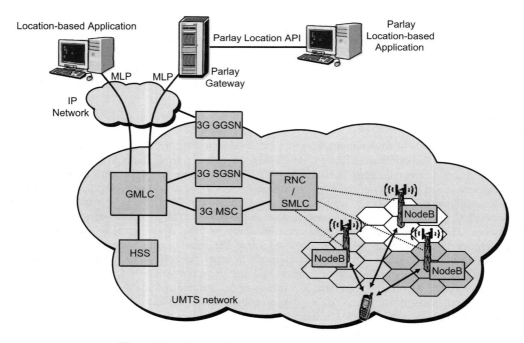

Figure 25.1   Control Plane Location in GSM/UMTS networks

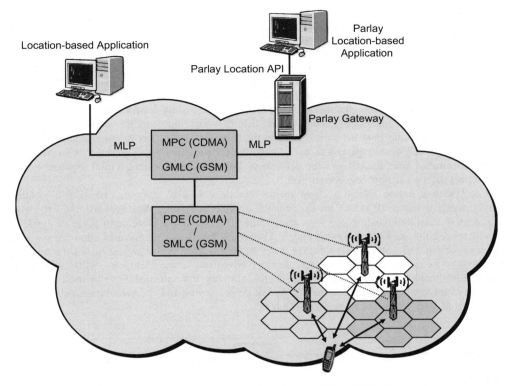

Figure 25.2 Simplified Control Plane Location in GSM and CDMA networks

It is well beyond the scope of this book to describe in detail the Control Plane Location Architectures for various networks including CDMA and GSM. Instead of describing all the network elements involved in this architecture, we will simplify the diagram by illustrating the major concepts in a nutshell. Suffice to say that such architectures support network elements as a Mobile Positioning Center (MPC) which communicates with Position Determining Equipment (PDE) in CDMA networks, or, in a GSM environment, a Gateway Mobile Location Center (GMLC) which communicates with Serving Mobile Location Centers (SMLCs) (see Figure 25.2). The SMLC (or PDE) may be integrated with the cellular base station and performs the actual location measurements, such as for example the triangulation calculations. The GMLC (or MPC) is the central contact point for location-based applications, serving as the intermediary or gateway toward the network. It may perform authentication and authorization (to ensure that privacy sensitive location information is distributed to authorized principals only), billing, and provisioning, and is responsible for routing the location query to the SMLC (or PDE) currently serving the mobile device. Applications may gain access to the functionality provided by the GMLC/MPC using network protocols like the Mobile Location Protocol (MLP), originally defined by the LIF (which is now affiliated with the OMA) or using APIs like Parlay APIs.

25.2.2 User Plane Location

We discussed the Control Plane Location Architecture based on the rather simplified view in Figure 25.2. The more complicated representation in Figure 25.1 shows that the SMLC (or PDE)

resides in the Radio Access Network (RAN) and interacts with entities in the RAN, such as the NodeBs. The GMLC (or MPC) resides in the CN and has interfaces to many of the elements in both the packet switched and the circuit-switched domains of the CN. In fact, there hardly is a network entity that is not impacted by the Control Plane Location Architecture. Being so deeply entwined with the signaling network, the control plane approach is highly reliable and secure. But this significant impact on the network operator's deployed infrastructure is extremely costly, which may be seen by some as prohibitive for the cost-effective roll out of LBS. To address this issue, an alternative approach has emerged that does not involve the signaling network and mobile switching elements, but instead consists of establishing a basic IP connection from the mobile device across the operator's existing data network to access the location server. The location data exchanged using this approach merely appears as user data to the network, hence this approach is termed User Plane Location. Figure 25.3 shows the differences between the two architectural approaches and the impact on the existing network entities.

User Plane Location allows a client on the mobile device to communicate with a location server across a secure IP tunnel set up over the operator's existing data network. No expensive upgrades to existing signaling networks are required. By bypassing the control plane designed to handle voice calls and everything that entails, User Plane Location Architectures allow for low cost implementation and faster time-to-market. User Plane Location is not dependent on the network architecture or radio access technology. Another advantage is the ability to swiftly update the location information locally on the mobile device, allowing this information to be used by device resident client applications. Predominantly, mobile device centric and end-user initiated applications benefit from User Plane Location Architectures.

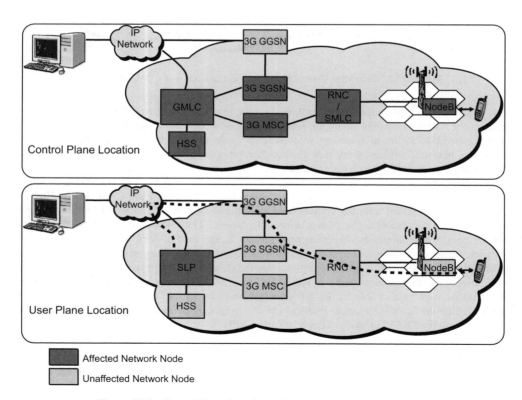

Figure 25.3   Control Plane Location and User Plane Location compared

25.3   The Mobile Location Services Enabler

The previous section has introduced two architectural solutions for LBS. This section will focus on the OMA enabler for Control Plane Location, that is, the OMA MLS enabler [MLS ERP]. The MLS consists of three protocols, each of which will be introduced in the following subsections.

25.3.1 OMA Mobile Location Protocol

We will now succinctly cover the OMA MLP, which defines the application interfaces to the Control Plane Location Architectures. Succinctly only, as MLP came into OMA through affiliation of the LIF, and can now be viewed as an established technology.

The MLP is one of three protocol specifications that make up the OMA MLS enabler [MLS ERP]. MLP [MLP TS] describes the protocol between an LBS application and the location server (which is either an MPC or a GMLC). For example in a 3GPP context, the MLP protocol is the technology realization of choice for the Le reference point [3GPP TS 23.271]. MLP defines XML content, in the form of Document Type Definition (DTD) elements, which can be carried over various transport protocols, including HTTP and Simple Object Access Protocol (SOAP). MLP supports several query patterns. The most straightforward pattern is the synchronous request. This pattern supports a simple request and response exchange, as well as an immediate answer in case of errors. The Standard Location Immediate Service, which is used to request the location of one or more mobile subscribers when a response is required within a set time interval, is an example of the synchronous request pattern. Another query pattern is called triggered reporting, where the Triggered Location Reporting Service is one of the examples. The Triggered Location Reporting Service is used when the location of the device should be reported at a specific time interval or when a specific event of interest occurs in the network. This pattern is somewhat more involved as it supports messages to start and stop the triggered reports, as well as a message for the report itself.

Table 25.1 lists the MLP basic services, and their supported messages. We introduce them briefly here because, as we shall see, the MLP protocol is re-used by the SUPL and some of these messages make an appearance in the SUPL flow diagrams later on in this chapter.

25.3.2 OMA Privacy Checking Protocol

Like the MLP, the Privacy Checking Protocol (PCP) [PCP TS] is part of the protocol specifications that make up the OMA MLS enabler [MLS ERP]. PCP is an application-level protocol for asserting those privacy settings of an end-user that are specific to LBS. PCP may be used as the protocol between a network server such as the MPC or GMLC and an external privacy policy resource. An end-user may not wish to make her whereabouts known to just about anyone. For example, Alice may only allow her direct colleagues in the office and her friends on her buddy list to see her location. Such preferences are stored in Alice's privacy profile. PCP provides operations to access the privacy profile of a positioning target before obtaining or releasing any of the location data. PCP can also be used to establish pseudonyms that conceal the true identity (i.e. Mobile Subscriber ISDN Number (MSISDN) and International Mobile Subscriber Identity (IMSI)) of a positioning target from the requesting location application.

The privacy considerations for MLS are mentioned here, as privacy is an important service requirement and often a mandatory regulatory requirement for OMA enablers like Location. In addition, we make mention of PCP here as it is referenced in Chapter 22. For further details on the PCP, the reader is referred to [PCP TS].

25.3.3 OMA Roaming Location Protocol

In the case where an LBS application in the home network needs to obtain location information for a subscriber who happens to be roaming in another network, an exchange needs to take place between the Location server in the visited network and the Location server in the home network. Such inter-Location server communication is also required in the case where a Location server in

Table 25.1 MLP basic services

Standard Location Immediate Service	
• Standard Location Immediate Request (SLIR) • Standard Location Immediate Answer (SLIA) • Standard Location Immediate Report (SLIREP)	Standard location query, followed by one (SLIA) or more (SLIA plus several SLIREP) immediate asynchronous location responses
Emergency Location Immediate Service	
• Emergency Location Immediate Request (EME_LIR) • Emergency Location Immediate Answer (EME_LIA) • Emergency Location Immediate Report (EME_LIREP)	Location query for a mobile device that has placed an emergency call, followed by one (EME_LIA) or more (EME_LIA plus several EME_LIREP) immediate asynchronous location responses
Standard Location Reporting Service	
• Standard Location Report (SLR) • Standard Location Report Answer (SLRA)	Location query where the mobile subscriber wants the LBS to receive the location of the device, that is, the opposite direction from SLIR/SLIA
Emergency Location Reporting Service	
• Emergency Location Report (EMEREP)	Emergency location report initiated by the network
Triggered Location Reporting Service	
• Triggered Location Reporting Request (TLRR) • Triggered Location Reporting Answer (TLRA) • Triggered Location Reporting Report (TLREP) • Triggered Location Reporting Stop Request (TLRSR) • Triggered Location Reporting Stop Answer (TLRSA)	Location query requesting location responses triggered at a certain time interval or by certain events

a network other than the home network of the subscriber wishes to obtain the subscriber's location information, while the Location server in the home network is performing the privacy checks. The MLS enabler contains a technical specification for the Roaming Location Protocol (RLP) [RLP TS] for such inter-Location server communication. In the 3GPP context, this specification will be an instantiation of the Lr reference point as defined in [3GPP TS 23.271]. RLP is based on MLP, and [RLP TS] refers to [MLP TS] where applicable. For further details on the RLP, the reader is referred to [RLP TS].

25.4 The Secure User Plane Location

Where we have seen that location architectures for the control plane have been developed by the standards organizations responsible for defining those control planes, the specification of User Plane Location technology is developed by the OMA. In the remainder of this chapter therefore, the focus will be on OMA SUPL. We will start this section by gradually building up the OMA SUPL Architecture, introducing all the architectural entities, their functions, and the interfaces they support. Once we have that under our belt, we will take a more detailed look at the SUPL interface specification, and conclude with an example SUPL sequence flow.

25.4.1 SUPL 1.0 Architecture

The SUPL 1.0 Architecture is defined in [SUPL-V1_0 AD]. SUPL is an enabler that defines the use of a User Plane data bearer for the exchange of positioning protocol operations and location assistance information (including A-GPS data) between a mobile device and the network. Such a mobile device is called a SUPL Enabled Terminal (SET), which is an A-GPS-capable device that supports the SUPL defined interface and can host a location requesting application, or SUPL agent. At the other end of the data bearer is the location server or SUPL Location Platform (SLP). The SUPL agent, requesting location information on behalf of an LBS application, can reside on the SET (SET-Initiated Location Procedure) or in the network (Network-Initiated Location Procedure). In its simplest form, the SUPL Architecture is shown in Figure 25.4. The SUPL defined reference point that demarcates the boundary between SET and SLP is the Lup reference point. Note that in Chapter 2 we argued for the use of interfaces over reference points. However, since the definition of location architectures started with the Control Plane Location Architectures in 3GPP and 3GPP2, which use reference points, the OMA LOC WG chose to continue to use reference points. Several interfaces are supported across the Lup reference point, as we shall see in the remainder of this section.

The SLP corresponds with the MPC and GMLC in 3GPP2 and 3GPP networks respectively and is responsible for two main functions, Service Management and Positioning Determination.

- Service Management deals with control functions such as setting up a session with the SET, which involves locating the SET by obtaining routing info and establishing Quality of Service (QoS) parameters for the connection.
- Positioning Determination deals mainly with positioning calculation (using any of the technologies introduced in Section 25.1) and with obtaining and delivering assistance data for A-GPS.

As these two functions are quite different in nature, the SUPL Architecture introduces two dedicated entities. The SUPL Location Centre (SLC) is in charge of the Service Management function, whereas the task of the SUPL Positioning Centre (SPC) is carried out by the Positioning

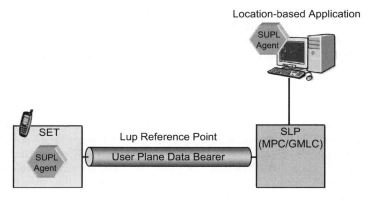

Figure 25.4   Basic SUPL Architecture

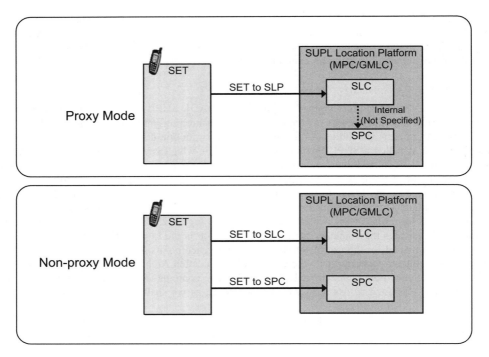

Figure 25.5 Operation modes for the SLC and SPC

Determination function. The SLC co-ordinates the operations of SUPL in the network and manages the SPC. The SPC provides GPS assistance data to the SET, and calculates the position of the SET.

There are two operation modes for the SLC and SPC. As the SLC manages the SPC, it can communicate with the SET on the SPC's behalf. This is called the proxy mode. In the proxy mode, the SET to SLP interface is used. The proxy mode is used in the GSM/UMTS Architecture defined by 3GPP. In a non-proxy mode, the SPC may communicate with the SET directly. For this scenario, SUPL has introduced the SET to SLC interface and the SET to SPC interface. The separation of the SPC and SLC is used in the CDMA Architecture defined by 3GPP2. A separate security association is used for each of the entities. Reasons to separate the SPC from the SLC may include the fact that each is a specialized, dedicated function. In addition, the Positioning Determination function can reside in an external domain, and hence requiring the separate security association. These two operation modes are depicted in Figure 25.5. The interface between the SLC and SPC, in case of proxy-mode configuration is not specified in SUPL Version 1.0, and hence marked as a dotted arrow.

As mentioned earlier, the SUPL agent acting on behalf of the location-based client application, can reside in two entities in the User Plane Architecture. In the case of the Network-Initiated Location Procedure, the SUPL agent resides in the network, or at a third party application server. This being the User Plane approach, the SUPL transaction will take place over a User Plane data bearer. However, in most 3G networks such as GPRS/UMTS networks, setting up a data connection toward a mobile device is not straightforward, as there could be no Packet Data Protocol (PDP) context open for the mobile device, or the mobile device might currently be detached from the data network altogether. So, as a first step the mobile device has to be triggered to attach itself to the data network. The SUPL Version 1.0 Architecture supports two mechanisms to initiate this trigger toward the SET, that is, the Short Message Service (SMS) or the Wireless Application Protocol (WAP). Figure 25.6 introduces these two mechanisms.

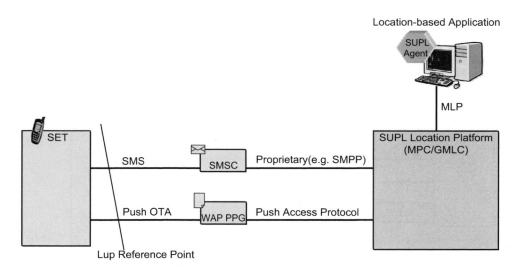

Figure 25.6 Network-Initiated Location Request

In case of SMS, the protocol used across the Lup reference point is the SMS tele-service. The protocol between the SMS Center (SMSC) and the SLP is proprietary, and may be realized using Short Message Peer-to-peer Protocol (SMPP). In case of WAP, the protocol across the Lup reference point is the Push Over-the-air (Push OTA) Protocol [PushOTA TS]. The protocol between the WAP Push Proxy Gateway (WAP PPG) and the SLP is the WAP Push Access Protocol (WAP PAP), as dictated by the WAP specifications [PushAP TS].

Before we put all the piece parts together, there are a number of other reference points included in the SUPL Architecture. These reference points, or interfaces that run across them, are not specified by OMA, but help place SUPL in the proper context. First of all, the SLP (in its realization as an MPC or GMLC) of course has its place in the overall LCS Control Plane Architecture. This is represented by the Lg and Lh reference points [3GPP TS 23.271] toward the control plane cloud. To support scenarios where the SET is roaming, the Lr reference point is shown between the SLP and SLPs in other networks. Now we can combine Figures 25.4–25.6 to compose the complete SUPL Version 1.0 Architecture, in Figure 25.7.

25.4.2 SUPL 2.0 Architecture

SUPL Version 1.0 has reached Approved Enabler Release status in June 2007. At the time of writing this book, SUPL Version 2.0 is nearing completion with the OMA LOC WG starting to look at even further extensions in SUPL Version 3.0.

The following is a summary of some of the extensions supported in SUPL Version 2.0 [SUPL-V2_0 AD]:

- Extension to allow all possible Navigation Satellite System assisted positioning technology to be utilized, for example, GPS, GALILEO, and so on.
- Support for SETs connected to a Wireless Local Area Network (WLAN). Location data such as the WLAN access point information currently serving the mobile device may be used for positioning.
- Security Improvements. This includes security aspects such as improved Denial of Service (DoS) protection, but it also includes privacy aspects. For example, SUPL Version 2.0 adds support for

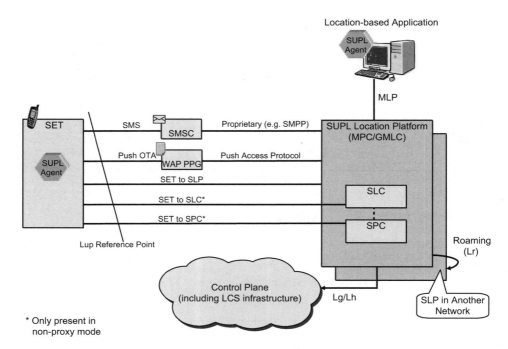

Figure 25.7   Completed SUPL 1.0 Architecture

notification and authorization for positioning based on the SET's location, to supports scenarios where the SET may not be positioned when it is located within a specific geographic area.

- Support for additional location request patterns. In Section 25.3.1 and Table 25.1 we have seen that MLP supports a number of MLP basic services, which in essence are location query patterns. SUPL Version 1.0 only supported the Standard Location Immediate Service. SUPL Version 2.0 adds support for other MLP basic services as well, that is, periodic location requests (e.g. for tracking) and triggered location requests (e.g. for event-based service invocation). Furthermore, SUPL Version 2.0 adds support for Enhanced Mobile Originated Requests, to locate other target devices (e.g. friend finder).

- Introducing the E-SLP, an Emergency SLP that handles the positioning for emergency call services in the serving network. An SLP dealing with emergency call services has some special requirements. Because of how emergency services are defined, the E-SLP has to be an SLP that either resides in or is associated with the mobile network that is currently serving the SET that initiated the emergency call. So in case of roaming scenarios, it cannot be the SLP in the home network.

- Specification of the Internal Location Protocol (ILP) between SLC and SPC. As shown in Figure 25.5, in SUPL Version 1.0 this interface was not specified. ILP is the protocol-level instantiation of the reference point between SLC and SPC.

- Introducing two additional options to contact the SET for the Network-Initiated Service mode.

  – Session Initiation Protocol (SIP) Push, an OMA Enabler where SIP is used as the transport bearer to push messages over the air [SIPPush RD];
  – User Datagram Protocol (UDP)/IP, in case the IP address of the SET is known.

Out of this list of extensions for SUPL Version 2.0, we will look at two in a little more detail. Figure 25.8 depicts the two additional triggering mechanisms for network-initiated location queries.

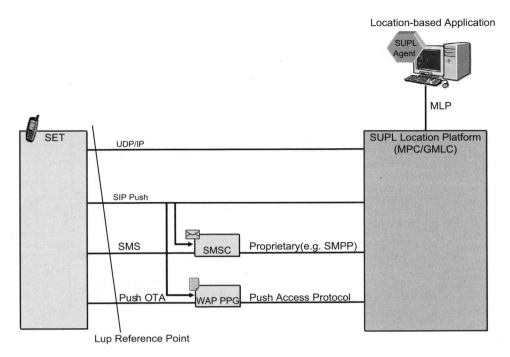

Figure 25.8 Network-Initiated Location in SUPL V2.0

These additional mechanisms allow the SLP to use more of the capabilities of the SET to trigger the SET to attach itself to the data network. In IP Multimedia Subsystem (IMS) or other SIP deployments, the IP address of the mobile device may be known at the SLP (as the SLP is involved in authentication of the SET and obtaining routing info). In this case, the SET can be triggered using a plain UDP/IP bearer. In addition, the SLP may make use of the SIP Push OMA enabler to trigger the SET. The SIP Push enabler uses the SIP/IP CN to transfer push content from the SLP (acting as the push sender agent) to the SET (acting as push receiver agent) using SIP messages. As shown in Figure 25.8, the SMSC or WAP PPG may also take on the role of a push sender agent.

In the first release of the OMA SUPL enabler, the reference point between the SLC and SPC was considered out of scope. In SUPL 2.0, a protocol instantiation of this reference point is introduced as the ILP. Section 25.4.3.2 provides further details on ILP. Here, we present Figure 25.9 to show ILP between the SLC and SPC.

If we now extend the SUPL Version 1.0 Architecture in Figure 25.7 with the additional functionality in Figures 25.8 and 25.9, we arrive at the SUPL Version 2.0 Architecture, as outlined in Figure 25.10. This architecture now includes the support of additional triggering mechanisms, as well as the protocol instantiation of the SLC to SPC reference point.

25.4.3 SUPL Technical Specifications

The previous two sections have described the SUPL 1.0 and 2.0 Architectures. This section will provide a concise description of the two technical specifications produced for the SUPL 2.0 enabler. It is beyond the scope of this book to delve into any of the protocol details. A flavor of the protocols, and the messages they support, is included though, to be able to understand the main SUPL sequence flow presented in Section 25.4.4.

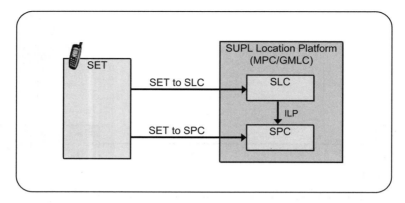

Figure 25.9 Internal Location Protocol – ILP

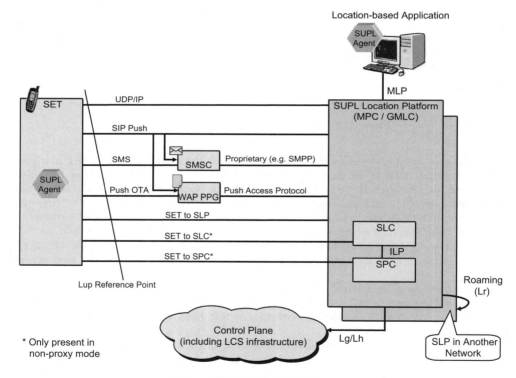

Figure 25.10 SUPL 2.0 Architecture

25.4.3.1 UserPlane Location Protocol (ULP)

The UserPlane Location Protocol (ULP) is specified in [ULP TS]. The transport protocol for ULP is TCP/IP, with of course the exception of the message used for the Network-Initiated Location Procedure, SUPL INIT. If you recall, separate mechanisms to trigger the SET to attach itself to the data network are used (i.e. SMS, Push OTA, SIP Push, and UDP/IP). All other ULP messages however are transported using TCP/IP.

Table 25.2 ULP Service Management (ULP SM) interface messages

Message name	Description
SUPL INIT	The SUPL INIT message is used by the SLP to initiate a SUPL session with the SET. This message is used in network-initiated SUPL services
SUPL SET INIT	The SUPL SET INIT message is used by the SET to initiate a SUPL session to locate the other SET
SUPL START	The SUPL START message is used by the SET to start a SUPL session with the SLP
SUPL TRIGGERED START	The SUPL TRIGGERED START message is used by the SET to start a triggered SUPL session with the SLP
SUPL RESPONSE	The SUPL RESPONSE message is used by the SLP as a response to a SUPL START message in a SET-initiated location request
SUPL TRIGGERED RESPONSE	The SUPL TRIGGERED RESPONSE message is used by the SLP as a response to a SUPL TRIGGERED START message
SUPL TRIGGERED STOP	The SUPL TRIGGERED STOP message is used by the SLP or SET to end an existing SUPL TRIGGERED session
SUPL END	The SUPL END message is used by the SLP or SET to end an existing SUPL session
SUPL AUTH REQ	The SUPL AUTH REQ message is only used in non-proxy mode for authentication of SET and SPC
SUPL AUTH RESP	The SUPL AUTH RESP message is only used in non-proxy mode for authentication of SET and SPC
SUPL NOTIFY	The SUPL NOTIFY message is only used by the SLP in notification based on the current location of the SET
SUPL NOTIFY RESPONSE	The SUPL NOTIFY RESPONSE message is used by the SET as a response to a SUPL NOTIFY message

ULP carries messages across the reference point between the SET and the SLP. As we have seen in Section 25.4.1, the SLP is responsible for two main functions Service Management and Positioning Determination. Two separate interfaces are supported across this Lup reference point for these two main functions. Table 25.2, reproduced from [ULP TS], lists the messages supported by the ULP Service Management (ULP SM) interface.

Table 25.3, reproduced from [ULP TS], lists the messages supported by the ULP Positioning Determination (ULP PD) interface.

The SUPL Report message is the actual location information report sent from the SLP to the SET. The message structure in Table 25.4, reproduced from [ULP TS], gives an indication of what type of location information is available to the LBS application. The main mandatory (M) parameter of interest is the 'position' parameter, which carries the calculated position of the SET, along with a time stamp. The data definition for the 'position' parameter is listed in Table 25.4. Fields like latitude and longitude, altitude (i.e. elevation), and velocity speak for themselves. The field 'uncertainty ellipse' may require a little more explanation.

As the precise geometric shape of the earth is highly irregular, with the earth's surface consisting of mountain ranges and the ragged bottom of the ocean, topographic and positioning applications make use of mathematical models of the physical earth. For this purpose, the WGS84 (World

Table 25.3 ULP Positioning Determination (ULP PD) interface messages

Message name	Description
SUPL POS	The SUPL POS message is used between the SLP and SET to exchange positioning procedure messages used to calculate the position of the SET
SUPL POS INIT	The SUPL POS INIT message is used by the SET to initiate the positioning protocol session with the SLP
SUPL REPORT	The SUPL REPORT message is used by the SLP or SET to report position estimate result
SUPL END	The SUPL END message is used by the SLP or SET to end an existing SUPL session
SUPL POS	The SUPL POS message is used between the SLP and SET to exchange positioning procedure messages used to calculate the position of the SET

Table 25.4 SUPL REPORT message

SUPL REPORT Message		
Parameter	Presence	Description
ReportDataList	O	SUPL REPORT contains the Report Data List as the only parameter. Additional parameters may be added in the future.
• Report Data	M	A sequence of N Reports each including Position Data and/or Measurement Data and/or Result Code.
– Position Data	O	A calculated position and the respective positioning mode used (optional).
• Position	M	The calculated position of the SET (including a time stamp).
• Posmethod	O	Positioning method with which the position was calculated (e.g. SET Based A-GPS, autonomous GPS, etc.).
– Measurement Data	O	Multiple Location ID.
– Result Code	O	Result Code describing why no position or measurement could be reported, for example, Out of radio coverage.
– Time Stamp	O	Time Stamp indicating when the SUPL REPORT message is sent.

Geodetic System 1984) uses geospatial data collected from triangulation, satellites, radar, and various other measuring sources to define a mathematically defined surface that approximates the shape of the physical earth. This surface is called a reference ellipsoid. A reference ellipsoid is defined in terms of a number of axes which we will not further explain in this book, but which you will see represented in the data type definition of 'uncertainty ellipse' in Table 25.5.

Table 25.5 Position data type

Parameter	Presence	Value/Description
Position	–	This parameter describes the position of the SET
• Time Stamp	M	Time when position fix was calculated
• Position Estimate	M	–
– Sign of Latitude	M	Indicates north or south
– Latitude	M	The latitude
– Longitude	M	The longitude
– Uncertainty Ellipse (semi-major, semi-minor, major axis)	O	The location expressed in terms of a WGS84 reference ellipsoid
– Confidence	O	Represents the confidence by which the position of a target entity is known, and is expressed as a percentage
– Altitude Information	O	Optional, present only for 3D position information
• Altitude Direction	M	Indicates height (above the WGS84 ellipsoid) or depth (below the WGS84 ellipsoid)
• Altitude	M	Provides altitude information in meters
• Altitude Uncertainty	M	Contains the altitude uncertainty
• Velocity	O	Speed and bearing values

25.4.3.2 Internal Location Protocol (ILP)

The ILP, introduced in SUPL 2.0, is a protocol instantiation of the SLC to SPC reference point [ILP TS]. The protocol is used between the SLC (SUPL Location Center) and a SPC (SUPL Positioning Center) for those operators who wish to use an open, defined interface between the SLC and the SPC. As in the ULP section, a brief overview of the messages supported by ILP is provided, for the purpose of understanding the sequence flow in Section 25.4.4.

Like with ULP and Lup, there are two interfaces supported across the reference point between the SLC and SPC. The ILP Positioning Control (ILP PC) interface is used for managing the session between the SLC and SPC, that is, establishment, maintenance and clearing of sessions. The messages supported by the ILP PC interface are listed in Table 25.6.

The ILP Positioning Data (ILP PD) interface is used to transport information used for the position calculation. The messages supported by the ILP PD interface are listed in Table 25.7. This interface is used in proxy mode only, since there is no direct communication between the SPC and the SET. The SLC will forward the location information received in a PMESS message to the SET on behalf of the SPC, in the ULP PD message SUPL POS.

25.4.4 SUPL Sequence Flow

The SUPL technical specifications for ULP and ILP contain an extensive collection of detailed call flow diagrams, covering a wide range of scenarios. The call flows address cases where the SET is roaming in a visited network or residing in the home network, using the proxy mode or the non-proxy mode, using the SET-Initiated or Network-Initiated mode, as well as a number of exception procedures for rainy day scenarios. Here, we describe one sunny day scenario to put all the various elements and their interfaces into perspective. The sequence flow diagram in Figure 25.11 depicts a Network-Initiated scenario, using the proxy mode for a non-roaming SET. It is not the intention to cover all possible exchanges or scenarios. Rather, this particular sequence flow aims to give the reader a good feel of the OMA Location enabler's capabilities and demonstrates how the various entities interact and how the various protocols and interfaces are engaged.

Table 25.6 ILP Positioning Control (ILP PC) interface messages

Message name	Description
PREQ	Used by the SLC to request a SUPL session of the SPC
PRESP	Response to a PREQ message and sent by the SPC to the SLC
PRPT	Used by the SPC to report a position estimate or an error to the SLC
PCANCEL	Used by the SLC to cancel an ongoing SUPL session in the SPC
PBORT	Used by the SPC to indicate to the SLC the abortion of a SUPL session
PLREQ	Used by the SLC (or SPC) to request a cell ID translation into coarse position estimate from the SPC (or SLC)
PLRES	Used by the SPC (or SLC) to report a coarse position estimate based on cell ID translation to the SLC (or SPC)
PAUTH	Used by the SLC to send SUPL authentication parameters to the SPC
PALIVE	Used by the SLC to verify the operational status of the SPC. The SLC may send the PALIVE message at any time. The SPC must then respond with a corresponding PALIVE message
PEND	Used by the SLC (or SPC) to inform the SPC (or SLC) about the end of a SUPL session

Table 25.7 ILP Positioning Data (ILP PD) interface messages

Message name	Description
PMESS	Bi-directional message used to carry the positioning payload
PINIT	Used by the SLC to initiate the positioning protocol session with the SPC

(1) The network resident SUPL Agent submits a location query for a given SET, by invoking the Standard Location Immediate Request (SLIR) message from the MLP Protocol (see Table 25.1).

(2) Upon receiving the SLIR message, the SLC engages in an ILP PC exchange with the SPC, in order to request service from the SPC, using the PREQ message. The SPC accepts the service request by responding with a PRES message. The positioning method (e.g. A-GPS) is now established.

(3) The SLC now initiates a location session with the SET. It needs to trigger the SET to connect itself to the data network, using the SUPL INIT message from the ULP SM interface. The SUPL INIT is sent using one of the supported triggering mechanisms (i.e. SMS, Push OTA, SIP Push, and UDP/IP).

(4) The SET now attaches itself to the data network and establishes a User Plane data bearer connection between itself and the SUPL agent.

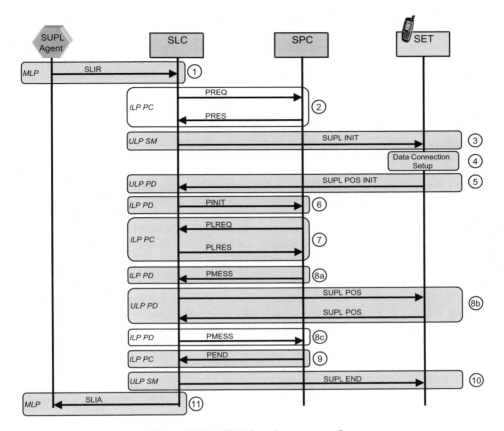

Figure 25.11 OMA Location sequence flow

(5) The SET initiates the positioning session by invoking the SUPL POS INIT message of the ULP PD interface. As the proxy mode is used, the SUPL POS INIT is destined for the SLC.

(6) In the proxy mode, the SLC communicates with the SET on the SPC's behalf. The SLC will engage in an ILP PD session with the SPC, by sending the PINIT message. If a position has been recently received or calculated by the SPC that matches the request in the PINIT message, the position is immediately returned to the SLC and no further positioning session exchange is required with the SET. In this scenario however, this is not the case, and hence some further set up is required between SLC and SPC.

(7) The SLC and SPC exchange the PREQ and PRES messages on the ILP PC interface to set up the SUPL session.

(8) Now the SPC and SET can engage in the positioning session exchange.

    (a) As this is the proxy mode, the SPC first sends a PMESS message to the SLC.

    (b) The positioning data is then exchanged between SLC and SET using a SUPL POS exchange over the ULP PD interface.

    (c) The positioning data is then relayed back to the SPC by the SLC again using the PMESS message.

(9) Once the positioning calculation process is completed, the SPC sends a PEND message to the SLC.

(10) The SLC can now terminate the positioning session with the SET by sending the SUPL END message.
(11) The SLC then returns the calculated position estimate to the network resident SUPL agent using the MLP Standard Location Immediate Answer (SLIA) message. This terminates the entire session and all resources can be released.

25.5 Summary

Location information can be gainfully deployed to enrich applications and enhance the end-user experience. In this chapter we have looked at two architectural approaches to location, that is, User Plane Location and Control Plane Location, and discussed where each of these is most suitable. So with all the benefits in terms of cost, performance and convenience that User Plane Location has over Control Plane Location, is there still a need or future for the latter? We have seen that Control Plane Location was well suited to support emergency services, where location information is required within the context of an emergency call. To achieve the same with User Plane Location, the deployed network has to support simultaneous voice and data with the ability to correlate the two, in order to provide concurrent emergency calls and associated location information. Until simultaneous voice and data will be widely deployed, there continues to be a role for Control Plane Location. The bulk of the attention in this chapter though was aimed at User Plane technologies, in particular the OMA SUPL enabler. We have introduced the high-level idea, gradually built up the architecture, introduced the various interfaces and their protocol realizations, and finally brought everything together in a sequence flow diagram. Hopefully this chapter leaves the reader with a good grounding in location technologies developed by the OMA.

26

The Mobile Application Environment

We see it all around us; mobile devices becoming ever more capable. Phones more often than not resemble PDAs, whereas the capabilities of PDAs come within reach of laptop computers. However, the fact remains that there is a literally incalculable number of less capable mobile devices out there. These are characterized by less powerful CPUs, less available memory Both Read-Only Memory (ROM) and Random Access Memory (RAM), restricted power consumption, smaller displays, and restricted input devices (such as a phone keypad). Yet we expect to be able to access our applications using these devices as well. We want to access the same web resources, be able to send and receive e-mail, and have access to our calendar.

However, if the applications are the same, while the devices are less capable, it must mean that something else has to give. You cannot have your cake and eat it too. The common technique to resolve such issues in the industry is to introduce a proxy server. The proxy engages with the application servers on behalf of the mobile device, using the existing protocols and interfaces, exchanging data objects defined for those protocols. The proxy then performs some transformation on the data and communicates with the mobile devices across a dedicated protocol optimized for the limitations of the device and the wireless bearer. Various Open Mobile Alliance (OMA) specifications address such characteristics of the mobile device as well as the network by adapting existing network technology to the special requirements of mobile devices. New technology may be introduced where appropriate.

A lot of the work in this field has been performed in the Wireless Application Protocol (WAP) Forum, and many good books on WAP have already seen the light of day. However, since the affiliation of the WAP Forum with the OMA, the Mobile Application Environment (MAE) sub-working group of Browser and Content Working Group (BAC WG), which evolved into the MAE *ad hoc* group of the Browser Technology Working Group (BT WG), has continued many of the specifications initiated in the WAP Forum and made significant progress. The field has advanced both in terms of new releases of former WAP specifications as well as new technologies in this space. As a result, these books describing WAP technologies have become somewhat outdated. For example, the focus of several WAP books has been on markup technologies like Wireless Markup Language (WML) and WMLScript, whereas the mobile profile of the Extended HyperText Markup Language (XHTML) has recently gained a lot more traction. And even though it is not the objective of this book to become the next WAP reference, no book on the OMA would be complete without

The Open Mobile Alliance   M. Brenner and M. Unmehopa
© 2008 Alcatel-Lucent. All Rights Reserved

at least a cursory review of the various BAC/BT MAE enablers. And so this brief chapter will do exactly that. Software developers of applications for mobile devices will not find the level of programmatic detail required to start using the described specifications. Rather, this chapter may serve as a cheat sheet to quickly identify the novel technologies and navigate to the particular specification of interest for the type of hands on information required. Other more recent enablers specified by the working groups that spawned from the BAC WG have already been covered in depth in Chapters 19–21.

26.1   The Mobile Web Architecture

Loosely spoken, MAE enables the World Wide Web (WWW) for the mobile environment. The general model for the WWW consists of applications and content that are presented in standard data formats, and are accessed and viewed using web browsers. The web browser sends requests for named data objects to a network server across a standard protocol, and the network server responds with the data encoded using the standard formats. Mobile enabling the WWW then means to introduce a proxy with the task of adapting the data objects such that they are suitable for transport across the wireless domain and processed by a mobile device [WAP AD]. This architecture is shown in Figure 26.1.

In such a proxy approach, it is important for the adapted requests and content formats to be based on well-known WWW technologies. The benefits are twofold. First, those technologies have been battle-hardened after years of commercial deployment in high-performance network environments. Leveraging existing protocols and techniques may hopefully lead to fewer growing pains and interoperability concerns. Secondly, the programming model and data formats will be familiar to the score of WWW application developers out there. This would instantly enable this entire Internet-savvy developer community to start developing applications for mobile devices.

The perceptive reader has of course recognized this proxy configuration from the description of the direct and indirect architecture models in Chapter 11, A Web Services Technology Realization of the OSE. The architecture in Figure 26.1 identifies a number of technology areas required to enable the WWW for mobile environments. There is a need for adjusted communication protocols to carry the adapted request. There is a need for adapted data formats for content objects, and content typing specific to the mobile environment. And there is a need for a mobile browser. The

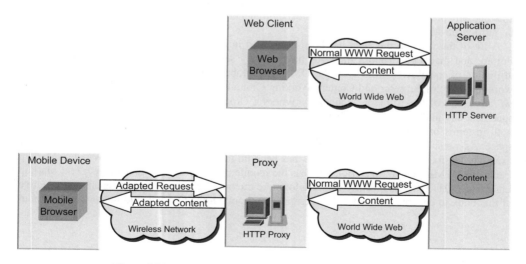

Figure 26.1   Mobile Application Environment Proxy Architecture

following sections will briefly introduce some of the various enablers that have been defined for the last two of these three categories. A description of the specific protocols, like the Wireless Datagram Protocol [WDP], Wireless Transport Protocol [WTP TS], and Wireless Session Protocol [WSP TS], is considered legacy information and hence outside the scope of this book.

26.2   Mobile Browser

Simply put, a browser is an application that allows you to locate and display web content. For ease of presentation, the content is annotated using a markup language. Mobile browsers differ from normal web browsers in that they access web content across a wireless bearer and present this content on a constrained device, with limited processing and display qualities. Accessing and transferring content across a wireless bearer requires adapted content data formats, which will be the topic of Section 26.3. This section deals with the markup languages used to render content on restricted devices, and the scripting languages used to augment the markup content.

26.2.1 Precursors

The first generation markup language for mobile browsers defined by WAP was WML. WML offered a scaled down version of HTML consisting of a subset of procedural elements more suitable for mobile devices. Like any markup language, WML allows one to define how content should be represented, for example, with text, images, and bullet lists. More elaborate display features are supported as well, such as selection lists, drop down menus, and forms. Nevertheless, all this content is static. Features like the ability to perform user input validation or advanced capabilities like access to functions of the device (e.g. to make a call, or access the Subscriber Identity Module (SIM) memory) cannot be supported by a markup language without modifying the markup itself. For this, you would have to include procedure logic within the WML markup. This is what WMLScript does. A scripting language complements the markup language with programmable features. WML and WMLScript have been around for a while, and have been the topic of numerous publications. The more respected among these publications, presented here for the interested reader, include [Singhal 2001, Foo 2001].

Another legacy technology covered here is Cascading Style Sheets (CSSs). Only a brief description is included as we will use this technology to highlight some of the salient points of other concepts presented later on in this section. Using a markup language to describe content as well as its presentation has been a cornerstone Web technology. A downside however is that when you wish to change the presentation, you need to change the markup, and hence change the content. CSSs allow you to separate the content (still described using the markup language) from the presentation (now described using the CSS). The single most important benefit of CSS is that it allows the same markup content to be rendered differently depending on the device. WAP Cascading Style Sheets (also referred to as Wireless Cascading Style Sheets (WCSS)) is defined as a simplified version of CSS with the addition of some specific extensions for use on wireless devices.

26.2.2 OMA Extensions

Since the publication of WML and WMLScript, both the capabilities of mobile devices as well as the developments of HTML have progressed significantly. This has led to the next generation of mobile markup and scripting languages, which will eventually bring about the deprecation of WML and WMLScript.

26.2.2.1 Markup Language Evolution

When it comes to data representation, the XML has undoubtedly emerged as the leading technology. This success has had its impact on other markup technologies as well. To capitalize on this trend, the World Wide Web Consortium (W3C) has defined XHTML by reformulating HTML as an application of XML. This implies that XHTML is conformant to XML, which brings along a number of benefits. The new language brings the extensibility of XML to HTML, while XHTML can take advantage of the extensive tool support for XML.

As with many specifications, XHTML provides developers with a myriad of features and options. To introduce a common denominator between implementations, W3C has defined XHTML Basic as a simplified version of XHTML. XHTML Basic includes the minimal set of language modules required to compose a valid XHTML document for browsers that do not support the full set of XHTML features. XHTML Basic is designed as a common base that may be extended.

OMA has taken the common denominator provided by XHTML Basic, and extended that base to offer a content authoring language that addresses the requirements from the mobile environment. The result is the XHTML Mobile Profile (XHTMLMP). The XHTMLMP is defined as a subset of XHTML and a superset of XHTML Basic. This implies that XHTMLMP content can be processed by XHTML browsers, and XHTML Basic content can be processed by XHTMLMP browsers [XHTMLMP TS].

For example, XHTML Basic removed the support for CSSs, frames, and scripting from the full version of XHTML. The support for CSSs was restored by introducing the use of WCSS, allowing different presentations of XHTMLMP authored content. Other elements and attributes from the full version of XHTML such as <i>, <b>, <small>, <big>, and <hr> were re-introduced as well. The support for forms including file upload was included as well.

XHTMLMP also brings back support for including a script within a markup document. The scripting capabilities are further elaborated in the next section.

26.2.2.2 Scripting Language Evolution

As XHTMLMP is set to replace WML as the markup language for mobile browsers, the support for scripting also needs to be revisited. The key scripting functionalities lost in the transition from WML to XHTML will have to be restored somehow. And here MAE has followed the pattern we have seen emerging throughout this chapter; re-using and profiling specifications defined elsewhere. A technology called ECMAScript is a widely used scripting language for XHTML. So where the markup language XHTML was profiled for mobile environments, it makes sense to also profile the scripting language to operate in concert with the XHTMLMP. This effort is called ECMAScript Mobile Profile (ESMP) [ESMP TS]. ESMP is to XHTMLMP what WMLScript is to WML. Semantically, ESMP will support all functionality present in WMLScript.

Profiling ECMAScript for mobile environments consisted of defining a subset language that left out a number of operators and constructors such that scripts do not need to be compiled on the mobile device itself. Dropping the need for compilation is a lot friendlier in terms of CPU cycles and memory, which are typically in short supply on resource constrained devices. In addition, the language subset reduced the number of requests the browser needs to make across the network to access online content, resulting in further efficiency gains.

In addition to subsetting, ESMP adds some functionality compared to ECMAScript as well. ECMAScript does not provide an execution environment. In order to provide the script with the ability to dynamically access and adapt the content and structure of a loaded document, the mobile browser provides a number of objects to ESMP, from the W3C Document Object Model [DOM2CORE]. This Document Object Model is a set of interfaces and objects used to represent and manipulate well-formed XML documents. Language-wise however, ESMP represents a proper subset of ECMAScript, which is supported by all major web browsers. Consequently, scripts written in ESMP should run on normal web browsers as well as mobile browsers.

Now that we have provided a cursory review of the markup and scripting capabilities of the mobile browser, let's take a look at the data formats for adapted content objects in the next section.

26.3 Mobile Content Data Formats

In order to deliver data to mobile devices, the proxy performs the function of transcoding. Transcoding is defined as the adaptation of content to different device capabilities or network conditions, and hence will change the actual representation of the data objects obtained from application servers on behalf of the mobile device. This section will present a selection of the mobile-specific data formats.

26.3.1 vObject

We have seen the use of profiles when describing the OMA Web Services Enabler Release in Chapter 11, and also in the previous section while discussing XHTMLMP. Profiles constrain implementation choices in a base specification, thereby providing guarantees for minimum interoperability. In addition, by clarifying ambiguities, profiles further contribute to increased interoperability. The vObject minimum interoperability profile [vObject TS] takes a set of three base specifications from two industry consortia and adapts them for use in a mobile environment. The three base specifications are [vCard2.1] for the exchange of electronic business cards, [vCal1.0] for the exchange of electronic calendaring and scheduling information, and [vBook1.0] for the exchange of electronic bookmarks. Collectively, these electronic formats are referred to as vObjects.

An example of an interoperability issue resulting from an ambiguity in the specification is the manner in which to specify all-day events in vCalendar. Although all-day events are a common feature in commercial calendar or scheduler implementations, the specification does not provide a standard way to express these. The vObject minimum interoperability profile has resolved this ambiguity by agreeing to define an all-day event as one starting at midnight (00:00) and ending at midnight on the following day (24 h). This may seem rather trivial but because of the ambiguity, equally valid implementations might specify such events using (24h00–23h59) or (00h00–00h00), leading to incompatibilities when performing synchronization.

Another example becomes evident when looking at the various options for content types that are supported, for example by [vCard1.2]. To account for a choice of electronic message formats, a vCard object can be defined in terms of so-called 'plain' content type when transferred as a legacy Simple Mail Transfer Protocol (SMTP) e-mail message, or of the specific 'vCard' content type when transferred as a Multipurpose Internet Mail Extensions (MIME) entity. When downloaded to a mobile browser as part of a synchronization operation, these different content types for the object can result in interoperability issues.

The observant reader might ask if there is anything mobile-specific about the vObject profile as specified by the OMA. After all, an all-day event is an all-day event, whether you synchronize your calendar on your mobile phone or on your laptop. There are two considerations, however, that are particularly relevant in a mobile environment. In desktop environments, where resources are generally not an issue, implementations are often seen to implement all or most features specified, mandatory, as well as optional. This reduction in optionality leads to fewer interoperability issues. In mobile environments however, resource restrictions and reduced capabilities require careful consideration of what feature subset to support. A minimum subset of the more basic functions is often selected, leaving out the more exotic and less used features. Interoperability is then facilitated by an agreed common subset, which is what the vObject minimum interoperability profile provides. The second consideration is the multitude of devices in the market. Pair-wise testing between the server and each of the devices supported in a given network is simply not a scaleable solution. This enormous plurality of clients is much less of an issue in other environments. Having said all this though, environments other than the mobile space would be wise to take note of the OMA vObject specifications as well, as the value of removing ambiguities extends beyond constrained mobile devices.

26.3.2 SVG for the Mobile Domain

Interactive multimedia content on mobile devices is an attractive way to enrich the end-user experience of mobile applications and appreciably enhances the attraction of the device. Many technologies exist to encode images and define the operations to manipulate that image. One such technology, Scalable Vector Graphics (SVG), is an XML-based graphics language that describes high-quality two-dimensional graphics with vector shapes, text, and embedded raster graphics, in a compact manner. Vector images can be scaled continuously in that they are not limited to a single, fixed, pixel size. Being vector-based, content can be manipulated without any loss in image quality, for example, when zooming in or resizing. And perhaps more importantly in wireless networks, where radio resources are a scarce commodity, content can be adapted without having to collect any new data from the content server. For example, map images can be panned or rotated by the user. This is a major difference with, for instance, bitmap images.

SVG specifications were developed and published by the W3C, and were predominantly aimed at graphics displayed on web pages. SVG is defined such that domain-specific profiles can be defined by listing the SVG capabilities they allow as a subset of the total SVG specification. Two examples of such profiles are the mobile profiles SVG Basic (SVGB) and SVG Tiny (SVGT), where the first focuses on high-end mobile devices like PDAs while the latter is directed at less capable devices such as most cell-phones. These mobile SVG profiles attempt to maximize compatibility with SVG 1.2 to allow for the display of existing web content, limiting the need for content adaptation to a minimum.

SVG provides support for basic graphic attributes like shapes (e.g. circles, ellipses, polygons) and color, and also for more sophisticated attributes. For example, SVG includes provisions for so-called 'pointer-events' that allow developers to specify under what circumstances a given graphics element can be the target of a pointer event (like a mouse click). Other examples include color attributes like 'gradient', which defines continuous color transitions within an SVG element, or 'animation' which includes motion effects like fade-in and fade-out, growing, and shrinking, etc.

The OMA enabler 'SVG for the Mobile Domain' takes as input the W3C SVGT 1.2 specification and ensures that these profiles meet the requirements of OMA members [SVG RD]. For example, what are the requirements on WCSS when supporting an SVG profile and what are the interaction modes needed to support SVG within the XHTMLMP document environment? The technical specification contains a set of tables with normative references to the SVGT 1.2 specification [W3CSVGT], and identifies the elements and attributes that are either mandatory or optional to fulfill OMA requirements. 'SVG for the Mobile Domain' thus allows an OMA SVG client to be embedded in the mobile browser, bringing a significant new look-and-feel to the applications on mobile devices.

26.3.3 SMIL for the Mobile Domain

One of the more obvious ways to adapt content for the mobile domain is to make it smaller. And a trivial way to make one big file smaller is to break it up into pieces. In case of multimedia content, an audiovisual object can be broken up into separate files and streams (audio, video, text, and images), each sent to the mobile device separately. Once available on the mobile device, the individual pieces are assembled and displayed together as if they were one single multimedia stream. It is important to make sure the parts are synchronized, when assembling the piece parts into a single stream. For example, audio should be in lip sync with the video, animated slide presentations should have well-timed build ups, etc.

When left to individual enablers dealing with transporting, rendering, or presenting multimedia content, the support for synchronization may be realized in vastly different ways. Such diversity would lead to increased implementation cost and increased complexity in authoring multimedia content. The W3C therefore has produced a single multimedia synchronization technology called the Synchronized Multimedia Integration Language (SMIL, pronounced as 'smile'). SMIL is an

XML-based language that allows for the authoring of interactive audiovisual presentations, which integrate streaming audio and video with images, text or any other media types. These media types may be obtained from separate content servers, where SMIL provides functions for defining sequences and duration of elements from all these sources, and functions for defining position and visibility of such elements. SMIL supports a number of modules, each introducing a set of semantically related elements, properties, and attributes. For example, there are elements for both basic duration-related functions such as repeating an animation for a number of iterations, as well as more involved functions such as accelerating or decelerating certain elements, or restarting and freezing animations.

The OMA enabler 'SMIL for the Mobile Domain' takes as input the W3C SMIL 2.1 specification and defines a profile that meets the requirements of OMA members [SMIL RD]. The enabler identifies the subset of features and modules of SMIL 2.1 that are appropriate for the mobile environment and less capable mobile devices. Profiling will also be based on the assessment what features of SMIL 2.1 are aligned with OMA SVG for Mobile Domain for its SMIL animation use.

26.3.4 Where Browser and Content Meet

We have seen that SMIL has been defined using a modular language structure, based on XML. This fosters the integration of SMIL constructs into other XML-based languages. For example, basic timing and animation modules from SMIL can be integrated into the other XML-based content data format we have described, that is, SVG. And moreover, the same modular language structure makes it possible to incorporate SMIL and SVG data objects into XHTMLMP markup content documents, providing a rich mobile browsing experience.

26.4 Multiple Interaction Modalities and Devices

So far, we have looked at MAE activities from the perspective of the capabilities of the mobile device and the wireless bearer, both of which have certain restrictions when compared to client devices in a wired environment. We have seen the use of a proxy for content adaptation or transcoding (Section 26.3), and technologies for a mobile browser capable of accessing and presenting the transcoded data objects (Section 26.2). Let us now take the point of view of the end-user.

There are two aspects to consider here, again related to the resource constraints of mobile devices. The first aspect is that of modality, or modes of interaction with the device. Interaction modes for mobile devices have evolved beyond the keyboard and small display of the most basic mobile phones. More advanced methods like a mouse, a stylus, a click-wheel, or even voice recognition capabilities are available on many devices to provide input. Among the more sophisticated output modes you may find audio recordings and speech synthesis. The end-user should be able to freely take advantage of the modality best suited or most appropriate in a particular situation.

For example, during your morning commute in a crowded train, common courtesy for your fellow passengers may urge you to use the keypad when selecting an address to send a text message, rather than opting for the voice-activated address book. In the confines of your own car however, you are your own audience and other considerations will apply. For example, when inputting large volumes of text, traffic safety is best served by using the speech recognition feature of your device rather than the limited numeric keypad. However, the choice of modality may not only be based on circumstance or preference. For example, the visually impaired may have to rely on only a subset of available modalities for interacting with common devices in the market. Specialized devices may be equipped with dedicated modalities like Braille features or touch sensitive interfaces.

The second aspect is that of multiple devices. Not only do end-users switch from one device to another, but also often they carry more than one device at the same time, or carry a mobile device while sitting at their desktop. Multidevice applications combine input and output on more than one device. For example, a route-finder application may provide spoken directions on your phone, while printing a map on your printer.

These user-centric requirements for Multimodal and Multidevice (MMMD) services are described in [MMMD RD]. With multimodal access and multidevice capabilities, end-users have the flexibility to pick and choose the right mode and most appropriate device for a particular task and particular situation. MMMD applications provide a compelling user interface which exploits the advantages of each modality or device type without being constrained by their limitations, allowing for ubiquitous, peripheral interaction.

This is a very attractive value proposition, but it does introduce an interesting problem. To account for input using different modalities, possibly originated from multiple devices, the content and services somehow need to be synchronized. Brute force solutions could be conceived whereby slightly different instances of the same application or the same content are offered via different channels for each of the modalities and devices, but such solutions are simply not scaleable. A better solution would be to have the same application delivered and rendered for each modality and every device. The synchronization and interaction with the various modalities and devices needs to happen in such a way that the application and any involved OMA enabler remain blissfully unaware. Remember the OMA neutrality principles?

Figure 26.2 shows the logical architecture for the MMMD enabler. The MMMD Back-end is an amalgamated component consisting of the application logic and the OMA enablers support-ing that application, without any consideration of multiple modalities or devices. To perform the synchronization of the data flows and the co-ordination of the data itself in a way transparent to the MMMD Back-end, a new component called the Interaction and Multimodal Synchronization Manager (IM/SM) is introduced. The IM/SM resides between the MMMD Back-end and the user agents, a component that logically represents a modality for a given device.

The IM/SM communicates with the MMMD Back-end via I2 interfaces, that is, interfaces not defined by the MMMD enabler. In fact, these are the interfaces that provide the content streaming

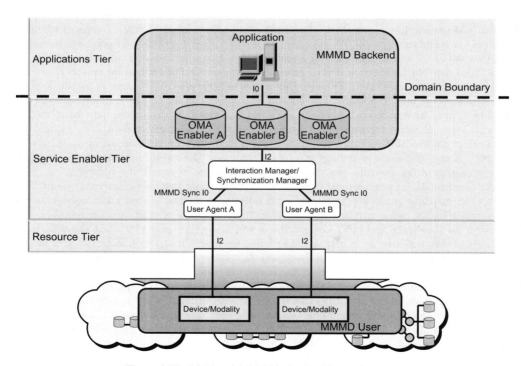

Figure 26.2 Multimodal, Multidevice Enabler Architecture

toward the user. The IM/SM is inserted on that path to transparently perform its functions. The multimodal synchronization protocol between the IM/SM and the user agents on the other hand is an I0 interface, defined by the MMMD enabler. It is responsible for synchronizing the exchanges among modalities and devices.

Before interaction and synchronization for multiple modalities can take place, configurations of user agents need to be registered in the MMMD Registry. A second I0 interface, the Multimodal and Multidevice Configuration Protocol (MMCP) is used for this purpose. For reasons of simplicity, the Registry and the MMCP interface are not shown in Figure 26.2, nor are the various deployment configurations or details of the user agent. Further details can be found in [MMMD AD].

26.5 Summary

The review of MAE specifications and the mobile web architecture in this chapter present a rather gross oversimplification. To do justice to the vast array of specifications produced first in the WAP Forum and continued and further enhanced in BAC MAE, and subsequently in BT MAE, would warrant a book in itself, and in fact many have been published. Nevertheless, we have attempted to provide the reader with an appreciation for the work, with a focus on the more recent topics. We have introduced a proxy architecture to deal with less capable mobile devices, and the specifications for adjusted content types and format as well as the mobile browser capabilities that are required in such an architecture. We have also taken the point of view of the end-user and introduced the MMMD enabler currently under specification by BT MAE.

The material presented in this chapter has hopefully served to provide an update of the work on the MAE, since the affiliation of the WAP Forum with the OMA. The objective is to equip the reader with a quick reference and navigational aid to the more detailed specifications in the vast area addressed by the BT MAE *ad hoc* group.

27

Recent Topics

As outlined in the preface, when describing technology that is still very much in the process of being defined or standardized, it is inevitable that one takes a snapshot of a moving target. The same holds true for this book, as new versions of Open Mobile Alliance (OMA) specifications are being continuously published. At the time of writing the book, many other topics are progressing. It was impossible, or at least impractical, to cover all of the work in detail. Not only because of the constraints of time and space, but especially because some of the more recent work has not matured enough to warrant a detailed chapter. However, some of the on-going work will result in enablers that may have significant impact going forward, and a sneak preview of what this work is all about may be welcomed by the reader. The following sections will describe some of the more recent OMA activities.

27.1 The General Service Subscription Management Enabler

Like any other for-profit organizations, service providers derive main revenues from a solid, loyal customer base to which they sell services. Subscription services are a preferred way to offer services to their customer base, since they allow for a much more accurate forecast of the revenue. What are subscription services? These are long-term services where a consumer is billed periodically on an on-going basis. The typical services in this category are volume-based or unlimited messaging services such as Short Message Service (SMS), Multimedia Messaging Service (MMS), content-related services such as ring tones, wallpaper, daily news, cartoons, pop trivia, music and video alerts, weather updates, daily news, sports results, horoscopes, topic-specific messages (e.g. motivational, religious), targeted advertisements, or services that facilitate access to other on-demand services (e.g. Wi-Fi® access in different locations, or location-based services). And although pre-paid is gaining grounds, the plain old, tried and tested voice telephony service is still bringing in revenue as a subscription service as well.

Subscription services have many things in common, which leads to the conclusion that a common management model for subscriptions is not only possible, but also desirable. Common characteristics include the occurrences of service per subscription per interval and frequency of alerts, and the ability to customize preferences related to the subscription. However, they also include the fact that subscription services are charged at a set price, at regular intervals, and share flexibility in the way those services are subscribed to and paid for. For example, mobile services may be subscribed to at the mobile network operator, or directly at the service provider (e.g. content provider), although the charges may show as added on the consumer's monthly bill for cellular phone services.

The Open Mobile Alliance   M. Brenner and M. Unmehopa
© 2008 Alcatel-Lucent. All Rights Reserved

With multiple actors (service provider, network operator, subscriber, end-user) involved in interactions for creating, delivering, and consuming subscription services, which share certain characteristics, service subscription management becomes a necessity, and doing it in a standard way becomes a true possibility.

27.1.1 Prior Work – Subscription Management

Subscription Management (SuM) specifications work has captured the attention of several standards and/or specifications organizations. SuM is defined in a manner consistent with the generic management architecture for 3GPP networks, which is a hierarchical system. The network is modeled as consisting of Network Elements (NEs). Examples of NEs include the radio base station controllers, the switches, the subscriber databases, etc. These NEs are then managed by Network Managers (NMs) that are responsible for the management of a set of functionally related NEs. Standardized interfaces are supported between NE and NM. Some of the NEs deal with provisioning of services, and may store or manage parts of the data required for provisioning. A specific type of provisioning data is called the subscription profile. This subscription profile, required by service providers, value added service providers and Mobile Operators in order to provision, control, monitor, and bill the configuration of services that they offer to their subscribers, is the focus of 3GPP SuM.

The SuM Architecture is defined in [3GPP TS 32.141], and it addresses the management of Subscription Profile Components (SPCs) stored in NEs for the purpose of providing services to specific subscribers. While, in general, SPCs are outside the jurisdiction of Home Subscriber Server (HSS), certain SPCs can be associated with the HSS for those services that are controlled by the HSS. SPCs are located either in the NEs themselves or in the NMs. Operations System Functions (OSF) functionality, therefore, can be implemented in the NEs or in the NMs. SuM OSFs for network management and service management are located in network/service management systems. The SuM Integration Reference Point (SuM IRP) is the particular integration reference point of interest. It is composed of a SuM IRP agent (included in an NE) and a SuM IRP manager (included in an NM).

SuM IRP solution sets may re-use 3GPP General User Profile (GUP) specifications stage 3 [3GPP TS 29.240], which describe a network protocol for accessing user-related information located in different entities in the network.

SuM configuration management requirements are in [3GPP TS 32.171], which mandates following the 3GPP configuration management requirements as applicable to the Integration Reference Point (IRP). Finally, [3GPP TS 32.172] describes the requirements for the Network Resource Management (NRM) IRP, containing the Information Object Classes (IOCs), attributes, relations etc. for SuM.

Other organizations that invest efforts in this topic include the Telecommunications & Internet Services & Protocols for Advanced Networking (TISPAN) and the TM Forum (see Section 27.3.1).

27.1.2 New Work – General Service Subscription Management

The OMA General Service Subscription Management (GSSM) enabler regards service subscription as the information that describes the commercial relationship between a subscriber and the service provider (e.g. operator). The use of the term commercial relationship is a very strong indication of the importance of this work for service provider (see Chapter 5). It is, therefore, not very surprising to see that service providers in the OMA, eager to get a handle on having a standard way to conduct SuM for the growing variety of online services, are not ready to wait or settle for work performed in other standards organizations, at a time when it may not be crystal clear to them what they may get, or when they will get the results.

What distinguishes OMA GSSM work from the SuM work in 3GPP and TISPAN, and the information model work in TM Forum? GSSM's goals are consistent with the broader OMA goals: develop general service subscription management functions compliant to the principles of exposing re-usable interfaces, neutral to underlying networks and realization technologies, in order to avoid SuM to be handled locally by each enabler (a dangerous trend leading to costly silo-architecture), or handled in a way that only works when deployed over a specific network bearer. The functions GSSM plans to expose via interfaces include the following:

- service subscription handling (e.g. subscribe/unsubscribe, suspend/resume/renew subscription, query for subscription information);
- service subscription validation (e.g. verifying subscription before granting a service request, verifying service request against service usage directives);
- service subscription profile access.

GSSM will also send subscription notification and confirmation (e.g. notification of change of service subscription to affected principals, asking for conformation on notifications), using interfaces defined by other resources for this purpose.

With all the work going on in other standards bodies, the bottom line is that the service providers still do not have standard interface, and protocols realizations to support those functions. It may also have something to do with subtle differences in what different standards bodies mean by service (see Chapter 5 for a broad definition). So, the attraction for the service provider to do this work in OMA is the mentality of how OMA members approach any body of work in OMA: the focus is on how to get data (defined in OMA or elsewhere) exchanged between resources that have a well-defined role and behavior, regardless of how that behavior is modeled or realized.

To be specific, while GSSM work is still in its infancy, we don't think that the focus will be on the service subscription management information model. Although such model will have to be subsumed, OMA GSSM would probably re-use an information model provided by another standards body, rather than create their own. However, GSSM will focus on the information that is provisioned or obtained, and supported by the information model. Where such information is not yet available from other standards bodies, GSSM will have to define it (and probably liaise with those standards bodies to ensure that it gets represented in the information model). For example, GSSM assumes that there is a relationship between the Subscription Profile and the Service Preferences, but that one does not have to subsume the other (they can be separate pieces of information). And that is because the Subscription Profile's main contributor and beneficiary is the Subscriber, while in the case of the Service Preferences it is the end-user (which may or may not be the same as the Subscriber).

Another good example of GSSM focus (or lack thereof) is the protocol to be used. If available, GSSM would prefer to re-use protocols specified by other standard bodies, rather than create their own or even have to be in the position to select between several candidates. The question is: are the protocols from other standards bodies appropriate for binding the GSSM messages to them? For example, currently, 3GPP is only looking into the use of GUP specifications for 3GPP's SuM work. GUP specifications can help provision and/or retrieve user data deemed as 'user profile' from pretty much anywhere in the network. However, that does not solve the requirements for subscription checking, subscription pausing/suspending/resuming, or service subscribe/unsubscribe.

27.1.3 Related Activities

The TM Forum produced recommendations that are very much in scope for SuM. TM Forum's Shared Information/Data (SID) model (see [TM Forum GB 922]) defines the SID Framework, used to model the SID model business view content. Among other concepts defined, SID also defines business entities such as 'Product' and 'Service' and the relationship between them. This is interesting because using the case of GSSM, the Subscription Profile relates to the SID 'Product' business entity, while the 'Service Preferences' relates to the 'Service' business entity. As we discussed before, Subscription Profile could include Service Preferences, but does not have to, and certainly does not have to include all Service Preferences. The fact that in SID there is a defined relationship between 'Product' and 'Service' makes the GSSM assumptions consistent with the SID model.

Other related activities in the industry include work in progress in the Working Group8 (WG8) in TISPAN. While the broader charter of the group is Network Management, the group started working in 2006 on SuM, with specifications in progress for requirements, information model, architecture, and solution set (see [ETSI DTS 188 002-2]). The work is supposed to cover interactions between service provider and subscriber, support validation (registration, authentication, authorization) of a service subscriber request, collection, distribution, and storage of Service Profile information for the user, and management of access and delivery resources needed by the service. The Next Generation Networking (NGN) SuM intent is to leverage 3GPP specifications mentioned before, while questions remain about harmonizing requirements for fixed/mobile convergence (3GPP is focused on mobile services), and about solution sets using newer technologies (e.g. Web Services). TISPAN's WG8 also is a strong supporter of the TM Forum's Enhanced Telecom Operations Map (eTOM), and would like to see 3GPP's SuM IRP evolve in a manner consistent with eTOM.

In the final analysis, it may well become evident that work in the different standards bodies discussed is more complementary than overlapping, in particular, because of the different focus (i.e. focus on mobile network services in 3GPP, focus on fixed/mobile convergence information models in TISPAN, and focus on re-usable interfaces and components, neutral to underlying networks and realization technologies, to support building of new applications and services, in OMA).

27.2   Device Profile Evolution

One of the aims of OMA is to grow the market for applications delivered to devices in a mobile environment. When designing such applications, developers cannot assume homogeneity of such devices, as device capabilities vary greatly. Not only is there great diversification from one device to another, the capabilities of any one given device may also change dynamically over time, sometimes even within a single session. The number of different devices supported by an application is an important factor in determining whether the application will be a commercial success or not. Consequently, developing applications requires application rendering and content adaptation. And the process of content adaptation and application rendering requires knowledge of the device's capabilities and properties.

27.2.1 Prior Work – Static Properties

There are two existing and compatible standards available in the industry that deal with device capabilities. The World Wide Web Consortium (W3C) has developed the Composite Capabilities (CC)/Preferences Profile (PP) specification, which defines a structured set of information (a list of attribute names and associated values) describing the capabilities of the device. The second existing standard is the OMA specification for User Agent Profile (UAProf), inherited through the affiliation of the Wireless Application Protocol (WAP) Forum. Like CC/PP, UAProf defines the schema and a base vocabulary of property descriptions for the use in device profiles. The structure of the schema is defined in terms of device attribute definitions and the semantics for those attributes. All this information is maintained in a repository of device capabilities. The repository can then be browsed and queried for device capabilities and properties, based on specific search criteria.

Device capabilities may include input and output capabilities such as the support of a keyboard, stylus or click-wheel, or display characteristics like height and width dimensions, resolution and color support. Other characteristics like Operating System, processor type, browser, and markup language support can be part of the device profile as well. These capabilities of the device are determined by its hardware characteristics, user settings, and installed software components. What is common about these capabilities is that they are static properties, that is, they do not change over time. CC/PP and UAProf lack the ability to allow applications to respond in real-time to changes in the device's properties. The real issue is that, while most nominal physical properties of the device exposed via CC/PP and UAProf may not change, some of the actual visible and usable properties may change.

27.2.2 New Work – Dynamic Properties

Many of the new devices entering the market sport capabilities of an increasingly dynamic character. The model of a device with pre-configured static capabilities, as assumed by CC/PP and UAProf, is no longer applicable. Mobile devices may be equipped with Wireless Local Area Network (WLAN) capabilities, an MPEG-1 Audio Layer 3 (MP3) player, a camera, Bluetooth adapters, and the like. Plugging in one of the adapters or powering off the WLAN radio causes an instantaneous change in the capabilities of the device. Consequently, these actions dynamically change the content appropriate for delivery to the device.

The OMA Device Profile Evolution (DPE) enabler is being developed to manage the publication of a device's hardware, software, and network properties as they change over time, possibly even during the course of an ongoing session. Dynamic device properties are those attributes that may change their value as a result of hardware, software, or configuration changes on the device. Such dynamic device properties may be gainfully deployed by applications to adapt and render content appropriately for the target device. The goal of the OMA DPE enabler is to define an enhanced device profiles mechanism that allows a device to convey dynamic device properties to an application in real-time, thereby ensuring that the application can provide content best suited to the capabilities of the device at that time [DPE RD]. Such an enhanced device profile will also enable rapid categorization of devices in classes based on their capabilities, thus significantly facilitating content distribution to large audiences that use devices with a similar dynamic profile (i.e. expose a common subset of dynamic device properties for a reasonable amount of time).

27.2.3 DPE Examples

A straightforward example of a dynamic property is the condition of the network. Consider an end-user who is engaged in a streaming session and is presented with content that is adapted to the particular capabilities of that device. When the device's network bandwidth changes during the ongoing streaming session, the application may want to subsequently adapt the content to these new network bandwidth conditions.

The following, more involved use case is taken from [DPE RD]. Consider an end-user who has selected the device's speaker as the preferred audio output mode. The end-user accesses an application that plays audio clips of the latest sports headlines. The application gets notified by the DPE client software running on the device of the device's capabilities (its current software, hardware, and content rendering capabilities), as well as any end-user settings that may apply (in this case the selected speaker audio mode). The application receives the end-user request for sports headlines along with the device profile, and proceeds to adapt the content and delivery mechanism according to the end-user audio playback capabilities. Halfway through the session, the end-user enters a quiet environment and places the device's loudspeaker on mute. The DPE client software running on the device notifies the application of this dynamic change in audio output modality. The application can now use this information in its content adaptation process, for example, by converting the sports clips to a text format for presentation on the device's display. This dynamic adaptation provides the end-user with a seamless service experience, while conserving resources by avoiding the continuous sending of audio clips that cannot be consumed anyway using the new audio modality. The end user now leaves the quiet environment and starts to drive in her car. The device's Bluetooth feature detects the presence of in-car speakers, and the device's audio stream is automatically routed through to these speakers. The DPE client software running on the device notifies the application that the device's audio output modality has changed once more. The application thus reverts to sending the sports clips in audio format. This use case shows how real-time knowledge of the device's dynamic properties is of value to applications in their effort to offer a seamless, context-aware service experience.

27.2.4 DPE Related Activities

Related activities in the industry are taking place in the W3C Device Descriptions Working Group (DDWG) and Device Independence Working Group (DIWG). To ensure interoperability, a common base vocabulary for device capabilities and properties among these two activities and the DPE activity would be very beneficial. DDWG, DIWG, and DPE are engaged in a liaison dialogue to develop such a vocabulary in close collaboration.

27.3   Converged IP Messaging Enabler

Messaging has been a core activity in OMA since the early days of its predecessor, the WAP Forum. Many market requirements have been fulfilled by the development of messaging capabilities in the OMA. The main approach taken has been one of analyzing the market requirements and developing something new to cater to all perceived market requirements for a given service. This has been a useful approach so far, as it has provided drivers for the OMA to develop specifications that can be deployed in the market to bring benefits to the mobile community.

More recently it has been realized that the more we develop 'something new' to cater to the 'current' requirements, the more the shelf of enabler products creaks with all the new things added, and the harder it is for the mobile community to decide which enablers to deploy. Market demands in practice dictate that a given operator will not need everything in one enabler and sometimes needs to 'mix and match' features. If the core transport capabilities are incompatible, then the right feature set cannot be delivered to the market without significant proprietary deviation from the standards.

Together with the general mobile community drive for Session Initiation Protocol (SIP) based services, in general, and application of the OMA Service Environment (OSE) principles, this has led to re-thinking in the OMA about how we develop new messaging services, and the birth of a new enabler called Converged IP Messaging (CPM) that aims to deliver a single platform with 'mix and match' capabilities so that operators can rely on the following:

* single core platform;
* expansion capabilities to cover many different messaging experiences;
* handsets with single client.

This chapter discusses how OMA has set about achieving this vision.

27.3.1 Multimedia Messaging Service

The Multimedia Messaging Service (MMS) was born from discussions in the European Telecommunications Standards Institute (ETSI) about Third Generation Mobile (3G) and what the messaging needs would be in the 3G. The thinking then was that 3G would be all about multimedia experience, and therefore, a new 3G messaging service would be needed to replace the 2G Short Message Service (SMS). The intention was to have something that could carry any type of media, including text, and to provide the capability to completely supersede SMS so that SMS would not be needed in the 3G era and operators could focus on a single 3G messaging platform.

Requirements were developed in the Third Generation Partnership Project (3GPP). It was decided that each operator would handle incoming and outgoing messages for their own customers, unlike SMS where each message is handled by a single operator (the operator whose customer sends the message). An architecture for delivering this service was developed in 3GPP and then the WAP Forum was asked to handle the detailed specifications.

In the WAP Forum, work was already underway on mobile browsers. To expedite the development of MMS, it was decided that an appropriate mechanism for communication between the device and network would be to re-use a form of HTTP. This would work well for a device wanting to send a message, or a device knowing that there was a message to receive; however, there was no mechanism inherent in HTTP to tell the device that there was a message waiting. So, a mechanism had to be developed to advise the mobile about messages waiting. It had to be a simple mechanism which was available at the application layer so that the MMS service could make use of it. Again, to expedite delivery of the MMS service it was decided to re-use SMS to alert the device to waiting messages.

So, while the original aim had been for SMS to be unnecessary in the 3G era, due to the split of responsibility between standards bodies and the need for a quick solution, we ended up needing to have SMS platforms to support MMS in the 3G era. Also, the solution for MMS was complicated and expensive to deploy, which meant that for simple text messaging it did not make sense to use MMS rather than SMS.

27.3.2 Instant Messaging and Presence Service

During the period where 3G services were being developed, access to the Internet was becoming more and more common and a new type of service started to emerge on personal computers. The 'instant message' service was a way to send text to someone else's computer who was also connected to the Internet. This was not a new concept – even in the 1980s there were messaging capabilities in mainframe computers such that short messages could be sent from one user to another. However, it was new to the decentralized computing world of the Internet. Unlike SMS, which delivers immediately or stores the message for later delivery, Instant Messaging (IM) on the Internet would only work if both users were online at the same time, and thus the popularity of this service was inherently limited until there was a large enough user base online for much of the day. In order to know which users would be worthwhile contacting, it was necessary to have a list of 'online' contacts. So, the first Presence services on the Internet were developed to support IM. Again, this type of capability was also inherent in 1980s mainframe computers but not available to a mass consumer market until provided on the Internet.

As these services became more and more popular on the Internet, and as packet data capabilities became a core function of mobile networks it became possible for mobile users also to be 'online' for long periods of time and, therefore, the market for mobile IM was considered to be viable.

To fill the need for a mobile IM standard, a new industry forum called Wireless Village started with the WAP Browser capabilities used by MMS and developed a set of specifications for Mobile Instant Messaging based on HTTP and SMS. When the OMA appeared on the scene in 2002, Wireless Village was incorporated and the specifications were renamed as OMA Instant Messaging and Presence Service (IMPS).

27.3.3 SIP and IMS introduce SIMPLE Instant Messaging

The increase in popularity of the Internet over the past decade has led to increasingly bigger markets for services based on Internet Protocol (IP). The sheer market sizes, in turn, lead to lower price points and more demand for IP-based protocols. In the late 1990s, a group of Mobile Operators and vendors called Third Generation Internet Protocol Forum (3G.IP) developed a set of mobile specification principles aimed at delivering all mobile services, including voice and messaging, over IP. The principles were fed into 3GPP and led to the creation of the 3GPP IP Multimedia Subsystem (IMS) specification set. IMS is based on the use of the Internet Engineering Task Force (IETF)'s Session Initiation Protocol (SIP). Once the principle was established for the development of an IP-based mobile infrastructure using SIP, it became clearer that it made more sense for new services to re-use the SIP infrastructure of IMS rather than some other incompatible protocol.

The IETF had already developed SIMPLE Instant Messaging based on SIP and 3GPP had developed 'IMS Messaging' also based on SIP but neither of these could fulfill all the requirements of IMPS. So, the OMA enhanced the work in the IETF and 3GPP, coming up with a specification for IM, which would work over a SIP/IP core like IMS.

27.3.4 Push-to-Talk over Cellular

In the USA, the Nextel™ network has been very successful at delivering walkie-talkie type services to blue collar industries but also more recently to white collar industries and even to consumers. Sometimes, the ability to send short packets of voice to multiple recipients wherever they are (not just within walkie-talkie ~2 mile range) is very appealing. The OMA recognized this trend and developed a set of specifications to provide this capability over a SIP-based cellular network. In addition to the exchange of voice packets between individuals or groups, OMA has provided for short text interchange in the same application.

In Push-to-talk over Cellular Version 2, the OMA has expanded the capabilities of this enabler to include sending pictures and videos along with network-based storage capabilities (see also Chapter 15).

27.3.5 OMA's Approach to Enablers

Part of the OMA's industry vision is to enable users to communicate, access, and exchange information independent of device and network. This is the focus of everything new created by OMA. However, to achieve real gains for the users, increase market use, and thereby add significant value for the industry, it is necessary to provide interoperability between enablers as well as between devices and networks.

So, just as the industry, in general, is re-focusing on IP-based capabilities, and telecommunications services are re-focusing on SIP-based enablers. The OMA needs to ensure that its enablers are provided as component building blocks that can be used in different ways but still deliver interoperability.

The OMA has a number of legacy capabilities that are in the portfolio because they were created before the OMA existed, in one or other of OMA's affiliates. The general approach of standardizing enablers was one where an idea for a set of features was brought to the table, and everyone focused on delivering that set of features to the marketplace as quickly as possible, pretty much ignoring overlap with existing capabilities or the potential for delivering innovative services based on more than one enabler.

In today's OMA, this approach is called a 'silo' approach because people focus on getting the current job done as quickly as possible, without thinking 'outside of the silo'. Using some of the multiple messaging technologies discussed, an example of the complexity in the network, and the effects of the 'silo' approach on the Quality of Experience of the end-user, is illustrated in Figure 27.1.

There will always be different technologies, but how far do the differences have to be exported? Do we need to have a separate client on the mobile phone to handle each messaging technology? Do all clients have to behave differently with respect to the end-user? And what about the network side? Do service providers have to continually add different servers for different messaging experiences, and handle provisioning, maintenance, and upgrades differently for each of them? As OMA's thinking has matured, the desire by companies to have advanced building blocks has increased, and this has led to the thinking about converging enablers. We already have transport convergence around IP and service convergence around SIP, so this higher-level convergence drive is really the next phase.

27.3.6 Converged IP Messaging

Early in 2006, O2 (now Telefónica O2 Europe) made a presentation to OMA's Technical Plenary (TP) calling for a more industrial thinking on how to provide an integrated approach to messaging.

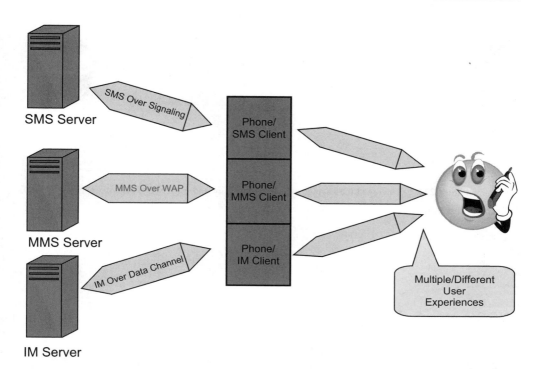

Figure 27.1 Silo messaging: complex deployment and less-than-ideal user experience

What was becoming increasingly obvious was that the increase in the number of messaging clients in handsets, coupled with the increase in messaging platforms in mobile networks, was unsustainable. Users were confused about which messaging client to use, and network operators were unable to install a myriad of new platforms when the individual market demand for any of them was unclear.

Although there is clearly a market for new messaging services, it is far better for the industry to focus on a core client and messaging platform with expansion capabilities. Following this activity and other proposals made to the OMA by member companies, the OMA agreed a work item called Converged IP Messaging (CPM), with the objective to specify an enabler with a single device client and a single network-based messaging platform.

As usual with a new idea, the community has to come to a common understanding about what the work actually means. This is much harder for a cross-functional enabler which tries to break out of very focused, tangible silos. The first question to be answered was 'what is a message'? Clearly this includes text, graphics, pictures, and can be easily extended to cover voice and other data files. But what about real-time streams? It is very hard to draw a line between transferring a video clip file and transferring a video stream from the user perspective.

So the OMA has ended up describing requirements for CPM, which include real-time voice and video – to the extent that some have suggested that this work really means Converged IP Everything.

The OMA CPM enabler will provide for the deployment of a single messaging client in a mobile device. This client will use SIP to interact with the mobile network and provide all existing messaging experience. Other options may have to be explored, but in either case, the mobile phone clients need to expose a single/same user experience. As illustrated in Figure 27.2, a single logical CPM entity is needed to interact with this single client, and new messaging technology functions may be exposed by this entity, thus reducing the network complexity.

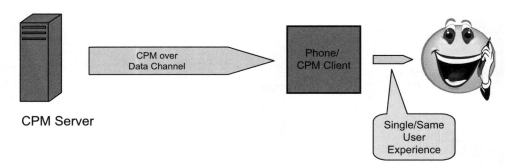

Figure 27.2   Converged messaging: reduced complexity and improved user experience

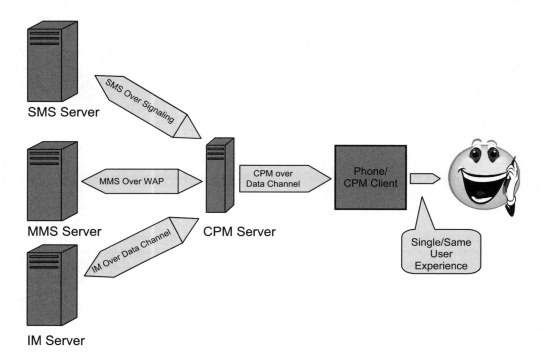

Figure 27.3   Converged messaging: interworking with legacy messaging systems

This will make it possible to enter some text, a mobile number and send this to another user, whether they have a CPM facility or not. The network will work out the appropriate delivery mechanism based on the known facilities of the recipient, the content of the message, and the availability of appropriate network connectivity. In the reverse path, if an SMS message, for example, is sent to a CPM user then the network will intercept this and deliver it through the CPM Framework.

This principle can be extended to other legacy messaging technologies. In this way, there is no need for any legacy messaging client in the device, yet the CPM user can communicate, access and exchange information with others, no matter what technology the others are using. Figure 27.3 illustrates how CPM can achieve the promise of less complexity for new messaging services and improved user experience, while also supporting interworking with legacy messaging systems.

In addition to providing a person to person rich messaging capability, including interworking with non-CPM networks, CPM provides several ways to add value, as follows:

- Messaging within groups – the ability to send to more than one user at a time, have group chats, manage group membership, etc.
- Network-based storage – if a user is unavailable, messages are stored until the user can take delivery. Even after delivery, a network-based store is available so that users can review messages on different devices.
- Storage sharing – users can make content in their network-based store available to other users.
- Network-based address book – CPM can access and manage a network-based address book for use with messaging features.
- Presence – although CPM does not need Presence to send and receive messages, Presence can be integrated into the client and network.
- Multiple devices – CPM can deliver messages to more than one device, for example, it can send a voice message to a mobile phone and a video clip to a PC device.
- Application interface – third-party services can be built on top of CPM so that users can exchange CPM messages with external applications.

27.3.7 CPM Summary

CPM is one of the most significant application projects undertaken by OMA in recent years. It aims to break through the silo approach which has so far limited the uptake of more advanced messaging services than SMS, providing advanced native features while retaining connectivity to older technologies without increasing client complexity. History has shown that advanced mobile messaging technologies have had a rough time but CPM offers the hope of a different approach which does work, so that the users and the industry will make the jump and facilitate richer, more inclusive mobile messaging dialogue!

27.4 Mobile Advertising

We challenge you to name three objects that you use on an average (open/close, pick/drop, start/stop, you get the picture) inside and/or outside your home, more than 10 times a day for a total of over half-an-hour or more. One of those objects is likely to be your mobile phone. Then consider that over two billion people do that everyday. With their interactive and unique personalization capabilities, the frequency of use and the rate of increase of subscribers worldwide, the mobile phones convey an image of the promised land of opportunities for advertisers.

A little icon, a couple of lines of text sandwiched in between other text messages, and that is all it may take to reach a huge audience. If it would only be that easy . . .

How many of the two billion plus subscribers see any such attempt as annoying spam? How many of them go a step further and consider it an intrusion into their privacy? How many are complaining to their service providers, and how many switch over to another service provider which may be more considerate with respect to their privacy privileges? The answer in all cases is: enough to have all actors in the mobile advertising value chain scramble to find solutions that will make this market work and grow.

However, before we look further into challenges and solutions, let's step back for a moment and define what we mean by mobile advertising, and its value chain.

Advertising is a controlled form used by an identified sponsor to deliver messages (text-based, image-based, etc.) to consumers, in an effort to influence and persuade them to take some action (buy, try, talk about, etc.) in relation to the sponsor's products and/or services. Mobile advertising uses mobile devices (e.g. mobile phones, Personal Digital Assistants (PDAs)) as a unique advertising channel, and can achieve efficiency by reaching a target group anytime and anywhere, with personalized and customized advertisements.

In such a nascent market, actors and roles are constantly evolving, and the same entity can assume the roles of multiple actors. The current view is that the mobile advertising value chain comprises the following actors:

- Advertiser: a company, institution, organization, or individual who pays for advertising space or time to present an advertisement to consumers. The advertiser ideally wants the advertisement to reach as many 'right' consumers as possible, at the 'right' time. The advertiser usually pays for its advertisement to be advertised.
- Advertising Agency: the link between the product being advertised and the market. An advertising agency needs to understand the advertiser's requirements and the characteristics of mobile services. Based on that understanding, it creates the advertising campaign and strategy, and selects the target audience. The advertising agency is usually paid by the advertiser.
- Content Provider: the entity that provides rich and attractive content for subscribers, which can create a suitable opportunity for attaching an advertisement. The content provider may either sell its content to other actors in the chain, or derive revenue by placing the advertisement as part of or attached to its content.
- Service Provider: the entity that offers services (e.g. a streaming media service, a Multimedia Messaging Service (MMS)) through which advertising content can be delivered, using service platforms and service enablers that the entity owns. The service provider earns revenues from service charges to customers. When the services are used to also deliver mobile advertisements, a key issue is to do that in a way that avoids degradation of the user experience.
- Technology Provider: a telecommunication equipment and/or device manufacturer and/or IT vendor and/or application integration solution provider. The technology provider sells equipment and/or solutions to operators and service providers.
- Operator: an entity that maintains control over the distribution of mobile services and maintains important subscriber information that can help in the targeting of advertisements. The operator establishes partnerships with other actors in the value chain, in order to derive revenues related to mobile advertising from the use of the resources it offers.
- User and/or Subscriber: the user is the principal who receives the mobile service, whereas the subscriber is the particular user that has the billing relationship with the service provider and the operator. Users that are actively looking for certain products (e.g. avid collectors) may even pay for a mobile advertising service. However, the majority of the users may not be interested, in general, and many would actually be opposed to receiving advertisements through the mobile terminal channel. Hence, there is an on-going debate about whether offering the subscriber incentives (e.g. discounts on some other subscribed services) will remove such user's adversity to mobile advertisements. But then, the question remains as to why send advertisements to a mobile user that is not interested to receive them, and would only accept them just because other incentives were offered?

The user experience of mobile advertising is a lot different from the experience with traditional advertising service (e.g. TV advertising). The mobile user can receive personalized advertisements and, possibly, interactively select products by using the mobile device, and this may be done at a time and in a place where the user may actually welcome the advertisement. A user may welcome an advertisement (sometimes accompanied by a coupon) from a nearby restaurant if she is looking for one in the area, while a user who is searching for a specific fashion style or hobby may be supplied with information in the form of an advertisement that may save searching time. This may change consumers' behavior.

A further degree of advertisement personalization could be achieved by taking advantage of user Presence-based and/or user Location-based services accessible through mobile applications. For example, a user being out on the town and looking for place to shop, dine or entertain may be offered mobile advertisements targeted to those needs, and the ability to find out more details and/or make reservations or purchases.

Some providers may partner with search engine providers to emulate the success Google had with the use of e-mail and search keywords to find out the topics of interest for users – a model that has taken off successfully in Asian countries, in particular. This model seems to suggest that people find it acceptable for advertisements to be presented to them, if they have a sense of having invited the advertising pitch by their actions (e.g. search on a topic), while push marketing and spam are not very successful strategies.

Typically, the choice of receiving mobile advertisements is left to the subscribers. To soften their potential resistance to accept the offer of delivery of free targeted interactive advertisements, they are being offered discounted subscriptions to other services. Those who are already inclined to receive such targeted advertisements will jump at the opportunity, while others may just go along for the ride and give it a try. The model tries to capitalize on human nature: most people are willing to try something if they receive something useful (at times, just something) in return, and the jury is still out on whether the model works. While initially mobile advertisements were accessible indirectly through websites where a mobile user was looking for other content, operators are beginning to consider capitalizing on their huge subscriber information base for the delivery of targeted and personalized mobile advertisements. Taking notice of their subscriber's dislike of spam, operators have to execute with surgeon-like precision, when using their subscriber's information in the targeting process. Advertising agencies may have to change the way they advertise as well, not only to better fit the mobile device footprint and other characteristics, but also to fit the behavior of different subscriber segments. The bottom line is that one cannot simply extrapolate from existing advertising methods, and apply them using the mobile channel. New ways to advertise via the mobile channel may require new service enablers, and those may require new enabler specifications.

Now that we have provided a view into the landscape of the topic on mobile advertising, we will describe in the next section what is being done today in terms of guidelines, best practices, and standards to help guide the industry in creating successful mobile advertising models and solutions.

27.4.1 Prior Work – Mobile Advertising Landscape

While the topic of mobile advertising is a relatively new area for the OMA, it has already been explored in several industry fora. Even before the proliferation of mobile applications, advertisement through electronic means has captured the interest of industry fora. While some fora have provided and continue to provide studies and/or are profiled toward stimulating the growth of the mobile advertising market, others are providing or planning to provide guidelines and recommendations, or even some specifications that apply to the mobile advertising industry. In addition to fora specialized on the Internet and/or mobile advertising, many specifications that support the handling of generic content are either directly applicable to mobile advertising, or may be applicable when some extensions are provided.

The Mobile Marketing Association (MMA) [MMA] has the goal of stimulating the growth of mobile marketing and its associated technologies. It sees itself as clearing obstacles to market development, establishing standards and best practices for sustainable growth and evangelizing the mobile channel for use by brands and third-party content providers. Standards created by the MMA are yet to emerge, and technical specifications from this source are unlikely, given its focus on marketing. However, the MMA has published mobile advertising guidelines, a glossary of applicable terms and best practice guidelines for consumers, and is working on a Mobile Marketing Code of Conduct.

The Mobile Entertainment Forum (MEF) [MEF] drives the mobile entertainment industry's evolution and its commercial potential, reducing entry barriers to an innovative entertainment market. It offers a platform for the mobile entertainment industry to raise its public profile by promoting its offerings and facilitates the development of commercial standards and best practices. No standards are yet available from this forum as far as we can tell, but the forum has produced numerous white papers and has on-going initiatives, including one that focuses on best practices for achieving Quality of Experience, and another one that focuses on defining a certification process for 'realtones' (or ring tones, defined as tones that one can use when the phone rings).

The Interactive Advertising Bureau (IAB) [IAB] proves and promotes the effectiveness of interactive advertising, encourages the growth of the advertising marketplace, and ensures secure transactions in interactive advertising processes. The IAB is focusing on educating both advertisers and publishers on security and operational best practices, and although not specifically focused on the mobile advertising market, has published numerous guidelines that, with some constraints or extensions, should be applicable to mobile advertising. The topics on which IAB has published guidelines include, among others, advertisement campaign measurement and auditing, privacy, rich media, broadband video commercial measurements, and lead generation data transfer. The IAB has also launched the interactive industry's first centralized database of specifications for advertisement units from 88 major publishers within the interactive space.

The GSM Association (GSMA) [GSMA] and the MMA have agreed in June 2007 to work jointly on accelerating the development of mobile advertising, by exploring new mobile advertising techniques and leading standardization efforts. While the MMA will focus on leading development of guidelines, formats, and best practices for mobile advertising, the GSMA will focus on the development of inventory types, as well as commercial and measurement models that will support advertisers in creating new propositions. However, neither the MMA nor the GSMA is expected to create the technical specifications supporting these new techniques and new commercial models. They would have to rely on existing technical specifications, or identify fora that have the expertise to create new technical specifications supporting the newly created requirements and models.

The CDMA Development Group (CDG) [CDG] is another forum that could show interest in developing new requirements for mobile advertising in Code Division Multiple Access (CDMA) networks.

Mobile advertising specifications cannot simply be reduced to one enabler (otherwise it would be a very complex one). It may be more appropriate to refer to a Mobile Advertising Framework that will rely on existing and new technical specifications, where the newer specifications are dictated by gaps uncovered when architecting this framework. When all is said and done, a complete Mobile Advertising Framework may involve a very large number of OMA enablers, some of them described in previous chapters. It seems natural that such a framework will have to rely on existing specifications related to handling content, such as OMA DRM (see chapter 19), OMA BCAST (see chapter 20), and OMA DCD (see chapter 21). It should also make use of services offered by Presence (see chapter 14), Location (see chapter 25), CBCS (see chapter 23), GPM (see chapter 22), GSSM (see chapter 27.1) and CPM (see chapter 27.3). Since no framework that involves mobile devices can survive without Device Management (DM), a Mobile Advertising Framework would also rely on DM (see chapter 18). And the list can go on.

So one may rightfully ask, if all these specifications already exist, what else is missing? The next section will try to tackle the answer to this very question.

27.4.2 New Work – Mobile Advertising

OMA member companies representing a cross-segment of OMA membership got together in late 2006 in the Mobile Advertising Birds of a Feather (MobAd BoF) activity, with the goal of gaining a common understanding of the mobile advertising industry landscape, and creating recommendations to OMA based on that understanding. The MobAd BoF handled the activity through two parallel approaches: (i) a typical OMA approach of creating and discussing use cases related to mobile advertising; and (ii) another investigative approach at looking at the industry as a whole and understanding how it deals with this topic. The second approach involved understanding the contribution of other industry fora to this space (e.g. MMA, MEF, IAB, GSMA, CDG) and what technical specifications may be available (e.g. OMA specifications), as well as a general understanding of the actor chain that participates in a Mobile Advertising ecosystem. The relatively good understanding of specifications available helped in the analysis of the use cases. As a result, it was possible to eliminate quickly the need to focus on some issues (relegating those to possible extensions of existing enablers), and instead document issues that did not seem to have a technical specification in place, while one may be needed to complete a Mobile Advertising Framework. Such issues were documented in a list of high-level gaps. The MobAd BoF was closed in May 2007, but not before creating a white paper that describes the Mobile Advertising Landscape [MobAd WP] and a series of recommendations to the OMA TP. The recommendations encouraged OMA members to create a new work item to focus on some of the more visible gaps identified by the MobAd BoF.

Subsequently, a Mobile Advertising Work Item was created with the initial goal of focusing on Mobile Advertising requirements and a Mobile Advertising Framework Architecture, focused on addressing the main gaps identified during the MobAd BoF activity. These include the following:

- Personalization of the Advertisements: one of the keys to the commercial success of mobile advertising is the degree of the advertisement's personalization. In order to achieve this, an enhanced user profile that includes more information about the user's preferences is needed. At the same time, such preferences have to be matched against a wealth of advertisements, so a better way to characterize the advertisements themselves is also necessary (e.g. ad metadata that accurately describes the advertisement). Finally, ensuring that the advertisement is presented as expected by the advertiser leads to the need of specifications for ad formats.
- Interactivity of Advertisements: in order to reap the benefits of presenting the advertisement, mechanisms need to be made available to allow a user that is presented with an advertisement to interact with it. Such mechanisms are not only useful to assess the user's reaction, but may be critical in different payment models.
- Technology to Facilitate the Collection of Advertising Metrics: advertising campaigns need to have the ability to measure the advertisement's impact and user behavior, in order to verify the effects of the advertisement relative to the targeted audience. Data correlated across large groups after collection from targeted audiences can provide additional feedback to the mobile advertising value chain. Missing specifications include technologies dealing with the defining, reporting, and collecting the needed advertising metrics, and the handling of group statistics results.

At the time of writing the book, work was in progress on writing the Mobile Advertising Requirements Document, and the work on Mobile Advertising Architecture was yet to start. However, early discussions in the requirements phase seem to point toward the basic model for advertisement delivery illustrated in Figure 27.4.

The Ad Selector is an actor identified by the OMA MobAd Requirements Document that is responsible for selecting and serving appropriate advertisements to the user via the user agent and application. For example, a gaming application is enabled with interactive advertisements by the MobAd user agent, (also know as the Ad Engine). The user agent is envisaged to be device resident but could also be located in the network. It serves multiple purposes, for example, 'fetching' ad content from the Ad Selector and reporting ad metrics back to the Ad Selector or other authorized entities. Examples of such metrics include the identity of the application that used the ad, context it was presented and information about how the user interacted with the advertisement.

Further discussion is required to fully scope the requirements on the interfaces between the Ad Selector and the Ad Engine (user agent) and between the Ad Manager and ad-enabled application.

One of the thornier issues that has to be addressed is how to reconcile the increasing pressure of finding effective ways to make advertisements much more targeted and effective, while ensuring that privacy of any involved actors is preserved.

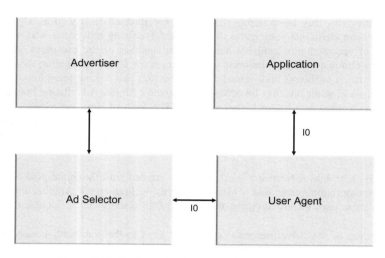

Figure 27.4   Basic model for mobile advertisement delivery

While the initial work item started with the assumption that requirements created may be neatly organized in topics already covered by other enablers, and handed over to those groups for extending their current activities, at this point in time it is not clear anymore whether this will be the final approach. Given that many more companies are involved in the requirements phase, than were in the MobAd BoF activity, it is not surprising that some companies are already advocating the need for a full-blown Mobile Advertising enabler as a more appropriate approach.

Some of the users may like the idea of mobile advertising (or the discounts or freebies they may receive if going along with it) and some other users will never like it. Regardless, mobile advertising is viewed as one of the potential 'killer applications' for the mobile industry. In this particular case, the lack of specifications will not break such a trend, but may create delays. As discussed, the mobile advertising value chain involves many actors, from diverse industries. Without specifications and with a proliferation of proprietary solutions as a result, it will be difficult for all actors in the value chain to be profitable and that carries a risk for the entire model. The OMA MobAd work seems to have chosen to work on technical aspects that will bring about welcomed solutions to identified gaps. On the other hand, it is much too early to assess whether the solutions for the identified gaps are true 'silver bullets' for the issues facing mobile advertising. And that has little to do with decisions made by OMA, it has to do with the fact that a perfect viable business model for mobile advertising is yet to emerge and gain momentum. When that time arrives, a different array of needs may have to be addressed, in addition to the ones currently identified.

Part IV

Conclusions

It took a little working on, but we have just spent the better part of this book describing the exciting field of service enablers for next generation applications, as addressed by the Open Mobile Alliance. We have covered a lot of ground on a whole slew of topics. This last part of the book will wrap things up with a few concluding remarks and some projections on possible next steps.

The Open Mobile Alliance   M. Brenner and M. Unmehopa
© 2008 Alcatel-Lucent. All Rights Reserved

28

Concluding Remarks, and What's in Store Next?

'Next-Generation Applications, sounds interesting, but where are they defined?'

'Can't I get an overview of how things relate, rather than just traverse a bunch of individual enabler specifications?'

'Standards specifications make for such dry reading.'

'Only a seasoned standards veteran can navigate the web sites of standards fora or industry consortiums.'

These are the questions and statements we started this book with, questions and statements that inspired us to begin writing. This book, like many other technical books we can think about, intends to educate the target audience on specific topics, that, without guidance are difficult to recognize as an explored topic, difficult to identify in a sea of seemingly similar topics, difficult to untangle from the slew of dependencies, difficult to comprehend, and bottom-line just difficult. Specifications are indeed dry, and it is somewhat ironic that they seem to appear especially dry for somebody thirsty to understand how they fit into the proverbial 'bigger picture'. Not all product managers are well versed in the nitty-gritty details related to the bits and bytes of the protocols, why to package data in a certain format rather than another, or how to pick the best way to encode data to be transmitted over the wire. Yet, they are the ones who ultimately make the big decisions on what gets built, or what gets deployed.

28.1 Project Post-mortem

The main goal of the book you just finished reading (unless you skipped straight to the concluding remarks) was to hit the sweet-spot for those readers who are definitely interested in knowing a lot more about service enablers for Next-Generation Services than just marketing sound-bites, but do not personally plan to start writing code the very next day. Let's explore if we achieved this goal, and some others that we had on our mind, and may have explicitly committed to in the introductory chapter. This may sound a little like a project post-mortem, not surprising, since quite a project this was!

First of all, we wanted the reader to walk away with a good, and perhaps new understanding and recognition of what service enablers are, and the comprehension and, hopefully, conviction

The Open Mobile Alliance   M. Brenner and M. Unmehopa
© 2008 Alcatel-Lucent. All Rights Reserved

that building services using service enablers is a sound, effective, beneficial long-term approach for all actors in the industry chain (service providers, operators, vendors, content providers to name just a few). We then introduced the reader gradually to the issues and solutions, building up the knowledge about service enablers, the OMA Service Environment (OSE) architecture, and the critical components such as the Policy Enforcer, until we could finally break through and delve into the architecture and some specification details of horizontal topics and a broad selection of OMA enablers. We did so by arming the reader in advance with sufficient knowledge on how the OMA is organized, and what processes it uses in its development activities, since such knowledge is often key to understanding why enablers were developed in a certain way and took a certain direction, and how the interfaces they expose relate to the ones exposed by some other enabler (i.e. enablers that depend on them or are themselves dependent on).

OK, let's say we met our goals, although you, the reader will be the ultimate judge of that. Project well done, one might say. But did we go beyond that, did we go the extra mile, did we exceed the expectations? We can only address this question in terms of our own expectations, and we think we exceeded every expectation we ourselves had, by leaps and bounds. As in any good post-mortem, some metrics may help.

The book was started by 'two men and a napkin'. It ended up with over 400 pages of solid information, as accurate and as detailed as possible while still digestible by our targeted audience. Of course, the publisher was not going to accept the napkin, no matter how hard we would have tried, but truth be said, neither did we plan on such a comprehensive reference book at the outset. And though it all started with just 2 people, it ended up with 15 of them, who each contributed at least one chapter or section in the book. Of course, such a significant effort requires the review by even more people. In total, representatives of 18 companies (18!) from 3 different continents (Europe, North America, and Asia) contributed to this project either by writing, or reviewing and providing valuable feedback, or both. The 18 companies include a complete cross-section of major operators/service providers, telecommunication equipment vendors, mobile phone manufacturers, and IT vendors, with the contributors being deeply and directly involved in creating the specifications explained in the book. While we were hoping to convince a few to contribute to the book, we never expected or even hoped to be able to engage so many. The book is so much the better for it.

It is more than worth to mention that some of the contributors work for a company that competes with ours. Fierce debates have taken place in the OMA Working Groups, on specifications where we jointly work with some of the very same contributors invited to take part in this project. It is fair to say that for some chapters, if written by ourselves, we would have most definitely approached the topic from a completely different angle than the one that was provided by the invited contributor. It was our intent, a mere hope when we started writing, to create a piece of work that was company-neutral, and therefore more objective, more interesting, and more valuable – more long-lasting maybe, and less brittle. Not unlike the OMA, that is neutral to programming language, operating system, or network bearer.

The initial intent was to cover just a handful of enablers in-depth, primarily those we have been involved with ourselves, and for which we were very comfortable that we possessed the knowledge and the insight to cover them in detail. We ended up describing the activities in every Working Group and Committee, and at least one enabler created by each one of the OMA Working Groups, with one sole exception. And in that particular case, that work is covered implicitly by its re-use in other enablers.

More than 400 pages covering over 30 enablers, provided by 15 expert contributors from 8 different companies and verified by as many reviewers from even more companies. Quite a project indeed.

28.2   What's Next?

And now, to something completely different. What's up next? Or put in a different way: so what?

So what if we now understand what service enablers are, so what if academically we have even proven that this is a valuable approach to help building new cool services? The cynics may say: 'you only explained what each enabler does and what it exposes, and waved at us the promise that, because of open interfaces and focus on intrinsic functions and re-use of others, and because of this Policy Enforcer, it's going to be so much easier to build services. But you have shown nothing about how it all comes together'. And the cynics would have it right, at least this time. The book has not shown that. But we have not shown it deliberately, because it was not one of our goals to do so. The goal was to talk about the OMA, and how this forum delivers building blocks for the creation of services, called OMA service enablers. The OMA explicitly does not address end-to-end services, and leaves the architecture of end-to-end services, and solutions to meet them, as a differentiating factor that allows vendors on one hand, and service providers on the other hand, to fairly and innovatively compete with each other in their respective markets. Hence the book also does not talk about, or evangelize specific services or applications, no matter how much of a killer they may be.

Having said that, hints about 'what could be' were dropped in several chapters (e.g. Chapter 7, with insights on the Policy Enforcer and beyond), and those readers who were interested in finding all those hints, have done so for sure. While the OMA may or may not go any further in combining enablers into more complex end-to-end architecture specifications, and technical specifications to support them, other standards fora may do so. And in the industry as a whole, such activities have started for a while. There is a lot of talk in the industry about Service Delivery Environments (SDEs), Service Delivery Frameworks (SDFs), and Service Delivery Platforms (SDPs). While not completely synonymous, the different terms deal with the problem of creating an environment and the mechanisms in such an environment for easier blending of applications, deployed on emerging

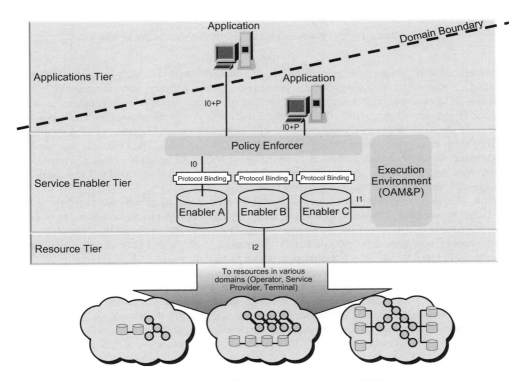

Figure 28.1   The OMA Service Environment (OSE)

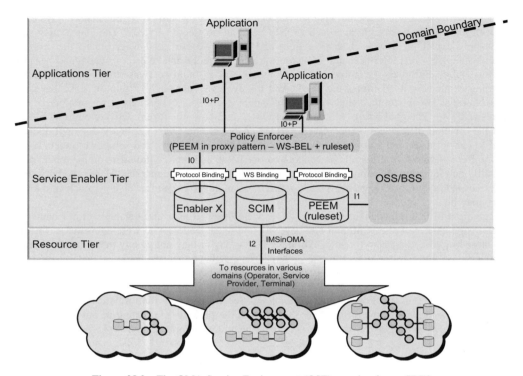

Figure 28.2   The OMA Service Environment (OSE) – recipe for an SDE?

converged network architectures (e.g. IP Multimedia Subsystem (IMS)). SDE concerns itself with creating an appropriate architecture to encourage the creation, delivery, and management of new services, an architecture that fuses the best technologies from the telecommunications industry and the IT industry [Brenner2007]. SDF concerns itself with designing an as-complete-as-possible toolbox in the SDE, while SDP concerns itself with creating a specific instance of such a toolbox.

Well then, this may have something to do with the OSE after all. The OSE was presented as a blueprint for allowing the creation and mixing-and-matching of granular enablers produced by OMA Working Groups, but also interacting with resources not defined by OMA. Let's recall the OSE generic diagram presented in Chapter 2 (see Figure 28.1).

Now let's allow our creativity to wander a little bit further (for those who have read the entire book and, in particular, Chapter 7, this will be a trivial exercise). The picture becomes a little more clearer when we populate the OSE with some specific OMA enablers and non-OMA resources, and use notions by now popular to the avid reader: the notions of I0, I1, and I2 interfaces explained in Chapter 2. Figure 28.2 shows a potential path for an SDE, built on an OSE recipe.

Some of the non-OMA resources we refer to are part of the IMS architecture, others are resources built by combining specifications from multiple standards bodies – but not necessarily fully specified per se in any of these bodies. Such resources could be what are referred to in 3GPP as Application Servers (ASs). One of the more interesting ones for this discussion, the Service Capability Interaction Manager (SCIM), in practical terms a Session Initiation Protocol (SIP) Service Broker, uses I2 interfaces to interact with IMS resources using Utilization of IMS in OMA (IMSinOMA). But would it be farfetched for a SCIM to expose an OMA-defined I0 interface, possibly with a Web Service binding? Possibly, but why that would be important is that this would facilitate a Policy Enforcer using an orchestration workflow instance deployed by a service provider, to create/blend new services capitalizing on the converged IMS architecture. The workflow enforced by the Policy Enforcer is whatever the service provider wants it to be. Hence it could end up delegating functions not only to the SCIM, but also to any other OMA Service Enabler. The Policy Enforcer would focus on macro-orchestration of service enablers to create new user-visible services, while the SCIM would focus on the low-latency micro-orchestration needed in coordinating IMS resources. Add a Policy Evaluation, Enforcement, and Management (PEEM) engine that helps in managing user preferences. Fulfill the promise of the I1 interfaces that will allow Operations Support System/Business Support System (OSS/BSS) to manage each and every OMA enabler. We may now have the basic building blocks to create new services. For example, throw in a Television Application Server, a Presence Server, and a Voice Mail Application Server and you may have most components needed in the Service Enabler Tier to build a triple-play solution. Of course, you would need a lot of underlying network infrastructure. And of course, we won't explore this any further here.

Recent efforts in standards fora show that there is an overall industry interest in exploring the possibility of standardizing an SDF, or at least provide guidelines on how to achieve one. The TM Forum has started a broad SDF initiative, and is inviting the collaboration of other industry fora, including OMA.

So the question 'is the OSE a recipe for an SDE?' is a valid one to ask. But that does not make it less hard to answer, because it requires work beyond the reading of the book. The book was not supposed to provide the answer to this question, but it did suppose to give the reader the keys to unlock the door and let creativity break free. We can only hope that the book has provided those keys that will help in tackling the future of the SDE, and of OMA service enablers in this environment. Our last words are: watch that space!

Annex A

Supplementary Tables to Chapter 14

For ease of readability, a number of the tables referenced in Chapter 14 'The Presence and List Management Enablers' are included in this annex.

Table A.1 Basic IETF RFCs relevant to the Presence enabler

Name	WG, Specification	Description
A Model for Presence and Instant Messaging	IMPP RFC 2778	Explains the presence service, how it could work, and its use by applications like instant messaging
Instant Messaging/Presence Protocol Requirements	IMPP RFC 2779	Defines core protocol requirements for instant messaging and presence
SIP: Session Initiation Protocol	SIP RFC 3261	Defines the SIP protocol
SIP specific event notification	SIP RFC 3265	Defines event notification in SIP, specifically, the SUBSCRIBE and NOTIFY constructs
An event state publication extension to SIP	SIP RFC 3903	Describes how event state publication can be done in SIP, defines the PUBLISH method
A mechanism for content indirection in SIP messages	SIP RFC 4483	Explains content indirection and how it can be supported in SIP. This concept is also leveraged in the OMA reference architecture
SIP extension for instant messaging	SIP RFC 3428	Defines a new SIP MESSAGE method to support page mode IM exchanges

The Open Mobile Alliance   M. Brenner and M. Unmehopa
© 2008 Alcatel-Lucent. All Rights Reserved

Table A.2   Summary of IETF SIMPLE WG RFCs (RFCs are proposed standards in the IETF)

Name	Specification	Description
A Presence event package for SIP	RFC 3856	
A watcher information event template package for SIP	RFC 3857	Defines the winfo event package and explains how watcher information can be propagated to presentities
An XML-based format for watcher information (winfo)	RFC 3858	Provides an XML-based document representation of winfo notifications to presentities
Indication of message composition for Instant Messaging (IM)	RFC 3994	Describes the SIP support for message composition indicators (e.g. to tell Alice that Bob is typing an IM once a chat is in progress)
Timed Presence extensions to the PIDF to indicate status information for past and future time intervals	RFC 4481	Explains how calendar events can be propagated to interested, authorized watchers using PIDF documents, defines necessary extensions
RPID: Rich Presence extensions to PIDF	RFC 4480	Indicates how the basic structure of the PIDF can be extended to include additional information of interest to watchers
CIPID: Contact Information for PIDF	RFC 4482	PIDF extensions for additional address book contact information like icons, homepages, maps etc.
A data model for Presence	RFC 4479	Defines a data model for the presence service, also explains how various entities like person, service and device relate to each other and the system as a whole
A SIP event notification extension for resource lists	RFC 4662	Describes the RLS function and list presence
An XML-based format for event notification filtering	RFC 4661	Defines XML documents used to support the notion of filtering
Functional description of event notification filtering	RFC 4660	Explains filtering and SIMPLE support for the same, with examples
XML Configuration Access Protocol (XCAP)	RFC 4825	Defines the XCAP Protocol used for list management operations
XML formats for representing resource lists	RFC 4826	Defines how lists may be represented in XML for use by various services

Table A.3 Summary of IETF SIMPLE WG drafts (Internet drafts are works in progress as of this writing)

Name	Specification	Description
Message Session Relay Protocol (MSRP)	draft-ietf-simple-message-sessions-19	Defines the MSRP protocol for SIMPLE session-based IM
SIP extensions for partial notification of presence information	draft-ietf-simple-partial-notify-09	Explains partial presence notifications and SIMPLE protocol support for the same. Partial presence limits the number of bits that transit the client-server interface
PIDF extensions for partial Presence	draft-ietf-simple-partial-pidf-format-08	XML extensions to PIDF to enable partial presence
SIP user agent capability extensions to PIDF	draft-ietf-simple-prescaps-ext-08	XML document format extensions to express device capabilities, etc.
Presence authorization rules	draft-ietf-simple-presence-rules-10	Explains how authorization rules for allow, deny, polite block, and confirm may be encoded into XML documents
XCAP usage for manipulating presence document contents	draft-ietf-simple-xcap-pidf-manipulation-usage-03	Explains how XCAP can be used actively to tweak presenty published presence information
Relay extensions to MSRP	draft-ietf-simple-msrp-relays-10.txt	Describes MSRP relays that regulate the flow of MSRP messages between end points with MSRP sessions
Publication of partial Presence information	draft-ietf-simple-partial-publish-06	Explains how RFC 3903-defined publication mechanisms can be extended to also support partial presence publication
An XML document format for indicating change in XCAP resources	draft-ietf-simple-xcap-diff-05	Defines XCAP diff capabilities – the ability to represent list changes or deltas in smaller documents called change logs
An XML representation for expressing policy capabilities	draft-ietf-simple-common-policy-caps-02	Describes a generic XML document structure that can be used to represent policies.
An XML representation for expressing Presence policy capabilities	draft-ietf-simple-pres-policy-caps-02	Defines how the XML document described in the previous row can be used to represent presence-specific policies, so a presenty can indicate what subset of presence status information should be shared with which watchers, for example
An XML Patch Operations Framework Utilizing XML Path Language (XPath) selectors	draft-ietf-simple-xml-patch-ops-03	Defines XPath-based extensions to perform additional list management operations.

(*continued overleaf*)

Table A.3 (*continued*)

Name	Specification	Description
Instant message disposition notification	draft-ietf-simple-imdn-04	Explains how IM disposition notifications (e.g. when a recipient has read an IM) may be implemented in SIMPLE
Advanced IM requirements for SIP	draft-ietf-simple-messaging-requirements-01	Defines new requirements and capabilities to make SIP IM more useful and usable. Extensions discussed include disposition notifications, composition indicators, support for additional types of content, and group messaging

Table A.4 3GPP2 specifications and equivalent TIA Standards for the 3GPP2 Presence Service

Name	3GPP2 specification	TIA equivalent standard	Description
Presence for wireless systems stage 1 requirements	3GPP2 S.R0062-0	Not available yet	Functional requirements of the 3GPP2 Presence service
Presence Service; architecture and functional description	3GPP2 X.S0027-001-0	TIA-1032-001	Functional architecture to support the 3GPP Presence service in CDMA networks
Presence security	3GPP2 X.P0027-002-0	TIA-1032-002	Defines the security architecture, features, and mechanisms for Presence security
Presence Service using IP multimedia core network subsystem; stage 3	3GPP2 X.P0027-003-0	TIA-1032-003	Protocol details using the SIP, SIMPLE, and XCAP framework for support of presence in MMD
Network presence	3GPP2 X.P0027-004-0	TIA-1032-004	Defines how presence information from network entities can be collected

Table A.5 3GPP specifications and equivalent European Telecommunications Standards Institute (ETSI) Standards for the 3GPP Presence service

Name	3GPP specification (Release 6)	ETSI standard equivalent	Description
Presence service; stage 1	3GPP TS 22.141	RTS/TSGS-0122141v650	Functional requirements of the 3GPP Presence Service
Presence service; architecture and functional description	3GPP TS 23.141	RTS/TSGS-0223141v690	Functional architecture to support the 3GPP Presence service in GSM/UMTS
Presence service using the IP Multimedia Subsystem (IMS) Core Network (CN) subsystem	3GPP TS 24.141	RTS/TSGS-0123141v670	Protocol extension to 3GPP IMS and IETF specifications to support 3GPP Presence service
IP Multimedia System (IMS) messaging and Presence; media formats and codecs	3GPP TS 26.141	RTS/TSGS-0426141v630	Defines the minimal baseline and optional media codecs that can be used in Presence service
Presence service; security	3GPP TS 33.141	RTS/TSGS-0300141v620	Defines the security architecture, the security features, and security mechanisms for the Presence services

Table A.6 OMA specifications for IMPS

Name	OMA specification	Description
OMA IMPS delta requirements	OMA-RD_IMPSDelta-V1_3	Defines the requirements for IMPS1.3
IMPS architecture	OMA-AD-IMPS-V1_3	Defines the architecture for IMPS1.3
Client-server protocol XML syntax	OMA-TS-IMPS-CSP-XMLS-V1_3	
Client-server protocol transport bindings	OMA-TS-IMPS-CSP_Transport-V1_3	Describes the bindings for the client-server protocol covering WSP, SMS, HTTP, HTTPs, and TCP
Client-server protocol data types	OMA-TS-IMPS-CSP_Data_Types-V1_3-20051011-C.pdf	Defines the data types in the client-server protocol
Client-server protocol plain text syntax	OMA-TS-IMPS-CSP_PTS-V1_3-20051011-C.pdf	Describes the encoding of primitives, information elements, and the contained values in plain text format

(*continued overleaf*)

Table A.6 (*continued*)

Name	OMA specification	Description
Client-server protocol binary XML definition and examples	OMA-TS-IMPS-CSP_WBXML-V1_3-20051011-C.pdf	Defines the binary XML tags and associated tokens
Client-server protocol session and transactions	Client-server protocol session and transactions	Defines the transactions and the information elements of the client-server protocol
Presence attributes	OMA-TS-IMPS-PA-V1_3	Defines the presence attributes as part of IMSP1.3
Presence attributes XML syntax	OMA-TS-IMPS-PA_XMLS-V1_3	Defines the XML DTDs for the presence attributes defined as part of IMPS 1.3 carried over the client-server protocol.
Management Object	OMA-TS-IMPS-MO-V1_0	Describes the management object syntax that allows configuration deployment of IMPS clients
Server-server protocol semantics document	OMA-TS-IMPS-SSP-V1_3	Defines the semantics for the server to server protocol
Server-server protocol XML syntax document	OMA-TS-IMPS-SSP_XMLS-V1_3-20051011-C.pdf	Defines the XML DTSs carried over the server to server protocol
server-server protocol transport binding	OMA-TS-IMPS-SSP_Transport-V1_3-20051011-C.pdf	Describes the binding for the server-server protocol over HTTP, HTTPS or TCP.
Application characteristic for IMPS	OMA-TS-wA-Application-Characteristic-for-IMPS-V1_0-20051011-C.txt	Describes the application characteristics for IMPS

List of Abbreviations and Acronyms

1×RTT	1 times Radio Transmission Technology
2.5G	2.5th generation of wireless technology for mobile phones (e.g. GPRS, EDGE)
2G	Second Generation
3D	Three-dimensional
3G	Third generation of wireless technology for mobile phones
3G.IP	Third Generation Internet Protocol Forum
3GPP	Third Generation Partnership Project
3GPP/2	3GPP and 3GPP2
3GPP2	Third Generation Partnership Project 2
AAA	Authentication, Authorization and Accounting
AAC	Advanced Audio Coding
ABNF	Augmented Backus-Naur Form
ACA	Accounting Answer
ACR	Accounting Request
AD	Architecture Document
A-GPS	Assisted GPS
AHG	Ad hoc Group
AI	Application Instance
AJAX	Asynchronous JavaScript and XML
AKA	Authentication and Key Agreement
AMR	Adaptive Multi-Rate
AMR-WB	Adaptive Multi Rate – Wide Band
AOL	America Online
AP	authentication proxy
API	Application Programming Interface
AppID	Application ID
ARC WG	Architecture Working Group
ARC	Architecture
ARPU	Average Revenue Per User
AS	Application Server -or- Actor Session
ASA	Abort-Session-Answer
ASID	Actor Session ID
ASP	Application Service Provider
ASR	Abort-Session-Request

The Open Mobile Alliance   M. Brenner and M. Unmehopa
© 2008 Alcatel-Lucent. All Rights Reserved

ATIS	Alliance for Telecommunications Industry Solutions
AUID	Application Usage Identity
AVP	Attribute Value Pair
AWSP	ACORD Web Services Profile
B2B	Business-to-Business
BAC	Browser and Content
BAC WG	Browser and Content Working Group
BCAST	Broadcast -or- Mobile Broadcast -or- OMA Broadcast Enabler
BCMCS	Broadcast/Multicast Services
BDS	Broadcast Distribution System
BER	Basic Encoding Rules
BLOB	Binary Large Object
BoD	Board of Directors
BoF	Birds of a Feather
BPEL	Business Process Execution Language
BSA	BCAST Service Application
BSD/A	BCAST Service Distribution/Adaptation
BSF	Bootstrapping Server Function
BSM	BCAST Subscription Management
BSS	Business Support System
BT	Browser Technologies
BT WG	Browser Technology Working Group
CADE	Client Application Data Exchange
CAMEL	Customized Application for Mobile Enhanced Logic
CAP	CAMEL Application Part
CAPEX	Capital Expenditure
CAR	Client Application Registration
CBCS	Categorization Based Content Screening
CC/PP	Composite Capabilities/Preference Profile
CCR	Credit-Control Request
CD	Compact Disc -or- Content Delivery
CDG	CDMA Development Group
CDMA	Code Division Multiple Access
CDMA2000	Hybrid 2.5G/3G mobile telecommunications standards that use CDMA
CD-ROM	Compact Disc Read-Only Memory
CEA	Capability-Exchange-Answer
CEK	Content Encryption Key
CER	Capability-Exchange-Request
CF	Controlling PoC Function
CI	Content Issuer
CIM	Common Information Model
CIO	Chief Information Officer
CMIP	Common Management Information Protocol
CMISE	Common Management Information Service Element
CN	Core Network
ConnMO	Connectivity Management Object
CORBA	Common Object Request Broker Architecture
CP	Client Provisioning -or- Content Protection
CPDE	Content Provider Data Exchange

CPIM	Common Profile for Instant Messaging
CPM	Converged IP Messaging
CPP	Common Presence Profile
CPR	Content Provider Registration
CPU	Central Processing Unit
CR	Change Request
CRL	Certificate Revocation List
CRM	Customer Relationship Management
CSCF	Call State Control Function
CSI	Client/Server Interface
CSIM	CDMA Subscriber Identity Module
CSP	Client-Server Protocol
CSS	Cascading Style Sheet
DCD	OMA Dynamic Content Delivery Enabler -or- Dynamic Content Delivery
DCF	DRM Content Format
DCMO	Device Capability Management Object
DDF	Device Description Framework
DDWG	Device Descriptions Working Group
DiagMon	Diagnostics and Monitoring
DIG	Developers Interest Group
DIWG	Device Independence Working Group
DLDRM	Download and Digital Rights Management
DM	Device Management
DMC	Device Management Client
DMP	The Digital Media Project
DMR	Domain Model Relationship
DMS	Device Management Server
DM-SC	Device Management Smart Card
DMTF	Distributed Management Task Force, Inc.
DMTF/CIM	Distributed Management Task Force/Common Information Model
DM-WSI	Web Services Interface for Device Management
DNS	Domain Name Service
DoS	Denial of Service
DPA	Disconnect-Peer-Answer
DPE	Device Profile Evolution
DPR	Disconnect-Peer-Request
DPWS	Devices Profile for Web Services
DRM	Digital Rights Management
DS	Data Synchronization
DSN	Delivery Status Notification
DS WG	Data Synchronization Working Group
DTD	Document Type Definition
DVB	Digital Video Broadcasting
DVB-H	Digital Video Broadcasting – Handhelds
DVB IPDC	Digital Video Broadcasting IP Datacast
DWA	Device-Watchdog-Answer
DWR	Device-Watchdog-Request
E	Evaluation (or Evaluation and Enforcement)
E911	Enhanced 911

eBNF	extended Backus–Naur form
ECMA	European Computer Manufacturer Association
EDGE	Enhanced Data Rates for GSM Evolution
EICS	Enabler Implementation Conformance Statement
EM	Element Manager
EME-LIA	Emergency Location Immediate Answer
EME-LIR	Emergency Location Immediate Request
EME-LIREP	Emergency Location Immediate Report
EMEREP	Emergency Location Report
EMN	E-Mail Notification
ENTBoF	Enterprise BoF
ERP	Enterprise Resource Planning
ESB	Enterprise Service Bus
ESG	Electronic Service Guide
E-SLP	Emergency SLP
ESMP	ECMAScript Mobile Profile
ESMTP	Enhanced SMTP
ET_RPT	Enabler Test Report
ETG	Enabler Test Guidelines
eTOM	enhanced Telecom Operations Map
ETR	Enabler Test Requirements
ETS	Enabler Test Specification
ETSI	European Telecommunications Standards Institute
EVDO	Evolution-Data Optimized or Evolution-Data only
EVP	Enabler Validation Plan
EVRC	Enhanced Variable Rate CODEC
FAB	Fulfillment, Assurance, Billing
FCAPS	Fault, Configuration, Accounting, Performance, Security
FCC	Federal Communications Committee
FD	File Distribution
FTP	File Transfer Protocol
FUMO	Firmware Upgrade Management Object
GAA	Generic Authentication Architecture
GBA	Generic Bootstrapping Architecture
GCC	Generic Call Control
GCF	Global Certification Forum
GGSN	Gateway GPRS Support Node
GLMS	Group List Management Server
GMLC	Gateway Mobile Location Center
GPM	Global Permissions Management
GPRS	General Packet Radio Service
GPS	Global Positioning System
GS	Game Services
GSM	Global System for Mobile communication
GSMA	GSM Association
GSSM	General Service Subscription Management
GUI	Graphical User Interface
GUP	General User Profile
GS WG	Game Services Working Group
HLR	Home Location Registry
HSS	Home Subscriber Server

HTML	HyperText Markup Language
HTTP	HyperText Transfer Protocol
HTTPS	Secure HyperText Transfer Protocol
I/O	Input/Output
IAB	Internet Advertising Bureau
IANA	Internet Assigned Numbers Authority
ICRA	Internet Content Rating Association
I-CSCF	Interrogating CSCF
ID	Identifier -or- Identity
IDC	International Data Corporation
ID-FF	Identity Federation Framework
IDL	Interface Definition Language
ID-WSF	Identity Web Services Framework
IEEE	Institute of Electrical and Electronics Engineers
IETF	Internet Engineering Task Force
IIOP	Internet Inter-ORB Protocol
ILP	Internal Location Protocol
ILP PC	ILP Positioning Control
ILP PD	ILP Positioning Data
IM	Instant Messaging
IMAP	Internet Message Access Protocol
IMPP	Instant Messaging and Presence Protocol
IMPS	Instant Messaging and Presence Service
IMS	IP Multimedia Subsystem
IMSI	International Mobile Subscriber Identity
IMSinOMA	Utilization of IMS in OMA
IM/SM	Interaction and Multimodal Synchronization Manager
IN	Intelligent Networking
IOC	Information Object Class
IOP	Interoperability
IOP_RPT	Enabler IOP Report
IOP WG	Interoperability Working Group
IP	Internet Protocol
IPDC	IP Datacast
IP MM BoF	IP Multimedia BoF
IPR	Intellectual Property Rights
IPSec	Internet Protocol Security
IPTV	IP Television
IR	Infrared
IrDA	Infrared Data Association
IRP	Integration Reference Point
ISC	IMS Service Control
ISDN	Integrated Services Digital Network
ISO	International Standards Organization
ISUP	ISDN User Part
IT	Information Technology
ITU	International Telecommunication Union
ITU-T	International Telecommunication Union – Telecommunication Standardization Sector
J2EE	Java 2.0 Enterprise Edition
J2ME	Java 2 Platform, Micro Edition

JR	Java Realization
JSR	Java Specification Request
KMC	Key Management Centre
KMC-IF	Key Management Centre Interface
LAN	Local Area Network
LBS	Location Based Services
LCM	Life Cycle Management
LCS	Location Services
LDAP	Lightweight Directory Access Protocol
LEMONADE	License to Enhance Messaging Oriented Network Access for Diverse Endpoints
LIF	Location Interoperability Forum
LOC	Location -or- OMA Location working group
LTKM	Long-Term Key Message
LUAD	Liberty enabled User Agents and Devices
M	Management -or- Mandatory
MAE	Mobile Application Environment
MAP	Mobile Application Part
MBMS	Multimedia Broadcast/Multicast Service
MBS	Multicast and Broadcast Service
MCC	Mobile Commerce and Charging
MCC WG	Mobile Commerce and Charging Working Group
MD5	Message-Digest algorithm 5
MEF	Mobile Entertainment Forum
MEM	Mobile E-mail -or- Mobile E-Mail
MGIF	Mobile Games Interoperability Forum
MIB	Management Information Base
MIME	Multipurpose Internet Mail Extensions
MLP	Mobile Location Protocol
MLS	Mobile Location Service
MMA	Mobile Marketing Association
MMCP	Multimodal and Multidevice Configuration Protocol
MMD	Multi-Media Domain
MMMD	Multimodal and Multidevice
MMOG	Massively Multiplayer Online Game
MMORPG	Massively Multiplayer Online Role Playing Game
MMS	Multimedia Messaging Service
MMS-IOP	Multimedia Messaging Service Interoperability
MNO	Mobile Network Operator
MO	(device) Management Object
MobAd BoF	Mobile Advertising Birds-of-a-Feather
MobAd	Mobile Advertising
MO ID	(device) Management Object Identifier
MP3	MPEG-1 Audio Layer 3
MPC	Mobile Positioning Center
MPCC	Multi Party Call Control
MPEG	Moving Pictures Expert Group
MS	Mail Store
MSC	Mobile Switching Center
MSISDN Mobile	Subscriber ISDN Number
MSN	Microsoft Network

MSRP	Message Session Relay Protocol
MTA	Message Transfer Agent
MTOM	Message Transmission Optimization Mechanism
MWG	Messaging Working Group
MWG-CPM	MWG Converged IP Messaging
MWG-IM	MWG Instant Messaging
MWG-MEM	MWG Mobile E-mail
MWG-MMSG	MWG Multimedia Messaging Group
MWIF	Mobile Wireless Internet Forum
MWS	Mobile Web Services
MWS WG	Mobile Web Services Working Group
NAF	Network Application Function
NAP	Network Access Point
NDA	Non Disclosure Agreement
NE	Network Element
NEBS	Network Equipment-Building System
NEM	Network Equipment Manufacturer
NGN	Next Generation Network -or- Next Generation Networking
NGOSS	Next Generation Operations Support System
NM	Network Management -or- Network Manager
NMS	Network Management System
NRM	Network Resource Management
NW	Network
O	Optional
OA&M	Operations, Administration and Maintenance
OAM&P	Operation, Administration, Maintenance and Provisioning
OASIS	Organization for the Advancement of Structured Information Standards
OBEX	OBject EXchange
OBKG	On Board Key Generation
OCS	Online Charging System
OCSP	Online Certificate Status Protocol
OCSPMP	Online Certificate Status Protocol Mobile Profile
OCSPMP TS	OCSP Mobile Profile Technical Specification
ODP	On-Device Portal
ODRL	Open Digital Rights Language
OEM	Original Equipment Manufacturer
OMA	Open Mobile Alliance
OMA CP	OMA Client Provisioning
OMA DM	OMA Device Management
OMA DM WG	OMA Device Management Working Group
OMA MEM	OMA Mobile E-Mail
OMA MWS WG	OMA Mobile Web Services working group
OMG	Object Management Group
OMNA	Open Mobile Naming Authority
OPEX	Operational Expenditure
OPS	Operations and Processes
OSA	Open Service Access
OSE	OMA Service Environment

OSF	Operations System Function
OSG	OMA Security Gateway
OSGi	Open System Gateway Initiative
OSI	Open Systems Interconnection
OSPE	OMA Service Provider Environment
OSS	Operations Support System
OTA	Over The air Activation -or- Over-the-Air
OWP	OMA Work Program
OWSER	OMA Web Services Enabler Release
OWSER-NI	OMA Web Services Enabler Release Network Identity
P2P	Peer-to-Peer
PAG	Presence and Availability Group -or- Presence, Availability and Group Management
PAN	Personal Area Network
PAP	Push Access Protocol
Parlay	The Parlay Group
PC	Personal Computer
PCIM	Policy Core Information Model
PCP	Privacy Checking Protocol
P-CSCF	Proxy Call State Control Function
PDA	Personal Digital Assistant
PDE	Positioning Determining Equipment
PDF	Policy Decision Function
PDP	Packet Data Protocol -or- Policy Decision Point
PDSN	Packet Data Serving Node
PE	Policy Enforcer
PEEM	Policy Evaluation, Enforcement, and Management
PEEM RD	PEEM Requirements Document
PEF	Policy Evaluation and Enforcement
PEK	Programme Encryption Key
PEL	Policy Expression Language
PEM-1	PEEM specified callable interface
PEM-2	PEEM specified management interface
PEP	Policy Enforcement Point
PER	Packed Encoding Rules
PF	Participating PoC Function -or- Policy Enforcement
PIDF	Presence Information Data Format
PIM	Personal Information Manager
PIOSE	Parlay in OSE
PKI	Public Key Infrastructure
PLS	Presence List Server
PM	Policy Management
PNA	Presence Network Agent
PoC	Push-to-talk over Cellular
POC	Push-to-Talk Over Cellular Working Group
POP	Post Office Protocol
POS	Point-of-Service
PPG	Push Proxy Gateway
PPR	Privacy Profile Register
PRM	Partner Management

PS	Presence Server
PSK-TLS	Pre-Shared Key Transport Layer Security
PSTN	Public Switched Telephone Network
PTCRB	PCS Type Certification Review Board
PTT	Push-to-Talk
Push OTA	Push Over-the-air
PV	Policy Evaluation
QoE	Quality of Experience
QoS	Quality of Service
R&A	Review and Approval
RAA	Re-Auth-Answer
RACS	Resource and Admission Control Subsystem
RAM	Random Access Memory
RAN	Radio Access Network
RAR	Re-Auth-Request
RD	Requirements Document
RDF	Resource Description Framework
REK	Rights Encryption Key
REL	Release Planning and Management
REQ	Requirements
REQ WG	Requirements Working Group
RF	Radio Frequency
RFC	Request for Comments
RFI	Request for Information
RFID	Radio-Frequency Identification
RFP	Request for Proposals
RFQ	Request for Quotation
RI	Rights Issuer
RLP	Roaming Location Protocol
RLS	Resource List Server
RMF	Rich Media Format
RMI	Remote Management Invocation
RNC	Radio Network Controller
RO	Rights Object
ROAP	Rights Object Acquisition Protocol
ROI	Return on Investment
ROM	Read-Only Memory
RRP	Reference Release Package
RSAC	Recreational Software Advisory Council
RSS	Really Simple Syndication
RTCP	Real Time Control Protocol
RTP	Real Time Protocol
R-UIM	Removable User Identity Module
SAML	Security Assertion Markup Language
SAS	Personal Information Manager
SC	Smart Card
SCE	Secure Content Exchange
SCF	Service Capability Feature
SCF API	Service Capability Feature Application Programming Interface

SCIM	Service Capability Interaction Manager
SCOMO	Software Component Management Object
SCR	Static Conformance Requirement
S-CSCF	Serving-Call State Control Function
SCWS	Smart Card Web Server
SD	Stream Distribution
SDE	Service Delivery Environment
SDF	Service Delivery Framework
SDO	Standards Development Organization
SDP	Service Delivery Platform -or- Session Description Protocol
SEC	Security
SECA	Security Agent
SEC-CF	Security Common Functions
SEC WG	Security Working Group
SEK	Service Encryption Key
SET	SUPL Enabled Terminal
SG	Service Guide
SGCC	Service Guide Content Creation
SGML	Standard Generalized Markup Language
SGSN	Serving GPRS Support Node
SGW	Service Gateway
SI	Service Interaction
SID	Shared Information/Data -or- Shared Information/Data Model -or- Session ID
SIM	Subscriber Identity Module
SIMPLE	SIP for Instant Messaging and Presence Leveraging Extensions
SIP	Session Initiation Protocol
SLA	Service Level Agreement
SLC	SUPL Location Center
SLF	Service Locator Function
SLIA	Standard Location Immediate Answer
SLIR	Standard Location Immediate Request
SLIREP	Standard Location Immediate Report
SLP	SUPL Location Platform
SLR	Standard Location Report
SLRA	Standard Location Report Answer
SLT	Service Level Tracing
SMAC	Service Model and Catalog
SMASH	Systems Management Architecture for Server Hardware
SMCNP	Server to Mobile Core Network Protocol
SMI	Storage Management Initiative
SMIL	Synchronized Multimedia Integration Language
SMK	Subscription Management Key
SMLC	Serving Mobile Location Center
SMM	Service Model Management
SMPP	Short Message Peer-to-peer Protocol
SMS	Short Messaging Service
SMSC	SMS Center
SMTP	Simple Mail Transfer Protocol

SNMP	Simple Network Management Protocol
SOA	Service Oriented Architecture
SOAP	Simple Object Access Protocol
SP	Service Provider
SPC	Subscription Profile Component -or- SUPL Positioning Center
SPR	Service Provisioning
SRM	OMA Secure Removable Media Enabler -or- Secure Removable Media
SS7	Signaling System number 7
SSL	Secure Socket Layer
SSP	Server to Server Protocol
STI	Standard Transcoding Interface
STKM	Short-Term Key Message
SuM	Subscription Management
SuM IRP	SuM Integration Reference Point
SUP	Secure User Plane
SUPL	Secure User Plane Location
SVG	Scalable Vector Graphics
SVGB	SVG Basic
SVGT	SVG Tiny
SWG	Sub Working Group
SyncML	Synchronization Markup Language
TCP	Transmission Control Protocol
TCP/IP	Transmission Control Protocol/Internet Protocol
TDM	Time-Division Multiplexing
TDOA	Time Distance Of Arrival
TEK	Traffic Encryption Key
Telco	Telecommunication
TINA	Telecommunications Information Networking Architecture
TISPAN	Telecommunications and Internet Services and Protocols for Advanced Networking
TLRA	Triggered Location Reporting Answer
TLREP	Triggered Location Reporting Report
TLRR	Triggered Location Reporting Request
TLRSA	Triggered Location Reporting Stop Answer
TLRSR	Triggered Location Reporting Stop Request
TLS	Transport Layer Security
TNA	Technology Neutral Architecture
TNDS	Tree and Description Serialization
TOM	Telecommunications Operations Map
TP	Technical Plenary
TS	Technical Specification
TS_RPT	Test Session Report
TTFF	Time To First Fix
UA	User Agent
UAProf	User Agent Profile
UDDI	Universal Description, Discovery and Integration
UDP	User Datagram Protocol
UE	User Equipment

UICC	Universal Integrated Circuit Card
ULP	UserPlane Location Protocol
ULP PD	ULP Positioning Determination
ULP SM	ULP Service Management
UMTS	Universal Mobile Telecommunications System
URI	Uniform Resource Identifier
URL	Uniform Resource Locator
USB	Universal Serial Bus
USIM	Universal Subscriber Identity Module
UTC	Coordinated Universal Time
UTF-8	8-bit UCS/Unicode Transformation Format
VAS	Value Added Service
VASP	Value Added Service Provider
VCR	Video Cassette Recorder
VPN	Virtual Private Network
W3C	World Wide Web Consortium
WAP	Wireless Application Protocol
WAP PAP	WAP Push Access Protocol
WBEM	Web-based Enterprise Management
WBXML	Wireless Binary XML
WCDMA	Wideband CDMA
W-CDMA	Wideband Code Division Multiple Access
WCSS	WAP Cascading Style Sheet
WDP	Wireless Datagram Protocol
WG	Working Group
WGS	World Geodetic System
WGS84	World Geodetic System 1984
WID	Work Item Document
WiFi	Wireless Fidelity
WIM	Wireless Identity Module
WiMAX	Worldwide Interoperability for Microwave Access
WiMAX MBS	WiMAX Multicast and Broadcast Service
winfo	Watcher information
WKPI	Wireless Public Key Infrastructure
WLAN	Wireless Local Area Network
WML	Wireless Markup Language
WS	Web Service -or- Web Services
WS-AT	Web Services Atomic Transaction
WS-BA	Web Services Business Activity
WS-BPEL	Web Services Business Processes Execution Language
WSDL	Web Services Description Language
WS-I	Web Services Interoperability organization
WS-I BP	WS-I Basic Profile
WSP	Web Service Provider -or- Wireless Session Protocol
WSR	Web Service Requestor
WTA	Wireless Telephony Application
WTP	Wireless Transport Protocol
WV	Wireless Village
WWW	World Wide Web
XACML	eXtensible Access Control Markup Language
XCAP	XML Configuration Access Protocol

XDM	XML Document Management
XDMC	XDM Client
XDMS	XML Document Management Server
XER	XML Encoding Rules
XHTML	Extended HyperText Markup Language
XHTMLMP	XHTML Mobile Profile
XKMS	XML Key Management Specification
XML	eXtensible Markup Language
XMPP	Extensible Messaging and Presence Protocol
XPath	XML Path Language
XSD	XML Schema Definition

References

[3GPP] 3rd Generation Partnership Project, (November 2007), URL: http://www.3gpp.org/
[3GPP_specs] 3GPP Specification Status Report, (November 2007), URL: http://www.3gpp.org/ftp/Specs/html-info/status-report.
htm
[3GPP2] 3rd Generation Partnership Project2, (November 2007), URL: http://www.3gpp2.org
[3GPP2_specs] 3GPP2 Specifications, (November 2007), URL: http://www.3gpp2.org/public_html/specs/index.cfm
[3GPP TS 20.198-13] 3GPP TS 29.198-13, 3rd Generation Partnership Project, 'Technical Specification Group Core Network and Terminals; Open Service Access (OSA); Application Programming Interface (API); Part 13: Policy management Service Capability Feature (SCF) (Release 6)', Version 6.4.1 (July 2006) URL: http://www.3gpp.org/
[3GPP TS 22.071] 3GPP TS 22.071, 3rd Generation Partnership Project, 'Technical Specification Group Services and System Aspects; Location Services (LCS); Service Description; Stage 1 (Release 7)', Version 7.4.0 (December 2005), URL: http://www.3gpp.org/
[3GPP TS 22.228] 3GPP TS 22.228 3rd Generation Partnership Project, 'Technical Specification Group Services and System Aspect; Service Requirements for the IP Multimedia; Core Network Subsystem (Stage 1)', Version 7.5.0 (September 2006), URL: http://www.3gpp.org/
[3GPP TS 23.125] 3GPP TS 23.125, 3rd Generation Partnership Project, 'Technical Specification Group Services and System Aspects; Overall high level functionality and architecture impacts of flow based charging; Stage 2 (Release 6)', Version 6.5.0 (June 2005), URL: http://www.3gpp.org/
[3GPP TS 23.140] 3GPP TS 23.140, 3rd Generation Partnership Project, 'Technical Specification Group Core Network and Terminals; Multimedia Messaging Service (MMS); Functional description; Stage 2 (Release 6)', Version 6.14.0 (September 2006), URL: http://www.3gpp.org/
[3GPP TS 23.141] 3GPP TS 23.141, 3rd Generation Partnership Project, 'Technical Specification Group Services and System Aspects; Presence Service; Architecture and functional description (Release 7)', Version 7.2.0 (September 2006), URL: http://www.3gpp.org/
[3GPP TS 23.228] 3GPP TS 23.228, 3rd Generation Partnership Project, 'Technical Specification Group Services and System Aspects; IP Multimedia Subsystem (IMS); Stage 2 (Release 7)', Version 7.7.0 (March 2007)
[3GPP TS 23.246] 3GPP TS 23.246, 3rd Generation Partnership Project, 'Technical Specification Group Services and System Aspects; Multimedia Broadcast/Multicast Service (MBMS); Architecture and functional description (Release 7)', Version 7.3.0 (June 2007), URL: http://www.3gpp.org/
[3GPP TS 23.271] 3GPP TS 23.271 V7.8.0 (2007–03), 3rd Generation Partnership Project, Technical Specification Group Services and System Aspects; Functional stage 2 description of Location Services (LCS), (Release 7), URL: http://www.3gpp.org/
[3GPP TS 24.109] 3GPP TS 24.109, 3rd Generation Partnership Project, 'Technical Specification Group Core Network and Terminals; Bootstrapping interface (Ub) and network application function interface (Ua); Protocol details (Release 6)', Version 6.7.0 (September 2006), URL: http:www.3gpp.org/
[3GPP TS 24.167] 3GPP TS 24.167, 3rd Generation Partnership Project, 'Technical Specification Group Core Network and Terminals; 3GPP IMS Management Object (MO); Stage 3 (Release 7)', Version 7.1.0 (March 2007), URL: http://www.3gpp.org/
[3GPP TS 26.235] 3GPP TS 26.235, 3rd Generation Partnership Project, 'Technical Specification Group Services and System Aspects; Packet switched conversational multimedia applications; Default codecs', Version 7.1.0 (March 2006), URL: http://www.3gpp.org/

[3GPP TS 26.236] 3GPP TS 26.236, 3rd Generation Partnership Project, 'Technical Specification Group Services and System Aspects; Packet switched conversational multimedia applications; Transport protocols (Release 7)', Version 7.1.0 (September 2006), URL: http://www.3gpp.org/

[3GPP TS 26.346] 3GPP TS 26.346, 3rd Generation Partnership Project, 'Technical Specification Group Services and System Aspects; Multimedia Broadcast/Multicast Service (MBMS); Protocols and codecs (Release 7)', Version 7.4.0 (June 2007), URL: http://www.3gpp.org/

[3GPP TS 29.198-14] 3GPP TS 29.198-14, 3rd Generation Partnership Project, 'Technical Specification Group Core Network and Terminals; Open Service Access (OSA); Application Programming Interface (API); Part 14: Presence and Availability Management (PAM) Service Capability Feature (SCF) (Release 7)', Version 7.0.0 (March 2007), URL: http://www.3gpp.org/

[3GPP TS 29.240] 3GPP TS 29.240, 3rd Generation Partnership Project, 'Technical Specification Group Core Network and Terminals; 3GPP Generic User Profile (GUP); Stage 3; Network (Release 7)', Version 7.0.0 (June 2007), URL: http://www.3gpp.org/

[3GPP TS 32.141] 3GPP TS 32.141, 3rd Generation Partnership Project, 'Technical Specification Group Services and System Aspects; Telecommunication management; Subscription Management (SuM) architecture (Release 7)', Version 7.0.0 (June 2007), URL: http://www.3gpp.org/

[3GPP TS 32.171] 3GPP TS 32.171, 3rd Generation Partnership Project, 'Technical Specification Group Services and System Aspects; Telecommunication management; Subscription Management (SuM) Network Resource Model (NRM) Integration Reference Point (IRP): Requirements (Release 7)', Version 7.0.0 (June 2007), URL: http://www.3gpp.org/

[3GPP TS 32.172] 3GPP TS 32.172, 3rd Generation Partnership Project, 'Technical Specification Group Services and System Aspects; Telecommunication management; Subscription Management (SuM) Network Resource Model (NRM) Integration Reference Point (IRP): Information Service (IS) (Release 7)', Version 7.0.0 (June 2007), URL: http://www.3gpp.org/

[3GPP TS 32.272] 3GPP TS 32.272, 3rd Generation Partnership Project, 'Technical Specification Group Charging Management; Charging Architecture and Principles', Version 7.4.0 (June 2007), URL: http://www.3gpp.org/

[3GPP TS 32.299] 3GPP TS 32.299, 3rd Generation Partnership Project, 'Technical Specification Group Service and System Aspects; Telecommunication management; Charging management; Diameter charging applications (Release 7)', Version 7.6.0 (June 2007), URL: http://www.3gpp.org/

[3GPP TS 33.220] 3GPP TS 33.220, 3rd Generation Partnership Project, 'Technical Specification Group Services and System Aspects; Generic Authentication Architecture; Generic bootstrapping architecture (Release 6)', Version 6.10.0 (September 2006), URL: http:www.3gpp.org/

[3GPP TS 33.222] 3GPP TS 33.222, 3rd Generation Partnership Project, 'Technical Specification Group Services and System Aspects; Generic Authentication Architecture; Access to network application functions using Hypertext Transfer Protocol over Transport Layer Security (HTTPS) (Release 6)', Version 6.6.0 (March 2006), URL: http:www.3gpp.org/

[3GPP TS 33.246] 3GPP TS 33.246, 3rd Generation Partnership Project, 'Technical Specification Group Services and System Aspects; 3G Security; Security of Multimedia Broadcast/Multicast Service (Release 7)', Version 7.4.0 (June 2007). URL: http://www.3gpp.org/

3GPP2 S.R0062-0 3GPP2 S.R0062-0, 3rd Generation Partnership Project 2, 'Presence for Wireless Systems, Stage 1 Requirements', Version 1.0 (30 October 2002), URL: http://www.3gpp2.org/

[3GPP2 S.R0061-0] 3GPP2 S.R0062-0, 3rd Generation Partnership Project 2, 'Wireless Immediate Messaging, Stage 1 Requirements', Version 1.0 (22 October 2002), URL: http://www.3gpp2.org/

[3GPP2 S.R0100-0] 3GPP2 S.R0100-0, 3rd Generation Partnership Project 2, 'Push-to-talk over Cellular (PoC): System Requirements', Version 1.0 (September 2005), URL: http://www.3gpp2.org/

[3GPP2 S.S0083-A] 3GPP2 S.S0083-A, 3rd Generation Partnership Project 2, 'Broadcast-Multicast Service Security Framework', Version 1.0 (26 August 2004), URL: http://www.3gpp2.org/

[3GPP2 S.S0109] 3GPP2 S.S0109-0, 3rd Generation Partnership Project 2, 'Generic Bootstrapping Architecture (GBA) Framework', Version 1.0 (30 March 2006), URL: http://www.3gpp2.org/

[3GPP2 X.S0013.4] 3GPP2 X.S0013.4, 3rd Generation Partnership Project 2, 'All-IP Core Network Multimedia Domain: IP Multimedia Call Control Protocol Based on SIP and SDP Stage 3', Version 1.0 (December 2003), URL: http://www.3gpp2.org/

[3GPP2 X.S0013-008] 3GPP2 X.S0013-008, 3rd Generation Partnership Project 2, 'Technical Specification Group Core Network; All-IP Core Network Multimedia Domain: IP Multimedia Subsystem – Accounting Information Flows and Protocol', X.S0013-008-A v1.0 (November 2005), URL: http://www.3gpp2.org

[3GPP2 X.S0013-015] 3GPP2 X.S0013-015, 3rd Generation Partnership Project 2, 'Technical Specification Group Core Network; All-IP Core Network Multimedia Domain: IP Multimedia Subsystem – Online Charging System', X.S0015-015-0 v1.0 (November 2005), URL: http://www.3gpp2.org/

[3GPP2 X.S0022-A] 3GPP2 X.S0022-A, 3rd Generation Partnership Project 2, 'Broadcast and Multicast Service in cdma2000 Wireless IP Network', Version 1.0 (16 February 2007), URL: http://www.3gpp2.org/

[3GPP2 X.S0016.31] 3GPP2 X.S0016.31, 'MMS MM1 Stage 3 Using M-IMAP for Message Submission and Retrieval', Version 1.0.0 (May 2003), URL: http://www.3gpp2.org/

[Acord] 'ACORD Insurance Data Standards', (November 2007), URL:http://www.acord.org/

[ARC BP] Open Mobile Alliance, 'Architecture Best Practices', Draft Version 1.0 – (13 September 2007), URL: http://www.openmobilealliance.org

[BCAST AD] Open Mobile Alliance, 'Mobile Broadcast Services Architecture', Candidate Version 1.0 – (03 September 2007), URL: http://www.openmobilealliance.org/

[BCAST ERELD] Open Mobile Alliance, 'Enabler Release Definition for Mobile Broadcast Services', Candidate Version 1.0 – (29 May 2007), URL: http://www.openmobilealliance.org/

[BCAST RD] Open Mobile Alliance, 'Mobile Broadcast Services Requirements', Candidate Version 1.0 – (29 May 2007), URL: http://www.openmobilealliance.org/

[BLOB] JCA, 'Interface Blob', java.sql, J2SE v.1.4.2, URL: http://java.sun.com/j2se/1.4.2/docs/api/java/sql/Blob.html

[Bluetooth] Bluetooth Special Interest Group, 'Specification of the Bluetooth System', Core Package Version 2.1 (July 2006), URL: http://www.bluetooth.com/

[BPEL] Alves, A., Arkin A., Askary S., et al., Editors, 'OASIS Web Services Business Process Execution Language (WSBPEL)', Version 2.0 (11 April 2007), OASIS Standard, URL: http://www.oasis-open.org/

[Brainerd1974] Brainerd, W.S. and Landweber, L.H., 'Theory of Computation', John Wiley & Sons, (1974), pp. 358, ISBN-10: 0471095850, ISBN-13: 978–0471095859

[Brenner2007] Brenner, M.R., Unmehopa, M.R. and Grech, M.L.F, 'The Service Delivery Environment – a Standards-Driven Melting Pot', ICIN 2007, (7–10 October 2007)

[BusinessWeek2007] MacMillan, D., Business Week, 'Gaming Goes Business Casual', (22 March 2007), URL: http://www.businessweek.com/

[Camarillo2006] Camarillo, G. and García-Martí, M-A., 'The 3G IP Multimedia Subsystem (IMS): Merging the Internet and the Cellular Worlds', 2nd edn, John Wiley & Sons, (10 February 2006), pp. 456, ISBN: 0470018186

[CBCS AD] Open Mobile Alliance, 'Categorization Based Content Screening Framework Architecture', Draft Version 1.0 – (30 August 2007), URL: http://www.openmobilealliance.org/

[CBCS RD] Open Mobile Alliance, 'Categorization Based Content Screening Framework Requirements', Candidate Version 1.0 – (11 July 2006), URL: http://www.openmobilealliance.org/

[CBDI] Wilkes, L., 'The Web Services Protocol Stack', CBDI Forum Report, (February 2005), URL: http://roadmap.cbdiforum.com/reports/protocols/

[CDG] CDMA Development Group, (November 2007), URL: http://www.cdg.org/

[CHG AD] Open Mobile Alliance, 'Charging Architecture', OMA-AD-Charging-V1_0, Candidate Version 1.0 – (26 September 2006), URL: http://www.openmobilealliance.org/

[CHG BP] Open Mobile Alliance, 'Whitepaper of Charging Specification Best Practices', (May 2006), URL:http://www.openmobilealliance.org/

[CHG OFFLINE TS] Open Mobile Alliance, 'OMA Offline Charging Interface', OMA-TS-Offline_Charging_Interface-V1_0, Candidate Version 1.0 – (22 May 2007), URL: http://www.openmobilealliance.org/

[CHG ONLINE TS] Open Mobile Alliance, 'OMA Online Charging Interface', OMA-TS-Online_Charging_Interface-V1_0 (May 2007), Candidate Version 1.0 – 22 URL:http://www.openmobilealliance.org/

[CHG RD] Open Mobile Alliance, 'Charging Requirements', OMA-RD_Charging-V1_0, Candidate Version 1.0 – (18 November 2004), URL: http://www.openmobilealliance.org/

[CHG WP] Open Mobile Alliance, 'White Paper on Charging Deployment Scenarios', (December 2006), URL:http://www.openmobilealliance.org/

[ConnMO TS] Open Mobile Alliance, 'Standardized Connectivity Management Objects For use with OMA Device Management', Draft Version 1.0 – (14 December 2006), URL: http://www.openmobilealliance.org/

[CoreMedia] CoreMedia, 'CoreMedia DRM', URL: http://www.coremedia.com/

[CP ERP] Open Mobile Alliance, 'OMA Client Provisioning Enabler Release Package', Candidate Version 1.1 – (28 April 2005), URL: http://www.openmobilealliance.org/

[DCD AD] Open Mobile Alliance, 'Dynamic Content Delivery Architecture', Draft Version 1.0 – (08 August 2007), URL: http://www.openmobilealliance.org/

[DCD RD] Open Mobile Alliance, 'Dynamic Content Delivery Requirements', Candidate Version 1.0 – (16 July 2007), URL: http://www.openmobilealliance.org/

[DIG WP] Open Mobile Alliance, 'White Paper on Developer Guidelines For OMA Namespace Encoding', Draft – (25 October 2006), URL: http://www.openmobilealliance.org

[DLOTA ERP] Open Mobile Alliance, 'OMA Download Over The Air Enabler Release Package', Candidate Version 2.0 – (07 September 2006), URL:http://www.openmobilealliance.org/

[DMTF CIM] DMTF, 'Common Information Model (CIM) Infrastructure Specification', DSP0004, Version 2.3 Final, (4 October 2005), URL: http://www.dmtf.org/

[DMTF CIM HTTP] DMTF, 'Specification for CIM Operations over HTTP', DSP0200, Version 1.2, (9 December 2004), URL: http://www.dmtf.org/

[DMTF WS Managementt] DMTF, 'Web Services for Management (WS-Management)', DSP0226, Preliminary Release, (April 2006), URL: http://www.dmtf.org/

[DMTF CIM Schema] DMTF, 'Common Information Model (CIM) Specification', Version 2.13.1, (16 November 2005), URL: http://www.dmtf.org/

[DMTF CIM XML] DMTF, 'Specification for the Representation of CIM in XML', DSP0201, Version 2.2, (9 December 2004), URL: http://www.dmtf.org/

[DM-V1.1.2 ERP] Open Mobile Alliance, 'OMA Device Management Enabler Release Package', Approved Version 1.1.2 – (13 January 2004), URL: http://www.openmobilealliance.org/

[DM-V1.2 ERP] Open Mobile Alliance, 'OMA Device Management Enabler Release Package', Approved Version 1.2 – (09 February 2007), URL: http://www.openmobilealliance.org/

[DM-Security TS] Open Mobile Alliance™, 'OMA Device Management Security', Approved Version 1.2 – (09 February 2007), URL:http://www.openmobilealliance.org/

[DM TNDS TS] Open Mobile Alliance, 'OMA Device Management Tree and Description Serialization', Approved Version 1.2 – (09 February 2007), URL: http://www.openmobilealliance.org/

[DMP] The Digital Media Project, (November 2007), URL: http://www.dmpf.org

[DMTF WS Management] DMTF, 'Web Services for Management', DSP0226, Preliminary Release, (April 2006), URL: http://www.dmtf.org/

[DPE RD] Open Mobile Alliance, 'Device Profile Requirements', Candidate Version 1.0 – 09 Open Mobile Alliance, (February 2007), URL: http://www.openmobilealliance.org/

[DPWS] Devices Profile for Web Services, (February 2006), URL: http://specs.xmlsoap.org/ws/2006/02/devprof/DevicesProfile.pdf

[DReaM] Sun Labs Research Project, 'Project DReaM', URL: http://research.sun.com/

[DRM AD] Open Mobile Alliance, 'DRM Architecture', Approved Version 2.0.1 – (31 July 2007), URL: http://www.openmobilealliance.org/

[DRM DCF] Open Mobile Alliance, 'DRM Content Format', Approved Version 2.0.1 – (31 July 2007), URL: http://www.openmobilealliance.org/

[DRM DRM] Open Mobile Alliance, 'DRM Specification', Approved Version 2.0 – (03 March 2007), URL: http://www.openmobilealliance.org/

[DRM RD] Open Mobile Alliance, 'OMA DRM Requirements', Approved Version 2.0 – (03 March 2006), URL: http://www.openmobilealliance.org/

[DRM REL] Open Mobile Alliance, 'DRM Rights Expression Language', Approved Version 2.0.1 – (31 July 2007), URL: http://www.openmobilealliance.org/

[DRM TS] Open Mobile Alliance, 'DRM Specification', Approved Version 2.0.1 – (31 July 2007), URL: http://www.openmobilealliance.org/

[DRM XBS] Open Mobile Alliance, 'OMA DRM v2.0 Extensions for Broadcast Support', Candidate Version 1.0 – (07 September 2007), URL: http://www.openmobilealliance.org/

[DS-V1.1.2 ERP] Open Mobile Alliance, 'Enabler Release Package for Data Synchronization', Approved Version 1.1.2 – (21 June 2004), URL: http://www.openmobilealliance.org/

[DS-V1.2 ERP] Open Mobile Alliance, 'Enabler Release Package for Data Synchronization', Approved Version 1.2.1 – (10 August 2007), URL: http://www.openmobilealliance.org/

[ENTBOF TR] Open Mobile Alliance, 'Technical Report – OMA Enterprise BOF', Draft Version 1.0 – (08 August 2004), URL: http://www.openmobilealliance.org/

[Erl2005] Erl, T., 'Service-Oriented Architecture: Concepts, Technology, and Design', Prentice Hall PTR, (2005), pp. 792, ISBN-10: 0131858580

[ESMP CR] Open Mobile Alliance, 'Crypto Object for ECMA Script Mobile Profile', Candidate Version 1.0 – (22 March 2005), URL: http://www.openmobilealliance.org/

[ESMP TS] Open Mobile Alliance, 'ECMAScript Mobile Profile, A Wireless Markup Scripting Language', Candidate Version 1.0 – (13 September 2006), URL: http://www.openmobilealliance.org/

[ETSI] European Telecommunications Standards Institute, (November 2007), URL: http://www.etsi.org/

[ETSI DTS 188 002-2] ETSI, DTS 188 002-2, 'Telecommunications and Internet Converged Services and Protocols for Advanced Networking (TISPAN); NGN Management; Subscription Management Information Model', V0.0.5 (March 2007), URL: http://www.portal.etsi.org/

[ETSI EN 300 468] ETSI, EN 300 468, 'Digital Video Broadcasting (DVB); Specification for Service Information (SI) in DVB systems', V1.5.1 (May 2003), URL: http://www.portal.etsi.org/

[ETSI TISPAN] ETSI TISPAN, (November 2007), URL: http://portal.etsi.org/

[ETSI TS 102 005] ETSI, TS 102 005, 'Digital Video Broadcasting (DVB); Specification for Use of Video and Audio Coding in DVB Services Delivered Directly Over IP Protocols', V1.2.1 (April 2004), URL: http://www.portal.etsi.org/

[ETSI TS 102 470] ETSI, TS 102 470, 'Digital Video Broadcasting (DVB); IP Datacast over DVB-H: Program Specific Information (PSI)/Service Information (SI)', V1.1.1 (April 2006), URL: http://www.portal.etsi.org/

[ETSI TS 102 471] ETSI, TS 102 471, 'Digital Video Broadcasting (DVB); IP Datacast over DVB-H: Electronic Service Guide', V1.2.1 (November 2006), URL: http://www.portal.etsi.org/

[ETSI TS 102 472] ETSI, TS 102 472, 'Digital Video Broadcasting (DVB); IP Datacast over DVB-H: Content Delivery Protocols', V1.2.1 (December 2006), URL: http://www.portal.etsi.org/

[ETSI TS 102 474] ETSI, TS 102 474, 'Digital Video Broadcasting (DVB); IP Datacast over DVB-H: Service Purchase and Protection', V1.1.3 (July 2006), Draft, URL: http://www.portal.etsi.org/

[Exchange] Microsoft Exchange Server, (November 2007), http://www.microsoft.com/

[find_RFCs] IETF RFC Index Search Engine, (November 2007), URL: http://www.rfc-editor.org/rfcsearch.html

[Foo 2001] Foo, S.M., Hoover, C., Lee, W.M., 'Dynamic WAP Application Development', Manning Publications, (August 2001), pp. 900, ISBN: 1930110081

[FUMO TS] Open Mobile Alliance, 'OMA Firmware Update Management Object ERP', OMA-ERP (February 2007), Approved Version 1.0 – 9 URL:http://www.openmobilealliance.org/

[Game Services AD] Open Mobile Alliance, 'Game Services Architecture', Candidate Version 1.0 – (03 March 2006), URL: http://www.openmobilealliance.org/

[Game Services CSI TS] Open Mobile Alliance, 'OMA Game Services Client/Server Interface Specification', Candidate Version 1.0 – (07 March 2006), URL: http://www.openmobilealliance.org/

[Game Services RD] Open Mobile Alliance, 'OMA Game Services Requirements', Candidate Version 1.0 – (10 February 2006), URL: http://www.openmobilealliance.org/

[Game Services WP] Open Mobile Alliance, 'White Paper on Mobile Gaming Evolution', Candidate – (25 June 2007), URL: http://www.openmobilealliance.org/

[Gaming Platform] Open Mobile Alliance, 'Gaming Platform Version 1.0', Candidate Version 1.0 – (12 June 2003), URL: http://www.openmobilealliance.org/

[Gaur2006] Gaur, H., Zirn, Markus, eds, 'BPEL Cookbook: Best Practices for SOA-Based Integration and Composite Applications Development', Packt Publishing Limited, (2006), pp. 199, ISBN: 1904811337

[GBA Profile TS] Open Mobile Alliance, 'OMA GBA Profile', Draft Version 1.0 – (07 June 2007), URL: http://www.openmobilealliance.org/

[GPM AD] Open Mobile Alliance, 'Global Permissions Management Architecture', Draft Version 1.0 – (13 August 2007), URL: http://www.openmobilealliance.org/

[GPM RD] Open Mobile Alliance, 'Global Permissions Management Requirements', Candidate Version 1.0 – (28 September 2006), URL: ttp://www.openmobilealliance.org/

[GSMA] GSM Association, (November 2007), URL: http://www.gsmworld.com/

[Hirsch2006] Hirsch, F., Kemp, J., Ilkka, J., 'Mobile Web Services – Architecture and Implementation', John Wiley & Sons, (March 2006), pp. 338

[IAB] Interactive Advertising Bureau, (November 2007), URL: http://www.iab.net/

[IDC2006a] IDC Market Analysis, 'U.S. Wireless Gaming 2005–2009 Forecast', (January 2006)

[IDC2006b] IDC, 'Predictions for the Telecoms Market 2006', (January 2006) IDC Report (Doc # AP201202M)

[IETF] The Internet Engineering Task Force, (November 2007), URL: http://www.ietf.org/

[IETF Draft2007a] Rosenberg, J., 'Presence Authorization Rules', IETF Internet Draft (work in progress), Expires: (10 January 2008), URL: http://www.ietf.org/

[IETF Draft2007b] Gregorio, J. and de Hora, B., eds, 'An Atom Publishing Protocol', IETF Internet Draft (work in progress), Expires: (10 January 2007), URL: http://www.ietf.org/

[IETF P-IMAP] Maes, S., Lima, R., Kuang, C., Comwell, R., Hav, V., Chiu, E., Day, J. and Sini, J., 'Push Extensions to the IMAP Protocol (P-IMAP)', IETF Internet Draft (work in progress), Expired (September 2004)

[ILP TS] Open Mobile Alliance, 'Internal Location Protocol', Draft Version 2.0 – (14 September 2007), URL: http://www.openmobilealliance.org/

[IMF RD] Open Mobile Alliance, 'Identity Management Framework Requirements', Candidate Version 1.0 – (02 February 2005), URL:http://www.openmobilealliance.org/

[IMPP] IETF Instant Messaging and Presence Protocol (IMPP) working group charter, (November 2007), URL: http://www.ietf.org/html.charters/OLD/impp-charter.html

[IMPS AD] Open Mobile Alliance, 'IMPS Architecture', Approved Version 1.3 – (23 January 2007), URL: http://www.openmobilealliance.org/

[IMS GLC] IMS Global Learning Consortium, (November 2007), URL:http://www.imsglobal.org/

[IMSinOMA AD] Open Mobile Alliance, 'Utilization of IMS Capabilities Architecture', Approved Version 1.0 – (09 August 2005), URL: http://www.openmobilealliance.org/

[IMSinOMA RD] Open Mobile Alliance, 'Utilization of IMS capabilities Requirements', Approved Version
    1.0 – (09 August 2005), URL: http://www.openmobilealliance.org
[IMSinOMA TR] Open Mobile Alliance, 'Technical report on the usage of 3GPP/3GPP2 IMS in OMA',
    Approved Version 1.0 – (12 September 2003), URL: http://www.openmobilealliance.org
[Informa2006] Coffman, C., Informa Media and Telecom, 'Mobile Games', (July 2006)
[INTERTRUST] Intertrust Technologies Corp., (November 2007), http://www.intertrust.com/
[ISO/IEC 9595] ISO/IEC, 'Information Technology – Open Systems Interconnection – Common Management
    Information Service Element', ISO/IEC 9595:1998, published (1998), URL: http://www.iso.org/
[ISO/IEC 9899] ISO/IEC, International Standard ISO/IEC 9899, 'Programming Languages – C', 2nd edn, (01
    December 1999), URL: http://www.iso.org/iso/en/
[ITU] International Telecommunication Union, (November 2007), URL: http://www.itu.int/
[ITU M.3050] ITU, 'Enhanced Telecommunications Operations Map', ITU Recommendations M.3050.0M.
    3050-1, M.3050-2, M.3050-3, M.3050-4 and M.3050, (April 2004), URL: http://www.itu.int//
[Java] Sun Microsystems, 'The Java Language Specification', 3rd edn, (November 2007), URL:
    http://java.sun.com/
    docs/books/jls/
[J2SEBLOB] Sun Microsystems, java.sql, 'Interface Blob', Java 2 Std. Ed. v.1.4.2, URL: http://java.sun.com/
    j2se/1.4.2/docs/api/java/sql/Blob.html
[JSR 94] Java Community Process, JSR 94, 'Java Rule Engine API', (04 August 2004), URL:
    http://jcp.org/en/jsr/
[JSR 116] Java Community Process, JSR 116, 'SIP Servlet API', (07 March 2003), URL: http://jcp.org/en/jsr/
[JSR-172] Java Specification Request JSR-172, 'J2ME Web Services', 1.0 Final Release, (October 2003), URL:
    http://jcp.org/en/jsr/
[JSR 289] Java Community Process, JSR 289, 'SIP Servlet v1.1', (30 January 2007), URL: http://jcp.org/en/jsr/
[Kaye2003] Kaye, D., 'Loosely Coupled, The Missing Pieces of Web Services', RDS Press, (2003), pp. 332,
    ISBN 1881378241
[LEMONADE] IETF Working Group Charter, 'Enhancements to Internet email to Support Diverse Service
    Environments (lemonade)' (accessed September 2007), [online], http://www.ietf.org/html.charters/lemonade-
    charter.html
[LEMONADE bis] Cridland, D., Melnikov, A., Maes, S., 'The Lemonade Profile', IETF Internet Draft (work
    in progress), expires: (05 October 2007
[Liberty-AuthnContext] 'Liberty Authentication Context Specification', Version 1.2, Liberty Alliance Project,
    URL: http://www.projectliberty.org
[Liberty-BindProf] 'Liberty Bindings and Profiles Specification', Version 1.2, Liberty Alliance Project, URL:
    http://www.projectliberty.org
[Liberty-IDWSF-AuthnSSO] 'Liberty ID-WSF Authentication Service and Single Sign-on Service Specifica-
    tion', Version 1.1, Liberty Alliance Project, URL: http://www.projectliberty.org
[Liberty-IDWSF-Client-Profiles] 'Liberty ID-WSF Profiles for Liberty Enabled User Agents and Devices',
    Version 1.1, Liberty Alliance Project, URL: http://www.projectliberty.org
[Liberty-IDWSF-Disco] 'Liberty ID-WSF Discovery Service Specification', Version 1.2, Liberty Alliance
    Project, URL: http://www.projectliberty.org
[Liberty-IDWSF-DST] 'Liberty ID-WSF Data Services Template Specification', Version 1.1, Liberty Alliance
    Project, URL: http://www.projectliberty.org
[Liberty-IDWSF-Interaction-Svc] 'Liberty ID-WSF Interaction Service Specification', Version 1.1, Liberty
    Alliance Project, URL: http://www.projectliberty.org
[Liberty-IDWSF-Security-Mechanisms] 'Liberty ID-WSF Security Mechanisms', Version 1.2, Liberty Alliance
    Project, URL: http://www.projectliberty.org
[Liberty-IDWSF-SOAP-Binding] 'Liberty ID-WSF SOAP Binding Specification', Version 1.2, Liberty Alliance
    Project, URL: http://www.projectliberty.org
[Liberty-ProtSchema] 'Liberty Protocols and Schema Specification', Version 1.2, Liberty Alliance Project,
    URL:http://www.projectliberty.org
[MCOM WP] Open Mobile Alliance, 'MCommerce Landscape', OMA-WP-McommerceLandscape, Approved,
    (December 2005), URL:http://www.openmobilealliance.org/
[MEF] Mobile Entertainment Forum, (November 2007), URL: http://www.m-e-f.org/
[MEM AD] Open Mobile Alliance, 'Mobile Email Architecture Document', Draft Version 1.0 – (14 June 2007),
    URL: http://www.openmobilealliance.org/
[MEM RD] Open Mobile Alliance, 'Mobile Email Requirements', Candidate Version 1.0 – (18 October 2005),
    URL: http://www.openmobilealliance.org/
[MLP TS] Open Mobile Alliance, 'Mobile Location Protocol 3.2', Candidate Version 3.2 – (24 November
    2005) URL: http://www.openmobilealliance.org/

[MLS ERP] Open Mobile Alliance, 'Enabler Release Package for Mobile Location Service (MLS)', Candidate Version 1.0 – (24 November 2005), URL: http://www.openmobilealliance.org/

[MMA] Mobile Marketing Association, (November 2007), URL: http://www.mmaglobal.com/

[MMMD AD] Open Mobile Alliance, 'OMA Multimodal and Multi-device Enabler Architecture', Draft Version 1.0 – (11 October 2006), URL: http://www.openmobilealliance.org/

[MMMD RD] Open Mobile Alliance, 'Multimodal and Multi-device Services Requirements', Candidate Version 1.1 – (13 November 2003), URL: http://www.openmobilealliance.org/

[MMS-V1.2 ERELD] Open Mobile Alliance, 'Enabler Release Definition for MMS', Candidate Version 1.2 – (23 June 2004), URL: http://www.openmobilealliance.org/

[MMS-V1.3 ERELD] Open Mobile Alliance, 'Enabler Release Definition for MMS', Candidate Version 1.3 – (27 October 2005), URL: http://www.openmobilealliance.org/

[MobAd WP] Open Mobile Alliance, 'White Paper on Mobile Advertising – Framework, Scope and Initiatives', Approved – (15 May 2007), URL: http://www.openmobilealliance.org/

[Motorola2006] Vasudevan, V. Motorola, 'Collaborative Mobile Gaming', Motorola Position Paper, (June 2006), URL: http://www.motorola.com/

[MPEG-LA] MPEG Licensing Authority, (November 2007), URL: http://www.mpegla.com/

[Newcomer2002] Newcomer, E., 'Understanding Web Services: XML, WSDL, SOAP, and UDDI', Addison-Wesley Professional, (May 2002), pp. 368, ISBN: 0201750813

[Nokia2006] Nokia, 'Evolution of Mobile Gaming', (December 2006), URL: http://sw.nokia.com/

[OASIS WS BPEL] OASIS, 'Web Services Business Process Execution Language', Version 2.0, URL: http://www.oasis-open.org/

[OASIS XACML] OASIS, 'XACML – eXtensible Access Control Markup Language', Version 2.0, URL: http://www.oasis-open.org/

[OBEX] Infrared Data Association, 'IrDA Object Exchange (OBEX) Protocol v1.2', URL: http://www.irda.org/standards/pubs/OBEX1p2_Plus.zip

[ObjEmail TS] Open Mobile Alliance, 'Email Data Object Specification', Approved Version 1.2.1 – (10 July 2007), URL: http://www.openmobilealliance.org/

[ObjFile TS] Open Mobile Alliance, 'File Data Object Specification', Approved Version 1.2.1 – (10 August 2007), URL: http://www.openmobilealliance.org/

[ObjFolder TS] Open Mobile Alliance, 'Folder Data Object Specification', Approved Version 1.2.1 – (10 August 2007), URL: http://www.openmobilealliance.org/

[OBKG RD] Open Mobile Alliance, 'On-Board Key Generation Requirements', Candidate Version 1.0 – (22 March 2005), URL: http://www.openmobilealliance.org/

[OCSPMP TS] Open Mobile Alliance, 'Online Certificate Status Protocol Mobile Profile', Approved Version 1.0 – (03 March 2007), URL: http://www.openmobilealliance.org/

[ODRL] The Open Digital Rights Language Initiative, 'Open Digital Rights Language (ODRL)', Version 1.1 (08 August 2002), URL: http://odrl.net/

[OMNA] Open Mobile Alliance, 'Open Mobile Naming Authority (OMNA)', URL: http://www.openmobilealliance.org/tech/omna/index.htm

[OSA] ETSI Overview & Status of OSA API Specifications, (November 2007), URL: http://portal.etsi.org/docbox/TISPAN/Open/OSA/Overview.html

[OSE AD] Open Mobile Alliance, 'OMA Service Environment', Approved Version 1.0.4 – (01 February 2007), URL: http://www.openmobilealliance.org/

[OSPE RD] Open Mobile Alliance, 'OMA Service Provider Environment Requirements', Candidate Version 1.0 – (14 June 2005), URL: http://www.openmobilealliance.org/

[OSPE AD] Open Mobile Alliance, 'OMA Service Provider Environment Architecture', Draft Version 1.0 – (30 August 2007), URL: http://www.openmobilealliance.org/

[Ovum2007] Ovum, 'Gaming', Japan: Wireless Multimedia Market, (March 2007)

[OWSERCore] Open Mobile Alliance, 'OMA Web Services Enabler (OWSER): Core Specifications' Approved Version 1.1 – (28 March 2006), URL:http://www.openmobilealliance.org/

[OWSERNIArc] Open Mobile Alliance, 'OMA Web Services Network Identity Architecture', Approved Version 1.0 – (28 March 2006), URL:http://www.openmobilealliance.org/

[OWSERNI-FF] Open Mobile Alliance, 'OMA Network Identity Federation Framework', Approved Version 1.0 – (28 March 2006), URL:http://www.openmobilealliance.org/

[OWSERNIReq] Open Mobile Alliance, 'MWS Identity Management (OWSER NI) Requirements', Approved Version 1.0 – (28 March 2006), URL: http://www.openmobilealliance.org/

[OWSERNI-WSF] Open Mobile Alliance, 'OMA Network Identity Web Services Framework', Approved Version 1.0 – (28 March 2006), URL: http://www.openmobilealliance.org/

[OWSEROvw] Open Mobile Alliance, 'OMA Web Services Enabler (OWSER): Overview', Approved Version 1.1 – (28 March 2006), URL: http://www.openmobilealliance.org/

[OWSERReq] Open Mobile Alliance, 'OMA Web Services Enabler (OWSER): Requirements', Approved Version 1.1 – (28 March 2006), URL: http://www.openmobilealliance.org/

[OWSERWSDL] Open Mobile Alliance, 'OMA Web Services Enabler (OWSER) Best Practices: WSDL Style Guide', Approved Version 1.1 – (28 March 2006), URL: http://www.openmobilealliance.org/

[Parlay] The Parlay Group, URL: http://www.parlay.org

[Parlay TS] The Parlay Group, 'Parlay Specifications', (November 2007), URL: http://www.parlay.org/en/specifications/

[Parlay X] ETSI OSA Parlay X, 'Parlay X 2.0 Specifications', URL: http://portal.etsi.org/docbox/TISPAN/Open/OSA/parlayx20.html

[PCP TS] Open Mobile Alliance, 'Privacy Checking Protocol', Candidate Version 1.0 – (20 October 2006), URL: http://www.openmobilealliance.org/

[PEEM RD] Open Mobile Alliance, 'Policy Evaluation, Enforcement and Management Requirements', Candidate Version 1.0 – (12 January 2005), URL: http://www.openmobilealliance.org/

[PEEM AD] Open Mobile Alliance, 'Policy Evaluation, Enforcement and Management Architecture', Draft Version 1.0 – (25 June 2006), URL: http://www.openmobilealliance.org/

[PEM-1 TS] Open Mobile Alliance, 'Policy Evaluation, Enforcement and Management Callable Interface (PEM-1) Technical Specification', Draft Version 1.0 – (12 August 2007), URL: http://www.openmobilealliance.org/

[PEM-2 TS] Open Mobile Alliance, 'Policy Evaluation, Enforcement and Management – Management Interface (PEM-2) Technical Specification', Draft Version 1.0 – (12 August 2007), URL: http://www.openmobilealliance.org/

[PEL-TS] Open Mobile Alliance, 'PEEM Policy Expression Language Technical Specification', Draft Version 1.0 – (12 August 2007), URL: http://www.openmobilealliance.org/

[PIOSE AD] Open Mobile Alliance, 'Parlay in OSE Architecture', Draft Version 1.0 – (22 June 2007), URL: http://www.openmobilealliance.org/

[PIOSE RD] Open Mobile Alliance, 'Parlay/OSA in OSE Requirements', Candidate Version 1.0 – (15 June 2007), URL: http://www.openmobilealliance.org/

[POC-V1_0 RD] Open Mobile Alliance, 'Push to Talk over Cellular Requirements', Approved Version 1.0 – (09 June 2006), URL: http://www.openmobilealliance.org/

[POC-V1_0 AD] Open Mobile Alliance, 'Push to Talk over Cellular (PoC) Architecture', Approved Version 1.0.2 – (05 September 2007), URL: http://www.openmobilealliance.org/

[POC-V1_0 UserPlane TS] Open Mobile Alliance, 'PoC User Plane', Approved Version 1.0.2 – (05 September 2007), URL: http://www.openmobilealliance.org/

[POC-V2_0 AD] Open Mobile Alliance, 'Push to Talk over Cellular (PoC) Architecture', Draft Version 2.0 – (08 August 2007), URL: http://www.openmobilealliance.org/

[POC-V2_0 ControlPlane TS] Open Mobile Alliance, 'OMA PoC Control Plane', Draft Version 2.0 – (24 August 2007), URL: http://www.openmobilealliance.org/

[POC-XDM-V1_0 TS] Open Mobile Alliance, 'PoC XDM Specification', Approved Version 1.0 – (09 June 2006), URL: http://www.openmobilealliance.org/

[Poikselka2006] Poikselka, M., Niemi, A., Khartabil, H., Mayer, G., 'The IMS: IP Multimedia Concepts and Services', 2nd Edition John Wiley & Sons, (10 March 2006), pp. 466, ISBN: 0470019069

[Presence AD] Open Mobile Alliance, 'Presence SIMPLE Architecture', Draft Version 2.0 – (03 September 2007), URL: http://www.openmobilealliance.org/

[Presence-V1_0 TS] Open Mobile Alliance, 'Presence XDM Specification', Approved Version 1.0 – (25 July 2006), URL: http://www.openmobilealliance.org/

[Privacy RD] Open Mobile Alliance, 'Privacy Requirements for Mobile Services', Approved Version 1.0.1 – (07 August 2007), URL: http://www.openmobilealliance.org/

[Prov AD] Open Mobile Alliance, 'Provisioning Architecture Overview', Candidate Version 1.1 – (28 April 2005), URL:http://www.openmobilealliance.org/

[Push ERP] Open Mobile Alliance, 'OMA Push Enabler Release Package', Candidate Version 2.1 – (22 November 2005), URL:http://www.openmobilealliance.org/

[PushAP TS] Open Mobile Alliance, 'Push Access Protocol', Candidate Version 2.1 – (22 November 2005), URL: http://www.openmobilealliance.org/

[PushEMN TS] Open Mobile Alliance, 'E-Mail Notification Version 1.0', Candidate 1.0 – (14 June 2004), URL: http://www.openmobilealliance.org/

[PushOTA TS] Open Mobile Alliance, 'Push Over The Air', Candidate Version 2.1 – (22 November 2005), URL: http://www.openmobilealliance.org/

[PushSIP TS] Open Mobile Alliance, 'Push using SIP', Draft Version 0.10 – (10 September 2007), URL: http://www.openmobilealliance.org/

[RFC 822] Crocker, D.H., 'STANDARD FOR THE FORMAT OF ARPA INTERNET TEXT MESSAGES', IETF RFC 822, (August 1982), URL: http://www.ietf.org/

[RFC 0959] Postel, J. and Reynolds, J., 'FILE TRANSFER PROTOCOL (FTP)', IETF RFC 0959, (October 1985), URL: http://www.ietf.org/

[RFC 1157] Case, J. 'A Simple Network Management Protocol (SNMP)', IETF RFC 1157, (May 1990), URL: http://www.ietf.org/

[RFC 1939] Myers, J., Rose, M., 'The Post Office Protocol Version 3', IETF RFC 1939, (May 1996), URL: http://www.ietf.org/

[RFC 1945] Fielding, R., Frystyk, H. and Berners-Lee, T., 'Hypertext Transfer Protocol – HTTP/1.0', IETF RFC 1945, (May 1996), URL: http://www.ietf.org/

[RFC 2045] Freed, N., Borenstein, N., 'Multipurpose Internet Mail Extensions (MIME) Part One: Format of Internet Message Bodies', IETF RFC 2045, (November 1996), URL: http://www.ietf.org/

[RFC 2246] Dierks, T., Allen, C., 'The TLS Protocol Version, 1.0.', IETF RFC 2246, (January 1999), URL: http://www.ietf.org/

[RFC 2278] Day, M., Rosenberg, J., Sugano, H., 'A Model for Presence and Instant Messaging', IETF RFC 2278, (February 2000), URL: http://www.ietf.org/

[RFC 2279] Day, M., Aggarwal, S., Mohr, G., Vincent, J., 'Instant Messaging/Presence Protocol Requirements', IETF RFC 2278, (February 2000), URL: http://www.ietf.org/

[RFC 2401] Kent, S. and Atkinson, R., 'Security Architecture for the Internet Protocol', IETF RFC 2401, (November 1998), URL: http://www.ietf.org/

[RFC 2406] Kent, S. and Atkinson, R., 'IP Encapsulating Security Payload (ESP)', IETF RFC 2406, (November 1998), URL: http://www.ietf.org/

[RFC 2560] Myers, M., Ankney, R., Malpani, A., Galperin, S., and Adams, C., 'X.509 Internet Public Key Infrastructure Online Certificate Status Protocol – OCSP', IETF RFC 2560, (June 1999), URL: http://www.ietf.org/

[RFC 2616] Fielding, R., Gettys, J., Mogul, J., Frystyk Nielsen, H., Masinter, L., Leach, P., Berners-Lee, T. 'Hypertext Transfer Protocol – HTTP/1.1', IETF RFC 2616, (June 1999), URL: http://www.ietf.org/

[RFC 2617] Franks, J., Hallam-Baker, P, Hostetler, J., Lawrence, S., Leach, P., Luotonen, A., Stewart, L., 'HTTP Authentication: Basic and Digest Access Authentication', (June 1999), URL: http://www.ietf.org/

[RFC 2753] Yavatkar, R., Pendarakis, J., Guerin, R., 'A Framework for Policy-based Admission Control', IETF RFC 2753, (January 2000), URL: http://www.ietf.org/

[RFC 2778] Day, M., Rosenberg, J., Sugano, H., 'A Model for Presence and Instant Messaging', IETF RFC 2778, (February 2000), URL: http://www.ietf.org/

[RFC 2779] Day, M., Aggarwal, S., Mohr, G., Vincent, J., 'Instant Messaging/Presence Protocol Requirements', IETF RFC 2779, (February 2000), URL: http://www.ietf.org/

[RFC 2817] Khare, R., Lawrence, S., 'Upgrading to TLS Within HTTP/1.1', IETF RFC 2817, (May 2000), URL: http://www.ietf.org/

[RFC 2821] Klensin, J., 'Simple Mail Transfer Protocol', IETF RFC 2821, (April 2001), URL: http://www.ietf.org/

[RFC 2828] Shirey, R., 'Internet Security Glossary', IETF RFC 2828, (May 2000), URL: http://www.ietf.org/

[RFC 3060] Moore, B., Ellesson, E., Strassner, J., Westerinen, A., 'Policy Core Information Model – Version 1 Specification', IETF RFC 3060, (February 2001), URL: http://www.ietf.org/

[RFC 3198] Westerinen, A., Schnizlein, J., Strassner, J., Scherling, M., Quinn, B., Herzog, S., Huynh, A., Carlson, M., Perry, J., Waldbusser, S., 'Terminology for Policy-Based Management', IETF RFC 3198, (November 2001), URL: http://www.ietf.org/

[RFC 3261] Rosenberg, J., Schulzrinne, H., Camarillo, G., Johnston, A., Peterson, J., Sparks, R., Handley, M. and Schooler, E., 'SIP: Session Initiation Protocol', IETF RFC 3261, (June 2002), URL: http://www.ietf.org/

[RFC 3265] Roach, A.B., 'Session Initiation Protocol (SIP)-Specific Event Notification', IETF RFC 3265, (June 2002), URL: http://www.ietf.org/

[RFC 3267] Sjoberg, J., Westerlund, M., Lakaniemi, A., Xie, Q., 'Real-Time Transport Protocol (RTP) Payload Format and File Storage Format for the Adaptive Multi-Rate (AMR) and Adaptive Multi-Rate Wideband (AMR-WB) Audio Codecs', IETF RFC 3267, (June 2002), URL: http://www.ietf.org/

[RFC 3460] Moore, B., Editor, 'Policy Core Information Model (PCIM) Extensions', IETF RFC 3460, (January 2003), URL: http://www.ietf.org/

[RFC 3501] Crispin, M., 'Internet Message Access Protocol – Version 4rev1', IETF RFC 3501, (March 2003), URL: http://www.ietf.org/

[RFC 3550] Schulzrinne, H., Casner, S., Frederick, R., Jackobson, V., 'RTP: A Transport Protocol for Real-Time Applications', IETF RFC 3550, (July 2003), URL: http://www.ietf.org/

[RFC 3588] Calhoun, P., Loughney, J., Guttman, E., Zorn, G., Arkko, J., 'Diameter Base Protocol', IETF RFC 3588, (September 2003), URL: http://www.ietf.org/

[RFC 3605] Huitema, C., 'Real Time Control Protocol (RTCP) attribute in Session Description Protocol (SDP)', IETF RFC 3605, (October 2003), URL: http://www.ietf.org/

[RFC 3629] Yergeau, F., 'UTF-8, a Transformation Format of ISO 10646', IETF RFC 3629, (November 2003), URL: http://www.ietf.org

[RFC 3975] Huston, G., Leuca, I., 'OMA-IETF Standardization Collaboration', IETF RFC 3975, (January 2005), URL: http://www.ietf.org/

[RFC 3986] Berners-Lee, T., Fielding, R., Masinter, L. 'Uniform Resource Identifier (URI): Generic Syntax', IETF RFC 3986, (January 2005), URL: http://www.ietf.org/

[RFC 4005] Calhoun, P., Zorn, G., Spence, D., Mitton, D., 'Diameter Network Access Server Application', IETF RFC 4005, (August 2005), URL: http://www.ietf.org/

[RFC 4006] Hakala, H., Mattila, L., Koskinen, J.P., Stura, M., Loughney, J., 'Diameter Credit-Control Application', IETF RFC 4006, (August 2005), URL: http://www.ietf.org/

[RFC 4279] Eronen, P. and H. Tschofenig, 'Pre-shared Key Ciphersuites for Transport Layer Security (TLS)', IETF RFC, (December 2005), URL: http://www.ietf.org/

[RFC 4287] Nottingham, M and Sayre, R., Editors, 'The Atom Syndication Format', IETF RFC 4287, (December 2005), URL: http://www.ietf.org/

[RFC 4550] Maes, S., Melnikov, A., 'Internet Email to Support Diverse Service Environments (Lemonade) Profile', IETF RFC 4550, (June 2006,2005), URL: http://www.ietf.org/

[RFC 4745] Schulzrinne, H., Morris, J., Tschofenig, H., Cuellar, J., Polk, J., Rosenberg, J., 'Common Policy: A Document Format for Expressing Privacy Preferences', IETF RFC 4745, (February 2007), URL: http://www.ietf.org/

[RFC 4825] Rosenberg, J. 'The Extensible Markup Language (XML) Configuration Access protocol (XCAP)', IETF RFC 4825, (May 2007), URL: http://www.ietf.org/

[RIM] Research In Motion, (November 2007), http://www.blackberry.com/

[RLP TS] Open Mobile Alliance, 'Roaming Location Protocol', Candidate Version 1.0 – (24 November 2005), URL: http://www.openmobilealliance.org/

[RSS] Really Simple Syndication, 'RSS 2.0 Specification', (June 2007), URL: http://www.rssboard.org/rss-specification/

[SAMLConf] OASIS 'Conformance Program Specification for the OASIS Security Assertions Markup Language', OASIS Standard, (05 November 2002), URL:http://www.oasis-open.org/

[SCE RD] Open Mobile Alliance, 'Secure Content Exchange Requirements', Candidate Version 1.0 – (20 October 2006), URL: http://www.openmobilealliance.org/

[SCOMO TS] Open Mobile Alliance, 'Software Component Management Object', Draft Version 1.0 – (03 September 2007), URL:http://www.openmobilealliance.org/

[SCWS TS] Open Mobile Alliance, 'Smartcard-Web-Server', Candidate Version 1.0 – (09 February 2007), URL: http://www.openmobilealliance.org/

[SECCF AD] Open Mobile Alliance, 'Security Common Functions Architecture', Draft Version 1.0 – (13 August 2007), URL: http://www.openmobilealliance.org/

[SIMPLE] IETF SIP for Instant Messaging and Presence Leveraging Extensions (simple) working group charter, (November 2007), URL: http://www.ietf.org/html.charters/simple-charter.html

[Singhal 2001] Singhal, S., Bridgman, T., Suyranarayana, L., Manuey, D., Chan, J., Bevis, D., Hild, S., Alvinen, J., 'The Wireless Application Protocol: Writing Applications for the Mobile Internet', 1st Edition Addison Wesley Longman; (15 January 2001), pp. 678, ISBN: 0201703114

[SIPPush RD] Open Mobile Alliance, 'SIP Based Push Requirements', Approved Version 1.0 – (29 November 2004), URL: http://www.openmobilealliance.org/

[SMIL RD] Open Mobile Alliance, 'Mobile Domain SMIL Requirements', Candidate Version 1.0 – (09 February 2006), URL: http://www.openmobilealliance.org/

[SOAP1.1] W3C Note, 'Simple Object Access Protocol (SOAP)', Version 1.1, (08 May 2000), URL: http://www.w3.org/TR/soap/

[SOAP1.2] W3C Note, 'Simple Object Access Protocol (SOAP)', Version 1.2, (24 June 2003), URL: http://www.w3.org/TR/soap/

[SOAPwAtt] W3C Note, 'SOAP Messages with Attachments', (11 December 2000), URL: http://www.w3.org/TR/SOAP-attachments/

[SPRULES] Rosenberg, J. 'Presence Authorization Rules', IETF Internet Draft (work in progress, expires: January 10, 2008), URL: http://www.ietf.org/internet-drafts/draft-ietf-simple-presence-rules-10.txt

[SRM RD] Open Mobile Alliance, 'OMA Secure Removable Media Requirements', Candidate Version 1.0 – (10 October 2006), URL: http://www.openmobilealliance.org/

[SSL3.0] 'The SSL Protocol Version 3.0', URL:http://wp.netscape.com/eng/ssl3/draft302.txt

[STI ERP] Open Mobile Alliance, 'Enabler Release Package for Standard Transcoding Interface', Approved Version 1.0 – (15 May 2007), URL: http://www.openmobilealliance.org/

[SVG RD] Open Mobile Alliance, 'SVG in the Mobile Domain Requirements', Candidate Version 1.0 – (12 January 2005), URL: http://www.openmobilealliance.org/

[SUPL-V1_0 AD] Open Mobile Alliance, 'Secure User Plane Location Architecture', Approved Version 1.0 – (15 June 2007), URL: http://www.openmobilealliance.org/

[SUPL-V2_0 AD] Open Mobile Alliance, 'Secure User Plane Location Architecture', Draft Version 2.0 – (31 August 2007), URL: http://www.openmobilealliance.org/

[SyncML ERP] Open Mobile Alliance, 'OMA SyncML Common Specification Enabler Release Package', Approved Version 1.2.1 – (13 August 2007), URL:http://www.openmobilealliance.org/

[SyncML-HTTP TS] Open Mobile Alliance, 'SyncML HTTP Binding', Approved Version 1.2 – (21 February 2007), URL:http://www.openmobilealliance.org/

[SyncML-OBEX TS] Open Mobile Alliance, 'SyncML OBEX Binding', Approved Version 1.2 – (21 February 2007), URL:http://www.openmobilealliance.org/

[SyncML-RepPro TS] Open Mobile Alliance, 'SyncML Representation Protocol', Approved Version 1.2 – (21 February 2007), URL:http://www.openmobilealliance.org/

[TelecomTV2007] TelecomTV/Mobile World TV, Daniels, G., 'Is the Fun going out of Mobile Gaming?' (March 2007), URL: http://www.telecomtv.com/

[TINA] Telecommunications Information Networking Architecture Consortium, URL: http://www.tinac.com/

[TM Forum GB 922] TM Forum, 'Shared Information/Data (SID) Model, Business Views Concepts, Principles and Domains', Release 6.0, GB922, V6.2, (December 2005), URL: http://www.tmforum.org/

[TLS Profile TS] Open Mobile Alliance, 'OMA TLS Profile', Draft Version 1.0 – (07 June 2007), URL: http://www.openmobilealliance.org/

[UDDI] 'UDDI Version 2.04 API Specification', UDDI Committee Specification, (19 July 2002), URL: http://uddi.org/

[UDDIData] 'UDDI Version 2.03 Data Structure Reference', UDDI Committee Specification, (19 July 2002), URL: http://uddi.org/

[ULP TS] Open Mobile Alliance, 'UserPlane Location Protocol', Draft Version 2.0 – (05 September 2007), URL: http://www.openmobilealliance.org/

[Unmehopa2006] Unmehopa, M., Vemuri, K. and Bennett, A., 'Parlay/OSA: From Standards to Reality', John Wiley & Sons, (January 2006), pp 322, ISBN: 0470025956

[vBook1.0] Infrared Data Association, 'IrDA Infrared Mobile Communications v1.1', URL: http://www.irda.org/

[vCal1.0] Internet Mail Consortium, 'vCalendar – The Electronic Calendaring and Scheduling Exchange Format', Version 1.0, (18 September 1996), URL: http://www.imc.org/pdi/

[vCard2.1] Internet Mail Consortium, 'vCard – The Electronic Business Card', Version 2.1, (18 September 1996), URL: http://www.imc.org/pdi/

[vObject TS] Open Mobile Alliance, 'vObject Minimum Interoperability Profile', Candidate Version 1.0 – (18 January 2005), URL: http://www.openmobilealliance.org/

[W3C DOM2CORE] W3C Recommendation, 'Document Object Model (DOM) Level 2 Core Specification', Version 1.0, (13 November 2000), URL: http://www.w3.org/TR/2000/REC-DOM-Level-2-Core-20001113/

[W3C MWBP] W3C, 'Mobile Web Best Practices 1.0', http://www.w3.org/TR/mobile-bp/

[W3C RDF] W3C, 'Resource Description Framework', http://www.w3.org/

[W3C SGML OVW] W3C, 'Overview of SGML Resources', URL: http://www.w3.org/

[W3C SVGT] W3C Recommendation, 'Mobile SVG Profiles: SVG Tiny and SVG Basic', (14 January 2003), URL: http://www.w3.org/TR/SVGMobile/

[W3C WS Glossary] W3C, 'Web Services Glossary', W3C Working Group Note, (11 February 2004), URL: http://www.w3.org/

[WAP AD] Open Mobile Alliance, 'WAP Architecture', Version 12 (July 2001), Wireless Application Protocol Architecture Specification, URL: http://www.openmobilealliance.org/

[WDP] Open Mobile Alliance, 'Wireless Datagram Protocol', Open Mobile Alliance, WAP-259-WDP, URL:http://www.openmobilealliance.org/

[Weerawarana2005] Weerawarana, S., Curbera, F., Leymann, F., Storey, T., Ferguson, D.F., 'Web Services Platform Architecture', Prentice Hall PTR, (March 2005), pp. 456, ISBN: 0131488740

[WIM TS] Open Mobile Alliance, 'Wireless Identity Module', Candidate Version 1.0 – (22 March 2005), URL: http://www.openmobilealliance.org/

[WKPI DF] Open Mobile Alliance, 'Wireless Protocol Key Infrastructure Definition', Candidate Version 1.1 – (22 March 2005), URL: http://www.openmobilealliance.org/

[WS-Arch] W3C Working Group Note, 'Web Services Architecture', (11 February 2004), URL: http://www.w3.org/TR/ws-arch/

[WS-AT] OASIS, 'Web Services Atomic Transaction (WS-AtomicTransaction) 1.1', (16 April 2007), URL: http://docs.oasis-open.org/

[WS-BA] OASIS, 'Web Services Business Activity (WS-Business Activity) 1.1', (16 April 2007), URL: http://docs.oasis-open.org

[WS-BPEL] OASIS, 'Business Process Execution Language', Web Services Business Process Execution Language Version 2.0, URL: http://docs.oasis-open.org

[WS-Federation] OASIS, 'Web Services Federation Language (WS-Federation)', Version 1.2, Editors Draft – 01, (18 June 2007), URL: http://docs.oasis-open.org

[WS-Policy] W3C, Web Services Policy Working Group, (November 2007), URL: http://www.w3.org/2002/ws/policy/

[WS-RM] OASIS, 'WS-Reliability 1.1', OASIS Standard, (15 November 2004), URL: http://docs.oasis-open.org/

[WS-SecureConversation] OASIS, 'WS-SecureConversation 1.3', OASIS Standard, (01 March 2007), URL: http://docs.oasis-open.org/

[WS-Trust] OASIS, 'WS-Trust 1.3', OASIS Standard, (19 March 2007), URL:http://docs.oasis-open.org/

[WSDL1.1] 'Web Services Description Language (WSDL) 1.1', Erik Christensen, Francisco Cubrera, Greg Meredith, Sanjiva Weeravarana, W3C NOTE, (15 March 2001), URL:http://www.w3.org/TR/wsdl.html

[WSI-Ovrvw] 'Interoperability: Ensuring the success of Web Services, An Overview to WS-I', Web Services Interoperability Organization, URL: http://www.ws-i.org/docs/20041130.introduction.ppt

[WSI BP1.0] Web Services Interoperability Organization Basic Profile Version 1.0, Final Material, (April 2004), URL: http://www.ws-i.org/Profiles/BasicProfile-1.0.html

[WSP TS] Open Mobile Alliance, 'Wireless Session Protocol 1.0', Candidate Version 1.0 – (20 September 2002), URL: http://www.openmobilealliance.org/

[WTP TS] Open Mobile Alliance, 'Wireless Transaction Protocol', Version 1.0, (10 July 2001), URL: http://www.openmobilealliance.org/

[XACML] Moses, T., Editor, 'OASIS eXtensible Access Control Markup Language (XACML)', Version 2.0, (01 February 2005), OASIS Standard, URL: http://docs.oasis-open.org/xacml/2.0/

[XDM AD] Open Mobile Alliance, 'XML Document Management Architecture', Candidate Version 2.0 – (24 July 2007), URL: http://www.openmobilealliance.org/

[XDM Core 1.0 TS] Open Mobile Alliance, 'XML Document Management (XDM) Specification', Approved Version 1.0 – (12 June 2006), URL: http://www.openmobilealliance.org/

[XDM Shared 1.0 TS] Open Mobile Alliance, 'Shared XDM Specification', Approved Version 1.0 – (12 June 2006), URL: http://www.openmobilealliance.org/

[XHTMLMP TS] Open Mobile Alliance, 'XHTML Mobile Profile', Candidate Version 1.2 – (18 January 2005), URL:http://www.openmobilealliance.org/

[XKMS] W3C Recommendation, 'XML Key Management Specification (XKMS 2.0)', Version 2.0, 28 (June 2005), URL: http://www.w3.org/TR/xkms2/

[XML-Canon] W3C Recommendation, 'Canonical XML', Version 1.0, (15 March 2001), URL: http://www.w3.org/TR/xml-c14n

[XML-ENC] W3C Recommendation, 'XML Encryption Syntax and Processing', (10 December 2002), URL: http://www.w3.org/TR/xmlenc-core/

[XML-SIG] W3C Recommendation, 'XML-Signature Syntax and Processing', (12 February 2002), URL: http://www.w3.org/TR/xmldsig-core/

[XML-XCanon] W3C Recommendation, 'Exclusive XML Canonicalization', Version 1.0, (18 July 2002), URL: http://www.w3.org/TR/xml-exc-c14n/

[XML1.0] W3C Recommendation, 'Extensible Markup Language (XML) 1.0 (4th Edition)', (16 August 2006), URL: http://www.w3.org/TR/xml

[XMLInfoSet] Cowan, J. and Tobin, R. W3C Recommendation, 'XML Information Set', (October 2001), URL: http://www.w3.org/TR/2001/REC-xml-infoset-20011024/

[XMLNS] W3C Recommendation, 'Namespaces in XML 1.0 (2nd Edition)', (16 August 2006), URL: http://www.w3.org/TR/xml-names

[XMLSchema1] W3C Recommendation, 'XML Schema Part 1: Structures 2nd Edition', (28 October 2004), http://www.w3.org/TR/xmlschema-1/

[XMLSchema2] W3C Recommendation, 'XML Schema Part 2: Datatypes 2nd Edition', (28 October 2004), http://www.w3.org/TR/xmlschema-2/

[XMPP] http://www.ietf.org/html.charters/OLD/xmpp-charter.html

[YahooMail] T-Mobile Yahoo® Mail Service, (accessed September 2007), [online], http://www.t-zones.co.uk/en /Messaging/chat/yahoo.html

[Yankee2004] Davis, M., Yankee Group, 'Korea Points the Way to the Future of Broadband', (October 2004)

[Yankee2006a] Goodman, M., Yankee Group, 'Video Games Are the Next Frontier for Advertisers', (March, 2006)

[Yankee2006b] The Yankee Group, 'Consumers Demand a Very Different Mobile Email Experience', (02 October 2006)

Index

18Crypt, 306
1×RTT, 239
2.5G, 329
2G, 416
3G, 329, 416
3GPP (*see* Third Generation Partnership Project)
3GPP Presence service, 215
3GPP vendor id, 265
3GPP/3GPP2 (3GPP/2), 53, 198, 211, 215
3GPP2 (*see* Third Generation Partnership Project 2)
4-pass, 297

Access, 210
Access configuration, 274
Accessg control, 178, 182
Access point name, 283
Account management, 252
Account object, 279
Accounting Answer (ACA) message, 264
Accounting Request (ACR) message, 264
Acquirer, 253
Act whenever (game), 369
Action, 95, 343
Active (component), 284
Actor, 59, 326, 339, 370, 412
Actor Session, 370
AD (*see* Architecture Document)
Ad Engine, 425
Ad Hoc Group (AHG), 29, 31
Ad hoc PoC group, 226
Ad hoc session, 230
Ad Manager, 425
Adaptation of content, 405
Adaptation to the underlying BDS, 308
Adaptive content delivery, 333
Adaptive Multi-rate (AMR), 226
Adaptive Multi-rate Wide Band (AMR-WB), 227
Add command, 278, 280
Address resolution, 204
Addressing, 242
Ad-enabled application, 425
Administration functions, 244
Administrative filter, 247
AdSelector, 425
Advanced Audio Coding (AAC), 293
Advanced revocation alert function, 231
Advertisement personalization, 422
Advertiser, 422

Advertising Agency, 422
Advertising campaign measurement and auditing, 424
Advertising channel, 421
Advertising guideline, 423
Affiliate, 22, 205
Affiliation, 401
Agent, 196, 204
Aggregate management operation, 279
Aggregate operation, 278
Aggregated one-time event, 261
Aggregating presence updates, 199
Aggregation function, 258
Aggregation Proxy, 209, 212, 214
Aggregation Proxy of Remote Network, 211
Aggregator, 321
A-GPS (*see* Assisted GPS)
A-GPS-capable device, 389
AHG (*see* Ad Hoc Group)
Air interface, 308
Alert, 227
Alias, 204
Allow, 199
Allow list, 198
Almanac data, 382
Analog media, 301
Anonymous call, 230
Anti-piracy, 290
API (*see* Application Programming Interface)
Application, 323, 370
Application agnostic, 15
Application dispatching, 69
Application domain, 220
Application instance, 370
Application interface, 421
Application Programming Interface (API), 204, 369, 370
Application Provider, 47, 59
Application rendering, 414
Application Server, 204, 432
Application Usage Identity (AUID), 211
Applications Tier, 23
Application-specific Management Object, 285
Approved Enabler Release, 35, 391
Approved enabler specifications, 233
Approved state, 35
Approved status, 282
Architectural configuration, 130

Architecture Document (AD), 26, 37, 51
Architecture Working Group (ARC WG), 27, 43, 51, 53
Ask, 340, 346
Ask for consent, 345
Ask Request, 341, 345, 347
Ask Target, 341, 345, 347
Assigned session ID, 331
Assisted GPS (A-GPS), 382, 389, 398
Asynchronous distribution, 300
Asynchronous JavaScript and XML (AJAX), 322
Asynchronous notification, 197, 199, 201, 205
Asynchronous operation, 278
Asynchronous subscribe/notify model, 204
Atom Syndication Format, 321, 326
Attachment conversion and compression, 240
Attribute provider, 147
Attribute query, 150
Attribute sharing, 147
Attribute Value Pair (AVP), 97, 264
Augmented Backus-Naur Form, 98
Authentication, 152, 185, 212, 214
Authentication and Key Agreement (AKA), 214
Authentication assertion, 147, 149
Authentication challenge, 186
Authentication context, 150
Authentication context classes, 150
Authentication credentials, 182, 186, 283
Authentication Proxy (AP), 181
Authentication, Authorization and Accounting (AAA), 204, 257
Authentication-related policies, 86
Authenticity, 178
Author creation, 353
Authorization, 152, 219
Authorization enabler, 347
Authorization policies, 181, 198, 211
Authorization rules, 209
Authorized, 343
Authorized principal, 178, 182, 271, 345
Authorized watcher, 197
Automatic answer, 223
Automatic answer mode, 224
Availability, 178, 195, 218
AVP code administration, 265

BAC (see Browser and Content Working Group)
Back-door device, 270
Backup Rights Object, 293
Balance Check Request, 262
Bandwidth limited, 242
Bandwidth management, 79
Barring, 227
Basic (QoE profile), 232
Basic message format, 277
Battery life constraint, 306
BCAST (see Broadcast)
BCAST Architecture, 306, 313
BCAST Architecture Document (BCAST AD), 306
BCAST CP, 313
BCAST enabler, 30, 304
BCAST enabler component, 307

BCAST Management Object, 320
BCAST RD (see BCAST Requirements Document)
BCAST Requirements Document (BCAST RD), 304, 307
BCAST service, 304, 308, 315
BCAST Service Application (BSA), 304, 308, 310, 318
BCAST Service Distribution/Adaptation (BSD/A), 308, 319
BCAST SG Adaptation function, 310
BCAST SG fragment, 310
BCAST SP, 313
BCAST Subscription Management (BSM), 308, 313, 319
BCAST-1, 308
BCAST-8, 308
BCMCS (see Broadcast/Multicast Services)
BDS (see Broadcast Distribution System)
BDS Service Distribution/Adaptation, 308, 319
BDS transparent mode, 311, 313
BDS-assisted mode, 311, 313
Bearer independence, 304
Bearer-independent notification mechanism, 245
Bearer-neutral, 283
Best practices, 26, 142, 155
Bi-directional unicast, 304
Billing, 251
Binary Large Object, 70, 81, 96
Binding, 63, 126, 205, 263
Birds of a Feather (BoF), 33
Blended service, 7
BLOB (see Binary Large Object)
BLOB interface, 97
Blocking, 354
Bluetooth, 276, 285, 415
BoD (see OMA Board of Directors)
Body, 277
Boolean value, 79
Bootstrap, 188, 274
Bootstrapping, 276
Broadcast, 266, 294, 303
Broadcast (BCAST), 252, 299, 304, 311, 320, 424
Broadcast channel, 304, 307, 310, 319
Broadcast Delivery client, 330
Broadcast Distribution System (BDS), 304, 309, 319, 330
Broadcast Network, 308
Broadcast service, 303
Broadcast/Multicast Services (BCMCS), 305, 310, 319
Browser and Content enablers, 193
Browser and Content Working Group (BAC WG), 28, 193
Browser Technology (BT), 29
Browser-based PoC service, 230
Browser-based PoC service, 233
Browser-based service, 321
Browsing, 291, 323
BSA (see BCAST Service Application)
BSD/A (see BCAST Service Distribution/Application)
BSM (see BCAST Subscription Management)
Buddy, 218

Buddy list, 195, 198
Building block, 66, 128, 431
Built-in trigger, 240
Bundle, 68
Business model, 51
Business process, 108
Business Process Execution Language, 81, 95, 145
Business process language, 69
Business process orchestration, 95
Business relationship, 253
Business Support System (BSS), 15, 63
Business transformation, 160
Business-to-Business (B2B), 48

Call attribute, 251
Call barring, 251
Call control, 223
Call details, 251
Call forwarding, 251
Call identifier, 231
Call waiting, 251
Callable mode, 70
Callable pattern, 344, 346, 358
Callable PEM-1 interface, 132
Callable usage pattern, 70, 359, 363
Called party, 251
Calling party, 251
Call-party identifier, 251
Candidate enabler, 233, 343
Candidate Enabler Release, 35
Candidate state, 35
Candidate status, 219, 266, 281
Capital Expenditure (CAPEX), 9
Cascading Style Sheet (CCS), 403
Categorization Based Content Screening, 112, 193,
    353, 365, 424
Categorization Based Content Screening (CBCS), 27
Categorization information, 361
Categorization Rules, 356
Categorization Rules management, 363
Category, 354
CBCS (*see* Categorization Based Content Screening)
CBCS architecture, 356
CBCS architecture (CBCS AD), 358
CBCS enabler, 360
CBCS flow, 362
CBCS proxy, 363
CBCS Proxy function, 362
CBCS requirements, 356
CBCS requirements (CBCS RD), 354
CBCS service, 354
CBCS Service Provider, 354
CBCS solution, 354
CBCS Target Request Requestor, 359
CBCS usage pattern, 359
CBCS user profile, 354, 359, 365
CBCS-1 interface, 359, 361, 363
CBCS-2 interface, 361
CBCS-3 interface, 361, 363
CC/PP, 415
CDMA (*see* Code Division Multiple Access), 42
CDMA 2000, 213, 305, 384

CDMA 3G, 200
CDMA Development Group (CDG), 424
CEK, 297
Cell ID, 196
Cell identifier (cell ID), 382
Cell sector, 196
Cell tower range, 382
Cellular base station, 382, 385
Cellular network, 304, 307, 309
Censorship, 352
Centralized call accounting, 223
Centralized database of specifications for
    advertisement units, 424
Certificate based trust management, 301
CF (*see* Controlling PoC Function)
CH-1 interface, 258, 261, 264
CH-1 message, 263
CH-2 interface, 258, 261, 264
CH-2 message, 264
Channel configuration, 331, 334
Channel ID, 331
Channel update notification, 332
Channel update request, 331, 334
Chargeable event, 258
Charging, 328
Charging Architecture Document (CHG AD), 256
Charging criteria, 255
Charging data transaction, 252
Charging Deployment Scenarios (CHG WP), 266
Charging enabler, 30, 121, 193, 252, 255, 265, 377
Charging enabler Requirements Document (CHG
    RD), 254
Charging Enabler User, 256, 260, 264
Charging event, 255, 257, 263
Charging event reporting, 258
Charging flow, 258
Charging for e-mail, 244
Charging model, 255, 258
Charging PEL, 95
Charging record, 263
Charging request, 263
Charging Requirements (CHG RD), 255
Charging session, 260
Charging Specifications Best Practices whitepaper
    (CHG BP), 266
Charging transaction, 258
Charging-related policies, 86
Charter, 24
CHG OFFLINE, 257
CHG OFFLINE TS, 263
CHG ONLINE, 257
CHG ONLINE TS, 264
Choreography, 108
CI (*see* Content Issuer)
CIPID, 436
Circuit-based wireline telephony, 251
Circuit-switch technology, 218
Client accounting state machine, 263
Client application, 323, 325
Client Application Data Exchange (CADE), 328
Client Application Registration (CAR), 328
Client Provisioning (CP), 274, 281
Client side filtering, 244

Client status attributes, 207
CLIENT, EVENT BASED, 264
Client/Server Interface (CSI), 370
Client-generated alert, 277
Client-Server Protocol (CSP) Access, 205
Client-side filtering, 239
Client-side polling, 197
CN (*see* Core Network)
Code Division Multiple Access (CDMA), 23, 42, 51,
    200, 274, 283, 385
Collection of Advertising Metrics, 425
Command codes, 97
Command language, 279
Committee, 24, 34
Common enabler, 10
Common function, 10
Common Information Model (CIM), 165
Common Management Information Protocol (CMIP),
    165
Common Management Information Service Element
    (CMISE), 165
Common Object Request Broker Architecture
    (CORBA), 48
Common Policy, 81, 95, 343
Common Presence Profile (CPP), 201
Common Profile for Instant Messaging (CPIM), 201
Compatibility with firewalls, 240
Component dependency information, 169
Component tracing, 170
Component, 145
Composable, 287
Composed interface, 84
Composite Capabilities (CC), 414
Composition, 108
COMPRESSION, 247
Concurrent list writers, 199
Condition, 95, 340, 343
Conditional grant, 347
Conditional header, 199
Confidentiality, 152, 178
Confirm, 198
Confirm list, 198
Confirmation request, 199
Confirmed indication of session acceptance, 223
Confirmed mode, 224
Conformance requirement, 282
Conformance test case, 37
Connectivity API, 370
Connectivity Management Object (ConnMO), 282
ConnMO, 283
Consistency Review, 26, 35
Constrained device, 403
Constrained mobile device, 405
Consumer market, 217
Contact identity, 197
Contact list, 219
Contact-level presence, 198
Content adaptation, 414
Content attribute, 310
Content bundle, 299
Content categorization, 352, 356, 358, 364
Content Categorization Component, 360, 363
Content Categorization Provider, 355

Content Categorization Requestor, 360
Content Categorization Rules, 354, 360
Content category, 352, 359, 361, 363
Content Creation, 308
Content Creation Source, 310, 312, 318
Content delivery, 306, 376
Content Delivery (BAC CD), 28
Content Delivery (CD), 29
Content delivery model, 322
Content Delivery Protocol, 306
Content distribution, 299
Content Encryption Key (CEK), 296
Content Identifier, 297
Content indirection, 202
Content Issuer (CI), 295, 301
Content labeling system, 356
Content metadata, 326, 353, 361
Content protection, 308
Content protection, 313
Content Protection (CP), 305, 308, 311, 315
Content protection management, 308
Content provider, 25, 41, 47, 59, 291, 323, 326, 331,
    353, 375, 422
Content Provider Data Exchange (CPDE), 328
Content Provider Registration (CPR), 328
Content rating, 352
Content reference, 360, 364
Content Screening, 329, 352, 356, 359, 364
Content Screening Component, 358, 360, 362
Content Screening Requestor, 359
Content Screening Rules, 354
Content Server, 209
Content Service Element, 207
Content source, 355, 361
Content syndication, 322
Content syndication service, 326
CONTENT TRANSFORMATION, 247
Context model, 377
Continuous media clip, 294
Control different user experiences, 229, 232
Control infrastructure, 14
ControlPlane, 224
Control Plane, 381, 383, 388
Control Plane Architecture, 384
Control Plane Architecture, 391
Control Plane Location, 381, 384, 387, 400
Control Plane Location Architecture, 385, 389
Controlling PoC Function (CF), 221, 223
Controversial (content), 351
Converged IP Everything, 419
Converged IP Messaging (CPM), 193, 234, 416, 419
Converged network-based address book, 234
Converged service environment, 302
Convergence, 48
Cooperation agreement, 24
Cooperation framework, 24
Copyright, 290
Copyright holder, 289
Copyright theft, 299
Core Network (CN), 384, 386
CoreMedia, 301
Corporate network, 120
Correlation function, 258

Correlation/aggregation function, 257
Contact presence, 199
CP (*see* Client Provisioning), 281
CP (*see* Content Protection)
CP functional architecture, 313, 315
CPM Framework, 420
CPM user, 420
Create, 210
Create (permissions rule), 345
Creation, 212
Credit check, 257
Credit-Control Answer (CCA) message, 264
Credit-Control Request (CCR) message, 264
Cryptographic binding, 295
CSCF, 214
CSI specified events, 375
CSI specified operations, 375
Custom PEM-1 Template, 97
Customer, 47, 57, 59, 232, 254
Customer Relationship Management (CRM), 49, 59, 73, 269
Cypher suite, 187

DATA, 240
Data representation, 277
Data Synchronization (DS), 245
Data Synchronization protocol, 30
Data Synchronization Working Group (DS WG), 30
Database-like (storage model), 280
DCD (*see* Dynamic Content Delivery)
DCD AD, 326
DCD administration action, 329
DCD architecture, 328
DCD client, 326
DCD enabler, 327
DCD entity, 327
DCD interface, 327, 330
DCD server, 326, 334
DCD service, 331
DCD-1 (pull interface), 328
DCD-2 (push interface), 328
DCD-3 (administration interface), 328
DCD-CADE, 328
DCD-CAR, 328
DCD-CPDE, 328
DCD-CPR, 328
DCD-defined administration, 334
DCD-enabled client application, 332
DCD-provided storage management, 334
DCF (*see* DRM Content Format)
DDF, 280, 284
Debit Request, 262
Debit units, 260
Decision, 346, 355
Decision making, 359
Decomposition, 66
Default disposition, 198
Delegate, 14, 20, 215, 342, 350, 362
Delegated Resource, 92, 344, 363
Delegation, 14, 69, 82, 87, 342
DELETE, 209, 212
Delete, 210

Delete (permissions rule), 345
Delete command, 278, 280
Deletion, 212
Delivered (sub-tree), 284
Delivered catalog, 284
Delivery, 253
Delivery method, 322
Denial of Service (DoS), 391
Deny, 199, 340, 346
Deny always, 341
Deny list, 198
DENY permission, 345
Deny this time only, 341
Deployed (sub-tree), 284
Deployment model, 68
Deposit filter, 247
Derived from, 361
Description, 144
DevDetail, 275, 282
Developer Interest Group (DIG), 31, 33, 155
Device Capability Management Object (DCMO), 285
Device Descriptions Working Group (DDWG), 416
Device firmware, 273
Device Independence Working Group (DIWG), 416
Device management, 274
Device Management (DM), 21, 30, 52, 211, 270, 280, 286, 306, 318, 320, 424
Device Management Client (DM Client or DMC), 209
Device Management enablers, 193, 212
Device Management Server (DM Server or DMS), 209
Device Management Smart Card (DM-SC), 286
Device Management Working Group (DM WG), 30
Device manufacturer, 42, 270
Device marking, 163
Device Profile, 328, 414
Device Profile Evolution, 193, 416
Device state, 279
Device vendor, 286
DevInfo, 275, 282
Diagnostics and Monitoring (DiagMon), 286
Diameter, 261, 266
Diameter Accounting, 263
Diameter Base Protocol, 255, 263
Diameter binding, 97
Diameter Charging Applications, 255
Diameter client, 263
Diameter Credit-Control Application, 255, 264
Diameter Credit-Control client, 264
Diameter Credit-Control server, 264
Diameter Network Access Server Application, 255
Diameter server, 263
Differentiated device, 270
DIG (*see* Developer Interest Group)
DIG WP, 32
Digital broadcast system, 303
Digital certificate, 144, 178
Digital content, 289
Digital expression, 289
Digital key, 291
Digital media, 290
Digital media object, 296

Digital music, 290
Digital Restrictions Management, 290
Digital Right, 289
Digital rights glossary, 289
Digital Rights Management (DRM), 29, 291, 296,
    320, 328, 424
Digital Rights Management enabler, 193, 377
Digital signature, 144
Digital Video Broadcasting (DVB), 45
Digital Video Broadcasting – Handhelds (DVB-H),
    306
Digital Video Broadcasting IP Datacast (DVB
    IPDC), 305, 320
Direct Model, 140, 155
Discounted subscription, 423
Discovery, 146
Discovery service, 151
Discovery service provider, 147
Discrete text-style media, 234
Dispatcher, 230
Display (right), 294
Distributed Management Task Force (DMTF), 165,
    288
Distributed multiplayer environment, 368
DM (see Device Management)
DM account credentials, 275
DM architecture, 271, 275
DM Bootstrap, 282
DM client, 271, 275, 280
DM client Bootstrap, 275
DM client-server session, 286
DM command, 278
DM component, 272
DM credentials, 273
DM DDF, 282
DM enabler, 271, 279, 281, 288
DM Large Object, 284
DM object, 282
DM protocol, 275
DM protocol, 282
DM Scheduling, 286
DM server, 271
DM session, 275
DM system, 273
DM tree, 279
DM Tree and Description, 282
DMAcc, 275, 282
DM-bootstrap OTA interface, 275
DMC, 211
DM-Notify, 275
DMP, 301
DMS, 211
DM-Security, 276
Document template, 26
Document Type Definition (DTD), 387
Domain Model Relationship (DMR), 373
Domain Name Service (DNS), 281
Domain profile, 292
Domain-specific profile, 156
Download (sub-tree), 284
Download and Digital Rights Management (BAC
    DLDRM), 28
Download catalog, 284

Download content, 291
Download mechanism, 284
Downloadable offline game, 368
DPE (see Device Profile Evolution)
DPE client, 415
DReaM, 301
DRM (see Digital Rights Management)
DRM AD, 302
DRM Agent, 292, 295, 299, 301
DRM content distribution, 306
DRM Content Format (DCF), 292, 295
DRM DCF, 302
DRM enabler, 30
DRM extension profile, 300
DRM profile, 302, 314
DRM RD, 302
DRM REL, 297, 302
DRM Requirements Document (DRM RD), 294
DRM specification, 290
DRM TS, 302
DRM XBS, 300
DRM-enabled device, 301
DRM-enabled handset, 300
Drop-box, 279
DS protocol layer, 245
DS server, 245
DS user interface layer, 245
DVB bitstream, 305
DVB-H (see Digital Video
    Broadcasting – Handhelds)
DVB-H IPDC (see Digital Video Broadcasting IP
    Datacast)
Dynamic Content Delivery (DCD), 29, 299, 320,
    326, 333, 424
Dynamic Content Delivery (enabler), 377
Dynamic Content Delivery enabler, 193
Dynamic property, 415

E Requestor, 93
ECMA Script Mobile Profile (ESMP), 180
ECMAscript, 180, 404
ECMAscript Mobile Profile (ESMP), 404
EDGE, 213
Electronic Service Guide (ESG), 306
E-mail client, 240
E-mail composition and sending, 239
E-mail data object (ObjEmail), 245
E-Mail Notification (EMN), 237, 239
E-mail reception, 239
E-mail server, 240
E-mail server-side layer, 245
Emergency call, 383
Emergency preparedness, 232
Emergency services, 384
Emergency SLP (E-SLP), 392
EMN (see E-Mail Notification)
Employee service, 57, 58
Enabler, 52
Enabler composition, 84
Enabler Implementation Conformance Statement
    (EICS), 37, 42
Enabler instance, 118

Enabler IOP Report (IOP_RPT), 38
Enabler Release, 35
Enabler Release Package, 26
Enabler specification, 36
Enabler Test Guidelines (ETG), 37
Enabler Test Report (ET_RPT), 38
Enabler Test Requirements (ETR), 37
Enabler Test Specification (ETS), 37
Enabler Validation Plan (EVP), 37
Enabler-specific XDMS, 211
Encrypted content, 291
Encryption, 178, 185, 247
End-to-end service, 431
End-user, 53, 208, 354, 412
End-user experience, 198
End-user privacy policies, 86
Enforcement, 15
Enhanced 911 (E911), 383
Enhanced Data Rates for GSM Evolution (EDGE), 23
Enhanced Mobile Originated Request, 392
Enhanced SMTP (ESMTP), 240, 247
Enhanced Telecom Operations Map (eTOM), 166, 414
Enhanced Variable Rate Codec (EVRC), 226
Enrollment, 275
ENTBOF, 60
ENTBoF Technical Report (ENTBOF TR), 59
Enterprise, 57, 120, 270
Enterprise Birds of a Feather (ENTBoF), 59
Enterprise Chooser, 59
Enterprise developer community, 126
Enterprise ecosystem, 58
Enterprise employee, 269, 350
Enterprise mobilization, 60, 239
Enterprise needs, 57, 59, 60
Enterprise network, 120
Enterprise Resource Planning, 73
Enterprise Service Manager, 59
Enterprise User, 58
Entertainment industry, 290
Entity tag (e-tag), 199, 212
Ephemeris data, 382
Equipment vendor, 286, 333
ESMTP (see Enhanced SMTP)
Essential IPR, 298
ETSI (see European Telecommunications Standards Institute)
European Telecommunications Standards Institute (ETSI), 23, 41, 44, 47, 305, 416
Evaluation, 346
Evaluation Requestor, 93
Event charging, 264
Event package, 197, 199
Event-based charging interface, 118
Event-based charging model, 258, 260
Event-based model, 262
Event-based service invocation, 392
Event-based specification, 370
Event-driven bi-directional synchronization, 239
Event-driven schedule, 286
EventRecord, 261
Evolution-Data Optimized (EVDO), 283

Exec AccessType, 279
Exec command, 279, 284
Executable policy, 71
Execute (right), 294
Execution Environment, 168
Execution management subsystem, 285
Explicit presence, 196
Explicit user-defined presence, 207
Export of Rights Object, 293, 295
Export permission, 295
Extended Hypertext Markup Language (XHTML), 401, 403, 404
Extended presence information, 207
Extended right, 300
EXtensible Access Control Markup Language, 81
EXtensible Markup Language (XML), 30, 198, 201, 209, 242, 245, 247, 255, 271, 277, 280, 287, 302, 326, 343, 348, 356, 373, 403, 406
EXtensible Markup Language Configuration Access Protocol (XCAP), 199
EXtensible Messaging and Presence Protocol (XMPP), 200
External entity, 219, 326
External liaison committee, 25
External PTT network, 232
Externally delivered game, 368

Fault, Configuration, Accounting, Performance, Security (FCAPS), 164
FD (see File Distribution)
FD functional architecture, 310
FD-1, 310
FD-2, 310
FD-5, 310
FD-6, 310
FD-B1, 310
Federal Communications Commission (FCC), 383
Federation termination notification, 150
Feeds, 321
Fetch, 204
Fetcher, 197
File (ObjFile), 245
File distribution, 308
File Distribution (FD), 304, 308, 310
Filter criteria, 213
Filtering, 239, 245, 354
Finance committee, 25
Firewall Traversal, 247
Firmware Update Management Object (FUMO), 282, 284
First responder community, 383
Fixed (storage model), 280
Fixed-tree device, 280
Flat rate, 252
Fleet member, 230
Flexible content scheduling, 322
Floor, 226
Floor control, 218
Folder (ObjFolder), 247
Folder management, 240
Folksonomy, 353
Follow-on call, 231

Forward lock, 291, 299
Forward without download, 242, 244
Forwarding, 240
Fragment, 212
Front-door device, 270
Full duplex, 217, 234
Full PoC session, 223
Full-duplex call follow-on proceed, 230
Fully Dynamic (storage model), 280
FUMO (*see* Firmware Update Management Object)
Functional area, 304
Funds transfer, 252

GAA Authentication proxy, 214
GALILEO, 391
Game communities, 367
Game CSI, 371
Game hosting, 367
Game interoperability, 377
Game networking, 367
Game portability, 377
Game server, 371, 373
Game Services, 379
Game Services AD, 368
Game Services Architecture, 370, 371
Game Services Client/Server specification, 370
Game Services CSI, 372
Game Services enabler, 193, 371, 377
Game Services requirements, 370, 379
Game Services specifications, 376
Game Services whitepaper, 375, 379
Game Services Working Group (GS WG), 30
Game software, 367
Game-capable phone, 368
Game-enabled phone, 368
Gaming platform, 368, 370, 373
Game Services Architecture, 379
Gateway Mobile Location Center (GMLC), 343,
    385, 389, 391
GBA credentials, 188
General Packet Radio Service (GPRS), 23, 213, 239,
    283
General Service Subscription Management (GSSM),
    27, 53, 193, 413, 424
General User Profile (GUP), 412
Generic Authentication Architecture (GAA), 182,
    214
Generic authorization enabler, 348
Generic Bootstrapping Architecture (GBA), 182,
    185, 188
Geo-fence, 383
Geospatial data, 396
GET, 209, 212
Get command, 278
Gifting, 293, 299
GLMS (*see* Group List Management Server)
Global Certification Forum (GFC), 38
Global Permissions Management (GPM), 27, 54,
    111, 342, 348, 424
Global Permissions Management enabler, 193
Global Positioning System (GPS), 381, 390
Global System for Mobile communication (GSM),
    23, 42, 47, 51, 200, 213, 275, 283, 385

Gm, 213, 214
GMLC (*see* Gateway Mobile Location Center)
Government regulations, 352
GPM (*see* Global Permissions Management), 338
GPM Administrator, 342
GPM architecture (GPM AD), 344
GPM enabler, 340
GPM interface, 347
GPM permissions checking flow, 346
GPM Permissions Rule management flow, 347
GPM requirements, 341, 348
GPM Requirements Document (GPM RD), 339
GPM Work Item, 347
GPRS (*see* General Packet Radio Service), 213
GPS (*see* Global Positioning System)
GPS-enabled device, 382
Grant, 340, 346
GRANT permission, 345
Grant this time only, 341
Granular specification, 52
Group, 204
Group advertisement function, 226
Group chat and thread mechanism, 201
Group communication style, 219, 225
Group list, 219
Group list management, 201, 218
Group List Management Server (GLMS), 198, 200,
    209
Group list URI, 209
Group management enabler, 210
Group Service Element, 207
Group Usage List XML Document, 211
Group XML Document, 211
GSM (*see* Global System for Mobile
    communication)
GSM Association (GSMA), 424
GSM/UMTS, 384
GSM-CDMA (inter-working), 241
GSM-GSM (inter-working), 241
GSSM (*see* General Service Subscription
    Management)
Guaranteed Quality of Service, 79
GUP (*see* General User Profile)

Half static SIP session, 223
Half-duplex, 217, 234, 276
Half-duplex style, 226
Harmful (content), 351
Header, 277
Hierarchical synchronization, 245
High latency, 242
History capability, 215
Home Location Register (HLR), 208
Home network, 181, 184
Home OSG, 186
Home Subscriber Server (HSS), 118, 257, 412
Horizontal enabler, 347
Horizontal function, 52
Horizontal service architecture, 1, 5, 7, 13, 15, 20,
    28, 125, 238
Horizontalization, 52
Hosting operator, 42

HTML, 403
HTTP, 17, 48, 209, 214, 242, 245, 271, 276, 283, 294, 329, 373, 387, 417
HTTP command, 212
HTTP Digest, 181, 185
HTTP POST, 277
HTTP proxy, 212, 283
HTTP URI, 212
HTTP/HTTPS, 240, 277
HTTPS, 276, 329
Hybrid device, 274

I/O signature, 81
I0 interface, 15, 63, 129, 215, 243, 271, 326, 343, 347, 357, 371, 432
I0 Web Services binding, 133
I0 Web Services interface, 153
I0+P interface, 15, 17, 65, 92, 220
I1 category interface, 168
I1 interface, 15, 63
I2 interface, 15, 63, 119, 129, 266, 272, 326, 343, 357, 379, 408
ICRA, 356
I-CSCF (*see* Interrogating-Call State Control Function)
Identification, 204
Identifier-value pair, 346
Identity, 196, 204, 226
Identity data federation, 146
Identity federation, 146
Identity Management Framework (IMF), 152
Identity management model, 146
Identity privacy, 219
Identity provider, 147
Identity service, 147
Identity theft, 337
ID-FF, 146
ID-WSF, 148
IETF (*see* Internet Engineering Task Force)
Illegal content, 352, 354
Illegal copying, 291
ILP (*see* Internal Location Protocol)
ILP PC (*see* ILP Positioning Control interface)
ILP PD (*see* ILP Positioning Data interface)
ILP Positioning Control (ILP PC) interface, 397
ILP Positioning Data (ILP PD) interface, 397, 399
IM (*see* Instant Messaging)
IM/SM (*see* Interaction and Multimodal Synchronization Manager)
IMAP (*see* Internet Message Access Protocol)
IMAP4rev1, 240
Implementation de-composition, 109
Implicit presence, 196
Implicit presence information, 208
Implicit user-defined presence, 207
Implicit-Add, 279
IMPP (*see* Instant Messaging and Presence Protocol)
IMPS (*see* Instant Messaging and Presence Service)
IMPS client, 205
IMPS server, 205, 207
IMS (*see* IP Multimedia Subsystem), 204
IMS – Accounting Information Flows and Protocol, 255

IMS – Online Charging System, 255
IMS architecture, 203
IMS capabilities, 116
IMS core, 119
IMS core network, 209
IMS infrastructure, 116
IMS mobile devices, 118
IMS network, 214
IMS reference point, 213
IMS services, 119
IMS terminals, 119
IMSinOMA (*see* Utilization of IMS in OMA)
Inactive (component), 284
Inappropriate content, 352, 354, 365
Inbox, 279, 282
In-building penetration, 382
Incoming Personal Alert Barring, 227
Independent media control, 231
Indirect Model, 140, 155
Individual consumer, 269
Information Object Class (IOC), 412
Information Technology (IT), 22
Infrared (IR), 285
Infrared Data Association (IrDA), 276
Infrastructure framework, 135
Initial content, 331
Initial provisioning, 270, 273
Initial Request, 263
Input BLOB, 97
Instant message, 227, 417
Instant Messaging (enabler), 377
Instant Messaging (IM), 195, 201, 205, 234, 269, 417
Instant Messaging and Presence Protocol (IMPP), 201, 435
Instant Messaging and Presence Service (IMPS), 31, 44, 205, 418, 439
Instant Messaging Service Element, 207
Instant Personal Alert, 227
Instant talk burst, 218
Institute of Electrical and Electronics Engineers (IEEE), 45
Integrity, 178
Integrity of session state, 244
Integrity protection, 185
Intellectual property, 289
Intellectual Property Rights (IPR), 24, 297
Interaction, 308, 339
Interaction and Multimodal Synchronization Manager (IM/SM), 408
Interaction channel, 304, 307, 310, 314, 318
Interaction Network, 304, 308
Interaction service, 151
Interactive advertisement, 423
Interactive Advertising Bureau (IAB), 424
Interactive multimedia content, 406
Interactivity of Advertisements, 425
Interceptor, 71
Interface, 7, 11, 15, 18, 210, 256, 258, 306, 308, 389
Interface to Other Resources, 92, 346, 362
Interim charging request, 258
Interim request, 260
InterimRecord, 261
Interior node, 277, 380

Inter-Location server communication, 387
Intermittent connectivity, 239
Internal Location Protocol (ILP), 392, 397
International Mobile Subscriber Identity (IMSI), 387
International Telecommunication
    Union – Telecommunication Standardization
    Sector (ITU-T), 44
International Telecommunication Union (ITU), 23
Internationalization Character Encoding, 98
Internet, 351
Internet Assigned Numbers Authority, 98
Internet Content Rating Association (ICRA), 353
Internet E-mail Messaging Model, 242
Internet Engineering Task Force (IETF), 24, 51, 198,
    221, 237, 255, 265, 306, 326, 335, 343, 417
Internet Message Access Protocol (IMAP), 238, 240,
    242, 247
Internet Protocol (IP), 219
Interoperability, 19, 35, 41, 57, 218, 227, 241, 255,
    281, 286, 298, 320
Interoperability (IOP), 233, 266
Interoperability committee, 25
Interoperability Recognition Program, 40
Interoperability test case, 37
Interoperability Working Group (IOP WG), 28
Interrogating-Call State Control Function (I-CSCF),
    204, 214
Inter-working capabilities, 229, 232
Inter-working function, 233
Intrinsic function, 17, 307, 338, 431
Invited party, 230
IOP champion, 45
IOP WG, 42
IP datacast, 306, 309
IP flow, 304
IP multicast datagram, 305
IP Multimedia BoF, 116
IP Multimedia Subsystem (IMS), 42, 53, 68, 115,
    200, 211, 219, 252, 266, 285, 335, 377, 393,
    417
IP TV, 298
IP-based services, 252
IP-broadcast/multicast, 304
IPDC (see Digital Video Broadcasting IP Datacast),
    306
IPR policy, 25
IPSec, 186
IPV4, 283
IPV6, 283
ISC, 213
ISDN User Part (ISUP), 48
Issuer, 253
IT Company, 25
IT infrastructure, 239
IT vendor, 47

J2EE container, 73

Key management, 144
Key Management Center (KMC), 181, 185
Key Management Center Interface (KMC-IF), 186
KMC (see Key Management Center), 185

LAN, 294
Latency, 226
Lawful interception, 232
Layered architecture, 138
LBS (see Location Based Services)
LCS (see Location Services)
Leaf node, 277
Legacy system, 7
Legal and trademark committee, 25
LEMONADE, 240
LEMONADE profile bis (LEMONADE bis), 243,
    247
Liaison, 24
Liaison Statement, 26
Liberty Alliance Framework, 154
Liberty Alliance Project, 146
Liberty Alliance Project Web Services Framework,
    148
Liberty enabled User Agents and Devices (LUAD),
    152
License to Enhance Messaging Oriented Network
    Access for Diverse Endpoints (LEMONADE),
    238
LIF (see Location Interoperability Forum)
Life Cycle Management (LCM), 160
Life-cycle management, 15, 270, 281
Lightweight mobile profile, 297
Limited XQuery over HTTP, 212
List (permissions rule), 345
List change update, 199
List Management, 195, 199
List management operations, 200, 216
List notification, 208
List of contacts, 195, 198, 209
List presence, 199
List subscription, 208
List update notification, 199
Local Area Network (LAN), 240
Local policies, 352
Location, 29, 328, 347, 424
Location assistance information, 389
Location enabler, 193, 339, 377, 383, 397
Location estimate, 383
Location information, 381, 343
Location Interoperability Forum (LIF), 22, 49, 381,
    385
Location PEL, 95
Location server, 386, 388
Location Services (LCS), 381, 391
Location Working Group (LOC WG), 31
Location-aware call, 384
Location-based application, 385
Location-based client application, 390
Location Based Services (LBS), 382, 386, 395
Logging API, 371
Logical architecture, 68
Long-term key, 313
Long-term Key Message (LTKM), 313
Loose coupling, 12, 14, 19, 145
LTKM (see Long-term Key Message)

M Requestor, 93

Macro-orchestration, 433
MAE (*see* Mobile Application Environment)
MAE enablers, 402
MAIL, 240
Mail Store (MS), 242
Maintain PoC session, 218
Malicious content, 354
Manage associations, 361
Managed network element, 164
Managed object, 165
Management action, 276, 286
Management agent, 165
Management application, 168
Management authority, 273, 282
Management client, 166
Management command, 278
Management function, 359
Management Information Base (MIB), 164, 282
Management infrastructure, 166
Management Object (MO), 271, 275, 278, 281
Management Object ID (MO ID), 278
Management Requestor, 93, 345
Management rights, 342
Management tree, 277
Mandatory codec, 311
Mandatory feature, 37
Manual answer, 223
Manual-answer mode, 224
Manual-answer-override mode, 223
Marked component, 163
Market service, 57, 60
Marking, 163
MARLIN, 301
Massively Multiplayer Online Game (MMOG), 376
Massively Multiplayer Online Role Playing Game
    (MMORPG), 377
Master Application Instance, 370
Maximum transmission time, 231
MBMS (*see* Multimedia Broadcast/Multicast
    Service)
MBMS bearer service, 305
M-Commerce, 255
Mcommerce Landscape Whitepaper (MCOM WP),
    232
ME-1, 243
ME-2, 243
ME-2, 245
ME-3, 243
ME-4, 243
Media burst, 231
Media codec, 226, 305
Media control, 219, 226
Media control handling, 229, 231
Media conversion, 244
Media duplication, 223
Media encoding, 308
Media filtering, 227
Media floor control, 230
Media handling, 221
Media path, 223
Media player, 293
Media relay function, 223
Media traffic optimization, 231

Media-floor arbitration, 223
MEM AD, 243
MEM architecture, 243
MEM client, 243
MEM enabler, 243, 250
MEM proxy function, 243
MEM server, 243
MEM server, 244
Memory card, 294
Merchant, 253
MESSAGE, 202
Message access, 242
Message binding, 261
Message correlation, 152
Message formatting, 242
Message integrity, 144
Message level security, 144
Message routing, 242
Message Session Relay Protocol (MSRP), 201, 437
Message Transfer Agent (MTA), 242
Message type, 261
Message viewing, 239
Message-digest Algorithm 5 (MD-5), 271
Messaging, 143, 266, 372
Messaging enabler, 377
Messaging within groups, 421
Messaging Working Group (MWG), 31
Messaging-based game, 368
Metadata, 240, 247
Metadata schema, 271
Meta-information, 277
Metered usage, 292
Metered-time, 299
Metering API, 370
Metrics, 258
Micro-orchestration, 433
M-IMAP, 240
MIME (*see* Multipurpose Internet Mail Extension)
MLP (*see* Mobile Location Protocol)
MLP basic services, 392
MLS enabler, 381, 388
MM1, 241
MM3, 241
MMA (*see* Mobile Marketing Association)
MMCP interface, 409
MMMD enabler, 408
MMMD Registry, 409
MMS (*see* Multimedia Messaging Service)
MMS client, 242
MMS MM1, 240
MMS Proxy-Relay, 242
MO (*see* Management Object)
MO ID, 285
MobAd BoF, 425
MobAd user agent, 425
Mobile advertisement, 423
Mobile Advertising (MobAd), 27, 193, 326, 376, 421
Mobile Advertising Architecture, 425
Mobile Advertising Birds of a Feather (MobAd
    BoF), 424
Mobile Advertising enabler, 426
Mobile Advertising Framework, 424

Mobile Advertising Landscape Whitepaper (MobAd WP), 425
Mobile Advertising Requirements, 425
Mobile advertising value chain, 422
Mobile Application Environment (MAE), 28, 29, 193, 401
Mobile Application Part (MAP), 203
Mobile Broadcast, 304
Mobile Broadcast (BCAST), 28, 29, 303
Mobile Broadcast enabler, 193
Mobile browser, 403, 405
Mobile browser-based game, 368
Mobile Commerce, 252, 265
Mobile commerce (m-commerce), 30
Mobile Commerce and Charging (MCC), 253
Mobile Commerce and Charging Working Group (MCC WG), 30
Mobile data application, 334
Mobile Device, 273
Mobile device constraints, 326
Mobile device vendor, 333
Mobile DM, 281
Mobile domain, 140
Mobile e-mail, 250
Mobile E-mail enabler, 30, 193, 238
Mobile Entertainment Forum (MEF), 423
Mobile environment, 304, 322. 402, 414
Mobile games, 368
Mobile Games Interoperability Forum (MGIF), 22, 369
Mobile gaming devices, 367
Mobile Gaming Evolution, 375
Mobile handset, 49, 293
Mobile Internet Wireless Forum (MWIF), 22
Mobile local address book, 245
Mobile Location Protocol (MLP), 139, 385, 387, 392, 398, 400
Mobile Location Service (MLS), 381, 387
Mobile Marketing Association (MMA), 423
Mobile Marketing Code of Conduct, 423
Mobile Network Operator, 269, 274, 322, 329, 333, 376, 383
Mobile Operator, 25, 47, 50, 58, 237, 250, 253, 273, 286, 291, 354, 412, 417
Mobile phone, 421
Mobile Positioning Center (MPC), 385
Mobile profile, 401
Mobile Service, 48
Mobile service enabler, 21
Mobile Services ecosystem, 49, 51
Mobile social network, 230
Mobile subscription, 3
Mobile Web Services, 135, 139, 155
Mobile Web Services (MWS), 21
Mobile Web Services Working Group (MWS WG), 31, 135
Mobile-oriented IMAP, 241
Mobile-specific data format, 405
Mobility, 48, 323
Mobility management, 381
Modality, 407
Modification, 212
Modify, 210

Modify permissions rule, 345
Mood, 196, 207
MP3 (see MPEG-1 Audio Layer 3)
MPC (see Mobile Positioning Center)
MPEG-1 Audio Layer 3 (MP3), 293, 415
MPEG-2 transport stream, 306
MPEG4, 293
MPEG-LA, 298
MSRP (see Message Session Relay Protocol)
Multicast, 293
Multidevice capabilities, 408
Multimedia Broadcast/Multicast Service (MBMS), 305, 310, 319
Multimedia Domain (MMD), 117, 219
Multimedia Messaging Service (MMS), 44, 234, 241, 280, 294, 298, 304, 315, 323, 346, 362, 411, 416
Multimedia Messaging Service Interoperability (MMS-IOP), 22, 241
Multimodal access, 408
Multimodal and Multidevice (MMMD), 408
Multimodal and Multidevice Configuration Protocol (MMCP), 409
Multiplayer game, 367, 376
Multiple clients, 244
Multiple devices, 407, 421
Multipurpose Internet Mail Extension (MIME), 245, 247, 250
Multi-vendor environment, 51
Mutual authentication, 181, 244
MWG Converged IP Messaging (MWG-CPM), 31
MWG Instant Messaging (MWG-IM), 31
MWG Mobile E-mail (MWG-MEM), 31
MWG Multimedia Messaging (MWG-MMSG), 31
MWS WG (see Mobile Web Services Working Group)

Name registration, 149
NAP (see Network Access Point)
NAP MO, 283
National security, 232
Navigation Satellite System, 391
Network Access Point (NAP), 273, 283
Network data bearer, 274
Network Element (NE), 412
Network Equipment Manufacturer, 122
Network equipment vendor, 42, 47
Network Equipment-Building System (NEBS), 38
Network identity, 146
Network Management (NM), 165
Network Management System (NMS), 164
Network Manager (NM), 412
Network Operator, 42, 47, 60, 411
Network proxy, 283
Network Resource Manager (NRM), 412
Network-based address book, 421
Network-based storage, 421
Network-Initiated Location Procedure, 389, 394
Network-initiated location query, 384
Network-initiated scenario, 397
Network-to-user (content delivery), 325
Neutrality principle, 23

New support features, 232
New support functions, 229
Next generation application, 7
Next Generation Networking (NGN) , 414
Next Generation Operations Support System (NGOSS), 166
NodeB, 386
Nomadic service, 48
Non Disclosure Agreement (NDA), 43
Non-BCAST entity, 307
Non-PoC solution, 233
Non-proxy mode, 390, 397
Non-real-time charging, 257
Non-repudiation, 178
Non-roaming SET, 397
Non-specified interfaces, 361
Normal mode, 224
Northbound, 129
Northbound interface, 66
Notification (NT), 240, 305, 308, 318
Notification Agent, 169
Notification delivery, 308
Notification filter, 250
Notification Generation Component, 318
Notification Initiated Session, 276, 282
Notification protocol, 242
Notify authorized principal, 345
NT (*see* Notification)
NT functional architecture, 318
NT-1, 318
NT-3, 319
NT-4, 319
NT-5, 319
NT-6, 319
NT-7, 319
NT-B1, 319
NW PoC Box, 228

OAM&P (*see* Operation, Administration, Maintenance, and Provisioning)
OASIS (*see* Organization for the Advancement of Structured Information Standards)
Object Exchange (OBEX), 245, 276
Objectionable (content), 351
OCSP Mobile Profile, 180
ODRL (*see* Open Digital Rights Language)
Official Governmental Use (QoE profile), 232
Offline charging, 118, 252, 256
Offline Charging Interface (CH-1), 261
Offline charging request, 261
Off-line usage, 239
OMA AD, 27
OMA Architecture Best Practices (ARC BP), 309
OMA Architecture Principles, 27
OMA authorization enabler, 350
OMA Board of Directors (BoD), 25, 35
OMA Broadcast (BCAST), 335
OMA Categorization Based Content Screening (CBCS), 353
OMA Client Provisioning (OMA CP), 274, 276, 281
OMA Committee, 26
OMA Content Delivery Working Group, 335

OMA CP (*see* OMA Client Provisioning), 276
OMA CPM enabler, 419
OMA Data Synchronization (DS), 242, 277
OMA Device Profile Evolution (DPE), 350, 415
OMA Digital Rights Management (DRM), 289, 291, 301, 306
OMA DM Device Description Framework (DDF), 277
OMA DM enabler suite, 282
OMA Download (DLOTA), 284
OMA DRM (*see* OMA Digital Rights Management)
OMA DRM 2.0 Extensions for Broadcast Support (DRM XBS), 306
OMA DRM Content Format (DCF), 306
OMA DRM licensing, 297
OMA DRM Rights Expression Language (DRM REL), 306
OMA EMN (EMN), 242
OMA enabler release, 25
OMA Game Services, 350, 369
OMA GBA Profile, 188
OMA General Service Subscription Management (GSSM), 412
OMA Global Permissions Management (GPM), 338
OMA goal, 23
OMA Horizontal Working Group, 27
OMA Instant Messaging and Presence (IMPS), 417
OMA interoperability program, 25
OMA IOP Testing Process, 36
OMA Location, 338
OMA Location Architecture, 342
OMA MEM (*see* OMA Mobile E-mail)
OMA MEM Architecture Document (MEM AD), 237
OMA MEM Requirements Document (MEM RD), 237
OMA mission, 23
OMA MLP (*see* Mobile Location Protocol)
OMA MLS enabler (*see* Mobile Location Service)
OMA Mobile E-mail (OMA MEM), 237, 241
OMA Mobile Location Services (MLS), 343
OMA namespace, 26
OMA namespace encoding, 32
OMA neutrality principle, 408
OMA Organizational structure, 21, 24
OMA Policy Evaluation, Enforcement and Management (*see* Policy Evaluation, Enforcement and Management)
OMA portal, 34
OMA Presence, 338
OMA Presence model, 207
OMA Presence service, 213
OMA Presence SIMPLE (Presence), 205
OMA Privacy Checking Protocol (PCP), 343
OMA Privacy Requirements (Privacy RD), 342
OMA Process Document, 26, 33
OMA Push (PUSH), 240, 242, 275
OMA Push Proxy Gateway, 273
OMA RD, 27
OMA Secure Removable Media (SRM), 301
OMA Secure User Plane Location (*see* Secure User Plane Location)
OMA Security Gateway (OSG), 185

OMA Service Environment (OSE), 5, 13, 27, 52,
    125, 219, 238, 255, 271, 338, 357, 416, 430
OMA Service Provider Environment (OSPE), 15, 27,
    53, 160
OMA STI (*see* Standard Transcoding Interface)
OMA SUPL (*see* Secure User Plane Location)
OMA Technical Plenary (TP), 25, 26, 34, 418
OMA Technical Working Group (WG), 22 24, 27, 34
OMA Test Festival (TestFest), 36
OMA TLS Profile, 187
OMA Vertical Working Group, 28
OMA Web Services Enabler Release (OWSER), 31,
    33, 135, 140, 180, 405
OMA WG (*see* OMA Technical Working Group), 22
OMA Work Item, 26
OMA Work Program (OWP), 25, 26, 34
OMA-specific AVP, 265
OMNA (*see* Open Mobile Naming Authority)
On-board Key Generation (OBKG), 180
On-demand content, 309
On-demand mode, 223
On-Device Portal (ODP), 324
One-many-one Dispatcher group session, 230
One-to-many, 217
One-to-many session, 225
One-to-one, 217
One-to-one session, 225
Online Certificate Status Protocol (OCSP), 44, 144,
    180
Online charging, 118, 252, 256, 260, 262
Online Charging Interface (CH-2), 262
Online charging request, 262
Online Charging System (OCS), 252
Open Digital Rights Language (ODRL), 289, 297,
    302
Open Mobile Alliance (OMA), 21
Open Mobile Naming Authority (OMNA), 26, 32,
    264, 278, 285
Open Security Framework, 306
Open Service Access (OSA), 48, 68, 200
Open source, 290
Operations, Administration and Maintenance
    (OA&M), 49
Operations, Administration, Maintenance, and
    Provisioning (OAM&P), 15, 160, 164
Operational Expenditure (OPEX), 9
Operations and Process Working Group, 51
Operations and Processes (OPS), 26
Operations Support System (OSS), 15, 63, 160, 174
Operations Support System/Business Support
    Systems (OSS/BSS), 54, 73, 172, 433
Operations System Function (OSF), 412
Operator, 41, 54, 422
Operator-specified warning message, 232, 233
OPEX (*see* Operational Expenditure)
Option, 36
Optional feature, 37
Optional codec, 311
Orchestrate, 14
Orchestrated workflow, 71
Orchestration, 66
Orchestration expression language , 71
Orchestration workflow, 432

Order, 253
Organization for the Advancement of Structured
    Information Standards (OASIS), 51, 138
Original Equipment Manufacturer (OEM), 274
Originating client, 225
OSA Gateway, 204
OSA PAM (*see* OSA Presence and Availability), 205
OSA Presence and Availability (PAM), 204
OSE (*see* OMA Service Environment), 5, 13, 15, 17,
    19, 35, 54, 63, 135, 153, 167, 183, 205, 219,
    228, 256, 272, 326, 338, 343, 347, 357
OSE blueprint, 63, 68
OSPE agent, 168
OSPE agent layer, 168
OSPE Data Management interface for SMAC, 169
OSPE LCM request interface, 169
OSPE notification interface, 169
OSPE provisioning interface, 169
OSPE Requestor, 169
OSPE server, 167
OSPE server layer, 168
OSPE SLT request interface, 169
OSPE tracing interface, 169
OSPE-1, 169
OSPE-2, 169
OSPE-3, 169
OSPE-4, 169
OSPE-5, 169
OSPE-6, 169
OSS (*see* Operations Support System)
OSS/BSS (*see* Operations Support System/Business
    Support System), 73, 172, 433
OTA (*see* Over The Air Activation)
Other Resource, 344
Out-band client I0 interface, 243
Out-band server I0 interface, 243
Out-of-band handling, 317
Out-of-coverage, 326
Output BLOB, 97
Over The Air Activation (OTA), 29, 237, 270, 274,
    281, 293
OWP (*see* OMA Work Program)
OWSER (*see* OMA Web Services Enabler Release)
OWSER Network Identity (OWSERNI), 31, 146,
    154
OWSER realization of the OSE, 154
OWSER WSDL style guide, 33
OWSERNI (*see* OWSER Network Identity)
OWSERWSDL, 33

P parameters, 15, 16, 64, 154
P2P Gaming, 379
Package, 277
Package creation, 285
Packet Data Protocol (PDP), 390
Packet Data Serving Node (PDSN), 213
Packet-technology, 218
Parameter P (*see* P parameters)
Parent-most interior node, 278
Parlay, 18, 48, 68, 125, 196, 205
Parlay API, 126, 395
Parlay architecture, 126

Parlay Framework, 126, 131
Parlay Gateway, 126
Parlay in OSE (PIOSE), 27, 53, 125, 128
Parlay policy framework, 73
Parlay X, 205
Parlay X Web Services, 128, 135
Parlay/OSA, 49, 53
Participants notification, 223
Participating Function, 223
Participating PoC Function (PPF), 221
Partner, 59
Partner Management, 73
Partner service provider, 168
Password, 178
Patent holder, 298
Pattern matching, 352, 359
Pattern recognition, 351
Pattern searching, 352
Payment, 253
Payment credentials, 253
Payment instrument, 254
Pc, 203
PCS Type Certification Review Board (PTCRB), 38
P-CSCF (*see* Proxy-Call State Control Function)
PE (*see* Policy Enforcer)
PE execution model, 65
PE logical concept, 89
PE logical entity, 100
PEEM (*see* Policy Evaluation, Enforcement and
     Management)
PEEM AD, 346
PEEM callable interface, 91
PEEM callable usage pattern, 99
PEEM enabler, 377
PEEM enabler implementation, 90
PEEM flow, 362
PEEM logical architecture, 90
PEEM management interface, 92
PEEM proxy interface, 93
PEEM proxy usage pattern, 100
PEEM Rules, 360
Peer-to-peer (content delivery), 325
Peer-to-Peer (P2P), 379
Peer-to-peer distribution, 292
Peer-to-peer sharing, 293
PEL (*see* Policy Expression Language)
PEL construct, 95
PEM-1 interface, 91, 95, 344, 346, 350, 356, 360
PEM-1 parameter, 346
PEM-1 Standard Template, 364
PEM-1 Template, 96, 347
PEM-1 Template bindings, 97
PEM-2 binding, 99
PEM-2 interface, 92, 344, 346, 350, 356, 361
Pen, 204
Pep, 213
PEP-PDP model, 80, 87
Periodic location request, 392
Permissions Rule, 339, 340
Permissions Checking and Management, 345
Permissions Checking interface, 339, 346, 349
Permissions Checking Request, 340, 345
Permissions Checking Requester, 345

Permissions Checking Response, 341
Permissions control, 338
Permissions management mechanism, 338
Permissions Manager, 342
Permissions Rule, 340
Permissions Target, 339, 342
Persistent group, 230
Persistent SIP session state, 223
Personal Area Network (PAN), 379
Personal Communication Service (PCS), 38
Personal Computer (PC), 240
Personal Digital Assistant (PDA), 28, 240, 270, 401
Personal Information Manager (PIM), 239, 242, 245
Personal mobile device, 59
Personalization capabilities, 421
Personalization of advertisements, 425
Peu, 204
Pex, 204
Ph, 203
Phishing, 337
Pi, 203
PIDF (*see* Presence Information Data Format)
PIM (*see* Personal Information Manager)
P-IMAP, 240
PIOSE (*see* Parlay in OSE)
Pl, 203
Place-type, 196
Plain voice, 48
Play (right), 294
PLS (*see* Presence List Server)
PMESS message, 397
PNA (*see* Presence Network Agent)
PoC (*see* Push-to-talk over Cellular)
PoC architecture, 220, 221
PoC Box, 228, 231
PoC chat group, 225
PoC client, 219, 220, 229
PoC enabler, 31, 218, 219, 220, 233
PoC group, 229
PoC remote access, 232
PoC server, 219, 220, 226
PoC service, 218
PoC service subscription, 232
PoC session, 209, 223, 229, 232
PoC session establishment model, 223
PoC session identifier, 226
PoC session management, 221
PoC session policies, 220
PoC session set-up, 222
PoC signaling control layer, 219
PoC user access expression language, 95
PoC XDM server, 220
POC-1, 221
POC-2, 221
POC-2/XDM-2, 221
POC-2/XDM-6, 221
POC-3, 221
POC-5, 221
POC-8, 221
PoC-specific user preferences, 220
Point of sale, 255
Point-of-Service (POS), 254
Point-to-multipoint channel, 300

Point-to-multipoint service, 305
Point-to-point, 330
Point-to-point communications, 315
Policies, 198
Policy, 79, 326, 338
Policy action, 80
Policy condition, 80
Policy control, 79
Policy control component, 70
Policy Core Information Model, 80
Policy Decision Function, 74
Policy Decision Point, 71
Policy Enforcement, 66, 154
Policy Enforcement Point, 71
Policy Enforcer (PE), 14, 20, 27, 82, 131, 184, 272,
    326, 343, 357, 430, 432
Policy enforcer process, 64
Policy engine, 79, 360
Policy evaluation, 69, 83
Policy evaluation and enforcement, 69, 78, 87
Policy Evaluation, Enforcement and Management
    (PEEM), 15, 27, 53, 69, 78, 145, 342, 347, 356,
    358, 364, 433
Policy expression, 86
Policy Expression Language (PEL), 71, 80, 346,
    356, 359, 364
Policy language, 69
Policy management, 79, 88, 300
Policy Management SCF, 132
Policy processing, 69, 345
Policy processing invocation, 81
Policy rule, 80
Policy server, 79
Policy topology, 69, 91, 104
Policy type, 72
Policy universe, 73
Policy-based Admission Control, 80
Policy-based control, 79
Policy-based management, 80
Policy-based network, 79
Polite block, 198
Poll request, 197
Poller, 197
Polling, 197
POP, 242
POP3, 240
Position Determining Equipment (PDE), 385
Position parameter, 395
Positioning Determination, 389, 395
Positioning protocol operations, 389
Positioning target, 387
Post Office Protocol (POP), 240
Post-paid charging, 252
Post-retail bootstrap, 275
Post-service delivery, 255
PPR (see Privacy Profile Register)
Pre-arranged group, 230
Pre-arranged PoC group, 225
Pre-categorized (content), 354
Pre-defined label, 352
Pre-emption, 232
Pre-established credentials, 181
Pre-established mode, 223

Preferences, 343
Preferences Profile (PP), 414
Premium (QoE profile), 232
Pre-paid charging, 251
Presence, 21, 41, 195, 199, 205, 215, 218, 328, 347,
    350, 372, 421, 424
Presence and Availability Working Group (PAG
    WG), 31
Presence and Group Management enablers, 193
Presence Architecture, 207, 210, 213
Presence aspects, 196
Presence authorization PEL, 95
Presence authorization rules, 81, 210
Presence data management, 216
Presence enabler, 121, 213, 216, 219, 234, 339, 377
Presence filter, 198
Presence information, 201, 203, 205, 343
Presence Information Data Format (PIDF), 198, 436
Presence List Server (PLS), 198, 208
Presence model, 203
Presence Network Agent (PNA), 203, 204
Presence PEL, 95
Presence rules, 343
Presence Server (PS), 197, 200, 203, 207+B1820,
    213
Presence service, 202, 417
Presence Service Element, 207
Presence SIMPLE architecture, 207
Presence source, 208, 219
Presence state publication, 196
Presence User Agent (PUA), 204
Presence XDMS, 209, 214
Presence-enabled service, 199
Present Authorization Rules, 343
Presentity, 196, 199, 208, 214
Presentity interface, 197
Presentity Presence proxy, 204, 213
Pre-service delivery, 255
Pre-Shared Key Transport Layer Security
    (PSK-TLS), 181
Programmed content, 309
Price Inquiry Request, 262
Principal, 47, 79, 146, 196, 204, 305
Print right, 294
Prioritization, 232
Prioritize permissions rule, 345
Priority call enforcement, 224
Privacy, 218, 226, 230, 290, 352, 381, 421, 425
Privacy Checking Protocol (PCP), 387
Privacy concerns, 352
Privacy management, 342
Privacy profile, 387
Privacy Profile Register (PPR), 342
Privacy protection, 342
Private information, 178, 338, 348
Private wireless network, 323
Product, 413
Professional (QoE profile), 232
Professional creation, 353
Profile, 36, 139, 148, 155
Program Encryption Key (PEK), 313
Program Specific Information/Service Information,
    306

Property, 278
Protection profile, 306
Protocol binding, 17, 81
Protocol layers architecture, 264
Prov AD, 274
Provisioning Agent, 169
Provisioning bootstrap, 281
Provisioning smart card, 281
Provisioning user agent behavior, 281
Proxy, 357, 405
Proxy interface, 92, 358, 362
Proxy mode, 70, 390, 397, 399
Proxy pattern, 344, 358
Proxy server, 401
Proxy usage pattern, 70, 359, 362
Proxy-Call State Control Function (P-CSCF), 204,
    213
PRS-1, 213
PRS-13, 214
PRS-2, 214
PS (see Presence Server)
Pseudonym, 204
PSK-TLS, 186
PTT service, 218
Public chat room, 226
Public communication network, 120
Public key, 180
Public Key Infrastructure (PKI), 295
Public wireless network, 323
Publication method, 331
PUBLISH, 202
Pull method, 330
Pull content, 352
Push, 285, 294, 323
Push method, 330
Push content, 352
Push e-mail, 242
Push enabler, 377
Push marketing, 423
Push mechanism, 291
Push Over-the-air (Push OTA), 291, 297, 299, 391,
    394
Push protocol, 29
PUSH Protocol (2-pass), 297
Push Proxy Gateway, 334
Push Proxy Gateway (PPG), 42
PushOTA (see Push Over-the-air), 291
Push-to-talk (PTT), 217
Push-to-talk over Cellular (PoC), 21, 31, 44, 121,
    193, 205, 212, 214, 219, 228, 233, 266, 269,
    285, 418
PUT, 209, 212
Pw, 204, 214

QoE profile, 232
Quality of Experience (QoE), 161, 232, 299, 319,
    418, 424
Quality of Service (QoS), 18, 53, 145, 232, 389
Query pattern, 387
Queuing, 231
Quick mailbox synchronization, 242
Quota, 257

Quota management, 257

Radar, 396
Radio Access Network (RAN), 386
Radio coverage, 307
Radio Frequency (RF), 42
Radio resource, 304
Radio tower, 381
Rating, 257
Rating function, 258
Rating label, 353
RCPT, 240
RD (see Requirements Document)
RDF (see Resource Description Framework)
Reactive authorization, 198
Real time game, 369
Real Time Protocol/Real Time Control Protocol
    (RTP/RTCP), 221, 226
Really Simple Syndication (RSS), 321, 326
Real-time charging, 257
Real-time content channel, 293
Real-time streamed content, 293
Real-time streaming, 294
Recreational Software Advisory Council (RSAC),
    353
Reference context, 278
Reference ellipsoid, 396
Reference model, 200
Reference point, 203, 214, 306, 389
Reference Release, 35
Refund Request, 262
Refunding, 257
Register operation, 331
Registration, 207
Registration and Discovery enabler, 153
Registration state, 219
Regulatory Body, 355
Regulatory policy, 343
Relay function, 256
Release Planning and Management (REL), 26
Remote Presence Network, 209
Remove node, 285
Replace command, 278
Replay protection, 182
Reply without download, 244
Report, 261
REQ WG (see Requirements Working Group)
Request for Proposal (RFP), 286
Request for Quotation (RFQ), 42
Request message, 261
Request pattern, 392
Request Type, 261
Requirements Document (RD), 26, 37
Requirements Working Group (REQ WG), 27, 34
Reserve units request, 260
Reserved units, 260
Reserving units, 258
Resource of interest, 197
Resource, 11, 13, 18, 355
Resource admission control, 79
Resource Admission Control Function, 74
Resource Description Framework (RDF), 356

Resource List Server (RLS), 198, 200, 208, 214
Resource List Server XDMS, 209
Resource Tier, 129, 205, 220
Resource usage, 252
Restore RO, 293
Result Code, 262
Resume, 245
Resume permissions rule, 345
Retrieval, 212
Returned result, 340
Re-usable service layer component, 67
Reverse proxy, 212
Review and Approval (R&A), 34
Review Report, 26, 35
RI (see Rights Issuer)
RI portal, 297
Rich media, 292
Rights binding, 293
Rights Encryption Key (REK), 297, 313
Rights expression language (REL), 297
Rights Issuer (RI), 292, 295
Rights management, 299
Rights Object (RO), 291, 294, 297, 300, 301
Rights Object Acquisition Protocol (ROAP), 297, 300, 302, 306
Rights protection, 290, 292
Right-to-speak, 231
Ring tone, 251, 291, 411, 424
RLS (see Resource List Server)
RO (see Rights Object)
Roaming, 226, 387
Roaming Location Protocol (RLP), 388
Roaming scenario, 392
ROAP (see Rights Object Acquisition Protocol)
ROAP sequence, 297
ROAP trigger, 297
Roster management, 201
RSS (see Really Simple Syndication)
RTP payload format, 227
RTP/RTCP (see Real Time Protocol/Real Time Control Protocol)
Rule, 95, 198, 343
Rule-based constraint, 294
Rules evaluation logic, 358
Rules expression language, 356
Rules Managers, 354
Ruleset, 95, 132
Ruleset engine, 73
Ruleset language, 69, 132

Sampling frequency, 227
Satellite, 396
Scalable Vector Graphics (SVG), 406, 407
SCE import function, 301
SCE RD, 301
Schematic configuration structure, 277
SCOMO (see Software Component Management Object)
Scores and Competition Management API, 371
Scoring API, 370
Screening, 354
Screening Rules, 356, 358, 361, 366

Screening Rules management, 363
Screensaver, 291
S-CSCF (see Serving-Call State Control Function)
SD (see Stream Distribution)
SD functional architecture, 311
SD-1, 312
SD-2, 312
SD-5, 312
SD-6, 315
SD-B1, 312
Search folders without download, 240
Search Proxy, 211
SEC-1, 185
SEC-2, 186
SEC-3, 186
SEC-CF (see Security Common Functions)
Second Generation (2G), 42
Secure connection, 181
Secure Content Exchange (SCE), 301
Secure dynamic provisioning, 286
Secure Socket Layer/Transport Layer Security (SSL/TLS), 271
Secure User Plane Location (SUPL), 44, 287, 349, 381, 387, 389, 392
Security, 152
Security Agent (SECA), 184
Security Assertions Markup Language (SAML), 143
Security association, 188, 390
Security Common Functions (SEC-CF), 28, 179, 347
Security enabler, 179
Security framework, 179
Security gateway, 182
Security Working Group (SEC WG), 28, 179
Selection, 253
Selective user experience, 233
Self-described MO instance, 280
Self-regulating ecosystem, 351
Self-regulating nature, 352
SEND, 240
Serialization, 144
Serialized MO, 279
Server accounting state machine, 263
Server Alert Synchronization (SAS), 245
Server authentication, 181
Server certificate, 181
Server to Mobile Core Network Protocol (SMCNP) Access, 207
Server to Server Protocol (SSP) Access, 207
Server, session and event based, 264
Server, stateless accounting, 263
Server-as-master protocol, 276
Server-side e-tag, 199
Server-side filtering, 239, 244
Server-side polling, 197
Server-side transaction state, 279
Service, 47, 57, 413
Service Access Point, 205
Service aggregation, 308
Service Assurance, 164
Service attribute, 169
Service Billing, 164
Service Broker, 432
Service building block, 11

Service Capability Feature (SCF), 126, 204
Service Capability Interaction Manager (SCIM), 68, 432
Service catalog, 163
Service chaining, 171
Service choreography co-ordinator, 84
Service component, 3, 163
Service composition, 145
Service configuration, 191
Service control option, 227
Service delivery, 48
Service Delivery Environment (SDE), 431
Service Delivery Framework (SDF), 431
Service Delivery Platform (SDP), 68, 108, 431
Service Deployment cycle, 162, 172
Service deployment instance, 168
Service element, 205
Service enabler, 1, 3, 7, 10, 14, 18, 47, 193, 429, 431
Service enabler tier, 129
Service Encryption Key (SEK), 313
Service environment, 4
Service Fulfillment, 164
Service Fulfillment, Service Assurance, Service Billing (FAB), 164
Service Guide (SG), 304, 309, 312, 335
Service Guide Content Creation (SGCC), 310
Service guide delivery, 308
Service guide generation, 308
Service information model, 173
Service Interaction (SI), 304, 308, 315
Service Level Agreement (SLA), 18, 48, 64, 84, 132
Service level policy framework, 73
Service Level Tracing (SLT), 53, 161
Service Life-cycle Management, 53
Service logic, 14
Service maintenance, 163
Service Maintenance cycle, 162
Service Management, 389, 395
Service model, 168
Service Model and Catalog (SMAC), 168
Service Model Management (SMM), 162
Service Oriented Architecture (SOA), 19, 65, 137, 179
Service package, 161, 168
Service policies, 230
Service Preference, 413
Service Profile information, 414
Service Protection (SP), 305, 308, 313
Service protection management, 308
Service provider, 3, 9, 15, 18, 47, 52, 57, 60, 64, 147, 215, 266, 282, 286, 295, 298, 303, 319, 329, 333, 339, 349, 353, 364, 367, 376, 411, 421
Service provider policies, 14, 144, 179, 184, 258
Service provider preferences, 344
Service Provider Resource, 341
Service provider rules, 258
Service Provisioning (SPR), 305, 308, 316
Service Purchase, 306
Service registry, 73
Service session, 163
Service Set Identifier (SSID), 283
Service silo, 1

Service Subscription, 335
Service subscription handling, 413
Service subscription profile access, 413
Service subscription validation, 413
Service usage, 257
Serving Mobile Location Center (SMLC), 343, 385
Serving-Call State Control Function (S-CSCF), 204, 213
Session charging, 264
Session control, 219
Session control and management, 221
Session duration, 258
Session establishment, 229
Session handling, 229
Session Initiation Protocol (SIP), 117, 198, 200, 209, 219, 242, 335, 343, 393, 416, 435
Session Management API, 370
Session mode, 201
Session triggering, 273
Session-based charging model, 258, 260, 263
SET (see SUPL-Enabled Terminal), 390
SET-Initiated Location Procedure, 389
Set-up PoC session, 218
SG (see Service Guide)
SG functional architecture, 309
SG generation/adaptation, 309
SG-1, 310
SG-2, 310
SG-4, 310
SG-5, 310
SG-6, 310
SGML (see Standard Generalized Markup Language)
Shared Content, 205
Shared Group XDMS, 211
Shared Information/Data (SID), 166, 413
Shared key, 181
Shared key mechanism, 181
Shared list of contacts, 209
Shared List XDMS, 211
Shared Policy XDMS, 211
Shared Profile XDMS, 211
Shared secret, 178
Shared XDM Server (Shared XDMS), 209, 215, 219
SHG-B1, 310
Short message, 48
Short Message Peer-to-Peer Protocol (SMPP), 391
Short Message Service (SMS), 19, 42, 234, 240, 273, 298, 304, 315, 323, 346, 362, 390, 411, 416
Short-term Key Message (STKM), 313
SI (see Service Interaction)
SI functional architecture, 315
SI-8, 316
SID (see Shared Information/Data)
SIEVE, 247
Signaling System number 7 (SS7), 48, 383
Silent rights renewal, 292
Silo, 8, 10, 13, 15, 347, 418
Silo architecture, 18, 413
Silo syndrome, 7, 9, 18
Silo system, 18
SIM (see Subscriber Identity Module)
SIMPLE (see SIP for Instant Messaging and Presence Leveraging Extensions)

SIMPLE Instant Messaging (SIMPLE IM), 205, 212, 215, 418
Simple Mail Transfer Protocol (SMTP), 240, 242, 283, 405
Simple Network Management Protocol (SNMP), 164, 282
Simple Object Access Protocol (SOAP), 255, 373, 387
SIMPLE RFCs, 202
Simultaneous PoC communication, 227
Single core platform, 416
Single device client, 419
Single frequency, 217
Single logical CPM entity, 419
Single media control for multiple media, 231
Single messaging client, 419
Single network-based messaging platform, 419
Single player (soloplay), 375
Single sign-on, 146, 149
Single sign-out, 150
Single/same user experience, 419
SIP (see Session Initiation Protocol)
SIP 200 OK, 225
SIP ACK, 225
SIP Application Server, 68
SIP authentication, 219
SIP compression, 219
SIP Event Package, 210, 212
SIP for Instant Messaging and Presence Leveraging Extensions (SIMPLE), 200, 205, 343, 436
SIP INVITE, 224
SIP protocol, 221
SIP proxy, 211, 219
SIP PUBLISH, 207
SIP Push, 346, 362, 392
SIP registrar, 219
SIP signaling, 219
SIP SUBSCRIBE, 214, 362
SIP URI, 214
SIP/IP Core, 115, 122, 205, 209, 211, 219, 221, 225, 290, 379, 393, 418
SIP-based reference point, 211
SIPinOMA, 122
SLC (see SUPL Location Centre)
Slow update, 369
SLP (see SUPL Location Platform)
Small business owner, 269
Smart card, 180, 188, 275, 286, 315
Smart card profile, 314
Smart Card Web Server (SCWS), 180
Smart phone, 270
SMIL for the Mobile Domain, 406
SMS (see Short Message Service)
SMS Center (SMSC), 391, 393
SMS tele-service, 391
SMSC (see SMS Center)
SMTP (see Simple Mail Transfer Protocol)
SMTP-Submit, 240
SNMP agent, 164
SOA composition, 65
SOAP binding, 97, 144
SOAP/XML, 267
Software catalog, 285

Software Component Management Object (SCOMO), 282, 284
Software package, 284
Soloplay game, 368, 377
Southbound, 128
SP, 308
SP functional architecture, 313
SP-2, 313
SP-4, 313
SP-5-1*, 314
SP-5-2*, 314
SP-6-1*, 314
SP-7*, 315
SP-9, 315
Spam, 421
Spamming, 337
SPC (see SUPL Positioning Centre)
Special series handset, 218
Specialized device, 270
Specification options, 51
Spectral efficiency, 326
Speech codec, 226
SPR (see Service Provisioning)
SPR functional architecture, 316
SPR-7, 316
SPR-8, 317
SSL, 276, 282
Standard Generalized Markup Language (SGML), 353, 356
Standard Location Immediate Request (SLIR), 398
Standard Location Immediate Service, 387, 392
Standard PEM-1 Template, 97, 346
Standard Transcoding Interface (STI), 28, 243, 247
Standards Development Organization (SDO), 36, 44
Start charging request, 258
StartRecord, 261
State machine, 264
Stateless RO, 295
Static Conformance requirement (SCR), 37
Static property, 414
Statistics, 44
STKM, 314
Stop charging request, 258
Stop session request, 261
StopRecord, 262
Storage sharing, 421
STORE, 247
Stovepipe architecture, 7
Strategic planning committee, 25
Stream Distribution (SD), 305, 308, 311
Streaming content, 293
Structural Query, 279
Style guide, 33
SUBMIT, 247
SUBSCRIBE/NOTIFY, 202
Subscribed channel, 331
Subscribed watcher, 197
Subscriber, 3, 326, 354, 412, 422
Subscriber Identity Module (SIM), 42, 271, 273, 319, 403
Subscriber ISDN Number (MSISDN), 387
Subscriber Management Key (SMK), 313
Subscriber's account, 251

Subscriber's location information, 388
Subscription Management (SuM), 53, 293, 308, 412
Subscription profile, 412
Subscription Profile Component (SPC), 412
Subscription service, 411
Sub-Working Group (SWG), 28, 31
SuM (*see* Subscription Management)
SuM Architecture, 412
SuM Integration Reference Point (SuM IRP), 412,
    414
SuM IRP (*see* SuM Integration Reference Point)
SuM IRP Agent, 412
SuM IRP Manager, 412
Super-distribution, 293, 295
Super-group, 230
SUPL (*see* Secure User Plane Location)
SUPL agent, 389, 398, 400
SUPL Architecture, 389, 391
SUPL enabler, 381, 393, 400
SUPL INIT, 394
SUPL Location Centre (SLC), 389, 397
SUPL Location Platform (SLP), 389
SUPL Positioning Centre (SPC), 389, 390, 392, 397
SUPL Report Message, 395
SUPL sequence flow, 393, 397
SUPL-Enabled Terminal (SET), 389
Supplier, 41, 59
Suspend, 245
Suspend (permissions rule), 345
SVG (*see* Scalable Vector Graphics)
SVG Basic (SVGB), 406
SVG for the Mobile Domain, 406
SVG Tiny (SVGT), 406
SWG (*see* Sub-Working Group)
Symmetrical encryption key, 292
Synchronization Markup Language (SyncML), 22,
    30, 50, 237, 245, 271, 276, 287
Synchronization operation, 405
Synchronized media, 231
Synchronized Multimedia Integration Language
    (SMIL), 406
Synchronized release, 52
Synchronizing e-mail over-the-air, 240
Synchronous request, 387
SyncML (*see* Synchronization Markup Language),
    30
SyncML Common Protocol, 277
SyncML Data Synchronization, 30
SyncML Initiative, 242, 271, 277, 281
SyncML Representation Protocol, 277, 282
Syndicated content delivery, 332
Syndicated service, 322
Syndication, 321

T(I0), 66
Talk burst, 225
Target Attribute Consumer, 339
Target Attribute Requestor, 339
Target enabler, 92
Target Information, 339
Target Request, 340
Target resource, 92, 169

Target Resource Requestor, 92
Target user attributes, 344
Taxonomy, 353
TCP/IP, 271, 394
Tear-down PoC session, 218
Technical Specification (TS), 24, 25, 37
Technology Provider, 422
Technology realization, 135
Telecom Operations Map (TOM), 166
Terminal, 308, 315, 318
Terminal Provisioning (TP), 305, 306, 308, 318
Terminal Provisioning functional architecture, 317
Termination Request, 263
Terrestrial channel, 382
Test Campaign, 42
Test Plan, 35
Test Session Report (TS_RPT), 37
Test tool, 41
TestFest, 1, 23, 25, 28, 37, 41, 233, 286, 298, 320
Text-based alert, 238
Texting, 196
The Parlay Group, 381
Third Generation Internet Protocol Forum (3G.IP),
    417
Third Generation Partnership Project (3GPP), 24, 50,
    196, 200, 219, 241, 252, 255, 265, 283, 291,
    305, 384, 389, 412, 416
Third Generation Partnership Project 2 (3GPP2), 24,
    50, 200, 202, 219, 240, 255, 265, 305, 384, 389
Third party application server, 390
Third party content provider, 423
Third-party application provider, 237, 269
Third-party Application Service Provider, 86
Third-party content provider, 298
Third-party content vendor, 7
Three-layer brick model, 200, 207
Time Distance of Arrival (TDOA), 382
Time to First Fix (TTFF), 382
Time-based schedule, 286
Timers API, 371
Time-to-market, 159
TISPAN, 74, 412, 414
TLS (*see* Transport Layer Security)
TM Forum, 54, 166, 412, 433
TNDS (*see* Tree and Description Serialization)
TP (*see* OMA Technical Plenary)
TP-7, 318
Trace, 163
Tracing Agent, 169
Tracing instance, 163
Tracing session, 171
Tracing token, 163
Traffic Encryption Key (TEK), 313
Traffic-based charging, 220
Transaction Credentials, 254
Transaction details, 253
Transactions, 145
Transcoding, 405
Transcoding/adaptation, 244
Transformation, 66, 343
Transformed interface, 65
Transparent interception, 93
Transparent redirection, 84

Transport, 142
Transport binding, 276
Transport Layer Security (TLS), 182, 276, 282
Tree and Description Serialization (TNDS), 280, 282
Tree-pruning, 279
Tree-structured collection, 275
Triangulation, 396
Triangulation calculation, 385
Triangulation method, 382
Triggered Location Reporting Service, 387
Triggered location request, 392
Triggering reporting, 387
Troubleshooting, 162
Trust domain, 147
Trust model, 292, 295
TS (*see* Technical Specification)
Turing complete, 69
Turn based (game), 369
Two-way radio, 217
Type, 278
Type of device, 58
Type registry, 278
Type-specific, 283

UAProf (*see* User Agent Profile)
UDDI, 146
UDP/IP, 392, 394
UDP/IP bearer, 393
UE PoC Box, 228
UIM/CSIM, 319
ULP (*see* UserPlane Location Protocol)
ULP PD (*see* ULP Positioning Determination)
ULP Positioning Determination (ULP PD) interface, 395, 399
ULP Service Management (ULP SM) interface, 395, 398
ULP SM (*see* ULP Service Management)
UMTS (*see* Universal Mobile Telecommunications System)
Uncertainty ellipse, 395
Unconfirmed indication of session acceptance, 223
Unconfirmed mode, 224
Undesirable content, 354
Unidirectional channel, 300
Unidirectional media stream transmission, 231
Unidirectional one-to-many, 304
Uniform Resource Identifier (URI), 197, 209, 271,278, 360
Unique list identity, 197
Universal Mobile Telecommunications System (UMTS), 23, 213, 239, 275
Universal Serial Bus (USB), 285
Unused quota, 257
Update Request, 263
Urban canyon, 382
URI (*see* Uniform Resource Identifier)
URI List XML Document, 211
URL, 207, 209, 214, 284, 295, 297
Usage directive, 151
Usage pattern, 239
Usage rights, 294

Usage volume, 258
Used quota, 263
User, 326, 370, 422
User Access Policy XML Document, 211
User Agent (UA), 242, 258, 260, 409
User Agent Profile (UAProf), 28, 414, 415
User creation, 353
User Datagram Protocol (UDP), 373
User experience, 231, 241, 291, 300, 322, 337, 372, 406, 420, 422
User identity, 254
User information, 53
User permission, 338, 340
User Plane, 227, 381, 383
User Plane Architecture, 390
User Plane data bearer, 389, 398
User Plane Location, 381, 386, 388, 400
User Plane Location Architecture, 386
User preferences, 243, 344, 352
User privacy, 53
User Profile XML Document, 211
User service profile, 219
User status attributes, 207
User subscription, 53
User-created content, 291
UserPlane Location Protocol (ULP), 394, 395, 397
User's attribute, 348
USIM, 319
Ut, 214
Utilization of IMS in OMA (IMSinOMA), 27, 53, 115, 202, 213, 219, 377, 432

Value Added Service Provider (VASP), 333
Value chain, 47
vBook, 405
vCal, 405
vCalendar, 405
vCard, 405
Vending machine, 254
Vendor-defined Management Object, 285
Vendor-specific Diameter application, 97
Verification of access, 348
Version number, 212
Vertical integration, 1, 7, 4, 19, 22, 40
View filter, 247
Virtual POS, 255
Visited network, 181
vObject, 405
vObject minimum interoperability profile, 405
Voice communication, 219
Voice telephony service, 411
Voice-call distribution system, 383
Voluntary rating, 352

W3C (*see* World Wide Web Consortium), 138, 335, 406, 414, 416
W3C Document Object Model (DOM2CORE), 404
Walkie-talkie, 217, 227, 418
WAP (*see* Wireless Application Protocol)
WAP Browser, 417
WAP Cascading Style Sheet (WCSS), 403

WAP client, 238
WAP Client Provisioning (CP), 274
WAP CP, 281
WAP device, 276
WAP Forum, 22, 28, 49, 51, 242, 274, 281, 401, 409, 416
WAP Gateway, 42, 334
WAP PPG, 393
WAP Proxy, 242, 281, 283
WAP Push, 273, 324, 329, 346
WAP Push Access Protocol (WAP PAP), 391
WAP PUSH Proxy, 242
WAP Push Proxy Gateway (WAP PPG), 391
WAP Session Protocol (WSP), 242
Watcher, 197, 208, 214, 219
Watcher information, 199
Watcher Information Subscriber, 208
Watcher interface, 197, 204
Watcher Presence proxy, 204
Watcher subscription, 197
Waterfall model, 33
W-CDMA, 42, 283
WCSS, 406
Web browser, 402
Web content filtering, 351
Web mail, 240
Web Service binding, 153, 432
Web Service description, 136
Web Service environment, 137
Web Service Provider, 136
Web Service Registry, 136, 146
Web Service Requestor, 136
Web Service technologies, 135
Web Service triangle, 137
Web Services (WS), 17, 19, 31, 33, 136, 192, 205, 286, 288
Web Services API, 140
Web Services deployment, 135
Web Services Description Language (WSDL), 32
Web Services infrastructure framework, 137
Web Services Interface for Device Management (DM-WSI), 285
Web Services Interoperability , 139
Web Services Interoperability organization (WS-I), 138, 156
Web Services platform architecture, 138
Web Services realization, 189
Web Services stack, 138
Web services technology, 179
Web-based e-mail, 238
Web-Based Enterprise Management (WBEM), 165
WG (see OMA Technical Working Group), 24
Wi-Fi, 274, 283, 323
WiMAX Multicast and Broadcast Service (WiMAX MBS), 320
Winfo, 199
Wired network, 323
Wireless Application Protocol (WAP), 237, 241, 245, 281, 291, 323, 346, 390, 403, 414
Wireless Area Network (WLAN), 283
Wireless browsing, 21

Wireless Datagram Protocol (WDP), 403
Wireless emergency service, 383
Wireless Fidelity (WiFi), 23
Wireless Identity Module (WIM), 180
Wireless Local Area Network (WLAN), 391, 415
Wireless Markup Language (WML), 242, 401
Wireless operator, 282
Wireless Public Key Infrastructure (WPKI), 180
Wireless Session Protocol (WSP), 245, 281, 294
Wireless Telephony Application (WTA), 281
Wireless Transport Protocol (WTP), 403
Wireless Vendor, 25
Wireless Village (WV), 22, 31, 50, 205, 417
WML, 403
WMLScript, 401, 403
Work Item Document (WID), 34
Workflow, 95, 108, 145, 155
Workflow language, 69
World Wide Web (WWW), 287, 402
World Wide Web Consortium (W3C), 138, 335, 356, 403, 406, 414, 416
Worldwide Interoperability for Microwave Access (WiMAX), 23
WS (see Web Services)
WS BPEL, 69
WS-*, 137, 287
WS-AtomicTransaction, 145
WS-BusinessActivity, 145
WS-I (see Web Services Interoperability organization)
WS-I Basic Profile, 140
WS-Management, 288
WSP (see Wireless Session Protocol)
WS-Policy, 145
WV (see Wireless Village)

XACML, 95
XCAP (see XML Configuration Access Protocol), 98, 209, 214, 343, 436
XCAP client, 214
XCAP server, 211
XDM (see XML Document Management)
XDM Architecture, 209
XDM Client (XDMC), 209, 211
XDM component, 210
XDM document, 214
XDM enabler, 210, 213, 219, 228, 234
XDM Management Object (MO), 211
XDM Server (XDMS), 209, 210, 212, 343
XDM-1, 211
XDM-3, 211, 214
XDMC (see XDM Client)
XDMS (see XDM Server)
XHTML (see Extended Hypertext Markup Language), 403
XHTML Basic, 404
XHTML browser, 404
XHTML Mobile Profile (XHTMLMP), 404, 405
XHTMLMP (see XHTML Mobile Profile)
XHTMLMP browser, 404
XML (see eXtensible Markup Language)

XML attribute, 212
XML Configuration Access Protocol (XCAP), 81,
    98, 209, 214, 221, 343, 436
XML document, 212
XML Document Management (XDM), 31, 44, 54,
    121, 205, 210, 212, 215, 219
XML Document Management Server (XMDS), 207,
    343

XML element, 212
XML namespace, 326
XML schema, 211
XMPP (*see* eXtensible Messaging and Presence
    Protocol)
Xpath, 437

Zero policy, 68